CASES IN STRATEGIC MANAGEMENT

CASES IN STRATEGIC MANAGEMENT

David W. Grigsby
Clemson University

and

Michael J. Stahl
University of Tennessee

First published 1997

First published in USA 1997
2 4 6 8 10 9 7 5 3 1

Blackwell Publishers Ltd
108 Cowley Road
Oxford OX4 1JF
UK

Blackwell Publishers Inc
238 Main Street
Cambridge, Massachusetts 02142,
USA

Library of Congress Cataloging -in -Publication Data

Grigsby, David W.
    Cases in strategic management / David W. Grigbsy and Michael J.
  Stahl.
      p.   cm.
    Includes bibliographical references and index.
    ISBN 1–55786–651–1 (alk. paper)
     1. Strategic planning.   2. Strategic planning—Case studies.
  I. Stahl, Michael J.   II. Title.
  HD30.28.G753   1996
  658.4'012—dc20   96–29124
                                               CIP

British Library Cataloguing in Publication Data

A CIP catalogue record for this book is available from the
British Library.

Commissioning Editor: Catriona King
Desk Editor: John Taylor
Production Manager/Controller: Lisa Parker

Typeset in 10 on 12 pt Photina
by Graphicraft Typesetters Ltd., Hong Kong
Printed in the USA

This book is printed on acid-free paper

Contents

PREFACE

Cases in Strategic Management is designed to provide students with the best means for developing their decision-making skills. This edition contains 25 comprehensive, timely cases featuring a wide range of organizations that are undergoing, or have undergone, strategic change. Although we have included a number of "classic" case studies, most of the cases are entirely new. All cases feature actual organizations, with real people, real accomplishments, and real problems. They range in size from small businesses to industry giants. In order to provide a realistic appraisal of situations, many of the case writers have included a wealth of industry data. All of the cases have been "classroom tested," and most have been critically reviewed by members of the North American Case Research Association. As the name of the book implies, the emphasis is on strategic decisions, particularly those involving quality issues and global competition. Most of the cases are grouped with others that deal with issues in the same industry or in closely related industries. This affords the opportunity for students to study industries in depth, and to understand strategic issues in the broader context of the firm's competitive environment. The combined result of these features is an appealing casebook that can be used in both undergraduate and graduate strategic management courses. It may be used with the companion text *Strategic Management: Total Quality and Global Competition*, by Michael J. Stahl and David W. Grigsby, or with other texts or books of readings.

The leadoff case, "Harley-Davidson, Inc.," chronicles the turnaround of this almost legendary American company, including its successful quality-enhancement strategy. ETA Corporation's strategic response to structural changes in the global wristwatch industry, which led to the first high-quality low-priced Swiss watch, is the focus of "The Swatch in 1993." Strategic issues in the global pharmaceutical industry and corporate social responsibility questions are emphasized in the case "Hoechst-Roussel Pharmaceuticals, Inc.: RU 486." "The rise and fall of Yugo America, Inc." chronicles one of the most publicized cases in recent years of failure due to low quality.

A three-case grouping, beginning with case 5, features strategic issues in industrial products businesses. All three cases deal with companies that have extensive international operations, and quality issues figure prominently. A struggling joint venture is the setting for "GM Allison Japan Ltd." A small Canadian company's struggle with US trade regulations is the focus in "Kenhar Products, Inc." Another feature of this case is the company's unique strategy of producing a low-technology product (steel fork-lift arms) using high-technology manufacturing processes. In "Calox Machinery Corporation" a USA based maker of construction equipment must make decisions about its distribution strategy in New Zealand.

The next two cases feature strategic issues in the global passenger airline industry. The cases are "American Airlines International Strategy" and "Korean Air: Challenges and Opportunities in the Growth of a Korean Firm." The issues covered in this group of cases range from growth issues and competing in a newly deregulated environment to corporate strategy formulation and management succession.

The following case addresses issues in the global home appliance industry, which has undergone a significant amount of restructuring in recent years, and focuses on one of the most successful competitors, Whirlpool.

Retailing companies are featured in the next four cases, all of which deal with successful innovation in the industry. "Cosmetics and Activism: Anita Roddick and The Body Shop" not only tells the fascinating story of this unique entrepreneurial effort, but focuses on social responsibility issues as well. "IKEA (Canada) Ltd" explains this well known Swedish furniture company's low-cost, high-quality strategy and presents the competitive situation faced in a new market. An updated version of a classic case, "Toys 'R' Us, 1993," yields insight into the remarkable strategies that led this firm to industry dominance, and the case "Wal-Mart, 1992" follows the story of the world's fastest growing retailer.

Three food and beverage industry cases form the next group. Industry dynamics in the global candy and soft drinks markets make "Cadbury Schweppes plc" an interesting to this section. "Kentucky Fried Chicken in China" analyzes KFC's entry strategy in the world's largest market. Accompanying "LaBatt Breweries of Europe" is an extensive industry note which aids in analyzing the Canadian brewer's strategy. The next case, "Dibrell Brothers, Inc.," presents a merger decision in the leaf processing segment of the tobacco industry.

Textile and apparel industry companies form a three-case unit. "Liz Claiborne, Inc., 1994" is an updated version of a classic case which traces the meteoric rise of the company and its subsequent decline following the retirement of its founders. Strategic management of the world's largest athletic shoe company is the subject of "Nike, Inc." "Lee Jing Textile Company Ltd" looks at problems developing in a traditional Taiwanese company from increased competitive pressure by low-wage nations.

All the cases in the final group feature strategic decisions in companies that were publicly owned and have been privatized. In the first, "Amtrak: Is This Any Way to Run a Railroad?," management of the still partially subsidized railroad system in the United States must deal with a multitude of issues. The recently reprivatized banking industry of Portugal has created some unique issues, dealt with in "UNICRE

SA and the Credit Card Industry in Portugal." In "Transvit of Novgorod, Russia," a producer of small electrical transformers must learn to compete with global producers to survive.

The book's introduction provides comprehensive advice on how to prepare for class discussions, oral reports, and written assignments. It also contains an extensive outline that can serve as a checklist for a strategic audit when conducting analyses of these and other cases. A complete instructor's manual accompanies the casebook. It contains detailed teaching notes for each case arranged in a standardized format. For each case there is a summary of the case's important aspects, teaching suggestions for alternative ways of using the case, thought-provoking questions that can be used either as discussion starters or for testing, and a step-by-step analysis, including financial analysis when it is appropriate. Many of the case notes contain updated information on the companies and the situations featured in the case.

Whether used alone or with an accompanying text such as *Strategic Management: Total Quality and Global Competition*, we feel that this casebook can provide a very appealing incentive for you to study and develop management skills. We hope you enjoy using it.

Introduction: Preparing and Presenting Effective Case Analyses

This book was designed to be used in courses which make extensive use of case analysis. You will study business strategy cases, which are accounts of actual business situations, and be placed in the role of a top-level decision-maker. By introducing a variety of situations, the case method provides a wide range of opportunities for you to apply the skills learned in business courses and to begin building confidence in your decision-making ability.

Although case study may be a new experience for you and therefore confusing at first, you will quickly see that it can increase your understanding of the complex world of strategic decision-making and sharpen your analytical skills. Case study will also enhance your knowledge of the strategic conditions in different industries. Although there is no substitute for real-world management experience, case study is "the next best thing to being there."

This case study guide is offered to familiarize you with the things that will be expected of you as a student. It will help guide you through your first cases and will show you how to prepare the analyses that will be required. The cases, which follow, represent a broad range of strategic decisions, all taken from real life. There are both large and small businesses in a variety of industries, ranging from manufacturing to service and distribution activities. There are successful organizations as well as organizations that are struggling. In some, the company and the names of managers have been disguised, but many of the organizations are ones that you will readily recognize. The majority deal with recent events, but there are also a few classic business strategy cases.

Reading and Studying the Case

Because you are expected not only to read cases as they are assigned, but to analyze them and develop sound, reasoned judgments that will lead to recommendations, the case method requires a level of preparation that often goes well beyond that required in a traditional lecture course. It is important, therefore, that you devote plenty of time to studying and analyzing each case.

To get the most out of a case, read it at least two times and, if possible, separate the two readings in time. On the first reading, go through the case rather quickly, without trying to take notes or underline. Read it as you would a magazine article or short story. Get a general idea of the situation the company is in – its industry, its position within the industry, and its competition. Note the date of the latest case information. Treat the tables and financial statements merely as illustrations rather than trying to analyze them at this time.

Before your second reading, stop and think about the case. Ask yourself, "What are the central issues?" and "What do I need to try and uncover in my analysis?" All business strategy cases revolve around one or, at most, two or three major problems or decision points. The earlier you can identify these the better, as they will guide your analysis. During your second reading of the case, take notes on the case facts that are important for analysis.

There will undoubtedly be instances when you feel that you do not have all the information you need to make the best decision. The information provided in case reports is often incomplete by design. Just as real-world managers are often called on to make decisions without extensive information, this aspect of the case method is not unlike real experience. One of the most important steps toward becoming an effective strategic decision-maker is knowing how to make the most of the limited amounts of information the environment provides.

The time frame for decisions is an important element in any case. That is, you should make decisions based only on information that was available to the managers at the time of the case date, although it may seem a bit artificial at times. You may even be required to ignore some information you may have about the company or its situation. For instance, if you are analyzing a 1986 case, your knowledge of the stock market crash of October 1987 should not affect your handling of the case. Although you are encouraged to do outside research, you should resist the temptation to second-guess the decision-makers on the basis of information they could not have had.

Your professor may assign you or other class members the responsibility of updating a case by researching recent information on the company. Examination of later information about the strategies that firms actually adopted and their subsequent outcomes often proves to be an interesting way to complete the study of a case. A company's actual strategy should not be taken as the "right" answer, however, even if it proved to be a very profitable one for the company, as any number of other recommended strategies might also have been successful.

Doing the Analysis

Organize the case facts

Cases sometimes present a bewildering number of names, titles, dates, and other facts that are hard to keep straight. Before proceeding with an in-depth analysis of the case, make sure you have a sufficient grasp of the facts. Sometimes it may be necessary to construct a chronology to help you keep in mind the sequence of significant case events and their relationships. To keep names, organizational titles, and relationships in focus, you may need to sketch a rough organization chart if one is not provided in the case. Once you have an adequate grasp of the case facts and the central issues, you are ready to begin an in-depth analysis.

Start with financial analysis

"Number crunching" is nearly always the best way to begin a case analysis, as it gives you an objective assessment of the company's performance and can help identify problem areas for further analysis. Key financial ratios must be calculated so that you can get a reading on the company's financial performance and condition. Exhibit I.1 provides a review of the most often used financial ratios (in case your ratio analysis skills are a bit rusty). Keep in mind that ratios should be interpreted only in light of the organization's situation, and remember that trends are always important. For that reason, two or more years of financial statements are usually included in the cases so that any trends in the ratios can be discerned. Industry averages with which to compare the key ratios are also helpful; if not contained in the case, these averages are available from a number of reporting services.

Converting the financial statements to "common-size" ones is also helpful. The balance sheet is common-sized by setting total assets equal to 100 percent and then calculating each balance sheet account as a percentage of total assets. Income statements are common-sized by setting net sales equal to 100 percent and then calculating each item as a percentage of net sales. With common-size statements, relative relationships among the various accounts can readily be seen and trends noted over time. These relationships and trends can indicate other problems to be investigated. Common-size statement information is best used in combination with other information. For example, a steadily increasing cost of goods sold as a percentage of net sales may indicate waste, loss of efficiencies in production, increased raw materials prices that have not been passed on to buyers, or some combination of these factors.

Financial analysis can be one of the most time consuming parts of your preparation. You can save yourself a lot of time if you do only those analyses that you need rather than using the same standard analyses for every case. Thus, you need to use your head at least as much as your calculator or computer spreadsheet. The focus should be on developing information to help you understand the company and to provide the basis for recommendations to solve its problems.

Exhibit I.1 Key financial ratios

Ratio	Formula	Expressed as
Profitability ratios		
Return on investment	$\dfrac{\text{Net income after taxes}}{\text{Total assets}}$	percentage
Return on stockholders' equity	$\dfrac{\text{Net income after taxes}}{\text{Total stockholders' equity}}$	percentage
Earnings per share	$\dfrac{\text{NIAT-preferred dividends}}{\text{No. common shares outstanding}}$	dollars
Gross profit margin	$\dfrac{\text{Sales} - \text{CGS}}{\text{Sales}}$	percentage
Operating profit margin	$\dfrac{\text{Net income before taxes and interest}}{\text{Sales}}$	percentage
Net profit margin	$\dfrac{\text{Net income after taxes}}{\text{Sales}}$	percentage
Liquidity ratios		
Current ratio	$\dfrac{\text{Current assets}}{\text{Current liabilities}}$	decimal
Quick (acid-test) ratio	$\dfrac{\text{Current assets} - \text{inventories}}{\text{Current liabilities}}$	decimal
Inventories to net working capital	$\dfrac{\text{Inventories}}{\text{Current assets} - \text{current liabilities}}$	decimal
Leverage ratios		
Debt to assets	$\dfrac{\text{Total debt}}{\text{Total assets}}$	percentage
Debt to equity	$\dfrac{\text{Total debt}}{\text{Total stockholders' equity}}$	percentage
Long-term debt to equity	$\dfrac{\text{Long-term debt}}{\text{Total stockholders' equity}}$	percentage
Times-interest earned	$\dfrac{\text{NI before taxes and interest}}{\text{Interest expenses}}$	decimal
Fixed-charge coverage	$\dfrac{\text{NI before taxes and interest} + \text{lease obligations}}{\text{Interest expenses} + \text{lease expenses}}$	decimal
Activity ratios		
Total asset turnover	$\dfrac{\text{Sales}}{\text{Total assets}}$	decimal
Fixed asset turnover	$\dfrac{\text{Sales}}{\text{Fixed assets}}$	decimal
Net working capital turnover	$\dfrac{\text{Sales}}{\text{Current assets} - \text{Current liabilities}}$	decimal
Inventory turnover	$\dfrac{\text{Sales}}{\text{Average inventory of finished goods}}$	decimal
Collection period for receivables	$\dfrac{\text{Average accounts receivable}}{\text{Annual credit sales/365}}$	days
Investment ratios		
Price-earnings ratio	$\dfrac{\text{Market price per share}}{\text{EPS}}$	decimal
Dividend payout	$\dfrac{\text{Annual dividends per share}}{\text{EPS}}$	percentage
Common stock dividend yield	$\dfrac{\text{Annual dividends per share}}{\text{Market price per share}}$	percentage

Focus your analysis

Effective case analysis must include both an internal analysis of the firm and an external analysis of the firm's operating environment. Internal analysis is usually handled by taking a functional approach, first making sure you understand the organization's top management and its corporate- and business-level objectives and strategies, and then moving on to analyze each of the company's functional-level objectives and strategies. Part II of the case analysis outline (appendix) contains a step-by-step internal analysis plan.

External analysis can best be accomplished by breaking the environment down into sectors and analyzing the influence of each sector separately. Consider the possible effects of the economy, demographics, and social change. Analyze the regulatory environment, resource availability, and technological change. Above all, do a thorough analysis of the competitive environment. Part III of the case analysis outline (appendix) lists some questions to consider in external analysis.

The analysis process can be very time consuming if one tries to analyze every aspect in detail. For that reason, you should let the key issues in each case indicate which aspects of the case you will treat in detail. The case analysis outline (appendix) can help you through the analytical process. Keep in mind that it is intended as a comprehensive resource rather than a structured checklist. You will probably want to emphasize different aspects of analysis for each individual case, as the focal points in each case are different.

Make recommendations

The end result of your analyses will be your recommendations. These should be based solely on the findings of your analysis and should include supporting evidence for any judgmental elements included. Although real-world business decisions are often subject to intuitive processes, more analytical processes are always preferred unless the decision-makers have a great deal of first-hand experience with the type of strategic problems encountered in the case. Therefore, a statement such as "My analysis shows the following . . ." is always better than "I believe the company should. . . ."

Most professors prefer that you prepare a list of several feasible alternatives to the case problems. This process allows you to compare competing solutions from which you select your recommendations. In the drafting of the solution, implementation issues should not be ignored, especially financial ones. A recommendation is always strengthened considerably if you can show that the company has the resources to accomplish it and if you present a well laid out implementation scheme including as much detail as facts allow. If you recommend a strategic change, include a timetable and budget for accomplishing the new strategy, assign specific managers the responsibility for carrying it out, and tell how the company should follow up to make sure the new strategy is successful.

Perhaps one of the hardest adjustments to make to the case method is the realization that there is no such thing as the "right" answer or even the "right" approach. After all the work you put in, there is a natural tendency to wonder, "Did I get it right?" Remember that strategic decision-making is not an exact science. Just as two businesses that adopt completely different courses of action while competing in the same markets are often both successful, different approaches and solutions to the same case also are often both "right." (It is exactly that quality that makes strategic management a challenging and interesting field.) Although no single solution or approach is the only "right" one, there are always some decisions that are better than others and some ways to approach a decision situation that are superior to other approaches. As you develop and refine your case analysis skills, you will also increase your ability to identify the conditions under which different approaches and solutions may be successful. The important thing to remember in case analysis is to justify and support your recommendations with thorough analysis.

Class Discussions

Instructors have a number of ways of handling case discussions in class. These range from structured discussion, in which specific questions about the case are asked and sometimes distributed in advance, to unstructured discussions, in which the students are given some latitude in identifying the important issues in the case and in presenting their analyses and recommendations. As most business strategy courses utilize the unstructured approach, and few students have encountered it before, we discuss it here.

A good case discussion can be a very rewarding class experience for everyone, but its success depends on good preparation by you and the right set of expectations. Keep the following points in mind.

1 Before class, reduce your analysis to two or three pages of notes. Your notes should include your list of the key issues in the case, a SWOT summary (identifying strengths, weaknesses, opportunities, and threats), key financial ratios, a list of two or three feasible alternatives, and your recommendations. Refer to these notes often during the discussion, and add any new ideas that come up.

2 One of the most important things to bring to class with you is an open mind. Once the discussion starts, you will undoubtedly find that there are nearly as many approaches to the case as there are class members. Although there is merit in standing by your convictions, keep in mind that most complicated management problems can best be approached by the refinement process, which requires decision-makers to be open to a variety of views.

3 Make the classroom time count by not rehashing case facts. Assume that everyone is familiar with the facts and get right into identifying key issues and problems and analyzing them. Strive to reach the decision-making level of participation (see exhibit I.2)

4 Remember that you cannot test your ideas if you remain silent. In an active class, that may mean that you have to assert yourself to get the floor. Be careful not to equate "air time" with participation, however. Do not dominate the conversation, especially if you have little to add.

5 If a class discussion is going well, you will discover that the professor has done very little of the talking. His or her role in the discussion is to keep the flow of

Exhibit I.2   Four levels of case discussion

Fact sharing
The lowest level of discussion. The class simply goes over case facts without really analyzing them. Symptoms of underlying problems are discussed without uncovering the problems themselves.

Problem finding
A step above fact sharing. The class goes through a structured analysis of the company.
Strengths, weaknesses, opportunities, and threats are uncovered, and the problems
underlying the symptoms are identified.

Problem solving
The third level of class discussion. Attention is directed to the problem areas, problems are
prioritized, and recommended solutions are developed for each problem area.

Decision making
The highest level of class discussion. Organizational problems are seen as a whole.
Solutions are merged into an overall strategic plan, and implementation considerations
are included.

---

ideas coming, challenge opinions that are offered, insist on reasons behind your
statements, and occasionally summarize the analysis.

Oral Presentations

Students are sometimes assigned cases to present orally, usually in teams of three
or four students. The degree of formality in the presentation is up to the professor,
but regardless of the formality, preparation for the presentation and the actual
conduct of the case in class will differ markedly from informal class discussion.
Thorough preparation will naturally be important, as the entire presentation of
issues, analysis, and decision may be up to you and the other members of your team.
Here are some points to keep in mind if you are assigned an oral case presentation:

1   Make sure the audience knows the case facts. If the case has not been assigned
    to the rest of the class to read, the first part of the presentation will have to be
    devoted to factual material. Although this step is important, keep it brief to
    allow time for your analysis. Handing out fact sheets is a good way to move this
    step along quickly.
2   It often helps to identify a role for yourself. The role of outside analyst or consult-
    ant is usually preferable to the role of corporate official, as it allows you to speak
    more objectively.
3   Organization is important, and communicating the organization of your talk
    early in the presentation is a good idea. Identify the issues early in the presenta-
    tion so you can focus on them throughout the analysis. Summarize at several
    points to remind the audience of where you are in the talk.
4   Visual aids can significantly improve a presentation, but they also can be

overdone. Prepare a few good charts and graphs to help tell the story, but don't bury the audience in needless detail.

5 Make your recommendations as thorough as you can. Always include financial and staffing plans for the implementation of your recommendations and provide for evaluation and follow-up.

6 Take questions from the floor if allowed. They are a good way to demonstrate your knowledge of the case and depth of thinking. You should set up ground rules for questions at the beginning, however, so you won't be interrupted at unwanted times.

Written Case Assignments

A written case analysis may be assigned, either as a structured paper in which you are asked to address specific issues or topics in the case, or as a comprehensive analysis. To prepare a written analysis, you should go through much the same preparation as for class discussions, but here your analysis would probably need to be more thorough.

The written format of your paper will vary according to the particular case and the wishes of your professor. If the assignment is a structured one, you may want to address the questions one by one and present your recommendations. If the unstructured approach is taken, you may need some suggestions as to how you should organize the contents of the paper. The outline in exhibit I. 3 is offered as an example that applies to most business strategy cases in your textbook.

Doing Additional Research

Case analysis sometimes requires research to find additional information about the firm or its industry in order to recommend a course of action. You may, for example, want to update the information in a case that is several years old or to investigate more thoroughly the firm's environment or competition. You may also use the library to develop your own business strategy case from secondary sources.

Fortunately, most college and university libraries and public libraries are well equipped to provide the necessary resources. The companies themselves also can be important sources of current information, and many of them will willingly provide you with copies of their quarterly and annual reports as well as other information. Company sources should not be relied on exclusively, however, as information that is unfavorable to the company is unlikely to be obtained that way.

Keep in mind that sometimes the cases use disguised company names and are therefore impossible to research directly. Also, most privately held companies do not make it a practice to share financial information with the public, as publicly held companies are required to do. This limitation can make it difficult to obtain the latest information on some companies, although you can usually obtain information about their industries. The major financial reporting services often report estimates of the sales, profits, and key ratios for private companies, and their estimates are considered quite accurate.

It is generally true that the larger the company is, the more information you

Exhibit I.3   Suggested outline for written cases

I   Introduction. Give a brief statement of the purpose of the report and how the report is organized. You might also include some basic facts about the company as a way of introduction.

II   Internal analysis.
   A   Present situation. Discuss the firm's present strategy. Describe its markets, products or services; its competitive orientation; and the scope of its activities. What is being attempted, and how? How well is it working?
   B   Financial resources. Describe the financial condition of the company and assess its ability to meet the demands of its environment and to provide for future growth.
   C   Strengths and weaknesses. Discuss the company's strong and weak points as uncovered in your analysis of the various functional areas.

III   External analysis.
   A   General environment. Describe any feature of the economic, technological, regulatory, physical, and social environments that is relevant to the organization's future.
   B   Operating environment. Describe the competitive environment. Who are the competitors? What are their strengths and weaknesses?
   C   Opportunities and threats. Summarize all of the relevant issues uncovered by your external analysis.

IV   Key decisions. Identify the main points at issue in the case. What are the problems and decisions the company faces? What should be the focus of the recommendations?

V   Alternatives. Describe each of the possible strategies the firm could adopt. Discuss each one and include its strong and weak points.

VI   Recommended decisions. Tell what you think the company should do. What should its strategy be? Justify your choice on the basis of analysis. Discuss implementation, evaluation, and follow-up. Include time estimates for implementation and financial staffing plans where appropriate.

VII   Appendices, tables, and graphs.

will find. Most of the Fortune 500 size companies discussed in the cases are the subjects of many news articles, industry analyses, and trade reports, and therefore make excellent subjects for secondary case research.

Working in Teams

Just as strategic decisions in real businesses are often the products of teams of managers working together, professors frequently assign class members to teams for the preparation of case reports in order to provide a more realistic experience in the decision-making process. Teamwork may be a new experience for you and the other members of your team. The following points may make your team experience a more successful and satisfying one:

1. Determine the relative strengths and skills of team members and divide the work to take advantage of them. Breaking the analysis down into distinctive parts will avoid duplication of effort.

2. Meet often and work as a team. Remember that your performance on the assignment depends on each other. Make sure that meetings are scheduled when all members can attend and that meetings are planned ahead of time.

3. Use consensus processes and make decisions jointly. Make sure the final product is consistent throughout. Teams often make the mistake of presenting a final paper or presentation that is simply an accumulation of parts instead of a single analysis with a unified set of recommendations.

Summary

This chapter presents a general framework for analyzing strategic management cases and developing case reports. These guidelines may seem long to you now, but as you become more familiar with the process, much of it will become automatic. The purpose is to get you started on the road to formulating effective strategic decisions and communicating the results of your analyses.

Case analysis, like any other valuable skill, takes time to develop and requires concentration and hard work. The rewards are plentiful, however. In addition, case analysis is very personal. Every successful decision-maker eventually adopts a style that is his or her own. For that reason, you will probably find it necessary to modify the framework presented in this chapter to fit your own work habits and decision style. We suggest that you follow this guide closely until you feel comfortable with the process, and then use it only occasionally to review your own procedure and analyses.

APPENDIX: CASE ANALYSIS OUTLINE

I The present situation

A *Mission, Objectives, Strategies, Policies*

1. Mission. What business(es) is the company in? Is the mission relatively stable or undergoing change.

2. Objectives. What is the company trying to accomplish? Are corporate-level, business-level, and functional objectives consistent with the corporate mission and with each other? Are objectives written down, or must they be inferred from performances?

3. Strategies. How is the company attempting to achieve its objectives? Are the strategies consistent with the mission and objectives? Are strategies coordinated, or do they appear to be developed piece-meal?

4. Policies. Does the corporation have well-developed guidelines for carrying out its strategies? Do they seem to enhance or hinder goal accomplishments?

B   *Corporate Performance*

    1 Financial performance. Is the company's financial performance adequate? What is its net profit margin, its return on investment, and earnings per share? What are the trends in these overall measures of performance?

    2 Goals. How well is the organization meeting its objectives? Does present performance match expectations?

    3 Competitive stance. Is the company remaining competitive in its industry? Is it maintaining or enhancing its market share?

II Internal analysis – strengths and weaknesses

A   *Organizational Structure and Corporate Culture*

    1 Type. What type of organizational structure does the firm have: simple, functional, divisional, horizontal, or matrix?

    2 Centralization. Is decision making centralized at top management levels, or decentralized throughout the organization?

    3 Culture. Is there a well-defined culture? Is the culture market-oriented, product-oriented, or technology-oriented?

    4 Consistency. Are the company's structure and culture consistent with the firm's objectives and strategies?

B   *Top Management and Board of Directors*

    1 The CEO. How would you rate the CEO in terms of knowledge, skills, and abilities? Is his or her overall management style autocratic or participative?

    2 The board. Is the board of directors directly involved in the strategic management process, or is it a "rubber-stamp" board?

    3 Top managers. How would you rate the overall capability of the top management team? Is there an adequate plan for executive succession and training for top management positions?

C   *Financial Management*

    1 Functional objectives and strategies. Does the company have clearly stated financial objectives and strategies? Are they consistent with the company's overall objectives?

    2 Profitability. How is the company performing in terms of profitability ratios? How does this performance compare with past performance and industry averages? Does a common-sized income statement reveal any discrepancies in the components of net income?

    3 Liquidity and cash management. How is the firm performing in terms of its liquidity ratios? Are cash-flow problems indicated? How do the ratios compare with past performance and industry averages?

    4 Leverage and capital management. Is the firm's leverage appropriate, as evidenced by its leverage ratios? Is the amount of leverage in keeping with the industry and the company's strategies for expansion?

    5 Asset management. Are inventories, fixed assets, and other resources being effectively managed as indicated by the activity ratios? How do these ratios compare with the firm's past performance and other firms in the industry?

    6 Financial planning and control. What individuals are involved in the firm's financial planning? How often are budgets prepared? How closely are spending decisions monitored, and who has the authority to control financial resources? How sophisticated are the financial and asset management systems of the firm?

D   *Operations Management*

1   Technical core. Does the technical core of the organization center on production, service, or merchandising?
2   Capacity. Is the productive capacity of the firm adequate for present needs and for future growth in operations?
3   Quality. Is the quality of the product or service in keeping with customers' expectations and the company's goals? Are quality assurance systems in place and functioning properly?
4   Efficiency. Is operating efficiency adequate? Can it be improved?

E   *Marketing Management*

1   Product. What is the company's present mix of products and/or services? At what stages in their product life cycles are they? Who are the firm's target customers? Is there a readily identifiable product-mission philosophy?
2   Price. Are prices competitive and in keeping with product quality and the target market? Is price determination demand-based, competitive, or on a cost-plus basis?
3   Place. Is the distribution system adequate? Does the company maintain its own sales team or depend on outside firms? Is it an integrated part of the company or separately controlled? Are relations with the sales force and distributors good? Do compensation systems provide the right amount of incentives?
4   Promotion. How does the company advertise and promote its products or services? Is the promotion effective? Is promotion designed in-house or by outside firms?
5   Marketing information systems. How does the company identify new markets or target groups? Is the marketing department involved in the development of new products? How does the company exchange information with the distribution system?

F   *Human Resources Management*

1   Human resources planning. Is there an effective human resources planning effort? Are personnel requirements included in strategy formulation and facilities planning?
2   Obtaining personnel. Are adequate processes in place for obtaining qualified personnel? How are personnel recruited and selected?
3   Retaining and improving human resources. Are training programs effective? Are performance evaluation and improvement managed effectively? Are grievances handled well?
4   Compensation. Is the compensation system effective and fair? Is pay generally competitive or above competitive levels? Are fringe benefits high or low for the industry? Does the firm have a profit-sharing plan?

5 Labor relations. If the company is unionized, are relations with labor organizations congenial or combative?

G *Research and Development*

1 Organization. Is there one centralized R&D department, or is R&D decentralized?

2 Level of R&D effort. What percentage of the firm's resources are devoted to the R&D effort? How does this compare with competitors?

3 Control. How is the R&D effort controlled? Where in the organization is policy established for R&D?

4 Product development. How effective is R&D in bringing new products to market?

H *Management Information Systems*

1 Is a management information system in use at all levels – operational, middle management, and top management?

2 Is the system adequate to meet information needs at each level?

3 Does the organization use a centralized MIS or independent decentralized systems for various departments and functions?

4 Is the MIS cost-effective?

5 Does the strategic management process make use of a decision support system (DSS) to aid in strategic analysis?

III External analysis – opportunities and threats

A *Economic Environment*

What is forecast for the industry, and how are economic events likely to affect this firm? How would an inflationary period or a recession affect product demand?

B *Technological Environment*

What innovations are likely to occur that will affect either products and services or production processes? Is the rate of change in technology increasing or slowing?

C *Regulatory Environment*

Are there any present or expected government and/or industry regulations that present either threats or opportunities? Are there ongoing efforts to monitor or actively participate in the regulatory process?

D *Physical Environment*

Can we expect any significant depletion of needed resources? Will there be any changes in the physical surroundings of the organization that might affect the accomplishment of its goals or present opportunities?

E *Social/Demographic Environment*

Are any important demographic changes in customers, suppliers, or the labor pool expected? Are tastes and preferences changing in a way that might affect this firm?

F *Competitive Environment*

Who are the firm's competitors? What are their market shares? How effective are they? How likely is the entrance of new competition? Are there close substitutes for the company's products or services?

G *Customer Environment*

Who are the current and future customers. What are their requirements? How does the firm provide value to current customers? How will the firm provide value to future customers?

HARLEY-DAVIDSON, INC.

Sexton Adams and Adelaide Griffin

Company History

The year was 1903. Henry Ford introduced the first Model A, the Wright brothers flew over Kitty Hawk, and, in a shack near Milwaukee, Wisconsin, a machine called the Silent Grey Fellow was born. Three brothers, William, Walter, and Arthur Davidson, had invented a machine that would exemplify "the American desire for power, speed and personal freedom" – the Harley-Davidson motorcycle.

The Davidsons' first crude machines found a ready market among both individuals and law enforcement agencies, and by 1907, production had reached 150 motorcycles per year. Two years later, a new engine, the V-twin, enabled motorcycles to attain top speeds of 60 m.p.h. Motorcycles were fast becoming the primary source of transportation in the United States.

The Harley-Davidson Motorcycle Company took pride in America. When the USA joined Europe in the First World War, Harley-Davidson motorcycles helped the US Army chase the Kaiser across Germany. After the First World War, however, it was the automobile, not the motorcycle, that gained popularity as America's principal means of transportation. Harley's annual production plunged from 28,000 to 10,000 units immediately after the war. After a decade of struggle, Harley-Davidson again reached prewar production levels, only to be ravaged by the Great Depression. In 1933, only 3700 motorcycles were produced by Harley-Davidson.

This case was prepared by students Scott Draper, A. Scott Dundon, Allen North, and Ron Smith under the supervision of Professor Sexton Adams, University of North Texas, and Professor Adelaide Griffin, Texas Woman's University, as a basis for classroom discussion and not to illustrate either effective or ineffective handling of administrative situations. © 1990, Sexton Adams and Adelaide Griffin.

The economic boost provided by the Second World War and the military's high demand for motorcycles enabled Harley-Davidson to again match its 1920 production level. But after the Second World War, the motorcycle industry crashed. As America's heroes returned, their focus was on housing and family necessities, not motorcycles. At one time Harley-Davidson was one of 150 US motorcycle manufacturers, but by 1953, the weak motorcycle market had eliminated Harley's final US competitor, Indian Motorcycle Company. Harley-Davidson stood alone as the sole manufacturer of motorcycles in the United States.

The AMF reign

Harley-Davidson made its first public stock offering in 1965, and shortly thereafter, the struggle for control of Harley-Davidson began. In 1969, Bangor Punta, an Asian company with roots in the railroad industry, began acquiring large amounts of Harley-Davidson stock. At the same time, AMF, an international leader in the recreational goods market, announced its interest in Harley-Davidson, citing a strong fit between Harley-Davidson's product lines and AMF's leisure lines. Bangor Punta and AMF entered a bidding war over Harley-Davidson. Harley's stockholders chose AMF's bid of $22 per share over Bangor Punta's bid of $23 per share because of Bangor Punta's reputation for acquiring a company, squeezing it dry, and then scrapping it for salvage. AMF's plans for expansion initially were perceived as more favorable for Harley-Davidson's long-term existence.

AMF's plans did not, however, correspond with Harley-Davidson's ability to expand. Much of Harley-Davidson's equipment was antiquated and could not keep up with the increase in production. One company official noted that "quality was going down just as fast as production was going up." These events occurred at a time when Japanese motorcycle manufacturers began flooding the US market with high-quality, low-cost motorcycles that offered many innovative features.

Many of Harley's employees felt that if AMF had worked with the experienced Harley personnel instead of dictating orders for production quotas, many of the problems could have been properly addressed. One Harley senior executive stated that "the bottom line was that quality went to hell because AMF expanded Harley production at the same time that Harleys were getting out of date, and the Japanese were coming to town with new designs and reliable products at a low price." Unlike their Japanese competitors, whose motorcycles failed to pass inspection an average 5 percent of the time, Harley's motorcycles failed to pass the end-of-assembly-line inspection at an alarming 50–60 percent rate.

After a $4.8 million annual operating loss and 11 years under AMF control, Harley-Davidson was put up for sale in 1981. A management team led by Vaughn Beals, vice-president of motorcycles sales, used $81.5 million in financing from Citicorp to complete a leveraged buyout. All ties with AMF were severed and Harley-Davidson, Inc. was created.

The tariff barrier

Harley-Davidson had managed to obliterate its US competition during the 1950s and 1960s, but the company took a beating from the Japanese in the 1970s. Japanese competition and the recession presiding over the nation's economy had taken nearly all of Harley-Davidson's business. The company's meager 3 percent share of total motorcycle sales led experts to speculate whether or not Harley-Davidson would be able to celebrate its eightieth birthday. Tariff protection appeared to be Harley-Davidson's only hope. Fortunately, massive lobbying efforts finally paid off in 1983, when Congress passed a huge tariff increase on Japanese motor-cycles. Instead of a 4 percent tariff, Japanese motorcycles would now be subject to a 45 percent tariff. The protection was to last for five years.

Slowly, Harley-Davidson began to recover market share as the tariff had its impact on competitors. Management was able to relinquish its ownership with a public stock offering in 1986. Brimming with confidence, Harley-Davidson asked Congress to remove the tariff barrier in December 1986, more than a year earl-ier than originally planned. It was time to strap on the helmet and race with the Japanese head to head.

Acquisition and diversification

Holiday Rambler was purchased in 1986 by Harley-Davidson, a move that nearly doubled the size of the firm. As a wholly owned subsidiary, the manufacturer of recreational and commercial vehicles provided Harley-Davidson with another business unit that could diversify the risks associated with the seasonal motorcycle market. That move gave Harley-Davidson two distinct business segments, Holiday Rambler Corporation and Harley-Davidson Motorcycle Division. In addition, dur-ing the late 1980s, Harley-Davidson attempted to capitalize on its manufacturing expertise by competing for both government and contract manufacturing oppor-tunities in an attempt to further increase the proportion of revenues derived from nonmotorcycle sources.

Holiday Rambler Corporation

Harley-Davidson implemented many new management techniques at Holiday Rambler. The Yadiloh program was created in 1989. Yadiloh was "Holiday" spelled backwards and an acronym for "Yes Attitude, Deliver, Involvement, Leadership, Opportunity, Harmony." The goal of Yadiloh was to address cost and productivity problems facing Holiday Rambler. The employees of Holiday Rambler seemed to favor the program. "This program will help us solve a lot of problems in the long run. So I think it's a really big step, a positive step," said Raud Estep, a quality con-trol inspector for Holiday Rambler. Another employee, Vickie Hutsell, agreed: "I think that most of the people who've gone through the Yadiloh training session are 'pumped up' about it."

But Holiday Rambler's new owners did more than get employees excited. They built a new, centralized facility, scheduled to be completed in late 1990, to handle all of the company's manufacturing needs. They also installed more computer aided design (CAD) equipment to support the research and development staff, which led to a $1.9 million increase in operating expenses.

Observers, however, felt that the success of Holiday Rambler was mixed at best. Several strong competitors had entered the recreational vehicle (RV) market in 1988. Holiday Rambler responded by discontinuing its Trail Seeker line of RVs after the unit experienced a $30 million sales decline in 1988. Holiday Rambler continued to trim poor performing areas. In October 1989, Parkway Distribution, a recreational vehicle parts and accessories distributor, was sold. A $2.8 million decline in revenues from the business units of Creative Dimensions, Nappanee Wood Products, and B & B Molders was recorded in 1989. Holiday Rambler enacted competitive pricing measures and a lower-margin sales mix in 1989. The result was a decrease in gross margin percentage, from 19 percent to 18.2 percent.

Some industry experts recognized a possible recovery for the sluggish RV market in 1990. However, the message of H. Wayne Dahl, Holiday Rambler president, was unclear. "Whether our business is RVs, commercial vehicles or a related enterprise, we intend to keep it strong and growing by keeping in close touch with its customers."

In 1986, Harley executives claimed that the acquisition of Holiday Rambler would help diversify the risks associated with the seasonal motorcycle market. However, some industry experts questioned whether such an acquisition was a wise move for Harley. They pointed out that although the acquisition smoothed seasonal fluctuations in demand, cyclical fluctuations caused by the economy were unaffected. One expert asserted, "Because both items [motorcycles and recreational vehicles] are luxury goods, they are dependent on such key economic factors as interest rates, disposable income, and gasoline prices."

In addition to the economy, the demographics of the RV market presented a challenge to Harley. The main consumer of RVs in the 1970s was the blue-collar worker who worked a steady 40 hours per week. However, economic trends led to a switch from manufacturing to a more service-oriented economy. The trends left most consumers with little time on their hands for recreational activities. Statistics revealed in 1989 that the typical owner of an RV was between 35 and 54 years old with an average income of $39,800. Census projections also indicated that the American population was growing older at the end of the 1980s. The high incomes and older ages gave RV manufacturers the opportunity to include extra features that allowed them to raise total vehicle prices by $20,000 and more.

The RV industry had support from nonconsumer groups that existed specifically to accommodate the RV owner. The Escapees, for instance, offered insurance and cash handling services to members driving RVs. The Good Sam's Club provided road service to RVs in need of repair. RV owners were even treated to their own television program to watch while on the road – *Wish You Were Here*. The show, broadcast via satellite by the Nashville channel, highlighted RV lifestyles through interviews with owners across the country.

Management

Vaughn Beals's outward appearance was far removed from the burly image that many might have expected of a Harley chief executive. The middle-aged Ivy Leaguer graduated from MIT's Aeronautical Engineering School and was known in manufacturing circles as a productivity guru. But, on the inside, Vaughn Beals was a "Hog" (a Harley fanatic) in the truest sense of the word. He began working with Harley-Davidson as vice-president of motorcycle sales with AMF. Disgruntled with AMF's declining attention to quality, Beals led a team of 12 others that successfully completed a leveraged buyout from AMF.

But Beals had a difficult mission ahead. Even after receiving tariff protection, Harley-Davidson had to find a way to restore confidence in its products. So Beals decided to hit the high road – literally. He drove Harley-Davidson motorcycles to rallies, where he met Harley owners. In doing so, Beals was able to learn about product defects and needed improvements directly from the consumer. Industry experts believed that these efforts were vital to the resurgence of the company.

Willie G. Davidson, grandson of the company's founder, rode along with Vaughn Beals on Harley's road to recovery. "Willie G." provided a sharp contrast to Beals. If Vaughn Beals looked more at home in a courtroom, Davidson might have looked more at home behind the bars of a jail cell. His appearance was that of a middle-aged remnant of the 1960s. A Viking helmet covered his long, stringy hair, and his beard hid the hard features of a wind-parched face. He wore a leather jacket that, like his face, showed the cracks of wear and tear that the miles of passage over US highways had caused. Nonetheless, Willie G. was named the new vice-president of design for Harley in 1981. Industry observers believed that he was instrumental in instigating much-needed improvements in the Harley Hog.

Beals stepped down as CEO in 1989, passing the reins to Richard Teerlink, who was then serving as chief operating officer for Harley-Davidson Motorcycle Division. Beals, however, retained his position as chairman of the board. After the transition, Harley-Davidson retained a long list of experienced executives. The organizational chart in exhibit 1.1 highlights the depth of the Harley-Davidson management team.

In a somewhat ironic turn of events, Beals and other executives of Harley-Davidson had traveled to Japan in 1981 to visit the factories of their competition in an attempt to uncover any secrets. What they found was surprising. The Japanese did not run a low-cost production facility with sophisticated machinery; instead, they simply used effective management techniques to maximize productivity. Armed with a new management perspective from the Japanese, Harley-Davidson began implementing quality circles, statistical operations controls, and just-in-time (JIT) inventory.

The first dramatic change implemented by Harley management was to divide each plant into four to seven profit centers. The managers of each profit center were assigned total responsibility within their particular area. The increase in responsibility gave plant managers more authority and allowed Harley-Davidson to greatly reduce the staff functions previously needed to assist production. Harley-Davidson was able to reduce its employee work force by 40 percent after implementing these changes. In 1982 the company adopted a JIT system for control of "in-plant" manufacturing and a materials-as-needed (MAN) system that dealt with control of all inventories both inside and outside the plants.

Next, Harley-Davidson attempted to increase employee involvement through the formation of quality circles (QCs). Thomas Gelb, Harley's executive vice-president of operations, noted that even though QCs were only a small part of employee involvement' programs, they played a significant role in helping to break down the communication barriers between line workers and supervisors. Line workers who

Exhibit 1.1 Harley-Davidson organizational chart

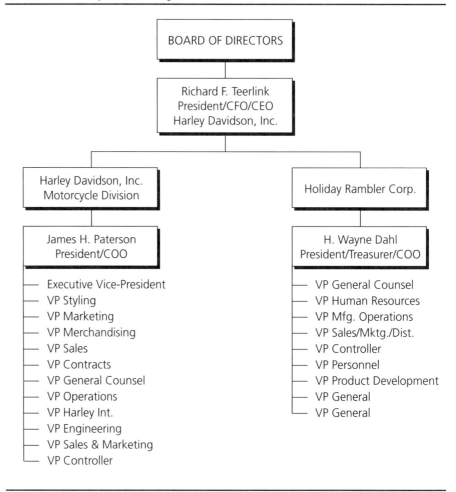

Source: Harley-Davidson, Inc.

were previously given quotas from high-level management became involved, through the use of QCs, in setting more realistic quotas based on actual production capacity and needs. Employee involvement gave workers a real sense of ownership in meeting these goals, according to Gelb. Employees were viewed as links in a chain, and through employee involvement programs they could drive quality throughout the organization. Employees were involved, by direct participation, in discussions and decisions on changes that affected them in the performance of their own work. Also, management trained employees on ways to recognize and eliminate waste in the production process. According to 1986 figures, Harley's tab for warranty repairs, scrap, and reworking of parts had decreased by 60 percent since 1981.

Employee involvement was further increased through a program called statistical operator control (SOC). SOC gave employees the responsibility for checking the quality of their own work within a predetermined range. Employee quality checks took place on the production floor, and on many occasions, the workers themselves were given the responsibility for making the proper correcting adjustments. SOC helped to identify errors in the production process on a timely basis and gave line workers more responsibility.

Although employees became more involved at Harley, labor relations remained strained. Management implemented an open-door policy to improve labor relations and increased stock options to include a broader base of employees. Management took a more sensitive stance toward the opinions of all employees. Union relations also improved when management voluntarily agreed to put the union label on all motorcycles produced and to share financial information with union leaders. Harley attempted to deal with all employees, even those affected by layoffs, in a humane way. Several employee assistance programs were put into place. Among these were outplacement assistance to cushion the blow of layoffs, early retirement (age 55) or voluntary layoffs, and drug abuse programs administered by the Milwaukee Council on Drug Abuse.

In order for these changes to work, Harley developed several overall goals. As stated in the annual report, Harley's 1989 management goals included improvement of quality, employee satisfaction, customer satisfaction, and shareholder return. The company's long-term focus would address four major areas of concern for the 1990s: quality, productivity, participation, and flexibility.

- *Quality.* Management efforts in the late 1980s attempted to overcome the company's reputation for poor quality. Because most of Harley's upper management believed that quality improvement was an ongoing process, they made a commitment to a long-term goal.
- *Participation and productivity.* These two areas were overlapping objectives, according to Harley executives. Because of this connection, the company emphasized employee involvement programs throughout the firm.
- *Flexibility.* The diminishing domestic marketplace and the slowing US economy created the need for flexibility. Harley-Davidson management hoped to explore other options for the firm.

Management hoped to lead rather than follow the competition. In 1990, Harley cultivated the phrase "Do the right thing and do that thing right."

Production and Operations

After the leveraged buyout, manufacturing was still a major problem. According to one Harley executive, fewer than 70 percent of motorcycles were complete when they reached the end of the assembly line. Motorcycle production schedules were often based on the parts that were available instead of the planned master schedule. According to industry experts, "Japanese manufacturing techniques were yielding operating costs 30 percent lower than Harley's." How did the Japanese do it? Though Beals and other managers had visited Japanese plants in

1981, it was not until they got a chance to tour Honda's assembly plant in Marysville, Ohio, after the buyout that they began to understand Japanese competion. Beals said, "We were being wiped out by the Japanese because they were better *managers*. It wasn't robotics, or culture, or morning calisthenics and company songs – it was professional managers who understood their business and paid attention to detail." Harley managers attributed most of the difference to three specific Japanese practices: quality circles, the use of statistical operations controls to ensure consistently high quality, and just-in-time manufacturing. The company quickly began to initiate the Japanese techniques.

The just-in-time inventory method

A pilot JIT manufacturing program was quickly introduced in the Milwaukee engine plant. Tom Gelb, senior vice-president of operations, called a series of meetings with employees and told them bluntly, "We have to play the game the way the Japanese play or we're dead."

Gelb's program was met with extreme skepticism. The York, Pennsylvania, plant, for instance, was already equipped with a computer-based control system that utilized overhead conveyors and high-rise parts storage. In a meeting with the workforce of the York facility, Gelb announced that the JIT system would replace these effects with push carts. The production floor erupted with laughter. Surely, this was a joke. Plant managers mumbled that Harley-Davidson was returning to 1930.

Observers noted that the overriding principle of the JIT method was that "parts and raw materials should arrive at the factory just as they are needed in the manufacturing process. This lets the manufacturer eliminate inventories and the costs of carrying them." Anne Thundercloud, the York plant quality circle facilitator, stated that "it is the Harley employees who make JIT work, by having an investment in seeing it work." The same men and women who laughed out loud over the implementation of JIT began to believe in JIT's "exacting discipline." Their belief was justified: nearly 60,000 square feet of warehouse space were freed, and costs of production plummeted. In 1986, Harley was able to lower its break-even point to 35,000 units, down from 53,000 in 1981.

Supplier cooperation was also critical to JIT success, but Harley-Davidson had a poor track record with its vendors. As one industry observer noted, "Harley was notorious for juggling production schedules and was one of the worst customers when it came to last-minute panic calls for parts." Furthermore, suppliers were wary of their role in the JIT picture. Edward J. Hay of Rath & Strong, a Lexington, Massachusetts, management consulting firm, stated, "The big problem is that companies treat just-in-time as a way of getting the suppliers to hold the inventories." One expert noted that Harley had to "abandon the security blanket that inventory often represented for them and learn to trust their suppliers."

Critics believed that Harley erred initially by taking a legalistic approach in trying to sign up suppliers for a JIT system. The company insisted on contracts that were 35 pages long, devoted largely to spelling out suppliers' obligations to Harley. This strategy was ambitious and too pretentious. Early results did not meet management's expectations, and the animosity was growing between Harley and its suppliers. One Harley supplier contended, "They're constantly renegotiating contracts, and tinkering with the layout of the plant."

Finally, the company took positive steps to improve vendor relations. Contracts were reduced to two pages. According to one Harley executive, "We need to get out of the office and meet face-to-face." Experts noted, "Teams of its buyers and engineers fanned out to visit suppliers: they began simplifying and improving designs and helping suppliers reduce setup time between jobs by modifying equipment to permit quick changes of dies. To improve the quality of the parts, Harley gave suppliers courses in statistics to teach workers how to chart small changes in the performance of their equipment. The practice provides early tip-offs when machines are drifting out of tolerance."

In 1986 Harley-Davidson began pressing some of its suppliers to start passing up the line more of the cost savings that JIT afforded. "It's time," said Patrick T. Keane, project engineer at Harley's York, Pennsylvania, plant, "to enter an era of negotiated price decreases. And right now we are holding meetings to accomplish that."

After five years of using JIT, reviews poured in. Between 1981 and 1988 the following results were achieved:

1 Inventory had been reduced by 67 percent.
2 Productivity climbed by 50 percent.
3 Scrap and rework were down two-thirds.
4 Defects per unit were down 70 percent.

Some industry experts believed that "the results for Harley and its suppliers have been good, although the company still has not achieved all its goals." "We are very inefficient," said Keane, "but the comparison of where we were five years ago is phenomenal."

Materials-as-needed

Harley's MAN system was tailored after that of Toyota's and was driven by "Kanban" technology – a control system that used circulating cards and standard containers for parts. The system provided real-time production needs information without the use of costly and complex resources that were typically needed for planning and support. Tom Schwarz, general manager of Harley-Davidson Transportation Company, developed a strategically controlled inbound system for dealing with suppliers. As one executive noted, "Harley's ultimate goal is to control all inbound and outbound shipments themselves. They prefer to keep a minimum [number] of carriers involved. That reduces the chance of delays." Harley-Davidson used its own leased fleet of 26 tractors and 46 trailers for the bulk of its road miles and used contract carriers only to supplement direct point service to its 700 dealers.

Harley-Davidson then began to evaluate its present suppliers based on manufacturing excellence and ability to provide small and frequent deliveries instead of evaluating suppliers strictly on price. Harley's trucks made daily, timed pickups from five to six suppliers on a predetermined route. Over the course of a week, the truck brought in all inbound shipments from 26–30 important vendors within a

200-mile radius of the plant. This type of system also allowed for frequent, small deliveries while helping to reduce freight costs. From 1981 to 1986, MAN cut York's inbound freight costs (mostly from vendor billing) by $50,000.

Other important elements in keeping freight costs down were the elimination of nonproductive travel and Harley's new purchase order system. The company reported in 1986 that only 4 percent of the two million miles that its fleet traveled in the past year were empty. Harley changed its purchase order system in 1986 so that the only prices it would acknowledge were FOB vendors' shipping docks. This prevented suppliers from including freight in their prices and in turn discouraged them from using their own carriers for shipments to the motorcycle maker's plants.

Quality

In the 1970s, the running joke among industry experts was "If you're buying a Harley, you'd better buy two – one for spare parts." After the buyout from AMF, Harley-Davidson strove to restore consumer confidence by raising the quality of its motorcycles. Harley-Davidson's quality improvements did not go unnoticed. John Davis, a Harley dealer mechanic, stated, "I've been wrenching on Harley-Davidson motorcycles for 26 years. I think the main key to their success is quality. And since '84 they have been very good." Teerlink boasted in his 1990 letter to shareholders that Harley-Davidson would be competing for the Malcolm Baldrige National Quality Award in 1991. "We will follow the example established by the 1990 winner [Cadillac]."

Harley's commitment to quality may have led management to opt not to carry any product liability insurance since 1987. One Harley executive commented, "We do not believe that carrying product liability insurance is financially prudent." Instead, Harley created a form of self-insurance through reserves to cover potential liabilities.

Other production

In 1988, Teerlink proudly stated, "Capitalizing on is reputation as a world class manufacturer, Harley-Davidson is developing a strong contract manufacturing business. In April of 1988, the company became the first Army Munitions and Chemical Command (AMCCOM) contractor to be certified under the US Army's Contractor Performance Certification Program. The company achieved the certification for its application of advanced manufacturing techniques in the production of 500-pound casings for the US Army. Additionally, the company is the sole supplier of high-altitude rocket motors for target drones built by Beech Aircraft."

Harley-Davidson formed an agreement with Acustar, Inc., a subsidiary of Chrysler Corporation, in early 1988 to produce machined components for its Marine and Industrial Division. Harley also manufactured small engines for Briggs & Stratton. The company planned to further broaden its contract manufacturing business by aggressively marketing its proven and innovative manufacturing efficiencies to the industrial community. For 1990, management placed a goal of nonmotorcycle production to reach 25–30 percent. Teerlink felt strongly that "this goal is actually quite conservative and can be easily accomplished."

International operations

The international markets of England, Italy, and other European countries were hardly uncharted territory for Harley-Davidson. Since 1915, Harley-Davidson had been selling its products in these overseas markets. Harley-Davidson's international efforts increased significantly during the mid-1980s. In 1984, the company produced 5000 motorcycles for export; projections for 1990 called for production in the 20,000 unit range.

Several international markets exploded for Harley-Davidson in the late 1980s. In 1989, Harley motorcycle sales grew in France by 92 percent, England by 91 percent, and Australia by 32 percent. Europeans also bought other Harley products, such as T-shirts and leather jackets. Clyde Fessler, director of trademark licensing for Harley-Davidson, said, "In Europe we're considered Americana."

Marketing

> *When it comes to pleasuring the major senses, no motorcycle on earth can compare to a Harley. That's why I've tattooed my Harley's name on the inside of my mouth.*
>
> Lou Reed

Probably not every Harley-Davidson owner has Lou Reed's loyalty. Nonetheless, loyalty to Harley-Davidson has almost always been virtually unparalleled. According to the company's research, 92 percent of its customers remain with Harley. Even with strong brand loyalty, however, Harley's marketing division did not reduce its advertising. Harley-Davidson limited its advertising focus to print media, opting not to explore a radio or television campaign. The company used print ads in a variety of magazines, including trade magazines and the company's own trade publication, *The Enthusiast*. The advertising department, headed by Carmichael Lynch, had the benefit of a very well known company name. Unfortunately, the company name also carried serious image problems.

One major problem that plagued Harley's marketing efforts was that bootleggers were ruining the Harley-Davidson name by placing it on unlicensed, unauthorized goods of poor quality. Furthermore, society was turning away from the attitudes of the 1960s. With antidrug messages becoming a prevalent theme in American society, Harley-Davidson found itself linked to an image of the pot-smoking, beer-drinking, women-chasing, tattoo-covered, leather-clad biker. One industry expert observed, "When your company's logo is the number one request in tattoo parlors, it's time to get a licensing program that will return your reputation to the ranks of baseball, hot dogs, and apple pie." This image problem was not ignored by management. Kathleen Demitros, who became director of marketing in 1983, stated, "One of our problems was that we had such a hard-core image out there that it was basically turning off a lot of people." Demitros was speaking from experience. The Milwaukee native had been with the company since 1971. Like many of the company executives, she owned a Harley. By her own admission, Demitros chose not to ride her "Hog" to work. She saved it for the weekends.

Harley-Davidson took a proactive approach to solving the image problem. Managers created a licensing division responsible for eliminating the bootlegged products. This new division was led by John Heiman, formerly a mechanical accessories products manager. Goods with the Harley-Davidson logo would have to be sold by licensed dealers to be legal. Using warrants and federal marshals, Heiman went to conventions of motorcycle enthusiasts and began to put an end to the bootleggers.

Harley-Davidson then began to concentrate its efforts on a wide variety of products, ranging from leather jackets to cologne and jewelry, to supplement motorcycle sales. The concept was not new to Harley-Davidson. As far back as the 1920s, Harley had designed and sold leather jackets. The hope was that consumers would buy the other products, get comfortable with the Harley name, and then consider purchasing Harley motorcycles. One company executive said, "It helped pull us through the lean years." In 1988, he continued, "we sold 35,000 bikes and over 3 million fashion tops." For Harley-Davidson, these sales were crucial in offsetting the seasonal market of the motorcycle industry. Industry observers applauded Harley on this marketing ploy. "Historically, the winter months are tough on sales for the motorcycle industry. Harley-Davidson has been successful at selling fashion items." A Harley marketing executive went one step further. "If we can't sell someone a bike in the winter, we'll sell them a leather jacket instead."

Essentially, the licensing division had become an extension of marketing. Heiman said, "If you've got a 6-year-old boy wearing Harley pajamas, sleeping on Harley sheets and bathing with Harley towels, the old man's not going to be bringing home a Suzuki." In addition, retailers found that the licensed goods were popular. Major retail chains began selling Harley-Davidson products. The logic behind the selection Harley goods was simple: "Harley is the only motorcycle made in the United States today, and I thought with pride in America high, the time was right for the licensed goods," explained one major retailer. However, the hard-core biker image of Harley-Davidson was still a strong influence. For example, when Fifth Avenue Cards, Inc. decided to sell Harley items, it did so in a satirical manner. According to Ethel Sloan, the card store chain's vice-president of merchandising, "We were definitely shooting for tongue-in-cheek, selling this macho, all-black coloration merchandise to bankers in three-piece suits – it was a real hoot!" It may have been this cynical and virtually unexpected market that Vaughn Beals hoped to exploit. Beals predicted the emergence of a new breed of Harley customer. "We're on the road to prosperity in this country, and we'll get there on a Harley."

The customers he spoke of began to buy Harleys in record numbers. The new Harley consumers were bankers, doctors, lawyers, and entertainers who developed an affection for "Hogs." They became known as Rubbies – Rich Urban Bikers. The Rubbies were not frightened by the high price tags associated with the Harley-Davidson product line. The Sportster 883, which was Harley's trademark motorcycle, and the Nova, which was specifically designed to capture the college student market, sold in a price range of $14,000–15,000 in 1987.

Harley continued to expand its product line in 1988 with the addition of the Springer Softail, the Ultra Classic Electra Glide, and the Ultra Classic Tour Glide. James Paterson, president and chief operating officer of the Motorcycle Division, commented, "The Springer goes to the heart of Harley-Davidson, the custom-cruiser type of motorcycle. The Ultra Classics . . . are aimed at the touring market, . . . a market we couldn't reach previously." Product line expansion continued in 1989 with a move that several industry observers thought to be a questionable

Exhibit 1.2 US market share of super heavyweight motorcycles, 1989 (percent)

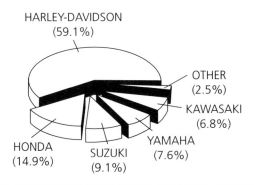

HARLEY-DAVIDSON
(59.1%)

OTHER
(2.5%)

KAWASAKI
(6.8%)

YAMAHA
(7.6%)

SUZUKI
(9.1%)

HONDA
(14.9%)

Source: R. L. Polk & Co.

marketing decision. Harley-Davidson introduced the Fat Boy, their largest motor-cycle with 80 cubic inches of V-twin engine.

The Rubbies brought Harley back into the forefront. By 1989, Harley-Davidson was again the leader in the US super heavyweight motorcycle market, with a nearly 60 percent market share (see exhibit 1.2). One consequence of the Rubbie market was the Rubbies' impact on the demographics of the Harley-Davidson consumer. According to an August 1990 *Wall Street Journal* article, "One in three of today's Harley-Davidson buyers are professionals or managers. About 60 percent have attended college, up from only 45 percent in 1984. Their median age is 35, and their median household income has risen sharply to $45,000 from $36,000 five years earlier."

Even with the growth of the Rubbie market, Harley-Davidson was careful not to lose touch with its grassroots customers. In 1990, roughly 110,000 members belonged to the Harley Owners Group (HOG). The fact that upper management continued to ride alongside the loyal throng was an important marketing tool. Paterson asserted, "Going to rallies and mixing with our customers has more value than you might initially expect. You begin to understand how important the motorcycle is and how important the Harley-Davidson way of life is to them. . . . At a motorcycle rally, everyone's part of the same family – sharing their love for motorcycling and life in general." Paterson's beliefs were shared by Harley owner Pat Soracino. "It's a family affair. My bike rides better with [wife] Vicki riding next to me. And our daughter has grown up with Harleys. It's more than a motorcycle to us. It's our lives."

HOG and Harley-Davidson combined their efforts often in 1989. One such venture was a series of national forest improvement projects. In addition, the First Annual National Poker Run motorcycle rally received the support of almost 160 Harley dealers nationwide. This rally and others raised about $1.7 million for the Muscular Dystrophy Association, a charity for which Harley-Davidson collected over $6.5 million during the 1980s.

Exhibit 1.3   Harley-Davidson's share of the US super heavyweight motorcycle market

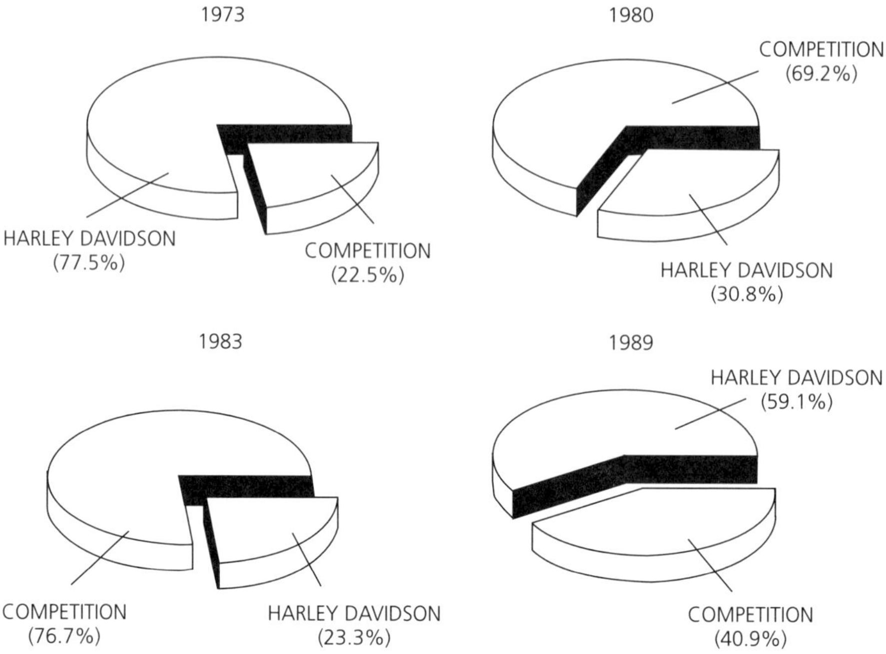

1973

HARLEY DAVIDSON
(77.5%)

COMPETITION
(22.5%)

1980

COMPETITION
(69.2%)

HARLEY DAVIDSON
(30.8%)

1983

COMPETITION
(76.7%)

HARLEY DAVIDSON
(23.3%)

1989

HARLEY DAVIDSON
(59.1%)

COMPETITION
(40.9%)

Source: R. L. Polk & Co.

Although high performance was not a strong selling point for Harley-Davidson motorcycles, the company did enhance its reputation on the racing circuit in 1988 and 1989. In both years, Harley's factory-sponsored rider, Scotty Parker, captured the Grand National and Manufacturer's Championship in the American Motorcyclist Association's Class C racing season.

Competition

Motorcycle competition

Harley faced stiff competition from Japan's big four motorcycle manufacturers – Honda, Yamaha, Suzuki, and Kawasaki (see exhibit 1.3). Industry analysts claimed that the Japanese manufacturers held a commanding lead in the world market, with 80 percent of total motorcycle production.

In 1990, Honda was the world's largest motorcycle manufacturer. The president of the company, Shoichiro Irimaziri, attributed Honda's success to his company's philosophy of producing products of the highest efficiency at a reasonable price. In every aspect of the design of both its cars and its motorcycles, the company's engineers endeavored to achieve a reasonable level of efficiency and obtain the last increment of performance. The president also placed a high value on the early involvement of production and engineering. In his vision, the marketing and production departments are part of engineering; production departments are part of a bigger unit aimed at achieving quality and efficiency.

Yamaha grossed $3 billion in sales in 1989, making it the second-largest producer of motorcycles in the world. For decades, Yamaha remained extremely diversified as the leading producer of outboard motors, sailboats, snowmobiles, and golf carts. At Yamaha Motor, many of the products were developed almost exclusively for overseas markets. Why so much diversification? First, Yamaha executives believed that the motorcycle business in the late 1980s was a shrinking one. Second, as voiced by the president of the company, "Diversification is a hobby of my father's. He gets bored with old businesses."

Suzuki made its name selling motorcycles, but in 1987 almost doubled its sales with the introduction of a jeep, the Suzuki Samurai. When it was first introduced, critics thought it would be a modern-day Edsel. "When these oddball vehicles first came out; nobody gave them a nickel's chance of success," said Maryann N. Keller, a vice-president and automotive analyst with Furman Selz Mager Dietz & Birney. But the critics were wrong. Suzuki sold a record 48,000 units in 1986. The Samurai was the best model launch in history of any Japanese auto manufacturer. Despite its success, however, the Samurai was hit with negative publicity in 1988. Specifically, the Consumers Union, a consumer protection organization, gave the Samurai a "not acceptable" rating and pleaded for the recall of 150,000 Samurais and full refunds to all owners. The union claimed that the vehicle was unsafe because it rolled over easily when turning corners. Although the negative publicity caused a temporary decline in sales, Suzuki rebounded in the second half of 1988 through utilization of dealer and customer incentives.

In 1988, Kawasaki's motorcycle sales increased 5 percent while the overall motorcycle market shrank 20 percent Kawasaki's management attributed much of this success to a new service in which dealers could make sales with no-money-down financing. A computer network, Household Finance Corporation, allowed dealers to get nearly instantaneous responses on credit applications. Kawasaki also focused efforts to accommodate its dealers. The K-share program was developed in 1986 to act as a sales support system for dealers. K-share allowed dealers to make payments electronically; as a result, interest expense was reduced and keying errors made by Kawasaki were virtually eliminated because the manual input of checks was no longer necessary.

Recreational vehicle competition

With its acquisition of Holiday Rambler, Harley nearly doubled its revenues. However, experts indicated that it also bought into a very troubled industry with declining demand. They further claimed that greater competition in the industry would lead to increasing marketing costs and decreasing profit margins. Harley faced three top competitors in the RV industry: Fleetwood, Winnebago, and Airstream.

Fleetwood Enterprises, Inc. was the nation's leading manufacturer of RVs in 1989. Its operations included 21 factories in 17 states and Canada. For 1989, its sales totaled approximately $719 million.

Winnebago was number one in sales, with $420 million in 1988. The company experienced financing problems in early 1990 when Norwest Bank cancelled a $50 million revolving credit line. This situation caused Winnebago to fall to number two in industry sales in 1990.

Airstream ranked third among the RV manufacturers with sales of approximately $389 million for 1989. Thor Industries bought the failing RV manufacturer from Beatrice Foods in 1980. Thor made assembly-line improvements and upgraded components to cut warranty costs and help the RV's image. In 1990, thousands of Airstream owners were members of the Wally Bran Caravan Club International. The club, started by Airstream, held regional rallies and caravans throughout the year. This cult-like following provided a loyal customer base, accounting for 60 percent of all of Airstreams sold.

The Impact of the Economy

Historically, the success of Harley-Davidson has hinged significantly on the performance of the US economy. The company suffered along with everyone else during the Great Depression, and the boom periods of both world wars represented times of prosperity for Harley-Davidson. Changing demands of consumers during the postwar years in the 1940s and 1950s had an adverse effect on the motorcycle industry, and, just when Harley was on the road to recovery in the early 1980s, the economy fell into a recession.

Harley-Davidson proved repeatedly that it was a survivor, having restored peak production levels after each economic downturn. The company reached its highest levels of output in 1989, but, once again, the threat of recession was looming on the horizon. *Standard & Poor's Industry Surveys* warned that "leading indicators have been roughly flat and pointing to little growth, . . . recent financial market activity alternates between fears of recession and inflation. Presently, inflation is a bigger worry for the markets, though recession is the larger worry for the moment."

As the summer of 1990 was reaching its peak, a major international crisis unfolded. On August 2, Iraq invaded Kuwait, unleashing a series of events that seriously affected the US economy. In its August 16, 1990, *Trends & Projections*, Standard & Poor's discussed some of the effects of the anxiety in the Middle East: "The economy looks a lot more vulnerable than it did only a month ago. That was true before the Iraqi invasion; it is even truer with oil prices climbing. . . . A very slow, sluggish economy is predicted for the second half of 1990."

Valueline offered some further insight into the risks of the Middle East situation to Harley-Davidson. "The chief cause for concern would be curtailment of fuel supply in case of a shooting war. In any event, higher oil prices mean more inflation, which increases the risk of recession and with that, a slump in spending for big-ticket recreational goods." Harley-Davidson's products traditionally carried a reputation of producing less fuel efficient bikes than their Japanese counterparts. "This is no touring bike . . . that will take you nonstop from Tucson to Atlantic City."

Other analysts predicted continued pessimism in the recovery of the recreational vehicle market. "Consumers are getting nervous about the economy; recent consumer sentiment reports show deteriorating trends. . . . In the consumer durables category, weak auto sales are not likely to be reversed soon . . . the prospect of higher oil prices means more pressure on consumer spending. Because it is difficult to reduce energy consumption in the short run, many consumers react to higher oil prices by reducing their spending on other items."

Legal and Safety Issues

Speed and helmets

In 1988, 21 states had laws that required motorcycles to be operated with their headlights turned on during the daytime as well as nighttime hours. In addition, 20 states required motorcycle riders to wear helmets. Motorcyclists argued that such laws were a violation of their constitutional rights and that helmets actually prevented them from hearing sirens and other important road noises. But such legislation was not without justification. The number of deaths on motorcycles reached 4500 in 1987 – a rate approximately 16 times higher than that for automobiles. Cycle enthusiasts had a tendency to push the blame on unobservant car drivers. However, statistics from the Insurance Institute for Highway Safety (IIHS) showed that 45 percent of these accidents involved only one vehicle. Of particular concern to the IIHS were the high-speed superbikes that became available to the general public. These bikes accounted for almost twice the number of fatalities of other cycles. Moreover, the IIHS blamed the motorcycle industry for marketing these bikes' high speed and power, claiming that this emphasis encouraged the reckless use of an already dangerous product. The president of IIHS stated, "The fact is motorcycles as a group have much higher death and injury rates than cars, so the last thing we need is this new breed of cycle with even higher injury rates."

But what did all this mean to Harley? With the high revs of the traditional Hog and the production of lighter-weight race-style cycles like the Nova, industry experts claimed that Harley was sure to be hit with the same adverse publicity and criticisms as its Japanese counterparts.

The Rubbie (rich urban biker) influence

I love riding the motorcycle. What a shame it nearly throws you into the jaws of death.

Billy Idol

Every motorcycle rider thinks about the possibility of an accident. But I figured I was sharp enough in my reactions not to have one. . . . But the fact is, on Sunday, December 4, 1988, there I was, sprawled at the feet of a policeman with paramedics on the way.

Gary Busey

Both Idol, the international rock star, and Busey, the Academy Award nominated actor, suffered near-fatal accidents while riding Harley-Davidson motorcycles. Neither Idol nor Busey was wearing a helmet at the time of his accident. An apparent disdain for the safety aspect of motorcycle riding was condoned by these role models. Busey, in fact, continued to be an opponent of helmet laws even after his ordeal. His stance remained with the throng of enthusiasts for whom "the decision to wear a helmet is a matter of personal freedom."

The Rubbies that helped revive Harley-Davidson were a double-edged sword. Well-known personalities such as comedian Jay Leno, actors Sylvester Stallone, Mickey Rourke, Lorenzo Lamas, Kurt Russell, Daniel Day-Lewis, and John Schneider, and Michael Hutchence of the rock group INXS were members of the Rubbie "fraternity." Their high-profile status drew attention to the helmet laws. Many of these celebrities were often seen in photos mounted on their Harleys without wearing helmets. Peter DeLuise, star of television's *21 Jumpstreet*, explained, "Biking is like sliding through the air. When you put a helmet on, it takes away part of the feeling." Ironically, DeLuise's show, which catered to an adolescent audience, often depicted teenagers cruising streets and highways without helmets.

Statistics showed that "142,000 Americans are injured in motorcycle accidents each year." In the early 1970s, Congress used its power over the states to enact legislation that required all motorcycle riders to wear helmets. Federal highway funds were cut in those states that did not pass the laws. Forty-seven states complied with the demand, but in the bicentennial year, aggressive lobbying efforts by biking groups succeeded in influencing Congress to revoke the sanctions. By 1980, 25 of the states had removed or weakened their helmet laws. Federal figures reported an increase in motorcycle fatalities of over 40 percent during this three-year period (1977–80). A 1986 study by General Motors revealed that one-quarter of the 4505 motorcyclists killed that year would have lived if they had worn helmets.

With models that can reach top speeds of 150 m.p.h., Harley-Davidsons continued to satisfy "the American desire for power, speed and personal freedom." The company was never in the business of manufacturing helmets, nor did it take a stance on the helmet issue. Although the contention of prochoice enthusiasts was that the decision was personal, statistics showed that society was absorbing the cost. According to *Time*, a 1985 survey in Seattle found that 105 motorcycle accident victims hospitalized incurred $2.7 million in medical bills, of which 63 percent was paid from public funds.

Financial Highlights

Harley-Davidson's financial position improved greatly from 1986 to 1989 (see exhibit 1.4). Even after the public stock offering in 1986, insiders continued to maintain some ownership of the company. *Valueline* reported in September 1990 that insiders owned 11.6 percent of Harley-Davidson's stock. Other major shareholders included FMR Corporation (7.2 percent) and Harris Association (6.7 percent). In June 1990, Malcolm Glazer reduced his ownership in Harley-Davidson from 7.29 percent to less than 1 percent, earning a $10 million profit in the process.

Management's concern for employee satisfaction impacted the company's financial statements when in April 1989 Harley paid a $1.3 million signing bonus to the Wisconsin labor unions. Harley lowered its debt–equity ratio considerably in 1989 with the repurchase of $37.1 million of debt during the year, which created

Exhibit 1.4   Harley-Davidson, Inc.: net income comparison, 1982–1989

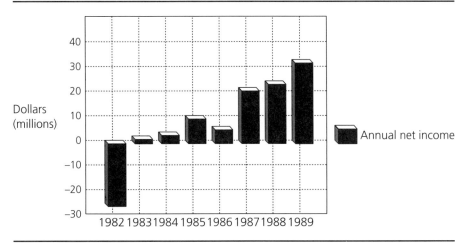

Source: Harley-Davidson, Inc.

a decrease in the debt–equity ratio from 55 percent to 40 percent. In 1990, Harley-Davidson's stock was pounded from a high of $34 to a low of $13 before recovering to $18 as 1990 drew to a close. (The company's financial position is shown in the appendix.)

APPENDIX

Harley-Davidson, Inc. consolidated balance sheets, 1988 and 1989

	December 31	
	1989	1988
	(In thousands, except share amounts)	
ASSETS		
Current assets:		
Cash and cash equivalents	39,076	52,360
Accounts receivable, net of allowances		
for doubled accounts	45,565	42,857
Inventories	87,550	89,947
Deferred income taxes	9,662	8,844
Prepaid expenses	5,811	4,795
Assets of discontinued operation	–	12,488
Total current assets	187,674	211,291

(*continued*)

	December 31	
	1989	1988
	(In thousands, except share amounts)	
Property, plant, and equipment, net	115,700	107,838
Goodwill	66,190	68,782
Deferred financing costs	2,356	4,495
Other assets	7,009	4,307
Noncurrent assets of discontinued operation	–	4,401
	378,929	401,114
LIABILITIES AND STOCKHOLDERS' EQUITY		
Current liabilities:		
Notes payable	22,789	21,041
Current maturities of long-term debt	4,143	12,188
Accounts payable	40,095	36,939
Accrued expenses and other liabilities	69,334	63,047
Liabilities of discontinued operation	–	3,172
Total current liabilities	136,361	136,387
Long-term debt	74,795	135,176
Accrued employee benefits	5,273	3,309
Deferred income taxes	6,253	4,594
Commitments and contingencies (Notes 4, 7, and 9)		
Stockholders' equity:		
Series A Junior Participating preferred stock, 1,000,000 shares authorized, none issued	–	–
Common stock, 9,155,000 shares issued	92	92
Additional paid-in capital	79,681	76,902
Retained earnings	77,352	44,410
Cumulative foreign currency translation adjustment	508	374
	157,633	121,778
Less:		
Treasury stock (447,091 and 520,000 shares in 1989 and 1988, respectively), at cost	(112)	(130)
Unearned compensation	(1,274)	–
Total stockholder's equity	156,247	121,648
	378,929	401,114

Source: Harley-Davidson, Inc.
The accompanying notes are an integral part of the consolidated statements.

Consolidated statements of income

	Year ended December 31		
	1989	**1988**	**1987**
	(In thousands, except share amounts)		
Net sales	790,967	709,360	645,966
Operating costs and expenses:			
Cost of goods sold	596,940	533,448	487,205
Selling, administrative, and engineering	127,608	111,582	104,672
	724,546	645,030	591,877
Income from operations	66,421	64,330	54,089
Interest income	3,634	4,149	2,658
Interest expense	(17,956)	(22,612)	(23,750)
Other-net	910	165	(2,143)
Income from continuing operations before provision for income taxes and extraordinary items	53,009	46,032	30,854
Provision for income taxes	20,399	18,863	13,181
Income from continuing operations before extraordinary items	32,610	27,169	17,673
Discontinued operations, net of tax:			
Income (loss) from discontinued operation	154	(13)	–
Gain on disposal of discontinued operation	3,436	–	–
Income before extraordinary items	36,200	27,156	17,673
Extraordinary items:			
Loss on refinancing/debt repurchase, net of taxes	(1,434)	(1,468)	–
Additional cost of 1983 AMF settlement, net of taxes	(1,824)	(1,776)	–
Benefit from utilization of loss carryforward	–	–	3,542
Net income	32,942	23,912	21,215
Per common share:			
Income from continuing operations	3.78	3.41	2.72
Discontinued operation	0.41	–	–
Extraordinary items	(0.38)	(0.41)	0.55
Net income	3.81	3.00	3.27

Source: Harley-Davidson, Inc.
The accompanying notes are an integral part of the consolidated financial statements.

Consolidated statements of cash flows

	Year ended December 31		
	1989	1988 (In thousands)	1987
Cash flows from operating activities:			
Net income	32,942	23,912	21,215
Adjustments to reconcile net income to net cash provided by operating activities			
Depreciation and amortization	20,007	17,958	15,643
Deferred income taxes	821	(1,375)	(2,875)
Long-term employee benefits	2,741	1,037	(439)
Gain on sale of discontinued operation	(5,513)	–	–
Loss on disposal of long-term assets	28	1,451	1,505
Net changes in current assets and curent liabilities	10,051	(30,346)	12,205
Total adjustments	28,135	(11,275)	26,039
Net cash provided by operating activities	61,077	12,637	47,254
Cash flows from investing activities:			
Capital expenditures	(24,438)	(23,786)	(17,027)
Less amounts capitalized under financing leases	819	2,877	–
Net capital expenditures	(23,619)	(20,909)	(17,027)
Proceeds on sale of discontinued operation and other assets	19,475	–	–
Other-net	(2,720)	(1,204)	901
Net cash used in investing activities	(6,864)	(22,113)	(16,126)
Cash flows from financing activities:			
Net increase in notes payable	1,748	1,083	5,891
Reductions in debt	(69,245)	(42,652)	(78,478)
Proceeds from issuance of common stock	–	35,179	18,690
Proceeds from additional borrowings	–	–	70,000
Repurchase of warrants	–	–	(3,594)
Deferred financing costs	–	–	(3,265)
Net cash provided by (used in) financing activities	(67,497)	(6,390)	9,244
Net increase (decrease) in cash and cash equivalents	(13,284)	(15,866)	40,372
Cash and cash equivalents:			
At beginning of year	52,360	68,226	27,854
At end of year	39,076	52,360	68,226

Source: Harley-Davidson, Inc.
The accompanying notes are an integral part of the consolidated financial statements.

Consolidated statements of changes in stockholders' equity

| | Year ended December 31, 1989, 1988, and 1987 (in thousands, except share amounts) | | | | | | |
| | Common stock | | Additional paid in capital ($) | Retained earnings (deficit) ($) | Cumulative foreign currency translation adjustment ($) | Treasury stock ($) | Unearned compensation ($) |
	Outstanding shares	Balance ($)					
Balance, January 1, 1987	6,200,000	62	26,657	(717)	287	(130)	–
Net income	–	–	–	21,215	–	–	–
Net proceeds from common stock offering	1,230,000	12	18,678	–	–	–	–
Repurchase of 230,000 warrants in connection with public debt and common stock offering	–	–	(3,594)	–	–	–	–
Cumulative foreign currency translation adjustment	–	–	–	–	443	–	–
Balance, December 31, 1987	7,430,000	74	41,741	20,498	730	(130)	–
Net income	–	–	–	23,912	–	–	–
Net proceeds from common stock offering	1,725,000	18	35,161	–	–	–	–
Cumulative foreign currency translation adjustment	–	–	–	–	(356)	–	–
Balance, December 31, 1988	9,155,000	92	76,902	44,410	374	(130)	–
Net income	–	–	–	32,942	–	–	–
Issuance of 72,909 treasury shares of restricted stock	–	–	2,779	–	–	18	(1,274)
Cumulative foreign currency translation adjustment	–	–	–	–	134	–	–
Balance, December 31, 1989	9,155,000	92	79,681	77,352	508	(112)	(1,274)

Source: Harley-Davidson, Inc.
The accompanying notes are an integral part of the consolidated financial statements.

REFERENCES

Advertising Age (1988) "Crisis communications," September 5, p. 29.

Airstream Corporation Annual Report (1989), p. 17.

Busey, Gary (1990) "A near-fatal motor crash changes an actor's life, but not his refusal to wear a helmet," *People*, May 15, p. 65.

Carey, David (1986) "Road runner," *Financial World*, November, pp. 16–17.

Fannin, Rebecca (1988) "Against all odds," *Marketing and Media*, March, pp. 45–7.

Fleetwood Corporation Annual Report (1989), p. 18.

Forbes (1983) "Thunder road," July 18, p. 32.

Forbes (1987) "Harley back in high gear," April 20, p. 8.

Greising, David (1990) "Unhappy campers at Winnebago," *Business Week*, May 8, p. 28.

Harley-Davidson, Incorporated Annual Report (1988).

Harley-Davidson, Incorporated Annual Report (1989).

Harley-Davidson News (1988).

Hutchins, Dexter (1986) "Having a hard time with just-in-time," *Fortune*, June 9, p. 66.

Irimaziri, Soichiro, "The winning difference," *Vital Speeches*, pp. 650–1.

Kitchen, Steve (1983) "More than motorcycles," *Forbes*, October 3, p. 193.

Ludlum, David (1989) "Good times roll," *Computer World*, August 7, p. 51.

Marvel, Mark (1989) "The gentrified Hog," *Esquire*, July, pp. 25–6.

Parola, Robert (1989) "High on the Hog," *Daily News Record*, January 23, p. 74.

Popular Mechanics (1989) "The Harley priority," June 9, p. 24.

Purchasing (1986) "At Harley-Davidson JIT is a fine tuned cycle," April 24.

Reid, Peter C. (1988) "Well made in America: lessons from Harley-Davidson on being the best," Harley-Davidson, Inc.

Roberts, John Madock (1985) "Harley's Hogs," *Forbes*, December 7, p. 14.

Rolling Stone (1990) "Billy Idol," July, p. 174.

Rose, Robert L. (1990) "Vrooming back," *Wall Street Journal (Southwestern Edition)*, August 31, p. 1.

Saathoff, John A. (1989) "Workshop report: maintain excellence through change," *Target*, Spring, p. 2.

Schwartz, Joe (1986) "No fixed address," *American Demographics*, August, pp. 50–1.

Serafin, Raymond (1988) "RV market puzzled," *Advertising Age*, July, p. 52.

Spadoni, Marie (1985) "Harley Davidson revs up to improve image," *Advertising Age*, August 5, p. 30.

Standard and Poor's Industry Surveys (1990) August 16, p. 4.

Standard and Poor's, Trends and Projections (1990) August 16, p. 3.

Stores (1986) "Greeting card chain scores big with macho 'biker' promotion," February, p. 21.

Tanzer, Andrew (1987) "Create or die," *Forbes*, April 6, pp. 55–9.

Time (1988) "High gear," December 19, p. 65.

Willis, Rod (1986) "Harley-Davidson comes roaring back," *Management Review*, March, pp. 20–7.

THE SWATCH IN 1993

Arieh A. Ullman

The Swiss Watch Industry in the Late 1970s

In 1978, when Dr Ernst Thomke became managing director of ETA after a 20-year leave of absence from the watch industry, the position of this Swiss flagship industry had changed dramatically. Just like other industries suffering from the competitive onslaught from the Far East, the Swiss watch industry faced the biggest challenge in its 400 years of existence. Once the undisputed leaders in technology and market share – which the Swiss had gained thanks to breakthroughs in mechanizing the watch manufacturing process during the nineteenth century – the Swiss had fallen on hard times.

In the late 1970s, Switzerland's share of the world market, which in 1952 stood at 56 percent, had fallen to a mere 20 percent of the finished watch segment while world production had grown from 61 million to 320 million pieces and movements annually. Even more troubling was the fact that the market share loss was more pronounced in finished watches compared to non-assembled movements (exhibit 2.1). Measured in dollars, the decline was not quite as evident, because the Swiss continued to dominate the luxury segment of the market while withdrawing from the budget price and middle segments.

The Swiss, once the industry's leaders in innovation, had fallen behind. Manufacturers in the United States, Japan and Hong Kong had started to gain market share, especially since the introduction of the electronic watch. Although in 1967 the Swiss were the first to introduce a model of an electronic wristwatch at

Exhibit 2.1 World watch production and major producing countries 1980

Country	Production (million pieces)			Market
	Electronic	Mechanic	Total	Share (%)
Switzerland: watches	10.4	52.6	63.0	20
incl. non-assembled movements	13.0	83.0	96.0	30
Japan: watches	50.4	17.1	67.5	21
incl. non-assembled movements	53.8	34.1	87.9	28
United States: watches & movem'ts	2.0	10.1[a]	12.1[a]	
Rest of Europe: watches & movem'ts	4.5	57.2[a]	61.7[a]	42[b]
Rest of Asia: watches & movem'ts	76.0	31.3[a]	107.3[a]	
Latin America: watches and movem'ts	–	2.7[a]	2.7[a]	

[a] Includes unassembled movements.
[b] Without unassembled movements.

Source: Swiss Watchmanufacturers Federation.

Exhibit 2.2 Switzerland's 1975 share of world production by type of technology

Technology	Year of introduction	Stage of product life cycle	Swiss share (%)
Simple mechanical	Pre-1939	declining	35
Automatic	1948	mature	24
Electric	1953	declining	18
Quartz (high freq.)	1970	growing	10
Quartz (solid state)	1972	growing	3

Source: Swiss Watchmanufacturers Federation.

the Concours de Chronometrie of the Neuchatel Observatory (Switzerland), smashing all accuracy records, they dismissed the new technology as a fad and continued to rely on their mechanical timepieces where most of their research efforts were concentrated. While the Swiss dominated the watch segments based on older technologies, their market shares were markedly lower for watches incorporating recently developed technologies (exhibit 2.2). Thus, when electronic watches gained widespread acceptance, the Swiss watch producers found themselves in a catch-up race against the Japanese, who held the technological edge (exhibit 2.3).

The situation in the industry, which exported more than 90 percent of its production, was aggravated by adverse exchange rate movements relative to the US dollar making Swiss watches more expensive in the USA – then the most important export market. Until the early 1970s, the exchange rate stood at US$1 = SFr 4.30; by the end of the decade it had dropped to about US$1 = SFr 1.90.

Exhibit 2.3   Share of electronic watches in annual output

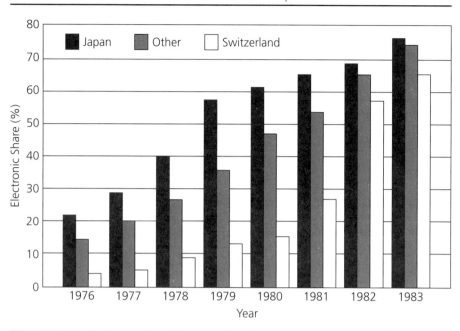

Structural Change in the Industry

Throughout its history the Swiss watch industry was characterized by an extreme degree of fragmentation. Until the end of the 1970s, frequently up to thirty independent companies were involved in the production of a single watch. Skilled craftsmen called suppliers manufactured the many different parts of the watch in hundreds of tiny shops, each of them specializing on a few parts. The movements were either sold in loose parts (*ébauche*) or assembled to *chablons* by *termineurs*, which in turn supplied the *établisseurs*, where the entire watch was put together. In 1975, 63,000 employees in 12,000 workshops and plants were involved in the manufacture of watches and parts. Each *établisseur* designed its own models and assembled the various pieces purchased from the many suppliers. Only a few vertically integrated manufacturers existed which performed most of the production stages in-house (exhibit 2.4). The watches were either exported bearing the assembler's or manufacturer's brand name (factory label) via wholly owned distributors and independent importers, or sold under the name of the customer (private label). By the late 1970s, private label sales comprised about 75 percent of Swiss exports of finished watches. In addition, the Swiss also exported movements and unassembled parts to foreign customers (exhibit 2.5).

This horizontally and vertically fragmented industry structure had developed over centuries around a locally concentrated infrastructure and depended entirely

Exhibit 2.4 Traditional structure of Swiss watch industry

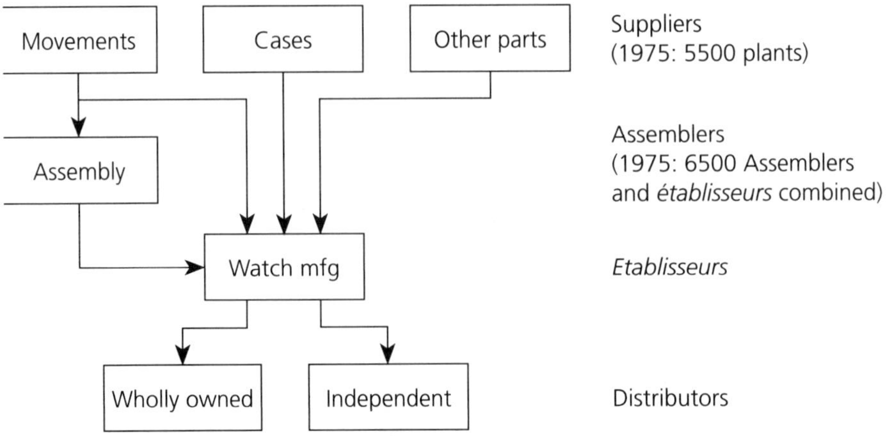

Source: Bernheim, 1981.

on highly skilled craftsmen. Watchmaking encompassed a large number of sophisticated techniques for producing the mechanical watches and this complexity was exacerbated by the extremely large number of watch models. The industry was highly specialized around highly qualified labor, requiring flexibility, quality, and first-class styling at low cost.

This structure was, however, poorly suited to absorb the new electronic technology. Not only did electronics render obsolete many of the watchmaker's skills that had been cultivated over centuries, it also required large production volumes to take advantage of the significant scale and potential experience effects. Whereas the traditional Swiss manufacturing methods provided few benefits from mass production, the extreme fragmentation from the suppliers to the distributors prevented even these. Furthermore, the critical stages in the value added chain of the watch shifted from parts and assembly – where the Swiss had their stronghold – to distribution, where the Japanese concentrated their efforts. Encasement, marketing, wholesale, and retail distribution, which the Japanese producers emphasized, represented over 80 percent of the value added.

Sales of mechanical watches in the budget and middle price segments dropped rapidly when electronic watches entered the market. Initially these were introduced by US producers which had electronic capability, such as Texas Instruments Inc., National Semiconductor Corp., Hughes Aircraft, Intel, and Time Computer. Due to rapidly increasing production and sales volumes of electronic watches, prices dropped dramatically, from $1000 to $2000 in 1970 to $40 in 1975 and less than $20 by the end of the 1970s. At this time most of the early American digital watch producers had started to withdraw from the watch business and it was the cheap digital watch from Hong Kong that flooded the market. As an indication of the eroded market power of the Swiss, the sale of assembled and unassembled

Exhibit 2.5   Swiss exports of watches, movements, and parts, 1960–1992

Year	Finished pieces[a]	Watches francs[b]	Assembled pieces[a]	Movements francs[b]	Unassembled pieces[a]	Movements francs[b]
1960	16.7	767.2	8.2	192.7	n.a.	n.a.
1965	38.4	1334.4	14.8	282.7	n.a.	n.a.
1970	52.6	2033.8	18.8	329.5	n.a.	n.a.
1975	47.2	2391.2	18.6	329.1	5.4	44.0
1976	42.0	2262.4	20.0	343.0	8.0	54.2
1977	44.1	2474.5	21.9	381.3	15.8	94.8
1978	39.7	2520.0	20.6	380.3	18.7	103.5
1979	30.3	2355.6	18.6	371.1	20.2	121.0
1980	28.5	2505.8	22.5	411.8	32.7	189.2
1981	25.2	2880.2	19.9	382.5	27.5	160.5
1982	18.5	2754.6	12.7	256.4	14.5	81.0
1983	15.7	2676.6	14.6	247.1	12.7	76.8
1984	17.8	3063.9	14.5	235.0	14.6	98.5
1985	25.1	3444.1	13.4	220.4	18.8	138.9
1986	28.1	3391.0	13.3	213.4	19.4	133.3
1987	27.6	3568.0	11.1	179.4	20.9	122.8
1988	28.0	4128.8	12.2	202.8	31.9	162.1
1989	29.9	5080.0	12.6	217.7	28.4	136.3
1990	30.2	5808.7	12.1	204.9	35.6	122.4
1991	32.1	5882.8	8.4	163.2	50.6	163.6
1992	40.1	6403.2	8.0	173.3	49.9	141.5

[a]   In millions.
[b]   In millions of current Swiss francs.

Source: Swiss Watchmanufacturers Federation.

movements started to rise while exports of finished watches declined (exhibit 2.5) – a trend which negatively affected domestic employment.

The industry's misfortune caused large-scale layoffs, and bankruptcies started to increase steeply in the 1970s. Because the watch industry was concentrated around a few towns in the western part of Switzerland, the ensuing job losses led to regional unemployment unknown in Switzerland since the 1930s (exhibit 2.6).

ETA, where Dr Thomke became managing director, was a subsidiary of Ebauches SA, which, in turn, was a subsidiary of ASUAG (General Corporation of Swiss of Horological Industries Ltd). ASUAG had been created in 1931 during the first consolidation period in the industry. It was Switzerland's largest watch corporation (total sales 1979: SFr 1212 million) and combined a multitude of companies under its holding structure, including such famous brands as Certina, Eterna, Longines, and Rado. Ebauches, of which ETA was part, was the major producer of watch movements for ASUAG and most of the other Swiss etablisseurs. The other large Swiss manufacturer was SSIH (Swiss Watch Industry Corporation Ltd) which also was a creation of the same 1931 consolidation whose flagships were Omega and

Exhibit 2.6   Swiss watch Industry: plants and employment

Year	Number of plants	Employment
1960	2,167	65,127
1965	1,927	72,600
1970	1,618	76,045
1975	1,169	55,954
1976	1,083	49,991
1977	1,021	49,822
1978	979	48,305
1979	867	43,596
1980	861	44,173
1981	793	43,300
1982	727	36,808
1983	686	32,327
1984	634	30,978
1985	634	31,949
1986	592	32,688
1987	568	29,809
1988	562	30,122
1989	564	32,208
1990	572	33,923
1991	575	32,970
1992	534	31,909

Source: Swiss Watchmanufacturers Federation.

Tissot. During the second half of the 1970s ASUAG suffered from deteriorating profitability and cash flow, poor liquidity, rising long-term debt, and dwindling financial reserves due to sluggish sales of outdated mechanical watches and movements which comprised about two-thirds of ASUAG's watch sales. Diversified businesses outside the watch segment contributed less than 5 percent of total sales.

Turnaround at ETA

Ernst Thomke grew up in Bienne, the Swiss capital of watchmaking. After an apprenticeship in watchmaking with ETA, he enrolled at the University of Berne, where he first studied physics and chemistry and later medicine. After his studies, he joined Beechams, a large British pharmaceuticals and consumer products company, as a pharmaceutical salesman. In 1978, when his old boss at ETA asked him to return to his first love, he was managing director of Beecham's Swiss subsidiary and had just been promoted to Brussels. However, his family did not wish to move and so, after 20 years, he was back in watches.

When he took over, morale at ETA was at an all-time low due to the prolonged period of market share losses and continued dismissals of personnel. ETA's engineers and managers no longer believed in their capabilities of beating the competition from Japan and Hong Kong. Although ETA as the prime supplier of watch movements did not consider itself directly responsible for the series of failures, it was equally affected by the weakened position of the Swiss watch manufacturers. When Thomke assumed his position he clearly understood that for a successful turnaround his subordinates needed a success story to regain their self-confidence. But first a painful shrinking process had to be undertaken in order to bring costs under control. Production, which used to be distributed over a dozen factories, was concentrated in three centers and the number of movement models reduced from over 1000 to about 250.

As *a first step*, a project called "Delirium" was formulated with the objective of creating the world's thinnest analogue quartz movement – a record which at that time was held by Seiko. When Thomke revealed his idea to ETA's engineers, they were quick to nickname it "Delirium Tremens" because they considered it crazy. But Thomke insisted on the project despite his staff's doubts. To save even the tiniest fraction of a millimeter some watch parts were for the first time bonded to the case instead of being layered on top of the watch back. Also, a new extra thin battery was invented. In 1979, the first watch was launched with the Delirium movement which was only 1.98 millimeters thick – and ETA had its first success in a long time. In that year, ASUAG sold more than 5000 pieces at an average price of $4700, with the top model retailing for $16,000.

The Delirium project not only helped to boost the morale of ETA's employees, it also led to a significant change in strategy and philosophy with ETA's parent, Ebauches SA. No longer was Ebauches content with its role as the supplier of movement parts. In order to fulfill its primary responsibility as the supplier of technologically advanced quality movements at competitive prices to Switzerland's *établisseurs*, Ebauches argued, it was necessary to maintain a minimum sales volume that exceeded the depressed domestic demand. Therefore, in 1981, ETA expanded movement sales beyond its then current customers in Switzerland, France, and Germany. This expansion meant sales to Japan, Hong Kong, and Brazil. Ebauches thus entered into direct international competition with Japanese, French, German, and Soviet manufacturers. In short, ETA claimed more control over its distribution channels and increased authority in formulating its strategy.

As *a second step*, the organizational culture and structure were revamped to foster creativity and to encourage employees to express their ideas. Management layers were scrapped and red tape was reduced to a minimum. Communication across departments and hierarchical levels was increased, continued learning and long-term thinking encouraged, playful trial-and-error and risk-taking reinforced. The intention was to boost morale and to create corporate heroes.

The third step consisted of defining a revolutionary product in the medium or low price category. By expanding even farther into the downstream activities, Thomke argued, ETA would control more than 50 percent instead of merely 10 percent of the total value added. Since 1970 the watch segments below SFr 200 had experienced the highest growth rates (exhibit 2.7). These were the segments the Swiss had ceded to the competitors from Japan and Hong Kong. As a consequence, the average price of Swiss watch exports had steadily risen, whereas the competitors exported at declining prices. Given the overall objective to reverse the

Exhibit 2.7 World watch production by price category, 1970s versus 1980

Price category (million pieces)	1970 sales	1980 sales	Growth (%)
Less than 100 SFr	110	290	264
100–199 SFr	33	50	52
200–500 SFr	20	20	0
More than 500 SFr	7	10	43

Source: Thomke, 1985.

long-term trend of segment retreat, it was crucial to reenter one or both of the formerly abandoned segments. Thomke decided to focus on the low price segment. "We thought we'd leave the middle market for Seiko and Citizen. We would go for the top and the bottom to squeeze the Japanese in the sandwich."[1] Thomke's strategy received welcome support from a study conducted by Hayek Engineering, a consulting house, which had been commissioned by ASUAG's top management to aid in the turnaround. The new concept was summarized in four objectives:

1 *Price:* quartz-analogue watch, retailing for no more than SFr 50.00.
2 *Sales target:* 10 million pieces during the first three years.
3 *Manufacturing costs:* initially SFr 15.00, less than those of any competitor. At a cumulative volume of 5 million pieces, learning and scale economies would reduce costs to SFr 10.00 or less. Continued expansion would yield long-term estimated costs per watch of less than SFr 7.00.
4 *Quality:* high quality, waterproof, shock resistant, no repair possible, battery only replaceable element, all parts standardized, free choice of material, model variations only in dial and hands.

The objectives were deliberately set so high that it was impossible to reach them by improving existing technologies; instead, they required novel approaches. When confronted with these parameters for a new watch, ETA's engineers responded with "That's impossible," "Absurd," "You're crazy." Many considered it typical of Thomke's occasionally autocratic management style, which had brought him the nickname "Ayatollah." After all, the unassembled parts of the cheapest existing Swiss watch at that time cost more than twice as much! Also, the largest Swiss watch assembler – ETA's parent ASUAG – sold 750,000 watches annually scattered over several hundred models. In an interview with the *Sunday Times Magazine* Thomke told the story: "A couple of kids, under 30, said they'd go away and look at the Delirium work and see if they could come up with anything. And they did. They mounted the moving parts directly on to a molded case. It was very low cost. And it was new, and that is vital in marketing."[2] The concept was the brainchild of two engineers. Elmar Mock, a qualified plastics engineer, had recommended earlier that ETA acquire an injection molding machine to investigate the possibilities of producing watch parts made of plastic. Jacques Muller was a horological engineer and specialist in watch movements. Their new idea was systematically evaluated and improved by interdisciplinary teams consisting of the inventors, product and manufacturing engineers, and specialists from costing, marketing, and accounting, as well as outside members not involved in the watch industry.

The fourth step required that ETA develop its own marketing. In the 1970s and early 1980s it did not have a marketing department. Thomke turned to some independent consultants and people outside the watch industry with extensive marketing experience in apparel, shoes, and sporting goods to bring creative marketing to the project. Later, as Swatch sales expanded worldwide, a new marketing team was built up to cover the growing marketing, communications and distribution activities.

Product and Process Technology

A conventionally designed analogue watch consisted of a case in which the movement was mounted. The case was closed with a glass or crystal. The movement included a frame onto which the wheels, the micromotor needed for analogue display and other mechanical parts as well as the electronic module were attached with screws. First the movement was assembled and then mechanically fixed in the case. Later the straps were attached to the case.

The Swatch differed with regard to both its construction and the manufacturing process.

Construction

First, the *case* was not only an outer shell, it also served as the mounting plate. The individual parts of the movement were mounted directly into the case – the Delirium technology was perfected. The case itself was produced by a new very precise injection molding process which was specifically developed for this purpose. The case was made of extremely durable plastic which created a super-light watch.

Second, the number of *components* was reduced significantly from 91 parts for a conventional analogue quartz watch to 51. Unlike in conventional watch assembly, the individual parts of the movement – the electronic module and the motor module – were first assembled in subgroups before mounting and then placed in the case like a system of building blocks.

Third, the *method of construction* differed in that the parts were no longer attached with screws. Components were riveted and welded together ultrasonically. This eliminated screws and threads, reduced the number of parts and made the product rugged and shock-resistant. As the crystal was also welded to the case, the watch was guaranteed water-resistant up to 100 feet.

Fourth, the tear-proof *strap* was integrated into the case with a new, patented hinge system which improved wearing comfort.

Fifth, the *battery* – the only part with a limited life expectancy of about three years – was inserted into the bottom of the case and closed with a cover.

Production

First, as a special advantage the Swatch could be assembled from one side only.

Second, because of this it was possible to fully automate the watch mounting process. Ordinary watches were assembled in two separate operations: the mounting of the movement and the finishing. The Swatch, however, was produced in one single operation. According to representatives of the Swiss watch manufacturers, this technology incorporated advanced CAD/CAM technology as well as extensive use of robotics and was the most advanced of its kind in the world.

Third, due to the new design, the number of elements needed for the Swatch could be significantly reduced and the assembly process simplified. As a prerequisite for incorporating this new product technology new materials had to be developed for the case, the glass and the micromotor. Also, a new assembly technology was designed and the pressure diecasting process perfected.

Fourth, quality requirements had to be tightened, because the watch could not be reopened and therefore except for the battery could not be repaired. Given these constraints, each step in the manufacturing process had to be carefully controlled, including the parts, the pre-assembled modules, and the assembly process, as well as the final product. This was especially important because in the past high reject rates of parts and casings indicated that many Swiss manufacturers had difficulties with quality control which damaged their reputation.

Overall, the new product design and production technology reduced the costs significantly and raised product quality above watches in the same price category produced by conventional technology.

Marketing

The new marketing team came up with an approach that was unheard of in this industry dominated by engineers.

- *Product positioning.* Contrary to conventional wisdom in the industry, it was not the product, its styling and technical value that were emphasized but its brand name. Quality attributes such as waterproofness, shock resistance, color and preciseness were less important than the association of the brand name with positive emotions such as "fun," "vacation," "joy of life." The watch was positioned as a high fashion accessory for fashion conscious people between 18 and 30. As it turned out many people outside this range started buying the Swatch. Jean Robert, a Zurich based designer, was responsible for Swatch's innovative designs. The fact that the watch was made from plastic made it easy to change colors and thus helped greatly in developing a stream of innovative designs based on a constant technical concept.
- *Price.* The price was set at a level that allowed for spontaneous purchases yet provided the high margins needed for massive advertising.
- *Distribution.* As a high fashion item competing in the same price range as some Timex and Casio models the Swatch was not sold through drugstores and mass retailers. Instead, department stores, chic boutiques, and jewelry shops were used as distribution channels. Attractive distributor margins and extensive training of the retailers' sales personnel combined with innovative advertising ensured the unique positioning of the product.
- *Brand name.* In 1982, 20,000 prototypes of 25 Swatch models were pretested in the United States, which was viewed as the toughest market that set the

trend for the rest of the world. The unisex models only differed in color of the cases and straps and the dial designs. It was during these pretests that Franz Sprecher, one of the outside consultants of the marketing team, came up with the name "Swatch" (Swiss + Watch = Swatch) during a brainstorming session with the New York based advertising agency concerning the product's positioning and name. Up until then Sprecher's notes repeatedly mentioned the abbreviation S'Watch. During this meeting Sprecher took the abbreviation one step further and created the final name.

The Swatch Team

Besides Thomke, three individuals played a crucial role in the successful launch of the Swatch: Franz Sprecher, Max Imgrueth, and Jacques Irniger.

Franz Sprecher obtained a masters in economics and business from the University of Basle. Following one year as a research assistant and PhD student he abandoned academia and entered the international business world as a management trainee with Armour Foods in Chicago. After six months he returned to Switzerland and joined Nestlé in international marketing. Two years later he became sales and marketing director of a small Swiss/Austrian food additives company. Later Sprecher moved to the positions of International Marketing Director of Rivella and then Account Group Manager at the Dr Dieter Jaeggi Advertising Agency in Basle. Sprecher took a sabbatical at this point in his career and planned to return to the international business world as a consultant within a year. Towards the end of his sabbatical, while considering the offer to become a professor at the Hoehere Wirtschafts- and Verwaltungshochschule in Lucerne, he received a phone call from Dr Thomke concerning the new watch. Thomke told Sprecher: "You've got too much time and not enough money, so why don't you come and work for me." Sprecher took over the marketing of the as yet unnamed product as a freelance consultant.

Another important person involved in the creation of the Swatch was Max Imgrueth. Max Imgrueth was born in Lucerne, Switzerland. Following graduation from high school in St Maurice, a small town in the Valais surrounded by high mountains, he went to Italy and studied art history in Florence and fashion and leather design in Milan. After a brief stint in linguistics he enrolled in business courses at the Regency Polytechnic in England and the New York University. In 1969, he left the United States because he had difficulties in obtaining a work permit and started to work in a women's specialty store in Zurich, Switzerland. Two years later he switched to apparel manufacturing and became manager for product development and marketing. In 1976, he was recruited by SSIH, owners of the Omega and Tissot brands. From 1976 to 1981 he was in charge of product development and design at Omega's headquarters in Bienne. Conflicts with the banks – which at that time *de facto* owned SSIH due to continued losses – over Omega's strategy led him to resign from his job and to start a consulting business. One of his first clients was ETA, which was getting ready to test market the Swatch in San Antonio, Texas. He convinced ETA that San Antonio was the wrong test market and that the Swatch as a new product required other than the traditional distributors. New York and Dallas were chosen as primary test sites and TV advertising and unconventional forms of public relations were tried out. While working on debugging the introduction of the Swatch he was offered the position of President of Swatch USA, a job which initially consisted of an office on Manhattan's Fifth Avenue and a secretary. In this position he involved himself actively in promoting the Swatch. He appeared as Mad Max IV the Merchant Warrior adorned with black leather, Swatch watches and a can of dog food on posters and in sales promotions in famous department stores such as Bloomingdale's.

The third individual involved in the early phase of the Swatch was Jacques Irniger, who joined ETA in 1983 as Vice-President Marketing and Sales for both ETA and Swatch worldwide. In 1985, he was a board member of the Swatch SA, Vice-President Marketing-Sales of ETA SA Fabriques d'Ebauches and President of Omega Watch Corp., New York. Irniger received his doctorate in economics from the University of Fribourg, a small city located in the French speaking part of Switzerland. After training positions in marketing research and management at Unilever and Nestlé he became a marketing manager at Colgate Palmolive in Germany. After Colgate, he moved on to Beecham Germany as Vice-President Marketing. Before joining ETA he was Vice-President of Marketing and Sales for Bahksen International.

Market Introduction

The Swatch was officially introduced in Switzerland on March 1, 1983 – the same year that ASUAG and SSIH merged after continued severe losses that necessitated a SFr 1.2 billion bailout by the Swiss banks. During the first four months 25,000 Swatch pieces were sold – more than a third of the initial sales objective of 70,000 for the first year. According to some distinguished jewelry stores located on Zurich's famous Bahnhofstrasse, where Switzerland's most prestigious and expensive watches were purchased by an endless stream of tourists from all over the world, the Swatch did not compete with the traditional models. On the contrary, some jewelers reported that the Swatch stimulated sales of their more expensive models. The success of the Swatch encourage other Swiss manufacturers to develop similar models which, however, incorporated conventional quartz technology.

Subsequent market introductions in other countries used high-powered promotion. In Germany, the launching of the Swatch was accompanied by a huge replica of a bright yellow Swatch that covered the entire facade of the black Commerzbank skyscraper in Frankfurt's business district. Later, the same approach was used in Japan. On Christmas Eve 1985, the front of a high story building in Tokyo was decorated with a huge Swatch that was 11 yards long and weighed more than 14,000 pounds. Japan, however, turned out to be a difficult market for the Swatch. The 7000 yen Swatch competed with domestic plastic models half the price. Distribution was restricted to 11 department stores in Tokyo only and carried out without a Japanese partner. After six months it became obvious that the original sales target of SFr 25 million for the first year could not be reached. The head of the Japanese Swatch operation, American Harold Tune, resigned. His successor was a Japanese.

In the United States, initial sales profited from the fact that many American tourists coming home from their vacation in Switzerland helped in spreading the word about this fancy product, which quickly became as popular a souvenir as Swiss army knives. US sales of this $30 colorful watch grew from 100,000 pieces in 1983 to 3.5 million pieces in 1985 – a sign that Swatch USA, ETA's American subsidiary, was successful in changing the way time pieces were sold and worn. No longer were watches precious pieces given as presents on special occasions such as confirmations, bar mitzvahs and marriages to be worn for a lifetime. "Swatch yourself" meant wearing two or three watches simultaneously like plastic bracelets. Swatch managers travelling back and forth between the United States and Switzerland wore two watches, one showing EST time, the other Swiss time.

The initial success prompted the company to introduce a ladies' line one year after the initial introduction, thus leading to 12 models. New Swatch varieties were created about twice a year. Also, special models were designed for the crucial Christmas season: in 1984 scented models were launched, a year later a limited edition watch called Limelight with diamonds sold at $100. The Swatch was a very advertising-intensive line of business. For 1985, the advertising budget of Swatch USA alone was $8 million, with US sales estimated at $45 million (1984 sales: $18 million). In 1985, Swatch USA sponsored MTV's New Year's Eve show; the year before it had sponsored a breakdancing festival, offering $25,000 in prizes, and the Fresh Festival '84 in Philadelphia.

Swatch managers were, however, careful not to flood the market. They insisted that in 1984 an additional two million watches could have been sold in the United States. In the UK, 600,000 watches were sold in the first year and the British distributor claimed he could have sold twice as many.

Continued Growth and Success

The marketing strategy called for complementing the $30 dollar timepiece with a range of Swatch accessories. The intention was to associate the product with a lifestyle and thereby create brand identity and distinction from the range of lookalikes which had entered the market and were copying the Swatch models with a delay of about three months. In late 1985, Swatch USA introduced an active apparel line called Funwear. T-shirts, umbrellas, and sunglasses would follow in the hope of adding an extra $100 million in sales in 1986. Product introduction was accompanied by an expensive and elaborate publicity campaign including a four-month TV commercial series costing $2.5 million, an eight-page Swatch insert featuring a dozen Swatch accessories in *Glamour*, *GQ*, *Vogue*, and *Rolling Stone*, and a $2.25 million campaign on MTV. The Swatch bonanza continued through the 1980s and early 1990s, only constrained by shortages in production capacity.

In January 1985, Swatch AG was spun off from ETA. The purpose of the new Swatch subsidiary was to design and distribute watches and related consumer goods such as shoes, leather and leather imitation accessories, clothes, jewelry and perfumes, toys, sports goods, glasses and accessories, pens, lighters and cigarettes. Swatch production, however, remained with ETA. Furthermore, licenses were being considered for the distribution of the products. All of these products as well as the watches were designed in the United States with subsequent adaptations for European markets.

Broadening the product line was, however, not without risks, because it could dilute the impact of the brand name. *Forbes* magazine mentioned the example of Nike, which failed miserably when it tried to expand from runningwear to leisure wear, as did Levis when it attempted to attach its brand recognition to more formal apparel.[3] Yet Max Imgrueth was quick to point to other examples such as Terence Conran, a designer and furniture maker who succeeded in building a retail empire ranging from kitchen towels to desk lamps around his inexpensive, well-designed home furnishings aimed at the young. However, in 1988 the Swatch accessories line was discontinued due to unmet profit objectives and negative impact on the Swatch brand image.

By the end of 1985, 45,000 Swatch units were produced daily and annual sales were expected to reach 8 million pieces (1984: 3.7 million). The Swatch was so successful that by the end of 1984 Swatch profits above recovering all product related investments and expenditures contributed significantly towards ETA's overhead. The Swatch represented 75 percent of SMH's unit sales of finished watches and made it SMH's number one brand in terms of unit sales and the number two brand in terms of revenues topping such prestige brands as Longines and Rado. SMH (Swiss Corporation for Microelectronics and Watchmaking Industries Ltd) was the new name of the Swatch parent after the ASUAG–SSIH merger in 1983. Thanks to the Swatch SMH was able to increase its share of the world market (1985: 400 million units) from 1 to 3 percent within four years. The success also invigorated the Swiss industry at large (exhibit 2.5).

In 1986, the Maxi-Swatch was launched, which was ten times the size of the regular Swatch. Before the start of the ski season during the same year the Pop-Swatch was launched, which could be combined with different color wristbands. As a high-technology extravaganza the Pop-Swatch could also be worn in combination with a "Recco-Reflector" which had been developed by another SMH subsidiary. The Recco reflected radar waves emitted from a system and thus helped to locate skiers covered by avalanches.

In 1987, Swatch wall models and the Swatch Twinphone were introduced. The latter was not just colorful. It had a memory to facilitate dialling and, true to its origin, provided an unconventional service in that it had a built-in "party line," so that two people could use it simultaneously. Flik Flak, a colorful watch designed for children, was another offspring of the Swatch. The name of the new model came from the two characters Flik and Flak which formed the hands of the watch.

The year 1988 saw the successful introduction of the Twinphone in the USA, Japan, and the airport duty-free business, as well as the expansion of the Pop-Swatch product line. While Swatch sales continued to increase overall, sales in the USA stagnated due to distribution problems.

In its 1989 annual report, SMH reported cumulative sales of over 70 million Swatch pieces (exhibit 2.8). Over 450 models of the original concept had been introduced during the first 7 years. The Swatch had also become a collector's item. Limited edition models designed by well-known artists brought auction prices of SFr 1600, SFr 3900 and SFr 9400 – about 25 to 160 times the original price. Flik

Exhibit 2.8   Swatch sales (millions of units)

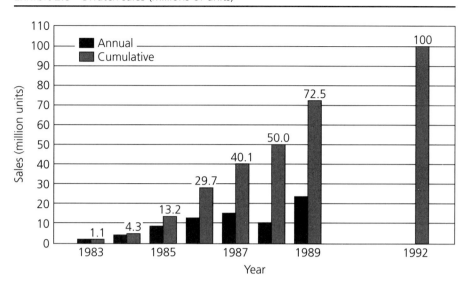

Flak, which until then had been housed in ETA, became an independent profit center and represented the second largest unit of SMH after the Swatch in terms of watches produced.

In May 1990, the "Swatch-Chrono" was launched to take advantage of the chronometer fashion. Except for the basic concept – plastic encasement and battery as the only replaceable part – it had little in common with the original model and represented a much more complex instrument. It had four micromotors instead of only one due to the added functions, and was somewhat larger in diameter. Despite the added complexity it claimed to be as exact and robust as the original Swatch. As a special attraction the watch, which was available in six models, retailed for only SFr 100. The designers of the Swatch-Chrono received a special recognition when Contrôle Officiel Suisse the Chronomètres, the agency in charge of controlling quality standards of chronometers, awarded the Certificate of Chronometer Quality to 4843 out of 5000 Chronos tested. The Chrono was received with incredible enthusiasm by the market. Very quickly, a black market developed, with prices a multiple of the official SFr 100. The company was also experimenting with a mechanical Swatch to be marketed in developing countries where battery replacement posed a problem. In this way the company hoped to boost sales in regions which represented only a minor export market for the Swiss. During the summer of that year, the 75 millionth Swatch left the fully automated plant in Switzerland. In view of the growing number of Swatch collectors throughout the world, the "Swatch Collectors of Swatch" club was founded on August 15, complete with an oversized colorful newsletter, "The Swatch World Journal," produced by the company.

The year 1991 saw the introduction of another two Swatch models – the Scuba diving Swatch and the Automatic, a mechanical Swatch. The latter model was a big hit among young buyers who were unaccustomed to the ticking of mechanical timepieces and who could see the moving part in the watch through the transparent back. Technologically, the Automatic was more complex than the original Swatch, since it contained 200 parts compared to 55. Another new model was the Swatch Stop-Watch, which looked like a conventional watch but which enabled the owner to use the hands of the watch to measure periods of time. In August, Swatch celebrated Switzerland's 700th anniversary with a series of four special Art Swatch models designed by artists from the four regions of Switzerland. In December, Swatch introduced the Swatch Piepser, a pager which combined watch and telecommunication technology within a plastic encasement and was the smallest pager on the market. Retailing for SFr 250, it was considered very inexpensive. The development of the Piepser required several technological breakthroughs. The sophisticated electronics demanded an integrated circuit with 120 square millimeters of silicium compared with 3.5 sq. mm of a regular watch. The much higher energy consumption of the pager was fueled by its own replaceable lithium battery hidden in a drawer-like encasement. The pager's antenna was placed on the inside of the watch glass and resembled the defroster on automobile rear windows. In the USA, the pager was distributed in cooperation with Mobile-Comm, a subsidiary of BellSouth Corp. The company also announced a joint venture with Volkswagen, Europe's largest car maker, to produce an electric "Swatch-Mobile" to be launched in 1996. The battery powered car would have a range of about 125 miles and cost around $6300. At the contract signing ceremony SMH CEO Nicolas Hayek stated: "This is not just a contract. It is a new dimension in the car industry."[4] Also, the company made a renewed effort to transfer its brand recognition to other products with the introduction of "Swatch Eyes", a collection of sunglasses. By the end of the year, the Swatch Collectors of Swatch Club reported a membership of 50,000. Collecting Swatches had become a serious hobby; two Swatch models from the "Art Collection" series were sold at an auction in Hong Kong for $46,000 apiece.

In 1992, the demand for the Swatch-Chrono and the other Swatch models continued to outstrip supply, so much so that the company placed advertisements in newspapers expressing its satisfaction about the success and apologizing for the stockouts. On April 7, the 100 millionth Swatch, the Spring 1993 model "Fresh Fish," came off the production line and was signed by the CEO of SMH, Nicholas Hayek, under the cameras of dozens of reporters from all over the world. In September, SMH celebrated this milestone with a multimedia spectacle "Swatch the World" and 1200 invited guests and 40,000 visitors in Zermatt, at the bottom of the Matterhorn, Switzerland's most famous mountain peak. In July, the Swatch MusiCall was launched, which had an alarm. In addition to the usual buzzer sound a rhythmic melody could be replayed which was composed by the famous French electronic composer and artist Michel Jarre, who was also responsible for the "Swatch the World" show. During the same year, the Twintam, an integrated answering machine, was added to the Twinphone. Flik Flak, which in the meantime had added an alarm clock, introduced a "Fantasy" collection and celebrated the 5 millionth Flik Flak watch.

In January 1993, Volkswagen withdrew from the joint venture. Swatch's parent, SMH, indicated that it would search for another partner while continuing the work on the Swatch-Mobile. In December, SMH/Swatch Chairman and CEO Nicolas Hayek in Lausanne (Switzerland), the CEO for the Atlanta Committee for the Olympic Games, Billy Payne in Atlanta, and the US Olympic Committee Executive Director, Dr Harvey Schiller in Colorado Springs, announced in a video teleconference that Swatch would be the Official Timekeeper for the 1996 Olympic Games in Atlanta. Thus, after Seiko had snapped away this opportunity from the Swiss in 1992 in Barcelona, Swatch, together with its sister subsidiary Swiss Timing, was resuming a tradition the Swiss had maintained since 1932, when Omega was entrusted with this prestigious job.

Supporting Growth

Besides quality and price – the latter had remained the same for almost ten years – design was crucial in securing the appeal of the Swatch. Each year, two Swatch collections were introduced of 70 styles each – a total of 140 models, not counting the special limited editions for special occasions such as Christmas, Switzerland's 700 year anniversary, etc. The main Swatch Design Lab was located in Milan, a center of fashion design. The art director was Alessandro Mendini, a well-known leader in European design. The Lab was staffed by about 20 designers recruited from all over the world with varying backgrounds. While the size and shape of the product remained the same, the ideas for new varieties came from all sources imaginable – art exhibits, fashion shows, books, movies, etc.

Given the intended emotional appeal, the Swatch relied heavily on event sponsorship. These included sports events such as the Freestyle World Cup in Breckenridge (Colorado) in 1984 and 1985, and in Tignes (France) in 1986; the World Solar Challenge, a race for solar powered cars in Australia (1990), Arizona (1991), and Japan (1992); and a competition for paper kites in Haarlem (the Netherlands) in 1987. Increasingly, the Swatch also found its way into art exhibits or organized its own art shows. A few examples: in 1985, the Centre Pompidou in Paris featured a Swatch exhibition as part of the Art Spectacular; early on in 1984 and 1985, Swatch organized street painting happenings in Paris and London; in 1986, Pierre Boulez and Swatch teamed together for a concert tour; in the same year, Swatch and London's Royal College of Art organized an exhibition, "Time and Motion," and the Geneva Musée d'Horlogerie et d'Emaillérie held a Swatch retrospective; in the late 1980s the Swatch Newseum, an exhibit of all Swatch models toured Europe; in 1992, the Blackbox in Berlin, Germany's first Swatch retrospective, showed all 900 models ever produced since 1983.

The success of the Swatch at the market front was supported by a carefully structured organization. Just like the other major brands of SMH, the Swatch had its own organization in each major market, responsible for marketing, sales, and communication. These regional offices were supported by SMH country organizations

Exhibit 2.9 SMH: financial data

		1984	1985	1986	1987	1988	1989	1990	1991[1]	1992
	Except for share prices all monetary values in million SFr									
	A. Income statement data									
Sales	Gross sales	1,665	1,896	1,895	1,787	1,847	2,146	2,139	2,373	2,346
Revenues	Operating revenues	1,582	1,855	1,879	1,772	1,805	2,101	2,089	2,299	2,854
Costs	Materials	714	812	759	670	681	793	755	554	683
	Other external charges	286	360	356	335	331	346	361	120	175
	Wages and salaries	541	556	593	577	580	646	665	568	622
	Social security costs	n.a.	n.a.	n.a.	n.a.	n.a.	n.a.	n.a.	147	166
	Depreciation (fixed assets)	60	61	68	73	71	80	90	93	111
	Depreciation (current assets)	n.a.	n.a.	n.a.	n.a.	n.a.	n.a.	n.a.	20	13
	Other operating expenses	n.a.	n.a.	n.a.	n.a.	n.a.	n.a.	n.a.	501	592
	Total operating costs	1,601	1,789	1,776	1,655	1,663	1,865	1,871	2,003	2,362
Profits	Operating profit (loss)	51	66	103	117	142	236	218	296	492
	Income before taxes	38	72	82	90	126	209	223	291	509
	Net income	26	60	70	77	105	175	191	246	413
	B. Balance sheet data									
Assets	Total current assets	1,049	1,070	1,080	1,103	1,065	1,194	1,348	1,548	1,844
	Cash, securities & short-term investments	102	111	80	176	111	166	234	414	649
	Inventories	524	513	568	528	562	602	658	616	654
	Receivables	334	371	361	331	337	373	385	516	541
	Long-term loans & fixed assets	451	456	507	533	510	529	576	712	773
	Property, plant & equipment	435	440	487	512	499	522	566	623	696
	Total assets	1,500	1,526	1,587	1,636	1,575	1,723	1,924	2,260	2,617
Liabilities	Short-term debt	501	524	503	442	384	367	379	414	431
and	Long-term debt	898	862	801	798	302	295	335	327	324
stockholders'	Total liabilities	1,399	1,386	1,304	1,240	686	662	714	741	755
equity	Total shareholders' equity	420	490	648	697	760	892	1,050	1,262	1,575
	Total liabilities & shareholders' equity	1,500	1,526	1,587	1,636	1,575	1,723	1,924	2,260	2,617
	C. Other data									
	Personnel: in Switzerland	8,982	9,173	9,323	8,526	8,385	8,822	9,017	8,834	9,441
	: abroad	2,311	2,353	2,611	2,597	2,893	2,963	3,754	5,412	4,863
	: total	11,293	11,526	11,934	11,123	11,278	11,785	12,771	14,246	14,304
	Stock price[2]: high	4	410	700[3]	490	382	560	730	668	1,600
	low		127	375	150	178	378	380	416	690
	Unit sales watches and movements (1,000)	n.a.	n.a.	n.a.	n.a.	n.a.	n.a.	n.a.	77,567	86,920

[1] Change in presentation to conform with 4th and 7th Directive of the EC.
[2] Nominal value SFr/share.
[3] Trading moved from Basle to Zurich on July 17, 1986.
[4] No shares publicly traded.

Exhibit 2.10   World production of watches and movements, 1992

	Volume (millions of units)			Value (millions of SFr)		
	Mechanical	Analogue	Digital	Mechanical	Analogue	Digital
Switzerland	7	138	0.4	3548	4422	40
Japan	20	314	39	194	2648	388
Hong Kong	–	–	175	–	–	1225
Others	102	72	10	985	532	650
Total	129	524	224	4727	7602	2303

Source: Swiss Watchmanufacturers Federation.

which handled services common to all brands such as logistics, finance, controlling, administration, EDP, and after-sales service.

The Swatch also meant a big boost for Dr Thomke's career. He was appointed general manager of the entire watch business of the reorganized SMH and became one of the key decision makers of the new management team that took over in January 1985. The "Swatch Story" was instrumental in the turnaround of SMH, which only six years after the merger of two moribund companies showed a very healthy bottom line and continued to thrive (exhibit 2.9).

Future

Despite the smashing success of the Swatch and its contribution to the reinvigoration of the Swiss watch industry (exhibit 2.10), future success was by no means guaranteed.

First, competition remained as fierce as ever. The 1980s and early 1990s were characterized by an oversupply of cheap watches because many manufacturers had built capacity ahead of demand. Prices dropped, especially for the cheapest digital watches, a segment that the Swiss avoided. However, several competitors switched to the more sophisticated analogue models and thus created competition for the Swatch. Many look-alikes with names such as Action Watch, A-Watch, etc. flooded the market.

Second, the Swiss had to guard their brand recognition – not just because of the diversification of the Swatch line. It was not clear whether the Swatch brand name was strong enough to create a sustainable position against the imitations. Also, the quality advantage of the Swatch was neither evident to the consumer nor a top priority for the purchasing decision.

A third issue was for how long the Swatch could maintain its technological advantage. By the late 1980s all imitations were welded together. In addition, many competitors, especially the Japanese, were larger than SMH and therefore able to support larger R&D budgets.

Fourth, there was a good chance that the second effort of transferring the Swatch brand to other products could flop again.

A fifth threat was market saturation. While countries with a GDP per capita of over $5000 comprised only 17 percent of the world's population, they absorbed

87 percent of Swiss watch exports. The changes in watch technology and pricing during the last 15 years had increased watch consumption. In England, consumption grew from 275 watches per 1000 inhabitants in 1974 to 370 watches 10 years later. In the United States the respective figures were 240 and 425 units, of which 90 percent was made up of low price electronic models. While the average life of a watch was much shorter today and consumers had started to own several watches, market saturation could not be ruled out. Also, given the trendy nature of the Swatch, it could fall out of fashion as quickly as it had conquered the market. For this situation SMH was not as well prepared as, say, Seiko or Casio, whose non-watch businesses were much stronger and contributed more in terms of overall sales and profits. However, the company remained optimistic that the political changes in China and Central and Eastern Europe would open large new markets for the Swatch.

A sixth threat was the continued rapid development of technology, especially in the field of communications. Increasingly, time measurement was but one of several features of an integrated communication system. Watches were already integrated in a wide variety of products, including household durables, computers, and telephones. Several SMH subsidiaries involved in microelectronics, electronic components, and telecommunications were developing products in this area and searching for applications in other markets as well. In spite of recent successes it was not clear how SMH and its Swatch subsidiary would fare in this turbulent era characterized by intense technological innovation and very short product life cycles. SMH's high-technology business was much smaller than those of its new competitors in the area of telecommunications (exhibit 2.11).

Finally, despite of the success of the Swatch and of several mid-priced models under other brand names such as Tissot, the Swiss continued to experience higher than average unit prices for their watches. This was partially due to the success of their luxury mechanical watch pieces, which were frequently encased in precious metal and adorned with precious stones. However, executives of Swiss companies expressed concern about this trend.

Exhibit 2.11 SMH subsidiaries (1992)

Company name, registered offices	Field of activity	Share capital in millions		SMH shareholding direct of indirect (%)
SMH Swiss Corporation for Microelectronics and Watchmaking Industries Ltd, Neuchâtel	Holding	CHF	331.3	
Asulab AG, Biel	Research and development	CHG	0.05	100
Atlantic Uhrenfabrik AG, Bettlach	Real estate	CHF	0.7	100
Blancpain SA, Le Brassus	Watches	CHF	0.1	100
—Swiss Prestige Uhren GmbH, Reutlingen (DEU)	After sales service of watches	DEM	0.15	100
Certina, Gebr. Kurth AG, Grenchen	Watches	CHF	3.5	100
Chronométrage Suisse SA (Swiss Timing), Biel	Sports timing	CHF	0.05	100

Exhibit 2.11   (Cont'd)

Company name, registered offices	Field of activity	Share capital in millions		SMH shareholding direct of indirect (%)
Demier Batz SA, Neuchâtel	Real estate	CHF	0.05	100
Diantus Watch SA, Castel San Pietro	Watches, movements	CHF	0.4	100
EM Microelectronic-Marin SA, Marin	Microelectronics	CHF	25.0	100
Endura SA, Biel	Watches	CHF	2.0	100
ETA SA Fabrique d'ébauches, Grenchen	Watches, movements, components and systems	CHF	6.2	100
—ETA (Thailand) Co Ltd, Bangkok (THA)	Movements, components	THB	165.0	100
—Leader Watch Case Co Ltd, Bangkok (THA)	Inactive	THB	20.0	100
Flik Flak SA, Itingen	Inactive	CHF	0.05	100
ICB Ingénieurs Conseils en Brevets, Biel	Patents	CHF	0.2	100
Lascor SpA, Sesto Calende (ITA)	Watch cases and bracelets	ITL	800.0	100
Compagnie des Montres Longines Francillon SA, Saint-Imier	Watches	CHF	10.0	100
—Columna SA, Lausanne	Retailing	CHF	1.5	100
—Longines de Venezuela C.A., Caracas (VEN)	Distribution (Longines, Rado, Swatch)	VEB	27.9	100
—SMH Watches & Microelectronics (Malaysia) Sdn Bhd, Kuala Lumpur (MYS)	Distribution (Longines, Certina)	MYR	0.0	100
—SMH Watches & Microelectronics (Singapore) Pte Ltd, Singapore (SGP)	Distribution (Longines, Certina)	SGD	1.0	100
—SA Longines pour la vente en Suisse, Saint-Imier	Distribution (Longines)	CHF	1.5	100
Maeder-Leschot SA, Biel	Real estate	CHF	0.7	100
Meco AG, Grenchen	Watch crowns	CHF	0.5	100
Micromechanics (Malaysia) Sdn Bhd, Ipoh (MYS)	Assembly, watch components	MYR	3.0	67
Mido G. Schaeren & Co SA, Bienne	Watches	CHF	1.2	100
—SMH do Brazil, Industria e Comercio de Relogios Ltda, Sao Paulo (BRA)	Distribution (Omega, Longines, Mido, Swatch)	CHF	2.6	100
—SMH do Amazonas SA, Manaus (BRA)	Assembly	CHF	0.86	99
Omega SA, Biel	Watches	CHF	50.0	100
—O.N. Center B.V., Amsterdam (NLD)	Inactive	NLG	1.54	100
Omega Electronics SA, Biel	Sports timing equipment, information display systems	CHF	1.5	100
Piguet Frédéric SA, Le Brassus	Movements	CHF	0.3	100
Rado Uhren AG, Lengnau	Watches	CHF	2.0	100
Ruedin Georges SA, Bassecourt	Watch cases	CHF	2.4	100
SMH Advertising Pte Ltd Singapore, Singapore	Advertising	SGD	0.2	100
SMH Australia Ltd, Prahran (AUS)	Distribution (Omega, Longines, Rado, Tissot, Swatch, Flik Flak, Balmain)	AUD	0.4	100

Exhibit 2.11 (Cont'd)

Company name, registered offices	Field of activity	Share capital in millions		SMH shareholding direct of indirect (%)
SMH Belgium SA, Bruxelles (BEL)	Distribution (Omega, Longines, Rado, Tissot, Certina, Flik Flak, Balmain)	BEF	84.0	100
SMH España SA, Madrid (ESP)	Distribution (Omega, Rado, Tissot, Swatch, Flik Flak)	ESP	200.0	100
SMH France SA, Paris (FRA)	Distribution (Omega, Longines, Rado, Tissot, Certina, Swatch, Flik Flak, Balmain)	FRF	16.2	100
—Frésard Composants SA, Charquemont (FRA)	Watch components	FRF	1.0	100
SMH (HK) Ltd, Hong Kong (HKG)	Distribution (Longines, Swatch, Flik Flak, ETA)	CHF	1.5	100
SMH Immeubles SA, Neuchâtel	Real estate and project management	CHF	0.5	80
SMH Ireland Ltd, Dublin (IRL)	Inactive	IEP	0.1	100
SMH Italia SpA, Rozzano (ITA)	Distribution (Omega, Rado, Tissot, Swatch, Flik Flak, Balmain)	ITL	6300.0	100
SMH Japan KK, Tokyo (JPN)	Distribution (Longines, Tissot, Certina, Hamilton, Swatch)	JPY	200.0	100
SMH Management Services SA, Biel	Services and licenses	CHF	0.05	100
SMH Sweden AB, Stockholm (SWE)	Distribution (Omega, Longines, Rado, Tissot, Certina, Swatch, Flik Flak)	SEK	0.5	100
SMH Trading Far East Ltd, Hong Kong (HKG)	Distribution (Omega)	CHF	0.002	100
SMH Uhren and Mikroelektronik GmbH, Bad Soden (DEU)	Distribution (Omega, Longines, Rado, Tissot, Certina, Hamilton, Swatch, Flik Flak, Balmain)	DEM	2.5	100
—Pforzheimer Uhrenrohwerke PORTA GmbH, Pforzheim (DEU)	Movements	DEM	10.0	100
SMH (UK) Ltd, Eastleigh (GBR)	Distribution (Omega, Rado, Tissot, Swatch, Flik Flak)	GBP	2.0	100
—Omega Electronics Ltd, Eastleigh (GBR)	Distribution	GBP	0.006	100
SMH (US) Inc., Dover, Delaware (USA)	Distribution (Omega, Rado, Tissot, Hamilton, Swatch, Flik Flak, ETA)	USD	115.9	100

Exhibit 2.11   (Cont'd)

Company name, registered offices	Field of activity	Share capital in millions		SMH shareholding direct of indirect (%)
—Unitime Industries Inc., Virgin Island V.I. (USA)	Assembly	USD	0.1	100
SMH-Volkswagen AG, Biel	Automobile project	CHF	14.0	50
Société Européenne de Fabrication d'Ebauches d'Annemasse (SEFEA) SA, Annemasse (FRA)	Watch components and electronic assembly	FRF	4.4	100
SSIH Management Services SA, Biel	Inactive	CHF	0.05	100
Swatch AG, Biel	Watches	CHF	2.0	100
Tissot SA, Le Locle	Watches	CHF	5.0	100
Pierres Holding SA, Biel (in liquidation)	Holding	CHF	24.0	78
—Rubistar Sàrl, Thun	Real estate	CHF	0.2	100
Technocorp Holding SA, Le Locle	Holding	CHF	6.0	100
—A. Michel AG, Grenchen	Industrial components	CHF	2.0	100
—Baume SA, Les Breuleux	Real estate	CHF	0.2	100
—Comadur SA, La Chaux-de-Fonds	Products in hard materials	CHF	7.9	100
—Fabrique de fournitures de Bonnétage FFB, Bonnétage (FRA)	Watch components and precision parts	FRF	1.9	99
—Farco SA, Le Locle	Real estate	CHF	2.0	100
—Jeanneret-Wespy Louis SA, La Chaux-de-Fonds	Real estate	CHF	0.05	100
—Lasag AG, Thun	Laser for industrial applications	CHF	1.5	100
—Lasag Corp., Arlington Heights, Ill. (USA)	Distribution	USD	0.001	100
—Meseltron SA, Corcelles	High precision length measurement (Cary) and automatic size control (Movomatic)	CHF	2.0	100
—Nivarox-FAR SA, Le Locle	Watch components and thin wires	CHF	4.0	100
—Oscilloquartz SA, Neuchâtel	High stability frequency sources	CHF	2.0	100
—OSA-France Sàrl, Boulogne-Billancourt (FRA)	Distribution	FRF	0.2	100
—Renata AG, Itingen	Miniature batteries	CHF	0.5	100
—S.I. Grand-Cemil 2, Les Brenets SA, Les Brenets	Real estate	CHF	0.1	100
—S.I. Grand-Cemil 3, Les Brenets SA, Les Brenets	Real estate	CHF	0.1	100
—S.I. Rue de la Gare 2, Les Brenets SA, Les Brenets	Real estate	CHF	0.2	100
—SMH Engineering AG, Grenchen	Machine tool construction and automation	CHF	1.0	100

NOTES

1 Moynahan, B. and Heumann, A. (1985) The man who made the cuckoo sing. *The Sunday Times Magazine*, August 18, 25.

2 Ibid.

3 Heller, Matthew (1986) Swatch Switches, *Forbes*, January 27, p. 87.

4 *Swiss American Review*, 49, July 17, 1991, p. 1.

REFERENCES

Bentivogli, Chiara, Hans H. Hinterhuber and Sandro Trento, "Die Uhrenindustrie: eine strategische Analyse," *Die Unternehmung*, No. 2 (1992).

Bernheim, Ronnie A., *Koordination in zersplitterten Märkten*. Berne, 1981: Paul Haupt Publ.

ETA S.A., "SWATCH. The Revolutionary New Technology." Company brochure.

Fédération de l'industrie horlogère Suisse (Swiss Watchmanufacturers Federation), *Annual Reports*, 1983–1992, Bienne.

Heller, Matthew, "Swatch Switches," *Forbes*, January 27, 1986, pp. 86–7.

Hieronymi, O., et al., *La diffusion de nouvelles technologies en Suisse*. Saint-Saphorin, 1983: Georgi.

Hill, Wilhelm, *Die Wettbewerbsstellung der schweizerischen Uhrenindustrie*. Report for the Swiss Federal Department of Economics, mimeo., Basle 1977.

Ludwig, Benoit D., "Innovation ist mehr als neue Produkte," *io Management-Zeitschrift*, no. 2 (1985), pp. 54–9.

Moynahan, Brian, and Andreas Heumann, "The man who made the cuckoo sing," *The Sunday Times Magazine*. August 18, 1985, pp. 23–5.

Müller, Jacques, and Elmar Mock, "Swatch. Eine Revolution in der Uhrentechnick," *Neue Zürcher Zeitung*, Fernausgabe Nr. 50, March 2, 1983.

Neue Zürcher Zeitung, various issues, 1980–1993.

SMH Swiss Corporation for Microelectronics and Watchmaking Industries Ltd, Annual Reports, 1984–1992.

Swiss American Review, "Swatch-Chef in Japan hat den Hut genommen," July 2, 1986, p. 9.

Swiss American Review, "Olympics in Atlanta: comeback for Swiss timing," July 17, 1991, p. 1.

Thomke, Ernst, "In der Umsetzung von der Produktidee zur Marktreife liegt ein entscheidender Erfolgsfaktor," *io Management-Zeitschrift*, no. 2 (1985), pp. 60–64.

Taylor, William, "Message and muscle: an interview with Swatch titan Nicolas Hayek," *Harvard Business Review* (March–April 1993), pp. 99–110.

Union Bank of Switzerland, *The Swiss Watchmaking Industry*. USB Publications on Business, Banking and Monetary Topics No. 100, Zurich, March 1986.

Hoechst-Roussel Pharmaceuticals, Inc.: RU 486

Jan Willem Bol and David Rosenthal

Introduction

In July, 1991, the management of Hoechst-Roussel Pharmaceuticals had, as yet, made no public announcement as to their plans for marketing RU 486 in the United States. The product had been available for testing in very limited quantities, but the steps necessary to bring the new drug to market had not yet been taken.

RU 486 was a chemical compound which was commonly referred to as "the morning after pill" in the press. The compound had the effect of preventing a fertilized egg from attaching to the uterine wall or ensuring that a previously attached egg would detach. The pill had been thoroughly tested in several European countries with significant success.

RU 486 had become the focus for a great amount of publicity, press coverage, and industry speculation. The compound was also the center of a series of United

This case was originally written by Laura Case, Gail Geisler, Chris Peacock, Sherri Thieman, and Elisabeth Wolf. Originally presented at a meeting of the North American Case Research Association, November 1991. This case was written from public sources, without the cooperation of management, solely for the purpose of stimulating student discussion. All incidents and individuals are real, although some names have been changed at the request of the individuals. Copyright © the *Case Research Journal* and Jan Willem Bol, 1993.

States Senate hearings. Activists, both in support of and in opposition to RU 486, had sought to influence the company's course of action since the product's inception.

Pharmaceutical industry observers suggested that the company was not marketing the product aggressively in order to "maintain a low profile." It was clear that the Hoechst-Roussel management had an ongoing and very complex issue to resolve as to the disposition of RU 486.

The Drug Industry

The drug industry consisted of three primary components: biological products, medicinals and botanicals, and pharmaceutical preparations. Pharmaceuticals were generally classified into one of two broad groups:

- ethical pharmaceuticals – drugs available only through a physician's prescription;
- over-the-counter (OTC) drugs, both generic and proprietary (drugs sold without prescription).

The pharmaceutical industry had grown steadily since 1970 as a result of rising health care costs throughout the world and continuing product innovations from manufacturers. From 1970 to 1980 worldwide sales grew at an average of 10 to 12 percent, in real dollars. In the 1980s growth was slightly lower, about 7 percent, and real growth rates were expected to decrease slightly during the early 1990s, the projected rate being from 6 to 8 percent. The growth rates varied considerably among countries and product categories. An estimated breakdown of 1987 worldwide sales of ethical pharmaceuticals by country or region, with projected growth rates, is shown in exhibit 3.1.

Exhibit 3.1   Leading pharmaceutical markets

Country	1987 sales US$ millions	1990–1995 growth potential
United States	23,979	Moderate
Japan	15,690	Moderate
Germany	6,527	Moderate
France	5,992	Moderate
China	4,890	Low
Italy	4,690	High
United Kingdom	3,370	Low
Canada	1,710	Moderate
South Korea	1,500	High
Spain	1,480	Moderate
India	1,400	High
Mexico	1,300	Declining
Brazil	1,180	Declining
Argentina	856	Declining
Australia	685	Moderate
Indonesia	590	Moderate
Others	33,200	High

Source: Thompson from Arthur D. Little Inc.

Exhibit 3.2 Twenty leading global pharmaceutical companies

Company	Country	1987 sales, US$ thousands
Merck & Co., Inc.	USA	5,060,000
American Home Products Corp.	USA	5,020,000
Pfizer Inc.	USA	4,910,000
Hoechst Corp.	Germany	4,610,000
Abbott Laboratories	USA	4,380,000
Smithkline Beckman Corp.	USA	4,320,000
American Cyanamid Co.	USA	4,160,000
Eli Lilly & Co.	USA	3,640,000
Warmer-Lambert Co.	USA	3,480,000
Schering Plough Co.	USA	2,690,000
Upjohn Co.	USA	2,520,000
Sterling Drug Inc.	USA	2,300,000
Squibb Corp.	USA	2,150,000
Schering Corp.	USA	1,900,000
E. R. Squibb & Sons Inc.	USA	1,800,000
Hoffman-LaRoche Inc.	Switzerland	1,500,000
Miles Inc.	USA	1,450,000
Glaxo Inc.	USA	937,000
Rorer Group Inc.	USA	928,000
A. H. Robins	USA	855,000

Source: Estimates based on various industry sources. The figures should be regarded as approximations due to differences in fiscal years of companies, and variations in data due to different definitions of pharmaceutical sales.

Size and composition

In the late 1980s the industry was not particularly concentrated; the top four firms comprised slightly less than 10 percent of the market. Within specific product categories, however, there were much higher concentration levels, the top four competitors often sharing 40 percent to 70 percent of total sales. Exhibit 3.2 lists 1987 pharmaceutical sales of the leading global pharmaceutical companies.

Research and development

The overall health of the pharmaceutical industry was measured by the number of products it developed, the value of its exports, and the high level of its profits. These factors were, in turn, directly affected by the amount of dollars spent on research and development.

The US drug industry spent some $6 billion on R&D in 1988, up from $5.4 billion in 1987 and $4.7 billion in 1986. As a percentage of sales, the drug industry spent more on R&D than any other major industry group. In 1988 research accounted for more than 15 percent of revenues. Exhibit 3.3 lists research and development expenditures for some of the leading pharmaceutical companies.

Exhibit 3.3 Research and development expenditures (sales in millions of dollars)

Company	1986		1987		1988	
	Sales	%	Sales	%	Sales	%
Abbot	295	8	361	8	455	8
Bristol-Myers	311	8	342	8	394	7
Johnson & Johnson	521	7	617	8	674	7
Hoechst Group	395	10	540	10	608	10
Eli Lilly	420	13	466	13	541	13
Merck	480	12	566	11	669	11
Pfizer	336	7	401	8	473	9
Rorer Group	70	8	82	9	103	10
Schering-Plough	212	9	251	9	298	11
SmithKline	377	10	424	10	495	10
Squibb	163	9	221	10	294	11
Syntex	143	15	175	16	218	17
Upjohn	314	14	356	14	380	14
Warner-Lambert	202	7	232	7	259	7

Source: Annual Reports.

The outlook in 1991

There were a number of positive factors affecting the industry at the beginning of the 1990s. The demographic growth trend in the over-65 segment of the population presented both a larger and more demanding market. The nature of the pharmaceutical business tended to make sales and revenues recession-resistant. High and increasing profit margins tended to attract capital in order to support the ambitious R&D needs of the industry.

Not all conditions were positive. Pharmaceutical firms had been increasingly criticized for their drug pricing policies. Critics argued that relatively low manufacturing costs should be reflected in the pricing of drugs, and that high profit levels proved their point. Generic (unbranded) drugs continued their trend of high growth, supplanting the higher-profit, proprietary segment of the market. Liability costs and the costs associated with compliance with increasingly complex and restrictive regulation continued to soar.

Drug companies in the United States were essentially free to price their products as they wished. This was contrary to the policies in many countries outside the United States, where pharmaceutical prices were strictly regulated by governmental agencies. However, as a result of the rapid increase of health care costs during the 1970s and 1980s, there was a movement toward a more restrictive pricing environment at both the state and federal levels. In order to make their operations more efficient and acquire economies of scale, many companies had chosen to form alliances with other firms. A trend toward consolidation through merger and acquisition resulted.

The growth of the generic drug segment posed a significant problem to the industry because generic products were priced much lower than proprietary products. The price of a generic drug was often as much as 50 percent lower than the price of the corresponding proprietary drug. All 50 states had laws that permitted substitution of generic drugs for proprietary drugs. As a result, the generic drug market doubled in sales from 1983 to 1987.

Pharmaceutical companies faced extensive product liability risks associated with their products. This was especially true for "high risk" products such as vaccines and contraceptives. The cost of liability insurance to cover these adverse effects had forced many companies to coinsure or curtail their research efforts in these areas. In 1991 liability insurance coverage for the manufacture and sale of contraceptives was in most cases impossible to obtain. As a result of this "insurance crunch," the industry had become polarized. Only small companies with few assets and large corporations with the ability to self-insure tended to market contraceptives.

The pharmaceutical industry's high profit levels and "heavy" expenditure on marketing made it a frequent target for attack by political figures and consumer advocates. Critics suggested that the pharmaceutical companies priced drugs so high that only wealthy patients could afford treatment. Marketing expenditures were blamed for "overprescribing," or the tendency for physicians to rely too heavily on drugs for treatment. Marketing was also blamed for hiding from physicians information regarding side effects and contraindications in order to boost sales.

Outpatient drug coverage

Regulation of health care played an important role in the pharmaceutical industry. Increasingly complex regulations at both the state and federal levels resulted in corresponding increases in costs of compliance. Further, the political nature of the regulatory system often resulted in uncertainty for the industry. For example, the outpatient drug coverage provision of the Medicare catastrophic health insurance bill was expected to have both a positive and negative impact on the US market, with the overall impact uncertain. Scheduled to begin a three-year phase-in period in 1991, the plan was to cover 50 percent of Medicare beneficiaries' approved drug expenditures, after an annual deductible of $600 was met. Although the new coverage was expected to expand the overall market, it also made the industry more dependent on the federal government, whose reimbursements were increasingly affected by cost constraints. Further, policies regarding other social issues, such as race or sex discrimination, abortion, and even environmental protection, came into play for those health care facilities which dealt with Medicare recipients. The documentation necessary to show compliance with the relevant regulation was sure to result in increased costs for facilities. Pharmaceutical company managers were uncertain what effect such regulation would have on specific products.

Hoechst Celanese

Hoechst Celanese was a wholly owned subsidiary of Hoechst AG of Frankfurt, Germany. Hoechst AG and its affiliates constituted the Hoechst Group, one of the world's largest multinational corporations, encompassing 250 companies in 120

Exhibit 3.4 Hoechst-Roussel's prescription drugs

Drug Name	Description
Lasix (furosemide)	A widely prescribed diuretic.
Clarofan (cefotaxime)	One of the largest selling third-generation cephalosporin antibiotics used to treat infections.
Topicort (desoximetasone)	A steroid applied to the skin.
Streptasea (streptokinase)	A product used to dissolve clots in blood vessels, e.g. in the treatment of heart attack.
Trental (pentoxifylline)	Improves arterial blood flow, and is used to treat intermittent claudication (leg pain associated with arteriosclerosis).
Diabeta (glyburide)	An oral antidiabetic agent used in the treatment of non-insulin-dependent diabetes.

Source: Hoechst AG, 1988 Annual Report.

nations. The Hoechst companies manufactured and conducted research on chemicals, fibers, plastics, dyes, pigments, and pharmaceuticals. The United States was the largest and fastest growing segment for the Hoechst product lines and was often the key to establishing worldwide marketing capability.

Within its Life Sciences Group, Hoechst Celanese, in affiliation with Roussel-Uclaf (a French pharmaceutical company), provided leading products to the prescription-drug markets in the United States. The division was referred to as Hoechst-Roussel Pharmaceuticals Incorporated (HRPI). Exhibit 3.4 lists the primary prescription drugs provided by HRPI to the United States health care market.

The company also marketed stool softeners and laxatives, including Doxidan and Surfak, directly to consumers, and was developing potential drugs for many conditions, including Alzheimer's disease, cardiovascular disease, some kinds of tumors, and diabetes. HRPI had not previously invested in research into contraceptives or abortion drugs.

Roussel-Uclaf

Roussel-Uclaf, founded in Paris, France, was engaged in the manufacturing and marketing of: chemical products for therapeutic and industrial use; perfumes; eyeglasses; and nutritional products. In addition, Roussel was one of the world's leading diversified pharmaceutical groups. Within its pharmaceutical group, Roussel poured its research dollars into a wide range of product categories, including antibiotics, diuretics, steroids, and laxatives.

Roussel employed 14,759 people, and its 72 subsidiaries yielded a total net income of over $84 million in 1988. Ownership was held by two groups: the German company Hoechst AG, with 54.5 percent of common stock, and the French government, with 36 percent.

In 1979, George Teutsch and Alain Belanger, chemists at Roussel-Uclaf, synthesized chemical variations on the basic steroid molecule. Some of the new chemicals blocked receptors for steroids, causing inhibition of the effects of the steroids, including the hormones involved in sexual reproduction. Because of the controversy surrounding birth control, Roussel had maintained a company policy not to develop drugs for the purpose of contraception or abortion and did not want to pursue research into the type of compounds that had been synthesized by Teutsch and Belanger. However, Dr Etienne-Emile Baulieu, one of Roussel's research consultants, argued persuasively that such compounds represented a revolutionary breakthrough and might have many important uses other than those involved with reproduction, and Roussel continued its research. The research led directly to the discovery, by Dr Baulieu, of RU 486, and Roussel began manufacturing the drug in the early 1980s.

History

The trade name for RU 486, a synthesized steroid compound, was Mifepristone. The company referred to the product as a "contragestive," something between a contraceptive and an abortifacient, and marketed it as an alternative to surgical abortion. Like birth control, it could prevent a fertilized egg from implanting on the uterine wall and developing. It could also ensure that an implanted egg "sloughed off" or detached, making the product more like a chemical abortion. Its use was primarily intended for first trimester pregnancies, because if taken up to 49 days after conception, it was 95 percent successful. In the office of the doctor or woman's health center a woman would take a 600-milligram dose of RU 486. She would return two days later for a prostaglandin injection or pill, which would result in a vaginal blood flow two to five days later which was comparable to that of a menstrual period and which lasted approximately one week. A follow-up visit to her doctor would then determine whether the abortion was complete and make sure the bleeding had been controlled. If the fertilized egg was not completely expelled, a surgical abortion could then be performed. Researchers believed that the success rate would approach 100 percent when dosage levels were more defined. A few patients did feel slight nausea and cramps. Complications were rare, but it was recommended that the drug be taken under a physician's care because of the potential for heavy bleeding or the failure to abort.

The drug was first offered to the French market in September 1988. During the time it was on the market, 4000 women used the drug, reporting a 95.5 percent success rate. However, during this period strong protests and proposed worldwide boycotts of Hoechst products (Roussel's German parent company) brought about the removal of RU 486 from the market and all distribution channels. Dr Baulieu said the company's decision was "morally scandalous." At this point the French government, which owned 36 percent of Roussel-Uclaf, intervened. Two days after the pill's removal, Health Minister Claude Evin ordered RU 486 back into production and distribution in France, saying, "The drug is not just the property of Roussel-Uclaf, but of all women. I could not permit the abortion debate to deprive women of a product that represents medical progress." Since then, the product had been sold only to authorized clinics. Over 100 French women took the drug each day. Thus, approximately 15 percent of all French abortions were conducted through the use of RU 486.

Because RU 486 triggered such strong emotion for and against its use, Roussel management was hesitant to make it available to the world. A Roussel researcher, Dr Eduoard Sakiz, commented: "We just developed a compound, that's all, nothing else. To help the woman. . . . We are not in the middle of the abortion debate." Roussel held the patent to the compound, but willingly supplied it for investigations around the world.

The only US research on RU 486 was a joint effort of the Population Council, a nonprofit research organization in New York City, and the University of Southern California. Early results showed a 73 percent efficacy rate. Shortly after the drug became legal in France, China was able to officially license the use of the drug and by 1991 was close to manufacturing the drug itself. In 1990, Roussel management decided to market RU 486 to Great Britain, Sweden, and Holland as well.

It was generally believed that groups opposed to abortion under any circumstances had been largely responsible for keeping the drug out of the United States. Similarly, interest in research on the drug in the United States had apparently been curtailed by the intimidating tactics of the anti-abortion groups. No US drug maker had sought a license from Roussel. However, other compounds, similar to RU 486, were in the process of development by pharmaceutical companies both in the United States and worldwide.

No long-term risks or effects had been found to result from continuous use of the drug, nor were any problems expected from its occasional use. There was no information about how the drug might affect a fetus if the woman decided to continue her pregnancy after RU 486 failed, because the limited number of reported failures had all been followed by surgical abortions. Some studies reported that the drug seemed to suppress ovulation for three to seven months after use. One medical journal did report that use of the drug created birth defects in rabbits, but the results could not be duplicated in rats or monkeys.

RU 486's primary function was obviously that of an abortifacient. It was thought that the drug was particularly beneficial for three segments of the population. First, it would be important in the developing nations, where many women lacked access to medical facilities and the anesthetics needed for surgical abortion. Second, it would be useful among teenagers, whose use of contraceptives was erratic at best. Third, it would be useful for women who for various reasons were unable to use other methods successfully.

Secondary markets were potentially available as well because RU 486 functioned by inhibiting progesterone. The drug could, therefore, be beneficial in the treatment of Cushing's disease, in which an overactive adrenal gland releases too much of a steroid similar to progesterone. The drug could also be used to treat types of cancer that depend on progesterone for growth, such as tumors of the breast and other cancers of the reproductive system and endometriosis (abnormal growth of uterine lining). In addition, RU 486 had potential for treatment of the nearly 80,000 women yearly who have ectopic pregnancies, a dangerous condition in which the egg develops outside the uterus.

In France, the availability of RU 486 was limited, and the product was used only under medical supervision. Because of these conditions the price was high, about $80 (US dollars). Industry analysts believed that with larger markets and an increased production scale, the cost of the drug could be reduced in the United States. US industry consultants believed that when drug companies identified the large profit potential associated with RU 486, US interest in the drug would grow.

Political and Legal Environment

The management of Hoechst-Roussel faced considerable problems with the introduction of RU 486 into the United States. The process of obtaining FDA approval was not likely to begin without the vocal support of American women who saw the drug as an important means to achieve more personal and political control over their fertility. The process of satisfying FDA requirements was likely to require considerable time and expense. Despite criticisms, the FDA had shown little inclination to reduce the time required for licensing new drugs, and the politically sensitive aspects of RU 486 were unlikely to speed the process.

Although the approval process for RU 486 could have in theory been significantly shortened because of the test data already generated by foreign researchers, no American company had yet petitioned the FDA to even begin the process. The standards required before the FDA would approve a new drug were (a) safety for the recommended use and (b) substantial evidence of efficacy. The clinical trials and testing occurred in three phases. Statistically, of 20 drugs which entered clinical testing under the FDA, only one would ultimately be approved for the market. It frequently cost a pharmaceutical company up to $125 million and 15 years to move a contraceptive from the lab to approval for the market.

With RU 486, the FDA had apparently resolved to be even more restrictive than normal. Special policies and exceptions to their normal FDA rules had been enacted. Under normal circumstances the FDA allowed patients to ship certain unapproved drugs into the country if the drugs were to be sued to treat life-threatening conditions. The agency refused to apply these rules to RU 486. FDA Commissioner Frank Young had written to a Congressional representative that the FDA would not permit RU 486 to be imported into the United States for personal use – for *any* reason.

The FDA did not, however, change an established rule that might permit RU 486 to be imported for the purpose of a "secondary use" such as the treatment of breast cancer. The FDA did not have jurisdiction to regulate the administration of a drug by a physician, so a doctor could theoretically prescribe the RU 486, which had been presumably imported for treatment of breast cancer, for the purpose of inducing abortions. However, the potential liability for a physician who chose to prescribe RU 486 in this manner was probably sufficient to render this possibility remote.

RU 486 was not without its advocates. The National Academy of Sciences recommended that RU 486 be marketed in the United States, but also reported that for that to be possible, the FDA would have to streamline its stringent rules for the approval of new contraceptives. It also recommended that pharmaceutical companies be given federal protection from liability suits so they would be encouraged to reenter the contraceptive business.

If the federal government approved the pill, an individual state could not limit a doctor's decision to prescribe it. The fundamental tenet of the United States Supreme

Court decision *Roe* v. *Wade* was that abortion in the first trimester should remain free from intrusive regulation by the state. Thus *Roe* v. *Wade* would permit US use of RU 486 as an abortifacient to be administered under close medical supervision. The remote possibility of use of RU 486 as a monthly antifertility drug would also be well within abortion law, and perhaps would allow RU 486 to be treated under law as a contraceptive.

Paradoxically, some observers argued that the United States was most likely to witness the appearance of RU 486 if the *Roe* v. *Wade* decision were overturned and abortion again became illegal. It was suggested that a black market for the pill would evolve to meet the need for illegal abortions. Dr Sheldon Siegel of the Rockefeller Foundation stated, "If there is a serious attempt to constrain further progress and further knowledge about RU 486, then it is likely that a black market manufacturer and supply system would develop."[1] The black-market scenario posed very serious health risks for women. Many could suffer side effects, especially in the absence of medical supervision. Still more frightening was the idea that women using the pill illegally would not have access to the backup of safe surgical abortion.

The Contraceptive Industry

As of 1991 there were nearly 6 million unwanted pregnancies each year in the United States, and as a result, there were 1.5 to 2 million abortions. Yearly, there were 500,000 pregnancy-related deaths and 200,000 of those were from improperly performed abortions.[2] Up to half of these unwanted pregnancies and deaths could have been prevented if women had more birth control options. In 1991 American contraceptive research had come to a virtual halt, causing the United States to fall far behind other countries in developing new techniques. In the early 1980s, 11 companies in the United States did research in the contraceptive field, but by 1991 only two were engaged in such studies. Political opposition and the possibility of large liability suits appeared to be the most important reasons for the decline in focus on these drugs.

In 1991 several "morning after" abortifacients had been approved by the FDA for use in the United States. These drugs, based on prostaglandins, which are powerful hormones that can cause serious side effects, were distributed only to hospitals approved by the manufacturer, the Upjohn Company. The drugs were only available by prescription and under the most controlled conditions. The FDA allowed the drugs to be used only for second trimester pregnancies. The drugs were neither advertised to the public nor promoted to physicians by company sales representatives. Likewise, samples of the drugs were not provided to the medical profession. Jessyl Bradford, spokeswoman for Upjohn, stated, "We believe that our commitment to provide a safe and effective alternative to saline and surgical procedures is a responsible one. However, we do not promote abortion. It is an individual decision, made in consultation with a physician. We make no effort to influence such decisions."[3]

The contraceptive market was relatively small, its value being about $1 billion yearly worldwide. Within this market, $700 million was accounted for by the use of oral contraceptives. There were, however, nearly 3 million women in the United States who used nonoral methods.[4] The profit margin on contraceptives was very high. To illustrate, the US government, buying in bulk for shipment overseas, was able to buy a monthly supply of birth control pills for about 18 cents, whereas the average consumer paid about $12 a month. The leader in the contraceptive field was a company named Ortho, which sold contraceptive pills, diaphragms, spermicides, and other products for family planning (e.g. home pregnancy kits). Ortho was continuing to develop improved oral contraceptives that would provide better cycle control and have fewer side effects; however, as mentioned previously, the estimated cost of development of a contraceptive from the laboratory to the market was estimated as $125 million.

Although pro-life forces attributed the decline in contraceptive development in the United States to their efforts, companies and outside experts argued that the reduction was the result of three main factors: high research costs, relatively low potential profit, and the enormous risk that liability suits presented. Robert McDonough, spokesman for Upjohn Company, said, "[Upjohn] terminated its fertility research program in 1985 for two reasons. There was an adverse regulatory climate in the US; it was increasingly difficult to get fertility drugs approved. And there was a litigious climate. . . . Litigation is terribly expensive, even if you win."[5]

In 1988 an $8.75 million judgment was passed against GD Searle in favor of a woman injured by the company's Copper-7 intrauterine device (IUD). Similarly, Dalkon Shield cases forced the AH Robbins Company into bankruptcy. In the late 1980s, AH Robbins was forced to establish a $615 million trust fund to compensate victims of IUD-caused pelvic infections and deaths. Such settlements made liability insurance for contraceptive manufacturers nearly impossible to obtain.

One of the few organizations in the United States that continued research on contraceptives was the Population Council, a nonprofit organization backed by the Rockefeller and Mellon foundations. The Population Council had been conducting US studies of RU 486 on a license from the French developer. Additional support for contraceptive development was evident in proposed legislation that would provide $10 million for the "development, evaluation, and bringing to the marketplace of new improved contraceptive devices, drugs, and methods." If passed, the legislation would put the federal government into the contraceptive marketing business for the first time.

Technical Issues

RU 486 acts as an antiprogesterone steroid. Progesterone is a hormone which allows a fertilized embryo to be implanted on the inner wall of the uterus. Progesterone also reduces the uterus's responsiveness to certain contractile agents which may aid in the expulsion of the embryo. Additionally, progesterone helps the cervix to become firm and aids in the formation of a mucous plug which maintains the placental contents. All of these steps are necessary for an embryo to properly develop into a fetus. Without progesterone, which initiates the chain of events, an embryo cannot mature.

RU 486 masks the effects of progesterone by binding to the normal receptors of the hormone and prohibiting a proper reaction. The embryo cannot adhere to the uterine lining, so the subsequent changes do not occur and the normal process of menstruation (shedding of the uterine wall) begins.

The Population Council sponsored two studies (1987 and 1988) at the University of Southern California which examined the efficacy of RU 486. The tests were all conducted on women within 49 days of their last menstrual cycle. In the 1987 study 100 milligrams per day for 7 days was 73 percent effective and 50 milligrams per day was 50 percent effective. In the 1988 study one 600-milligram tablet was 90 percent effective.

The studies were conducted without prostaglandin, a compound which dramatically increases the effectiveness of RU 486. With prostaglandin, RU 486 was tested at 95.5 percent efficacy.

The general conclusions drawn from the Population Council research were that RU 486 was more effective at higher doses and that the earlier it was administered in the gestational period, the greater its efficacy.

Opposition and Support

The National Right to Life Committee of the United States played an important role in keeping RU 486 from being introduced in the United States. The group referred to RU 486 as the "death pill," claiming that a human life begins at conception and that RU 486 intervenes after conception. A former vice president of Students United for Life said in 1990: "RU 486 is a poison just like cyanide or other poisons. Poisons are chemicals that kill human beings. . . . RU 486 is such a poison which kills the growing unborn human being."[6]

Antiabortionists also resisted the marketing of RU 486 because in clinical testing, women were required to agree to surgical abortions if the drug was unsuccessful. Pro-lifers also suggested that by simply taking a pill to end a pregnancy, a woman was evading the moral significance of the act. One antiabortion legislator, Republican Congressman from California Robert Dornan, wrote a letter to his colleagues in 1986 to gain support to curtail federal funding for the testing of the pill. He stated his concerns as follows: "The proponents of abortion want to replace the guilt suffered by women who undergo abortion with the moral uncertainty of self-deception. Imagine with the Death Pill, the taking of a pre-born life will be as easy and as trivial as taking aspirin."

Pro-life groups reacted strongly and even violently to prevent the drug's introduction into the US market. The US Right to Life group began its campaign by pressuring the French company which originated the pill, Roussel-Uclaf. At one point, as a result of the efforts and the influence of this group, which included bomb threats on Roussel executives, the company temporarily discontinued its production of RU 486. Subsequently the strategy of the group was focused on preventing the drug's introduction in the United States. The transfer of pressure to the US domestic market occurred as a result of RU 486's expansion into the British and Chinese markets and the resultant fear that the United States was the next logical market for introduction.

Pro-life groups continued their letter-writing campaign to Roussel and extended the campaign to Roussel's parent company, Hoechst AG. Further, they threatened to boycott Hoechst's American subsidiary, Hoechst Celanese. The right-to-life campaign succeeded in getting Hoechst to place a "quarantine" on the drug, limiting its distribution to current markets.

Another strategy used by antiabortionists included putting pressure on the US Congress to limit federal funding for research on the drug. Such limitations would strongly impede the Food and Drug Administration approval process. At the same time, pro-life members of Congress continued to lobby for legislation to prohibit further testing. The position of the President, and the increasingly conservative character of the Supreme Court, suggested that the introduction of RU 486 would meet stiff resistance.

In addition to the antiabortion concerns, pro-life groups and some feminist groups were concerned over the short- and long-term physical dangers associated with the use of the drug. Advocates for the pill stressed that a main advantage of the drug was that it was a "safe" method of abortion as compared to the probabilities of injury associated with surgical abortion. The safety claim was largely unsubstantiated, however, due to the lack of available objective test results. According to the *Yale Journal of Law and Feminism*, "The level of ignorance about the long-term effects of RU 486 makes it premature to apply the adjective 'safe.' "[7] Although Dr Baulieu stated that studies had been performed using rabbits and immature human eggs, no direct objective evidence from these tests had been provided to substantiate his claims of safety.

There were additional concerns that the drug could harm subsequent offspring or cause malformation in unsuccessful abortions. Baulieu admitted that there had been cases where the drug was unsuccessful in causing the abortion and the women had forgone surgical abortion. He indicated that there had been no evidence of maldevelopment. RU 486 was said to be "quickly flushed from a woman's system, making long-term effects less likely." This claim had not yet been proved through empirical evidence.

Although the efficacy of RU 486 was increased significantly when used in conjunction with a prostaglandin, the possibility of incomplete abortion remained. Such a condition was dangerous because of the potential for the tissue remaining in the uterus to cause infection. The threat to the health and life of the woman was, therefore, a reasonable concern.

The final concern that pro-lifers had about the dangers of RU 486 was that it had been proved to be ineffective on ectopic pregnancies, pregnancies which occur in the fallopian tubes or the ovary rather than in the uterus. The concern was that the number of ectopic pregnancies in the United States was on the rise and that women with ectopic pregnancies who used RU 486 and thus believed themselves no longer pregnant were in danger of dying if their fallopian tubes burst.

Gynecologists and obstetricians were mixed in their views toward the introduction of RU 486 into the United States. Pressure from doctors belonging to the World Congress of Obstetrics and Gynecology had forced the French government to require Roussel-Uclaf to resume distribution of the drug after its 1988 withdrawal.

However, some doctors considered the product to be unnecessary. One prominent gynecologist and obstetrician believed that there were other chemical alternatives available and stated:

> The drug will be a fiasco for whoever decides to market it due to the stink from Right to Life groups. . . . We already have similar forms of chemical abortifacients that are legal and are used in the US. For example, Ovral is used as a "morning after" pill. In residency . . . when a rape victim came into the emergency room, she was given one dose of Ovral then and another one in the morning. This makes the uterus incapable of conception which is similar to the effects of RU 486. This method is 95.5 percent effective whereas RU 486 alone [without prostaglandins] is only up to 90 percent effective. Not many people are aware that this goes on so there is not much publicity.[8]

RU 486 was not without supporters. The controversy surrounding the drug elicited the attention of many consumer and political groups. Family planning establishments such as Planned Parenthood Federation of America, World Health Organization, and the Population Council, and feminist groups such as the Committee to Defend Reproductive Rights, Boston Women's Health Book Collective, and the National Women's Health Network, all supported the drug. During the period that Roussel had stopped production and sales of RU 486, the World Congress of Gynecology and Obstetrics had planned to ask physicians to boycott Roussel products if the company did not reverse its decision. Kelli Conlin, president of National Organization for Women in New York, called for a campaign urging US pharmaceutical companies to test abortion drugs such as RU 486. She said, "Companies cannot let these (anti-abortion) groups push them around. And that group is really a minority."[9]

Right-to-life groups considered RU 486 to be a particular threat because one of their main avenues of action had been picketing abortion clinics and making the process more difficult for those people who chose to terminate their pregnancies. RU 486 could be used in a doctor's office, thus making pickets and public demonstrations less effective. Further, the drug was to be used within the first seven weeks of pregnancy, and the emotional appeal of showing developed fetuses in danger of abortion would be limited since all that is observed is bleeding similar to menstruation. One fear of pro-life groups was the if RU 486 became common, the very term "abortion" could become obsolete. Dr Baulieu told the *MacNeil-Lehrer News Hour* in September 1986 that "Abortion, in my opinion, should more or less disappear as a concept, as a fact, as a word in the future."

If RU 486 was authorized for use, it would be possible for a woman to take the pill safely and privately very soon after missing her period without ever knowing whether she was actually pregnant or not. In fact, if used monthly, there was some question whether it should actually be labelled an "abortion drug." Depending on when it was taken, RU 486 worked virtually the same way as the "pill" or an IUD. Normally, the pill prevented pregnancy by suppressing ovulation, but certain forms (containing lower doses of hormones to reduce the side effects) occasionally failed to suppress ovulation and instead prevented the fertilized ovum from implanting in the uterus. The IUD, too, worked by irritating the uterus and preventing implantation. If RU 486 was used within eight days of fertilization, it brought about the same effect.

One of the reasons given most often in support of RU 486 was safety. The United States had one of the highest percentages of accidental pregnancies in the industrialized world. According to the World Health Organization, "Surgical abortions [in the world] kill 200,000 women each year. Companies are retreating from research in abortion for fear of controversy, special interest pressure, and product liability questions – creating a major health care crisis."[10]

Likewise, there were increased safety problems when the abortion was postponed until later stages of pregnancy. Women facing an unwanted pregnancy often attempted to avoid the physically and emotionally painful abortion decision by ignoring it. If the abortion options were less harsh, it was thought that many women would face up to their situations more immediately and, therefore, more safely. Polls indicated that "Americans tend to oppose early abortions much less fervently and in fewer numbers than late abortions."[11]

Pro-life groups argued that conception is equivalent to fertilization, thus making RU 486 a form of chemical abortion. However, the federal courts and the American College of Obstetrics and Gynecology defined "conception" as implantation. In 1986, the Federal Appeals Court overturned an Illinois law that had used the pro-life definition in its legislation pertaining to abortion. The implantation definition was based on the fact that 40 to 60 percent of all fertilized ova fail to implant. Some pro-choice advocates suggested that if the pro-life argument were carried to its logical (but absurd) conclusion, women should be required to take progesterone to encourage implantation and prevent accidental death of the fertilized ova.

One of the most significant reasons for support for the introduction of RU 486 was the improvement it provided over other abortion options. With RU 486, there would be "no waiting, no walking past picket lines, no feet up in stirrups for surgery." In many cases, abortion clinics would be unnecessary. The clinics, instead, could be replaced by a few 24-hour emergency clinics that could treat any potential complications. It would make the abortion decision much more a personal matter. In some cases it would remove the psychological agony of deciding on an abortion at all. Women who took the pill just a few days after missing their period would never even know if they had been pregnant. Considering the extreme emotional trauma an abortion often caused, this was considered by supporters to be a great benefit. Finally, the cost of RU 486 would make it much more attractive than other methods. According to a *Newsweek* article, "If RU 486 is approved, Planned Parenthood plans to make it available free or 'at cost' at its family planning centers."[12]

A number of industry observers suggested that the availability of RU 486 in the US market was inevitable. They argued that there were enough people who supported RU 486 for a black market to develop. Such a market was even more likely because the drug was already legal and easily available in other countries. Some radical groups even called for their members to support the illegal use of RU 486. Norma Swenson of the Boston Women's Health Book collective argued that RU 486 would save so many women from death by "botched abortions" that it would be worth it for women's groups to encourage its underground use. According to Swenson, "Using RU 486 . . . would be a type of civil disobedience."

Conclusion

The management of Hoechst-Roussel held the legal and moral responsibility for the decision regarding introduction of RU 486 to the United States. It was clear that, regardless of its direction, the decision would have far-reaching implications for vast numbers of people – not only Hoechst-Roussel's stockholders and customers, but also US society as a whole. It was also evident that the pressures being brought to bear would continue to build.

REFERENCES

1 *60 Minutes*, April 9, 1989.

2 *Time*, February 26, 1990, p. 44.

3 "Letter to Columbia from Upjohn," 1987.

4 *Business Week*, April 1, 1985, p. 88.

5 "Letter to Columbia from Upjohn," 1987.

6 Personal telephone conversation, April 1990.

7 *Yale Journal of Law and Feminism*, 1(75), 1989, p. 96.

8 Personal telephone conversation, April 1990.

9 *The New York Times*, October 27, 1988, pp. A1, B18.

10 *Business Week*, November 14, 1988.

11 Mishel, D. R., *American Journal of Obstetrics and Gynecology*, June 1988, pp. 1307–12.

12 *Newsweek*, December 29, 1988, p. 47.

THE RISE AND FALL OF
YUGO AMERICA, INC.

Carolyn Silliman and Jeffrey S. Harrison

The five years that I invested in the Yugo project were rewarding and maturing for me, although I had a modest financial equity and a large amount of sweat equity invested in the company. In hindsight, there were areas where we failed, but I feel as though it all made a significant impact on the product and pricing aspect of the automobile industry.

William E. Prior, cofounder, former chief executive, and president of Yugo America, Inc., collected his thoughts and reflected on the past five years as he glanced across a crowded airport. It was June 1989, only five months after his company had declared bankruptcy. Looking back, he noted that the privately held company had traveled a rocky road, yet made the most significant impact on the automobile industry in the decade.

It was 1983 when Prior and his two partners, Malcolm Bricklin and Ira Edelson, stumbled upon the idea of a company featuring a low-priced import. Bricklin, who was probably best known for the flashy sports car prototype that bears his name, was heading up the project as its main financial backer. Prior was the former president and general manager of Automobile Importers from Subaru, the nation's second largest Subaru distributor, a company Bricklin had founded after the collapse of his sports car project. Edelson was Bricklin's accountant and financial advisor. The three men had been researching the automobile industry, looking for a niche in the already crowded new car market. From their research, the men

Prepared by Carolyn Silliman and Professor Jeffrey S. Harrison, University of Central Florida, as a basis for classroom discussion and not to illustrate either effective or ineffective handling of administrative situations. © Jeffrey S. Harrison, 1990.

came to the conclusion that there was no "entry level car;" that is, there was not a new automobile inexpensive enough for the average first-time buyer. Bricklin, Prior, and Edelson concluded that they had discovered "a market in search of a product."

Once the concept was conceived, the three entrepreneurs began their search for a low-priced, "no frills" mode of basic transportation. They determined that production costs would be too high in the United States, so they began evaluating the possibility of importing. In looking for a country which manufactured such a product, they wanted to meet three requirements:

1 The foreign company was not presently exporting to the United States, but desired to do so.
2 The overall quality of the car would be inferior to American and Japanese cars but could meet United States standards and consumer requirements.
3 The foreign company would be able to sell the cars at a low enough price for the new company to make marginal profits.

Bricklin, Prior, and Edelson spent four months investigating and traveling to countries in pursuit of the "right" country and product that met the three requirements. They researched manufacturing plants in Brazil, Japan, Mexico, Poland, France, Romania, Czechoslovakia, England, and the Soviet Union before they discovered the Zastava car factory in Yugoslavia. Zavodi Crvena Zastava, Yugoslavia's leading automobile manufacturer, had been producing the Yugo GV model for five years and was quite receptive to Bricklin's proposal. Bricklin, Prior, and Edelson toured the Yugoslavian plant in May 1984 and began discussing the terms of a contract that same month.

Yugoslavian officials were eager to hear of the Yugo America venture. The country's economy was weak, and it owed (in 1985) approximately $19 billion to the Western world. In order to purchase goods from the West, such as oil, steel, and electronics, Yugoslavia had to have "hard" currency (a universal currency of choice). The dinar, Yugoslavia's monetary unit, was not considered hard currency, so the country had to earn dollars by exporting. Yugoslavia's modest exports, including jewelry, tourism, furniture, leather, and sporting guns, did not contribute a significant sum in terms of national debt. Since cars are an expensive item, Yugoslavian officials saw the venture as a profitable method of increasing the supply of hard currency in their monetary economy.

Bricklin and Zastava agreed that 500 Yugos should be shipped to a Baltimore port in early August 1985, so that the cars would be in showrooms and ready to sell later that month. In addition, technicians would be trained at the Zastava's plant prior to the launch in America, in order to guarantee customer satisfaction when the cars were sold and serviced. Bricklin and his partners returned to the United States in late May 1984 and began setting up operations.

Competitive Strategy

Competitive maneuvering among car manufacturers revolves around such factors as innovative options and styles, pricing, and brand name/reputation. Of these factors, Yugo's strategy focused on pricing. Innovative options and styles were not considered important, since the car was an older model and had no fancy options included in the base price. The company could not rely on reputation, since the company did not have an established name.

Yugo America took advantage of a pricing scheme which set it apart from other automobile manufacturers. At $3995, it was the lowest priced car in America. Because price is important to most car buyers, Yugo felt that its low price strategy gave the company an advantage over other small cars. Major price competitors included the Toyota Tercel, Volkswagen Fox, Chevrolet Sprint, and, later, the Hyundai Excel; however, the Yugo GV was priced below all of these competitors. Instead of targeting families or status-conscious individuals, Yugo America made its car appealing to the first-time buyer looking for an economical subcompact.

Operations Begin

Four strategic decisions were made at the onset of operations:

1 The cars would be sold through "dual dealerships;" that is, Yugo would be a partner to an established retailer, such as Ford or Subaru. In this manner, Yugo America's executives hoped the public would associate its name with another successful manufacturer's name and reputation.
2 Prior, Bricklin, and Edelson decided that the company would import regionally rather than nationally. More specifically, Yugo America, with a home base in Upper Saddle River, New Jersey, would establish itself among Northeastern dealers. Approximately 23 percent of all import cars are sold in this region, and the Northeastern coast is the closest to Yugoslavia.
3 There would be a small number of dealers selling a large number of Yugos. The idea behind this decision was that the dealers would be making a substantial profit from the large number of cars, which would motivate them and encourage them to sell more.
4 The price of the car would be low, but the company would stress the fact that the car was of acceptable quality.

The first task to accomplish before announcing the introduction of the Yugo GV in America was to set up a management hierarchy. As mentioned previously, Malcolm Bricklin was Yugo America's chief financial backer. As chairman, he owned 75 percent of the company. William Prior, who would act as president and head of operations, owned 1 percent. Ira Edelson owned 2 percent of the company and held the title of financial administrator. The remaining 22 percent was held by investors who were not involved in the management of the company.

In February 1985, the company began recruiting automobile dealers. (The company's founders had been reviewing dealers for over four months, but the actual signing did not take place until February.) Tony Cappadona was hired as dealer development manager and given the responsibility of locating established dealers who were interested in selling the Yugo. In addition, extensive surveys helped Mr Cappadona determine the best area placement of Yugo franchises. By the end of July, the first 50 dealers were contracted in Pennsylvania, Massachusetts,

New York, New Jersey, Connecticut, Rhode Island, Delaware, Maryland, and Washington, DC.

Some dealers were hesitant to sign because of the financial commitment involved. Pressure from Manufacturers Hanover Trust Company required that Yugo America produce 50 letters of credit by December 1985. By the terms of agreement, dealers had to produce a $400,000 stand-by letter of credit to cover at least two months of vehicle shipments. The dealer also had to pay $37,000 for a start-up kit and arrange financing for a floor plan. A floor plan is an agreement between a financial institution and an auto dealership to finance the vehicles that are on the lot. The financial institution retains title to the automobiles until they are sold, which allows the financial institution to offer extremely attractive rates to the dealership, usually one to two percentage points above the prime lending rate. A typical floor plan would only require $600,000 of credit. However, the commitment of funds was excessive for such a risky operation. In response to these concerns, Yugo executives assured dealers that the Yugo GV would sell itself.

Bricklin contacted Leonard Sirowitz, a New York advertiser, to write and launch a $10 million campaign prior to the debut of the Yugo GV. Sirowitz, who helped to create the Volkswagen Beetle advertisements during the 1960s, expected the Yugo ads to reach a potential one million buyers via newspapers, magazines, and television. He hoped to convince Americans that, despite their views of communist Yugoslavia, the $3995 car was of sound quality.[1] Yugo's first slogan intended to catch the consumer's eye by asking, "The road back to sanity: why pay higher prices?"

In addition to trained technicians, Yugo's support system of quality parts and service was comprehensive. The company received 180 tons of spare parts to distribute among dealers during the summer of 1985. The company implemented the industry's first universal product code inventory system, which enhanced the accuracy and efficiency of inventory processing. In addition, service schools were developed so that technicians would have no problems or questions when repairing the cars. For the "do-it-yourself" consumers, Yugo America published its own repair manuals and included a toll-free telephone number for assistance.

The Yugo Arrives in America

The first shipment of 500 cars from the Zastava plant arrived in mid-August 1985 (the features of the Yugo are listed in exhibit 4.1). Ten cars were sent to each of the 50 dealers in the Northeast. Each dealer was instructed to reserve two cars as demonstration vehicles and to uphold this condition at all times. By the end of August, the cars were polished and ready for their national debut.

Yugo's official entry into the automobile industry was announced on August 26, 1985. It was a long-awaited moment, and consumers were equally excited about the car as the Yugo employees. The Yugo frenzy spread so quickly that 33 dealerships were added and 3000 orders were taken for cars by September 9. Customers paid deposits in order to reserve their cars, and by the end of 1985, a six-month waiting list was tallied. Indeed, Yugo's founders had discovered "a market in search of a product."[2]

Exhibit 4.1 Yugo GV standard features

VEHICLE TYPE
Front-engine, front-wheel drive, four passenger, three-door hatchback.

DIMENSIONS AND CAPACITIES
Wheelbase: 84.6 inches
Overall Length: 139.0 inches
Overall Height: 54.7 inches
Overall Width: 60.7 inches
Headroom: Front: 37.0 inches
          Rear: 36.0 inches
Legroom: Front: 39.0 inches
         Rear: 39.0 inches
Ground Clearance: 4.8 inches

Luggage Capacity: 18.5 + 9.0 cubic feet
Fuel Capacity: 8.4 gallons
Curb Weight: 1,832 pounds

ENGINE
Type: Single overhead cam, 1.1 liter + cylinder with aluminum cyl. head. Dual barrel
      carburetor
Bore & Stroke: 80×55.5 mm.
Displacement: 1116 cc.
Compression Ratio: 9.2:1
Horsepower: 54hp at 5,000 rpm.
Torque: 52 lbs. at 4,000 rpm.

DRIVE TRAIN
Transmission: 4-speed Manual
Final Drive Ratio: 3.7
Gear Ratios: 1st-3.5, 2nd-2.2, 3rd-1.4, 4th-1.0, Reverse-3.7

SUSPENSION
Front: Independent, MacPherson struts, anti-sway bar.
Rear: Independent, transverse leaf spring with lower control arms

BRAKES
Front: 8.0" disc, power-assisted
Rear: 7.2" drum, power-assisted
Rear brake proportioning valve

WHEELS AND TIRES
Wheels: Steel
Tires: Tigar 145SR-13, steel-belted radials with all-weather tread design.

ELECTRICAL
Bosch electronic ignition
Alternator: 55 amp
Battery: 12 volt, 45 amp

Exhibit 4.1   (Cont'd)

ECONOMY
City: 28 mpg
Highway: 31 mpg

STANDARD EQUIPMENT
1.1 liter 4-cylinder overhead cam engine
Front-wheel drive
4-wheel independent suspension
Power assisted brakes, disc front, drum rear
Front anti-sway bar
Rack and pinion steering
Color-coordinated fabric upholstery
Full carpeting, including carpeted luggage compartment
Reclining front seats
Folding rear seats – 27.5 cu. ft. luggage space
3 grab handles
2 dome lights
Visor vanity mirror
Analog instrument gauges
Low fuel warning light
Steel-belted radial tires (145 × 13)
Lexan bumpers
Plastic inner front fender shields
Bosch electronic ignition
Rear brake proportioning valve
Full-size spare tire
Front spoiler
Hood scoop
Hub caps
PVC undercoating
Opening rear quarter windows
Rear window electric defroster
Quartz halogen headlights
Body side molding
Special owner's tool kit
Cigarette lighter
Locking gas cap
Dual storage pockets
Concealed radio antenna
Spare fuse and bulb kit
Night/day rear-view mirror
Electric cooling fan
Console

Source: Yugo America, Inc. promotional materials.

During its first year of operations, which ended July 31, 1986, Yugo America, Inc. grossed $122 million from the sale of 27,000 automobiles and parts and accessories. The Yugo was hailed as the "fastest selling import car in the history of the US."[3] The company employed 220 dealers throughout the Southeast and East Coast, and it was estimated that the consumer credit divisions of Chrysler, Ford, and General Motors financed one-third of the Yugo retail sales.[4] At the end of July, Prior announced the expansion of the New Jersey home office to include a corporate planning department. He also informed reporters of Yugo's new slogan, "Everybody needs a Yugo sometime."[5]

Problems Begin

In February 1986, *Consumer Reports* published the first of two articles criticizing the Yugo GV. Reporters mocked Malcolm Bricklin for his other car ventures (the Subaru 360 and the Fiat Spider) which had recently failed. The writers pointed out that, after adding destination charges, dealer preparation fees, and a stereo, the price of the car exceeded $4600. The magazine's personal test evaluation was also published. It stated that the transmission was "sloppy," the steering was "heavy," the ride was 'jerky," and the heating system was "weak and obtrusive."[6]

The writers continued by criticizing almost every aspect of the car, from seat coverings to the "not-so-spacious" trunk. The safety of the car was questioned, but could not be verified by government crash tests. It was noted, however, that the impact of a collision at 3 m.p.h. and 5 m.p.h. severely twisted and crushed the bumpers. It was estimated that repairing the damage to the front and rear bumpers was $620 and $461, respectively.[7] Twenty-one other defects were discovered, ranging from oil leaks to squealing brakes. A survey by J. D. Power and Associates (included in the article) concerning customer satisfaction revealed that over 80 percent of Yugo buyers had reported problems. In short, the writers did not recommend the Yugo GV at *any* price.

The Yugo was facing increasing competitions as well. In late 1985 Hyundai Motor America, a subsidiary of the giant South Korean industrial company, announced the American introduction of the Hyundai Excel for $4995. The Excel was a hatchback model that included standard features which were comparable to the Yugo GV. Therefore, the Excel posed a direct threat to the Yugo GV in the lower priced automobile market.

By mid-October 1986, Yugo America responded to the *Consumer Reports* article and increasing consumer complaints by making 176 improvements to the car without raising its price.[8] Prior stated that Yugo spent between $2.5 and $3 million to improve its image through advertisements and national incentives. Independent dealers offered additional rebates, as well, in an effort to boost sagging sales.

Looking ahead, Yugo America had hoped to introduce some new models, all within the lower price range. For 1987, the Yugo GV would be given a "face lift" to take on an aerodynamic look, and a convertible GV would be available later in the year. In order to meet the needs of couples and small families, Yugo anticipated the 1988 debut of a five-door hatchback, which would compete with the Honda Accord. A four-door sedan would be added to the line between 1989 and 1990, and a two-seater sports car named "TCX" would be the highlight of 1990.[9]

During 1986, there were rumors that Yugo America was considering a move to "go public" by issuing common stock, since the company was beginning to experience financial tension. The proposal was later cancelled for two reasons. First, Bricklin did not want to surrender any of his equity (75 percent). Second, the company was starting to feel the effects of negative publicity, and financial consultants felt that the stock would not bring a fair price. For the time being, Yugo would remain a private company.

More Trouble

In April 1987, *Consumer Reports* released its annual survey of domestic and foreign cars, and once again, Yugo's image was tainted. The writers criticized the Yugo GV from bumper to bumper, stating that "the manual transmission was very imprecise . . . the worst we've tried in years." As for comfort, "small, insufficiently contoured front seats" contributed to an "awkward driving position." In addition, the ride of the car was described as "noisy" and "harsh."[10]

Besides the negative description of the car's driving performance, the article publicized the results of an independent crash test. This test, which was not mandated by law, disclosed the results of a crash at 35 miles per hour among domestic and foreign automobiles. (The National Highway Traffic Safety Administration requires that all cars pass the national standard impact at 30 miles per hour.) The Yugo GV was among the 40 percent which did not pass the test. In fact, it received the lowest possible ranking with respect to driver and passenger protection. The report indicated that the steering column "moved up and back into the path of the driver's head," and the seats "moved forward during the crash, increasing the load on occupants."[11]

Consumer Reports also reported that damage to the front and rear bumpers when hit at an impact of 3 and 5 m.p.h. was $1081, the highest in its class. This was particularly embarrassing to Yugo America, since many of its foreign competitors (including Toyota, Mazda, and Saab) escaped the collisions without a scratch.[12]

Before the second *Consumer Reports* articles, Yugo sold every car coming into its ports every month. Sales in 1987 were the highest to date. From there, Yugo's problems started to catch up with the company. The negative image of the Yugo was apparent, and dealers were forced to offer $500–750 rebates as an incentive to buy. In addition, several new programs and extended warranties were offered to entice customers. Monthly sales levels started to decline, and waiting lists became virtually obsolete.

Through all of these problems, William Prior remained an exemplary figure for all of the Yugo-Global employees. As Tony Cappadona stated, "Bill added a lot of charisma and dedication to the company. He let the employees know that everyone was working to achieve a mission. They (the employees) didn't mind working 10 or 12 hours a day, because they saw Bill putting in twice as much."

Changes in Ownership

The 1987 year was marked by the acquisition of Yugo America, Inc. by Global Motors, Inc., a company founded by Malcolm Bricklin. Bricklin established Global Motors as an umbrella corporation for importing cars worldwide. Gaining 91 percent of Yugo America, Global became its parent, distributor, and holding company, and it helped with the coordination and distribution of Yugos as they arrived at the Baltimore port.

By 1988, Yugo America and Global Motors began contemplating the sale of a substantial portion of the company in an effort to avoid bankruptcy. In April, Mabon Nugent and Company, a New York investment firm, purchased Global Motors for $40 million.[13] Bricklin sold 70 percent of his equity for $20 million, and a debenture was purchased from Global for an additional $20 million. A management group headed by Prior and Edelson agreed to contribute $2.1 million to obtain 5.5 percent of the company. The management group would be awarded stock options periodically over the following three years, to bring the group's total ownership to 22 percent. Prior was named chief executive officer during the acquisition.[14]

The Final Year

By April 1988, the company's operating problems had also increased. Not only had the *Consumer Reports* articles thrashed the Yugo GV again, but dealers were beginning to undermine the company as well. William Prior stated that dealers would often persuade buyers to purchase one of their other brands instead of a Yugo. To make things worse, consumers could only receive 36-month financing with the purchase of a Yugo. Conversely, Ford Motor Credit and other financiers offered 60-month plans on their own cars, which resulted in lower payments. The thought of lower monthly payments was incentive enough for a prospective Yugo buyer to change his or her decision to purchase. If the former tactic did not persuade the buyer, the salesperson would criticize the Yugo directly and accentuate the features of the other line. Higher commissions on more costly brands increased the motivation of salespeople to move away from the Yugo.

Even after deciding to buy a Yugo, many consumers ran into additional difficulties when they tried to obtain financing. Because the typical Yugo customer was a young, low-income, first-time buyer, lending institutions were hesitant to make high-risk loans to persons in this segment of the market. It was estimated that as many as 70 percent of all Yugo customers were declined for credit, since the majority had no previous credit history and a debt–income ratio of over 50 percent. This common scenario was discouraging for both the customers and dealers. Enticing advertisements lured customers in, yet many could not obtain financing. The dealers became frustrated because of the amount of time and effort contributed to "put the deal together." Prior described the situation as "an inefficiency in the market."

In an effort to hurdle these financing roadblocks, Yugo America announced in

June 1988 that it would design its own program for financing. The first-time buyer plan was administered through Imperial Savings Association, a $10-billion institution based in San Diego. Yugo and Imperial intended to protect themselves by charging a higher annual percentage rate – as much as four percentage points higher than those of other finance companies. In doing so, Yugo America could establish a "higher-than-average" reserve for loan defaults. Though the annual percentage rate was higher, buyers could finance the loan over 60 months so that monthly payments remained low.[15]

Approximately 50 dealers were enrolled in the program. Imperial was hesitant to allow all of the dealers to take advantage of Yugo Credit, since there were still some "bugs" in the system. Also, each state required separate licensing, and Yugo did not have the time to wait for acceptance in each state.

The financing program was terminated after 90 days. One of the provisions of the plan required Yugo America to be "in good standing" financially. Bills were accumulating at Yugo and company debt was becoming unmanageable. Imperial Savings had to pull out.

In November 1988, William Prior and 71 other employees were released from the company, leaving a skeleton crew of 71 remaining. Mabon Nugent's intentions were to cut costs in an effort to relieve cash-flow pressures and generate additional funds for product development. Marcel Kole, senior vice president and chief financial officer of Global Motors, temporarily replaced Prior as president and chief executive of Yugo America. Turnover within the company was high, and national advertising was brought to a halt.[16] Norauto LP of Ohio agreed to finance two shipments of Yugos backed by letters of credit. Norauto, a firm which aids bankrupt, terminated, or distressed companies, took possession of the cars until Yugo America could repay the $14.3 million letter of credit.[17]

Mabon Nugent and Company had written off $10.5 million as a loss in Global Motors by January 30, 1989. It was estimated that Global would need $10 million to get back on its feet, but Mabon Nugent did not feel that contributing more money to a dying company was a worthy investment. The firm's partners considered selling the company to Zastava or private investors, but neither of the ideas was pursued.[18] Global officially filed for Chapter 11 bankruptcy on January 30, 1989.[19] Global's unaudited balance sheet reported in the petition for bankruptcy is contained in exhibit 4.2.

A Hazy Future for Yugo America

After declaring bankruptcy in January 1989, parent company Global Motors, Inc. discharged 250 (of 300) Yugo America employees. Zastava, honoring the warranty of the cars, began seeking financial backing so that the company could remain afloat. By February 1989, three lawsuits had been filed against Global Motors and Mabon Nugent and Company. William Prior sued the companies for breach of contract and Turner Broadcasting System in Atlanta filed suit demanding $182,000 for unpaid bills. A third lawsuit, by Imperial Savings, alleged that Mabon Nugent was "involved in the day-to-day operations of the company"

Exhibit 4.2   Global Motors, Inc. balance sheet, December 31, 1988 (unaudited)

ASSETS	
Cash	0
Due to/from subsidiaries	27,145
Due from manufacturer	15
Inventories	0
Prepaid and other current assets	48
	27,208
Property, plant and equipment (at cost)	8
Less: Accumulated depreciation	(1)
	7
Investment in subsidiaries	223
Deferred charges	
Total Assets	27,438
LIABILITIES AND EQUITY	
Acceptances payable	0
Accounts payable and accrued expenses	1,429
Notes payable	11,825
Due to/from subsidiaries	0
Estimated warranty (current)	0
	13,254
Estimated warranty (long-term)	0
Long-term debt	11,000
Minority interest	0
Shareholders' deficiency	3,184
Total Liabilities and Equity	27,438
	0

Note: Amounts are given in thousands of dollars.

Source: Bankruptcy Docket Number 89 00680, filed January 30, 1989, United States Bankruptcy Court, District of New Jersey.

(Global) before it (Mabon Nugent) actually took control of Yugo-Global in 1988. Mabon Nugent denied the charge.[20]

John A. Spiech became Yugo's new president and chief executive, succeeding Marcel Kole. Spiech, a veteran of the automobile industry, had full confidence in the company and its product, stating, "Whatever happened wasn't the car's fault. It is still good, low-cost, reliable transportation."[21] He intended to take the company to the top, even though he was starting from the very bottom.

NOTES

Much of the information in this case is based on personal interviews with William Prior and Tony Cappadona, conducted in June 1989.

1 J. Fierman, "Can A beetle brain stir a yearning for yugos?" *Fortune* (May 13, 1985), 73.

2 "The Price is Right," *Time* (September 9, 1985), 58.

3 J. L. Kovach, "We don't overpromise," *Industry Week* (October 13, 1986), 73.

4 Ibid.

5 J. A. Russell, "Yugo grosses $122 Million in first year." *Automotive News* (September 1, 1986), 42.

6 "How much car for $3990?" Consumer Reports (February 1986), 84–6.

7 Ibid.

8 Kovach, "We don't overpromise."

9 J. A. Russell, "Zastava to construct plant for US Yugos," *Automotive News* (May 20, 1985), 2.

10 "The 1987 cars," *Consumer Reports* (April 1987), 200–15.

11 Ibid., 200.

12 Ibid., 208.

13 J. A. Russell, "Bricklin's import firm sold in $40 million deal," *Automotive News* (April 18, 1988), 1, 56.

14 Ibid.

15 J. Henry, "Low finance: Yugo offers loans to spur buyers," *Automotive News* (August 1, 1988), 1, 51.

16 C. Thomas, "Prior ousted: shaky Global trims ranks," *Automotive News* (November 14, 1988), 1, 58.

17 J. Henry, "Yugo, liquidator in accord," *Automotive News* (March 27, 1989), 1.

18 J. Henry, "Global struggles to remain afloat," *Automotive News* (January 30, 1989), 1, 257.

19 Henry, "Yugo, liquidator in accord."

20 J. Henry, "More Yugo grief – maker plans termination," *Automotive News* (February 20, 1989), 1, 51.

21 D. Cuff, "A car industry veteran will try to revive Yugo," *New York Times* (March 17, 1989), D4.

GM ALLISON JAPAN LTD

Richard T. Dailey

The decision by the Allison Division of General Motors Corporation (GM) to name James D. Swaim president of GM Allison Japan Ltd (GMAJ) in June 1987 was a significant departure from the way Allison had been dealing with its Japanese joint venture. Swaim, who arrived at GMAJ in October 1984, was not only the first American selected to run the company, but also the first employee sent to GMAJ from Allison on a long-term assignment. Even though GMAJ had been in operation since 1972, the business had not performed up to Allison's expectations. By the early 1980s some problems, particularly warranty problems, had become serious, and Allison's management realized that something had to be changed.

On his arrival in Tokyo, Swaim said his first goal was "to help try to fix the problems at GMAJ and learn if we also had product problems that were aggravating the basic issues." After his appointment as GMAJ's president he reflected on the need to change the way the Japanese company had been doing business. One of his primary concerns, he commented, "was how to make sure that Allison's Japanese customers understood that Allison was indeed committed to the Japanese market for the long term."

Allison Division

In the early 1970s, the Allison Division of General Motors Corporation and Isuzu Motors established GM Allison Japan Ltd as a joint venture company for the purpose of selling heavy-duty transmissions to Japanese truck manufacturers. Although

This case was prepared by the author as a basis for classroom discussion and not to illustrate either effective or ineffective handling of managerial situations. The generous cooperation of GM Allison Japan Ltd is gratefully acknowledged. © 1991, Richard T. Dailey.

General Motors Corporation had established a marketing organization to sell automobiles in Japan in the late 1920s, this was its first effort at selling components to Japanese original equipment manufacturers (OEMs).

Allison was a well-known US manufacturer of gas turbine engines for fixed-wing aircraft and helicopters and of heavy-duty transmissions for trucks and buses, mining and construction equipment, and industrial applications. In 1970, a major change took place in the transmission side of the business when the company began manufacturing a family of new automatic transmissions for trucks, buses, and certain types of off-highway construction and mining equipment. The initial members of this family of transmissions were designed primarily for use in highway vehicles equipped with gasoline engines.

The company manufactured transmissions in a variety of sizes for school buses, the largest intercity buses, small city delivery trucks, and the largest over-the-road tractors. This new line of transmissions represented a major shift in both product line and product development, and this shift would require extensive marketing efforts to gain acceptance by end users.

In September 1970, General Motors merged its Detroit Diesel and Allison divisions, which gave Allison full access to the Detroit Diesel worldwide distribution system. The new Detroit Diesel Allison Division permitted a smoother integration of the new line of transmissions into GM's Detroit Diesel products.

Establishing the Joint Venture Company

In early 1970, General Motors Corporation began discussions with Isuzu Motors, an OEM of automobiles, trucks, and buses, regarding the feasibility of GM assuming an equity position in Isuzu. Although Isuzu is not a major automobile manufacturer in Japan (its market share is about 3 percent), it is a major manufacturer of commercial vehicles, with a market share of around 16 percent (see exhibits 5.1 and 5.2). The idea of an automatic transmission for trucks intrigued Isuzu's management and was an incentive for them to join GM in the joint venture. The Japanese partners envisioned local manufacture when sales volume reached sustainable levels.

An equity position in Isuzu, GM executives reasoned, would provide GM with a foothold in the growing Japanese motor vehicle market, which grew at an average annual rate of 3.7 percent between 1973 and 1988 (see exhibit 5.3) and which GM, as well as other US manufacturers, had been unsuccessful in entering. Other US motor vehicle manufacturers were developing relationships with Japanese auto and truck manufacturers. Of necessity, the talks between Isuzu and GM were kept very quiet, because if word leaked out that a corporation the size of GM was negotiating with a company of Isuzu's size, the rumor would have a major impact on the price of Isuzu shares on the Tokyo stock exchange.

Japanese industrial organization

In order to smooth the development and operation of the new joint venture, GM needed to link up with one of Japan's industrial groups, known as *keiretsu*. A *keiretsu* consists of about twenty major companies, one in each industrial sector. The typical

Exhibit 5.1 Truck sales in Japan, 1984–1988: industry volume and Isuzu volume

	Model year				
	1984	1985	1986	1987	1988
Heavy duty					
Industry	116,236	111,374	109,243	126,925	165,419
Isuzu	30,214	28,492	28,215	33,055	42,460
10 ton					
Industry	39,647	37,227	36,958	44,624	58,375
Isuzu	9,768	8,471	8,487	10,641	13,644
4 ton					
Industry	65,237	63,767	62,749	72,256	93,729
Isuzu	17,965	17,781	17,514	20,278	26,193
Light duty					
Industry	701,783	706,683	728,097	784,682	927,786
Isuzu	87,617	88,451	82,171	84,813	102,408
2–3 ton					
Industry	154,876	158,869	160,835	170,112	207,551
Isuzu	49,120	50,798	48,576	53,310	65,260
1–1½ ton					
Industry	206,077	209,825	208,602	228,103	272,053
Isuzu	32,761	33,004	29,585	27,727	30,286

Source: Company records.

Exhibit 5.2 Japanese automobile production share by automaker, 1987

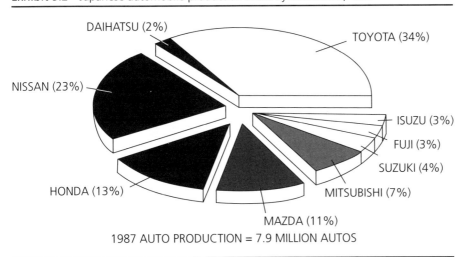

DAIHATSU (2%)

TOYOTA (34%)

NISSAN (23%)

ISUZU (3%)

FUJI (3%)

SUZUKI (4%)

HONDA (13%)

MITSUBISHI (7%)

MAZDA (11%)

1987 AUTO PRODUCTION = 7.9 MILLION AUTOS

Source: Japan Automobile Manufacturers' Association.

Exhibit 5.3   Motor vehicle sales in Japan

	Cars				Trucks				Buses			Grand total
	Large	Small	Mini	Total	Large	Small	Mini	Total	Large	Small	Mini	
1973	489,273		97,014	586,287	70,499	592,558	410,775	1,073,832	14,843		14,843	1,674,962
1974	9,064	1,652,855	713,170	2,379,137	164,086	986,672	538,743	1,693,502	10,256	17,572	27,828	4,100,467
1975	45,125	2,531,396	157,120	2,737,641	121,118	999,155	431,181	1,551,454	8,818	11,018	19,836	4,308,931
1976	46,592	2,224,783	178,054	2,449,429	128,501	1,043,467	459,395	1,631,363	9,415	13,044	23,259	4,104,051
1977	53,069	2,277,934	165,072	2,500,095	132,041	1,031,804	587,393	1,671,238	9,327	13,509	22,916	4,194,249
1978	64,428	2,620,069	172,213	2,056,710	156,764	1,094,590	549,022	1,800,376	10,496	14,281	24,777	4,681,063
1979	84,721	2,781,889	170,263	3,036,873	185,732	1,220,668	686,494	2,092,894	9,589	14,396	23,985	5,153,752
1980	74,931	2,608,215	174,038	2,854,176	154,472	1,144,167	839,308	2,137,947	9,414	13,973	23,381	5,015,518
1981	78,221	2,522,936	165,538	2,866,695	126,731	1,045,420	1,064,253	2,237,404	9,358	13,539	22,897	5,126,996
1982	63,697	2,794,789	179,786	3,038,272	113,136	933,321	1,154,909	2,201,366	8,705	13,088	21,793	5,261,431
1983	80,210	2,857,490	197,911	3,135,611	111,314	910,529	1,204,553	2,226,396	7,947	12,363	20,310	5,382,317
1984	82,068	2,019,540	193,546	3,095,554	120,717	935,031	1,265,190	2,320,938	7,688	12,579	20,267	5,436,759
1985	73,539	2,069,527	161,013	3,104,083	110,009	945,484	1,367,685	2,431,172	8,798	12,775	21,513	5,556,834
1986	81,178	2,926,590	138,255	3,146,823	109,676	954,918	1,475,580	2,540,174	8,826	12,791	21,617	5,793,014
1987	111,415	3,036,517	126,868	3,274,880	132,114	1,042,219	1,547,247	2,721,581	8,786	13,232	22,018	6,010,399
1988	166,054	3,397,628	153,677	3,717,359	169,036	1,214,847	1,596,220	2,900,103	9,177	14,365	23,542	6,721,004

Source: Japan Automobile Manufacturers' Association.

keiretsu contains a bank, a trading company, an insurance company, and a company in one of the basic industries, such as steel or motor vehicle manufacturing. Nearly all of the equity of the individual companies in the group is held by other members of the *keiretsu*, one of the characteristics of Japanese business culture that makes it difficult for outsiders to obtain a controlling ownership in a Japanese firm. A major purpose of the *keiretsu* is to help members of the group raise investment funds. General Motors chose to become associated with the *keiretsu* headed by Dai-Ichi Kangyo Bank (DKB) because GM had worked with DKB on previous occasions.

C. Itoh Trading Company

To ease any problems that GM might encounter in importing components to Japan, the company followed a suggestion that a Japanese trading company become a partner in the joint venture. GM chose C. Itoh, one of Japan's largest trading companies and a member of the DKB *keiretsu*, for this purpose. Isuzu Motors is also a member of this group of companies.

Kawasaki Heavy Industries

Kawasaki Heavy Industries (KHI), another member of the DKB group, became part of the joint venture because it manufactured manual transmissions for Isuzu. In addition, KHI was interested in the vehicular gas turbine engine Allison was developing. Kawasaki Heavy Industry executives thought the engine might have applications in Japanese heavy-duty trucks and construction equipment.

Equity shares in the joint venture

By 1972, the negotiations were completed and General Motors Allison Japan Ltd became a reality. It was formed as a joint venture company with General Motors holding 50 percent of the shares, Isuzu 20 percent, Kawasaki 20 percent, and C. Itoh the remaining 10 percent. The new company was capitalized at ¥90 million. General Motors Corporation, meanwhile, had purchased a 38 percent equity position in Isuzu Motors, which represented an infusion of new capital for Isuzu.

Unfortunately, a Detroit Diesel Allison distributor in Japan who had been buying transmissions from Allison and selling them to Japanese truck manufacturers lost his marketing rights as a result of the new joint venture.

Staffing the New Company

The agreement for staffing the new organization called for the president of the company to represent the Japanese partners of the joint venture and for the vice-president to represent the GM side of the business. Accordingly, GMAJ's first president was Japanese and came from Kawasaki Heavy Industries. The GM vice-president was an American who was also vice-president of GM Overseas Corporation – Japan Branch. His office was in Tokyo but was some distance from GMAJ's offices. All other members of the joint venture company were Japanese.

Source of employees for GMAJ

Some employees of GMAJ were "seconded" employees from other companies participating in the joint venture. It is common practice among the Japanese *keiretsu* for one company in the group, especially one of the lead companies, to provide employees to another company in the group. These employees may be lent on a short-term basis to work on technical problems or may be sent to the company for an indefinite period of time.

Employees seconded to a company for the long term are likely to be near retirement age with no possibility of advancing any further in their organization. Often they are moved to make room for younger employees, or they may be sent as a favor to a manager of one of the participating companies. Several employees seconded to GMAJ were in these two categories.

Isuzu had high hopes for the success of the joint venture and seconded some of its best people to the new company. For example, an engineer who was seconded was considered one of Isuzu's best transmission designers for manual transmissions. Allison executives in Indianapolis reasoned that since the Japanese knew the truck market in Japan better than they did, it would not take long for GMAJ to become a profitable company.

In 1974, GMAJ's first president returned to Kawasaki Heavy Industries, and Toshihiko Tamura of Isuzu Motors became GMAJ's second president. He remained in that position until 1987. Mr Tamura was trained as an electrical engineer, and although he had extensive experience in the marine engine business, he had none in the transmission business.

Staff training and support

GMAJ's product engineers and certain technical support people were sent to Allison's manufacturing headquarters in Indianapolis for two- to four-week training sessions. They were provided with the latest technical information about

Allison's automatic transmissions and had sessions on troubleshooting, the types of vehicles that were best suited for an automatic transmission, and the associated manuals and documentation that would assist them in answering their questions after they had returned to Japan. All technical manuals and other documentation provided to the GMAJ engineers were in English.

Periodically engineers from Indianapolis visited GMAJ to provide on-site technical support and service. Typically, these people visited Japan three or four times each year and stayed for two to three weeks.

A final support mechanism was provided by the Detroit Diesel Allison regional marketing organization headquartered in Singapore. Every four to six weeks, a Singapore-based sales representative, not necessarily an engineer, would visit GMAJ and spend one or two days providing whatever assistance he could to solve problems that could not be handled by the Japanese staff.

Product Marketing

GM Allison Japan was established as a Japanese company to sell truck and bus transmissions initially to Isuzu Motors and subsequently to other Japanese vehicle manufacturers. Although a US firm owned 50 percent of GMAJ, it conducted business as a Japanese firm. James Swaim pointed out that

> as a "child" company or captive firm, it serves at the pleasure of its owners, all of whom are represented on the board of directors. Japanese tradition for component suppliers required them to work only with the OEMs and leave all end user contact to the OEMs. Most US component manufacturers and distributors work with the end users of their products, encouraging them to specify their equipment from the vehicle manufacturers. In this kind of relationship the component manufacturers quite often become complementary engineering organizations to the end users, as well as marketing partners to the OEMs.
>
> In Japan, however, the situation is much different. Sales representatives of the component manufacturers do not call on the end users. Rather they work primarily with the OEMs and, to a limited extent, the dealers, when selling their products. Thus, the executives of GMAJ never established the type of relationships with the end users that would result in their specifying Allison transmissions.

The Japanese truck market
Over 95 percent of Japanese trucks are equipped with diesel engines, which tend to be more fuel efficient than gasoline engines. By comparison, approximately 45 percent of the US trucks in the medium-duty class had diesel engines in 1984. (By 1990, however, that figure was expected to approach 90 percent.) Another aspect of the Japanese market that makes it different from its US counterpart is that Japanese trucks are much smaller on average than those in the United States.

Marketing strategy
The marketing strategy Isuzu implemented at the outset of the joint venture was traditional for a Japanese company. It offered low option prices, special deals for fleet operators, and special programs to get the Allison product into the marketplace. Because of the relatively weak yen at that time (see exhibit 5.4), import prices for the transmissions were rather high. Isuzu, however, absorbed the higher costs internally in order to price the Allison product competitively.

Exhibit 5.4   Annual average rate of Japanese yen per US
dollar, 1971–1989

Year	¥/$
1971	347.48
1972	303.08
1973	270.89
1974	291.53
1975	296.69
1976	296.38
1977	267.80
1978	208.42
1979	218.18
1980	226.63
1981	220.63
1982	249.06
1983	237.55
1984	237.45
1985	238.47
1986	168.35
1987	144.60
1988	128.17
1989	138.07

Source: Federal Reserve Bulletin.

Price increases

Japanese captive companies such as GMAJ are unable to increase the product prices they charge to their parent firms solely on the basis of higher costs they may experience for labor, raw materials, energy, and the like. Instead, they are expected to improve productivity and manufacturing efficiency at least enough to hold the line on prices. They are expected to improve their production methods enough to reduce prices to their customers. If the captive firm is unable to develop programs that will reduce costs and thus prices, the parent firm will usually provide assistance by lending personnel, acquiring new technology, or whatever it may take to achieve productivity improvements. A price increase is considered a last resort.

Allison's costs were escalating due to a rapidly increasing rate of inflation in the USA during the late 1970s and early 1980s, and it was passing these costs on in the form of higher prices to its joint venture partner. In spite of these price increases, however, GMAJ was expected to do business in the Japanese manner. That meant minimal price increases to its customers. Even several years' losses were to be accepted as a normal part of doing business. (Exhibits 5.5, 5.6, and 5.7 show the company's financial position in the mid to late 1980s.)

Exhibit 5.5 Income statement (unit: yen)

	April 1, 1985 to March 31, 1986	April 1, 1986 to March 31, 1987
Sales	632,687,169	318,832,286
Cost of sales	499,902,770	277,039,435
SELLING PROFIT	132,784,399	41,792,851
Selling, general & admin. expenses:		
Salaries and bonus	45,635,054	61,913,065
Legal welfare expenses	8,106,522	16,986,979
Rent	13,338,798	18,421,354
Advertisement	727,249	5,680,796
Claim expenses	4,676,082	5,906,500
Travel expenses	2,185,202	1,349,040
Depreciation	2,465,829	7,525,619
Other expenses	16,123,811	19,261,665
TOTAL EXPENSES	93,258,547	137,045,018
OPERATING PROFIT (LOSS)	39,525,852	(95,252,167)
Non-operating profit:		
Interest income	2,719,680	2,177,422
Miscellaneous income	12,951,823	123,085,022
TOTAL NON-OPERATING PROFIT	15,671,503	125,262,444
GROSS PROFIT (LOSS) FOR THE TERM	55,197,355	30,010,277
Non-operating loss:		
Interest paid	9,202,363	8,474,853
Tax for interest on deposit	465,311	403,635
Miscellaneous loss	15,239,486	15,210,587
TOTAL NON-OPERATING LOSS	24,907,160	24,089,075
Recurring profit (loss)	30,290,195	5,921,202
Income tax	10,915,660	*5,700,000
Net profit (loss) after taxes	19,374,535	221,202
Profit (loss) brought forward	(16,730,732)	2,643,803
Unappropriated profit	2,643,803	2,865,005
*Remarks:		
Corporate Income Tax	4,540,000	
Municipal Inhabitant Tax	1,160,000	
TOTAL INCOME TAX	5,700,000	
DISPOSITION OF PROFIT		
Unappropriated profit	2,865,005 yen	
(Including profit for the term)	221,202 yen	
We would like to dispose the above amount as follows:		
Profit carried forward	2,865,005 yen	

Exhibit 5.6   Balance sheet (unit: yen)

	March 31, 1986	March 31, 1987
ASSETS		
Current:		
Cash, banks	94,982,382	81,304,533
Notes receivable	92,145,502	65,110,802[a]
A/C receivable	99,182,586	56,476,327
Inventory	89,034,191	94,361,413
Other current	84,701,978	112,277,592[b]
Allowance for doubtful A/C	(2,900,000)	(2,750,000)
TOTAL CURRENT ASSETS	457,146,639	406,780,667
Fixed:		
Buildings/structures	6,173,000	8,729,390
Machinery & equipment	11,124,742	11,274,742
Vehicles	5,874,450	8,320,000
Tools & office equipment	13,518,655	28,697,833
Telephone right	399,793	618,193
Telex right	25,938	–0–
Guarantee money	12,912,360	22,376,640
Accumulated depreciation	(28,655,767)	(32,428,476)
TOTAL FIXED ASSETS	21,373,171	47,588,322
TOTAL ASSETS	478,519,810	454,368,989
LIABILITY & EQUITY		
Current:		
S/T borrowings	155,000,000	155,000,000
Notes payable	120,738,452	124,857,421
Accounts payable trade	74,284,562	39,920,661
Accounts payable others, due within one year	3,741,888	2,549,810
Tax payable for business tax	3,120,000	150,000
Other current	780,136	7,170,129
TOTAL CURRENT LIABILITIES	357,665,038	329,648,021
Reserve:		
Reserve for corporation tax	11,021,960	–0–
Reserve for bonus	1,930,000	4,670,105
Reserve for retirement allowance	13,799,009	25,725,858[c]
TOTAL RESERVE	26,750,969	30,395,963
TOTAL LIABILITIES & RESERVE	384,416,007	360,043,984

Exhibit 5.6 (Cont'd)

	March 31, 1986	March 31, 1987
Equity:		
Common stock, ¥10,000 par value:		
authorized 36,000 shares,		
issues 9,000 shares	90,000,000	90,000,000
Profit (loss) brought forward	(16,730,732)	2,643,803
Profit (loss) for term	19,374,535	221,202
General contingency	1,460,000	1,460,000
TOTAL SHAREHOLDERS' EQUITY	94,103,803	94,325,005
TOTAL LIABILITY & SHAREHOLDER'S EQUITY	478,519,810	454,368,989

Notes:
[a] Balance of notes discounted – none.
[b] Outstanding accounts receivable others in US dollar denomination, US $691,931.94, is included in Other Current Assets. Conversion into yen with exchange rate as of fiscal year end results in ¥100,226,341; accordingly exchange loss of ¥9,211,176 has been incurred.
[c] Reserve for director's retirement allowance (based on commercial law article (287-2) ¥15,225,858 has been included in Reserve for Retirement Allowance.

Remarks: Important accounting principles
1 Inventories are stated at cost standard by FIFO.
2 Depreciation of fixed assets – declining balance method.
3 Provisions and reserves
    Reserve for bonus is reserved on tax regulation basis (matching to payment terms).
    Reserve for retirement allowance is provided on tax regulation basis; 40 percent of retirement allowance at the end of the term.
    Standard of provision for uncollectible accounts is provided on tax regulation basis.
4 Conversion of accounts receivable and payable on foreign currency basis into Japanese yen is rated by exchange rate at the time we received credit memorandum – received basis.

Product availability

Isuzu was so anxious to get Allison automatic transmissions into the market place that it sold one to anybody who requested it. This approach led to some technical difficulties because dealers often failed to select the proper options necessary for successful operation in certain applications and difficult operating conditions. For example, inner-city delivery trucks need transmissions that will stand up to stop-and-go conditions. Isuzu worked hard to overcome these initial growing pains and eventually was able to surmount most of the technical problems.

Market development

GM Allison Japan was established for the primary purpose of working with Isuzu Motors. Any programs with the other three truck manufacturers – Hino, Mitsubishi, and Nissan Diesel – would be secondary after the Isuzu market was established. By the end of 1973, the first transmissions were being tested under actual highway

Exhibit 5.7 Income statement (unit: yen)

	April 1, 1986 to March 31, 1987	April 1, 1987 to March 31, 1988
ORDINARY P/L		
Operating P/L:		
Sales	318,832,286	533,131,443
Cost of sales	277,039,435	464,796,986
Selling & admin. expenses	137,045,018	164,232,507
OPERATING LOSS	(95,252,167)	(95,898,050)
Non-Operating Income:		
Interest	2,177,422	1,219,775
Others, including Marketing Assistance	123,085,022	128,120,766
Non-Operating Expenses		
Interest	8,474,853	8,655,362
Others	15,614,222	24,526,493
ORDINARY PROFIT (LOSS)	5,921,202	250,636
EXTRA-ORDINARY P/L		
Profit		
Retirement reserve for director reverted	–0–	15,225,858
Loss		
Retirement gratuity paid	–0–	15,150,000
NET PROFIT BEFORE TAXES	5,921,202	326,494
INCOME TAX & RESIDENT TAX (CREDIT)	5,700,000	(3,330,380)
NET PROFIT AFTER TAXES	221,202	3,656,874
PROFIT BROUGHT FORWARD	2,643,803	2,865,005
UNAPPROPRIATED LOSS THIS TERM	2,865,005	6,521,879

Remarks: tax details (refund for the taxes paid for the previous term):

| Income tax | (3,004,730) |
| Resident tax | (325,650) |

and other working conditions. The program was about ready to launch on a commercial scale, and with growing confidence in the product, Isuzu began an active marketing campaign.

The 1978–9 Oil Shock

Just about when the market for the automatic transmission began to shown significant growth (see exhibit 5.8), the Organization of Petroleum Exporting Countries' (OPEC's) oil embargo stunned the world's industrialized nations. This second oil shock of the decade was to send oil prices as high as $47 per barrel, thus increasing energy costs substantially on a worldwide basis.

Extremely high oil prices in Japan resulted in a significant recession and an

Exhibit 5.8   GMAJ sales of Allison automatic transmissions

Fiscal year	Units
1973	10
1974	26
1975	114
1976	81
1977	299
1978	724
1979	1138
1980	977
1981	643
1982	481
1983	378
1984	445
1985	467
1986	600
1987	1034
1988	1050
1989	2753

Source: Company records.

annual rate of inflation that reached 18 percent. Commercial vehicle sales, as a result, declined to extremely low levels for the next several years (see exhibit 5.3), and fuel efficiency became of paramount importance. The drop in truck and bus sales in Japan led to lower sales for automatic transmissions. Another factor discouraging automatic transmission sales at this time was the perception among some end users that automatics were less fuel efficient than manual transmissions.

In spite of rapidly rising prices for raw materials and energy products, it was impossible for GMAJ to raise transmission prices because captive companies must find ways to reduce costs rather than to raise prices. Thus, GMAJ's president, Toshihiko Tamura, was forced to implement a cost-cutting drive that included greatly reduced funds for travel and telephone expenses. For example, GMAJ salesmen could not call on customers who were demanding on-site assistance.

Technical Problems

As a Japanese company, GMAJ was obliged to provide after-sales service to its end-user customers on a continuing basis. Allison provided the same warranty for its products to the Japanese original equipment manufacturers as it did for its US customers: a two-year warranty on parts and labor. The OEMs, in turn, provided a one-year warranty as their standard vehicle warranty. However, Japanese vehicle manufacturers are accustomed to providing generous coverage on power train components to their customers regardless of the published warranty provisions.

Escalating warranty costs

In 1979 Allison began experiencing serious technical problems with its automatic transmissions, nearly all of which had been installed in on-highway trucks and buses. The problems (and in many cases the complete failure of a unit) resulted in escalating warranty costs for the company. These problems were also experienced by GMAJ and were far more serious in the Japanese market than in the USA. Product quality and service are integral parts of the Japanese way of doing business. The goal is to establish long-term relationships between customers and suppliers. For example, contracts, if used, are usually written in a very broad manner with an opening date and automatic renewal. The principal concept of most agreements is to work together to resolve any conflicts in a mutually satisfactory manner.

Technical specification misunderstandings

GM Allison Japan was caught in the position of receiving a product with a fixed set of technical specifications and requirements from Allison in the United States and then representing those specifications to a third party, an OEM. In several instances, Japanese truck manufacturers wanted changes made in the transmission specifications to meet what they considered special Japanese operating conditions. Allison, however, was unwilling to agree to any changes in the technical specifications that GMAJ's engineers suggested or requested. Allison's marketing department took the position that since its transmissions were sold in several other countries without design changes, none were necessary for Japan. Furthermore, in the opinion of Allison's management, the Japanese market was not big enough to justify costly design changes.

As a result of the technical problems Allison was experiencing at this time, the Japanese OEMs were forced to deal with both application problems and product problems without recourse to technical improvements in the product. This left the Japanese manufacturers with the impression that Allison, a nonresident company attempting to sell automatic transmissions in Japan, was not interested in them. In short, they felt the Japanese market was not important to Allison.

Although GMAJ sales volume in its early years pointed toward a successful joint venture, more recent events placed the company in an unprofitable position. Managers at Allison's headquarters in Indiana, meanwhile, paid little attention to Japan. They recognized that sales in the Japanese market had become sluggish, but they were preoccupied with technical problems and the escalating warranty costs occurring in the US market.

Increasing Industry Competition

The worldwide automotive industry was becoming increasingly competitive in the 1980s, particularly in the United States. For a variety of reasons including exchange rates, productivity, quality, service, and marketing, US manufacturers of automotive products faced their stiffest competition from Japan.

In early 1984, Allison noted a shift developing in the US market for medium-duty trucks. US truck manufacturers had fallen behind their Japanese and European counterparts in the development and design of low-cab-forward or stub-nose trucks. In these vehicles the engine is behind or underneath the cab. Such trucks form the backbone of many inner-city delivery systems. Companies that needed fuel-efficient and maneuverable trucks were turning to Japanese and European models because of their superior designs and advanced dieselization.

Japan's entry into the US medium-duty truck market was of primary importance. Allison had a 25-percent penetration in this market segment, and to maintain its market share it needed to make its transmissions broadly available in Japanese imports. This realization prompted Allison's senior management to conclude that to protect the home market, Allison through GMAJ must battle the Japanese on their home turf.

The Early 1980s at GMAJ

Allison's technical problems with its automatic transmissions in the United States had an additional ramification in the Japanese market. There, GMAJ's engineers discovered, the automatic transmission was still not technically correct for vehicles equipped with diesel engines. Additionally, Tamura's cost-cutting drive only added to GMAJ's problems because its salesmen could not provide adequate customer service. Recognizing the need to solve the company's continuing warranty problems, Allison's management formed a special interdisciplinary team to address those issues in 1981. Team members were relieved of their regular responsibilities and given a six-month assignment to study and provide solutions for the whole range of problems Allison was having with its transmissions. Among the disciplines represented were engineering, service, marketing, warranty, manufacturing, finance, and reliability. The team was headed by the director of quality control at Allison's aircraft engine operation, and James Swaim represented the sales and service side of the business.

Swaim's background
After earning a degree in engineering from the General Motors Institute, Swaim joined Allison's aircraft service department. From there he moved through several other departments at Allison. His work included an assignment as a field service representative in Okinawa from 1964 to 1966. As a manager in the transmission service department, Swaim created an after-sales service infrastructure that permitted a smooth integration of the transmission line into the Detroit Diesel Allison distribution system. From that position he was named manager of the service operations organization in the transmission service department. His responsibilities included technical support for the field organization and manufacturers, customer contact, product liability, and product liability litigation. In addition, he was worldwide technical coordinator for Allison's transmission products, a position that required him to interact with all of the various disciplines in the transmission operation.

Allison's decision to assign an engineer to GMAJ
By the early part of 1984, Allison's senior executives had reached the conclusion that someone from the United States should be in Tokyo on a permanent basis.

Considerable thought went into Allison's decision regarding the type of individual who should be sent to Japan. Swaim was selected on the basis of his previous experience in Okinawa, his knowledge of Allison's product line, the wide range of positions he had held with the company, and the fact that he and his wife could adapt to the Japanese culture.

The Situation in 1984

When Swaim arrived in Tokyo in October 1984, his assignment was to provide technical and engineering support to the GMAJ staff. He reported to Allison's headquarters in Indianapolis rather than to anyone in Japan.

Swaim learned after his arrival in Tokyo that because GMAJ acted as a traditional Japanese company, no one from GMAJ was contacting the end-user customers. In that culture, only the manufacturers and dealers have direct customer contact. Although Allison managers had been urging GMAJ's president to make direct customer contact in order to convince them of the advantages of automatic transmissions, Tamura did not feel that was his responsibility. Japanese component manufacturers don't usually deal directly with end users except to handle technical questions. Allison's managers in Indianapolis did not fully appreciate the rigidity of these Japanese business practices. Thus, they were unable to understand fully the extent of the problems at their joint venture operation in Tokyo. Likewise, the managers at GMAJ had very little knowledge of how to work with US vendors or suppliers.

Swaim also learned that some GMAJ salesmen had little technical understanding of Allison's products. Furthermore, the joint venture OEM engineering groups often operated with insufficient technical data and on some occasions obsolete data. GMAJ management had decided to forgo supplying comprehensive technical data to some of its non-Isuzu Japanese manufacturers. Since GMAJ considered the data to be proprietary in nature, there was concern about it falling into the hands of "Isuzu competitors." In the vendor-subservient role required of Japanese component suppliers, GMAJ found it difficult to implement the new technical specifications developed by the task force in Indianapolis to correct the product problems.

Building relationships

Until Swaim's arrival, no American from Allison had stayed at GMAJ longer than six weeks. Swaim, therefore, set out to reassure the Japanese that "he was an Allison employee and that his company was committed to the Japanese market; that he was now resident in Japan and here to help GMAJ and its OEM customers solve their technical problems. Of primary importance was convincing the Japanese that he would indeed be in Japan for an extended period of time." Japanese managers strive to build long-term business relationships with suppliers, manufacturers, wholesalers, customers, and any others who may be a part of the distribution chain. Therefore, Swaim's long-term commitment was an essential factor in building trust.

Transmission Service Network

GMAJ sold Allison transmissions directly to the OEMs and thus acted as both wholesaler and distributor. It did not, however, provide company-owned, after-sales service to either the manufacturers or the end users. Instead, by contracting with an Isuzu dealer and an Isuzu dealer-related organization, GMAJ developed a service support network for Allison transmissions. Since the owner of a Nissan Diesel, for example, would be unwilling to take his truck to an Isuzu dealer for service, GMAJ arranged for an independent diesel repair shop to service Allison transmissions for end users who did not own Isuzu trucks.

Pricing

GMAJ purchased Allison transmissions for resale to its four OEM customers at a special discounted price from the Allison factory. GMAJ charged the OEMs prices ranging from ¥500,000 to ¥600,000, with no fixed, recognizable pricing policy. Because of the special relationship between GMAJ and Isuzu, however, GMAJ was able to charge Isuzu slightly higher prices than it charged the other three OEMs. To increase the sales volume of its child company, Isuzu elected to sell Allison transmissions in the market place as an option for ¥200,000 and absorb the cost difference. The other OEMs' option prices were ¥800,000. Because of this large disparity, the other OEMs concluded that GMAJ, with its close Isuzu relationship, offered preferential pricing to Isuzu.

The GMAJ staff in 1984

When Swaim arrived in Tokyo, the staff at GMAJ consisted of two engineers, a bookkeeper, a sales manager, and three salesmen, all of whom were seconded employees from Isuzu. The engineering manager, though a competent engineer, had little management experience. The sales manager had been in the sales promotion side of the business at Isuzu, was without technical ability, and had no experience in selling trucks or truck components. The group also included an employee seconded from C. Itoh. Most of these people were near retirement age and came to GMAJ expecting to be there three or four years. In addition, two young employees had been hired from outside the participant companies. None of GMAJ's 1984 employees had been there when the company was started in 1972.

A new president

Swaim had been in Japan for nearly three years when he was named president of GMAJ, and he realized that he must move the company in a new direction. He understood the need to develop a strategy that would expand Allison's share of the Japanese transmission market. He also was aware of the importance of developing the Japanese market in order to protect Allison's market share in the USA.

KENHAR PRODUCTS, INC.

Kenneth F. Harling

"Why should we lose our jobs because we are good at what we do? It's just not right!" a worker said to Bill Harrison, president of Kenhar Products, Inc. on December 12, 1985. The worker was obviously agitated and, along with Kenhar's other 133 employees, plainly puzzled. He had just learned from Harrison that Joseph Dyson & Sons, Inc., Kenhar's major competitor in the United States, was going to file a petition with the US International Trade Commission under Section 201 of the US Trade Act of 1974. In the petition, Dyson would ask for temporary tariffs of 35 percent on all imported steel fork arms while the US industry made itself more competitive. This move by Dyson had serious implications for Kenhar, whose sole product was steel fork arms used on forklift trucks. Kenhar manufactured them in Guelph, a small city an hour's drive west of Toronto, Ontario. From there, it exported 85 percent of its production to the United States, where it held 45 percent of that market.

Harrison had to determine what role, if any, Kenhar would play in the US International Trade Commission hearings. These hearings would be part of the investigation the commission had to conclude within 180 days of receiving the petition. The concluding report of the investigation would recommend whether the tariff should be applied. In the meantime, Kenhar would be allowed to export to the United States as usual. Harrison also thought he should review the company's

Written with the assistance of Alan DeRoo, University of Guelph. Management cooperated in the field research for this case which written with the financial support of the Laurier Institute. It was written solely for the purpose of stimulating student discussion. All incidents and individuals are real, although some financial data have been disguised at Kenhar's request. Copyright © the *Case Research Journal* and Kenneth F. Harling, 1993.

policy of manufacturing in Canada because it made Kenhar vulnerable to this and similar trade actions.

The Steel Fork Arm Industry

Steel fork arms (forks) were essentially bent and tapered steel bars manufactured primarily for use on forklift trucks and other powered lift equipment employed in the material-handling industry. Forks were used for lifting pallets on which a load (such as crates, boxes, and bricks) rested or for lifting a load (such as lumber, wallboard, or tires) directly. The key characteristics of forks were that they were discrete components that could be removed from the lift equipment, they were designed to support substantial weight (most were capable of lifting more than 2000 pounds), and they were forged. Forks were bought separately and attached to trucks. There were no substitutes for forks.

Forks were designed for specific applications: pallet forks lifted pallets, lumber forks lifted lumber, carpet forks or booms lifted carpet. Exhibit 6.1 illustrates the variety of forks. Ninety percent of all forks were used for pallets. Standards associations had specified 10 to 20 sizes of pallet forks to facilitate interchangeability between them and trucks made by different manufacturers. These sizes, which were called "standards" in the industry, ranged in thickness from 1.25 to 2.5 inches and in width from 4 to 7 inches, and had blades up to 96 inches long. Compliance with the standards was voluntary. All other forks were called "specials" and were manufactured to customer specification.

The configuration of a fork and the nomenclature associated with it are presented in exhibit 6.2. Forks were mounted on the lift carriage of trucks either by hooking them onto flat steel bars or by slipping them onto tubular steel bars. All forks were tapered for easier insertion under the load.

The most important aspect of a fork was its load capacity or strength. The most critical determinant was the strength at the bend or "heel," since this was where most of the stress of carrying the load was borne. Certain manufacturing processes, described below, appeared to produce stronger bends than others. Another factor affecting strength was width. Wider forks were stronger, although they cost more since they used more material. Still another factor was the type of steel used. Carbon steel was cheapest, but forks made of carbon steel needed to be larger in order to carry the same load as forks made from the stronger and more costly alloy and boron steels.

The Manufacturing Process

The production of a fork consisted of two major groups of operations (see exhibit 6.3). The first involved shaping bar steel into a fork and the second involved finishing the shaped fork. There were several ways of shaping bar steel into a fork. With the *full-in-forge process*, the billet was heated, then hammered into the shape of a fork and finally a bend was hammered into it. All other shaping processes started with bar steel. The bar was cut to length and then tapered by cutting and grinding it to the basic dimensions of a fork. It was then ground further to clean up the cut

Exhibit 6.1 Selected types of steel fork arms

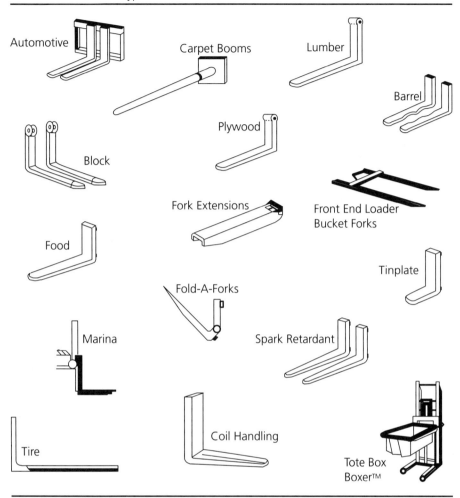

edges. Next the portion of the fork where the bend would be made was heated and bent in a horizontal press-brake. The sequence of the steps producing the bend differed, depending on when the "upset" step – thickening the bar at the bend to compensate for the thinning caused by the bending – was done. The upset was done by pushing the ends of the bar together. Manufacturers used one of three different approaches to bending and upsetting.

1 The *free bending method*. The bar was first bent and then upset.
2 The *upset-bend method*. The bar was first upset and then bent.
3 The *bend-upset-bend method*. The bar was first bent 89 degrees, then upset, and then the bend was finished.

Exhibit 6.2 Parts and ways of mounting forks

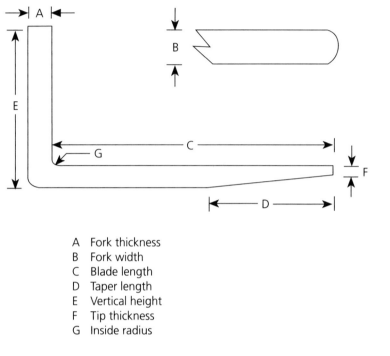

A Fork thickness
B Fork width
C Blade length
D Taper length
E Vertical height
F Tip thickness
G Inside radius

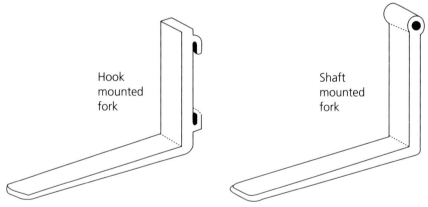

Hook
mounted
fork

Shaft
mounted
fork

Kenhar used the bend-upset-bend method.

After the fork had been shaped, it went through the second group of operations. First hangers (hooks or tubes) were welded to it so that it could be attached to a truck. Next it was heat-treated to improve strength and to give it a hard surface that would improve wear. Third, it was shot-blasted. Then it was examined and straightened where necessary. Finally it was painted.

Exhibit 6.3   Process for manufacturing a steel fork arm

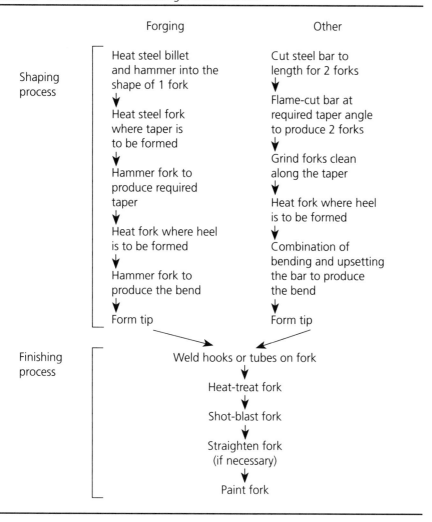

The Customer

Ninety percent of the forks sold were used on forklift trucks; the rest were used on cranes and construction equipment. The major US manufacturers of trucks (*original equipment manufacturers*, or *OEMs*) are listed in exhibit 6.4.

The customers who bought trucks generally used them for only one purpose, so each truck typically was paired with two forks for its life. This meant that the demand for forks depended heavily on the demand for new trucks: sales of forks for new trucks accounted for 70 to 80 percent of the annual sales of forks. The remaining sales were to replace worn or damaged forks or to allow conversion of a truck to a different use.

Exhibit 6.4   Manufacturers' shares of the US forklift truck market, 1985

	Share in percent
US companies	
Caterpillar Industries Inc.	11
Clark Material Handling Co.	19
Crown Controls Corp.	4
Hyster Co.	19
Raymond Corp.	5
Yale Materials Handling Corp.	11
	70
Foreign companies	
Kalmar AC	2
Mitsubishi	5
Nissan	9
TCM (Itoh)	4
Toyota	10
	30

Source: Compiled from industry sources.

Exhibit 6.5   Forklift trucks: US producers' domestic shipments, imports for consumption, and apparent consumption, 1981–1985

Year	US producers' domestic shipments[a]	Imports[b]	Apparent consumption	Ratio to consumption (%)	
				Producers' shipment	Imports
1981	49,784	11,826	61,610	80.0	19.2
1982	38,215	8,352	46,567	82.1	17.9
1983	39,549	13,978	53,527	73.9	26.1
1984	57,483	29,997	87,480	65.7	34.3
1985	55,219	37,039	92,258	59.9	40.1

[a] Based on responses of US producers accounting for more than 95 percent of domestic forklift truck production.
[b] Based on responses from importers accounting for more than 80 percent of imports under TSUS item 695.40, forklift trucks and similar industrial vehicles.

Source: Compiled from industry sources.

The demand for trucks followed the performance of the capital goods sector of the economy. A severe economic recession in the United States in the early eighties reduced demand for trucks considerably (see exhibit 6.5). The domestic truck industry never returned to its prerecession share of the market because of increased competition from imports.

As competition from imports drove truck prices down during the eighties, US truck manufacturers made cost-cutting their major priority. Some became importers themselves as they found that trucks could be produced more cheaply offshore. They either moved their production facilities overseas or set up joint ventures with foreign manufacturers to supply both the US and foreign markets. They imported the trucks, added forks to them, and then shipped them to customers. By 1985, 24,000 trucks a year were being imported from Japan. The trend toward importing appeared likely to continue into the future. Towmotor, a division of Caterpillar, had ceased production at its largest US facility in 1985, and Clark had announced in early 1985 that it would close its largest US plant in 1987 and then import half of its truck volume from Korea.

The OEMs also sought to reduce costs by replacing self-manufactured forks made by "captive" operations with cheaper ones from commercial manufacturers. Clark, for example, stopped making its own forks at the end of 1982 and Hyster stopped in June 1985. Other OEMs also increased the proportion of forks they bought commercially. The result was that US fork production had gone from being half self-manufactured and half commercial in 1980 to nearly all commercial by 1985.

Competition in the fork business also trended toward global production. Nine producers in five countries, including the United States, provided over 99 percent of the forks purchased in the United States (exhibit 6.6). By the end of 1985, the US fork industry had only two commercial producers (Dyson and GCN) and one self-manufacturer (Yale, which had an agreement with Kenhar that allowed it to use Kenhar's patented manufacturing process).

Although no government collected statistics on trade in forks, a US trade association had collected statistics from US truck manufacturers. It calculated that the number of imported forks had risen by 155 percent and their value by 45 percent from 1981 to 1985. Following the Tokyo Round of negotiations for the General Agreement on Tariffs and Trade in 1978, the tariff of 4.5 percent had been dropping at the rate of 0.5 percent per year. In 1985 it was only 1.0 percent and by 1987 it would be gone.

Truck manufacturers and users were greatly concerned over safety when buying forks. This meant that high quality – defined as a fork that would not fail in use – was a significant factor in the customer's mind. Other purchase criteria in order of decreasing importance were reliability of vendor firm, prompt delivery, availability of product, price, transportation costs, and proximity of the vendor firm.

Kenhar Products, Inc.

Kenhar Products, Inc. was founded in 1961 in Toronto, Ontario, by Livingston International, Inc. By 1975 it had achieved sales of $1.5 million and had 50 employees. In that year, the current owners purchased the company for $1.3 million. Following their purchase, Kenhar grew steadily and by 1985 it had sales of $14 million and 135 employees. In 1984 the company had moved its plant and office to the outskirts of Guelph, near Highway 401, a major transportation artery across Ontario that connected with the US interstate highway system.

Exhibit 6.6 Steel fork arms: US and foreign producers and selected industry information, 1985

Fork arm producer	Location	Share of 1985 US sales (%)[a]	Manufacturing process	Type of steel used	Types of forks produced	Customers
			United States			
Dyson	Painesville, Ohio	23	Upset and bend	Alloy	Standards and specials	OEMs, distributors, dealers, end users
GCN	Seattle, Wash.	2	Free bend and weld	Alloy	Standards and specials	OEMs, distributors, dealers, end users
Hyster[b]	Danville, Ill.	4[c]	Upset and bend	Boron	Standards and specials	Captive, very few to dealers
Yale	Greenville, N.C.	10	Bend and upset	Carbon	Standards	Captive, very few to dealers
		39				
			Foreign			
Erectoweld	Canada	5	Bend and upset	Alloy	Standards and specials	Dealers, distributors
Kenhar	Canada	45	Bend, upset, bend	Boron	Standards and specials	OEMs, distributors, dealers, end users
Industries Crown	Mexico	4	Bend and upset	Alloy	Standards	Crown Controls Corp.
Toyoshima	Japan	4	Rolling, upset, and bend	Alloy	Standards	Dyson, distributors
Falkenroth	West Germany	3	[d]	Boron	Standards and specials	OEMs, distributors, dealers, end users
		61				

[a] One percent of apparent US consumption is accounted for by imports from Great Britain and the Republic of Korea.
[b] Ceased production in 1985.
[c] Based on 6 months' production.
[d] Information not available.

Source: Compiled from industry sources.

Human resources

The senior management team at Kenhar included nine individuals (see exhibit 6.7). Management had kept itself lean so that people would not have to be laid off during economic downturns. This meant that managers were working a 50-hour week in 1985. Many of the Kenhar managers had previously worked for large industrial companies. They had been attracted to Kenhar because it lacked the bureaucracy of a larger company, it had a highly focused strategy, the president was a challenging leader, and the owners viewed their investment in long-run terms.

The company had 100 workers in the plant, which operated three shifts a day, five days a week. Each summer workers took vacation when the plant was shut down for two weeks. They were paid slightly more than the average industrial wage in the area and also shared 10 percent of the company's profits. The workforce was aging with the company because turnover was low. By 1985 the average

Exhibit 6.7 Kenhar's top management, 1985

Person	Title	Years with Kenhar	Previous experience
W. J. Harrison	Chief Executive Officer	10	John Deere, Allis Chalmers
D. Lewis	Vice-President: Operations	13	Massey Ferguson
B. Petts	Vice-President: Finance	3	Birks Jewellers
J. Hoy	Secretary Treasurer	8	Kearney National, Bank of Nova Scotia
R. Varilek	Director of Marketing	1	Allis Chalmers, Clark Material Handling, forklift truck dealership
H. Plumstead	Controller	20	Weston Bakeries
S. Hornung	Plant Engineer	22	Personal Business
A. Spinelli	Plant Manager	10	Allis Chalmers
A. Green	Manager, Quality Control and Metallurgy	4	Linread Canada

age of workers was 33 years. The workers had been unionized before the company moved to Guelph, but were no longer. A fifth of them were Portuguese immigrants who were productive workers though their knowledge of English was limited.

Finance

Kenhar's success in the market place was reflected in its financial statements (see exhibits 6.8 and 6.9). Three other financial aspects are of note. First, 54 percent of the inventory was raw materials, 34 percent was work-in-process, and 12 percent was finished goods. Second, when the company was bought in 1975, the current owners had financed it using an equal mix of debt, investment by venture capitalists, and investment by the current owners. Since then the owners had reinvested all profits back into the company. Third, the long-term debt on the balance sheet in 1985 had been created earlier that year when the venture capitalists had been paid off.

The company used a detailed standard cost system in which standard costs were set yearly based on industrial engineering data. When "specials" had to be estimated, their standard costs were set by extrapolating figures from the "standard" sizes. On average, 50 percent of the cost of making a fork was for materials, 15 percent for labor, and 35 percent for overhead.

Manufacturing

In 1984 the company had moved to a 100,000-square-foot plant that it had built in Guelph, Ontario. By 1985 it was operating at full capacity, manufacturing 450 to 500 forks a day, ranging from 90 to 400 pounds each. The operations manager, A. Spinelli, commented:

Exhibit 6.8 Balance sheet for Kenhar Products, Inc., 1985
(thousands of Canadian dollars)

Assets	
Cash and equivalents	112
Trade receivable	2,979
Inventory	1,964
Total current	5,055
Fixed assets (net)	5,288
Total assets	10,343

Liabilities	
Notes payable	0
Current long-term debt	110
Trade payables	2,509
Income tax payable	233
Total current	2,852
Deferred taxes	845
Long-term debt	4,055
Total long-term	4,900
Net worth	2,591
Total liabilities and net worth	10,343

We're very pleased with the layout of this plant. The only improvement, if we were to build a new one tomorrow, would be to install conveyor systems so that the forks could flow right through the plant without touching the floor. These systems would cost around $1 million. They would eliminate the cost of handling product as it moves between processes – around $4 a fork. Work-in-process inventories would also be cut in half.

The average age of the equipment in the Guelph plant was six years, but much of it could still be considered state-of-the-art. Furthermore, Kenhar had carefully maintained its equipment so that it continued to hold close tolerances. The equipment had come from many sources. A few of the machines had been specially built for Kenhar's needs, some in the company's machine shop and some by specialty manufacturers. Some equipment had also come from OEMs who had sold their equipment to Kenhar when they stopped manufacturing forks. After equipping the Guelph plant, Kenhar had enough used equipment in storage to half equip another plant of the same size.

The manufacturing process used by Kenhar had several advantages over those used by its competitors. The key difference was a special machine that Kenhar had developed and patented in the early 1970s. This machine bent, upset, and completed the bending of the fork with one heating of the bar. This provided numerous advantages. The cycle time was one-third faster than that of competitors, and die changes needed to make different-sized forks could be done in minutes while

Exhibit 6.9   Profit and loss statement for Kenhar Products, Inc., 1985
             (thousands of Canadian dollars)

Net sales		14,579
Cost of goods sold		8,921
Gross profit		5,658
Expenses		
Selling	787	
Administration	1,353	
Interest	588	
Depreciation	506	
Total Expenses		3,234
Operating profit before tax		2,424

the industry norm was hours. The result was that machinery worth $400,000 handled 40 percent more volume than that of competitors and used less labor. It also reduced energy costs because the fork had to be heated only once for both the bending and upsetting. These features lowered labor costs by $2.00 per fork and energy costs by $2.50 per fork. Finally, the Kenhar method appeared to produce bends of superior strength.

Kenhar was also unique in that it used robots to weld hooks on the forks; however, a considerable amount of hand-welding was necessary as well.

A major goal of management was to produce a high-quality product. The company strove to achieve this in several ways. First, the workforce was given the responsibility for both setting up their machines and checking the output they produced. Furthermore, Kenhar's welders were all fully certified. Management felt that Kenhar's all-certified welders did better work than their competitors' welders; in addition, certification gave the customers greater confidence in it. Finally, the company had kept material and process information on every fork it had ever made. This database was regularly analyzed to determine the optimal settings for the processes. It was also needed to satisfy the quality assurance programs of some of its major OEM customers.

The company also monitored quality at each of its processing steps. Every fork was tested for hardness following heat treatment, hardness being a proxy for strength. Each fork was also examined for cracks at the heel and improperly welded joints where parts had been attached. Finally, forks were tested randomly after painting to see that they withstood three times the specified load without any deformation occurring – a standard recommended by various standards associations.

An advantage that Kenhar and Erectroweld, another Canadian manufacturer of forks, had over US competition was that Canadian steel mills were among the best suppliers of bar steel in the world. They were able to provide high-quality steel in a wider variety of sizes than steel companies in other countries. Kenhar bought steel with 65 different cross sections in mill-run lots.

Engineering and development

Kenhar's management felt that a company could be competitive with a low-technology product if it applied high technology to its manufacture. Consequently, it had continually looked for ways to improve the product. Kenhar had used three-dimensional finite stress analysis to redesign its fork so that less steel was needed for the same strength. The chemical composition of the steel used had been modified, increasing the chromium content of its boron steel, again allowing Kenhar to use less material without sacrificing strength. These changes had lowered material costs by $5 per fork. They had also lowered labor and energy costs by $2 per fork because there was less material to be worked. Management estimated that these engineering improvements put Kenhar two to three years ahead of its competitors.

The company prided itself on its intellectual property. "We have more information on forks than anyone else in the world," remarked Varilek, Kenhar's director of marketing. "We do not have to worry about meeting customers' standards. The often ask us what their standards should be."

Quality was a major concern at Kenhar. The company had a full-time metallurgist who continually tested Kenhar's product to ensure that quality was being maintained. Kenhar also bought and tested forks made by competitors.

Marketing

Kenhar, which referred to itself as "the Fork Specialist," sold a full range of forks, both to OEMs and to dealers and distributors using personnel sent directly from Guelph. OEMs such as Hyster, Clark, and Caterpillar accounted for around 70 percent of its sales. Kenhar's marketers had worked hard to convince these OEMs to see the company as a partner who could help them in several ways.

- Kenhar's ability to supply high-quality forks on time was unsurpassed, because this was its only business.
- Specialization gave it economies of scale unavailable through self-manufacturing.
- Kenhar eased the OEMs' decision to discontinue making their own forks because Kenhar stood ready to buy their fork-making equipment. Kenhar then stored the equipment for potential use by itself.

Dealers and distributors accounted for 30 percent of Kenhar's sales. The company maintained inventories of standard forks so that it could guarantee delivery to buyers of this equipment within days. It ensured this by holding 70 percent of the company's finished goods inventory in three warehouses in the United States. It also supplied these customers with information to use when pricing forks to end users.

Kenhar's emphasis on OEM customers had been a conscious decision. OEMs gave Kenhar enough lead time to practice just-in-time manufacturing and delivery. This kept inventory down and allowed longer runs. The production of forks by Kenhar in 1985 is shown in exhibit 6.10.

Truck manufacturers viewed Kenhar's products as among the highest quality available. The company was also responsive to customer delivery needs, and would adjust its production schedules to meet their special requests. Kenhar stuck closely to its list prices, offering only modest discounts for volume buyers.

Exhibit 6.10   Kenhar fork production in 1985

	Standards			Specials	Total
	Small	Medium	Large		
Number (in thousands)	75	20	2	17	114
Total sales (in $ millions)	7.5	3.0	0.4	3.7	14.6
Total cost of sales (in $ millions)	4.8	1.9	0.2	2.0	8.9

Exhibit 6.11   Exchange rates in Canadian dollars per unit, 1976–1985

Year	US dollar	German mark	Japanese yen
1976	0.9861	0.3920	0.003327
1977	1.0635	0.4586	0.003980
1978	1.1402	0.5691	0.005480
1979	1.1715	0.6394	0.005375
1980	1.1690	0.6444	0.005183
1981	1.1990	0.5318	0.005450
1982	1.2341	0.5086	0.004966
1983	1.2324	0.4834	0.005190
1984	1.2948	0.4564	0.005457
1985	1.3652	0.4677	0.005767

Source: Average noon spot rates, *Bank of Canada Review*, Table I1.

Exchange rates

Through the eighties, the Canadian dollar depreciated against the US dollar (see exhibit 6.11). Kenhar's management tried to maintain a particular gross margin per dollar of sales and not lower its US prices as the Canadian dollar fell. Most of the exchange rate gains on US sales were taken in margins and then invested back in the business to that Kenhar's competitiveness was enhanced.

Joseph Dyson & Sons, Inc.

Joseph Dyson and Sons, Inc., the US company seeking protection from imports, was founded in 1884 as a blacksmith's shop in Cleveland, Ohio. In 1972, it moved operations to Painesville, Ohio. At the time of the move, it had six product lines: forks, sucker rods for the oil industry, industrial fasteners, forged rings, commercial forgings, and commercial heat treating. In 1981 Dyson became a manufacturer of trucks with its acquisition of Schreck Industries. Schreck was operated as a wholly owned subsidiary until 1983, when Dyson sold it. Dyson's total sales in 1985 were $14 million, with forks accounting for 64 percent of sales.

The company was a family-owned business that had been highly profitable into the seventies because it had dominated the US fork industry. Some of these earnings had gone into the Dyson Family Charitable Trust, allowing the family to play a major philanthropic role in Cleveland, Ohio. In recent years, the family's ownership had rested with two sisters; one, who held 51 percent of the company, lived in England and one lived in Canada. They expected the business to fund its own investment needs.

Dyson managers' assessment of the current situation was that the company was competitive with Kenhar, although Kenhar had some advantages. They thought the factor that had been hurting them most was the depreciating Canadian dollar, which, they felt, allowed price discounting by Kenhar. They estimated that this change had reversed the market shares of the two companies between 1980 and 1985.

Human resources

When Dyson had dominated the fork industry, a "country club" atmosphere had developed in the management echelons of the business. This was reflected in the company's reputation for big parties and a comment by a customer that the management "seemed more interested in spending money than making it." Many of the management team had aged with the company.

Dyson had 60 workers making forks. It kept its labor force small through extensive use of overtime during peak periods and by having it work on other products during slow periods. The workers' base pay was 15 percent more per hour than the wages paid by competitors making forks, though it was in line with wage rates for the products they worked on when they were not making forks. In addition, they were paid substantial incentive bonuses. They were unionized and had last gone out on strike for the first four months of 1983.

Finance

While Dyson was financially sound in 1985, it had suffered major difficulties in the early 1980s. A large number of operating problems had surfaced in Schreck after Dyson purchased it in 1981. These difficulties, coupled with a product recall, caused operating losses which brought Dyson's corporate net worth down from a substantial surplus to nearly zero by the end of 1982. The company was saved from a negative net worth of $700,000 that year by switching from last in first out (LIFO) to first in first out (FIFO) inventory valuation. Not until 1984 did profitability start to improve, and in 1985 it was the best it had been for years.

Kenhar's management estimated from its industry contacts that Dyson's fork business in 1985 had trade receivables of $1.6 million, inventories of $1.2 million, fixed assets of $2.0 million (half of which were used in its fastener business as well), and trade payables of $2.7 million. The whole of Dyson had long-term liabilities of $3.0 million and a net worth of $0.5 million. Kenhar had estimated Dyson's profit and loss as shown in exhibit 6.12.

Manufacturing

Dyson had invested $1 million in fork manufacturing equipment when it opened the Painesville plant in 1972. Since then this equipment had not been maintained,

Exhibit 6.12 Estimated profit and loss statement for J. Dyson and Sons steel fork arm operation, 1985 (thousands of Canadian dollars)

Net sales	9,100
Cost of goods sold	6,200
Gross profit	2,900
Operating expenses, other	1,900
Depreciation, depletion, amortization	200
Interest	150
Operating profit	650

Source: Kenhar managers' estimates.

upgraded, or replaced. Dyson's management felt that the market for forks had been shrinking and would continue to shrink in the future. Consequently, it had chosen to invest in other opportunities, including sucker rods, industrial fasteners, and Schreck, rather than in the fork business.

The apparent average age of equipment dedicated to manufacturing forks in 1985 was 13 years; much of this equipment was so worn that it had lost the precision necessary to produce forks to tight specifications. The actual average age of the equipment was lower, because some equipment had been bought in recent years for use in other businesses but was also used for manufacturing forks. A Hyster executive provided an overall evaluation of Dyson's equipment in 1985. After touring its plant to decide whether Hyster should rely on Dyson as its supplier of forks, the executive reported that the Dyson plant did not match the modernity and quality of the Hyster fork facility, which was 10 years old.

The manufacturing processes at Dyson differed from those at Kenhar in several ways. First, the methods and product flow in the plant were disorganized, in part because the plant made multiple products. This often resulted in mistakes in processing orders. Second, the processes were more labor-intensive than were Kenhar's. Third, Dyson's bending process for small and medium-sized forks used the upset-bend process common to most world producers of forks.

With the high demand for forks, Dyson found itself running considerable overtime in 1985. It supplemented its domestic production by importing; Dyson was the largest single importer of forks to the United States in 1985. Approximately 15 percent of its sales dollar volume came from the Japanese producer Toyoshima, which had already initiated a direct marketing program in the United States. Dyson recognized that Toyoshima, which had been modernizing its operations and working to lower its costs, planned to pursue the US market. By developing a joint venture with them, Dyson sought to control Toyoshima's marketing activities in the United States while at the same time satisfying Dyson's product needs.

Dyson had also signed a letter of agreement with Daewoo Heavy Industries, a

Korean firm. Under the agreement, Dyson would exchange technology for exclusive US marketing rights on Daewoo forks. This was an attractive source because the Korean won was soft against the US dollar. Dyson's management was concerned, however, that exchange rate movements might make imported forks too costly in the longer run.

Engineering and development

Dyson had significant research under way; however, resistance in the plant had slowed down adoption of many changes research findings had suggested.

Dyson had also had problems with quality and with the appearance of products. In 1981 its department of quality assurance discovered that a change in manufacturing methods had led to small cracks in the welds attaching the hangers to the arms. The company made a major product recall as a precaution "in view of the potential safety-related issues involved as a responsible manufacturer." This was done even though Dyson was never aware of any product failures or customer complaints about this problem. Quality suffered again following the strike in 1983. Most recently, there had been problems with the Japanese-supplied forks it sold; these forks were poorly finished, variable in dimensions, and their overall appearance was poor.

Marketing

Dyson sold its product only in the US market, mostly through distributors. The company's own sales staff consisted of five people in the office at the factory.

In its earlier years Dyson's domination of the industry had allowed it to charge high prices. As newer competitors producing high-quality forks entered the market, Dyson's market share eroded, and its switched to competing on price. Though it tried to offer lower prices than Kenhar, Dyson had lost several major OEM customers over the past three years and those remaining had reduced their purchases from Dyson.

Customers had complaints about Dyson. They said that its service was poor; that it seemed uninterested in small customers; that it did not respond to repeated requests for price quotations; that it did not always have standard forks available when requested; and that it had long delivery times (about three weeks longer than Kenhar's, which were four to six weeks for standards). Some customers described the company as having a bad attitude overall. Some OEMs had been further irritated by Dyson's purchase of Schreck, since this had put Dyson in direct competition with them. They also complained about the quality of Dyson's product.

Dyson's annual sales of its own product included 49,000 small, 12,000 medium, and 1000 large standard forks and 2000 special forks. In addition, it sold 6000 small and 5000 medium standard forks manufactured for Dyson by Toyoshima. All forks were priced to produce a 32 percent gross margin based on job cost estimates. To achieve this, Dyson's own standard fork prices averaged 5 percent higher than Kenhar's, and its specials were 11 percent higher. The forks supplied by Toyoshima were priced to match Kenhar's prices.

Kenhar's Current Situation

The petition

Dyson's petition for protection from trade came as a complete surprise to Kenhar's managers, as they had made a conscious effort to follow the rules of the General Agreement on Tariffs and Trade (GATT). Kenhar President Bill Harrison said, "We felt that we would never risk being excluded from the US market if we abided by the customs and regulations of GATT."

When the firm's Washington lawyers, retained to monitor shifting US regulations, told Harrison about the impending petition, he asked them what it might mean for Kenhar. They told him that it appeared that Dyson was going to ask for duties of 35 percent for two years, 25 percent for two more years, and then 20 percent for a year. Dyson was going to request this relief so that it could generate the funds it needed to invest in order to compete with foreign manufacturers.

The lawyers told Harrison that the petition was to be filed under Section 201 of the US Trade Act of 1974. The first step would be a hearing conducted by the US International Trade Commission. As this would be an analytical exercise, the key was to provide the investigators with information that supported Kenhar's case. For relief to be granted under Section 201, it had to be shown that the number of imported forks (either actual amounts or amounts relative to domestic production) were "a substantial cause of serious injury" or "threatened serious injury" to the US industry. This meant that the US International Trade Commission investigators would try to establish whether imported forks had caused significant idling of productive facilities, had made a significant number of firms unable to operate at reasonable profit, and had caused significant underemployment or unemployment in the industry. The lawyers sent an *aide-mémoire* to Harrison describing what they told him on the phone (see exhibit 6.13).

The lawyers felt that Kenhar had a good chance of winning the technical arguments, though they cautioned that victory was by no means assured. The US International Trade Commission had recently found that the US shakes and shingles industry had experienced serious injury in light of the considerable declines in production, employment, the number of firms, and production capacity, while demand had increased modestly in 1984. The lawyers suggested that Kenhar seek all the support it could get. Harrison should go to Washington immediately and meet everyone there who had any influence in the hearing process: lawyers, politicians, judges. They also suggested the Kenhar contact other offshore suppliers, since their interests would be affected equally by relief measures. The lawyers also raised the issue with External Affairs in Ottawa. Federal officials had said that the government would "give the fullest support they could" and would lobby the US President on Kenhar's behalf if the trade commission recommended that the US industry needed protection.

The lawyers estimated that the legal costs of fighting the petition would be around US$175,000. In addition, Kenhar would have to cover the cost of having its executives appear at the hearings in Washington, the costs of preparing documents, and incidental lobbying costs. When Harrison discussed the problem with

Exhibit 6.13 *Aide-mémoire* to W. J. Harrison, Kenhar's CEO

Meaning of a 201

Section 201 of the US Trade Act is called an "escape clause" and is common to the trade legislation of more than 30 countries that are members of the General Agreement on Trade and Tariffs (GATT). While the members of the GATT are, in principle, working toward reducing barriers to trade at their borders, the escape clause permits them to escape their obligations under the GATT and institute temporary import restrictions to allow them to modernize and adjust to competition.

Under Section 201, an industry or a company can seek remedies for relief: increased duties, quotas, a combination of the two, or quantitative limits needed for setting up an orderly marketing agreement. These remedies may last for an initial five years with an extension for another three. Relief granted for more than three years must be phased down after an initial three-year period, and an extension cannot increase it above the level in effect immediately before the extension.

Use of Section 201 is considered a political remedy because the section requires a decision by the President of the United States to provide relief. As a political decision, it may defy all economic logic while satisfying political needs.

Steps in the 201 Process

There are three steps to a 201 action:

Step 1. The US International Trade Commission (USITC) must investigate whether increased imports have injured US industry using an injury test that assumes fair trade. This must be done within 180 days of receiving a petition. The investigation includes sending questionnaires to importers and the US industry. Those providing information can request that trade secrets and other sensitive information be treated confidentially. It also includes a public hearing at which all interested parties can present evidence and file post-hearing briefs. The USITC's findings are published in a report that goes to the President and is also made public. If the USITC does not find injury or if it recommends the provision of adjustment assistance, the President has no discretion in the matter. If the USITC finds injury, the report concludes by recommending relief and the process goes to step two.

Step 2. An interagency committee recommends what relief should be provided. This committee is chaired by the US Trade Representative and includes the Departments of State, Commerce, Treasury, Labor, Defense and other agencies. It has 45 days from receipt of the USITC finding of injury until its recommendation must go to the President.

Step 3. The President decides what remedies he will use to provide relief, or alternatively, he can award adjustment assistance, or he can decide against any relief at all. The President must make his decision within 60 days of the USITC's finding of injury.

Kenhar's workforce, the workers said that they were willing to put 10 percent of the funds from their profit-sharing program toward financing the cost of fighting the petition.

Even if Kenhar were to defeat the petition, the lawyers indicated that Dyson had the right to appeal under Section 201 after one year. Furthermore, because US trade laws were uncoordinated and administered by a maze of agencies, Dyson might be able to bring action in some other way before then.

The new plant

In 1982 Kenhar's management had considered building its 10,000 square foot plant in the United States. Building costs would have been substantially less, with land cost 50 percent lower and construction costs 25 percent lower when dollars were converted at 1985 exchange rates. It had also considered building a plant half that size, which would have had 50 percent of the capacity of the larger plant but would have cost only 30 percent less to build. A municipal government had offered financing at 2 percent below prime. Operating costs would have been lower, as labor costs would have been 40 percent lower while the cost of steel and other materials and equipment only 5 percent higher.

In the end, management had decided to build the plant in Guelph. The land had cost $300,000 and the plant construction $2.5 million. The equipment in the plant had a book value of $3 million. By building in Guelph, Kenhar had the same energy costs as if it had built in the United States but better access to boron steel. Locating in Guelph also allowed the company to continue to use its highly experienced labor force. Recruiting and training a labor force to competitive levels would have taken one year and duplicating the current labor force would have taken three years. In addition, it satisfied the management team, many of whom had familial attachment to the Guelph area.

Harrison's view of the action

Harrison was furious over the petition. During the summer of 1985, the owners of Dyson had met with him three times to explore the possibility of selling their company to Kenhar. They had terminated the discussions without giving any reason. Now they had filed the petition. He commented to his colleagues about the petition, "Nobody in this industry makes a 35 percent profit. Raising the tariff to that level will effectively ban exports to the US, giving Dyson a monopoly. They say we're so strong and have done such a good job that they need duties so they can catch up. Well, they shouldn't have that opportunity!"

Given the petition, Harrison also reflected on the wisdom of Kenhar's decision to build its new plant in Canada. He certainly felt that the company's decision was questionable, especially now that Toyoshima, a Japanese competitor, was exploring the feasibility of building a plant in the United States. He wondered whether fighting the petition was enough. Perhaps Kenhar should try to purchase Dyson, or build a greenfield plant in the United States.

CALOX MACHINERY CORPORATION

Lester A. Neidell

Mike Brown, international sales manager, tapped his pencil on the notepad and contemplated his upcoming discussion with Calox's executive committee concerning the distributor situation in New Zealand. The Labor Day weekend break had not been especially conductive to his sorting out the conflicting information and varied opinions concerning the New Zealand predicament. After only three months on the job Mike had not expected to be involved in a decision that would have such far-reaching consequences.

On paper the decision looked simple: whether or not to adhere to his earlier decision to replace the original New Zealand distributor, Glade Industries, with a newly formed company, Calox New Zealand Ltd. Despite his newness to the company, Mike was confident that Calox's executive committee would agree with whatever recommendations he made in this situation, since he had been charged with "solidifying" the International Sales Division. If he decided to reverse his decision to terminate Glade Industries, could he "undo" any damage done so far?

Three previous faxes were spread on his desk along with the brief notes that he had jotted down during Thursday's conference call between Calox's executives and the company's legal counsel. Mike swung back to the PC behind his desk and began to draft what he hoped would be the definitive Calox policy for New Zealand.

The Company

Calox Machinery Company began in 1946 as a partnership between John Caliguri and William Oxley. The two engineers met during the Second World War and discovered mutual interests in mechanical engineering and construction. Both were natives of Kansas City, and at the end of the war they established a partnership with the expressed purpose of developing high-quality excavation equipment and accessories. Their first product was an innovative hydraulically operated replacement blade for a light-duty scraper.

Calox's principal customers were independent contractors engaged in excavation of building sites, and airport and highway construction and maintenance. Calox's products were primarily replacement items for OEM (original equipment manufacturer) parts and accessories. Some OEM sales were achieved; that is, contractors could order new equipment from OEMs with Calox blades and accessories already installed. Growth over the years was slow, but steady.

The product line expanded to include payloader buckets, a number of dozer and scraper blades, and parts for aerial equipment including construction forklifts and snorkels. A key to the company's success was its specialty status; its products were used to enhance the performance of expensive equipment produced by Caterpillar, Eaton, International Harvester, Case, and other OEMs. Calox's strategy was simply to provide a better part, often at a premium price, and to have it readily available in the field through a network of strong distributors. Direct competitors in the United States included small specialty producers such as Bobcat, Dresser, and Gradall, as well as the parts divisions of the large OEM manufacturers. Primary competitors in international markets included Terex, Deutsch, Takeuchi, and Hitachi. William Oxley compared Calox to the Cummins Engine Company, which had achieved a superior position in the diesel engine market through a similar strategy.

The partnership was replaced by an incorporated structure in 1970, when Bill Oxley Jr became CEO. Despite slow growth of the US economy, both 1990 and 1991 were very good years for Calox; annual sales increases of 12 percent were achieved, and the company set profit records each year. Sales for the 1991 fiscal year broke the $70 million barrier for the first time in the company's history. That year, approximately 280 people were employed at the single location in Kansas City, of which three-fourths were hourly workers engaged in fabrication.

International Sales

Calox's first international sale occurred in 1971, when the company responded to an unsolicited inquiry and shipped a small order to Canada. International sales languished throughout the 1970s, when a great deal of construction was put on hold due to the "energy crisis." Channels of distribution for international sales were much the same as for domestic sales. Independent distributors were given nonexclusive rights, although in practice most countries had only one distributor. Forty of Calox's 110 distributors were located outside the United States. In 1991 almost 25 percent of Calox's sales were generated internationally. In the 1988 to

1991 period, aided by the relative decline of the US dollar against most other currencies, international sales grew at an annual rate of 16 percent.

Prior to Mike's arrival, there was no uniform procedure by which Calox investigated foreign markets and appointed distributors outside the United States. Bill Lawrence, Mike Brown's predecessor, essentially ran export sales as a one-man operation. Since Calox had very limited international experience, and most international markets were relatively small compared to the United States, primary market research was considered to be an unnecessary expense. In those countries guesstimated to have large enough markets, Bill obtained a list of potential distributors by advertising in that country's construction journal(s) (if available) and principal newspapers. He then made a personal visit to interview and select distributors. In smaller markets, distributors were appointed through one of two methods. Most commonly, Bill appointed a distributor after receiving an unsolicited request. In a very few cases, distributor applications were solicited via advertisements as in "large" markets, which were then reviewed in Kansas City. In all cases in which personal visits were not made, distributor applicants had to submit financial statements. Efforts to interview distributor applicants by telephone were not always successful, due to time constraints and the lack of a suitable translation service.

The New Zealand distributorship

In 1986 Calox appointed G. W. Diggers Ltd as its agent for New Zealand. This arrangement was a novel one, for G. W. Diggers was also a producer of excavating equipment. Because of some earlier poor experiences in certain foreign markets, Calox had instituted a policy of not distributing through any company that also manufactured excavating equipment. This policy was not followed in New Zealand because of the limited distributorship options available. At the time of the appointment, the owner of G. W. Diggers, Geoffrey Wiggins, assured Calox that the two lines were complementary rather than competitive, and that he intended to keep it that way. During 1989, G. W. Diggers purchased $800,000 of equipment and supplies from Calox.

In 1990 an abrupt change occurred in what had been a very successful, if short, relationships. G. W. Diggers was purchased by a large New Zealand conglomerate, Excel Ltd, which gave a new name, Glade Industries, to its excavating facility. The former owner of G. W. Diggers, Geoff Wiggins, was not associated with Glade Industries. Mike Brown's predecessor felt that the acquisition by Glade could only help Calox's position in New Zealand, because the resources available through Excel, Glade's parent company, were so much greater than what had been available to G. W. Diggers.

However, it soon became apparent that working with Glade was going to be very challenging. Glade raised prices on all Calox products in stock. Then it complained that Calox products were not selling well and that a "rebate" was needed to make Calox's products competitive in the New Zealand market. Simultaneously, Glade began production of a line of products competitive with Calox, but of a substantially poorer quality. During 1991 sales to Glade were virtually zero, and market information obtained by Calox indicated that Calox's former position in the

Exhibit 7.1   Annual sales to G. W. Diggers and Glade Industries (thousands of US dollars)

Sales to G. W. Diggers					Sales to Glade		
							1992 (6 months)
1986	1987	1988	1989		1990	1991	
21	310	535	801		105	70	10

New Zealand market was being occupied by Wescot Industries, with products imported from Great Britain. Exhibit 7.1 gives annual sales of Calox products to G. W. Diggers and to its successor, Glade Industries.

Mike Brown began his new job as international sales manager for Calox in June 1992. A few weeks after arriving at Calox, Mike received a long letter from Geoff Wiggins. Geoff suggested that the situation in New Zealand was critical, and that he would be willing and able to establish a new distributorship, Calox New Zealand Ltd, to be exclusive distributors of the Calox product line. Mike then invited Geoff to come to Kansas City the last week of July to discuss the proposal. Mike found Geoff to be very affable, technically knowledgeable, and an excellent marketing person. In the time period since selling his business to Excel Ltd Geoff had been working as a general contractor. The 24-month "no-compete" clause Geoff had signed when he sold G. W. Diggers had expired. Geoff provided figures that indicated that New Zealand's 1991 imports of excavating equipment were roughly NZ$2 million, out of a total domestic market of nearly NZ$3 million. (In 1991, US$1=NZ$0.62.) He claimed that G. W. Diggers had achieved, at the height of its success, almost a 50 percent share of the New Zealand market. Geoff argued persuasively that with his personal knowledge of New Zealand's needs, Calox could once again achieve a dominant market position. With the blessing of the vice-president of marketing, Mike and Geoff shook hands on a deal, with the exact details to be worked out by mail and faxed over the next few weeks. Geoff urged that time was of the essence if Wescot's market advances were to be slowed, and left a $100,000 order for 75 units to be shipped in 120 days, but not later than November 15, 1992.

Communications with Glade

Mike began to prepare a letter of termination to Glade. However, before this was completed, Calox received three mailed orders from Glade, totaling $81,000. This was the first contact Mike had with Glade and the first order received from Glade in five months. Because the standard distributor's agreement required a 60-day termination notice, Mike felt the Glade orders had to be honored.

A short time later Calox received a letter in the mail from Glade stating that they had heard rumors that another company was going to supply Calox products to Glade's customers and that delivery had been promised within 150 days. The letter continued by saying that this information could not possibly be true because Glade had an exclusive distributor agreement. This was news to Mike as well as to others at Calox headquarters because it was against company policy to grant exclusive distributorships. A search of Bill Lawrence's files turned up a copy of the initial correspondence to Geoff Wiggins, in which Geoff was thanked for his hospitality and a sole distributorship arrangement was mentioned. However, the distributorship agreement signed with Wiggins was the standard one, giving either party the ability to cancel the agreement with 60 days' notice.

Mike and the other senior Calox executives assessed the situation at length. The letter mentioning the "sole distributor agreement" was in a file separate from all other New Zealand correspondence. It was nothing more than a statement of intent and probably not legally binding in the United States. However, New Zealand courts might not agree. Further, the distributorship agreement should have been renegotiated when Excel purchased G. W. Diggers, but this had not happened. Glade could make a case that the distributorship had endured for 2 years under the existing agreements, which included the letter in which exclusivity was mentioned.

Mike determined that the "sole distributorship" letter also contained "extenuating circumstances" language which Calox could use to justify supplying the new New Zealand distributorship:

> [T]here may be occasions in the future, when, due to unforeseen circumstances, some entity in your nation refuses to purchase any other way than direct from our factory. We do not want to lose any potential sales, however we pledge our best efforts to cooperate with you for any such possible sales should they present themselves and provided there is a reasonable profit to be made on such sales by us and cooperation can be worked out.

The letter also specifically stated that all agreements between Calox and G. W. Diggers were subject to the laws of Missouri. Furthermore, Mike felt that Glade had not lived up to the actual signed distributorship agreement in that Glade had not promoted Calox products, had not maintained adequate inventory, and had engaged in activities and trade practices that were injurious to Calox's good name.

Armed with this information, Mike sought legal counsel, in both the United States and New Zealand. After a week, Calox's US attorneys, based on their own investigations and those of a law firm in Christchurch, New Zealand, offered four "unofficial" observations:

1 New Zealand is a "common law" nation, whose commercial law is similar to that of the United States.
2 It was possible to argue that because G. W. Diggers had changed ownership, previous agreements might not be binding. However, the most likely court finding would be that there was an implied contract between Calox and Glade on the same terms as with G. W. Diggers, because numerous business dealings between Calox and Glade had occurred after the takeover.
3 Calox was required to give Glade 60 days' termination notice.
4 There was a possibility that a New Zealand court would agree to assume jurisdiction of the case.

After reviewing the above issues Mike suggested to Calox senior management that Glade be terminated. Mike reasoned that Glade would react in one of two ways. One possibility was that it would accept termination, perhaps suggesting some minor compensation. A second scenario was that Glade would attempt to renegotiate the distributorship agreement. Mike was instructed to draft and fax a termination letter to Glade. This letter, sent by fax on August 20, is reproduced in exhibit 7.2. The next day the first order for the new distributorship was shipped; the expected arrival date in New Zealand was October 10, 1992.

Glade's faxed reply, dated August 24, was not encouraging (see exhibit 7.3). It appeared that Mike and the rest of the Calox management team had miscalculated. Despite the tone of the Glade letter, and the expressed request to ship order 52557, Mike suggested to the executive committee that no additional product be shipped to Glade.

While Mike and the rest of Calox management was deciding how to respond to Glade's initial rejection of the termination letter, a longer fax, one with a more conciliatory tone, dated August 31, was received from Glade (see exhibit 7.4). In this letter Glade argued that Calox's best interest were served by working with Glade and mentioned an order for approximately ten times the "normal" amount of product. However, the order was not transmitted with the fax letter. Glade offered (for the first time) to come to Kansas City for a visit.

Glade's conciliatory letter created a great deal of consternation at Calox headquarters. Its arrival the week before Labor Day meant that holiday plans would have to be placed on the back burner while a suitable response was formulated. Two distinct camps developed within Calox.

One set of managers, whose position was supported by Mike Brown, felt strongly that despite potential legal risks, retaining Glade as a distributor would be a bad business decision. Although Glade had made promises and was offering to renegotiate, it was still producing a competitive line. Also, Glade's historical performance did not augur well for Calox's long-term competitive situation in New Zealand. The "extraordinary" order was viewed as a ploy to entice Calox into continuing the relationship. It was likely to take upwards of two years for all that machinery to clear the New Zealand market. Cognizant of Glade's earlier price manipulations, many of this group felt that Glade might resort to "fire sale" prices when confronted with a large inventory, further damaging Calox's reputation as a premier supplier.

This camp considered that Calox's long-term interests would best be served by terminating the Glade distributorship and completing a formal agreement with Geoff Wiggins. However, there was concern that outright rejection of the Glade order would add to potential legal problems.

These managers also suggested that any further correspondence with Glade should emphasize that Calox could and would exercise a unique product repurchase option upon termination of the distributorship. This provision in the distributorship contract provided that Calox, upon proper termination of the distributorship by either party, could repurchase all remaining Calox inventory from the distributor at 80 percent of its net sales price to the distributor. Thus, if Calox did produce and ship the large Glade order, Calox would, if the order were shipped normally via sea freight, be able to buy it back for 80 percent of the price paid by Glade before it ever reached New Zealand.

The alternative camp wanted to forestall any legal battles. Headed by the US sales manager and the comptroller, they argued that Glade had finally "gotten its act together" and that the new Glade team of three sales executives would provide

Exhibit 7.2   Fax from Calox to Glade, August 20, 1992

Calox Company, Inc.   August 20, 1992
P. O. Box 21110
Kansas City, MO 64002
USA

Mr Ian Wells
Group General Manager
Glade Industries
39 Ames Road
Christchurch, New Zealand 2221

Dear Mr Wells:

This letter is to inform you that Calox Company terminates any International Distributor's Sales Agreement or other Distribution Agreement that you may have or be a party to as Distributor expressly or impliedly with Calox Co. as Manufacturer. Said termination is effective 60 days from the date of this letter.

During the past year the following have gravely concerned us and effectively shut off our sales to the New Zealand market.

Reorganization of G. W. Diggers under Glade leading to continuous loss of personnel knowledgeable of the excavation business and difficulty for Calox's understanding with whom we are doing business. In June 1990, we were advised by telex that we were dealing with Excel Ltd., not G. W. Diggers or Glade.

Only $10,000 purchases for an eight-month long period from us, which we clearly found led to major loss of Calox sales to the marketplace and a complete domination of the excavation business by Wescot Industries, a major competitor.

Lack of effort on the part of Glade in promoting our product and maintaining effective selling facilities.

Numerous complaints to us from Customers in New Zealand about Glade continually changing policies, lack of stock, and wildly increasing prices have clearly pointed out that our reputation, as well as G. W. Diggers, has been badly hurt and will impair sales for some time to come.

No progress has been made in introducing our heavy industrial line to the New Zealand market despite assurances from Glade personnel that progress would be made.

We have thoroughly investigated the New Zealand Market and now have firmly decided that it is time for Calox to make a change in its distribution of products.

For the long term, this will allow us to best carve out a full niche in a market we and you have allowed competitors to dominate for too long. We must guarantee ourselves a consistent, aggressive sales effort in the market, which will not be subject to the effects of major policy changes such as those we have seen from Glade.

While two shipments are already en route to you, order number 52557 has not yet been completed for shipment. Since it will be ready imminently, please let us know immediately whether you wish, under the circumstances, to receive shipment or to cancel this order.

Sincerely,

Michael Brown
International Sales Manager

Exhibit 7.3   Fax from Glade to Calox, August 24, 1992

Glade Industries   24 August 1992
39 Ames Road
Christchurch, New Zealand 2221

Mr Michael Brown
International Sales Manager
Calox Company, Inc.
P. O. Box 21110
Kansas City, MO 64002
USA

Dear Sir:

We acknowledge receipt of your letter dated 20 August 1992.

We are currently discussing its contents with our solicitors. They are also reviewing the distribution agreement.

Please proceed with the shipment of order #52557.

Yours faithfully.

GLADE INDUSTRIES LTD.
Ian Wells
Group General Manager

Exhibit 7.4   Fax from Glade to Calox, August 31, 1992

Glade Industries   31 August 1992
39 Ames Road
Christchurch, New Zealand 2221

Mr Michael Brown
International Sales Manager
Calox Company, Inc.
P. O. Box 21110
Kansas City, MO 64002
USA

Dear Sir:

I refer to your letter dated 20 August 1992, terminating our agreement which was executed on 28 February 1986.

In accordance with this agreement and attached to this letter is our order #A1036, for 600 products and parts. We would be pleased if you would confirm this order in due course.

We respectfully ask that you reconsider your termination decision as we believe that it is not in your best interests for the following reasons:

1. G. W. Diggers/Glade were not achieving an adequate return on investment until June 1991. An unprofitable distributor certainly is not in your best interests as principal.

Exhibit 7.4   (Cont'd)

2. The individuals that contributed to that unprofitable performance are no longer working for our company. Incidentally I understand that you have appointed Mr Geoffrey Wiggins to a position as distributor in New Zealand. How can you justify appointing the person responsible for your market share decline over the past three years?

3. Our purchases certainly have been reduced the last nine months due to our need to get inventory down to lift overall return on investment. That situation has now been corrected with the order attached to this letter.

4. We now have a young aggressive marketing team, all highly experienced in marketing products of a similar nature to yours. When Bill Lawrence was in New Zealand, I advised him that I was restructuring our marketing group. A resume on our three senior marketing men is attached. These men have all commenced in the last four months. I am confident that this team will achieve market leadership in New Zealand and selected export markets with or without Calox's involvement. We have already commenced targeting Wescot's customers. Our recommendation is that you renegotiate your distribution agreement with us, with the inclusion of mutually agreed performance targets which will satisfy your objectives in terms of profitability and market share from the New Zealand market. I would like you to advise me a time which is convenient to you, for me to meet with you in Kansas City to commence negotiation of this distributor agreement.

Yours faithfully,

GLADE INDUSTRIES LTD
Ian Wells
Group General Manager

———

These are the three new men who have commenced to work for us:

Sean Cox, Sales Manager
35 years old. Formerly CEO of Sean Cox Industries of Christchurch. SCI was the chief contractor for the Auckland airport, but sold its business to Midland Industries. Mr Cox has fifteen years experience in the construction industry.

Joshua Dunn, Sales Representative, North Island
46 years old. Formerly an independent sales representative for various equipment manufacturers, including Hitachi and Ford New Holland.

Brian Muldoon, Sales Representative, South Island
23 years old. Construction engineering degree from New South Wales Institute of Technology (Sydney, Australia). Formerly a management trainee with our parent company, Excel Ltd.

greater market coverage than Geoff Wiggins's "one man show." This group introduced the possibility of reopening negotiations with Glade, supplying Glade by diverting the order already shipped to Geoff Wiggins, and producing the (yet unreceived) large Glade order.

By Wednesday, September 2, the two sides had hardened their positions. Mike was determined to break with Glade and begin anew in New Zealand. However, he was concerned about legal ramifications, and, on Thursday, September 3, Calox's executive committee and Mike conferred with their Kansas City attorneys via a conference call.

The lawyers agreed that any further business conducted with Glade would be detrimental to a termination decision. They warned that despite the termination letter (exhibit 7.2) any further shipments to Glade would likely yield a court ruling that the distributorship was still in effect and, furthermore, that the buyback provision could not be enacted. They also said that if all business with Glade were terminated, and Glade did come to the United States to file, the most they would be likely to receive if they won the court case were the profits on the new sales to Geoff Wiggins, which amounted to $10,000. This sum was probably not large enough to warrant legal action by Glade, especially considering the apparently poor financial situation at Glade and the expense of initiating legal action in the United States.

At the end of this conference call, which lasted about 30 minutes, Bill Oxley Jr turned to Mike and said, "Mike, I'm off to the lake now for the holiday. I'd like your recommendation Tuesday morning on this Glade thing."

AMERICAN AIRLINES INTERNATIONAL STRATEGY

Steve Bogner and Lester A. Neidell

As he returns to Dallas from a planning conference in London with American Airlines' European managers it is clear to Arnold Grossman, Vice-President of International Planning, that the airline industry is in turmoil. American Airlines lost money in 1990 and 1991, and 1992, as of November, looks like another unprofitable year. Most competitors are doing even worse. Pan American World Airways and Eastern Airlines are no longer in business. Trans World Airlines, America West Airlines, and Continental Airlines are all working their way out of bankruptcy. USAir and Northwest Airlines are trying to form alliances with foreign airlines to improve their finances and ensure survival. The "Big Three," American Airlines, United Airlines, and Delta Airlines, greatly expanded their international presence in the past few years, and are struggling to pull out of repeated losses and restore order to what some call the harshest operating environment in aviation history. Some niche airlines, most prominently Southwest Airlines, are making money, but these profits pale in comparison with the industry's losses.

Industry turmoil is not limited to the USA. Most European airlines are also suffering large losses and some require substantial government subsidies. The

Prepared by Steven Bogner, Senior Business Systems Analyst, American Airlines, and Professor Lester A. Neidell of the University of Tulsa, as a basis for classroom discussion and not to illustrate either effective or ineffective handling of administrative situations. Copyright © Lester A. Neidell, 1994.

European market is to be opened to more competition, which will weed out weaker airlines through bankruptcy and consolidation. Japan's primary airline, Japan Airlines, is losing money due to increasing costs, lower revenue, and competition from other airlines in that region. Japanese, German, and French governments seem to be taking steps to protect their airlines from the increasing international competition.

The meeting with European managers did not yield much positive information. At the request of the company's international planning committee, Grossman was reexamining the international aviation market and American's international strategy. Given all the changes in the world's aviation industry, and American's finances in particular, some think the current strategy's assumptions may no longer be valid. Some analysts and managers suggest retrenchment and concentration on the more familiar domestic market. Others believe the company should continue with strong growth in international routes to increase market share and lead the company back to profitability. A third view is that the problem is not in the strategy, but in how the company executed the strategy. "All these scenarios are possible," thought Grossman, "but what is really going on in the global commercial aviation market, and how should we capitalize on it? As unforgiving as this business has become, the wrong strategy could hurt us for a long time, but the right one could make us the global leader. I'd better make sure we choose the right one, whatever it is."

American Airlines' Current Situation

American Airlines is a subsidiary of AMR, a holding company for several airline-related companies. AMR's larger subsidiaries are listed in exhibit 8.1. All are based

Exhibit 8.1 Selected AMR subsidiaries

Subsidiary	Lines of business
American Airlines	Air passenger and cargo transportation. Sabre Travel Information Network, a computerized airline reservation business, is an operating division of American Airlines.
AMR Eagle	Four domestic regional airlines: Simmons, Executive, Flagship, and Wings West, serving over 160 cities.
AMR Services	Ground services for airlines and general aviation customers, both domestic and international.
AMR Information Services	Telemarketing, software development, data processing, reservation services.
AA Decision Technologies	Decision support tools for operations research, computer science, and industrial engineering applications.

Exhibit 8.2 AMR: 1991 revenue

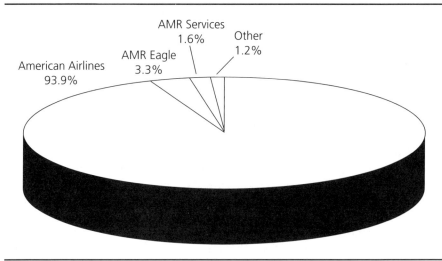

on particular strengths which originated from American Airlines. As exhibit 8.2 shows, American Airlines represents over 93 percent of AMR's consolidated revenue.

In addition to American Airlines' international flight operations, other AMR subsidiaries are active in international markets. AMR Services contracts with airlines to provide ground services such as fueling airplanes, handling cargo and luggage, and minor maintenance. Their latest international contract, one of the largest of its kind in the industry, provides cargo handling, passenger services, and ramp services for Lot Polish Airlines at the Warsaw hub airport. AMR Information Services is completing development of a computerized reservation system for France's SNCF, the national railroad system. AA Decision Technologies has international customers which include Airbus Industrie, Club Med, Lufthansa, Ansett Australia, and Britannia Airways. American Airlines' Sabre Travel Information Network, or STIN, is used in 57 countries on six continents by travel agents, hotels, airlines, and other companies.

Exhibit 8.3 illustrates that passenger sales dominate American Airlines' revenue. Airline ticket pricing is oligopolistic, and, except for the mid-1980s, revenue per passenger mile (the revenue from flying one passenger for one mile, called RPM) is not increasing as much as cost per available seat mile (or ASM; one seat, with or without passenger, flown one mile). Aircraft fuel prices, American's second largest expense, are higher for international than domestic operations. Overall, the industry's fuel price for international services was $0.705 per gallon international and $0.684 per gallon domestic. See exhibit 8.4 for ASM and RPM data, and exhibit 8.5 for financial statistics.

American's organization structure is divided into five major groups, as shown in exhibit 8.6: administration and general counsel, finance and planning, information systems, operations, and marketing. Both planning and marketing have

Exhibit 8.3   AA: 1991 revenue

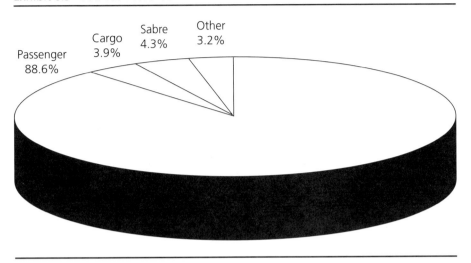

Exhibit 8.4   AMR operating statistics

	1991	1990	1989	1988	1987	1986	1985	1984	1983	1982	1981
Yield per RPM ($)	0.1301	0.1264	0.1203	0.1166	0.1083	0.1017	0.1130	0.1181	0.1139	0.1104	0.1213
Cost per ASM ($)	0.0905	0.0884	0.0801	0.0759	0.0750	0.0728	0.0783	0.0809	0.0817	0.0819	0.0857
RPMs	82,335	77,085	73,503	64,770	56,794	48,792	44,138	36,702	34,099	30,900	27,798
ASMs	133,472	123,773	115,222	102,045	88,743	75,087	68,336	58,667	52,447	48,792	45,264
Load factor (%)	61.7	62.3	63.8	63.5	64.0	65.0	64.6	62.6	65.0	63.3	61.4
Breakeven load factor (%)	61.6	61.8	57.9	56.0	58.5	59.3	57.3	57.1	60.4	63.7	60.5
Aircraft at year end	622	552	500	468	410	330	291	260	244	231	232

important roles in the development of AA's international business. The planning branch of finance and planning is responsible for controlling American's changes in aircraft, real estate, airport facilities, routes and route schedules. The actual international markets the company will serve are determined by international planning. The marketing organization manages advertising, customer relations, frequent flyer programs, flight services, food and beverage services, product design, reservations, sales development, pricing, and yield management. International marketing functions such as sales, sales development, and pricing are divided by region.

To ensure profitable growth, AA's international planning group requires all new routes to surpass a 15 percent internal rate of return (IRR) over a 15-year period. The hurdle rate applies to routes the company has applied for through the

Exhibit 8.5 AMR financial statistics

	1991	1990	1989	1988	1987	1986	1985	1984	1983	1982	1981
Total Operating Revenue	12,887	11,720	10,480	8,824	7,198	6,018	6,131	5,354	4,763	4,177	4,109
Passenger	10,714	9,743	8,839	7,555	6,150	4,960	4,986	4,336	3,885	3,414	3,377
Cargo	474	429	362	288	261	220	235	315	299	303	330
Total Operating Expense	12,882	11,596	9,736	8,018	6,737	5,607	5,594	4,985	4,482	4,168	4,037
Wages, Salaries, Benefits	4,030	3,609	3,234	2,821	2,400	2,053	1,952	1,748	1,601	1,473	1,417
Aircraft Fuel	1,782	1,899	1,367	1,094	1,008	837	1,142	1,092	1,039	1,070	1,116
Operating Income	5	124	744	806	461	411	537	369	281	9	72
Extraordinary Items	0	0	0	0	0	0	0	0	0	0	30
Net Earnings (Loss)	(240)	(40)	455	477	198	279	346	234	228	(20)	47
Total Assets	16,208	13,354	10,877	9,792	8,423	7,528	6,421	5,261	4,728	3,897	3,738
Long Term Debt	3,951	1,674	809	1,206	1,235	1,229	921	775	727	752	718
Capital Leases	1,928	1,598	1,497	1,543	1,547	1,183	910	767	785	765	799
Common Stock & Other Equity	3,794	3,727	3,766	3,148	2,681	2,485	2,181	1,513	1,300	836	731
Common Shares Outstanding	68,363	62,311	62,244	58,841	58,816	58,747	58,681	48,453	48,374	37,241	28,766
Common Share Book Value	55.50	59.82	60.50	53.50	45.58	42.30	37.00	30.98	26.59	22.07	24.88

Source: 1991 AMR Annual Report.

Note: All numbers, except Common Share Book Value, are in millions, no dividends have been paid.

Exhibit 8.6 AMR organization chart

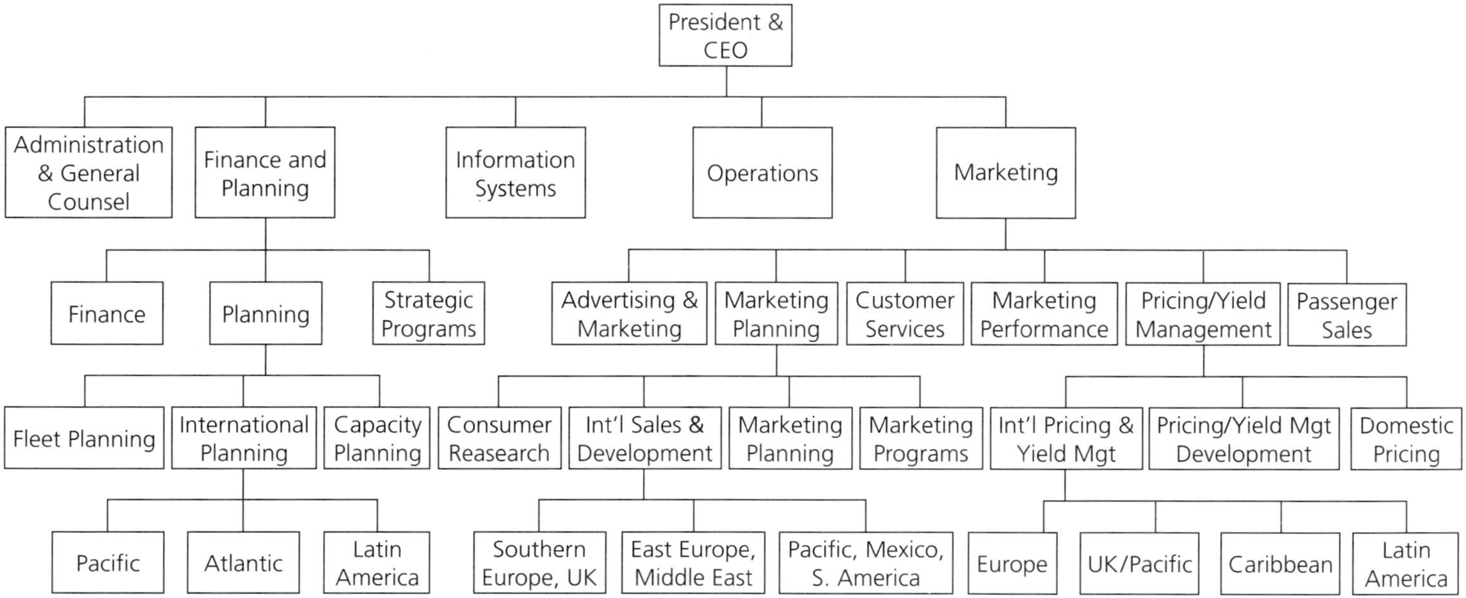

Department of Transportation (DOT) as well as any which are purchased. Factors such as traffic forecasts, economic trends, sales volume and growth, costs of establishing and maintaining service, changes in the aircraft fleet, costs of flight personnel and ground personnel, and government regulations all contribute to the analysis. If a route passes the hurdle it is presented to the international planning committee, chaired by Don Carty, Executive Vice-President of Finance and Planning. If passed by this group, the proposal is then forwarded to the corporate planning committee for final approval.

Sales of passenger tickets for domestic and international travel are made through travel agents, American Airlines Reservation Centers, and direct sales to groups and corporations. Travel agents earn about an 11 percent commission on international tickets and 10 percent for domestic trips. Incentives, including higher commissions and bonuses, can be much higher to promote certain routes.

To accomplish domestic and international expansion, AA's growth strategy in the 1980s was to expand airline operations in order to achieve higher market share and economies of scale. With the industry's and American's large losses in recent years, the company discarded a growth strategy for one that emphasizes a value concept. The company's attitude is that it must change in whatever manner needed to meet customers' new expectations product and price combinations for air travel.

Domestic Competitive Situation

The USA is the largest commercial aviation market in the world. Due to the United States' large size and economic prosperity, domestic airlines were able to grow profitably and serve their customers. The federal government, through the Civil Aeronautics Board (CAB) regulated competition "to the extent necessary to assure the sound development of an air-transportation system properly adapted to the needs of the foreign and domestic commerce of the United States, of the Postal Service, and of the national defense."[1] Formed in 1938, the CAB regulated fares, market entry and exit, accounting, and many other facets of commercial airline operations.

In October 1978, President Carter signed the Airline Deregulation Act, designed to free the airline industry from CAB governance by 1985. The CAB's authority over economic actions such as mergers, pricing, and market entry and exit was gradually phased out during this period, while concerns such as safety and international air service agreements were transferred to the Department of Transportation (DOT). Airlines in the USA are now free to set their prices, enter and exit markets, diversify, and offer other services without significant government interference.

As existing airlines pulled out of unprofitable routes they were forced to serve under CAB regulations, new regional airlines formed to serve those customers. The established airlines initiated new routes, eventually forming new, and enlarging existing, hub and spoke systems. These systems are designed to allow an airline to serve a larger number of city pairs than with point of point routes.

Exhibit 8.7 is an example of how a given airline's routes were connected before

Exhibit 8.7	Point to point service
From	**To**
Dallas	Tulsa
Dallas	Houston
Houston	New Orleans
Tulsa	Chicago
Chicago	Nashville

Exhibit 8.8	Hub and spoke service	
From	**Via**	**To**
Tulsa	Dallas	Houston
		Chicago
		New Orleans
		Nashville
Chicago	Dallas	Tulsa
		Houston
		New Orleans
		Nashville

deregulation. From Tulsa it was possible to fly directly to Dallas or Chicago. If a passenger wanted to go from Tulsa to Houston he or she would fly to Dallas and then get on another plane to go to Houston. Each *city pair* (Tulsa–Dallas, Dallas–Houston) is served by a *route*, and the change of planes in Dallas is a *connection*. Each route on a multiroute trip is called a *segment*. If the passenger wanted to go from Tulsa to New Orleans he or she would connect in both Dallas and Houston. Likewise, a person in Nashville would connect in Chicago and Tulsa to get to Dallas. Airline consumers generally wish to avoid three-segment trips and unnecessary connections, but the CAB limited city pairs an airline could serve. For example, American Airlines might have been allowed to have a direct route from Nashville to Dallas, giving it an advantage over those airlines which had to make connections. This built-in barrier served to limit competition among airlines in certain city pairs. The CAB's intentions were to provide service to cities rather than promote inter-airline competition.

After deregulation the airlines could serve whatever city pairs they wanted, subject to their own requirements for sufficient traffic, capacity, and profitability. To minimize three-segment trips and increase the number of city pairs served, a hub and spoke system evolved (exhibit 8.8). Now a Tulsa passenger could fly to New Orleans with only one connection, as could Chicago–New Orleans customers. The trade-off was redistribution of passenger traffic and discontinuance of some routes. For instance, the route from Tulsa to Chicago was discontinued in favor of connecting in Dallas.

Strategies such as the hub and spoke system enabled airlines to increase the number of cities they served, greatly enlarging their markets. It also helped to increase the ratio of filled to total seats, called *load factor*, on their airplanes. By increasing the load factor, the airlines moved more people while using the same number of airplanes.

Consolidation

As the larger airlines completed building their hubs, the economies of scope and scale made them very tough competitors for the smaller, regional carriers. Just as these smaller airlines took advantage of abandoned routes, the large airlines capitalized on their size by purchasing the regionals. The resulting *commuter* airlines continued to serve smaller cities, but their primary function was to feed the large hubs with additional passengers.

Not all large airlines fared well under deregulation. Those who could not adjust to increased competition and lower prices filed bankruptcy, liquidated, or merged. Carriers such as Pan American enjoyed large profits under CAB regulation, but failed to develop a hub system to feed its extensive international routes and eventually went bankrupt. Others, such as Air Cal and Piedmont, were purchased by stronger airlines.

International Competition

Domestic US airlines have free entry and exit to markets in the USA, which is not the case for international markets. Access to international locations is determined by treaties, called bilateral agreements, between two countries. These bilateral agreements determine how an airline can enter, exit and operate in a foreign market. DOT is responsible for negotiating, on behalf of all domestic carriers, bilateral aviation agreements with other countries. The department typically negotiates with foreign government aviation regulation agencies, not individual airlines. US airlines can apply to DOT for access to routes gained through a bilateral agreement or they may purchase another company's right to use a route. In addition to purchasing a carrier's right to use a route, the foreign operations may also be included in the transaction. Items such as foreign offices, personnel, and ground services may be transferred from one carrier to the other. Applying for route access costs very little, but may take years to finalize. Purchasing routes is much faster, but usually costly. In either case, both governments must usually approve the carrier to operate a route.

Codesharing is another method of providing international service to an airline's passengers. This is achieved by an agreement between two airlines to co-market a route and share the revenue generated on it. For instance, American Airlines has a codeshare agreement with South African Airlines (SA) to provide a service from Kennedy Airport (JFK) in New York to Johannesburg (JNB), South Africa. A passenger who wants to fly from Chicago to Johannesburg would fly AA to JFK and then switch planes to SA and continue to JNB. Although flying on two airlines, the passenger needs only one ticket for the trip. To the travel agent the ticket is handled in the same manner as a single airline ticket, instead of a multi-airline ticket which takes more time to book. After the trip is flown, AA and SA share the revenue from the ticket sale according to the codesharing agreement. American Airlines also has codesharing agreements with Lufthansa for the Chicago–Dusseldorf route and Malev Hungarian Airlines for Zurich–Budapest.

Internal markets within most foreign countries are regulated in the same style the CAB governed before its breakup. Prices, city pairs, and services are set within a framework determined by the national regulating agency. Many countries adhere to the concept of a single *flag carrier*, an airline they choose to carry out all or most international travel for the country. Domestic routes are then typically handled by a smaller airline on a point to point, instead of hub, basis. Foreign countries seek to protect their flag carriers for various reasons, including pride, national defense, jobs, or as a vehicle to gain hard currency. The USA has no single flag carrier: all domestic airlines are free to compete for international routes.

Although countries try to protect their flag carriers from losses and competition, the only way to get access to another country is to reciprocate access to your own. For instance, if the United Kingdom (UK) wants its flag carrier, British Airways (BA), to have access to Denver's Stapleton Airport, the USA will want something in return. The resulting negotiation may be long and arduous, perhaps resulting in access to Denver for BA, and access to London's Heathrow airport for one or two US carriers.

Access to a foreign country may be in several forms, called *freedoms. First freedom* allows an airline to fly over the air space of another country without landing. *Second freedom* is the right to make a stop in another country without taking on or letting off passengers. *Third freedom* is the right to take on home-country passengers and let them off in another country. *Fourth freedom* is the right to take on foreign passengers and let them off in the carrier's home country. *Fifth freedom* is the right to pick up passengers outside the carrier's home country and let them off at a destination which is not the carrier's home country. In addition to specifying these freedoms, a bilateral agreement may dictate specific city pairs which can be implemented. The USA may get first through fourth freedoms to Germany, but only on the city pairs of New York–Frankfurt, New York–Bonn, and Boston–Berlin. Each city pair may have a limited number of flights per day and may even restrict takeoff and landing times. Before the breakup of the former Soviet Union, few airlines enjoyed first freedom rights in that country. This forced the carriers to spend extra time and fuel flying around it. Bilateral agreements usually get very complex, with many more restrictions than outlined here.

International Air Transport Association

Just as the CAB regulated domestic airlines, there are agencies regulating international aviation activity. The International Air Transport Association (IATA) member airlines are responsible for about 98 percent of all air travel in the world. The group's principal purpose is ensure determine "fair" prices for international travel, which are agreeable to both the carriers and their governments. The association also provides a clearing house for international airline tickets, ensuring that the correct parties receive payment for multi-airline trips.[2] IATA also serves as a forum for discussion of other international airline issues.

A result of US deregulation was increased price competition in international markets. This forced many carriers to go beyond IATA's pricing guidelines to defend or gain market share. For hotly contested international markets this practice became the rule, not the exception, and forced IATA into a less significant role. IATA's price setting function is still more important in the developing countries than in Europe and North America. American's CEO, Robert Crandall, held IATA's top post, Director General, in 1993.

World airline regions

World airline operations are often grouped into six regions for comparing operations on a global scale: North America, Europe, Asia, Latin America/Caribbean, Middle East, and Africa. Exhibit 8.9 lists all airlines with revenue passenger kilometers (one passenger flown one kilometer, abbreviated RPK) over one billion in 1991 by region and country. Characteristics such as number of employees, regions served, load factor, and passengers served give a broad view of an airline's operations. Regional air traffic statistics, shown in exhibit 8.10, give an overall view of the world's commercial aviation markets. The exhibit lists international traffic only; domestic RPK's are not included.

Brief descriptions of the five regions outside North America follow.

Europe

Next to the USA, Europe is the largest commercial aviation market in the world. The North America–Europe routes, labeled the North Atlantic market, are where US and European airlines compete fiercely, and are one of the largest passenger markets in the world. Because many European countries are not large enough to support a sufficiently profitable domestic market, their carriers rely on and specialize in international routes.

Although some airlines are still owned by governments, the trend is toward full, or at least, partial privatization. British Airways, the largest European carrier, was privatized in 1987. Germany sold its majority stake in Lufthansa, and France is gradually reducing its ownership in Air France. Many governments continue to subsidize periodically their flag carriers, although the European Union's Competition Council is starting to criticize these practices.

Bilateral agreements between European countries and the USA vary in their restrictions. The Netherlands has an open skies agreement, which gives US and Dutch airlines free entry and exit, unrestricted capacity and frequency, and flexibility in setting fares in each other's countries. Most other bilateral agreements with Europe have more restrictive controls on frequency, capacity, city pairs, and fares.

Asia

The Asian region includes countries from India to Japan, and from China to New Zealand. It is growing quickly and now rivals the European region in international air traffic. Much of this growth has been fueled by the region's growing export economies and low-cost, high-quality airlines. Most of the wealth is centered in Japan, which also has the largest international passenger market in the region. Passenger traffic to the USA represents the largest traffic flow in this region.

Although bilateral agreements among countries in the region are somewhat liberalized, their relationships to Europe and the USA are traditionally restrictive. As developing economies grow, international trade, including international commercial aviation, could suffer if the industrial nations adopt more protectionist policies. Increased protection in Asian aviation markets would impede governments who want to negotiate access to this market for their carriers.

Exhibit 8.9   Major scheduled airlines of the world in 1991 (RPKs over one billion in 1991)

Airline	Country	Region	Govt Holding (%)	No. of Employees	Thousands of pass.	Millions of RPK	Load Factor (%)	Principal Routes Served
Air India	India	Asia	100	17,443	2,151	8,874	64	WW
Air Lanka	Sri Lanka	Asia	100	3,480	898	3,486	70	FE,AUST,ME,E,D
Air New Zealand	New Zealand	Asia	0	8,066	4,958	13,212	61	AUST,Asia,Pacific Islands, NA,E,D
All Nippon Airways	Japan	Asia	0	14,411	34,900	37,146	71	Asia,AUST,E,US
Ansett Australia	Australia	Asia	0	9,060	6,224	6,936	76	D
Australian Airlines	Australia	Asia	100	9,747	6,323	6,036	72	D
Cathay Pacific Airways	Hong Kong	Asia	0	12,747	7,391	24,433	74	E,Indian Ocean,AUST,NA
China Airlines	China	Asia	0	7,309	5,480	12,149	76	Asia,E,US South Africa,D
China Eastern	China	Asia	100	2,540	3,737		80	D,US
China Northern*	China	Asia	100		2,000			D
China Northwest*	China	Asia	100					D
China Southern*	China	Asia	100		4,700			D
China Southwest*	China	Asia	100					D
Dragon Air	Hong Kong	Asia	0	578	759	1,001	78	Regional
Garuda Indonesia	Indonesia	Asia	100	11,867	5,455	12,708	61	E,NA,ME,FE,AUST, Pacific,D
India Airlines	India	Asia	0	21,966	8,569	7,715	74	D,Regional
Japan Air System	Japan	Asia	0	5,056	14,622	9,236	70	D,Regional,Hawall
Japan Airlines	Japan	Asia	0	18,507	23,296	51,523	71	WW,D
Japan Asia Airways*	Japan	Asia	0	600	1,297	2,256	74	Regional
Korean Airlines	South Korea	Asia	0	14,580	13,470	19,956	70	Asia,NA,E,AF,AUST,D
Malaysia Airlines	Malaysia	Asia	65	16,149	11,837	14,225	69	FE,AUST,E,ME,US,D
Merpati Nusontana Airlines	Indonesia	Asia	0	3,360	3,795	3,651	60	D
Pakistan Int's Airlines	Pakistan	Asia	64	20,463	5,033	8,998	67	FE,ME,E,AF,NA,D
Philippine Airlines	Philippines	Asia	13	12,687	5,406	10,461	72	NA,E,ME,FE,AUST,D
Qantas	Australia	Asia	100	15,029	4,210	26,505	65	WW,D
Singapore Airlines	Singapore	Asia	54	14,113	8,131	34,894	74	NA,ME,FE,AUST,NZ,E
Thai International	Thailand	Asia	99	18,507	7,708	18,246	62	Asia,PAC,AF,ME,E,US,D
Aer Lingus	Ireland	Europe	100	5,197	4,311	3,786	68	E,NA,D
Aeroflot	CIS	Europe	100	14,838	85,640	148,998	83	WW,3000 Points Domestic
Air 2000	United Kingdom	Europe	0	980	2,772	7,525	91	Charter to E,East AF,NA,CAR,CA
Air Atlantis Sar	Portugal	Europe	0	369	539	1,081	75	Charter E,AF,ME
Air Europa	United Kingdom	Europe	0	750	2,138	5,226		Charter E,MED,MEX,US, FE
Air France	France	Europe	99	30,928	13,229	33,780	67	WW,D
Air Inter	France	Europe	0	10,821	15,787	8,911	65	D,E
Air Malta*	Malta	Europe	96	1,600	705	1,117	75	E,NA
Alitalia	Italy	Europe	0	21,306	17,281	21,710	62	WW
Austrian Air*	Austria	Europe	52	4,284	2,294	2,853	55	E,AF,ME,JAP,US
Avinco	Italy	Europe	67	1,860	5,004	2,328	67	D
Balkan Bulgarian Airways	Bulgaria	Europe	100	4,000	1,186	2,522	67	E,FE,AF,D
British Airways	United Kingdom	Europe	0	48,453	25,422	65,896	70	WW,D
British Midland Airways	United Kingdom	Europe	0	3,219	3,443	1,548	52	E,D

Exhibit 8.9 (Cont'd)

Airline	Country	Region	Govt Holding (%)	No. of Employees	Thousands of pass.	Millions of RPK	Load Factor (%)	Principal Routes Served
Broathems Safe Norway	Norway	Europe	0	2,858	3,481	1,303	54	D,E,
Caledonian Airways	United Kingdom	Europe	0	500	1,447	3,500	85	E,AF,NA,CAR,Charter
CSA	Czechoslovakia	Europe	60	4,126	877	2,103	61	E,ME,FE,NA,CA,D
Cyprus Airways	Cyprus	Europe	80	1,683	953	2,252	69	E,ME
Finn Air	Finland	Europe	70	7,768	4,325	4,775	58	E,NA,FE,D
Iberia	Spain	Europe	100	23,230	15,551	20,473	62	WW
Iceland Air	Iceland	Europe	0	1,277	774	1,728	67	E,US,D,Greenland
Jat-Yugaslavian Airlines	Yugoslavia	Europe	100	7,411	1,846	2,871	71	E,ME,FE,Austrialia,NA,D
KLM Royal Dutch Airlines	Netherlands	Europe	38	25,600	7,121	27,278	72	WW
Lauda Air	Austria	Europe	0	649	553	1,852	79	UK,FE,Medit,AF,CAR, Indian Ocean, AUST
Lot Polish Airlines	Poland	Europe	100	6,277	1,051	2,878	63	E,NA,ME,FE,AF,D
Lufthansa	Germany	Europe	51	50,826	23,324	42,258	62	WW
Malev Hungorian Airlines	Hungary	Europe	100	4,506	1,014	1,186	55	E,ME,NA,US-With Delta
Martin Air Holland	Holland	Europe	0	1,760	1,388	6,324		WW
Monarch Airlines	United Kingdom	Europe	0	1,776	2,583	5,728	85	E,Medit,AF,I,FE,NA
Olympic Airways	Greece	Europe	100	11,430	4,937	6,193	60	WW,D
Sabena Belgian	Belgium	Europe	55	11,254	3,018	6,223	61	E,ME,FE,AF,NA
SAS	Norway	Europe	50	38,940	13,917	15,416	63	Scandinavia,E,FE,NA,SA
Spanair	Spain	Europe	0	696	1,704	3,591	73	E,Medit,US,MEX, Charters
Sterling Airways	Denmark	Europe	0	1,000	1,438	3,925		E,Medit,NA,CAR,I, Charters
Swiss Air	Switzerland	Europe	0	20,915	7,292	15,099	62	E,NA,SA,AF,ME,FE
Tap–Air Portugal	Portugal	Europe	100	11,000	3,188	7,025	68	E,AF,NA,SA
Torom Romanian Air	Romania	Europe	100		1,711	2,666	67	E,AF,ME,FE,US,D
Turkish Airlines	Turkey	Europe	99	8,233	2,871	4,169	56	E,ME,FE,AF,NA,D
UTA	France	Europe	0	6,754	790	5,768	68	AF,ME,FE,AUST,US,D
Virgin Atlantic	United Kingdom	Europe	0	1,955	1,046	7,461	82	NA,FE
Aero Mexico	Mexico	LA/CAR	0	6,963	6,225	7,539	59	NA,E,D
Aerolineas Argentinas	Argentina	LA/CAR	5	8,792	3,236	81	61	NA,SA,E,D
Air Jamaica	Jamaica	LA/CAR	100	1,665	845	1,250	61	CAR,NA
Austral Lineas Aereas	Argentina	LA/CAR	0	1,609	1,183	1,083	65	D
Avianca		LA/CAR	0	5,900	3,270	3,421	64	NA,SA,E,CAR
Bwia Int'l	Trinidad, Tobago	LA/CAR	100	2,598	1,345	3,129	71	NA,CAR,SA,E,D
Cruzeiro	Brazil	LA/CAR	0	1,963	3,012	3,292	58	D
Cubana	Cuba	LA/CAR	100	2,665	842	1,597	72	NA,CA,SA,E,AF,D
Lab Airlines	Bolivia	LA/CAR	98	1,490	1,201	1,020	66	SA,CA,US
Ladeco Airlines	Chile	LA/CAR	0	1,467	589	1,040	60	SA,US,D
Lan Chile	Chile	LA/CAR	23	1,974	693	1,921	62	SA,CA,NA,PAC,E,D
Lap Paraquayan Airlines	Paraguay	LA/CAR	100	1,052	275	1,053	68	SA,US,E,D
Mexicana	Mexico	LA/CAR	0	11,150	8,549	10,743	60	US,CA,CAR,D
Trans Brasil	Brazil	LA/CAR	0	4,965	2,395	3,583	53	D,US

Exhibit 8.9 (Cont'd)

Airline	Country	Region	Govt Holding (%)	No. of Employees	Thousands of pass.	Millions of RPK	Load Factor (%)	Principal Routes Served
Varig	Brazil	LA/CAR	0	26,236	6,914	16,020	63	NA,SA,E,AF,JAP
Vasp	Brazil	LA/CAR	40	11,394	5,015	5,002	54	D,CAR
Viasa	Venezuela	LA/CAR	40	3,444	636	2,710	54	NA,SA,CAR,E
Air Algeria	Algeria	ME/AF	100	8,846	3,218	1,135	60	ME,NA,FE,E,D
Egypt Air	Egypt	ME/AF	100	12,782	2,601	8,370	59	AF,E,SA,ME,FE,D
El-Al	Israel	ME/AF		3,430	1,751	2,433	65	NA,E,ME,AF,FE
Emirates (UAE)	UAE	ME/AF		1,925	1,166	1,150	56	ME,E,AF,FE
Gulf Air (Bahrain)	Bahrain	ME/AF	100	4,961	3,502	1,241	31	AF,E,CAR,SA,D
Iran Air	Iran	ME/AF	100	10,609	5,235	588	13	ME,AF,E,D
Libyan Arab Airlines	Libya	ME/AF	100	6,122	1,883	15,585	66	ME,SE,AF,E,NA,D
Royal Air Maroc	Morrocco	ME/AF	93	5,063	1,430	2,532	59	E,AF,ME,NA,D
Saudia	Saudi Arabia	ME/AF	100	3,788	9,768	655	62	AF,INDIA,E,SA,D
South Africa Airways	South Africa	ME/AF	100	11,368	4,701	1,408	61	AF,ME,E,D
Tunia Air	Tunisia	ME/AF	45	4,210	1,201	1,390	54	AF,ME,E,US,D
Air Canada	Canada	NA	0	20,264	9,900	22,058	68	NA,CAR,E,SE. Asia,D
Alaska Airlines	United States	NA	0	6,800	5,810	7,963	56	Pacific US,MEX,Ussr
Aloha Airlines	United States	NA	0	1,900	4,925	1,070	63	Hawaiian Islands
American Airlines	United States	NA	0	97,900	75,994	132,313	62	D,E,CAR,SA,CA,MEX,JAP
American Trans Air*	United States	NA	0	2,200	2,388	4,610	65	E,FE,NA,CA,CAR,D
American West Airlines	United States	NA	0	11,696	16,907	20,777	64	D,Western Canada
Canadian Airlines Int'l	Canada	NA	0	15,400	8,036	20,467	64	Asia,AUST,E,NA,SA,D
Continental Airlines	United States	NA	0	33,730	36,970	66,680	63	D,CAN,CA,SA,E,FE,AUST
Delta Airlines	United States	NA	0	72,000	74,282	108,256	60	D,Bahamas,CAN,MEX,E, Asia
Hawaiian Airlines	United States	NA	0	2,500	4,054	4,150	64	Hawaii,Western US, S.Pacific
Northwest Airlines	United States	NA	0	45,200	41,117	85,786	66	NA,E,FE,AUST
Southwest Airlines	United States	NA	0	9,778	22,670	18,175	61	D
Sun Country Airlines	United States	NA	0	300	1,288	2,418	79	NA,CA,CAR,E,
Tower Air*	United States	NA	0	524	332	2,321	78	E, Israel
Transworld Airlines	United States	NA	0	29,027	20,736	45,271	65	NA,CAR,E,ME,
United Airlines	United States	NA	0	82,292	62,003	132,900	66	D,CAN,CA,SA,E,FE,AUST
US Air	United States	NA	0	45,284	55,600	54,900	59	US,CAN,CAR,E
World Airways*	United States	NA	0	350	481	1,648	59	WW

Source: Interavia, October 1992. Published by Aerospace Media Publishing, Geneva, Switzerland. Government holding and load factors have been rounded.

Notes: * means substantial number of passengers are on chartered flights, blank cells indicate no data available; RPK = revenue passenger kilometers
Key to Principal Route Abbreviations.

AF = Africa	E = Europe	MED = Mediterranean
AUST = Australia	FE = Far East	MEX = Mexico
CA = Central America	I = India	NA = North America
CAN = Canada	JAP = Japan	SA = South America
CAR = Caribbean	LA = Latin America	US = United States
D = Domestic	ME = Middle East	WW = Worldwide

Exhibit 8.10   World airline international traffic by region, 1990

	Passengers carried (thousands)	Passenger share (%)	RPK's (millions)	RPK share (%)	Load factor (%)
Europe + USSR	121,665	43	312,321	35	68
Europe − USSR	117,243		294,482		68
Africa	12,688	5	33,088	4	60
Middle East	13,857	5	38,155	4	64
Asia	58,864	21	237,821	27	72
North America	54,484	19	219,980	25	69
Latin America/Carib	18,925	7	52,131	6	65
Total, incl. USSR	280,483	100	893,496	100	

Source: Civil Aviation Statistics of the World, by International Civil Aviation Organization, 1990. Scheduled traffic only.

Latin America and the Caribbean

This region is divided into three sub-regions: the Caribbean, Central America/ Mexico, and South America. Airlines are highly regulated in this region, and many are owned by their government. These governments typically regulate airline capacity, allocating a predetermined amount to each airline for each city pair. However, some countries, such as Chile, are moving toward letting the market determine capacity. Although most foreign airlines operating in this region have only third and fourth freedoms, some enjoy fifth freedom. Most governments favor the concept of having a single flag carrier to transport all traffic to and from the country, but some have allowed foreign carriers to share the capacity. These foreign carriers are affected less by the region's damaging economic environment, which has made them a very competitive force.

Middle East

Air transportation in the Middle East countries is based on business travel to the region and as a refueling point for routes from Asia to Europe. The fortunes of its airlines rise and fall with the oil industry and political turmoil. As in Europe, most air travel is international because of a weak domestic traffic base. Many of the region's carriers are subsidized by their governments and protected by conservative bilateral aviation agreements.

Because of its central location between Europe and Asia, many Middle East airlines moved into the Europe–Asia routes. However, this opportunity is decreasing as the range of jet aircraft increases to the point where connections in the Middle East are no longer needed for refueling.

Africa

Although Africa is large in land mass and population, its financial position kept most countries, except South Africa, from prospering in commercial aviation. Many African governments have strict bilateral agreements intended to support

Exhibit 8.11 Financial statistics of industrial countries

		Average 1979–88	1989	1990	1991	1992	1993	Forecast average 1994–97
All industrial	Real GDP	2.7	3.4	2.5	0.8	1.8	3.3	3.1
	Current Acct	−0.5	−0.6	−0.6	−0.2	−0.3	−0.4	−0.4
Canada	Real GDP	3.2	2.5	0.5	−1.5	2.3	4.9	
	Current Acct	−0.9	−3.2	−3.3	−3.9	−2.9	−2.7	
United States	Real GDP	2.5	2.5	1.0	−0.7	1.6	3.5	
	Current Acct	−1.6	−2.0	−1.7	−0.2	−0.9	−1.1	
Japan	Real GDP	4.1	4.8	5.2	4.5	2.2	3.9	
	Current Acct	1.8	2.0	1.2	2.1	2.6	2.3	
France	Real GDP	2.1	3.9	2.8	1.2	1.8	2.6	
	Current Acct	−0.5	−0.5	−0.7	−0.5	−0.4	−0.3	
Germany	Real GDP	1.8	3.8	4.5	1.2	2.0	3.0	
	Current Acct	1.5	4.8	2.9	−1.2	−0.8	−0.5	
Italy	Real GDP	2.7	3.0	2.0	1.0	1.6	2.4	
	Current Acct	−0.6	−1.2	−1.3	−1.7	−1.7	−1.8	
United Kingdom	Real GDP	2.3	2.3	1.0	−2.2	0.8	3.1	
	Current Acct	3.0	−4.0	−2.8	−0.8	−1.4	−1.6	
Other industrial	Real GDP	2.3	3.8	2.5	8.0	2.0	2.7	3.0
	Current Acct	−1.2	−1.2	−0.8	−0.6	−0.6	0.5	−0.4

Source: *World Economic Outlook* (International Monetary Fund), 1992.
Real GDP is percentage change in real GDP.
Current acct is change in current account as percentage of GDP.

their flag carriers. They do this not only to ensure equal market access, but also to provide jobs and gain hard currency. The whole African market is highly protected to ensure their carriers survive in the global aviation market.

The global economy

As Eastern Europe and the former Soviet Union countries try to revive their economies, industrial countries are experiencing slow growth. In 1991, world GDP decreased by 0.05 percent. World output is expected to grow by about 1 percent in 1992 and 3 percent in 1993. As shown in exhibits 8.11 and 8.12, growth in developing countries should substantially outpace the industrial countries. Economic factors such as GDP growth, GDP per capita, and trade volume all contribute to the demand for international air transportation.

International competitors

The international competitive environment is changing rapidly; mergers and consolidations are the rule. British Airways is awaiting DOT approval to purchase 44 percent of USAir, the fourth largest US airline. Most governments, including the USA, limit foreign ownership of airlines so that the foreign owner does not have

Exhibit 8.12   Financial statistics of developing countries

		Average 1979–88	Average 1984–8	1988	1989	1990	1991	1992	1993	Forecast average 1994–97
All developing	Real GDP	3.8	3.9	4.1	3.2	1.3	−3.4	4.0	4.4	5.3
	Exports	−2.0	7.3	10.3	5.1	−0.2	3.6	6.4	8.4	8.3
	Imports	5.4	3.3	10.0	7.1	4.1	6.5	9.2	7.8	7.7
Africa	Real GDP	2.4	2.3	3.6	2.7	0.9	1.4	2.7	3.0	3.2
	Exports	−2.6	7.6	1.3	7.3	5.0	3.6	2.7	4.1	3.6
	Imports	2.4	0.5	6.1	2.8	1.5	1.9	4.0	4.0	4.6
Asia	Real GDP	5.9	7.8	8.9	5.3	5.6	5.8	5.5	5.7	6.2
	Exports	7.2	13.2	14.3	6.7	8.0	12.6	10.0		10.8
	Imports	8.0	10.4	20.1	9.5	8.1	14.7	9.9		10.3
Europe	Real GDP	4.1	3.3	4.7	2.3	−2.3	−16.0	−13.5	1.2	4.5
	Exports	3.1	4.2	5.4	−1.9	−19.4	−13.9	−7.9	6.8	6.8
	Imports	3.4	2.2	3.2	7.0	−2.0	−15.1	4.7	6.6	5.6
Middle East	Real GDP	3.0	0.2	−1.7	4.7	4.2	0.4	15.0	7.3	5.6
	Exports	−6.9	4.1	15.9	8.5	−0.5	−3.8	13.6	5.7	3.8
	Imports	11.5	−7.8	−1.2	5.5	1.1	2.5	13.6	3.6	1.9
Western hemis.	Real GDP	3.1	2.9	0.7	1.0	−0.1	2.8	2.7	4.2	5.0
	Exports	2.0	4.0	8.1	7.4	4.6	3.2	5.0	6.0	5.7
	Imports	0.2	3.0	6.0	2.4	6.0	15.6	10.5	5.8	5.3

Source: *World Economic Outlook* (International Monetary Fund), 1992.
All numbers are changes from period to period.

controlling interest. British Airways plans to purchase 25 percent of USAir in voting stock, with the remainder in non-voting stock. The two carriers plan to merge their services, making it appear as one airline. USAir, with very few international routes, would benefit from being able to provide international services. If combined, the two carriers would be the largest international airline in the world, serving 339 cities in 71 countries. British Airways would benefit from USAir's large US presence to feed its North Atlantic routes. The "Big Three" US airlines – AA, United, and Delta – are aggressively lobbying DOT to disapprove the deal. They want the US–UK bilateral agreement amended to allow US airlines the same freedoms currently enjoyed by British Airways. This would include not only greater access to the UK with third and fourth freedoms, but also fifth freedom rights. The additional freedom would allow US carriers to have routes which transport passengers from countries such as Germany and France to the UK, routes currently flown by BA.

   In addition to the USAir deal, BA is actively pursuing other carriers. It is trying to purchase Dan-Air, a British carrier providing service from the UK to the rest of Europe. This transaction is facing resistance from the UK's other carriers, and must be cleared not only by British officials but also by the European Union Competition Council. In a bidding competition with Singapore Airlines and Air New Zealand,

BA is pursuing part of Qantas, the Australian flag carrier. It also agreed to buy 49.9 percent of the French domestic carrier, TAT European Airlines.

KLM Royal Dutch Airlines (KLM) won DOT approval to merge its operations with Northwest Airlines, the fifth largest US airline. KLM, based in Amsterdam, Netherlands, currently owns 49 percent of Northwest Airlines. The two airlines plan to combine sales forces, inventory management, schedule planning, and pricing programs. As with the BA/USAir deal, the companies would make the two operations appear as one airline to the customer. KLM will benefit from increased access to the US market, and Northwest will benefit from increased passenger volume on routes which connect with KLM flights.

Other European carriers are not in the same shape as BA and KLM. Air France recently received a 1.25 billion franc subsidy from the French government. It is trying to become profitable by changing its fleet and route structure and by reducing costs. Lufthansa eliminated over 1700 jobs in 1992 and planned to eliminate 3600 more in 1993. Both Germany and France want to renegotiate and make their bilateral agreements with the USA more restrictive. Iberia, the Spanish flag carrier, received a 120 billion peseta subsidy from the government only after the European Union (EU) ruled that it would be the last bailout the airline could receive.

Japan Air Lines spent heavily in the 1980s to invest in new equipment and routes, and has the highest operating costs in the region. Some competitors are discounting tickets by as much as 30 percent, which reduced the company's return on sales to 1.2 percent in 1991. In contrast, Singapore Airlines had a return on sales of 24 percent for the same period.

Financial difficulties facing South America's airlines, particularly those in Brazil, will likely reshape its commercial aviation industry. Major airlines such as Transbrasil, VASP, and Varig are requesting about $2.2 billion in loans from the Brazilian government. It will be difficult, if not impossible, for Brazil to grant such an amount if it wishes to remain committed to its inflation reducing agreement with the International Monetary Fund.

American Airlines also competes with other domestic carriers such as United Airlines, Delta, and Northwest Airlines for international passengers. United developed strong route systems in the Pacific and South America when it purchased Pan Am's rights to those regions in the early 1990s. At the same time, Delta surpassed AA as the carrier with the most flights to Europe when it purchased Pan Am's rights to those routes and Pan Am's Frankfurt hub.

In summer 1992, AMR and PWA, the parent company of Canadian Airlines, began negotiations on an alliance between the two airlines. The agreement called for AMR to make an investment in PWA, joint marketing of the airlines' services, and a long-term services agreement. After very detailed discussions, and although AMR was willing to commit, PWA's board of directors rejected the agreement. PWA instead decided to merge with Air Canada. However, weeks after this decision was made PWA backed out of the merger. PWA and AMR are once again discussing the original agreement. PWA's financial condition worsened recently, and they received a temporary operating loan from the Canadian government.

In general, IATA expected the world's 200 international airlines to lose $2.6 billion on international routes in 1992. Cost reductions and traffic growth were projected to reduce the loss in 1993 and 1994. IATA expected passenger traffic to grow an average of 7.4 percent per year through 1996. The association's Director General, Gunther Eser, expected the membership to consolidate down to "about 50 very large entities" by the year 2000.

Political environment

US President Bill Clinton has "mixed feelings" about airline deregulation. His main concerns seem to be the existence of higher prices, lower quality service, service to smaller cities, and safety issues. He also opposed the BA–USAir merger; DOT said it would decide the issue before Clinton takes office.

In Europe, airline competition was likely to increase in 1993 when the EU's third package of civil aviation liberalization took effect. Under the new rules, which will be phased in by April 1, 1997, a licensed EU carrier is able to fly any route within the EU. The first phase of this transition restricts airlines to 50 percent of aircraft capacity on the foreign route. For example, Lufthansa could fly from Frankfurt to Paris and then on to Nice. However, the Paris to Nice segment is restricted to 50 percent of normal capacity. This means that if an airline uses an aircraft which seats 150 people on the Frankfurt–Paris–Nice route, only 75 people can be carried from Paris to Nice. After April 1, 1997, this restriction will be removed, allowing full freedom in loading the international segments of a flight. Pricing will be more liberal but still subject to restrictions intended to discourage excessively high or low fares and predatory pricing.

The EU would like to merge all member nations' bilateral agreements into a common EU policy. The EU would then negotiate aviation agreements between the community as a whole and other countries. This is being resisted by many member EU nations who do not want to lose control of their civil aviation agreements.

The Japanese government stated that its bilateral agreement with the USA, which dates to 1952, gives US carriers unfair advantages. It has put all USA–Japan routes on review, placing in jeopardy US carriers' routes to Japan and those which use Japan to connect to Australia and other points beyond. Germany and France would also like to renegotiate their bilateral agreements with the USA, with the intent of restricting US competitiveness in their markets.

China announced that it will restructure its airline industry to possibly allow for foreign investment in its airlines and airports. It has begun decentralizing its airlines into regional carriers. The largest of these are China Southern in Canton, Air China in Beijing, and China Eastern in Shanghai. China Southern, the most advanced of the three, planned to start issuing shares to domestic investors by 1993.

American Airlines' International Operations

Although the company has had routes to Canada, Mexico, and the Caribbean for many years, it only began aggressively pursuing other international routes after deregulation. In 1978, the year deregulation began, the company flew only 21 daily international non-stop routes to Mexico, Canada, and the Caribbean. In 1992 AA had over 100 non-stop routes to Mexico, the Caribbean, Canada, Europe, Japan, and Central and South America (see exhibit 8.13). Many of the routes have

Exhibit 8.13 American Airlines' International destinations

From	To	From	To
Chicago	Brussels, Belgium	San Juan	Anguilla
	London – Gatwick, England		Antigua
	London – Heathrow, England		Aruba
	London – Stansted, England		Freeport, Bahamas
	Manchester, England		Governor's Harbour, Bahamas
	Paris – Orly, France		Marsh Harbour, Bahamas
	Berlin, Germany		Barbados
	Frankfurt, Germany		Sao Paulo, Brazil
	Milan, Italy		Tortola, British Virgin Lslands
	Glasgow, Scotland		Virgin Gorda, British Virgin Lslands
	Stockholm, Sweden		Grand Gayman, Cayman Islands
	Zurich, Switzerland		Case de Campo, Dominican Republic
Dallas	London – Gatwick, England		La Romana, Dominican Republic
	Paris – Orly, France		Puerto Plata, Dominican Republic
	Frankfurt, Germany		Santo Domingo, Dominican Republic
	Tokyo – Narita, Japan		Grenada
	Acapulco, Mexico		Point-a-Pitre, Guadeloupe
	Cancun, Mexico		Port-au-Prince, Haiti
	Guadalajara, Mexico		Kingston, Jamaica
	Mexico City, Mexico		Montego Bay, Jamaica
	Puerto Vallarta, Mexico		Forte-de-France, Martinique
	Madrid, Spain		Nassau
Los Angeles	London – Heathrow, England		St Maarten, Netherlands Antilles
Miami	Buenos Aires, Argentina		St Kitts, Nevis
	Belize City, Belize		Aguadilla, Puerto Rico
	La Paz, Bolivia		Mayaguez, Puerto Rico
	Santa Cruz, Bolivia		Ponce, Puerto Rico
	Rio de Janeiro, Brazil		St Lucia
	Sao Paulo, Brazil		Treasure City
	Santiago, Chile		Port of Spain, Trinidad
	Barranquilla, Colombia	New York	Brussels, Belgium
	Bogota, Colombia		Bermuda
	Cali, Colombia		Sao Paulo, Brazil
	San Jose, Costa Rica		London – Heathrow, England
	Guayaquil, Ecuador		Manchester, England
	Quito, Ecuador		Paris – Orly, France
	San Salvador, El Salvador		Cancun, Mexico
	London – Heathrow, England		Zurich, Switzerland
	Paris – Orly, France	Boston	London – Heathrow, England
	Guatamala City, Guatemala	Seattle	Tokyo – Narita, Japan
	San Pedro Sula, Honduras	San Jose, CA	Tokyo – Narita, Japan
	Tegucigalpa, Honduras	Raleigh/Durham	Paris – Orly, France
	Cancun, Mexico		Cancun, Mexico
	Managua, Nicaragua		
	Panama City, Panama		
	Asuncion, Paraguay		
	Lima, Peru		
	Madrid, Spain		
	Caracas, Venezuela		

more than one flight per day. About 70 international destinations are served. Reflecting this, in 1981 AA flew about 28 million RPMs, while by 1991 the figure grew to 133 million RPMs (see exhibit 8.4). Most of the company's growth in the past ten years was in the international markets since AA almost saturated the domestic market.

In 1989 AA purchased Eastern Airlines' routes in Central and South America, giving it over 200 flights weekly to that region. American is now the major airline in that market. Before Delta Airline's purchase of Pan Am's North Atlantic routes, AA was also the largest carrier in that market. The airline currently flies to about 70 international destinations. Some of these routes were applied for and granted by the DOT, while others were purchased from rival airlines. For example, in 1991 American bought Trans World Airlines' routes from the USA to London's Heathrow airport. The $450 million transaction made AA one of the largest carriers to the UK, with over 90 flights weekly to London, Manchester, and Glasgow. Also in 1991, AA bought Continental Airlines' Seattle–Tokyo route and received DOT approval for a San Jose–Tokyo route.

Hubs such as Chicago, Dallas, Miami, San Juan and New York serve as major connecting points, or gateways, for AA's international traffic. Chicago and New York serve as gateways for Europe, Miami is the connecting point for Central and South America, and San Juan is the gateway for the Caribbean. Dallas is a gateway for several regions, including Mexico, Europe, and Japan. The company's other hubs in San Jose, Nashville, and Raleigh/Durham are newly developed and currently do not have substantial international traffic.

NOTES

1   CAB, Federal Aviation Act of 1958, Revised March 1, 1977, section 102(d).

2   For instance, AA sells a ticket for Dallas–London–Kuwait City. AA collects all the money and writes the tickets. But the tickets are AA from Dallas to London, transferring to British Airways (BA) from London to Kuwait City. In this case, AA owes BA that portion of the revenue for the London–Kuwait City segment. Although AA can write BA tickets, since they do not have a codesharing agreement, IATA distributes the revenue.

Korean Air: Challenges and Opportunities in the Growth of a Korean Firm

Chang Young-Chul

Introduction

I have long believed that business is much like an art. This is the guiding principle behind all our work.
(Cho Choong Hoon, Chairman and CEO, Korean Air[1])

The statement above reflects the philosophy of founder Cho Choong Hoon, Chairman and Chief Executive Officer of Korean Air (KAL) and its parent company, the Hanjin Group. He has been responsible for skilfully guiding KAL, which has evolved from a small domestic airline in 1969 to become one of the largest in the world today.

Since the transfer of the management of Korean Air to the Hanjin Group in 1969, the airline has registered remarkable growth, ranking fourth among the 200 airlines of the International Air Transport Association (IATA) in 1991, in terms of international scheduled services for cargo, and fifteenth in terms of passengers, freight, and mail. Its fleet size increased from a mere eight airplanes in

1969 to 85 modern aircraft by 1992, while the number of passengers who have enjoyed its services has grown from 380,000 to 15.2 million. The carrier's fleet of wide-bodied jets carried some 580,000 tons of cargo the world over in 1992, and its list of destinations includes 55 major cities in 25 countries. In addition, Korean Air strives continuously to upgrade its aircraft fleet and to apply the latest technology to enhance safety and efficiency. From 1983 to 1988, it ranked first in technical dispatch reliability of the Airbus Industrie A300s. With more than 12,000 well-trained employees, the airlines is setting new standards in transportation services to provide their customers with excellent service and convenient flight schedules.[2] It is presently one of the largest airline in Asia, and this unprecedented growth, which has taken place in just 24 years, is remarkable when compared to the 50-plus years of experience enjoyed by other major carriers in the world.[3]

Korean Air's development echoes the progress made by other Korean *chaebols* which mushroomed out of a war-stricken country in the middle of the twentieth century. The airline is the pride of the nation and symbolizes the advancement made by the Korean national aviation industry. With its network of routes around the world, it represents its country in air transportation around the globe. It was given the honor of being the official airline for the 1988 Seoul Olympics and played an important role in the successful execution of this international sports meet.

The achievements clocked by Korean Air so far cannot be understood completely without mentioning its affiliation to the Hanjin Group, the only *chaebol* in Korea which specializes in transportation services. The next section gives a brief description of the group, detailing its history and the business it is involved in.

The Hanjin Group

The Hanjin Group is one of the ten largest *chaebols* in Korea. It was founded in 1945, when Chairman Cho established the company as a trucking service. By 1965 it had included Air Korea Co., and in the years since, many companies have grown from the group's humble beginnings. Aside from taking over Korea's national airline in 1969, Hanjin Container Lines Ltd was also established in 1977, together with Korea Shipping Corporation, merged to form Hanjin Shipping Company Ltd in 1988 – one of the leading container/bulk carriers in the world. In 1989, the group added Hanjin Heavy Industry Co. to its list of affiliate companies. The high-sea transportation enabled it to play a pivotal role along with Korean Air in creating Korea's "miracle economy". The group's interests presently also include banking, securities, mining, architecture and construction, dredging, and shipbuilding.[4] Altogether, there are 25 affiliated companies, as well as the Inha University Foundation, Jungsuck Foundation, and Inha General Hospital. The goals of the Hanjin Group are clear and within reach – land transport to all corners of Korea, container shipping across all five oceans and in the air, the realization of the dream of an around-the-world service. Hanjin is Korea's only integrated air, land, and sea service organization. The services complement each other so that overall operations reach maximum efficiency.

Presently, the group has 38,000 employees, assets of approximately 9.3 trillion won and a total sales revenue of 4.2 trillion won. In 1993, its ranking within Korea was eighth by sales revenue and fifth by total assets. In the next section, the history of Korean Air will be detailed and an attempt will be made to analyze how the airline has managed to achieve the remarkable and unprecedented growth in its brief 24 years of civilian management history.

History of Korean Air

The history of Korean Airlines can be dated back to November 1948 when Korean National Airlines (KNA) became a full-scale civilian airline company. KNA suffered losses for 14 years before it was incorporated into Korean Airlines by the government in 1962 – the year when it also established domestic services. This company suffered chronic losses because government capital was not provided as had been forecast. The government, in search of a remedy, proposed to transfer the KAL management to Hanjin Transportation Co., as the latter had the experience of operating Air Korea and had been providing air services since 1960.[5] Korean Airlines, under the management of the Hanjin Group, was renamed Korean Air in 1987.

Establishment of civilian management

March 1, 1969 marked a new chapter in the history of Korean civil aviation, when the management of Korean Air was transferred from the government into the hands of civilian management. The Hanjin Group assumed the responsibility of operating the national airlines of Korea, which had up to 1969 suffered from chronic revenue losses, operating on eight outmoded aircraft with only six domestic and three Korea–Japan routes, and with no hope of progress materializing amid the country's general economic stagnation at that time. When Hanjin took over the management of the national airline, the carrier had accumulated liabilities of over 2.7 billion won.

The Hanjin Transportation Group was founded in 1945, and by 1969, when it assumed the national airline management, it had accumulated substantial experience in the transportation industry. Up to that time, it had gained experience in the fields of land transportation, shipping, operating air terminals, and, most importantly, experience in air services through its subsidiary Air Korea. Due to the group's specialization in the transportation industry, it was approached by the government to undertake the task of revitalizing the national airline. It was an opportunity not to be refused. Chairman Cho accepted this task and took the oath as the new President of Korean Air in March 1969. More importantly, this task was perceived as a contribution to national aviation development rather than for corporate or personal benefits.[6] Thus, the civilian Korean Air management concentrated all its efforts and honor on the future development of aviation, which was, and still is, considered an index of both national development and the service industries.

To achieve the goal of revitalizing the national airline, top management at that time had to formulate the vision, mission, and objectives which were to be manifested in the corporate philosophy. This will be detailed in the next subsection.

Corporate mission and philosophy

It can be inferred from the last subsection that the mission of Korean Air under Cho Choong Hoon was to uphold national pride in the aviation industry and to honor the future development of the aviation industry through its growth as the national flag carrier.

Korean Air's top management realized at that time that, to grow in the aviation industry, it had to focus its resources on certain elements of the industry. The three major elements considered indispensable to growth in this industry are aircraft, routes, and personnel. With these in mind, KAL laid its long-term objectives and ideals. Specifically, it strived to achieve the following long-term goals:[7]

- leading the airline industry in customer service;
- building the world's most creative and skilled workforce;
- applying the latest technology to enhance safety and efficiency;
- to be the world's best airline with a route network extending round the globe.[8]

These goals were typical of Chairman Cho, whose entrepreneurial ambitions and success were matched by few other present or past captains of industries. They were the seemingly unachievable strategic intentions of Korean Air when it first started out, but as the years went by, it seemed that the long-term goals could be realized. The chairman's philosophy for the Hanjin Group was to establish enterprise through trust and public credibility. It can also be inferred that his philosophy for Korean Air was to satisfy its publics by pursuing growth in a responsible manner. He believed that innovation was the best method to pursue this in the aviation industry. In particular, the carrier followed the philosophy of service excellence in an attempt to revolutionize the flying experience.

The corporate philosophy of Korean Airlines was manifested in their company motto of:

- innovate with conviction;
- act with sincerity;
- serve with responsibility.[9]

It should be highlighted that the corporate philosophy of service excellence had tremendous implications for the human resource management of Korean Air. This could only be brought about by good industrial relations, extensive training and development, motivation to maintain excellence and relevant reward structure. The airline had established this infrastructure from its early years and had placed great importance in human resource management. The employees were aptly named the "Korean Air Family." Its dedication to service excellence was echoed through its in-flight service motto of "The best service, to make our passengers feel all the comforts of home."[10]

The corporate philosophy, mission and long-term objectives of Korean Air guided its direction in the early years, which saw unprecedented growth taking place. The next subsection will detail how the airline has grown through its years of civilian management and its mission, philosophy, and objectives will be examined in this context.

Growth in the first two decades

The growth of Korean Airlines in the first 24 years of civilian management can be examined by analyzing the growth of the three major elements identified earlier, i.e. aircraft, routes, and personnel. In addition, other aspects of growth, such as cargo services and the use of technology, will be examined.

Aircraft

As mentioned, the civilian management inherited eight outmoded aircraft in 1969 when privatization took place. Since then, however, Korean Air has worked steadily and invested boldly in the modernization of its fleet. It purchased its first two modern jumbo jets, Boeing 747s, in 1973, and by the end of its second decade (1989) it had 65 up-to-date aircraft. At the end of 1992, its fleet size had increased to 85. Korean Air's dedication to the modernization of its fleet in its early years is thus congruent to its philosophy of service excellence by constantly upgrading the convenience and comfort of passengers through modern aircraft.

Routes

At the time of privatization of the national airline in 1969, its route structure comprised a meager six domestic routes and three Korea–Japan routes. By 1979 its route network had expanded to 22 cities, and at the end of its second decade it had a network of routes covering 38 cities in 18 countries. Presently, Korean Air flies to 55 cities in 25 countries. It attributes its aggressive expansion of routes as a sense of national duty contributing to the progress of the Korean aviation industry. This evidence further supports our inference that the mission is to honor the future development of the Korean aviation industry through the growth of Korean Air. Its fast pace in route additions also maintains the achievement of the long-term objective of "a route network extending round the globe" in the near future.

Personnel

When Hanjin acquired Korean Air in 1969, it employed only 500 employees.[11] The number has been increasing steadily over the years and, by the end of 1989, it had 12,000 employees in the "Korean Air family."

The two decades of growth in terms of the number of employees are complemented by an increase in the quality of the employees. Korean Air, guided by its philosophy of providing service excellence, sees the need to invest heavily in the training and development of its workforce throughout its period of growth. For example, as part of its flight training program, the airline operates simulators of its aircraft to train its pilots and also owns a training airfield on Cheju Island. The latter was established in 1989 and offers a complete two-year pilot training course which enables it to remain self-sufficient and also meet Korea's growing demand for commercial pilots.

One major strength of Korean Air that has helped to propel its growth is the excellence of in-flight services provided. In order for an airline to achieve this, it needs a crew of dedicated and spirited flight attendants. True to its in-flight service motto of "the best service to make our passengers feel all the comforts of home," Korean Air has added to the number of its flight attendants by recruiting from overseas (e.g. China, Japan, Thailand, and Hong Kong) so that international passengers can feel more at home while on board the plane. The flight attendants have to undergo intensive training to ensure that the services are excellently executed.

Besides the investment in the training and development of its pilots and flight attendants, Korean Airlines has dedicated itself to the training of its managers, navigators, technicians, and engineers, with the motive of developing technical skill and enhancing motivation. It has a very comprehensive training program that encompasses three broad categories:

- operation management training which aims at helping employees understand company policies and developing their management skills;
- professional training program which comprises curricular on all commercial and technical areas vital to airline operations;
- foreign language program which is designed to teach employees foreign language skills essential to an international airline.

Through its efforts placed in the training and development of its employees, Korean Air shows that it is moving in the right direction toward "building the world's most creative and skilled workforce" – one of its long-term goals.

Other aspects

Growth in the airline's cargo service volume is another important aspect of the airline's development. Korean Air has always placed great emphasis on freight.[12] The 380,000 tons of cargo carried by the airline in 1988 represented an incredible 198-fold increase over 1968, the year before the airline was transferred to civilian management. In 1991, it ranked fifth in the world in terms of cargo tonnage.

In accordance with its philosophy of enhancing efficiency, Korean Air utilizes the latest technology in every stage of its growth. The introduction of the IBM 370/145 computer system in 1974 marked its move toward fully computerized services. Another milestone in its technological history was the introduction of TOPAS in 1990, a passenger and ticketing system.

The above section describes the unprecedented development achieved by Korean Air in its 24 years and shows how the carrier's corporate philosophies and long-term objectives have guided its growth throughout this period. The next section will detail the airline's profile in the mid-1990s and will present a static picture of the company.

Profile of Korean Air

After 20 years of remarkable growth, Korean Air embraces the 1990s as one of the world's largest airlines. In this section, the profile of the company, such as its organizational structure, product line, marketing strategies, and financial structure, will be examined in the context of how it has developed to its present status and how well this company structure meets the needs and challenges of the new decade.

Organizational structure and management style

Korean Air adopts a very centralised organizational structure[13] (shown in exhibit 9.1) and has kept the control of top positions in the hands of the founder's family.

Exhibit 9.1 Organizational structure of Korean Air

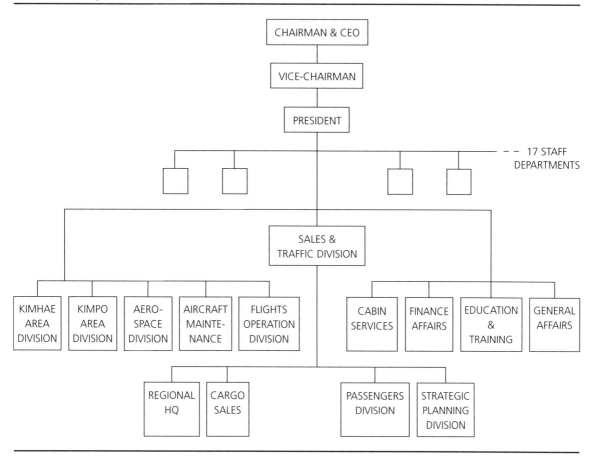

Chairman Cho, the founder of Hanjin Group and the first President of Korean Air, remains in control in Korean Air. The post of Vice-Chairman is delegated to his brother, Cho Choong Kun, who served as Korean Air's President until 1991. The Chairman's son, Cho Yang Ho, was appointed the President of Korean Air on February 27, 1992, and Chairman Cho regards this occasion as the passing of Korean Air to a younger management with "new ambition and a young spirit."[14] It is observed that Korean Air is controlled by the founder's immediate relatives and this mirrors the family-management style of the Hanjin Group, which is one of the best representations of a Korean *chaebol* where ownership lies in the sole possession of the owner and his family.[15]

From the organizational structure, it can be seen that the President has a very large span of control and is responsible for the daily operations of Korean Air. This structure suits the company well, as is evident in its phenomenal growth so far. Besides the centralized control and sole ownership which put tremendous power in the hands of top management, its success is also largely attributed to the dynamism and entrepreneurial ability of Chairman Cho, who is solely responsible for the functions of securing route rights, revising aviation agreements, and ensuring major loans for aircraft acquisition (e.g. obtaining a $500 million interest-free loan in 1979 to acquire ten Boeing 747s).

The Chairman's managerial philosophy is stated as "Business is an art. To make a good work of art, there should be harmony, just as good as an orchestra's."[16] Hence, his management style stresses harmonious relationships with workers. Employees of Korean Air are treated as assets and are viewed as belonging to the "Korean Air family." Aside from their training and development, which are taken very seriously, lifetime employment is also practiced. Korean Air believes that employees will only work as unofficial diplomats, i.e. properly representing both the airline and Korea, when there are harmonious relations between management and the employees. This is reflected in its mission, which is to uphold national pride in the aviation industry, where employees are expected to act as civilian diplomats.

Korean Air practices the philosophy of constantly looking ahead,[17] as Chairman Cho understands that a company will become obsolete if it fails to do so. Consequently, employees are requested to move ahead and not look back. This is manifested in the company motto – "Innovate with conviction" – which is translated into the recruitment policy of only selecting newcomers who are creative, responsible, and effective.[18] This policy is hence consistent with the rest of the company motto, which reads "serve with responsibility" and "act with sincerity."

Products and services
Korean Air derives more than half of its revenue from passenger transportation services, a quarter from freight transportation, and the rest from charter, mail, sales commission, sales manufacture, flight kitchen operations, etc.[19]

Passenger services
Passenger services is a very important aspect of the company services mix. Following its philosophy, the airline is committed to being excellent for its on-ground and cabin services and this is reflected in its outstanding record for on-time operations, which rose from 81.2 percent in 1990 to 90 percent in 1991. Its in-flight services stress comfort while its service motto proclaims that passengers should be made to feel all the amenities of home. In-flight services are divided into three categories – first class, prestige class (business class), and economy class – cash stressing different combinations of offerings with attentive service.

For passengers' convenience and travel options, Korean Air strives to add new routes every year. In 1993, Korean Air served 55 major cities in 25 countries and operated 11 domestic routes. It also added routes to Ho Chi Minh City, Bombay, Brisbane, and Penang (Malaysia) recently. To further develop the aviation industry through route development, the airline intends to establish flights to China in the near future.

Cargo services
Riding Korea's manufacturing and export boom, Korean Air has grown into one of the top six or seven scheduled airlines in terms of freight tonnage. Freight

operations remain a mainstay of the airline's operations, contributing to 35 percent of total revenue. Its cargo services ranked fourth in the world in terms of international freight ton-kilometers in 1992, and KAL is one of the few airlines that is still investing in all-cargo freighters to ensure prompt and reliable delivery. As the first airline also to offer a jumbo jet freighter service across the Pacific, Korean Air has its own cargo terminal at Los Angeles International Airport, the largest cargo terminal on the west coast of North America. Operating huge cargo terminals at New York's JFK and Tokyo's Narita International airports, its freighters make 50 cargo stops a week in 16 major cities worldwide. With continued computerization of cargo handling and the implementation of the automated cargo express system at a number of Korean Air terminals, the safety and reliability of all its cargo handling is further enhanced, especially through its cargo drop centre (CDC) facility.

One of Korean Air's competitive advantages which allows it to fulfill the distinct needs of air cargo customers is its association with the Hanjin Group's Land–Sea–Air Integrated Transportation System. This enables the airline to meet the special needs of its customers with reliable and timely service. This is an example of how a Korean company with a short history can compete with other well-established foreign companies through its synergistic relationship with the other companies in its affiliated *chaebol*.

Other services

Other services offered by Korean Air include group tours (Joyful Holidays), mail services, package express, and, more importantly, its flight catering services. Korean Air is the monopoly supplier of meals for all the 28 international airlines using Seoul Kimpo Airport, including rival Asiana Airlines.[20] But Asiana is setting up Asiana Catering, expected to begin operation in the second half of 1993, in a joint venture with Scandinavian Airlines System. This may present as a potential form of competition for Korean Air in the future.

Marketing strategies

Sales and distribution

Korean Air developed the fully integrated reservation and ticketing system, TOPAS (Total Passenger Automated Services), for travel agents in 1990, to replace their previous real-time reservation system, KALCOS. The TOPAS network is connected to service terminals in at least 40 countries and 104 cities around the world. With continuous effort to upgrade its services technology, Korean Air strives to develop a truly universal computerized reservation system (CRS) to be connected to terminals worldwide. This makes reservation and boarding procedures fast and convenient, and allows passengers to enjoy worldwide discounts from hotels and car rental agencies, as well as seating class upgrades and bonus tickets as Frequent Traveller Bonus System members. TOPAS typifies extreme convenience as it can be used to provide information on flight schedules of over 650 airlines, hotels, rental car companies, package tours, etc.

With this extensive CRS network, Korean Air is prepared to meet competition from foreign airlines when the Korean CRS market is opened in the near future.

Exhibit 9.2   Summary income statement (thousand US dollars)

Year	Operating revenue	Operating expenses	Operating income	Net income (loss)
1990	2,207,016	2,071,041	135,975	−10,302
1991	2,640,390	2,384,150	256,240	15,951
1992	2,965,151	2,095,644	259,286	1,493

This enduring effort to apply the latest technology in upgrading its reservation system reflects Chairman Cho's call for innovation as a means to survive in the transportation industry. The carrier's complex automated reservation system may be regarded as a strength and used to fight off other airlines' challenges.[21]

Advertising and promotional strategies

Korean Air's advertising theme centers mainly on the three important aviation elements, namely routes, aircraft, and service personnel. As an example, it has advertising campaigns focusing on its routes, i.e. "Fly Korean to Tokyo" or "Fly Korean, Explore Korea." With respect to the second element, some advertisements emphasize the airlines' commitment to state-of-the-art technology (e.g. investing in the most modern aircraft).

Korean Air has also changed its logo four times since 1969 to better represent itself as a national carrier to Korea and as an international airline to the rest of the world. To achieve the former goal, the current logo comprises of a *Taeguk*, as seen on the Korean flag. The symbol is comprised of two comma-shaped figures representing the principles of yin and yang, which indicate the interacting forces of heaven and earth, sun and moon, male and female, fire and water. To Koreans, the *taeguk* represents a basic philosophy of life – both material and spiritual.

In response to the worldwide use of the frequent-flyer program as a promotional tool for many airlines, Korean Air has developed its own Frequent Traveller Bonus System, as mentioned previously, and its Morning Calm Club, which offers members certain privileges, such as first class check-in service, a free baggage allowance of an extra 10 kilograms and priority baggage handling.

Financial performance

Exhibit 9.2 shows the summarized income statement of Korean Air in the early 1990s.[22]

Korean Air entered the 1990s with a net loss of US$10 million. But despite unfavorable conditions encountered, e.g. the Gulf War and increased competition, it rebounded to make a $16 million net profit in 1991. Chairman Cho attributes this turnaround to route expansion, efficiency of operations, improved safety level, and, most importantly, a heightened standard of service. In 1992, Korean Air achieved another outstanding year. Its operating revenue posted a 12.3 percent increase over 1991 and its operating income ranked seventh among all the world airlines.[23] In conclusion, it can be observed that operating revenues have been increasing since the early 1990s and this signifies the growth stage of the airline.

Korean Air has posted outstanding income showings year after year, and it is likely to remain profitable in the near future.

The Airline Industry Environment

Aside from high levels of capital expenditure, price sensitivity of customers (especially for economy class), and the intense rivalry for different routes, many other factors which are beyond the airline's control make this a tough industry to be in. Before we venture into the issues and challenges pertaining to Korean Air, the characteristics of the world aviation industry will be discussed. Some aspects of the Korean aviation industry will also be touched on.

Route network

An international airline's route network is its main asset. For every international route, an airline has to first obtain the right to fly that route from the government(s) involved. This is normally done through bilateral negotiations between the central authorities of the states involved, and the resulting agreements usually also cover the traffic rights and the freedoms of the air between the two countries. Although governments try to ensure that the distribution of capacity, traffic between countries and airline competitiveness is not heavily tilted in favor of other countries' airlines, they will sometimes resort to breaking these agreements when their national carriers fail to compete effectively.[24]

Route networks determine the size and type of the aircraft fleet. It is usually more cost efficient to utilize larger planes on heavily trafficked routes as fixed costs decline more quickly on these routes. Longer routes may also require utilizing airplanes which have large fuel storage or are fuel efficient, so that time taken for refueling can be cut down.[25]

Economic cycle of the airline industry

It is necessary for airlines to plan their capacity accurately in advance due to the high capital expenditure involved in matching aircraft to routes and the long lead times it takes to procure aircraft. Planning is very difficult as it is based on forecast customer demand. Airline supply and demand have their own cycles, which will always be out of sync with world economic conditions. For instance, it takes 18–24 months to build new aircraft to meet current demand. As a result, when the planes are ready, many countries might be experiencing a recessionary period instead. Airlines also cancel their contracts with aircraft manufacturers when the industry takes an unexpected downturn. The main drawback is that when demand picks up, they may be faced with insufficient capacity. According to Harry Forsythe, regional director for Australian aircraft-leasing company Ansett Worldwide Aviation Services, "Once people start scrambling to pick up aircraft to meet demand again, the whole thing will repeat itself." He believes the seeds of future destruction are sown when aircraft production is cut back to meet present or near-term demand.[26]

The industry is also susceptible to unexpected events such as the OPEC oil price increases in the 1970s, which led to increased industry costs. The US attack on

Libya in the 1980s and the Gulf War in the 1990s, on the other hand, led to decreased air travel.

Government relations

One characteristic of the aviation industry which makes it different from other industries is the large amount of government involvement in all major aspects. Government in many countries consider the aviation industry as their national pride, and this explains their high involvement in that particular industry. Most governments carefully select corporations to operate the national carriers and will usually only allow one or two airline companies to operate in the country. Exceptions to this are Japan and the USA, which admit plural civic airlines.[27]

More importantly, governments play a considerable role in the provision of funds, negotiation of international routes and frequencies, and regulation of air fares. There is direct involvement in the airline business even when the airlines are privately owned. The development of the aviation industry is considered by many developing countries as important to achieve the status of a developed nation. Governments will carefully chart the course of the industry, and private flag carriers are expected to adhere to these plans. Most governments also assist their private airlines to grow and be profitable. They take special interest in the "health" of their flag carriers, and will pump in funds to support them when financial difficulties arise.

The Korean aviation industry has its own characteristics. Chairman Cho was entrusted with the task of revitalizing the Korean National Airlines in 1969. As stated, the mission of Korean Air is to honor the future development of the Korean aviation industry through the growth of KAL. To achieve this mission, the airline has had to depend, to a large extent, on government support, which is displayed in various ways.

First, the government can be a major facilitator for funds. It offered its support to Korean Air by being its guarantor of loans of approximately US$4.9 million in 1992 through the government-run Bank of Development.

Second, in terms of route negotiations with other countries, the Korean government plays an even bigger role. It is involved in holding negotiations and making agreements with different countries with regard to the allotment of landing rights and flying frequencies between Seoul and foreign cities. The success of Korean Air (and Asiana Airlines) depends heavily on extensive international air routes, since domestic air fares are regulated by the government to be only about 40 percent of what they should be for the airline to generate a reasonable return. This is because the domestic air service is viewed as a social service to the Korean public an hence has to be made affordable to the majority. Both carriers make net losses on their domestic routes and depend heavily on their international routes to be competitive and profitable. It is thus vital that the Korean government makes full use of its diplomatic relations with other nations to secure beneficial agreements for its flag carriers and to ensure their competitiveness against foreign competitors.

For example, both Korean Air and Asiana Airlines have to depend on the government to hold negotiations with China before they can extend their route network to the country. China, in its effort to open up and industrialize, will prove to be a lucrative market if the airlines can schedule flights there. At the moment, negotiations between China and Korea have reached a standstill due to the issue of boundary definition.[28] As long as this issue is not resolved, both airlines may lose the opportunity to tap the Chinese market.

Airline costs

About half of an airline's costs consist of variable direct costs, of which fuel costs and wages are major components. In high-wage locations, up to 25 percent of total operating costs can be taken up by wages. Airlines such as Korean Air and SIA, which operate in countries in relatively low labour cost structures (as compared to the USA and Europe) and high productivity, are at an advantage. But this does not necessarily mean that the cost factor is not important to these airlines. They must still take measures to pare costs in different ways. For example, Cathay Pacific, aside from offering its almost entirely expatriate air crew offshore basing to escape paying expensive housing allowances in Hong Kong, is also extending a lower "B-scale" salary to new air crew. SIA is moving computer software development to Bombay while China Airlines has cut back on hiring staff and is accepting new aircraft more slowly than planned.[29]

Strategic alliances

There has been a growing trend toward strategic alliances in the form of equity tie-ups, such as the KLM–Northwest tie-up and British Airways' investment in USAir. Air China has also asked SIA to take a stake in the carrier, while Shanghai Airlines and United Airways are looking to forming a joint venture.[30]

On the whole, the industry has not been very profitable, with many airlines showing significant losses in times of recession and many being forced into bankruptcy. There was a record loss of US$4 billion for the industry in 1991. Overall industry growth in passenger traffic, which is estimated at 5.7 percent worldwide, hides regional differences, with the Asia Pacific region showing greater growth of as much as 9.7 percent as a result of strong regional economies, new airports, and the opening up of new destinations.[31]

Issues and Challenges

As mentioned, Korean Air's road to success was not entirely smooth. It faced some major challenges during its growth phase. Here, we present the issues Korean Air faces and how it might react to these challenges. These can be categorized mainly into five areas: world economic conditions, growth of the freight industry, prospects for new routes, competition, and company reputation and image.

World economic conditions

Growth of Asian economies

An analysis of the aviation industry environment shows some favorable trends for Asian airlines such as Korean Air. Specifically, Asian economies will grow strongly through the mid-1990s to the year 2000, and Asian airlines will generally continue to be profitable due to strong regional economies, increased tourism and foreign trade. Through the year 2000, Asian countries will lead the world in gross domestic product (GDP) growth, averaging more than 6 percent per year. According to Boeing forecasts, in seven years Asia will be as large a GDP block as North America, and surpass Europe in economic output. Asia's burgeoning economies will be responsible for much of the airline traffic expansion as air traffic growth historically follows GDP growth and economic prosperity means increases in air traffic. Rising regional business and personal income also mean more Asians will travel by air. Boeing predicts that, by the end of the century, 12 percent of all Asians will take at least one flight a year, compared with 6 percent now. Intra-Orient travel will represent much of the passenger traffic growth, increasing approximately 8 percent per year.[32] The vibrant Asian market and the strong financial health of most Asian carriers was demonstrated by their resilience to Gulf War related traffic drops and fuel price increases which caused many US and European carriers to experience deep losses in the same period. According to William M. Burke, managing director of Avmark-Asia, "things can only get better for Asian airlines. The strong carriers will get stronger, while the weak ones will be supported by their governments and not allowed to go under."[33]

Seoul, being long overshadowed by Tokyo and Hong Kong, is finally emerging as a hub for air transportation in East Asia. Korea is a lucrative market for local and foreign airlines and its link to Moscow and prospective routes to China are important.[34] Since the legalization of overseas travel in 1989, outbound Korean travellers in 1991 numbered 1.8 million, an increase of 20 percent over 1990. In 1992, more than 2.1 million Koreans ventured abroad, while the number of inbound travellers reached nearly 3.4 million. Korean Air should take advantage of this opportunity. It is likely to prosper through the mid-1990s owing to a strong national economy, increase in travel within the country, and solid financial backing by its corporate parent, the Hanjin Group.

Economic downturn in the USA, Europe, and Japan

Although it was mentioned in the previous section that the Asian economies are thriving, it is necessary to take into account the prolonged recession experienced by the rest of the world, especially Japan, Europe, and North America. A severe economic downturn in Japan kept many people there at home, and thus tourists and companies had to keep a much tighter reign on travel costs. But some big Asian airlines are optimistic about the industry's long-term outlook despite this turbulence. According to an SIA staff member, "What we're witnessing is a temporary situation. Airlines have to be optimistic, and travel in Asia is booming."[35]

This still does not reverse the trend for the increase in demand for heavily discounted economy class seats at the expense of the other types of airline seats. Some first class travellers have shifted back into business class while a lot of business class passengers have moved back to economy class. Even though some travellers will once again fly first class when the world economy brightens, it is widely believed by many people in the airlines industry that the "boutique" approach to pricing for air travel will not be accepted by the public, as most people basically want treasonable comfort at a reasonable price.

Korean Air must take world economic conditions into consideration, as these are likely to have a great impact on its performance. First and prestige (business) class seats provide the airlines with the highest profit margins, and the decrease in demand for these categories of seats will lead to declining yields, i.e. revenue per ton kilometer. In fact, 1992s decrease in net income of US$14,458,000 (refer to exhibit 9.2) may be an indicator of this situation. Although there still will be people demanding the more expensive seats, the majority will be more contented with the comfort of economy class seats, rather than the luxury of the former. It is hence necessary for Korean Airlines to correctly identify market segmentation and position itself clearly so as to cater to the needs of a particular group of people it wishes to target. In this way, the airlines will be better able to meet the needs of its travellers.

Growth of the freight industry

Many Asian airlines predict 6–8 percent yearly air cargo growth through the year 2000 as regional economies thrive and automation reduces costs and clearance times. Annual economic growth rates of on average 5 percent (in some developing countries significantly higher) will be the main driver of regional air freight development, while world economic growth rates, in contrast, are forecast to increase at a more leisurely 3 percent yearly average over the same time period. According to McDonnell Douglas forecasts, burgeoning Asia Pacific air routes will be responsible for a stunning 201 billion revenue ton kilometers, or 66 percent of the world's total air cargo traffic.[36]

Besides the increasing interdependence of Asian and worldwide economies which will further stimulate air freight shipments in the region, air cargo demand is predicted to be boosted significantly in the next decade due to international trends toward multinational manufacturing and just-in-time inventory practices. Many companies are sourcing parts and components overseas to reduce costs. The expense of having inventory tied up for six weeks while on a ship can easily offset air freight charges for many products. Computerization and automation will play a major factor in air cargo markets too in the late 1990s.[37] This will pose as an opportunity for Korean Air as it should expect its cargo operation to increase significantly.

As Korea's exports and imports have continued to increase over recent decades, the nation's air cargo industry has also grown at a fast pace. As it is moving towards exporting higher value-added and smaller products as well as high-tech products including electronics and machinery that require fast and careful delivery, prospects for the air cargo business are looking bright. The Ministry of Transportation (MOT) predicted that the country's air freight industry would continue its steady growth, forecasting an increase of 11.8 percent during the period from 1992 to 1996; 10.3 percent during 1997 to 2001; and 8.7 percent during 2002 to 2011.[38]

Although this is a positive trend for the freight operations of Korean Air, the carrier must recognize that the fast-growing market will be attracting more airlines to do business in Korea. Presently, there is a total of 40 airlines providing freight service in the country. Of them, the top five – Korean Air, Japan Air Lines, Northwest Airlines, Federal Express, and Cathay Pacific Airways – account for almost three-fourths of total volume.[39] Although Korean Air is clearly the leader, it must be wary that it might lose market share to freighter companies such as Federal Express and United Parcel Service, which have good reputations for their speedy courier service among the Koreans. To counter growing challenges to KAL's leadership efficiently, the flag carrier has become more market-oriented by introducing a variety of better services to customers by opening cargo drop centers, as mentioned before, in eight US cities. It is also offering sophisticated services such as small-package express transportation and specialized cargo transportation.

Prospects for new routes

An international carrier's route network can be its competitive advantage against other international airlines. Korean Airline is presently still limited to servicing a few routes. For example, under an accord signed in 1957 between Korea and the USA, KAL, on the one hand, is given the rights to fly on scheduled routes to only a few US destinations, and is not allowed to fly to other countries from the USA. On the other hand, US airlines are given less restrictive air rights. The MOT has declared its first priority as resolving the unfairness of the aviation agreement signed between the two countries. Potential Korean negotiating leverage includes Delta Air Lines' and United Airlines' plans to build Asian minihubs in Seoul. If talks of amendments are successful, Korean Air may be allowed to fly to additional cities, such as San Francisco, Dallas and Atlanta, and beyond the USA to other countries in Latin America, such as Mexico and Brazil (where a considerable number of Korean nationals live).[40] The airline will thus have to face up to the challenge of coping with the likely increase in demand for seats by domestic and international passengers as effectively as possible. With the revision of the accord, its cargo business will also be enhanced and this will possibly mean more profits for the company.

Besides possible addition to the number of Korea–USA routes, domestic traffic potential can also change rapidly following an improvement in relations with the hard-line communist government of North Korea. There is strong pent-up demand to visit relatives in the north, and tourism to North Korea will follow after the development of hotels, infrastructure, and industrial parks. Improving relations with China can result in the start of air service to the Middle Kingdom. Korean Air received permanent Beijing approval to overfly China in 1990. This move cut almost three hours off the weekly flight from Seoul to Bahrain.

Competition

Not many businesses operate without some sort of competition, and Korean Air is no exception. It faces surmounting competition from both local and foreign airlines in terms of passengers, cargo and landing rights. The underlying reasons for operating a business are survival, profits, and growth. To achieve these, Korean Air needs to brace itself to challenge its rivals so as to ensure its position in the aviation industry. For Korean Air, competition comes from: Asiana Airlines, which contends with the airline for domestic and international routes; and other international carriers. The next two subsections will analyze these two sources of competition in detail.

Local carrier – Asiana Airlines

The move to liberalize the nation's monopolistic 20-year-old private sector airline industry has ushered in a new era. To open its market to increased competition, the Korean government allowed the establishment of a second airline, Asiana Airlines (part of the Kumho Group, which has interests in tire manufacturing, ground transportation, petrochemical products, etc.) in 1989. This new chapter in the history of Korean air transport was written in response to Korea's increased role in global trade, to the increasing number of foreign airlines operating in Korea, and to the liberalization of overseas travel by Korean nationals.[41] Asiana was expected to provide domestic and overseas customers with a choice in air travel and to raise the overall competitiveness of Korea's air transportation industry.

While never pleased with the government's decision to launch a second carrier, Korean Air at first all but dismissed Asiana as a domestic rival. After all, there was more than enough domestic business for the two airlines, as demand was growing rapidly, and due to rigid government regulation on domestic fares virtually none of that business was profitable. Korean Air may well have supposed that, restricted to the domestic market, Asiana would soon go bust. However, the economic realities of the domestic market gave Asiana strong ground for an ultimatum to the government that had acted as a midwife in its birth: deregulate domestic air fares or support Asiana's efforts to launch and expand its international business. The government, to date, has chosen the latter option. Korean Air has realized that Asiana will not remain only as a domestic rival. Hence, a situation resulting in a hate–hate relationship has since emerged. The ongoing conflict between the two can be summarized in terms of international route allocations, raising of domestic fares, and poaching of pilots by Asiana Airlines from KAL.

International route allocations have been by far the major source of disagreement between Korean Air and Asiana Airlines. No longer silent or complacent, Korean Air charges that the government is being reckless in pursuing aviation agreements in the absence of a long-term aviation policy. One Korean Air manager argues that the trend in most countries is for single as opposed to multiple national airlines, and he warns that allowing two airlines to compete on the same international routes will spell financial disaster for both.[42] Asiana officials naturally reject these arguments. They remark that the government's aviation policy is already following a steady course of supporting a plural airline system and that to remain consistent, fairness in distributing landing rights is of paramount concern.

Right from Asiana's first jaunt into the international air space in December 1989 from Seoul to Sendai, Japan, where the Korean government awarded 19.6 of the 21 new 'passenger frequencies' (obtained from its new agreements with Japan) to Asiana, it could be foreseen that the battle between the two airlines might get fiercer. Due to this, guidelines for governing route service and flight frequency have become necessary. Hence, at the end of 1990, the MOT announced the setting up of Regulation 188, "Guideline for International Route Allocations," which is designed to govern issues of upcoming route allocations and flight frequencies. The two carriers agree on the need for government measures to promote the airline industry,[43] but both are strongly opposed to the actual content of the regulations.

In summary, Korean Air is basically not satisfied with the unequal allocation ratio of new routes in Southeast Asia (2:1 favouring Asiana), as well as the government's approval of Asiana's services to the USA, Japan, Southeast and Southwest Asia. It feels that these measures are clearly aimed at controlling and limiting its own development.

Kim Taek-Ho from Korean Air's public relations department points out, "In general, it is extremely advantageous to the second carrier. The problem lies in the fact that a company of more than 20 years is regarded in the same light with one that is only two years old. It is unreasonable to heavily allocate routes to the unprepared one."[44] Another official from KAL said, "Of course, we understand the government's intention to foster Asiana, but it should be done in a proper way. Korean Air has attained its present position by having survived harsh competition in the world market. Asiana must learn to survive the hardship already faced by Korean Air. Simply allocating them indigestible routes is not the proper way to achieve healthy growth or national profits."[45]

Asiana, on the other hand, feels that the destinations approved of in the guidelines are not sufficient at all, especially with the blocking of its operations in the European Union, the Middle East and certain parts of North America. It thinks that its growth has been vastly limited. In terms of route allocations, Asiana believes that it must be given new routes to ensure the sound development of the industry. This is because Korean Air has already occupied most of the main routes in the past 30 years. Few new routes will come into existence in the foreseeable future and hence equal allocation should be applied in terms of the whole routes available, rather than for new routes only.

Park Yong Tac of Asiana said, "Korean Air is a giant. Last year, its sales profits were over US$790 million, ranking it first in the world. But this giant is too sensitive to its younger brother. I wish big brother would embrace the virtues of a compromise. Our competition on international routes can be seen as self-defeating, but effect-wise, it boosts the market share by our nation's carriers."[46]

As can be seen, the result of the guidelines has caused considerable bitterness between the two carriers and an almost complete lack of cooperation. (Refer to the appendix for a synopsis of Regulation 188.)

Domestic airfares are regulated by the Korean government and are so low that both the carriers are making losses on their domestic routes, with Asiana recording a net operating loss of US$63 million in 1989 alone. For Korean Air, its losses are not so sensitively felt as its international business is sufficiently mature to more than make up for any losses incurred at home. Asiana clearly has more to lose from low domestic fares as domestic routes still account for the majority of its business.

To erase Asiana's red figures, the airline must expand its profits either through increasing its international routes or by charging higher fares on domestic routes, both of which have been opposed by Korean Air. In the context of raising domestic airfares, one Korean Air official commented, "We have tolerated a deficit on local routes for 15 years. Increasing fares now is not a reasonable settlement." He added that Korean Air's position does not stem from its opposition to Asiana, as it feels that local fares should promote public interest and customer service, not profit.[47] This can be related back to Chairman Cho's perspective in 1969, when he took over Korean Air as a form of contribution to the national aviation development, rather than for corporate profits.

Two years later, however, Korean Air realized that increasing domestic airfares would benefit its own performance as well, especially since it faced fierce competition from other airlines for its international routes and profits were thus squeezed. Hence, despite domestic fare increases of 22 percent in 1991 and 15 percent in 1992, both Korean Air and Asiana wanted to further raise the fares due to continuous losses incurred in serving the domestic routes.

The two flag carriers also conflict on the basis of employment of commercial pilots. Asiana recruits its pilots from Korean Air, the air force, and foreign countries. This has stirred up negative feelings in the Korean Air camp.

To counter this problem of poaching, Korean Air replaces its lost pilots with foreigners, and with air force fighter pilots. It also recruits by sponsoring *ab initio* at its own school on Cheju Island. There, the future pilots start from zero flying time to attain the minimum flying time required to fly a commercial aircraft. After graduation, they will be bounded to Korean Air for a prespecified period of time. This helps to ensure that Korean Air has a constant pool of pilots for its fleet. It is believed that although Korean Air treats its pilots well under the managerial philosophy of harmonious relationships, it is inevitable that a second Korean airline will poach these pilots through the offerings of better wages and benefits.

Foreign carriers

Korean Air faces very intense competition from foreign carriers on flights out of Korea. This fierce round of competition, especially among the regional airlines, was ignited by the sudden burst in demand after the liberalization of Korean overseas travel, as well as the development of Seoul as the hub of East Asia during a period of rapid Asian economic growth. Many foreign airlines are continuously offering better services and cheaper prices to attract local travellers. These efforts are often so extensive that they sometimes come in the form of "dumping" prices. The big loser in the competitive race is Korean Air. Cho Yoong-Eui, Director for Planning and Development of Information Systems at Korean Air, says, "When the Korean market was virtually closed to foreign airlines, we at Korean Air enjoyed very good performance. In 1986, we seized slightly below two-thirds of the market, but the market share declined to 46 percent in 1990." He attributes the lackluster business to heated competition with foreign airlines.[48] As of March 1992, there was a total of 26 foreign carriers aggressively vying for a larger slice of the Korean market, the most notable being Japan Airlines and Northwest Airlines, with each having 40 flights per week. These two carriers are the leading international carriers to and from Korea.

Japan Airlines has enjoyed a 100 percent occupancy seat rate over the past few years. Japanese travellers make up about 49 percent of inbound travellers to Korea and, likewise, Japan is a popular place for outbound travellers, mostly made up of Japanese and Koreans. Japan Airlines states that it plans to expand its capacity by a minimum of 6 percent annually through 1996.[49] In addition to introducing 30 more new aircraft, it intends to recruit more non-Japanese cockpit crew to cater to its increasingly diverse customer base.

Northwest Airlines, as a USA-based airline, can compete in the market with more airplanes and lower fares. In the Korean market, the carrier made great strides in 1990 to rank second in terms of international flight frequency, following Korean Air.[50] It plays a key role in the development of air routes to Korea and the introduction of new aircraft to the market. It also has an extensive network in the USA, which is a popular destination for many Koreans, and is also doing well in Europe and South America.

Cathay Pacific Airways, as one of the world's most profitable airlines, is another competitor for Korean Air. It links Hong Kong and Seoul twice a day and has provided the second longest lasting service to Seoul of any foreign airline. It also provides a cargo service once a week under a partnership arrangement with Korean Air. As a result of political constraints due to Hong Kong's colonial status, Cathay has become a strong regional carrier. Despite the airline industry slump experienced in certain countries, the carrier is continuing its expansion plans by purchasing new Boeing aircraft and expanding its route network to places such as Ho Chi Minh City and Johannesburg.[51]

The three airlines, along with the other 23, continuously challenge Korean Air's leadership in its own market. Furthermore, these foreign carriers intend to introduce their own versions of computerized reservation systems (CRSs) in the Korean aviation industry, which although weak, is growing. Such preemptive moves into Korea's growing market will enable them to capture and dominate the industry in the future.[52]

To counter the expected entrance of foreign CRSs, Korean Air, as mentioned, has developed its own modern version of the CRS named TOPAS. One advantage of TOPAS over the foreign airlines' CRSs is that it was developed to meet Korean customers' unique needs and can provide information in the native language. Language difference is a major barrier for foreign carriers who attempt to introduce their own CRSs, as seen from the case of United Airlines, which unsuccessfully introduced its APOLLO system in Japan and consequently had to cooperate with JAL in its AXESS system instead.[53] True to its philosophy of innovation, Korean Air strives continuously to upgrade TOPAS. It is seeking a foreign partnership to help to further upgrade its system, which will allow the airline to compete against other sophisticated CRSs.

Company reputation and image

The next major challenge faced by Korean Air were attacks made in the late 1980s and 1990s by the public on its reputation and image, which were caused by unfulfilled service expectations and poor safety records. This section presents an analysis with the corporate philosophy of establishing enterprise through trust and public credibility in mind.

Service quality level

Although Korean Air's service quality on its international routes is deemed one of the best by industry experts, its service on domestic flights is at times below customers' expectations. Before the birth of Asiana Airlines in December 1988, domestic passengers had no choice but to accept whatever Korean Air provided.

However, since the arrival of Asiana, many have switched to the new carrier for domestic flights.

Asiana appears to be winning the hearts of a large segment of Korea's flying public. Indeed, there is a note of revenge in the comments made by some domestic passengers who now prefer to fly Asiana. "They [Asiana] keep to their time schedule better. In the past, Korean Air sometimes disregarded the schedule without prior notice to the passengers," commented one passenger who prefers Asiana to Korean Air. The source, who is a frequent business flyer, added, "KAL's in-flight service on its domestic routes wasn't as nice as on its international routes. It's nonsense to ignore domestic passengers."[54] Another businessman who has been a frequent local passenger complained, "Surely you must have experienced the rude attitude of KAL staff."[55]

Korean Air can thus no longer remain complacent in its service quality on domestic flights since Asiana Airlines has come into play. If it remains slack in its domestic flight service, dissatisfied customers are likely to switch to Asiana Airlines for both domestic and international flights. In response, Korean Air has stepped up the service quality of its domestic flights. This is to ensure long-term customer satisfaction and loyalty, as well as to develop a strong competitive edge over competitors. This practice is consistent with its mission for service excellence and customer satisfaction.

Safety reputation

Equally, if not more, important is Korean Air's unfavourable safety reputation. For years, the airline has turned a deaf ear to howls of protest from passengers responding to rumours that the company has continually flouted safety regulations to save costs. Their objections intensified from mid-1989 after a series of crashes and other incidents that reignited public concern over the carrier's priorities. In a little more than five years, Korean Air reported four major tragedies which will be discussed in slight detail.

On September 1, 1983, a Soviet fighter shot down KAL flight 007 after it wandered into Soviet airspace. A total of 269 people lost their lives in the tragedy. In 1989, a US court ruled that Korean Air was partially responsible for the shooting-down, and the airline was ordered to pay US$50 million in compensation to the victims' families. The ruling was based on pilot negligence, and it was stated that the crew of Flight 007 had deliberately skirted Soviet airspace to save time and fuel, a charge that KAL has adamantly denied.[56]

In 1987, in the lead up to the 1988 Seoul Olympics, a KAL Boeing 707 was blown up by confessed North Korean spy Kim Hyon-Hui. All 115 passengers and crew died. This led Korean Air to come under fire for possible "security lapses."

Two years later, in August 1989, KAL flight 803 crashed during landing in Tripoli, Libya, killing 72 passengers and six people on the ground. The pilot, Captain Kim Ho-Jung, attempted to land in severe fog, despite knowing that the airport's landing guidance system had been out for a month. He ignored an advisory message from traffic controllers in Tripoli to divert to another airport. Eventually, he missed the runway by more than a mile and crashed into two farmhouses. Experts ruled out technical failure. The MOT revoked the cockpit licenses of the crew of three, filed criminal charges against Captain Kim and suspended KAL flights to Tripoli.

Critics of Korean Air said that Kim may have felt pressured by an overemphasis on timeliness and cost, both of which are important factors for bonuses and promotions for Korean Air pilots. It has long been rumoured among airline executives that Korean Air pilots are fined and can have their promotion prospects ruined by not keeping to schedules. As many of the cockpit crew are former top fighter pilots from the Korean Air Force, there apparently is a "do-or-die" spirit fostered by the fear of losing face by not attempting landing.[57]

Slightly more than two months after the Tripoli crash, another KAL jet (an F-28) on a domestic flight crashed at Seoul Kimpo International Airport during takeoff. Over 40 passengers were injured in the crash, one of whom later died in the hospital. Passengers blamed the cabin crew for failing to take command, and accused KAL of not carrying out proper emergency procedures. A Seoul businessman said that when the plane started to catch fire, the cabin attendants just moved about without trying to help the panic-stricken passengers. He added that the crew neither made any announcements about the accident nor demonstrated the use of the life vests and oxygen masks. One elderly man fumed from his hospital bed that the crew members and attendants of KAL were poorly trained to cope with emergencies.[58]

All these incidents show that Korean Air was responsible, to a large extent, for the disasters. In response to the crashes and many others which went unreported, the management has adopted a policy of "no comments." Thus, the airline's "strategy" for dealing with a major tragedy is to do nothing. Unlike other airlines, which usually impose a moratorium on all advertising after a crash, Korean Air's approach has been the opposite. The lack of decorum has left a bad taste in the mouths of the flying public. Many are disillusioned with the airline's priority of profits before safety, as well as its constant flouting of safety regulations to save cost (it was found that 58 regulations have so far been flouted).

The public feels that Korean Air has contradicted its corporate philosophy of trust and public credibility and has gone totally against its company's motto of "Act with sincerity" and "Serve with responsibility." But in all fairness, many of the disasters that have struck Korean Air were not entirely the airline's fault. Two of its worst disasters occurred when its planes were blown out of the sky, one shot down by the Russians and the other by a North Korean bomb planted by Kim Hyon-Hui and her male accomplice. The condition of provincial airports is sometimes quite dissatisfactory too. Many have runways shorter than required by international standards for safely landing and launching the smallest commercial aircraft used by KAL. Further, these airports, which are set in mountainous terrain, are regarded by pilots as being very difficult to approach. Many of them were originally built as air force bases. But Korean Air has not used these reasons as excuses for itself and shifted the responsibility for these crashes. By the early 1990s, the top management recognized the problem and consciously made efforts to repair the damage done by these incidents. Moreover by their own initiative, the airline's 300 or so pilots, who were aware of the slump in public confidence in the carrier, staged a morale-boosting rally at Kimpo a few months after the F-28 crash. They passed the resolution to fly more safely in the future. In a three-point resolution – the first in the history of the airline – the pilots vowed to strictly observe flight rules and regulations, learn and practise the most advanced flying technology, and perform safer flying operations.[59] True to their words, no major catastrophe has since occurred.

On the other hand, tragedy recently struck Asiana Airlines, when its Boeing 737–500 crashed near Mokpo Airport, killing 65 passengers and crew after the pilot Hwang In-Ki made an ill-advised third attempt to land the plane in a heavy rainstorm. Such third landing attempts are prohibited under international practices due to the danger that large passenger aircraft tend to lose "lift" – the ability to regain altitude – with each attempt. The plane was forced into a nearby island mountainside as it tried to regain altitude after its failed third landing attempt. It is widely speculated that the pilot was under similar pressure from Asiana Airlines to preserve fuel and to meet strict schedules, and had thus struggled with an attempt at a third landing so as to avoid loss of pride and punishment from the airline.[60]

Therefore, from the recent crash involving Asiana Airlines, it is concluded that Korean Air is not necessarily inferior to Asiana in terms of its safety practices. It is unfair to heavily penalize the former when the latter has an equally unfavorable safety record. What is important now is for Korean Air to clear its bad reputation by recognizing that passengers value security most and to start laying down concrete actions to make its flights safer.

Future Prospects for Korean Air

Before the future prospects of Korean Air are discussed, President Cho Yang Ho's strategies for the next few decades will be outlined. Under his management, Korean Air is to pursue the following five steps to achieve its long-term objectives:

- enhance safety (highest priority) by improving pilot training facilities and maintenance facilities;
- expand route network and modernize its fleet;
- establish alliances with other airlines for their CRSs and expand market coverage overseas;
- diversify and develop travel-related business;
- become more globalized by seeking to strengthen cooperation with other carriers in areas of ownership, coordinated operations and scheduling, and joint marketing programs.

An analysis of Korean Air's corporate profile/strategy and environment indicates that the airlines will continue to grow and be profitable at least until the year 2000. To be well prepared to face the challenges of the twenty-first century, it must pursue the philosophy of innovation.

A few specific points pertaining to Korean Air's future must be commented. First, the Asian aviation industry will grow at a faster rate than the rest of the world (due to the fast economic growth in the region) and Asian airlines are predicted to be the most profitable. Korean Air will continue to ride this tide of growth and this justifies the conjecture that it will remain profitable through the next few years. Second, top management of Korean Air must consciously make efforts to improve its safety reputation, as this will go a long way to regain the public's credibility. Third, management by the founder's family, specifically the passing of the presidency post to Chairman Cho's son, will ensure continuity of the corporate philosophy which has guided Korean Air successfully through the years.

Recommendations

To ensure that Korean Air maintains its path of growth, the airline must address certain issues carefully. First, the competition from Asiana must be addressed. It seems that in the long run, all-out conflict between Asiana and Korean Air will be detrimental to the Korean aviation industry as a whole. The key to success in the world market is to avoid encroachment on the domestic market by foreign carriers. Therefore, some type of organization or council must be established to engender peaceful coexistence of the two carriers, which must begin working toward mutually beneficial goals such as protecting the Korean market from foreign airlines' "invasion."

Second, Korean Air must address the issue of increasing competition from international carriers. It should try to differentiate itself from other international airlines by aggressively promoting excellence in its in-flight service. The success of Singapore Airlines can attest to the fact that outstanding in-flight services can command price premiums. Thus, Korean Air must not lose sight of its long-term objective of "leading the airline industry in customer service." The expected entrance of foreign CRSs into Korea as well as the introduction of Asiana Airline's own version of CRS, called ARTIS, should also motivate KAL to take action to avoid being left behind. One suggestion is for it to cooperate with foreign CRSs. Foreigners will not want to run independent systems by themselves for the time being due to the immature market in Korea. Instead, they will probably conduct business in cooperation with a local airline. Besides giving Korean Air a negotiating leverage, this will allow the flag carrier to take advantage of the other airlines' CRS technology, expand its own service base, and hence provide its customers with more relevant and up-to-date travel-related information. KAL can also look into offering a frequent-flyer program jointly with hotels, car rental firms, or credit card issuers. This will increase the loyalty of passengers (especially the Korean public) by increasing their switching costs, as they will try to accumulate more mileage by flying with only KAL. This is one method to thwart competitors' attempts to capture the Korean market.

Third, with regard to the airline's present poor reputation with the flying public, the airline should institute internationally recognized safety, reservations, and maintenance procedures. It should also limit its recruitment of pilots to only non-fighter pilots, because fighter pilots, although very well trained and skilful, are not necessarily safe airmen in the cockpit of a commercial passenger jet, where safety is everything. And to cope with the aftermath of any tragedy, there should be an efficient public relations department to oversee the proper handling of such a nerve-wrecking incident. Korean Air can no longer remain silent and adopt the policy of "no comments," as people will otherwise view the company as socially irresponsible. They may even resort to boycotting its services and this will be to the airline's detriment.

Fourth, there should be a steady investment in human resources and aircraft. This is one of the most important expenditures to be made by the airline. As mentioned, service quality is very important and it is must be perceived to be high before Korean Air can earn the loyalty of its passengers. Thus, the training and development of employees is a crucial aspect in the airline industry. Further, as airline demand and supply forces are usually out of sync with world economic conditions, many carriers tend to acquire aircraft on the basis of the present demand for plane seats, especially when they are cash-strapped. Due to the long lead times associated with the procurement of airplanes, demand and supply conditions are very different when the aircraft ordered is finally ready. It is hence necessary for Korean Air to avoid falling into this trap by continuously investing in its aircraft fleet.

Fifth, as the airline industry is particularly susceptible to unexpected events such as the Gulf War and oil crises, Korean Air should adopt a conservative financial policy, so as to enable itself to ride these unfavorable incidents better.

Sixth, it must continuously uphold its philosophy of innovation to remain competitive in the aviation industry. Specifically, it should strive to upgrade its computerized reservation system to match those of more established airlines. In addition, it should seek to continuously upgrade and modernize its aircraft fleet. This is presently practised by the airline as it pursues the policy of reducing its fleet age every year.

Seventh, Korean Air must continue its policy of adding new routes yearly to achieve a truly global route network. In particular, the China market is very lucrative. Although negotiations are currently under deadlock, the airlines must not be pressured into giving up on the negotiations.

Eighth, to strengthen its marketing position, Korean Air should explore strategic global alliances with other international airlines, as this will allow benefits such as the integration of routes and schedules, as well as the sharing of ground facilities. In this way, KAL will be able to offer its passengers travel to final destinations which itself does not serve.

Finally, it is concluded that the management-by-family style of Korean Air has been appropriate during the carrier's growth stage, but it is foreseeable that such a management orientation may not fit well once it reaches its maturity phase in the twenty-first century. Therefore, top management needs to continuously revise the company's corporate orientation to suitably adapt to the dynamic competitive environment.

Implications

Some lessons can be drawn from Korean Air's experience in its past 24 years.

It has been highlighted that the airline faces a serious problem regarding the safety issue, as many people complain that it places more priority on profit motives, rather than the safety of its passengers. With this, the company has earned itself a very unfavorable reputation with the public and many of them have decided to boycott the airline. This shows that it is very important for a company to operate in a socially responsible way and be a responsible corporate citizen. Even though it may cost more money to act in this manner, such behavior will allow the firm to gain the trust of its stakeholders, and in the long run this will pay off in the form of good reputation and increased profits. It must also take into consideration the necessary of an efficient public relations department which has the role of building up a favorable image of the corporation, especially one as large as Korean Air.

Among corporations, there should be a commitment to service quality. This is especially so for those in the service industry. With growing affluence among the general public, more people are willing to spend a larger sum of money in return for high quality goods and services. As judged from the Korean Air experience, perceived quality was low and this led some customers to fly with a less reputable airline like Asiana Airline, rather than with KAL, which was larger and had more years of flying experience.

The success of Korean Air is largely attributed to the abilities and entrepreneurial spirit of its dynamic leader Cho Choong Hoon, who led the carrier's growth from a small domestic airline in 1969 to one of the largest in the world today. Thus, it is very important for a company to have capable top management who are able to envision the corporate goals and mission, as well as formulate appropriate strategies for the particular sector it is in.

Further, in an industry such as the aviation industry, which is by nature a global one, it is necessary to take into account the competitive forces acting on it. In this new era of the 1990s, the world is becoming a smaller place to live in as more firms set up facilities abroad and become globalized. It is indispensable for companies such as Korean Air to view all foreign corporations as potential rivals and to take precautionary measures to preempt their actions. It is also essential to source supplies from the lowest-cost locations so as to remain competitive. Some forms of vertical integration may thus be necessary.

Conclusion

Civilian management has revitalized Korean Airlines, from an unprofitable company in the 1960s to an international success within 24 years. The airline's arrival can be attributed to the dynamism and foresight of Cho Choong Hoon, who guided its growth by overcoming many challenges along the way.

The path to success was not smooth. Although Korean Air virtually monopolized the Korean aviation industry for about 20 years, the emergence of Asiana Airlines in 1989 brought about the beginning of a pluralistic civic airline industry, and subsequently greater rivalry between the two airlines. KAL also faced serious threats to its safety reputation due to numerous crash incidents in the late 1980s, which many people attributed to the carrier's own negligence. Fortunately, by the early 1990s, Korean Air managed to overcome these stumbling blocks through top management's conscious efforts to remedy the situations and improve the company's competitive position.

It is concluded that with the guidance of the Cho family and KAL's corporate philosophy, the airline can continue to grow and remain profitable in the future. Under the skilfull guidance of Chairman Cho and his family, it is deemed to be prepared to face the challenges of the twenty-first century. In summary, Korean Air represents a successful Korean company that rose from the ashes to become a formidable international competitor in less than a quarter of a century. It has become the pride of Korea.

APPENDIX: POLICY AND POINTS OF VIEW

While the government's guidelines were intended to bring order to a potentially controversial issue, the preventative steps seem to have had the opposite effect. The following describes the government's guidelines and provides summaries of the positions taken by Korean Air and Asiana Airlines.

Synopsis of government's guidelines

Destination
Korean Air: worldwide.

Asiana: USA, Japan, Southeast Asia (Taiwan, Hong Kong, Philippines, Thailand, Singapore, Malaysia, Indonesia, Brunei, Papua New Guinea) and Southwest Asia (India, Pakistan, Afghanistan, Nepal, Burma, Bangladesh, Sri Lanka, Moldavia, Bhutan).

Allocation of new routes
Japan and Southeast Asia: 2 : 1 (Asiana : Korean Air).
USA and Southwest Asia: 1 : 1 (others : Korean Air).

Dual service and flight frequency
Dual service: annual passenger demand of more than 150,000 for minimum weekly frequency of seven flights per week with minimum seat occupancy of 70 percent.

Route forecast (number of routes available): 12 routes (Japan 4, Southeast Asia 5, USA 3).

Flight frequency: in favor of new carriers; three flights are allocated in priority in the initial stages, then equal allocation will follow.

Others: consultation with government authorities is required prior to aviation talks with foreign governments or carriers; and for the purchase of new aircraft, a proposal must be submitted for approval at least 90 days prior to commencing the contract. Aviation talks with China, USSR, and other specified countries will be handled on a case-by-case basis.

Korean Air's position

Destinations
With the second carrier's launching in 1988, the MOT clearly restricted possible international service by the second carrier to Japan and the USA. Now, even before the second carrier has established its operations to the USA, the MOT has approved service to Southeast Asia. These measures are clearly aimed at controlling the first carrier's development.

Allocation of new routes

They should be allocated equally. The present 2 : 1 ratio favouring Asiana in Southeast Asia is not reasonable at all.

Dual service and flight frequency

The report prepared by the Marine Industry Research Center on dual services indicated that the annual passenger demand should exceed 200,000. But this was later lowered to 150,000. This only served to open the door wider for the second carrier. According to this standard, Asiana can launch service to almost all main destinations in Japan and Southeast Asia. Another perogative measure giving Asiana priority is the right to obtain a maximum of three flights a week in additional route areas.

Other

Purchase of aircraft and talks on operational rights are all matters of strict confidentiality. If leaked, it hurts not only the concerned parties, but also the national interest. Therefore, the guideline that purchase contracts must be submitted to the government for approval 90 days before the actual contract is contrary to present aviation regulations.

Asiana's position

Destinations

It is not really a multi-system. The ratio of mileage supply is 95 : 1 and at best 99 : 5 for Korean Air and Asiana. This limits Asiana's growth. To block Asiana's operations to European Union countries is a great loss to both Asiana and the nation. Specializing each carrier based on destinations or routes is one idea, and before European Union unification occurs, Asiana should be permitted to operate to countries where Korean Air has not yet operated. Service to the USA should also be extended to all of North America, and the Middle East should be included on the list.

Allocation of new routes

For the past 30 years, Korean Air has occupied most of the main routes. Few new routes will come into existence in the foreseeable future. Equal allocation should be applied in terms of "the whole." For sound development of the industry, new routes must be given to Asiana.

Dual service and flight frequency

Seventy percent occupancy is too demanding. It should be lowered to 60 percent. And the 12-route limit for dual service is not sufficient for an international route network. If the minimum number of weekly flights required for dual service is seven, the allocation of new flights to Asiana must be seven flights per week. The equal allocation ought to be applied based on the actual flights, which means existing flights plus newly allocated ones. For example, Korean Air is operating 18 flights per week on the Seoul-Bangkok route. By 1992, it will be increased to 20 flights per week based on the recent guideline. But for Asiana, it will take at least four or five years to operate even seven flights per week. This is quite unbalanced.

Source: Extracted from: Competition for air travellers stirs controversy. *Business Korea*, February 1991.

NOTES

1 Hanjin Group Report, 1989.

2 *The Wings for the World: Korean Air 1969 to 1989*, Korean Air.

3 *Korean Air: Reaching for the Stars*, Business Korea, March 1992.

4 *The World of Korean Air*, Korean Air, 1993.

5 Hanjin Group Report, 1993.

6 Supra, note 2.

7 Supra, note 3.

8 *Korean Air: Still Riding the Tiger*, Air Transport World, June 1993.

9 Supra, note 3.

10 Supra, note 1.

11 *Korean Air, Present and Future*, Korean Air, 1993.

12 Supra, note 8.

13 Korean Air Annual Report, 1991.

14 Ibid.

15 Hattori, T., "Comparisons of large corporations in Korea and Japan," in Lee, H. and Chung, K. (eds), *The Structure and Strategy of Korean Corporations*. Seoul: Bupmunsa, 1986.

16 Yoo, S. and Lee, S. M., "Management style and practice of Korean chaebols," *California Management Review*, 29, 1987.

17 Lee, S. M., Yoo, S. and Lee, T. M., "Korean Chaebols: corporate values and strategies," *Organisational Dynamics*, December 1991.

18 Ibid.

19 Supra, note 13.

20 "Fly in the ointment," *Far Eastern Economic Review*, September 3, 1992.

21 "Computerized reservation system: foreign airline systems face uphill battle," *Business Korea*, February 1991.

22 Supra, note 11.

23 "World Airline Financial 1992," *Air Transport World*, June 1992.

24 Halstead, J. "Aerospace finance: trade doesn't always follow the flag," *Euromoney (UK) Aerospace Finance Supplement*, November 1987.

25 Ibid.

26 "Fasten seat belt," *Far East Economic Review*, August 26, 1993.

27 "Punches fly in local aviation war," *Korean Economic Report*, September 1989.

28 "Dividing line up in the air," *Far Eastern Economic Review*, September 3, 1992.

29 Supra, note 24.

30 "United, Chinese Airline plan joint venture," *Business Times*, January 12, 1993.

31 Proctor, P., "Regional economic growth to spur Asia-Pacific airline expansion in '90s," *Aviation Week and Space Technology*, February 24, 1992.

32 "Strong Asian economy boosts outlook for airlines, industry," *Aviation Week and Space Technology*, May 27, 1991.

33 Ibid.

34 "Homing in on Seoul," *Business Korea*, March 1992.

35 Supra, note 26.

36 "Thriving regional economies, automation spark growth of Asian cargo carriers," *Aviation Week and Space Technology*, February 24, 1992.

37 Ibid.

38 "On the way to market-oriented change," *Business Korea*, April 1991.

39 Ibid.

40 "Increasing air travel alternatives," *Business Korea*, April 1991.

41 "The maiden flight," *Korean Economic Report*, November 1990.

42 "Dog fights over international routes," *Korean Economic Report*, November 1990.

43 "Government controls aimed at long haul," *Business Korea*, February 1991.

44 Ibid.

45 Ibid.

46 Ibid.

47 "Up, up and away," *Korean Economic Reporter*, November 1990.

48 Supra, note 21.

49 Supra, note 32.

50 "Korea attracts retinue of foreign carriers," *Business Korea*, April 1991.

51 Ibid.

52 Supra, note 21.

53 Ibid.

54 "A 'flying David' goes international," *Korean Economic Report*, September 1989.

55 Supra, note 27.

56 "Flying in the face of danger," *Korean Economic Report*, March 1990.

57 "KAL safety record under attack," *Korean Economic Report*, December 1989.

58 Ibid.

59 Ibid.

60 "Danger in the air," *Korean Economic Report*, September 1993.

CASE

10

TEN

THE METAMORPHOSIS OF WHIRLPOOL CORPORATION

Arieh A. Ullman

The mood was upbeat as David Whitwam, President, Chief Executive Officer and Chairman of the Board of Whirlpool Corporation, emerged from the meeting with Whirlpool's senior management in January 1993. He and his associated had briefed the board on the results of the 1992 fiscal year. "Outstanding," "The best year in the company's 81-year history," were words used by the attenders to describe the accomplishments of the past year. Evidently, the strategy which had been formulated almost a decade ago was finally coming to fruition. Whirlpool's performance, measured in terms of shareholder value, the company's foremost objective, was clearly above average (exhibit 10.1).

The US Appliance Industry

Products, manufacturing and distribution[1]

Home appliances were generally classified as laundry (washers and dryers), refrigeration (refrigerators and freezers), cooking (ranges and ovens), and other (dishwashers, disposals and trash compactors) appliances. Many appliance manufacturers also make floor care goods such as floor polishers and vacuum cleaners.

Special thanks to Carol L. Sizer, Manager, Media and Community Relations, Whirlpool Corporation, for her helpful comments.

Exhibit 10.1   Five year cumulative return: Whirlpool, S&P index and S&P household
furniture and appliance group

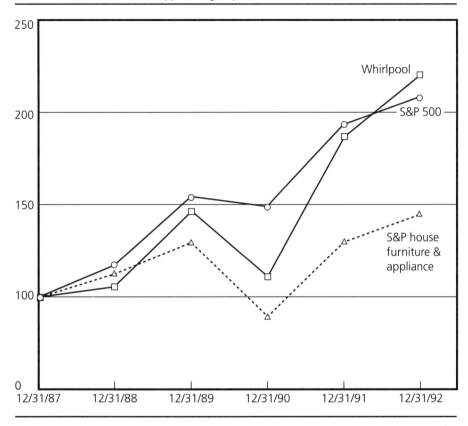

Assumes $100 invested on December 31, 1987 in whirlpool common stock, S&P 500, and S&P household furniture and
appliance group.
Cumulative total return is measured by dividing (i) the sum of (A) the cumulative amount of the dividends for the measurement
period, assuming dividend reinvestment, and (B) the difference between share price at the end and the beginning of the
measurement period; by (ii) the share price at the beginning of the measurement period.

Source: Whirlpool Corporation, 1992 Proxy Statement.

Manufacturing operations consisted mainly of preparation of a metal frame to
which the appropriate components were attached in automated assembly lines
and by manual assembly. Manufacturing costs comprised about 65–75 percent of
total operating cost with labor representing less than 10 percent of total cost.[2] Optimal
sized assembly plants had an annual capacity of about 500,000 units for most
appliances except microwave ovens. Unlike other industries such as textiles, variable costs played an important role in the cost structure; changes in raw material
and component costs were also significant. Component production was fairly scale
sensitive. Doubling compressor output for refrigerators, for instance, reduced unit

costs by 10–15 percent.[3] There were also some scale economies in assembly but the introduction of robotics tended to reduce those but also improved quality and performance consistency and enhanced flexibility.[4]

Distribution of major appliances occurred either through contract sales to home builders and to other appliance manufacturers predominantly directly or indirectly through local builder suppliers. Traditionally, these customers were very cost conscious and thus preferred less expensive appliance brands. Retail sales represented the second distribution channel with national chain stores and mass merchandisers such as Sears, department, furniture, discount and appliance stores acting as intermediaries. In recent years, independent appliance stores, which in the past sold about a third of all white goods, were being replaced by national chains such as Sears' Brand Central and mega-appliance dealers such as Circuit City. The consolidation of the appliance distributors led to the current situation where about 45 percent of the total appliance volume was being sold through 10 powerful mega-retailers with Sears leading with a market share of about 29 percent.[5] A third, less visible channel was the commercial market such as laundromats, hospitals, hotels, and other institutions.[6]

Consolidation

Before the Second World War, each company produced many varieties of one product. In the mid-1940s, there were over 250 firms manufacturing appliances in the United States, including all the major US automobile firms except for Chrysler. The industry experienced a period of mergers in the 1950s and 1960s while sales grew approximately 50 percent due to increased reliability, advances in technology, and a decline in prices. With the 1970s came high inflation and interest rates, but unit sales still continued to climb.

The last merger wave occurred in 1986 when in less than one year, Electrolux purchased White Consolidated, Whirlpool acquired KitchenAid, and Magic Chef was acquired by Maytag. Maytag's acquisition of Jenn-Air and Magic Chef increased its overall revenues by giving Maytag brand name appliances at various price points. Likewise, Whirlpool's acquisition of KitchenAid and Roper, respectively, broadened Whirlpool's presence at the high-end and low-end of the market.[7] In 1992, the number of domestic manufacturers varied by type of product between seven for home laundry appliances, fifteen for home refrigeration and room air conditioning equipment and five for dishwashers.[8]

Broad product scope

In the 1980s, the market continued to grow primarily thanks to the acceptance by the American people of the microwave oven. Microwave oven unit sales tripled from 1980 to 1989, while washers and dryers increased in sales 34 and 52 percent, respectively. Appliance manufacturers realized that they must offer a complete line of appliances even if they did not manufacture all of them themselves, which was one reason for the merger activity and practice of inter-firm sourcing. For example, Whirlpool made trash compactors for Frigidaire (Electrolux/White Consolidated) and In-Sink-Erator (Emerson Electric), as well as for Sears. General

Electric manufactured microwave ovens for Caloric (Raytheon), Jenn-Air, and Magic Chef (Maytag).[9]

In 1992, five major competitors controlled 98 percent of the core appliance market (cooking equipment, dishwashers, dryers, refrigerators, and washers) each of which offered a broad range of product categories and brands targeted to different customer segments. With 33.8 percent domestic market share, Whirlpool was ahead of GE (28.2 percent), a reversal of the leadership position compared to two years earlier. Electrolux (15.9 percent), Maytag (14.2 percent), and Raytheon (5.6 percent) followed, respectively. Whirlpool held market share leadership positions in several appliance categories (exhibit 10.2).

Market saturation

Throughout the 1980s and into the 1990s, competition in the United States was fierce. Industry demand depended on the state of the economy, disposable income levels, interest rates, housing starts, and consumers' ability to defer purchases. Saturation levels remained high and steady; over 70 percent of households had washers and over 65 percent dryers (exhibit 10.2). Refrigerators had become fully efficient at preserving food and the segment was saturated. Sales of electric ranges slowed as the microwave oven bloomed. Microwave sales, which had jumped from 3.5 million units in 1980 to over 10 million by 1989, started leveling out.[10] Sales of ranges had dropped off so drastically due to market maturation that it was not uncommon to find more than one gas or electric range in a home.

Factors of competition

In this environment all rivals worked hard at keeping costs down. Over four years, Electrolux spent over $500 million to upgrade old plants and build new ones for its acquisition, White Consolidated Industries. General Electric automated its Louisville, Kentucky, plant which, over ten years, halved the workforce and raised output by 30 percent. Had the appliance manufacturers been making automobiles, the price of a Chevrolet Caprice would have risen from $7209 in 1980 to $9500 in 1990 and not $17,370.[11]

Toward the end of the 1980s, it became even more important to lower costs, monitor margins and achieve economies of scale. The Big Four were renovating and enlarging existing facilities. Maytag built new facilities in the south to take advantage of lower cost, non-union labor. Others built twin-plants on the Mexican border to profit from cheap labor. A third trend was toward focus factories, where each plant produced one product category only covering all price points.[12]

Also, all competitors started to push into the high-end segment of the market, which was more stable and profitable. Once the domain of Maytag, it became increasingly crowded with the appearance of GE's Monogram line, Whirlpool's acquisition of KitchenAid and White's Euroflair models. This trend had its roots in the 1980s, which brought an increase in new home construction, home expansions and remodelings. It was estimated that each new home would purchase four to six new appliances. These recent developments emphasized more upscale models as compared to a previous tendency for builders to economize by buying the cheapest national brand appliances.[13]

Exhibit 10.2 Domestic market shares of major appliance manufacturers, 1991

Major producers	Market share (%)	Saturation (%)	Shipments (1000)
Refrigerators		99.9	7,273
GE	35		
Whirlpool	25		
Electrolux	17		
Maytag	12		
Freezers		33.0	1,414
Electrolux	70		
W. C. Wood	16		
Whirlpool	6		
Raytheon	3		
Washers		73.0	6,197
Whirlpool	51		
Maytag	18		
GE	16		
Electrolux	12		
Dishwashers		47.7	3,571
GE	40		
Whirlpool	33		
Electrolux	19		
Maytag	7		
Disposers		47.0	4,002
In-Sink-Erator	59		
Electrolux	29		
Waste King	7		
Electric ranges		56.7	2,900
GE	43		
Whirlpool	18		
Electrolux	17		
Maytag	12		
Gas ranges		45.7	2,132
Maytag.	25		
GE	24		
Electrolux	22		
Raytheon	21		
Electric dryers		50.6	3,295
Whirlpool	52		
GE	17		
Maytag	15		
Electrolux	14		
Gas dryers		16.1	1,018
Whirlpool	52		
GE	14		
Maytag	14		
Electrolux	12		
Microwave ovens		85.2	8,207[a]
Sharp	23		
Samsung	19		
Matsushita	16		
Goldstar	11		

[a] Domestic and imported units except combination microwave ovens/ranges.

Source: Appliance, September 1992.

Quality, too, became an important feature in the competitive game as symbolized by Maytag's lonely repairman. The number of service calls dropped across the board in the wake of rising consumer expectations. Defects rates dropped from 20 per 100 appliances made in 1980 to 10 twelve years later.[14] Relationships with suppliers changed as companies used fewer of them than in years past. Contracts were set up over longer terms to improve quality and keep costs low with just-in-time deliveries.[15]

A recent development was the demand by the powerful distributors for faster delivery. Distributors sought to curtail inventory costs, their biggest expense.

> We would like to carry even more brands, but we have to find a way to move product more quickly. Sharing information with manufacturers is critical. Logistics are more than distribution; they cover disposal of major appliances, next-day delivery guaranteed in a three-hour period, and emergency repairs. But we have to work with manufacturers to get the costs down,

declared Bernard Brennan, CEO of Montgomery Ward, at a meeting of the Association of Home Appliance Manufacturers.[16] As a consequence, manufacturers started to improve delivery systems. For instance, General Electric created its Premier Plus Program, which guaranteed three-day delivery. Also, sales departments were reorganized so that one sales representative would cover all of a manufacturer's brands of a given product category. Customer information services via 800 telephone lines were also strengthened.

Innovation

Two developments, government regulation and advances in computer software, when combined with intense competition, accelerated product innovation. New energy standards to be enforced under the 1987 National Appliance Energy Conservation Act limited energy consumption of new appliances with the objective to reduce energy usage in appliances by 25 percent every five years. At the same time, the possible ban on ozone-depleting chloro-fluorocarbons (CFCs) in refrigerators by 1995 was forcing the industry to redesign its refrigerators. Pressures were also exerted to change washer and dishwasher designs to reduce water consumption.

In 1989, the Super Efficient Refrigerator Program Inc. (SERP) was organized by the Natural Resources Defense Council, a few utilities, and the Environmental Protection Agency.[17] Because refrigerator makers had to revamp their product lines for EPA mandated improvements in energy efficiency and there was an impending ban on CFCs, the SERP organizers created a $30 million prize contest financed by 24 utilities to develop a refrigerator prototype free of CFCs and at least 25 percent more energy-efficient than the 1993 federal standards. The outcome of the competition would be announced in July 1993. The winner, who would take the entire $30 million, had to manufacture and sell over 250,000 refrigerators between January 1994 and July 1997.

Advances in computer technology represented the second development accelerating innovation. New programs called fuzzy logic or neural networks which mimicked the human brain's ability of detecting patterns were being introduced in many industries including white goods.[18] In Asia, elevators, washers and refrigerators using fuzzy logic to recognize usage patterns were already widespread.[19] In late 1992, AEG Hausgeräte AG, a subsidiary of Daimler Benz's AEG unit, introduced a washer using fuzzy logic to automatically control water consumption depending on the size of the load and to sense how much dirt remained in clothes.[20] United Technology was working on a line of air conditioners which automatically adjusted room temperature as a function of the number of people in a room, their preference for comfort, humidity, and air flow.[21]

Outlook

For the future, demand conditions in the United States continued to look unattractive with growth rates forecasted around 1 to 2 percent from a level which was 15 percent below 1988 industry shipments. At the prevailing saturation levels, demand was mostly restricted to replacement purchases (79 percent), with the remainder going to new housing and new household formation.[22]

The one positive element in this otherwise bleak outlook was a demographic trend, in that the aging baby boomers were demanding more stylish appliances with new features.[23] The late 1980s saw new technologies in cooking surfaces: ceramic-glass units, solid elements, and modular grill configurations. Other new customer-oriented features included the self-cleaning oven, automatic ice cube makers, self-defrosting refrigerators, pilotless gas ranges, and appliances that could be preset. Manufacturers' own brands normally were first accessorized, followed by the national retailers they outfitted. Sears and Montgomery Ward usually copied the previous year's most successful products. However, the industry was so competitive that no one manufacturer could keep an innovation to itself for more than a year without a patent. Finally, consumers became more concerned with the way appliances looked. Sleek European styling became fashionable, with smooth lines, rounded corners and a built-in look with electronic controls.[24] Another trend was the white-on-white look which suggested superior cleanability and made the kitchen look larger.[25]

The Globalization of the Appliance Industry

Foreign competition

The white goods industry was as American as baseball and apple pie. In 1992, 98 percent of the dishwashers, washing machines, dryers, refrigerators, freezers, and ranges sold in America were made in America. Exports represented around 5 percent of shipments. The manufacturing plants of the industry leaders were located in places such as Newton, Iowa (Maytag), Benton Harbor, Michigan (Whirlpool), and Columbus, Ohio (White Consolidated Industries). Each of the "Big Four" was nearer to a corn stalk than to a parking meter. Combined, these companies practically owned the market for each major appliance with one exception – microwave ovens. These represented the lion's share of imports which made up about 17 percent of total appliance sales.[26]

The acquisition of White Consolidated Industries by AB Electrolux of Sweden in 1986 marked a major change in the industry. Until then, foreign competition was largely restricted to imports of microwave ovens, a segment which was controlled by Far Eastern competitors from Korea (Goldstar, Samsung) and Japan (Sharp, Matsushita). Aware of the fate of other industries, many expected that it was only a matter of time before these companies would expand from their beachhead in microwave ovens and compact appliances into other segments. Indeed, the general manager of the overseas office of Matsushita, the market leader in Japan's white goods industry, stated: "Foreign makers are right to expect that Matsushita and other Japanese companies will enter the US and European markets soon enough. The traditional makers won't be number 1 and number 2 forever."[27]

Europe's promise

Of prime attractiveness to the US manufacturers was Europe. As a continent, Western Europe represented 27 percent of the global market and, if Eastern Europe and the Middle East and Africa were included, 43 percent. Asia's share was 27 percent, North America followed with 24 percent before Latin America with 6 percent.[28] Since 1985, Western Europe was rapidly moving toward a unified market of some 320 million consumers which was not nearly as saturated as Canada and the United States. Appliance demand was expected to grow at 5 percent annually. Political changes in Eastern Europe integrated these countries into the world trade system and thus added to Europe's long-term attractiveness.

During the 1970s and 1980s, the European white goods industry had experienced a consolidation similar to that in the United States. In the late 1980s, six companies – Electrolux Zanussi, Philips Bauknecht, Bosch-Siemens. Merloni-Indesit, Thompson and AEG – controlled 70 percent of the market (excluding microwave ovens and room air conditioners). Until the mid-1980s most companies were either producing and selling in only one national market or exporting to a limited extent to many European markets from one country. Observed Whirlpool CEO Whitwam: "What strikes me most is how similar the US and European industries are."[29] Research by Whirlpool also indicated that washers were basically alike in working components around the globe.[30]

However, the European market was very segmented and consumer preferences differed greatly from country to country with regard to almost every type of appliance. For example, the French preferred to cook their foods at high temperatures, splattering grease on oven walls. Thus, oven ranges manufactured for France should have self-cleaning ability. However, this feature was not a requirement in Germany where lower cooking temperatures were the norm.[31] In contrast to Americans, who preferred to stuff as many clothes into the washer as possible, Europeans overwhelmingly preferred smaller built-in models. Also, continental European "engineering" mentality disliked the US and British one-touch button models, but preferred the build-in concept, which was developed in the US where it failed to attract buyers.[32] In France, 80 percent of washing machines were top-loaders, while elsewhere in Western Europe, 90 percent were front-loaders. Also, European washers frequently contained heating elements and the typical European homemaker preferred to wash towels at 95 degrees centigrade. Gas ranges were common throughout Europe, except for Germany, where 90 percent were electric.

Given this situation, some observers were skeptical about the possibility of establishing pan-European models which would yield a sustainable competitive advantage through manufacturing, procurement, and marketing efficiencies. They claimed that the European market was actually many smaller individual markets made up of the respective countries. Furthermore, many of these national markets featured strong competitors.

AB Electrolux was a force practically in all of Europe, with an overall 25 percent market share.[33] Over 20 years the $14-billion multinational from Sweden had undertaken more than 200 acquisitions in 40 countries which spanned five businesses: household appliances, forestry and garden products, industrial products, metal and mining, and commercial services. Its expertise in managing acquisitions and integrating the newly acquired units into the organization was unequalled. For instance, in 1983, Electrolux took over the money losing Italian white goods manufacturer Zanussi with 30,000 employees, 50 factories and a dozen foreign sales companies. Within four years the Swedes turned a company which in 1983 lost 120 billion lire into an efficient organization netting 60 billion lire.[34] The acquisitions of Zanussi of Italy, Tricity in Britain, and three Spanish companies in anticipation of the changes in Western Europe marked the beginning of a new era in this mature industry. Industrial Design Centers and Research Centers were being established in Stockholm (Sweden), Venice (Italy), and Columbus (Ohio) to share product and operation ideas and to accelerate product development among the many brands. Instead of combining production, marketing, and sales on a market-by-market basis, a search for synergies began, first to establish pan-European brands for a unified Europe, and then to explore cross-Atlantic opportunities. The newly formed Electrolux Components Group was charged with taking advantage of the available integration opportunities, primarily by coordinating and developing strategic components worldwide. Parallel to this, a new organizational layer was created on the marketing side, combining sales and marketing of several countries on a regional basis.

In Germany Bauknecht (Philips) as well as Siemens-Bosch and AEG-Telefunken were dominant. In Britain, GEC's Hotpoint, and in France, Thomson-Brandt were forces to be reckoned with. Merloni from Italy pursued a different approach by flooding Europe with machines produced in Italy with lower cost labor. In 1987, Merloni acquired Indesit, an Italian producer in financial trouble, in order to enlarge its manufacturing base and take advantage of Indesit's marketing position in many European countries. However, in the late 1980s, no brand had more than 5 percent of the overall market, even though the top ten producers generated 80 percent of the volume.

General Electric was another important rival. In 1989, GE entered into an appliance joint venture with Britain's General Electric Corporation (GEC), which had a strong presence in the low-price segment of the European market, especially the UK, and thus complemented GE's high-end European products.

In the same year, Maytag also entered the European market. It had acquired the Hoover Division through the purchase of Chicago Pacific. Hoover, best known for its vacuum cleaners, also produced washers, dryers, and dishwashers in a highly integrated process in aging facilities in the UK. Hoover was also present in Australia and, through a trading company, serviced other parts of the world.

Exhibit 10.3   Core appliance market share of major competitors in the USA and Europe, 1991 versus 1989 (percentages)

USA	1991	1989	Europe	1991	1989
Whirlpool	33.9	32.7	Electrolux	19	20.5
General Electric	28.2	25.5	Bosch-Siemens	13	11.0
Electrolux	15.9	18.4	Whirlpool	10	11.5
Maytag	14.2	14.8	Miele	7	n.a.
Raytheon	5.6	n.a.	Thompson	6	n.a.
Other	2.2	8.6	AEG	5	n.a.
			Merloni		10.0
			Maytag		2.0
			Other	40	40.0

Sources: Bray, H. "Plugging into the world," *Detroit Free Press* (May 17, 1993), 10–11F; "A portrait of the US appliance industry 1992," *Appliance* (September 1992).

By acquiring Hoover, Maytag assumed a significant debt load and experienced a negative reaction from the stock market. However, the company's official strategy entailed continued globalization via expansion in Europe and in the Pacific Rim.

Thus, in spite of these concerns about differing consumer preferences in Europe, the largest US appliance manufacturers decided to set foot on the European market before the 1992 European Union Program became a reality. Within two years, General Electric, Maytag, and Whirlpool entered Western Europe and thus were closing the gap relative to the geographical scope of AB Electrolux (exhibit 10.3). European Union rules required 60 percent local content to avoid tariffs which, combined with the fear of a "Fortress Europe" protected by Community-wide tariffs after 1992, excluded exports as a viable strategy.

Within a very short time further agreements followed which greatly reduced the number of independent competitors in Europe. AEG started cooperating with Electrolux in washer and dishwasher production and development. Bosch-Siemens formed an alliance with Maytag, and the European Economic Interest Group combined several manufacturers with France's Thompson-Brandt as the leader. In spite of this trend toward consolidation, Whirlpool estimated that in 1992 the number of European manufacturers of home appliances was around 100.[35]

Asia

Asia, the world's second largest home appliance market, was expected to experience rapid economic growth in the near future primarily because of booming economies of the Pacific Rim countries. Home appliance shipments were expected to grow at least 6 percent per annum through the 1990s – more than in Europe or North America. The market was dominated by some 50 widely diversified Asian manufacturers, primarily from Japan, Korea, and Taiwan, with no clear leader emerging yet. The biggest promise of course was the huge markets of the world's most populous nations – China and India.

Exhibit 10.4   Milestones of Whirlpool's globalization

1957   Whirlpool invests in Brazilian appliance market through purchase of equity interest in Multibras SA, renamed Brastemp SA in 1972.

1969   Entry into the Canadian appliance market through 52 percent equity interest in Inglis, Limited. Sole ownership established in 1990.

1976   Increased investment in Brazil through purchase of equity interests in Consul SA, an appliance manufacturer, and Embraco SA, a maker of compressors.

1986   Purchase of majority interest in Aspera Srl of Fiat SpA, a manufacturer of compressors, located in Turin and Riva, Italy.

1987   Entry into the Indian appliance market through TVS Whirlpool Limited, a 33 percent ea. joint venture company formed with Sundaram-Clayton Limited of Madras.
Ownership in Inglis, Limited, increased to 72 percent.

1988   Vitromatic, SA de CV is formed with Vitro, SA, of Monterrey, Nuevo Leon, to manufacture and market major home appliances for Mexican and export markets. Whirlpool has a 49 percent interest.
Whirlpool operates a maquiladora, Componentes de Reynosa, in Reynosa, Tamaulipas, to manufacture components for final assembly in the United States.

1989   Whirlpool and N.V. Philips of the Netherlands consummate an agreement under which Whirlpool acquires a 53 percent interest in a joint venture company made up of Philips' former major domestic appliance division. The new company, Whirlpool International BV (WIBV), will manufacture and market appliances in Western Europe. The joint venture brand names are Bauknecht, Philips, Ignis and Laden.
North American Appliance Group (NAAG) formed from streamlined US, Canadian and Mexican operations.
Affiliates in Brazil, India and Mexico complete construction of facilities and start producing the "world washer."

1990   A program is launched to market appliances in Europe under the dual brands Philips and Whirlpool.
Formation of a joint venture company with Matsushita Electric Industrial Co. of Japan to produce vacuum cleaners for the North American market.
Creation of Whirlpool Overseas Corporation as a wholly owned subsidiary to conduct industrial and marketing activities outside North America and Western Europe.
Inglis Limited becomes a wholly owned subsidiary.

1991   Whirlpool acquires remaining interest in WIBV from Philips Electronics NV.
Creation of two new global business units: Whirlpool Compressor Operations and Whirlpool Microwave Cooking Business.

1992   Creation of Whirlpool Tatramat in the Slovak Republic. Whirlpool Tatramat a.s. will manufacture clothes washers for Slovakia and neighboring countries and import other WIBV major appliances for sale.
Begins gradual phase-out of dual-branded advertising to sole Whirlpool brand by removing the Philips name in Europe.
Whirlpool assumes control of SAGAD SA of Argentina from Philips.
Reorganization of Whirlpool Europe. The name is changed from WIBV to WEBV.
Didier Pineau-Valencienne, Chairman and CEO of Groupe Schneider SA, France, becomes a Whirlpool director, the first non-American on the board.

1993   Reorganization of NAAG. Start of the implementation of a new Asian strategy.
Sales subsidiaries are opened in Poland and the Czech Republic.
In May Whirlpool announced joint venture with Teco Electric & Machinery Co. Ltd of Taiwan to market and distribute home appliances in Taiwan.

Latin America

Another market promising attractive growth in appliances was Latin America once these countries would follow Chile's example and emerge from decades of political instability, economic mismanagement, and hyperinflation. Indeed, much of this was happening in the 1990s, accompanied by efforts to lower tariffs, which would stimulate trade. Whirlpool expected appliance shipments to expand at a faster pace than in North America and Europe.[36]

Whirlpool Corporation

Company background

Whirlpool Corporation, headquartered in Benton Harbor, Michigan, was one of the world's leading manufacturers and marketers of major home appliances. The company's plants were located in 12 countries and it distributed its products in over 120 countries under major brand names (exhibit 10.4).

Located two hours by car from Chicago, Whirlpool was founded in St Joseph, Michigan, in 1911. At the time, it was producing motor driven wringer washers under the name Upton Machine, with the hopes of selling them in large quantities to large distributors. In 1916, the first order was sold to Sears, Roebuck and Co. In 1992, this enduring relationship with its oldest and largest customer continued with Sears representing 19 percent of Whirlpool's sales. In 1929, Upton merged with Nineteen Hundred Corp. of Binghamton, New York, and plants operated in both locations until Binghamton was closed in 1939. In 1948, the Whirlpool brand automatic washer was introduced. This established the dual distribution system – one product line for Sears, the other for Nineteen Hundred. The Nineteen Hundred Corporation was renamed Whirlpool in 1950 with the addition of automatic dryers to the company's product line. In 1955, Whirlpool merged with Seeger Refrigerator Co. of St Paul, Minnesota, and the Estate range and air conditioning divisions of RCA. The company, now named Whirlpool-Seeger Corporation, established the RCA Whirlpool brand name (which was used until 1967). In 1957, the name was changed back to Whirlpool Corporation. In the same year, the Appliance Credit Corporation was established as a wholly owned finance subsidiary whose name later was changed to Whirlpool Financial Corporation. Also in 1957, Whirlpool for the first time entered the foreign market through the purchase of equity interest in Multibras SA of São Paulo, Brazil, later renamed Brastemp SA. In 1967, Whirlpool was the first competitor in the industry to take advantage of AT&T's new 800-line service and created the Cool-Line Telephone Service which provided customers a toll-free number to call for answers to questions and help with service. Over the years, Whirlpool consistently upgraded its manufacturing capacity by constructing new plants and closing old ones. In 1968, it completed the Elisha Gray II Research and Engineering Center in Benton Harbor, thereby establishing a solid R&D basis. In 1986, the KitchenAid division of Hobart Corporation was purchased from Dart & Kraft, which marked Whirlpool's entry into the upscale segment of the appliance market. In the same year, Whirlpool sold its central heating and cooling business to Inter-City Gas Corp. of Canada.

The year 1985 marked the company's sole effort to diversify. It purchased the assets of Mastercraft Industries Corp., a Denver based manufacturer of kitchen cabinets. A year later a second cabinet maker, St Charles Manufacturing Co., was acquired through the newly formed Whirlpool Kitchens, Inc. In March 1989, Whirlpool Kitchens was sold due to lack of fit. Whirlpool Kitchens had been losing money and had discontinued operations in 1988.

North American Appliance Group

In 1988, Whirlpool's North American operations were reorganized into four brand-oriented business units: Whirlpool Appliance Group (1988 sales $1678 million), KitchenAid Appliance Group (1988 sales $308 million), Kenmore Appliance Group (1988 sales $1440 million), and Inglis Limited (1988 sales $351 million). This structure was supposed to allow the company to capitalize on the success of its brands while at the same time reap scale effects through an integrated manufacturing network. KitchenAid served the upscale market based on its reputation for quality blenders and dishwashers, the Whirlpool brand served the mid-price segment, and the Roper brand name, which Whirlpool acquired in 1988 and which was part of the Whirlpool Group, focused on the lower segment and provided Whirlpool with gas range production capability. Thus, within the North American Appliance Group (NAAG) a clear market segmentation existed which ensured complete coverage and minimal overlap. NAAG's scope had been further extended in 1988 with the acquisition of Emerson Electric's dishwasher and trash compactor business.

In 1990, Whirlpool sold its vacuum cleaner business to a joint venture with Matsushita Electric Industrial Co. which would operate Whirlpool's Danville, Kentucky, vacuum cleaner plant.

In the early 1990s, the refrigerator business was streamlined by concentrating production of certain models in one plant and closing older facilities. Similar decisions also affected the production of dishwashers and trash compactors.

In 1992, as a result of a year-long strategic reassessment of the entire company, a new organizational structure was designed for NAAG. Effective January 1, 1993, the new organizational units focus on process management, branch management, customer management, product and service creation, manufacturing, and logistics. The new structure was intended to provide better support for a customer-oriented strategy. The sales and distribution organization was responsible for brand and customer management for the retail and contract sales business. Marketing focused on product and service creation and on enhancing brand awareness and loyalty. Logistics was responsible for managing availability and inventory through the warehouses, plants and vendors. A separate unit, the Kenmore organization, was charged with supporting Sears, Whirlpool's largest single customer.

In June 1993, Whirlpool was named the winner in the $30 million Super Efficient Refrigerator Program, a success which CEO Whitwam attributed to the multidisciplinary team which had been assembled from all over the world: "Each member of the Whirlpool team is an expert in his or her field," Whitwam said. "Their combined efforts and unrelenting focus on bringing a SERP refrigerator to market has resulted in the development of a superior product in a remarkably short time."[37] The first SERP model would be a 22 cubic foot side-by-side refrigerator/ freezer which would be introduced in early 1994. The SERP models eliminated CFCs completely by using a different refrigerant and blowing agent needed to expand foam insulation between the walls of the refrigerator liner and cabinet. Energy efficiency gains were achieved through better insulation, a high-efficiency compressor and an improved condenser fan motor in conjunction with a microchip controlled adaptive defrost control which incorporated fuzzy logic.[38] Jeff Fettig, vice-president, group marketing and sales for NAAG, declined to discuss details of the new technology but added: "I can say that these changes allowed us to surpass SERP's very tough requirement that the refrigerators be at least 25 percent more efficient than 1993 federal energy standards." Whirlpool had entered the SERP contest because it was consistent with the company's strategy to exceed customer expectations. Again, Fettig: "The SERP program allowed us to accelerate the development process and bring these products to the market sooner. Future products will be designed with these consumer expectations [regarding environmental friendliness] in mind, giving people even more reason to ask for a Whirlpool-built product next time they are in the market for a major home appliance."[39]

In its 1993 annual report, Whirlpool announced that since 1988, NAAG had increased its regional market share by nearly a third. The North American business remained Whirlpool's core group: "NAAG has been the source of much of the cash flow required to fund the company's expansion into new markets, and in 1992 accounted for nearly 60 percent of corporate revenues."[40]

Whirlpool's globalization

In 1992, Whirlpool's ongoing efforts to establish a global presence were more than ten years old. In its 1984 annual report, Whirlpool announced that it had concluded a two-year study and adopted a plan for the next five years. Among the steps mentioned were developing new international strategies and adding sound new businesses which would complement existing strengths. Whirlpool Trading Corporation was formed to consolidate existing international activities and explore new ventures. In January 1985, the company increased its equity interest in Inglis which dated back to 1969 from 48 percent to more than 50 percent. In the following year, Aspera Srl in Turin, Italy, a large compressor maker, was purchased from Fiat. Also, the company held talks with Philips about global opportunities. The 1986 annual report discussed the reasons for the emphasis on internationalization and explained the company's ambition to become an international leader: "against the backdrop of recent mergers and acquisitions that are both consolidating and globalizing our industry, we're determined to emerge as one of the few key players expected to prevail on the appliance scene, worldwide, by the year 2000."[41] Indeed, Whirlpool itself was actively involved in the market for companies, acquiring KitchenAid on January 31, 1986 for cash.

Already in the late 1950s, Whirlpool had undertaken the first expansion beyond the US borders when it entered Brazil, followed by Canada in 1969 (exhibit 10.5). In 1976 Whirlpool strengthened its position in Brazil. However, globalization truly took shape in the 1980s when Whirlpool added Mexico, India, and Europe through a series of joint ventures. The moves in South America and Asia were

Exhibit 10.5   Whirlpool's global presence

North America		Europe	
Principal products	**Major brand names**	**Principal products**	**Major brand names**
Automatic dryers	Acros*	Automatic dryers	Bauknecht
Automatic washers	Admiral (Canada)	Automatic washers	Ignis
Dehumidifiers	Crolls*	Dishwashers	Laden
Dishwashers	Estate	Freezers	Whirlpool
Freezers	Inglis	Microwave ovens	
Microwave ovens	KitchenAid	Ranges	
Ranges	Roper	Refrigerators	
Refrigerators	SpeedQueen (Canada)	Principal Locations	
Room air conditioners	Supermatic*	**Strategic and Group Center:**	**Parts Distribution Centers:**
Trash compactors	Whirlpool	Comerio, Italy	Comerio, Italy
	*Affiliate owned		Schorndorf, Germany
Principal locations		**Subsidiary:**	**Sales Subsidiaries:**
		Whirlpool Europe BV	Barcelona
Corporate:	**Parts Distribution Centers:**	Eindhoven, Netherlands	Brussels
Benton Harbor, Michigan	LaPorte, Indiana	**Affiliate:**	Budapest, Hungary
Subsidiaries:	Mississauga, Ontario	Whirlpool Tatramat a.s.	Comerio, Italy
Inglis Lt.	**Sales Divisions:**	Poprad, Slovakia	Dublin, Ireland
Mississauga, Ontario	Atlanta	**Manufacturing Facilities:**	Eindhoven, Netherlands
Whirlpool Financial Corp.	Boston	Amiens, France	Espoo, Finland
Benton Harbor, Michigan	Charlotte, North Carolina	Barcelona, Spain	Herlev, Denmark
Affiliates:	Chicago	Calw, Germany	Lenzburg, Switzerland
Matsushita Floor Care Co.	Dallas	Cassinetta, Italy	Lisbon, Portugal
Danville, Kentucky	Dayton, Ohio	Naples, Italy	London
Vitromatic SA de CV	Denver	Neunkirchen, Germany	Nürnberg, Germany
Monterrey, Mexico	Kansas City, Kansas	Norrköping, Sweden	Oosterhout, Netherlands
Manufacturing Facilities:	Knoxville, Tennessee	Poprad, Slovakia	Oslo, Norway
Benton Harbor, Michigan	Little Rock, Arkansas	Riva di Chieri, Italy	Paris
Cambridge, Ontario	Los Angeles	Schorndorf, Germany	Stuttgart, Germany
Clyde, Ohio	Miami	Siena, Italy	Wien, Austria
Columbia, South Carolina	New York City	Trento, Italy	
Evansville, Indiana	Orlando, Florida		
Findlay, Ohio	Philadelphia		
Forth Smith, Arkansas	Pittsburgh		
Greenville, Ohio	San Francisco		
La Vergne, Tennessee	Santurce, Puerto Rico		
Marion, Ohio	Seattle		
Montmagny, Quebec			
Oxford, Mississippi			
Reynosa, Mexico			

Exhibit 10.5 (Cont'd)

Latin America		Asia	
Principal products	Major brand names	Principal products	Major brand names
Automatic dryers	Buaknecht	Automatic dryers	Bauknecht
Automatic washers	Brastemp*	Automatic washers	Ignis
Freezers	Consul*	Cooking products	KitchenAid
Ranges	Ignis	Dishwashers	Roper
Refrigerators	KitchenAid	Microwave ovens	Whirlpool
Room air conditioners	Roper	Refrigerators	
	Semer*	Room air conditioners	
	Whirlpool	**Subsidiary:**	**Manufacturing Facility:**
	*Affiliate owned	Whirlpool Overseas Corp.	Pondicherry, India
Principal location		Benton Harbor, Michigan	**Sales Subsidiaries:**
Subsidiaries:	Joinville, Brazil	**Affiliate:**	Bangkok, Thailand
Whirlpool Argentina	Embraco S.A.	TVS Whirlpool Limited	Hong Kong
Buenos Aires, Argentina	Joinville, Brazil	Madras, India	Kuala Lumpur, Malaysia
Whirlpool Overseas Corp.	South American Sales Co.		Melbourne, Australia
Benton Harbor, Michigan	Sao Paulo, Brazil		Singapore
Affiliates:			
Brasmotor S.A.	**Manufacturing Facilities:**		
Sao Paulo, Brazil	Joinville, Brazil		
Brastemp S.A.	Sao Paulo, Brazil		
Sao Paulo, Brazil	San Luis, Argentina		
Consul S.A.			

motivated by the expectation that the climbing disposable incomes in these continents combined with better education and a broadening middle class would result in a growing demand for appliances that would "at least partially mirror the American consumer boom of the 1950s and 1960s."[42]

Among Whirlpool's top management David R. Whitwam was known as a champion of Whirlpool's globalization. Whitwam had succeeded Jack Sparks, who had retired in 1987 after 47 years of service, including five as CEO. Sparks had given Whirlpool the focus it had lacked. His legacy to the company was aptly summarized by the colleague: "He is a risk taker who challenges the status quo and a visionary who is value driven. He believes in people and recognizes and embraces a changing world."[43]

It was not an easy task to follow in the footsteps of such a distinguished leader. Born in Madison (Wisconsin), Whitwam graduated from the University of Wisconsin with a BS in economics with honors. After eight years in the United States Army and the Wisconsin National Guard, he joined Whirlpool as a marketing management trainee in July 1968. One year later he was named territory sales manager at the South California sales division and from there job descriptions did not change, only the locations. Whitwam spent time in New York and then in Southern California.[44]

A soft-spoken man with mid-western charm, Whitwam was never one to gloat, but his success in California was immense. His forward thinking and innovative spirit sparked Ed Herrelko, Vice-President of Marketing and Sales for Caloric, to exalt, "He's a legend out there."[45]

Whitwam moved to corporate headquarters in Benton Harbor in 1977 when he was named Merchandising Manger for Range Products. From that post came a promotion to Director of Builder Marketing, and then Vice-President. Whirlpool Sales, in 1983. In 1985, he was elected to the company's board of directors. On December 1, 1987, he assumed his current position as CEO and Chairman of the Board of Whirlpool Corporation. Since then, he has transformed a domestically oriented $4 billion company into a $7 billion global force.

Whirlpool Europe BV

Among those most strongly convinced of the promise of the European market was David Whitwam: "The only people who say you can't have a pan-European brand are the people who don't have one themselves."[46] In the 1987 annual report, Whitwam elaborated on the company's rationale for globalization:

> The US appliance market has limited growth opportunities, a high concentration of domestic competitors and increasing foreign competition. Further, the US represents only about 25 percent of the worldwide potential for major appliance sales.
>
> Most importantly, our vision can no longer be limited to our domestic borders because national borders no longer define market boundaries. The marketplace for products and services is more global than ever before and growing more so every day.
>
> Consumers in major industrialized countries are living increasingly similar lifestyles and have increasingly similar expectations of what consumer products must do for them. As purchasing patterns become more alike, we think that companies that operate on a broad global scale can leverage their strengths better than those which only serve an individual national market. Very likely, appliance manufacturing will always have to be done regionally. Yet the ability to leverage many of the strengths of a company on an international basis is possible only if that company operates globally.[47]

On August 18, 1988, Whitwam and Whirlpool made their boldest move so far towards global dominance in the white goods industry. They announced a joint venture with N. V. Philips, the second largest appliance manufacturer in Europe behind Electrolux. The deal for a 53 percent interest in Philips' worldwide Major Domestic Appliance Division was consummated on January 2, 1989 for $361 million in cash; the new company was called Whirlpool International BV.

Two years later, on the final day of July 1991, Whirlpool exercised its option to purchase from Philips the remaining interest in WIBV. With this move, Whirlpool became the world's largest appliance manufacturer, overtaking archrival AB Electrolux.

Philips' decentralized organization was phased out and WIBV split into two customer-focused business units – one for the Bauknecht brand, and the other for the dual-branded Philips/Whirlpool products, and Ignis and Laden products. Brands were thus positioned to fit the niches and conditions in Europe, an approach employed earlier in the USA, where each brand was given a particular segment. Bauknecht – Philips' most profitable brand – was aimed at the high end of the market, Philips/Whirlpool at the middle, and Ignis was designed for the lower end.

Sales and marketing were kept completely separate for the Bauknecht and Whirlpool appliance groups, yet non-marketing support from each of the 14 countries was combined. The manufacturing organization was also completely revamped. However, several plants located strategically were maintained – in contrast to Maytag. This turned out to be a significant advantage in a Europe with fragmented consumer tastes. Explained Lisa Mendheim of Maytag, referring to the company's Hoover operations: "We're very limited in adapting washers and dryers made in Wales to European standards."[48] Logistics, distribution, after-sales service, and information were tied together with assembly under one person. Distribution was reconfigured towards a pan-European approach and 10 out of 28 finished goods warehouses were closed.

A global outlook was instilled in the management team. Instead of having primarily Dutch managers, the top seven-member team comprised five nationalities. Managers were rotated between Europe and the United States to foster global thinking. This move paid off in late 1991 when the VIP Crisp microwave oven, developed by a new "advanced global technology unit" in Norrköping, Sweden, was introduced and quickly became Europe's best-selling model. The VIP Crisp has a heated base plate which allows Italians to bake crisp pizza crusts and the British to fry eggs. Now the company is starting to import the VIP Crisp to the United States.[49]

WIBV also made a series of moves to establish itself in the emerging markets of Central and Eastern Europe, which in 1991 represented about 11 percent of the world appliance market and promised attractive growth opportunities over the long term.[50] Bauknecht was first in setting up a distribution system in East Germany after the opening of the border. In early 1992, WIBV developed distribution networks in the entire region and established a wholly owned sales subsidiary in Hungary, Whirlpool Hungarian Trading Ltd. In May 1992, a 43.8 percent minority investment in Whirlpool/Tatramat as, a joint venture in Slovakia, was acquired, which in October started manufacturing and selling automatic washers and marketing products assembled at other WIBV locations. In 1993, sales subsidiaries were opened in Poland and the Czech Republic. By the end of 1992, WIBV with headquarters in Eindhoven, Holland, employed 14,000 people and maintained manufacturing facilities in six countries (exhibit 10.4).

In 1992, WIBV started redesigning its products in order to increase manufacturing efficiency and improve product quality and customer satisfaction. In September, WIBV, now called Whirlpool Europe BV (WEBV), was restructured. WEBV replaced the Bauknecht and Philips/Whirlpool Appliance Groups with centralized sales and marketing functions which supported all of Whirlpool's European brands. National sales subsidiaries were consolidated into three sales regions to take account of the growing European cross-border trade. The marketing function included separate, brand-oriented components to strengthen brand identity while at the same time ensuring coordination internally. Manufacturing and technology activities were reorganized around product groups and development centers, with Germany focusing on laundry and dishwashing products and Italy on refrigeration and cooking. Key support functions (consumer services, information technology, logistics, planning) were maintained as separate, centrally managed entities.[51] Explained WEBV president Hank Bowman: "The idea is to put systems support in place so we can deliver products more accurately and in a more timely manner."[52] A central account-management function was established to service transnational buying groups. WEBV also assumed responsibility for the Middle East and Africa, which formerly were housed in Whirlpool Overseas Corporation (WOC) and which accounted for $100 million in sales, mainly in the firm of kits in an attempt to boost local content and thus preempt the emergence of domestic-content rules. WEBV supported WOC by supplying products, components, and technology sold by WOC in its geographic domain. In June 1993, WEBV sold its refrigerator plant in Barcelona (Spain) to an Italian appliance maker in order to make better use of its remaining facilities.

By mid-1993, WEBV had become the third largest appliance manufacturer in Europe behind Electrolux and Bosch-Siemens and anticipated that by achieving increased efficiencies, coupled with volume growth, it would increase operating margins to the North American level.[53]

The world washer

Another initiative which encountered widespread skepticism in the industry was the development of a compact washer, dubbed the "world washer,"[54] which went into production in new manufacturing facilities in Brazil in late 1990, and in Mexico and India in early 1991. Lightweight, with substantially fewer parts than its US counterpart, it had good test scores and received favorable evaluations based on such features as stainless steel and porcelain baskets. According to Samuel J. Pearson, Director, International Engineering, its performance was equal to or better than anything on the world market while competitive on price with the most popular models in these markets.

Although many of the circumstances surrounding the decision to start world washer production in India, Brazil, and Mexico differed, all three countries saw a clear opportunity. In 1986, market penetration for washers in the targeted areas stood at only 6, 22, and 54 percent, respectively. Whirlpool estimated that about 10–15 percent of India's 840 million people could afford clothes washers while only about 250,000 lower quality machines were sold annually.[55] Further, a weakened US dollar provided the right "window" that Whirlpool and its partners needed to get the new design into production before competitors could capitalize on the same opportunities. The goal of the world washer effort was to develop a complete product, process, and facility design package versatile enough to satisfy conditions and market requirements in various countries but with low initial investment requirements. At the same time, the world washer established a beachhead, especially against the Far Eastern rivals.

The development was preceded by extensive market research and intensive analysis of almost every washer model marketed in Japan, Korea, Europe, New Zealand, and the USA. Originally it was planned to replicate the project design in each of the three countries. It eventually proved necessary to develop three slightly different variations. "Each of the affiliates presented different expertise both in the washer business and in working with various materials," said Lawrence J. Kremer, Senior Vice-President, Global Technology and Operations. "Our Mexican affiliate,

Vitromatic, has porcelain and glassmaking capabilities. Porcelain baskets made sense for them. Stainless steel became the preferred material for the others."

Costs also varied widely, further affecting both product and process decisions. "In India, for example, material costs may run as much as 200 to 800 percent higher than elsewhere, while labor and overhead costs are comparatively minimal," added Kremer. Another consideration was the garments to be washed in each country. "Saris – those beautiful, 18-foot lengths of cotton or silk with which Indian women drape themselves – posed a special challenge," recalled Pearson.

The plants also varied subtly from each other, although the goals were identical – minimizing facility investment, avoidance of big finish systems, and welding stations requiring extensive machinery for material cleanup and environmental safety. Brastemp, Whirlpool's Brazilian partner, put its new plant in Rio Claro, 100 kilometers northwest of São Paulo. Made of precast concrete, it was designed as a creative convention cooling system to address the high humidity. In India, the new facility was built in Pondicherry, just 12 degrees north of the equator. Although the plant looked similar to that in Brazil – except for the overhead fans – the method of construction was different. Concrete was hand mixed on location, then carried in wicker baskets to forms constructed right next to the building site. The Indian construction crew cast the concrete, allowed it to cure and then, using five or six men, raised each 3-ton slab into place using chain, block and tackle. Finally, two plants made up the facility in Monterrey. Internacional de Lavadores housed the flexible assembly lines as well as stamping and a few machine operations. Viplasticos, the adjacent facility, had injection molding and extrusion processes.

Pearson underscored the fact that the project resulted not only in new plants and a new product, but in team members from very different cultural backgrounds who have gained experience in how to manage a project differently, employing a small team with the authority to do many things. "Our foreign colleagues have become partners in every sense of the word," Pearson said. "When we make the final hand off to Gopal Srinivasan in India, to Francisco Fiorotto in Brazil, and to Luis Hernandez in Mexico, we will be placing the ventures in the hands of good people, good colleagues, good friends."

Whirlpool Overseas Corporation

Whirlpool Overseas Corporation (WOC) was formed in Spring 1990 as a wholly owned subsidiary to conduct marketing and industrial activities outside North America and Europe. It included US Export Sales, the Overseas Business Group acquired from Philips in the WIBV transaction and three wholly owned sales companies in Hong Kong, Thailand, and Australia. Industrial activities encompassed technology sale and transfer, kit and component sales, joint venture manufacturing, and project management for affiliates. WOC also oversaw the activities in Brazil and the joint venture in India.

One of the key responsibilities of WOC was to feed the new technologies from Whirlpool's bases in North America and Europe to its other units. A second responsibility was to ensure optimal brand positioning in each country and to analyze specific appliance designs for their suitability to various markets. Conditions could vary greatly from country to country. For instance, the company sold so-called giant ovens in Africa and the Middle East. These ovens were 39 and 42 inches wide compared to the standard 30 inches in the United States and were large enough to roast a sheep or goat.[56]

In January 1992, WOC strengthened its position in South America by taking over control of SAGAD, Philips' white goods operation in Argentina. In July, a joint venture was created with Whirlpool's affiliates to distribute Whirlpool's and the affiliates' products to independent distributors. As a result of these moves, Whirlpool and its affiliates were the leading marketers and manufacturers of major home appliances in the region.

WOC's activities were based on the belief that global leadership implied a strong presence in all major markets. Given the company's major presence in North America and in Europe and its 30-year history in South America, Asia represented the last, and what many believed biggest, challenge and opportunity. "In the US, we talk of households equipped with between seven and nine major appliance products. In Asia, which already accounts for 40 percent of the world market, it's more like four appliances per home," remarked Roger E. Merriam, Vice-President, Sales and Marketing, WOC. With growing income levels, significant market growth could be expected.[57]

In October 1992, WOC was reorganized by adopting a regional structure concentrating on Latin America and Asia which would go into effect in 1994. WOC Asia with headquarters in Tokyo was further subdivided into three sub-regions: Asia Pacific (South East Asia, India, Australia), Greater China (Hong Kong, People's Republic of China, Taiwan), and Japan. By adopting this regional structure, the company viewed itself as in a better position to expand from its infancy position in this region of a market share of 1 percent against the strong local manufacturers. This optimism was based on the fact that some of Whirlpool's products were being met with good customer acceptance. For instance, a top-load automatic washer sold in Hong Kong had about one-third of the market.[58] Whirlpool moved very quickly in Asia, creating a headquarters in Tokyo and establishing sales subsidiaries and regional offices. Whirlpool realized that a viable position implied more than selling imports from NAAG and WEBV and having kits assembled by licensees. This belief was also reinforced by the fact that consumer preferences in Asia were different from those in the USA and Europe. For instance, Japanese usually wash with cold water. But in order to get their clothes clean, Japanese machines have soak cycles which can range from 30 minutes to several hours. In May 1993, Whirlpool announced a joint venture with Teco Electric & Machinery Co. Ltd to market and distribute home appliances in Taiwan as an insider. Teco was Whirlpool's largest international distributor of Whirlpool products.

Fine Tuning the Strategy

With the new global structure established, Whirlpool fine tuned its strategy aimed at creating sustainable shareholder value. Comparisons with leading global firms established four areas essential for value creation: customer satisfaction, total quality, people commitment and growth and innovation. Excellence in these

Exhibit 10.6   Whirlpool's strategy for the 1990s

Overall Objective:	Create shareholder value by achieving a return on equity of about 18 percent.
Rationale:	"In order to attract investors in a rapidly changing world, it is not enough for Whirlpool to lead the developing global home-appliance industry. The company's financial performance must be competitive with the best of all large, publicly traded companies." (1991 Annual Report, p. 7)

Whirlpool believes that there are four areas in which it must excel in order to create sustainable value for its shareholders and, in turn, other stakeholders. For each area, the company has specific objectives which drive measurement, decisions and accountability. They are:

Customer Satisfaction	Through the intense customer focus of all Whirlpool people, we will measure and deliver the highest levels of customer satisfaction in all of our markets and with all of our products and services, assuring that we are the company of preference with our customers.
Total Quality	Our Worldwide Excellence System (WES) will deliver products and services that by measurement exceed customer expectations and outperform all of our competitors. We will achieve at least a 30-percent annual improvement in WES implementation through 1994. This will also improve our corporate total-cost productivity to a sustainable 5 percent per year improvement level as we assure that we are always doing the right things, the right way, the first time.
People Commitment	A high performance partnership with all of our people will encourage and enable contribution and commitment from each individual and team, and will provide a dynamic and diverse workplace environment which is valued by all.
Growth and Innovation	Our accomplishments and management systems will assure innovation in all areas of global business conduct, and create consistent internal growth in our revenues of at least six percent per year.

Source: Whirlpool Corporation, Annual Reports 1991, 1992.

four areas combined would lead to the targeted return on equity set at 18 percent (exhibit 10.6).

For each of the four areas, measures to track progress and drive decision making and accountability were developed and reported in the 1991 and 1992 Annual Reports to Shareholders.[59]

Concerning customer satisfaction, the company conducted extensive studies of dealer and customer satisfaction in North America and in Europe, resulting in a new "Quality Express" physical distribution system, product improvements and the creation of two Consumer Assistance Centers which greatly expanded the service compared to the Cool Line service and were designed to handle nine million consumer calls by 1995.

The total quality objective led to the introduction of the Worldwide Excellence System as a single framework to incorporate total quality standards, the Malcolm Baldrige National Quality Criteria and the ISO 9000 system. First successes were already being reported: The New Generation dishwasher models produced in Findlay, Ohio, reported a first-year service rate already lower than those they replaced. Quality improvements were also recorded in the automatic-washer manufacturing plant in Amiens, France, in the cooking products facility at Cassinetta, Italy, and in the Hong Kong subsidiary.

To show its commitment to people, Whirlpool in 1991 introduced Partner-Share, a stock option plan for its 22,000 US employees with the hope of encouraging employee ownership and dedication to building shareholder value. A gain-sharing program at the Benton Harbor components division slashed rework by 31 percent and total scrap cost by 62 percent and its parts-per-million rejection rate by 99 percent over three years. The program also provided each of the plant's 265 employees with an extra $2700 of pay in 1991.[60]

The growth objective had resulted in many acquisitions and joint ventures in recent years as well as the aggressive expansion of Whirlpool brands into new territories. The world washer and the SERP win were testimony of the company's growth and innovation orientation.

Besides optimizing the structure of its businesses, Whirlpool also adjusted the overall organization and board composition to support its strategy. In 1991, the position of Chief Technology Officer was created, which subsequently led to the creation of Whirlpool Compressor Operations and Whirlpool Microwave Cooking Business, two new business units with global responsibility. A fourth new entity with global responsibility was added in 1992 with the formation of the Water and Portable Appliance business unit charged with managing the company's small appliance business. Also, a centrally managed Global Technology Organization with system-wide responsibility was formed for advanced technology development, advanced product and manufacturing process creation, non-traditional new product opportunities and procurement. The objective was to better anticipate changes in technology and to enhance new product creation and the technology management process. Furthermore, Didier Pineau-Valencienne, Chairman and CEO of the Groupe Schneider, S.A., headquartered in Paris, France, joined the board to provide a broader perspective (exhibit 10.7).

At the beginning of 1993, Whirlpool's global direction and assembly of its geographic position was largely complete. However, by its own admission Whirlpool was not a truly global home-appliance company yet. It claimed to have made significant progress towards becoming the leader in the developing global home-appliance industry being the only player active in all four major regions:

But being a real global home-appliance company means more than just trading in countries around the world. It means identifying and respecting genuine national or regional differences in what

Exhibit 10.7   Directors and senior management, as of February 8, 1993

Directors		Senior management	

Directors

Victor A. Bonomo
Former Executive Vice-President, PepsiCo, Inc.
Committees: Audit, Organization, Strategic Planning

Robert A. Burnett
Former Chairman of the Board, Meredith Corporation Finance, Human Resources, Organization, Strategic Planning

Herman Cain
President and Chief Executive Officer Godfather's pizza, Incorporated Organization

Douglas D. Danforth
Former Chairman of the Board and Chief Executive Officer, Westinghouse Electric Corporation Finance, Human Resources, Organization, Strategic Planning

Allan D. Gilmour
Vice Chairman and Director, Ford Motor Company, and President, Ford Automotive Group Finance, Organization, Strategic Planning

William D. Marohn
President and Chief Operating Officer of the corporation

Miles L. Marsh
Chairman of the Board and Chief Executive Officer, Pet, Incorporated Audit, Organization, Strategic Planning

Didier Pineau-Valencienne
Chairman and Chief Executive Officer, Groupe Schneider S.A. and Societe Parisienne d'Entreprises et de Participation Organization

Philip L. Smith
Former Chairman of the Board, President and Chief Executive Officer, Pillsbury Company Finance, Organization, Strategic Planning

Jack D. Sparks
Former Chairman of the Board of the corporation Finance, Organization, Strategic Planning, Pension Fund

Paul G. Stern
Chairman, Northern Telecom Limited Human Resources, Organization, Strategic Planning, Technology

Janice D. Stoney
Former Executive Vice President, US WEST Communications Group, Incorporated Audit, Organization, Strategic Planning, Technology

Kenneth J. Whalen
Former Executive Vice President, American Telephone & Telegraph Company Finance, Organization, Strategic Planning, Technology

David R. Whitwam
Chairman of the Board and Chief Executive Officer of the corporation

Senior management

Executive Officers

David R. Whitwam
Chairman of the Board and Chief Executive Officer

William D. Marohn
President and Chief Operating Officer

Executive Vice Presidents

Harry W. Bowman
Whirlpool Europe B.V.

Michael J. Callahan
Chief Financial Officer

Robert Frey
Whirlpool Overseas Corporation

Ralph F. Hake
North American Appliance Group

Ronald J. Kerber
Chief Technology Officer

James R. Samartini
Chief Administrative Officer

Senior Officers
Vice Presidents

Ivan Menezes
Group Marketing, WEBV

Bradley, J. Bell
Treasurer

Bruce K. Berger
Corporate Affairs

E. R. (Ed) Dunn
Human Resources and Assistant Secretary

Jeff M. Fettig
Group Sales and Marketing, NAAG

Robert D. Hall
Global Procurement Operations

Stephen F. Holmes
Group Manufacturing and Technology, NAAG

Edward J. F. Herrelko
Sales and Distribution, NAAG

Daniel F. Hopp
General Counsel and Secretary

Halvar Johansson
Group Manufacturing and Technology, WEBV

Kenneth W. Kaminski
Kenmore Appliance Group

Jan Karel
Group Sales, WEBV

James E. LeBlanc
Chairman of the Board and Chief Executive Officer, Whirlpool Financial Corporation

Charles D. (Chuck) Miller Marketing, NAAG

P. Daniel Miller
President, Whirlpool do Brasil

Robert G. Thompson
Controller

Source: 1992 Annual Report.

customers demand from products and services – and simultaneously recognizing and responding to similarities across markets.[61]

The financial results for the first six months of 1993 showed continued improvement despite the unfavorable economic conditions worldwide (exhibits 10.8–10.14).

Exhibit 10.8 Consolidated income statement, year ended December 31 (millions of dollars except per share data)

		1992	1991	1990	1989	1988
Revenues	Net sales	7,097	6,650	6,424	6,138	4,314
	Financial services	204	207	181	136	107
	Total revenues	7,301	6,757	-6,613	6,274	4,421
Expenses	Cost of products sold	5,365	4,967	4,955	4,846	3,506
	Selling & administrative	1,323	1,257	1,180	932	607
	Financial services interest	82	91	85	65	47
	Intangible amortization	27	27	14	11	—
	Restructuring costs	25	22	22	9	—
	Total expenses	6,822	6,364	6,256	5,863	4,160
	Operating Profit	479	393	349	411	261
	Other income (expense)					
	Interest and sundry	38	49	19	19	25
	Interest expense	(145)	(138)	(148)	(122)	(53)
	Earnings before taxes and other items	372	304	220	308	233
	Income tax	154	130	110	132	87
	Earnings before equity earnings and other items	218	174	110	176	146
	Equity in net earnings of WFC	–	–	–	–	–
	Equity in net earnings (losses) of affiliated companies and other	(13)	(4)	(38)	38	15
	Loss from discontinued operations	–	–	–	–	(67)
	Net earnings	205	170	72	187	94
	Per share of common stock	$2.90	$2.45	$1.04	$2.70	$1.36
	Cash dividends	$1.10	$1.10	$1.10	$1.10	$1.10
	Avg. number of common stock outstanding (millions)	70.6	69.5	69.4	69.3	69.3

Exhibit 10.9 Consolidated balance sheet (millions of dollars)

		1992	1991	1990	1989	1988
Assets						
Current assets	Cash and equivalents	66	42	78	78	98
	Trade receivables less allowances	851	846	943	930	420
	Financing receivables less allowances	980	1,190	943	828	641
	Inventories	650	698	801	884	537
	Prepaid expenses and other	119	111	110	71	62
	Deferred income taxes	74	33	25	35	25
	Total current assets	2,740	2,920	2,900	2,889	1,827
Other assets	Investment in affil. companies	282	296	281	299	248
	Investment in WFC	–	–	–	–	–
	Financing receivables less allowances	912	828	628	497	387
	Intangibles, net	795	909	437	350	111
	Other	64	92	19	31	17
	Total	2,053	2,125	1,365	1,177	763
Property, plant,	Land	73	78	74	69	20
and equipment	Buildings	588	586	559	474	317
	Machinery and Equipment	2,052	2,026	1,823	1,289	888
	Accumulated Depreciation	(1,388)	(1,290)	(1,107)	(544)	(405)
	Total	1,325	1,400	1,349	1,288	820
	Total Assets	6,118	6,445	5,614	5,354	3,410
Liabilities and stockholders' equity						
Current liabilities	Notes payable	1,425	1,467	1,268	1,105	695
	Accounts payable	688	742	580	564	352
	Employee compensation	164	177	133	120	89
	Accrued expenses	495	478	506	399	198
	Income taxes	87	38	42	27	5
	Current maturities of long-term debt	28	29	122	36	
	Total current liabilities	2,887	2,931	2,651	2,251	1,374
Other liabilities	Deferred income taxes	213	166	167	184	139
	Accrued pensions and expenses	203	303	322	296	38
	Long-term debt	1,215	1,528	874	982	474
		1,631	1,997	1,363	1,462	651
	Minority interests	–	2	176	220	64
Stockholders' equity	Capital stock	76	75	74	74	74
	Paid-in capital	47	37	12	10	8
	Retained earnings	1,721	1,593	1,499	1,503	1,392
	Unearned restricted stock	(18)	(12)	–	–	–
	Cumul. translation adjustments	(49)	(1)	16	11	24
	Treasury stock – at cost	(177)	(177)	(177)	(177)	(178)
	Total stockholders' equity	1,600	1,515	1,424	1,421	1,321
	Total Liabilities and Stockholders' Equity	6,118	6,445	5,614	5,354	3,310

Exhibit 10.10 Consolidated statements of cash flows (millions of dollars)

		1992	1991	1990	1989
Operating activities	Net earnings	205	170	72	187
	Depreciation	275	233	247	222
	Deferred income taxes	9	3	(29)	16
	Equity in net losses (earnings) of affiliated companies incl. dividends received	16	(1)	35	(31)
	Gain on business disposition	–	–	(36)	–
	Provision for doubtful accounts	55	55	20	16
	Amortization of goodwill	27	27	14	11
	Minority interest	–	5	5	27
	Other	15	(19)	(9)	6
	Changes in assets and liabilities, net of effects of business acquisitions and dispositions	(83)	344	209	(72)
	Cash provided by operating activities	578	817	528	382
Investing activities	Net additions to properties	(288)	(287)	(265)	(207)
	Financing receivables originated and easing assets purchased	(2,497)	(3,129)	(2,749)	(2,268)
	Principal payments received on financing receivables and leases	2,655	2,409	2,506	1,938
	Business acquisitions less cash acquired	–	(595)	(134)	(345)
	Business disposition	–	–	80	–
	Other	(92)	(82)	1	(35)
	Cash provided by (used for) investing activities	212	(1,684)	(561)	(917)
Financing activities	Proceeds of short-term borrowings	12,066	9,268	10,611	10,084
	Repayments of short-term borrowings	(12,299)	(9,142)	(10,728)	(9,477)
	Proceeds of long-term debt	50	667	212	4
	Repayment of long-term debt	(73)	(134)	(41)	(36)
	Proceeds of non-recourse debt	–	269	–	45
	Repayment of non-recourse debt	(17)	(17)	(20)	(14)
	Dividends paid	(77)	(76)	(76)	(76)
	Other	8	(4)	75	(15)
	Cash provided (used for) financing activities	342	831	33	515
	Increase (decrease) in cash and equivalents	24	(36)	–	(20)
	Cash and equivalents at beginning of year	42	78	78	98
	Cash and equivalents at end of year	66	42	78	78

Exhibit 10.11   Revenues (millions of dollars)

	1992	1991	1990	1989	1988
Whirlpool appliance group	n.a.	1,819	1,795	1,691	1,678
Kenmore appliance group	1,050	1,000	1,011	1,110	1,447
KitchenAid appliance group	n.a.	447	400	344	308
Inglis Limited (Canada)	n.a.	315	327	337	357
Service and other, net of intercompany transactions	n.a.	335	357	368	–
Total North America	4,059	3,916	3,890	3,850	3,790
Whirlpool Europe	2,476	2,249	2,156	1,917	–
Whirlpool Overseas Corporation	336	223	178	–	–
Other, including export in 1989, net of intercompany transactions	226	162	200	371	495
Total appliance business	7,097	6,550	6,424	6,138	4,285
Whirlpool Financial Corp., net of intercompany transactions	204	220	189	136	136
	7,301	6,770	6,613	6,274	4,421

Revenues by line of product (millions of dollars)

		1992	1991	1990	1989	1988
Major Home Appliances	Home laundry appliances	2,489	2,300	2,220	2,108	1,485
	Home refrigeration and room air conditioning equipment	2,525	2,329	2,209	2,066	1,501
	Other home appliances	2,083	1,921	1,995	1,964	1,328
	Financial services	204	220	189	136	107

Exhibit 10.12   Geographic segment data (millions of dollars)

		1992	1991	1990	1989	1988
Revenues	North America	4,471	4,224	4,157	4,116	4,192
	Europe	2,645	2,479	2,405	2,169	244
	Corporate (and eliminations)	185	54	43	(11)	(15)
	Consolidated	7,301	6,757	6,605	6,274	4,421
Operating profit	North America	359	314	269	311	271
	Europe	101	82	86	101	(3)
	Corporate (and eliminations)	19	(3)	(6)	(1)	(6)
	Consolidated	479	393	349	411	262
Identifiable assets	North America	3,511	3,672	3,216	3,065	2,710
	Europe	1,917	2,284	1,905	1,678	210
	Corporate (and eliminations)	690	489	493	611	490
	Consolidated	6,118	6,445	5,614	5,354	3,410

Exhibit 10.12 (Cont'd)

		1992	1991	1990	1989	1988
Depreciation expense	North America	142	129	140	134	126
	Europe	132	104	107	88	17
	Corporate (and eliminations)	1	–	–	–	–
	Consolidated	275	233	247	222	143
Net capital expenditures	North America	174	183	158	135	171
	Europe	111	104	106	94	9
	Corporate (and eliminations)	3	–	1	–	–
	Consolidated	288	287	265	229	180

Exhibit 10.13 Industry segment data (millions of dollars)

		1992	1991	1990	1989	1988
Revenues	Major home appliances	7,097	6,550	6,424	6,138	4,315
	Financial services	235	233	210	163	136
	Corporate (and eliminations)	(31)	(26)	(29)	(27)	(29)
	Consolidated	7,301	6,757	6,605	6,274	4,421
Operating profit	Major home appliances	447	353	300	377	233
	Financial services	18	30	35	23	22
	Corporate (and eliminations)	14	10	14	11	7
	Consolidated	479	393	349	411	262
Identifiable assets	Major home appliances	3,612	3,835	3,513	3,438	1,865
	Financial services	1,941	2,143	1,632	1,337	1,049
	Corporate (and eliminations)	565	467	469	579	497
	Consolidated	6,118	6,445	5,614	5,354	3,410
Depreciation expense	Major home appliances	271	228	243	218	137
	Financial services	3	3	3	2	4
	Corporate (and eliminations)	1	2	1	2	2
	Consolidated	275	233	247	222	143
Net capital expenditures	Major home appliances	284	283	260	224	175
	Financial services	4	5	5	4	4
	Corporate (and eliminations)	–	(1)	–	1	1
	Consolidated	288	287	265	229	180
	Percentage of sales to Sears, Roebuck and Co.	19	19	20	23	38

Exhibit 10.14   Consolidated statement of earnings (millions of dollars)

		Six Months Ended	
		June 30, 1993	June 30, 1992
Revenues	Net sales	$3,633	$3,444
	Financial services	87	109
	Total revenues	3,720	3,553
Expenses	Cost of products sold	2,750	2,615
	Selling & administrative	708	645
	Financial services interest	32	46
	Intangible amortization	12	13
	Restructuring costs	8	7
	Total expenses	3,510	3,326
	Operating Profit (Loss)	210	227
Other income (expense)	Interest and sundry	(8)	15
	Interest expense	(57)	(71)
	Earnings before taxes, other items and accounting change	145	171
	Income tax	58	71
	Earnings before equity earnings, accounting change and other items	87	100
	Equity in net earnings of WFC	–	–
	Equity in net earnings (losses) of affiliated companies and other	5	(12)
	Net earnings (loss) before cumulative effect of accounting change	92	88
	Cumulative effect of accounting change for postretirement benefit	(180)	–
	Net earnings (loss)	$(88)	$88
Per share of common stock	Primary earnings before accounting change	$1.29	$1.25
	Primary earnings (loss)	$(1.23)	$1.25
	Cash dividends	$0.58	$0.55

NOTES

1 Hunger J. D. "The major home appliance industry in 1990: from US to global," mimeo, 1990.

2 Bower, J. L., and N. Dossabhoy. "Note on the major home appliance industry in 1984" (Condensed), Case 385–211, Harvard Business School, Cambridge, MA.

3 Ghoshal, S., and P. Haspeslagh. "The acquisition and integration of Zanussi by Electrolux: a case study," *European Management Journal*, Vol. 8, No. 4 (December 1990), pp. 414–33.

4 Hunger, J. D., op. cit.

5 "Poised for a moderate recovery," *Standard & Poor's Industry Surveys* (November 26, 1992), Vol. 2, pp. T96–101.

6 "Waiting for the next replacement cycle," *Standard & Poor's Industry Surveys* (November 1991), Vol. 2, pp. T102–105.

7 *Standard & Poor's Industry Surveys* (November 1992), op. cit.

8 Whirlpool Corporation, Form 10-K (1992).

9 Weiner, S. "Growing pains," *Forbes* (October 29, 1990), pp. 40–1.

10 Stewart, T. A. "A heartland industry takes on the world," *Fortune* (March 12, 1990), pp. 110–112.

11 Stewart, T. A., op. cit.

12 *Standard & Poor's Industry Surveys* (November 1992), op. cit.

13 *Appliance Manufacturer* (February 1990), pp. 36–7.

14 Bray, Hiawatha, "Plugging into the world," *Detroit Free Press* (May 17, 1993), pp. 10–11F.

15 DuPont, T. "Whirlpool's new brand name," *The Weekly Home Furnishing Newspaper* (April 11, 1988).

16 *Standard & Poor's Industry Surveys* (November 1992), op. cit.

17 *Standard & Poor's Industry Surveys* (November 1992), op. cit.; Treece, James B. "The great refrigerator race," *Business Week* (July 15, 1993), pp. 78–81.

18 Botskor, Ivan, Michel Chaouli and Bernhard Müller. "Boom mit Grauwerten," *Wirtschaftswoche*, No. 22 (May 28, 1993), pp. 64–75; Naj, Amal Kumar. "Air Conditioners learn to sense if you're cool," *Wall Street Journal* (August 31, 1993), p. B1; Bylinsky, Gene, "Computers that learn by doing," *Fortune* (September 6, 1993), pp. 96–102.

19 Botskor et al., op. cit.

20 Botskor et al., op. cit.

21 Naj, op. cit.

22 Bray, op. cit.

23 Fisher, J. D. "Home appliance industry," *Value Line* (December 22, 1989), p. 132.

24 *Standard & Poor's Industry Surveys* (November 1991), op. cit.

25 *Standard & Poor's Industry Surveys* (November 1992), op. cit.

26 *Standard & Poor's Industry Surveys* (November 1991), op. cit.

27 Ghoshal and Haspeslagh, op. cit.

28 Whirlpool Corporation, 1992 Annual Report.

29 Stewart, T. A., op. cit.

30 Kindel, S. "World washer: why Whirlpool leads in appliances: not some Japanese outfit," *Financial World*, Vol. 159, No. 6 (March 20, 1990), pp. 42–6.

31 Weiner, S., op. cit.

32 Tierney, Robin. "Whirlpool magic," *World Trade* (May 1993).

33 *Standard & Poor's Industry Surveys* (November 1991), op. cit.

34 Ghoshal & Haspeslagh, op. cit.

35 Whirlpool Corporation, Form 10-K (1992).

36 Whirlpool Corporation, 1992 Annual Report.

37 Whirlpool Corporation News Release, "Whirlpool Corporation named winner in $30 million super-efficient refrigerator competition," Benton Harbor, Mich. (July 1993).

38 Treece, op. cit.

39 Whirlpool Corporation News Release, op. cit. (1993).

40 Whirlpool Corporation, 1992 Annual Report, p. 9.

41 Whirlpool Corporation, 1992 Annual Report, p. 39.

42 Whirlpool Corporation, 1989 Annual Report.

43 Stewart, T. A., op. cit.

44 DuPont, T. "The appliance giant has a new president and a global vision," *The Weekly Home Furnishings Newspaper* (July 2, 1987), p. 1.

45 Zeller, W. "A tough market has Whirlpool in a spin," *Business Week* (May 2, 1988), pp. 121–2.

46 Stewart, T. A., op. cit.

47 Whirlpool Corporation, 1987 Annual Report.

48 Tierney, op. cit.

49 Bray, op. cit.; Tierney, op. cit.

50 Whirlpool Corporation, 1991 Annual Report.

51 Whirlpool Corporation, Form 10-K (1992).

52 Tierney, op. cit.

53 Whirlpool Corporation, 1992 Annual Report.

54 Whirlpool Corporation News Release, "Whirlpool 'world washer' being marketed in three emerging countries," undated.

55 Whirlpool Corporation, 1990 Annual Report.

56 *Appliance*, June 1991.

57 *Appliance*, June 1991.

58 Whirlpool Corporation, 1992 Annual Report.

59 Whirlpool Corporation, 1991 Annual Report.

60 Wartzman, R. "A Whirlpool factory raises productivity – and pay of workers," *Wall Street Journal* (May 4, 1992), p. A1.

61 Whirlpool Corporation, 1992 Annual Report.

Cosmetics and Activism: Anita Roddick and The Body Shop

David W. Grigsby, Alison M. Flynn, and Tanya Craig

On sleepless nights, Anita Roddick contemplates the future of The Body Shop and such ideas as setting up a school of business for young people so that the "culture of change and continuing education and social responsibility will carry on," how to use her shops as information centers for human rights abuses, and whether she should move into Cuba to help direct the social revolution into a business revolution. She also fears that The Body Shop is getting too large to "feel like a community" and wonders why "business people should be divorced from altruism."[1]

The Body Shop is an international manufacturer and retailer of cosmetics and toiletries bsed in the United Kingdom. Its products are made from natural ingredients and sold in plain, refillable bottles. In 1994, the company had shops in 45 countries and traded in over 23 languages.[2] Its products are sold exclusively through franchises rather than department stores or drug stores. The company is

---

not in business just to sell cosmetics, however, but also to educate. The Body Shop embraces awareness of social and environmental threats and promotes individual involvement and corporate responsibility through action. It supports trade relations with less fortunate communities internationally through its TRADE NOT AID program. In an industry that spends millions on advertising, the Body Shop spends nothing. Nevertheless, it experienced an explosive 50 percent compound growth throughout the 1980s.[3] By 1990, revenues had reached $143 million and profits had hit a record $15.3 million.[4]

Despite these earlier successes, much of what The Body Shop was doing in the early 1990s was damage control. The company faced a difficult period trying to stave off a negative press, handle the threatening effects of a lawsuit, maintain growth rates in the face of growing competition from Body Shop imitators, and placate disgruntled shareholders. In September of 1992, The Body Shop stock collapsed from $5.20 to $2.70 per share as shareholders responded to a disappointing earnings report.[5] The stock collapse resulted in The Body Shop receiving the number one billing in the *Financial Times* review of the top ten losers of 1992.

Prior to the stock collapse, a lawsuit, which lasted six weeks, was brought by The Body Shop against a television station which broadcast a report accusing The Body Shop of misleading its customers with its appeal for social consciousness by labeling its products "Against animal testing." It criticized the company for using ingredients that had ever been tested on animals. The Body Shop had changed its labeling in 1988 from "Not tested on animals" and does not use ingredients in its products that have been tested on animals within the past five years. This revelation resulted in hate mail to the Roddicks as well as lost sales and profits, and a decline of the company stock value. The Body Shop won the lawsuit, and received compensation of $415,000, but the lawsuit served to fuel rising skepticism among the press and customers. The effects of the lawsuit were compounded by Ms Roddick's appearance in a 1993 commercial for American Express Company where she discussed her activities in the company's TRADE NOT AID program. The advertisement confused loyal customers and angered others who accused Ms Roddick of compromising her pledge not to advertise.

A worldwide recession and a saturated market in the United Kingdom led to a reduction in profits for 1992, which were down 15 percent from $45 million to $34 million.[6] Analysts began questioning The Body Shop's ability to compete in the USA, where Americans are less brand loyal than Europeans and copycat stores are more common. Despite these troubles, The Body Shop's international retail sales rebounded, with a 48 percent increase to $115.7 million between February of 1993 and 1994,[7] indicating that the business of natural cosmetics and social reform may be more than just a passing trend.

The 51 year old feisty and energetic company founder was born of Italian immigrants and grew up in Littlehampton, England. With the pioneering spirit that ultimately resulted in The Body Shop becoming the progressive company that it is today, Anita Lucia Perella set out to first travel the world: working on an Israeli kibbutz, in Paris at a newspaper, and in Geneva for the United Nations. She then set route for New Hebrides, Tahiti, and New Caledonia as a "hippie" at the height of the sixties. After being thrown out of Johannesburg by police for attending a jazz club on "black night," Ms Perella returned to Littlehampton, where she met and married her husband and current Body Shop Chairman, Gordon Roddick.

In 1976, after Gordon Roddick left on a two-year adventure to fulfill his lifelong dream of riding horseback from Buenos Aires to New York City, Anita Roddick launched the first Body Shop in Brighton with $6500 in order to support her two daughters, then 6 and 4. While working at the United Nations, Ms Roddick learned that women in underdeveloped countries use organic potions to care for their skin. She opened up a cosmetics shop selling her own natural product line of 25 hair and skin products.[8]

The first product offerings included cocoa butter from Polynesia and pineapple facial wash from Sri Lanka. The store was painted bright green, not to reflect the color of plant life, but to hide the cracks in the walls. Products were sold in small, clear, plastic containers supplied by a local hospital for use in collecting urine samples. The container was later to win design awards for its simplicity. Customers were asked to come back to the store for refills so that the containers might be reused to cut down on costs, an effort that was to grow into a monumental recycling program. The round logo, said to represent the earth, was the least expensive logo available at the time that also allowed for the product name to be written in the center. Detailed information about the product ingredients and contents was hand printed and glued on to every container so that customers might understand why the products came in odd colors and were sometimes lumpy. Customers were enticed into the store by sweet smelling potpourri located throughout the shop and aromatic fragrances sprayed outside the door.

Ms Roddick learned the power of the press very early in her venture, when adjacent funeral parlor owners objected to the name of The Body Shop located so close to their business. She contacted the local newspaper and told the story of a young mother struggling to support her two daughters who was about to lose her business. The publicity supplied The Body Shop with many sympathetic customers, and Ms Roddick has relied upon a multitude of readily available, free publicity as a target of the press ever since. The first Body Shop was followed by a second store in Chichester within one year, and Anita Roddick quickly moved into franchising.

By 1984, The Body Shop consisted of 138 shops, 83 of which were located outside the United Kingdom.[9] The overseas expansion history of the company is shown in exhibit 11.1. Anita and Gordon Roddick took The Body Shop public in April of 1984 and its stock is traded on the London Stock Exchange. On the first day of trading, the share price rose from $1.30 to $2.30, increasing the company's value to over $11 million, of which the Roddicks retained 27.6 percent for a net worth of $2 million.[10] In 1985, Anita Roddick was named Business Woman of the Year, and in 1988, she was awarded the Order of the British Empire by the royal family. Before 1992, the company's value reached nearly $350 million.[11]

Disconcerted with the overwhelming public response to her newly acquired wealth and power, Ms Roddick decided to make her company a forum for social change, challenging the ethics of some common business practices, and leading the way toward environmental awareness and responsibility in the industry. Ms Roddick criss-crosses the world six months out of the year, channeling her energy into facilitating these causes, and locating new natural ingredients for her

Exhibit 11.1   The Body Shop International: overseas expansion

First shops opening in:

1976	United Kingdom		1986	Austria (Vienna)
1978	Belgium (Brussels)			Oman (Muscat)
1979	Greece (Athens)			Portugal (Lisbon)
	Austria (Vienna)			Kuwait
	Sweden			Spain (Madrid)
1980	Canada (Toronto)		1987	Antigua (St John's)
	Iceland (Reykjavik)			Malta (Sliema)
1981	Denmark (Copenhagen)			Qatar
	Finland (Tampere)			Saudi Arabia
	Ireland (Dublin)			Bermuda (Hamilton)
1982	The Netherlands (Leiden)		1988	USA (New York)
	France (Paris)			Gibraltar
1983	Australia (Melbourne)			Taiwan (Taipei)
	Cyprus (Limassol)		1989	New Zealand (Wellington)
	Germany (Cologne)			Cayman Islands
	Singapore		1990	Indonesia
	Switzerland (Zurich)			Japan (Tokyo)
	United Arab Emirates (Dubai)		1991	Luxembourg
1984	Hong Kong (Tsjmshatsue/Kowloon)		1993	Mexico
	Italy (Catania/Sicily)			Thailand
	Malaysia (Kuala Lumpur)			Macau
1985	Bahamas (Nassau)			Brunei
	Bahrain (Manama)			
	Norway (Oslo)			

Source: The Body Shop 1994 Annual Report and Accounts.

extensive product lines. The company has aligned itself with Greenpeace, Friends of the Earth, and Amnesty International, using its stores as a base for highly visible campaigns, such as stop the burning of the rain forests or protect the ozone.

Marketing

The Body Shop's mission is "to sell cosmetics with the minimum of hype and packaging," and "to promote health rather than glamour, reality rather than the dubious promise of instant rejuvenation."[12] Roddick's position is that cosmetic companies, having no social conscience, sell products by deceiving and exploiting women, telling them that they have some product that can give women back their youth. The Body Shop expressly promotes feeling good over looking good. The company prides itself on selling "well being."[13] The representative Body Shop customer is female and at the younger end of the baby boomers. A single customer typically spends an average of $14.00 per visit.[14] The latest market focus is on increasing store traffic among older women and the 17 to 25 year old segment, especially young mothers, as the company attempts to continue growth. The Body

Shop sells its products in individual franchised stores rather than department stores. Customers are encouraged to recycle or bring bottles back for refills.

The product line

Each Body Shop franchise stocks over 400 body care and cosmetic products and over 500 personal hygiene related products and accessory items.[15] The product line includes a full range of bath, skin, and hair care products, and colored cosmetics, including: Avocado Body Butter, Honey Stick Lip Balm, Brazil Nut Conditioner, a kit for expectant mothers including a flannel mopping brow cloth, soap bars shaped like endangered species, Elderflower Under Eye Gel, Sandlewood Shaving Cream, Pineapple Mango Bubble Bath, and Banana Hair Conditioner made from 15 percent pulped bananas. Additional product types include cleansers, skin refreshers, massage accessories, perfumes, sun care, and natural oils. Fifty new products were introduced in 1993, including the Watermelon Sun Care products and Tangerine Beer Shampoo. As is standard in the industry, each product has a tester or sample so that customers may try the product prior to buying. A men's product line named "Mostly Men" includes aftershave lotion, shaving cream, shampoo, and hair gel, as well as disposable razors. Back scrubbers woven from cactus fibers, foot rollers for massage, and facial scrub sponges represent an extension of the cosmetic product line as personal care products made available through the TRADE NOT AID program.

Additional product line extensions include limited edition cosmetics which are produced in limited quantities, and once sold out are not replenished. Gift baskets are available prearranged in price categories of $10 to $50, and may also be made up of various products as requested by the customer. Each store has a perfume bar where fragrances can be added to products at no additional charge. In 1992, The Body Shop introduced market specific product lines such as Blue Corn for the USA, and Tea Tree for Australia. The best selling products worldwide include the White Musk product line, Peppermint Foot Lotion, Banana Hair Conditioner, Vitamin E Cream, Cocoa Butter Hand and Body Lotion, and Black Mascara. A makeover service continues to grow, with over 8000 makeovers given in the United Kingdom during 1994.[16] Other nontraditional ways to reach new customers are continuously being developed, such as: seasonal shops, kiosks, and hospital gift shop and ferry shop displays.

Marketing strategy

The Body Shop marketing strategy is based on the premise that traditional marketing techniques are no longer successful with customers who are outhyped, overmarketed, and increasingly distrustful of corporate promises. The Body Shop focuses on building credibility with the understanding that customers want honest information given in a forthright manner. The company works to foster customer relationships by educating everyone who enters any one of its shops. It tells them all there is to know about every product: where it came from and what the ingredients are, as well as how the product was made and tested. Cards on every counter inform customers about ingredients and chronicle the century old history of some of the lotions. Leaflets offer tips about skin and hair care, pamphlets outline the company's view on animal testing and recycling efforts, and a manual of product information sits out on a counter for access by any customer interested in every one of the 1053 stores located worldwide. Some pamphlets even refer customers to their library for specific resources on a particular subject such as aromatherapy. The Body Shop does all this with a touch of humor, anecdotes, and bright graphics. Some stores even offer documentary videos played on televisions at low volumes discussing the product and the indigenous people from which the product originated or giving updated facts relative to a current social campaign.

In addition to offering information about what the Body Shop does do in making its products, it also provides brochures to explain what it doesn't do. It does not sell products with ingredients that have been tested on animals within the past five years. Nor does The Body Shop commission suppliers or outside testing organizations to test on animals. Rather, The Body Shop looks for innovative ways to test on humans. The Body Shop takes a basic customer concern such as cruel treatment of animals, and turns it into a powerful means of differentiating its products. Safety is closely tied to product development. The Body Shop develops its products from naturally based, biodegradable ingredients or from ingredients that have been used by human beings for decades, even centuries. However, when reviewing the ingredients carefully, it becomes apparent that polymers, alcohol, and other synthetic but non-hazardous chemicals are used in many of the products. Information about ingredients is used to further differentiate its products; the label on Rhassoul Mud Shampoo notes that it is made from "a traditional Moroccan Mud from the Atlas Mountains . . . which has astringent and toning properties."

In order to find such ingredients, Anita travels around the world and visits remote Third World countries, talking with native people about their methods of hair and skin care and all the while observing and respecting their customs. Her trips also produce the information used to educate customers. The Body Shop is marketing education, an approach that has always been extremely effective for the company, particularly since natural products cannot be patented. The strategy clearly differentiates the company from its major competitors and creates significant difficulties for potential copycats, who can't easily duplicate the type of information that only The Body Shop offers. Even if competitors provided the ingredient and manufacturing information as the Body Shop does, no competitor can duplicate the knowledge that Ms Roddick has acquired in all her travels. The understanding that a purchase is genuinely enhancing someone else's life creates excitement among customers, who actively promote the products to their friends, thereby fueling growth.

In 1994, The Body Shop authored and published a book entitled *The Body Shop Book on Skin, Hair, and Body Care*, providing recommendations for good health for men and women. The book is available only through The Body Shop franchises and Barnes and Noble bookstores. This is the second book to be published by Ms Roddick, the first being her autobiography, *Body and Soul*, published in 1993. The Body Shop Book provides readers with cultural information and photographs mixed with skin care guides, stories such as "The history of the shave," do-it-yourself facials and body massages, and factual tidbits such as the rhinoceros horn consisting of a dense tuft of hair. Clear photographs contrast with impressionistic illustrations in bright, sunny colors.

Prior to 1994, The Body Shop did not have an established marketing function; rather, it relied upon word of mouth promotion and the news media which are drawn to Anita Roddick's bold and unconventional approach to business. With the exception of the American Express commercial, the company has avoided advertising altogether. Even so, the Body Shop is considered an aggressive marketer. It promotes itself through good public relations, a highly trained staff, its unusual products, and an explicitly pronounced set of values. Two public relations firms, one in London and one in New York, are employed to make sure Ms Roddick keeps a high profile, giving The Body Shop access to approximately $3.5 million each year in free publicity from various appearances and articles written.[17] In 1990, a CBS film crew followed Anita's every move during a trip made to the USA, granting invaluable publicity and generating a great amount of public interest.

Franchisees act as surrogate marketers to local communities throughout the world. Store managers and salespeople are well versed on all of the store products. Dressed in The Body Shop T-shirts designed for the current campaign, they advise customers on which products are appropriate for them, inform customers on a social agenda as it relates to the product, and are knowledgeable about the history of the product and the roles of the natural ingredients. Once customers learn the details about specific product applications and are made aware of product history including the TRADE NOT AID program, they become more interested in the products. Customers also understand that their purchases support one of many good causes, and as a result, are more likely to buy.

Creating brand awareness

The Body Shop creates customer loyalty by making people feel good about buying Body Shop products because they can feel connected to a company that promotes social consciousness and environmental responsibility as a business in the 1990s. The Body Shop customers are buying principles as much as they are buying hair and skin care products. The Body Shop's agenda is much greater than just selling cosmetics, it embraces a philosophy of individual awareness, corporate responsibility, and social activism.

Before even entering a Body Shop store, customers are barraged with posters which adorn the storefront windows supporting a designated cause such as save the whales, fight for human rights, or protect endangered species. A 1994 campaign to protect endangered species had posters printed in black, white, and red that read: "The top three illegally traded goods in the world: drugs, guns, endangered species." Once inside the bright green shops, reflective of the original Body Shop in Brighton, customers are greeted by friendly sales people and rows of clear, plastic bottles with black caps and green labels in various sizes. Slogans and messages are scattered throughout the bottles of Blue Corn Cleansing Cream and Peppermint Foot Lotion where customers are sure to spot them. The stores are designed to be self-service. Should a customer want more information than that found in the folded cards, pamphlets, or the Product Information Manual, the customer must ask for help as sales people are strictly trained to not be pushy or overbearing. Often customers will stop by a store just to make conversation, connect with issues in the community, or see what the Body Shop is up to without making a purchase.

In the USA, stores have been used as voter registration centers and signed up 50,000 new voters. In Harlem, a store was opened which channels 50 percent of its profits back into the community. The Body Shop sponsored a "Have a Heart" campaign which urged Congress to spend less on defense to protect Europe and more money on caring for the elderly and the sick, fighting unemployment, and helping the homeless. Because 90 percent of The Body Shop customers are women, the company sponsored a campaign on AIDS education in 1993, as women are the fastest growing portion of the population to be infected with the HIV virus. Money from the sales of condoms was donated to AIDS charities.[18]

The Body Shop takes every opportunity to send a message that business can be for social change. Trucks are employed as billboards advocating individual involvement, with slogans such as "If you think you're too small to have an impact, try going to bed with a mosquito" or "The Indians are the custodians of the rain forest. The rain forests are the lungs of the world. If they die, we all die. The Body Shop says immediate, urgent action is needed."[19] Customers are encouraged to write letters supporting Amnesty International. T-shirts are sold in stores for each of the social and environmental campaigns. Proceeds in the amount of $1.00 per T-shirt sold are donated to The Body Shop Charitable Foundation, and $2.00 per specially designed T-shirts sold are contributed to the current campaign.

In 1993, The Body Shop contracted with Warner Brothers Records to compile a 16-track compact disc featuring environmentally active artists to be played in The Body Shop stores throughout the USA. More recently, it contracted with the musical groups 10,000 Maniacs and The Judybats for promotional purposes. The 10,000 Maniacs CD was made available in The Body Shop mail order catalog. The CD cover was packaged in handmade paper from Nepal bought through the TRADE NOT AID program. Among some of the most focal advocates of The Body Shop and its principles are Princess Diana and Sting. The Body Shop has become almost a way of life to its band of supporters.

Home shopping

The Body Shop entered the home shopping business in 1992 with the introduction of its mail order catalog. The catalog is characterized by its excellence in design, easy to scan copy, integrity, and attention to detail. The catalog combines good humor, hints for healthy skin and hair, and bold colored photographs giving it an entertainment value in addition to its product descriptions. The company charter is printed in the catalog so that customers who do not visit the shops will know what the business is all about. Throughout the catalog, customers find the familiar use of slogans. There is significant duplication between the catalog and the product line represented in the franchises. The catalog is made from uncoated recycled paper with edible and biodegradable soy ink, and is published only two times per year to reduce an intense use of paper. Before each mailing, the lists are purged of customers who request to be taken off the mailing list. Catalogs are only mailed to those customers requesting them, and The Body Shop asks that customers pass the catalogs on to friends when finished in order to prolong its useability and further ensure paper conservation.

Production/Operations

The Body Shop produces shampoos, conditioners, lotions, moisturizers, gels, and bubble bath products in its own Watersmead production facilities. The products come in simple plastic bottles or tubes and are offered in several different sizes. Each bottle is recyclable and refillable and can be taken back to any one of its stores for a $0.25 discount on the next purchase.

The Body Shop utilizes the most up-to-date production and supply facilities. Ten high-speed lines, capable of filling 215 bottles per minute, fill nearly one million bottles each week. Bottle filling is precisely scheduled, based on product and size needs. Each of the ten lines is almost identical, varying only in the type of filler. Although The Body Shop makes use of contract formulators and packers, it manufactures and fills most bottled liquids in-house. Approximately sixteen 24-ton batches are produced each day. Each batch is transferred from the mixer to 1000 liter, sturdy bags and later to primary packaging lines for shipping. These products account for only 35 percent of the company's product range but 70 percent of its total volume.[20] The company also blows and injection molds its own bottles and caps. Products manufactured elsewhere are shipped to The Body Shop Watersmead site, which is the central dispatch point for its worldwide distribution.

Products are formulated under extremely strict sanitary standards. No one is allowed to touch raw materials, fill products, or release packages until they have been cleared by the quality control department. Quality is a primary concern from the moment a product is conceived, not only in terms of the ingredients, but also the sourcing of these ingredients. The Body Shop boasts of its clean record in this area and has not had a customer complaint to date.

The Body Shop runs its manufacturing and retail firm with "planet friendly" practices. Public tours are given of the company's state-of-the-art environmentally conscious production factory, warehouse, and lab at its large Littlehampton, West Sussex, headquarters. Sensors automatically turn lights on and off, a windmill generates electrical power, and a waste water treatment plant is based in a traditional Sussex barn. Due to the company's rapid growth, in 1989 a new 200,000 square foot warehouse was opened in Watersmead. The new warehouse provides seven times the capacity of the old warehouse and allows for more frequent and efficient distribution to the stores. As a result, The Body Shop now has the ability to manufacture most of its products. This allows for greater control over the product mix and should prove instrumental in introducing new products. It also puts the company in a better position to satisfy growing international demand. However, the expansion of production and warehouse capacity has made it necessary to invest £10 million in upgrading the company's computer and management systems.[21]

The Body Shop develops products that are basic enough to be sold around the world as well as products that are geared to a specific market. This two-part focus allows the company to satisfy the needs of an international market and gain economies of scale by keeping its production costs low. This saving, coupled with its own packaging capabilities, helps The Body Shop price its products more competitively. The company's product development team is primarily responsible for evaluating opportunities in the marketplace. In addition, the team carries out research and development, technical evaluation and testing of new products, and redesigns and reformulates as needed. The technology used is often able to reinforce skin and hair rituals that humans have been practicing for centuries.

Cleaning up the Environment

The 1990s brought about a heightened awareness of the need to protect the environment. This "green direction" has many companies examining their processes to determine how they can eliminate waste and thus foster a cleaner and healthier environment. "If you are into manufacturing, then you are into producing more and more . . . all I do is clean up my own mess," says Anita Roddick.[22] Cleaning up is a key operation for The Body Shop. Its internal efforts to save the environment include eliminating unnecessary packaging for its products and using recycled paper for everything from stationery to toilet tissue.

The Body Shop outlets recycle packaging wastes, too. Along with the company's policy on refilling bottled products, customers can bring back any kind of Body Shop packaging and they will recycle it. Every customer that comes into one of the stores is made aware of this recycling service. Pamphlets scattered throughout the store give detailed information on The Body Shop's recycling efforts and a bin is provided in each store to collect the recyclable items. In 1994, the company introduced a refill discount card which offers the customer a free 60 ml product (from a limited selection) for every six refills. This offer is in addition to the usual discount for refills. Since 1992, some 73 percent of The Body Shop's core products now use recyclable packaging and 13 percent carry no packaging at all[23] in an industry known for huge amounts of wastes.

Corporate Culture/Human Resources

On the lobby walls of corporate headquarters are the messages: reinvent, reach, risk, refuse, resist, and reuse. Posters in the store cafeterias urge employees to "Break the rules" or "Think frivolously."[24]

Although The Body Shop offers the traditional company benefits, it realizes that it takes more than money to keep its employees motivated. People want work that will make a difference. The employees of The Body Shop believe that their small part contributes to the whole. As a result, there is a deep commitment to the company on the part of the employees and franchisees. The education, encouragement, and support given by the company generate a special kind of energy; one that doesn't come from sales or commissions but from empowerment. This empowerment promotes employee responsibility and creates excitement that is shared by the entire Body Shop team.

The company allows and encourages employees to spend a half day a month volunteering in some capacity for which they are compensated. In addition, after five years Body Shop International employees are allowed a six-month sabbatical. Many use the time to travel to Eastern Europe and volunteer to renovate orphanages in Romania and Albania.

The Body Shop franchises

There is a waiting list of 5000 people in England alone desiring a Body Shop franchise. Before a franchise is granted, each candidate is given a personality test to determine how well the candidate's personality fits in with the existing culture of The Body Shop. A key requirement is that candidates share Ms Roddick's concern for environmental issues. She wants franchisees who are politically aware and who want a livelihood that is led by values. In addition, she has the candidate work in one of The Body Shop stores where existing staff can evaluate how well the candidate would fit in. The candidate must then go through extensive interviews with Anita Roddick and other top executives at corporate headquarters.

Although most of The Body Shop stores are franchises and have some freedom in how the stores are run, corporate headquarters maintains tight control over store esthetics and the image it conveys. The majority of window display posters are designed and written at headquarters. Headquarters also controls store layouts and merchandising techniques, such as the way gift baskets are put together. Body Shop pamphlets and leaflets for products and causes are written by the Write Stuff department, consisting of five in-house writers and six staff graphic designers. This tight focus on details is important because Ms Roddick relies on national ad campaigns to build and maintain her company's image. As a result, storefronts and displays must be consistent and striking. She cannot afford to have her message diluted or confused by individual franchisees who execute a poor window display or use an unsophisticated store layout.

Training and development

All franchisees are thoroughly trained in London or one of the area development offices where they learn details of each product and the dos and don'ts of merchandising and running the stores. They learn where the products may have originated, what role each natural ingredient plays in cleansing and moisturizing as well as The Body Shop's social agenda as it relates to the product. Very little emphasis is placed on making money or selling. Instead, the company trains for knowledge. Ms Roddick keeps in close touch with franchisees through monthly videos and magazine mailings that contain company news, tips on window display techniques, and information on the company's latest social activities. The videos often highlight trips Ms Roddick has taken to find new ingredients and serve to motivate employees. She lets them know that she understands there is more to life than just selling a product.

Financial Outlook

Gordon Roddick is responsible for the financial management for the company. In 1994, The Body Shop was reviewing its operations in order to better position the company for long-term growth. Management planned to reduce operating

Exhibit 11.2   Body Shop expansion between February 28, 1993 and November 11, 1993

Australia	8 shops	Italy	6 shops
Austria	2 shops	Japan	2 shops
Belgium	2 shops	Malaysia	Net 1 shop
Canada	5 shops	New Zealand	2 shops
Denmark	1 shop	Norway	1 shop
France	7 shops	Saudi Arabia	2 shops
Germany	5 shops	Spain	4 shops
Greece	1 shop	Sweden	2 shops
Holland	5 shops	Switzerland	1 shop
Hong Kong	1 shop	United States	44 shops
Iceland	1 shop		

Total expansion: 103 shops in under eight months

Source: The Body Shop 1994 Annual Report and Accounts.

costs and capital expenditures, and consolidate the product line following a $30 million expansion program in 1993 (see exhibit 11.2). During 1993 pretax profits dropped by 15 percent despite a 14 percent increase in sales. Roddick planned to continue opening overseas stores beyond 1994, and increase the company's US manufacturing operations.

By October 1994, the implementation of this strategy, emphasizing expansion of overseas business, led to an increase of 20 percent in pretax profits over the same period in 1993.[25] The pretax profits reached $15 million, and were well ahead of projections for a 9–10 percent increase. Four new Body Shops were added in the United Kingdom during this period. Most analysts were happy with the interim results, but were critical of the company opening so many stores in one city. The new stores take 4 percent of sales away from other stores.[26]

The 1994 financial results turned around the negative trend of the early 1990s. Growth was achieved through the opening of 153 new stores in addition to existing shop sales increases. Worldwide total retail sales increased by 4 percent, up from a negative 6 percent the prior year, with the most significant growth occurring in the USA, up by 47 percent. Total international retail sales outside of the USA grew as follows: 38 percent in Asia of which Japan was the largest contributor, 24 percent in Europe, 16 percent in Australia and New Zealand, and 4 percent in North and South America (excluding the USA).[27] Principal growth in the short to medium term is expected to come from the USA, Japan, and Europe.

The Body Shop's fiscal year extends from February 28 of the year prior to February 28 of the current year. Pretax profits totaled $44.6 million (£29.7 million), up 16 percent from 1993, while operating expenses for 1994 rose over 15 percent. Average staff increased to 2456, up 16 percent due to hiring employees for the USA based operations. Earnings per share increased 39 percent to 15.5 cents (10.3p), and the net dividend was up 18 percent. The 1994 market value of

Exhibit 11.3   The Body Shop International: consolidated balance sheet as of February 28, 1994

	1994	1993	1992	1991	1990	1989
			In millions of pounds (£)			
Assets:						
Current assets	96.7	82.9	75.0	60.7	39.9	24.8
Fixed assets	71.6	70.0	58.6	45.6	31.4	15.6
Total assets	168.3	152.9	133.6	106.3	71.3	40.4
Liabilities:						
Current liabilities	35.6	31.2	54.1	36.1	38.4	16.2
Long-term debt	35.8	39.5	5.4	5.0	6.9	0.8
Total liabilities	71.4	70.7	59.5	41.1	45.3	17.0
Shareholders' equity	96.9	82.2	74.1	65.2	26.0	23.4

1994:   188,798,103 shares outstanding
1993:   187,267,908 shares outstanding

Source: The Body Shop 1994 Annual Report and Accounts.

Exhibit 11.4   The Body Shop International: consolidated profit and loss account for the year ended February 28, 1994 (millions of pounds except earnings per share data)

	1994	1993	1992	1991	1990	1989
Revenues	195.4	168.3	147.4	115.6	84.5	73.0
Profit before taxes	29.7	21.5	25.2	20.0	14.5	15.2
Less taxes	(10.1)	(7.6)	(8.3)	(7.3)	(5.5)	(6.3)
Net profit	19.4	13.8	16.4	12.1	8.5	8.5
(after deduction of minority interest)						
Dividends paid	3.8	3.2	3.0	2.3	1.6	1.4
Retained earnings	15.6	10.6	13.4	9.8	6.9	7.1
EPS	10.3p	7.4p	8.8p	6.7p	5.0p	5.1p

Source: The Body Shop 1994 Annual Report and Accounts.

the company was approximately $578 million (£385 million).[28] Financial statements for the years 1989 through 1994 are given in exhibits 11.3, 11.4, and 11.5.

The tour of The Body Shop manufacturing plant located in Watersmead is becoming more recognized by tour operators and continuing to attract an increasing number of international visitors, resulting in additional revenues. The Body Shop allows tours of the public with special group tours for students, journalists, corporate representatives, and special needs groups. The tour averages 250–300 people per day and attracts over 64,000 people each year.[29]

Exhibit 11.5   The Body Shop International: segment revenues and operating profit, February 28, 1994

	Revenues in millions of pounds (£)		Operating profit in millions of pounds (£)	
	1994	1993	1994	1993
United Kingdom	91.1	83.5	11.4	11.2
United States	50.4	37.8	6.2	2.1
Europe	30.9	28.2	5.9	5.7
Americas (excluding USA)	8.6	8.7	2.4	2.4
Australia and New Zealand	6.3	4.2	1.8	1.1
Asia	8.1	5.9	2.4	1.8
	195.4	168.3	30.1	24.3
Net interest			(1.5)	(2.8)
Profit on disposal of subsidiary				
Undertaking			1.1	0.0
Profit before tax			29.7	21.5

Source: The Body Shop 1994 Annual Report and Accounts.

Most recently, Anita and Gordon Roddick sold 2 percent of their total equity in The Body Shop to finance two charitable projects: the Healthcare Foundation, founded in 1987, and a television series called *Millennium*, which documents the lives of tribal people. A total of 3.5 million shares were sold, raising an amount of $13 million.[30]

Corporate Strategy

The Body Shop is structured as a "group" of subsidiaries divided along retail and operations lines as illustrated in exhibit 11.6. The Body Shop International plc oversees all of the subsidiary efforts: reviews and directs the R&D efforts, human resources, and communications, conducts quality improvement programs for operations, determines campaigns and designs posters and associated T-shirts, etc., establishes franchise design standards, and controls the franchising network. The company is decentralized in its structure only to the extent that international business is operated through head franchises who coordinate with the UK head-quarters, and offer the benefit of local expertise to their market. The head fran-chises operate all local company stores and subfranchise. The head franchises are responsible for the proper development of the domestic franchise network, includ-ing receiving, warehousing and distributing products, and selecting and manag-ing retail stores with final control over site locations, franchisees, and products sold in each shop. All retailers must conform to stringent guidelines established in order to maintain consistency in Body Shops throughout the world.

The Body Shop's corporate strategy has focused on high growth by means of

Exhibit 11.6   The Body Shop International: group structure as of November 1993

The Body Shop International plc
Exercises control of the group and provides
services including product development,
environmental, legal, design and corporate
communication functions

Retail subsidiaries	*Operating subsidiaries*	*Other subsidiaries*
The Body Shop Worldwide Ltd Responsible for all retail activities outside the UK and USA	The Body Shop Supply Company Ltd Manufactures bottle products and controls distribution to all retail outlets	Jacaranda Productions Ltd (80 percent owned) Video production for the Group and third parties
The Body Shop UK Retail Company Ltd Responsible for all UK retail activities	Cos-tec Ltd Manufactures color cosmetic, skin care and toiletry products including "Animals in Danger"	
The Body Shop Inc. (90 percent owned) Responsible for all US retail activities	Soapworks Ltd Manufactures soap products	
The Body Shop (Singapore) Pte Ltd Responsible for all retail activities in Singapore	Colourings Ltd Controls marketing of color cosmetic products	
The Body Shop Norway A/S Responsible for company shops in Norway		

Source: The Body Shop 1994 Annual Report and Accounts.

international expansion primarily through its franchising efforts. As of 1994, the
company had stores in countries as diverse as Argentina and the Arab Emirates;
239 stores are located in the United Kingdom alone. Of these 239 stores, 38 are
company owned, 21 are partnerships, and the remaining stores are franchises.[31]
Total company stores are located as follows: USA with 51 stores, UK with 38 stores,
Singapore with nine stores, and Norway with two company stores.[32] Anita Roddick,
as Managing Director, does not actually run the company. Gordon Roddick, as
Chairman, decides when and how The Body Shop can take advantage of growth
opportunities. This paired management strategy allows Anita Roddick to spend
the majority of her time generating publicity for The Body Shop, planning and
executing campaigns to promote social causes, and traveling the world looking for

new ingredients for products while avoiding the problems and stresses associated with unplanned growth.

With the United Kingdom nearly saturated, the Body Shop goal is to be represented throughout the world in the next decade. A new Body Shop opens every 2.5 days.[33] Gordon Roddick considers the company to be underrepresented in Germany, with only 39 stores, and also in Japan, with 17 stores there. France, Canada, Germany, and Japan are projected by Gordon Roddick to have the potential to support close to 200 stores each. The company's goal in the USA is to have 500 new stores by the end of the decade, expanding at a rate of 50 per year. Gordon Roddick estimates that 3000 stores globally will be the limit, and expects that The Body Shop's value will reach $1 billion in the next three years. "In five years time, we ought to be the best known international retailer with 3 main areas of strength – the USA, Europe, and the East."[34]

The Body Shop's corporate philosophy embraces environmental awareness, and applies it in all areas of business and functional strategies. When public skepticism of the company's testing and environmental policies reached a peak in 1992, The Body Shop put its own environmental audit into place. The audit complies with European Union Eco-Management and Audit Regulation, and evaluates every aspect of company operations, from waste management to energy efficiency. Three audits have been completed to date. The audit, entitled the Green Book, is independently verified and issued with the company's financial statements for the purpose of confirming to itself and its customers that The Body Shop truly practices what it preaches. An Environmental Projects department now exists to monitor the company's continual compliance with its principles. During 1994, a Social Performance Audit was implemented to examine involvement in community projects, corporate giving, testing procedures, TRADE NOT AID projects, and human resources issues. The company has recently announced plans to implement independent environmental reporting to be performed by Cos-tec at Wick and The Body Shop Inc. in North Carolina.

In an effort to be known as the leader for innovation in naturally based hair, skin and cosmetic products, The Body Shop views itself as a business that is not simply a creator of profits for its shareholders, but one that values an ability to make a difference to people and the world. The company takes a non-exploitative approach to generating its business, looking to minimize its own impact on the environment. Whereas most companies would put the shareholders' interests first, Anita Roddick openly declares that following her social conscience comes before any responsibility to shareholders. She refuses to be driven by whether the company's stock goes up or down or the bottom line, but by her values and those of top management, reflecting a "basic human understanding that business [is] an adjunct to life not a war to win at all costs, or a game to be played without severe consequences."[35] The Body Shop's long-term corporate goal is to become an "environmentally sustainable business."[36]

The Body Shop aims to integrate its business with its community and to support causes in the world at large. Causes that matter a great deal to the company include human and civil rights, the environment, protection of other species, and bringing an end to animal testing for non-medical purposes. Campaigns to promote education on these topics are carefully selected after intense factual research and are deliberately planned and executed. Twice per year, Body Shops are turned into "arenas of education" for causes to create publicity and excitement within local communities, ultimately leading to an increase in sales. The Body Shop actively participates in the campaigns, and will not promote a particular cause if all the facts are not known or there is any chance that it will come back to haunt the company. The Body Shop employees worldwide support over 600 projects.

TRADE NOT AID

The Body Shop launched its TRADE NOT AID program in 1987. It is a program set up for direct sourcing from producers. The purpose of the program is to help people in less fortunate countries develop a trade that will help them become self-sufficient. The company then buys many of these products at fair market prices, to be sold in The Body Shop stores. In Nepal, old paper making processes are used that have been adapted to employ people in economically depressed areas. The result is specially crafted writing paper, wrapping paper, and gift bags that are sold around the world. Other projects under this program include employing orphan boys in India and buying oil made from nuts harvested by the rain forest Kayopo tribe to make hair conditioner. Some examples of other projects are shown in exhibit 11.7.

Unlike traditional aid programs, which foster a dependence on charity, The Body Shop prefers to develop long-term trading relationships built on mutual benefit and trust. All TRADE NOT AID projects are carefully developed to ensure that they are sustainable and that they do not exploit an underprivileged community or cause environmental degradation. In addition, trading arrangements must be ethical and fair. Currently, direct sourcing represents a small percentage of the company's trade; however, efforts are being made to increase this practice wherever possible. Furthermore, the company is in the process of developing new projects in the United States.

Expansion into the United States

The Body Shop opened its first store in Manhattan on July 1, 1988. Over eight million customer transactions were recorded during the year of 1993 in the USA alone.[37] With 201 stores operational during the first half of the fiscal 1994 year, US sales grew by 47 percent to $44.6 million.[38] When first moving into the USA, Ms Roddick decided to own stores instead of immediately franchising. This was done in order to adjust to a new market where retail space is predominantly located in malls. Industry analysts have criticized this strategy as giving the competition time to catch up and develop their own images and marketing approaches.

The difference in operating environments is significant, however. Americans are used to shopping in malls, while The Body Shops have always been storefronts on local streets closely connected to the community. American competitors are much more likely to imitate the uniqueness of The Body Shop than anywhere else

Exhibit 11.7 TRADE NOT AID projects

SAMPLE PROJECTS

Brazil: The Body Shop has established a trading arrangement with the Kayopo Indians in the Eastern Amazon Basin on an invitation from the Indians themselves. The Kayopo produce Brazil nut oil from nuts harvested in the rain forest (used to make hair conditioner) and traditional beaded bracelets.

India: The Body Shop helped establish wood turning workshops in Tamil Nadu which produce the wooden foot massage rollers sold in many Body Shop stores. This helps the women to support themselves when their partners must leve the villages to find work in towns and cities.

Mexico: Five cooperatives employing some 350 Nanhu Indians produce plant fiber body scrub mitts sold in Body Shop stores. The company pays a premium into a community action fund which provides health care, education, and improved working conditions.

New Mexico: The Body Shop buys blue corn from the Santa Ana Pueblo Indians. This corn provides the basis for their Blue Corn line of face and body care products. The Santa Ana Tribal government reinvests the money into other agricultural businesses run by the tribe on their reservation.

Nepal: The Body Shop buys a range of handmade paper products in a village in the Katmandu Valley. This helps provide over 60 jobs for local people. The paper, which contains recycled organic materials, is made using skills which date from the eleventh century.

Solomon Islands: The Solomon, or ngali nut yields an oil which is used in The Body Shop's Self Tan Lotion.

Tanzania/Zambia: The organic honey used in Honey Stick is purchased from cooperatives in Tanzania and Zambia. The honey is harvested from traditional bark beehives hung throughout the forests that border these two countries.

LOCAL PROJECTS

The Candle Project: The Body Shop buys beeswax candles handmade by members of a self-help housing organization in New York City. Eleven homeless people are involved in this project; they use the money earned to support themselves while working towards purchasing and renovating abandoned tenement apartments which will become their homes.

Tico Enterprises: This Baltimore-based profit-making enterprise employs youth at risk to make products from recycled materials. Tico Enterprises supplies The Body Shop with its popular Soap Saver soap dishes, made from recycled pallets. Profits go into new business development and expansion, which permits the hiring of other youth at risk.

The Body Shop is investigating projects with communities in Ghana, Nicaragua, Russia, and Bangladesh.

Source: The Body Shop, Trade Not Aid broachure.

in the world. The company formed a Marketing Department for the first time in its history. The Marketing Department is expected to deal with the challenges of growing competition and focus on increasing US market share and building brand awareness as well as maintaining market share globally.

In some US markets, The Body Shop must also combat perceptions that it is in the business of exercise, such as a health center or gymnasium, or in the business of automotive repair, as there are companies with similar names incorporated and scattered throughout the USA. Ms Roddick is considering documercials in order to educate customers on the TRADE NOT AID program and still insists that The Body Shop will not advertise its products. Critics suggest that it will be difficult to cultivate awareness in the USA without media advertising and do not think that the non-traditional ways of marketing via publicity in the press will be as successful as it was in Europe. Once awareness is cultivated, the Roddicks feel that The Body Shop have a strategy in place that will sustain the business.

Regulations in the USA add about 5 percent to the costs of doing business. In addition there are compliance costs, up front costs, and time required to start a business. Franchise agreements and sales taxes differ from state to state, and legal issues such as zoning requirements also seem to bog down the development process. Franchisees must invest a $40,000 flat fee and an additional $250,000 to get the store stocked and running. In 1990, when The Body Shop began to accept applications for franchises in the USA, more than 2000 were received. US lawyers have cautioned The Body Shop that the liability associated with the recycling of containers is too great and that the company may lose its insurance. In 1990, Roddick proceeded with the recycling program anyway, including in-store supply of refills.

In mid-1993, The Body Shop completed its $1.3 million headquarters renovation of an abandoned fire extinguisher factory in Wake Forest, North Carolina, for the purpose of overseeing the aggressive expansion plans in the US market. The 40 acre site consists of 140,000 square feet of facilities for bottling, distribution, and office functions, including marketing.[39] Much of the furniture used at this site was made from The Body Shop's recycled plastic. There are over 150 employees located at the headquarters. The Body Shop also has a regional distribution center and its mail order business in New Jersey. Three other regional distribution centers are located in the USA: California, New York and Florida.

Competition in the USA

The Body Shop was one of the first companies to offer naturally based products. Since then, selling products made with natural ingredients has grown in popularity in the cosmetic industry. Consumers' increased awareness of and interest in environmental matters is becoming a part of life, as evidenced by community recycling programs. As a result, many companies are taking the environmental friendly approach to attract business and ultimately boost their bottom lines through the efforts of reducing waste and minimizing packaging.

The Body Shop's success in selling natural products has inspired many competitors to do the same. Companies like H2O Plus, Goodebodies, The Limited, Inc.'s Bath & Body Works, Estee Lauder's Origins, and Garden Botanika have developed their own naturally based products sold in plain bottles that are offered at prices competitive with or below The Body Shop prices. Even local drugstores have come up with their own generic naturally based products. Like The Body Shop, some competitors also emphasize non-animal testing and well being versus beauty, and donate money to various charities.

Anita Roddick sued Bath & Body Works when it started to look too much like The Body Shop in its display and use of colors. A Body Shop employee walked into a Bath & Body Works store to see one of The Body Shop's familiar slogans on the wall: "Stop the burning." Bath & Body Works claimed the slogan referred to sunburn rather than the rain forests and Ms Roddick felt this would lead to customer confusion. In addition, customers were bringing Bath & Body Works bottles into The Body Shop franchises for refills. Bath & Body Works eventually settled out of court with The Body Shop and agreed to distinguish themselves from The Body Shop and emphasize a country image using less of the color green.

Anita Roddick readily admits that this type of copycat competition was a surprise for her. Competition in Europe was not nearly as fierce. Companies there adopt a "live and let live" strategy. Ms Roddick believes that although the US market brings new challenges for The Body Shop, the key to success is to concentrate on its own business rather than on that of its competitors. A sign on her office door reflects the company's attitude towards competition: Department of The Future. "You can copy our past, but you can't copy our future," says franchisee Helen Mills, "No one can copy Anita's mind."[40]

NOTES AND REFERENCES

1 *Working Woman*, Feb. 1994, p. 95.

2 The Body Shop, 1994, Press release.

3 *Stores*, May 1991, p. 61.

4 *Stores*, May 1991, p. 61.

5 *Time*, Jan. 25, 1993, p. 54.

6 *Working Woman*, Feb. 1994, p. 30.

7 The Body Shop, 1994, Annual Report and Accounts.

8 The Body Shop, 1994, Press release.

9 *Working Woman*, Feb. 1994, p. 68.

10 *Time*, Jan. 25, 1993, p. 54.

11 *Time*, Jan. 25, 1993, p. 54.

12 *Inc.*, Jun. 1990, p. 37.

13 *Inc.*, Jun. 1990, p. 37.

14 *Stores*, May 1991, p. 61.

15 The Body Shop, 1994, Press release.

16 The Body Shop, 1994, Annual Report and Accounts.

17 *Working Woman*, Oct. 1990, p. 82.

18 *The New York Times*, Sept. 28, 1993, p. D4.

19 *Inc.*, Jun. 1990, p. 41.

20 *Packaging Digest*, March 1990, p. 78.

21 *Packaging Digest*, March 1990, p. 78.

22 *Working Woman*, Feb. 1994, p. 69.

23 The Body Shop, 1994, Annual Report and Accounts, p. 12.

24 *US News and World Report*, Dec. 12, 1988, p. 70.

25 *Working Woman*, Feb. 1994, p. 31.

26 *Working Woman*, Feb. 1994, p. 31.

27 The Body Shop, 1994, Annual Report and Accounts.

28 The Body Shop, 1994, Press release.

29 The Body Shop, 1994, Annual Report and Accounts.

30 *The New York Times*, Jul. 11, 1994, p. D7.

31 The Body Shop, 1994, Annual Report and Accounts.

32 The Body Shop, 1994, Annual Report and Accounts.

33 *Time*, Jan. 25, 1993, p. 52.

34 The Body Shop, 1994, Annual Report and Accounts.

35 *Business Quarterly*, Fall 1993, p. 16.

36 The Body Shop, 1994, Annual Report and Accounts.

37 The Body Shop 1994, Press release.

38 The Body Shop 1994, Annual Report and Accounts.

39 The Body Shop, 1994, Press release.

40 *Working Woman*, Feb. 1994, p. 73.

IKEA (Canada) Ltd (Condensed)

Paul W. Beamish and Peter Killing

Founded as a mail order business in rural Sweden in 1943, IKEA had grown to more than $1 billion (US) in sales and 70 retail outlets by 1985, and was considered by many to be one of the best-run furniture operations in the world. Although only 14 percent of IKEA's sales were outside Europe, the company's fastest growth was occurring in North America.

Success, however, brought imitators. In mid-1986, Bjorn Bayley and Anders Berglund, the senior managers of IKEA's North American operations, were examining a just-published Sears Canada catalogue, which contained a new 20-page section called "Elements." This section bore a striking resemblance to the format of an IKEA Canada catalogue and the furniture being offered was similar to IKEA's knocked-down, self-assembled line in which different "elements" could be ordered by the customer to create particular designs. Bayley and Berglund wondered how serious Sears was about its new initiative, and what, if anything, IKEA should do in response.

The Canadian Furniture Market

Canadian consumption of furniture totalled more than $2 billion in 1985, an average of well over $600 per household. Imports accounted for approximately 18 percent of this total, half of which originated in the United States. The duties on furniture imported into Canada were approximately 15 percent.

Furniture was sold to Canadian consumers through three types of stores: independents, speciality chains and department stores. Although the independents held a 70 percent market share, this figure was declining due to their inability to compete with the chains in terms of advertising, purchasing power, management sophistication, and sales support. The average sales per square metre in 1985 for furniture stores of all three types was $1666 (the figure was $2606 for stores which also sold appliances) and the average cost of goods sold was 64.5 percent.

While the major department stores such as Eaton's and Sears tended to carry traditional furniture lines close to the middle of the price/quality range, chains and independents operated from one end of the spectrum to the other. At the upper end of the market, specialty stores attempted to differentiate themselves by offering unique product lines, superior service and a specialized shopping atmosphere. The lower end of the market, on the other hand, was dominated by furniture warehouses which spent heavily on advertising, and offered lower price, less service, and less emphasis on a fancy image. The warehouses usually kept a larger inventory of furniture on hand than the department stores, but expected customers to pick up their purchases. Over half the warehouse sales involved promotional financing arrangements, including delayed payments, extended terms, and so on.

The major firms in this group – both of whom sold furniture and appliances – were The Brick and Leon's. The Brick had annual sales of $240 million from 15 Canadian stores, and was rapidly expanding from its western Canada base. With 30 additional stores in California under the Furnishings 2000 name, The Brick intended to become the largest furniture retailing company in the world. Leon's had annual sales of $160 million from 14 stores, and was growing rapidly from its Ontario base. These 14 stores were operated under a variety of names. Leon's also franchised its name in smaller cities in Canada. For part of their merchandise requirements, The Brick and Leon's often negotiated with manufacturers for exclusive products, styles and fabrics and imported from the USA, Europe, and the Far East. Although both firms had had problems earlier with entry to the US market, each intended to expand there.

Most furniture retailers in Canada purchased their products from Canadian manufacturers after examining new designs and models at trade shows. There were approximately 1400 Canadian furniture manufacturers, most of whom were located in Ontario and Quebec. Typically, these firms were small (78 percent of Canadian furniture plants employed fewer than 50 people), undercapitalized, and minimally automated. One industry executive quipped that one of the most significant technological developments for the industry had been the advent of the staple gun.

Canadian-produced furniture typically followed American and European styling, and was generally of adequate to excellent quality but was often more costly to produce. The reason for high Canadian costs was attributed to a combination of short manufacturing runs and high raw material, labor, and distribution costs. In an attempt to reduce costs, a few of the larger manufacturers such as Kroehler had vertically integrated – purchasing sawmills, fabric warehouses, fiberboard, and wood frame plants – but such practices were very much the exception in the industry.

The IKEA Formula

IKEA's approach to business was fundamentally different from that of the traditional Canadian retailers. The company focused exclusively on what it called "quick assembly" furniture, which consumers carried from the store in flat packages and assembled at home. This furniture was primarily pine, had a clean European-designed look to it, and was priced at 15 percent below the lowest prices for traditional furniture. Its major appeal appeared to be to young families, singles, and frequent movers, who were looking for well designed items that were economically priced and created instant impact.

According to company executives, IKEA was successful because of its revolutionary approach to the most important aspects of the business: product design, procurement, store operations, marketing, and management philosophy, which stressed flexibility and market orientation rather than long-range strategy. Each of these items is discussed in turn.

Product design

IKEA's European designers, not the company's suppliers, were responsible for the design of most of the furniture and accessories in IKEA's product line, which totalled 15,000 items. The heart of the company's design capability was a 50-person Swedish workshop which produced prototypes of new items of furniture and smaller components such as "an ingenious little snap lock for table legs which makes a table stronger and cheaper at the same time" and a "clever little screw attachment which allows for the assembly of a pin back chair in five minutes." IKEA's designers were very cost conscious, and were constantly working to lower costs in ways that were not critical to the consumer. The quality of a work top, for example, would be superior to that of the back of a bookshelf which would never be seen. "Low price with a meaning" was the theme.

Although it was not impossible to copyright a particular design or process, IKEA's philosophy was "if somebody steals a model from us we do not bring a lawsuit, because a lawsuit is always negative. We solve the problem by making a new model that is even better."

Procurement

IKEA's early success in Sweden had so threatened traditional European furniture retailers that they had promised to boycott any major supplier that shipped products to the upstart firm. As a result, IKEA had no choice but to go to the smaller suppliers. Since these suppliers had limited resources, IKEA began assuming responsibility for the purchase of raw materials, packaging materials, storage, specialized equipment and machinery, and engineering. What began as a necessity soon became a cornerstone of IKEA's competitive strategy, and by 1986 the firm had nearly 100 production engineers working as purchasers. Together with IKEA's designers, these engineers assisted suppliers in every way they could to help them lower costs, dealing with everything from the introduction of new technology to the alteration of the dimensions of a shipping carton.

Although IKEA sometimes leased equipment and made loans to its suppliers, the firm was adamant that it would not enter the furniture manufacturing business itself. In fact, to avoid control over – and responsibility for – its suppliers, the company had a policy of limiting its purchases to 50 percent of a supplier's capacity. Many products were obtained from multiple suppliers, and frequently suppliers produced only a single standardized component or input to the final product. Unfinished pine shelves, for example, were obtained directly from saw mills, cabinet doors were purchased from door factories, and cushions came from textile mills.

In total, IKEA purchased goods from 1500 suppliers located in 40 countries. About 52 percent of the company's purchases were from Scandinavia, 21 percent from other countries of Western Europe, 20 percent from Eastern Europe, and 7 percent elsewhere.

Store operations

IKEA stores were usually large one or two story buildings situated in relatively inexpensive standalone locations, neither in prime downtown sites nor as part of a shopping mall. Most stores were surrounded by a large parking lot, adorned with billboards explaining IKEA's delivery policy, product guarantee, and the existence of a coffee shop and/or restaurant.

On entering the store, the customer was immediately aware of the children's play area (a room filled with hollow multicolored balls), a video room for older children, and a receptionist with copies of IKEA catalogs, a metric conversion guide, index cards for detailing purchases, and a store guide. The latter, supplemented by prominent signs, indicated that the store contained lockers and benches for shoppers, a first-aid area, restrooms, strollers and a baby-care area, an "As-Is" department (no returns permitted), numerous checkouts, suggestion boxes and, in many cases, a restaurant. All major credit cards were accepted.

Traffic flow in most IKEA stores was guided in order to pass by almost all of the merchandise in the store, which was displayed as it would look in the home, complete with all accessories. Throughout the store, employees could be identified by their bright red IKEA shirts. Part-time employees wore yellow shirts which read "Temporary help – please don't ask me any hard questions." The use of sales floor staff was minimal. The IKEA view was that "salesmen are expensive, and can also be irritating. IKEA leaves you to shop in peace."

While IKEA stores were all characterized by their self-serve, self-wrapping, self-transport, and self-assembly operations, the company's philosophy was that each new store would incorporate the latest ideas in use in any of its existing stores. The most recent trend in some countries was an IKEA Contract Sales section, which provided a delivery, invoicing, and assembly service for commercial customers.

Marketing

IKEA's promotional activities were intended to educate the consumer public on the benefits of the IKEA concept and to build traffic by attracting new buyers and encouraging repeat visits from existing customers. The primary promotional vehicle was the annual IKEA catalog which was selectively mailed out to prime target customers, who in the Toronto area, for instance, had the following characteristics:

Income $35,000+
Owned condominium or townhouse
University degree
White collar
Primary age group 35–44
Secondary age group 25–34
Husband/wife both work
Two children
Movers

With minor variations, this "upscale" profile was typical of IKEA's target customers in Europe and North America. In Canada, IKEA management acknowledged the target market, but felt that, in fact, the IKEA concept appealed to a much wider group of consumers.

IKEA also spent heavily on magazine advertisements, which were noted for their humorous, slightly off-beat approach. In Canada, IKEA spent $2.5 million to print 3.6 million catalogs, $2 million on magazine advertising, and $1.5 million on other forms of promotion in 1984.

Management philosophy

The philosophy of Ingvar Kamprad, the founder of IKEA, was "to create a better everyday life for the majority of people." In practice, this creed meant that IKEA was dedicated to offering, and continuing to offer, the lowest prices possible on good quality furniture, so that IKEA products were available to as many people as possible. Fred Andersson, the head of IKEA's product range for the world, stated: "Unlike other companies, we are not fascinated with what we produce – we make what our customers want." Generally, IKEA management felt that no other company could match IKEA's combination of quality and price across the full width of the product line.

IKEA also made a concerted effort to stay "close to its customers," and it was not unusual for the General Manager of IKEA Canada, for instance, to personally telephone customers who had made complaints or suggestions. Each week an employee newsletter detailed all customer comments, and indicated how management felt they should be dealt with.

Another guiding philosophy of the firm was that growth would be in "small bites." The growth objective in Canada, for instance, had been to increase sales and profits by 20 percent per year, but care was given to sequence store openings so that managerial and financial resources would not be strained.

Internally, the company's philosophy was stated as "freedom, with responsibility," which meant that IKEA's managers typically operated with a good deal of

Exhibit 12.1   IKEA Canada sales by store (including mail order percentage)

	1981	1982	1983	1984	1985	1986 forecast	Mail order %
Vancouver	12,122	11,824	12,885	19,636	19,240	25,500	6.8
Calgary	7,379	8,550	7,420	7,848	9,220	11,500	8.6
Ottawa	5,730	6,914	8,352	9,015	10,119	12,500	1.8
Montreal			8,617	12,623	15,109	22,000[a]	2.2
Halifax	3,634	4,257	4,474	6,504	7,351	9,000	22.9
Toronto	11,231	13,191	16,249	18,318	22,673	30,500	1.8
Edmonton	6,506	7,474	8,075	8,743	9,986	16,000	15.4
Quebec City		5,057	8,284	9,027	10,037	12,000	6.1
Victoria					2,808	3,500	–
Total	46,602	57,356	74,176	91,714	106,543	142,500	6.7

Mail order: 1984 most recent data available.

[a]   Projected growth due to store size expansion.

autonomy. The Canadian operation, for instance, received little in the way of explicit suggestions from the head office, even in the one year when the budget was not met. The Canadian management team travelled to the head office as a group only once every several years. As Bjorn Bayley explained, "We are a very informal management team, and try to have everyone who works for us believe that they have the freedom to do their job in the best way possible. It's almost impossible to push the philosophy down to the cashier level, but we try."

IKEA in Canada

IKEA's formula had worked well in Canada. Under the direction of a four-person management team, which included two Swedes, the company had grown from a single store in 1976 to nine stores totalling 800,000 square feet and, as shown in exhibit 12.1, predicted 1986 sales of more than $140 million. The sales of IKEA Canada had exceeded budget in all but one of the past five years, and usually by a wide margin. Net profits were approximately 5 percent of sales. Profit and loss statements for 1983 and 1984, the only financial statements available, are presented in exhibit 12.2.

IKEA Canada carried just less than half of the company's total product line. Individual items were chosen on the basis of what management thought would sell in Canada, and if IKEA could not beat a competitor's price by 10–15 percent on a particular item, it was dropped. Most of the goods sold in the Canadian stores were supplied from central warehouses in Sweden. To coordinate this process a five-person stock supply department in Vancouver provided Sweden with a three-year forecast of Canada's needs, and placed major orders twice a year. Actual volumes were expected to be within 10 percent of the forecast level. As Bayley noted, "you needed a gambler in the stock supply job."

Exhibit 12.2   Statements of earnings and retained earnings, year ended August 31, 1984 (with comparative figures for 1983)

	1984	1983
Sales	$92,185,188	74,185,691
Cost of merchandise sold	49,836,889	38,085,173
Gross profit	42,348,299	36,100,518
General, administrative and selling expenses	28,016,473	23,626,727
Operating profit before the undernoted	14,331,826	12,473,791
Depreciation and amortization	1,113,879	1,066,286
Franchise amortization	257,490	257,490
Franchise fee	2,765,558	2,225,571
	4,136,927	3,549,347
Earnings from operations	10,194,899	8,924,444
Rental income	769,719	815,683
Less rental expense	245,803	258,296
	523,916	557,387
Interest expense	2,435,116	3,042,471
Less other income	438,683	65,757
	2,014,433	2,976,714
Earnings before income taxes	8,704,382	6,505,117
Income taxes:		
Current	3,789,773	2,716,645
Deferred	(70,400)	175,500
	3,719,373	2,892,145
Net earnings for the year	4,985,009	3,612,972
Retained earnings, beginning of year	5,501,612	1,888,640
Retained earnings, end of year	$10,486,621	5,501,612

Source: Consumer and Corporate Affairs, Canada.

Individual stores were expected to maintain 13.5 weeks of inventory on hand (10.5 weeks in the store and three weeks in transit), and could order from the central warehouse in Montreal, or, if a product was not in stock in Montreal, direct from Sweden. Shipments from Sweden took six to eight weeks to arrive, shipments from Montreal two to three weeks. In practice, about 50 percent of the product arriving at a store came via each route.

IKEA's success in Canada meant that the firm was often hard pressed to keep the best selling items in stock. (Twenty percent of the firm's present line constituted 80 percent of sales volume.) At any given time in Canada, IKEA stores might have 300 items out of stock, either because actual sales deviated significantly from forecasts or because suppliers could not meet their delivery promises. While management estimated that 75 percent of customers were willing to wait for IKEA products in a stockout situation, the company nevertheless began a deliberate policy of developing Canadian suppliers for high-demand items, even if this meant paying a slight premium. In 1984, the stock control group purchased $57 million worth of goods on IKEA's behalf, $12 million of which was from 30 Canadian suppliers, up from $7 million the previous year.

As indicated in exhibit 12.1, IKEA Canada sold products, rather reluctantly, by mail order to customers who preferred not to visit the stores. A senior manager explained, "To date we have engaged in defensive mail order – only when the customer really wants it and the order is large enough. The separate handling, breaking down of orders, and repackaging required for mail orders would be too expensive and go against the economies-through-volume approach of IKEA. Profit margins of mail order business tend to be half that of a store operation. There are more sales returns, particularly because of damages – maybe 4 percent – incurred in shipping. It is difficult to know where to draw the market boundaries for a mail order business. We don't want to be substituting mail order customers for store visitors."

In 1986, the management team which had brought success to IKEA's Canadian operations was breaking up. Bjorn Bayley, who had come to Canada in 1978, was slotted to move to Philadelphia to spearhead IKEA's entry into the US market, which had begun in June 1985 with a single store. With early sales running at a level twice as high as the company had predicted, Bayley expected to be busy, and was taking Mike McDonald, the controller, and Mike McMullen, the personnel director, with him. Anders Barglund, who, like Bayley, was a long-time IKEA employee and had been in Canada since 1979, was scheduled to take over the Canadian operation. Berglund would report through Bayley to IKEA's North American Sales Director, who was located in Europe.

New Competition

IKEA's success in Canada had not gone unnoticed. IDOMO was a well-established Toronto-based competitor, and Sears Canada was a new entrant.

IDOMO

Like IKEA, IDOMO sold knocked-down furniture which customers were required to assemble at home. IDOMO offered a somewhat narrower selection than IKEA but emphasized teak furniture to a much greater extent. With stores in Hamilton, Mississauga (across from IKEA), Toronto, and Montreal, IDOMO appeared to have capitalized on the excess demand that IKEA had developed but was not able to service.

The products and prices offered in both the 96-page IDOMO and 144-page IKEA catalogs were similar, with IKEA's prices slightly lower. Prices in the IKEA catalog were in effect for a year. IDOMO reserved the right to make adjustments to prices and specifications. A mail order telephone number in Toronto was provided in the IDOMO catalogue. Of late, IDOMO had begun to employ an increased amount of television advertising. IDOMO purchased goods from around the world and operated a number of their own Canadian factories. Their primary source of goods was Denmark.

Sears

The newest entrant in the Canadian knocked-down furniture segment was Sears Canada, a wholly owned subsidiary of Sears Roebuck of Chicago and, with $3.8 billion in annual revenues, one of Canada's largest merchandising operations. Sears operated 75 department stores in Canada, selling a wide range (700 merchandise lines comprising 100,000 stock keeping units) of medium price and quality goods. Sears Canada also ran a major catalog operation which distributed 12 annual catalogs to approximately four million Canadian families. Customers could place catalog orders by mail, by telephone, or in person through one of the company's 1500 catalog sales units, which were spread throughout the country.

A quick check by Bayley and Berglund revealed that Sears' Elements line was being sold only in Canada and only through the major Sears catalogs. Elements products were not for sale, nor could they be viewed, in Sears' stores. In the fall–winter catalogue that they examined, which was over 700 pages in length, the Elements line was given 20 pages. Although Sears appeared to offer the same "type" of products as IKEA, there was a narrower selection within each category. Prices for Elements products seemed almost identical to IKEA prices. One distinct difference between the catalogs was the much greater emphasis that IKEA placed on presenting a large number of coordinated settings and room designs.

Further checking indicated that at least some of the suppliers of the Elements line were Swedish, although it did not appear that IKEA and Sears had any suppliers in common. The IKEA executives knew that Sears was generally able to exert a great deal of influence over its suppliers, usually obtaining prices at least equal to and often below those of its competitors, because of the huge volumes purchased. Sears also worked closely with its suppliers in marketing, research, design and development, production standards, and production planning. Many lines of merchandise were manufactured with features exclusive to Sears and were sold under its private brand names. There was a 75 percent buying overlap for the catalog and store and about a 90 percent overlap between regions on store purchases.

Like any Sears product, Elements furniture could be charged to a Sears charge card. Delivery of catalog items generally took about two weeks, and for a small extra charge catalog orders would be delivered right to the consumer's home in a Sears truck. If a catalog item were out of stock, Sears policy was either to tell the customer if and when the product would be available, or to substitute an item of equal or greater value. If goods proved defective (10 percent of Sears Roebuck mail-order furniture purchasers had received damaged or broken furniture), Sears provided home pick-up and replacement and was willing, for a fee, to install goods, provide parts, and do repairs as products aged. Sears emphasized that it serviced what it sold, and guaranteed everything that it sold – "satisfaction guaranteed or money refunded." In its advertising, which included all forms of media, Sears stressed its "hassle-free returns" and asked customers to "take a look at the services we offer . . . they'll bring you peace of mind, long after the bill is paid."

In their assessment of Sears Canada, Bayley and Berglund recognized that the company seemed to be going through something of a revival. Using the rallying cry that a "new" Sears was being created, Sears executives (the Canadian firm had ten vice presidents) had experimented with new store layouts, pruned the product line, and improved customer service for catalog orders. Richard Sharpe, the Chairman of Sears Canada, personally addressed as many as 12,000 employees per year, and the company received 3000 suggestions from employees annually. Perhaps as a result of these initiatives, and a cut in the workforce from 65,000 to 50,000 over several years, Sears Canada posted its best ever results in 1985.

Conclusion

With the limited data it had on Sears, IKEA management recognized that comparison of the two companies would be incomplete. Nonetheless, a decision regarding the Sears competitive threat was required. Any solution would have to reflect Kamprad's philosophy: "Expensive solutions to problems are often signs of mediocrity. We have no interest in a solution until we know what it costs."

Toys 'R' Us, 1993

Caron H. St John

In 1948, Charles Lazarus began selling baby furniture in the back of his father's Washington, DC, bicycle repair shop, located below the apartment where the Lazarus family lived. Within a few months, and in response to customer requests, he added a few toys to his line of baby furniture. Before long he realized parents who bought toys returned for more toys – but parents who bought furniture rarely came back. "When I realized that toys broke," he said, "I knew it was a good business."[1] Soon his entire business was focused on toys.

After the success of his first store, he opened his second store in Washington as a self-serve, cash-and-carry business. In 1958, he opened his third store – a 25,000 square foot "baby supermarket" with discount prices and a large selection of products. Within a few years, a fourth supermarket-style store was opened. By 1966, the four stores in the Washington area were achieving $12 million in annual sales.

To get capital for continued growth, Lazarus sold his four stores in 1966 to Interstate Stores, a retail discount chain, for $7 million. Lazarus stayed with Interstate and maintained operating control over the toy division. Between 1966 and 1974, the Toys'R'Us division of Interstate Stores grew from 4 to 47 stores through internal growth and a merger with Children's Bargain Town.

In 1974, the parent company, Interstate Stores, filed for bankruptcy. When Interstate completed reorganization and emerged from bankruptcy in 1978, the new company name was Toys'R'Us (TRU) and Charles Lazarus was chief executive officer. Since then, all of the Interstate Stores have been divested and all creditors have been paid.

Between January 1979 and January 1984, Toys'R'Us grew from 63 stores with sales of just under $350 million to 169 stores with sales of over $1.3 billion, for a compound annual growth rate of 30 percent. During the same years, profits increased from $17 million to $92 million for a compound annual growth rate of 40 percent. TRU stock, which traded for $2 per share in 1978, split 3 for 2 for 4 years in a row and consistently traded above $40 per share. A $2 TRU stock investment made in 1978 was worth $200 in the spring of 1984.

After 1984, Toys'R'Us continued to grow and gain share of market in the US toy retailing market. By 1988 sales had more than doubled to $3.14 billion with earnings of $204 million. Between 1988 and 1992, TRU directed much of its expansion efforts to overseas markets by building retail stores in Europe, the Far East, and Canada. As of January 1993, Toys'R'Us was the largest toy retailer in the world with estimated sales of over $7 billion and an estimated US market share of between 22 and 25 percent. At that time, Toys'R'Us operated 540 US toy stores, 167 international toy stores, and 213 Kids'R'Us clothing stores.

Charles Lazarus has consistently been the motivating force behind the growth of Toys'R'Us. His vision is for Toys'R'Us to become the McDonald's of toy retailing: "We don't have golden arches, but we're getting there."[2] He credits his success in toy retailing to his love of the business. "What we do is the essence of America – making a business grow," he says. "If you're going to be a success in life you have to want it. I wanted it. I was poor. I wanted to be rich. . . . My ego now is in the growth of this company."[3]

Toy Industry

The US toy industry saw the best of times and the worst of times during the decade of the eighties. Between 1980 and 1984, sales growth in the toy industry, fueled by electronic games and Cabbage Patch Kids, was very strong. Including electronic games, sales growth in those years exceeded 18 percent per year. Excluding the electronic games category, industry sales growth averaged 11 percent. While electronic games accounted for 18.4 percent of total US toy sales in 1980, by 1982 they represented 30.9 percent – almost one-third – of total toy sales. During those same years, highly publicized toys such as Cabbage Patch Kid dolls, ET the Extra-Terrestrial toys, and the Trivial Pursuit board game accounted for 50 percent of nonelectronic game sales. Traditional toys such as Slinky and Etch-A-Sketch accounted for the remaining 50 percent.

In 1984 and 1985, interest in electronic games fell sharply. This trend, combined with a dearth of blockbuster new toys of the caliber of Cabbage Patch Kids and Trivial Pursuit, resulted in relatively flat sales for the industry from 1985 to 1987. Between 1988 and 1992, the toy industry was hurt further by the Gulf War and the ongoing recession. Increasing numbers of children and strong demand for Nintendo games could not offset the effects of the slow economy. Intense price competition coupled with soft demand forced many toy manufacturers and retailers out of business.

Toy manufacturing

During the slow growth years, many toy manufacturers suffered financially. Several companies posted losses in 1986 and 1987, and two large companies, Coleco and

Worlds of Wonder, were forced into Chapter 11 bankruptcy. In 1988, the industry turned much of its energy toward cost control. Hasbro and Mattel closed facilities to reduce overhead costs and Tonka shifted much of its production to contract vendors in the Far East. Product development efforts focused on traditional favorites with considerably less emphasis on promotional games and toys, and licensed dolls and action figures. The movement toward traditional toys and cost containment was fueled by the bankruptcies of Coleco and Worlds of Wonder, the creator of the talking Teddy Ruxpin bear. The consensus in the industry was that both companies had become overly dependent on their promotional toys and had neglected cost controls.

In the 1990s, the relationship between toy manufacturers and toy retailers began to change. As the toy manufacturing and retailing industries faced the poor economy, price pressures, and consolidation, the two groups began to cultivate partnerships, with more cooperative delivery and pricing arrangements. In 1992, industry analysts reported that the business prospects for the major toy manufacturers had improved substantially. All of the major companies were maintaining low debt structures, a strong position in stable toy lines, and tighter expense controls than in previous years. All of the major toy manufacturers were beginning to investigate overseas sales opportunities.

Toy retailing

There are thousands of retail toy outlets in the United States, with total sales in 1992 of approximately $14 billion. With 540 US toy stores in 1992, Toys'R'Us is the largest national toy chain with an estimated 22–25 percent share of US retail toy sales. Wal-Mart follows TRU with 12 percent of the market. K-Mart accounts for approximately 5 percent of toys sales and Kay-Bee, a specialty toy retailer usually located in shopping malls, is responsible for 4 percent of toy sales. Lionel Corporation, a large toy supermarket chain similar to Toys'R'Us, has 2.7 percent of the market. Lionel has been reorganizing under Chapter 11 of the Bankruptcy Act since the mid-eighties. Child World, another toy supermarket, experienced severe financial difficulties in the early 1990s and went out of business. In early 1993, Early Learning Centres Ltd closed its 73 US toy stores.

Although all categories of retailers compete with each other, they use different approaches to appeal to customers. The national toy chains offer a large selection of products at low prices with minimal in-store service. The discount stores frequently offer similar low prices and minimal service, but their selection is not as extensive as that of the toy warehouse chains. The small, independent toy stores provide personalized service and specialty items but ask higher prices. The larger department stores compete on the basis of convenience – the customer can purchase toys while shopping for other items. Toy departments in the large department stores are small, with minimum inventory and a limited product selection. Some large retailers such as J. C. Penney have dropped toy departments altogether.

Until the 1980s, discount stores were the primary outlet for toy sales in the USA. Beginning in 1980, toy supermarkets such as Toys'R'Us, Child World, and Lionel (now known as Kiddie City), made major inroads into the retail toy market. Throughout the 1980s, the three toy supermarkets competed head-on in several markets, pursued aggressive growth strategies, and constructed similar warehouse-style stores. With very few exceptions, however, TRU was the strongest competitor in those markets where the companies were in direct competition. Although all three competitors operated stores of similar size, TRU achieved an average of $8.4 million in sales a year per store compared to $4.4 million for Lionel and $4.9 million for Child World.

In 1987, Child World attempted a price war that undercut TRU across several product categories. The attack worked to increase sales at Child World stores at the expense of Toys'R'Us but profits were reduced so much at Child World that the company was unable to recover completely. Following the particularly difficult 1991 retail year, Child World declared bankruptcy and closed down. Lionel, operating under Chapter 11 protection, continued to experience problems as well. During 1992, 150 toy stores owned by Lionel and Child World were closed down. Toys'R'Us was expected to benefit by taking over as much as 50 percent of the $400 million sales volume previously accounted for by those stores.

In the late 1980s and early 1990s, general merchandise discount stores began to fight for toy retailing business. Wal-Mart, Kmart, and Target expanded their toy departments and promoted low-priced toys to attract customers into the stores. These more aggressive pricing postures by the discount chains helped the discounters increase their share of toy sales dramatically. For example, between 1988 and 1992, Wal-Mart doubled its share of toy sales to 12 percent. Since toys typically represent less than 5 percent of total store sales, discounters are able to use toys as "loss leaders" to attract customers without hurting overall store profits.

Some small "mom-and-pop" retailers are rethinking their approach to toy retailing as well. Rather than battle with Toys'R'Us and Wal-Mart on price or product line breadth, small independent retailers are taking the lead in introducing new items from small toy manufacturers. Specialty stores take toys out of the boxes and demonstrate how they are used. This personal approach appeals to many toy manufacturers and customers. When the producers of the PBS series "Shining Time Station" tried to sell the talking Thomas the Tank Engine through the large retail chains, sales were less than $2 million. The company withdrew the train from the large retailers and offered it exclusively to small retailers. Total sales of the Thomas line of toys and videocassettes were $200 million within two years.

Toy retailing is a very seasonal business. Well over 50 percent of toy sales are reported in the fourth quarter – with much of those sales generated in the six weeks before Christmas. To balance the unevenness of toy sales, some stores sell other less seasonal items such as party supplies and books, and they try to tie-in promotional items to summer activities (pools, lawn games) and other holidays such as Halloween and Valentine's Day.

Industry trends

Some demographic and industry trends that are expected to continue to influence demand for toys in the next several years are (exhibits 13.1 and 13.2).

(1) *Numbers of children.*   The number of households headed by people aged 35 to 44 grew by 51 percent between 1980 and 1990. Since the late seventies, many of

Exhibit 13.1   Population by age in 1980 and 1990 (thousands)

	1990	1980	Percent change
Total	249,870	226,546	10.3
Under 5	18,409	16,348	12.6
5 to 9	18,333	16,700	9.6
10 to 14	17,194	18,242	−5.7
15 to 19	17,521	21,168	−17.2
20 to 24	18,746	21,318	−12.1
25 to 29	21,592	19,521	10.6
30 to 34	22,359	17,561	27.3
35 to 39	20,080	13,966	43.8
40 to 44	17,481	11,669	49.8
45 to 49	13,838	11,090	24.8
50 to 54	11,496	11,710	−1.8

Source: Judith Waldrop and Thomas Exter, "What the 1990 Census Will Show," *American Demographics*, January 1990, p. 23.

these members of the baby boom generation, who delayed having children while in their twenties, started having babies. Consequently, the 2- to 5-year-old age group has grown steadily for several years. Although the number of married couples of child-bearing age is expected to increase through 1990, by 2000 the number will have dropped precipitously as the baby bust generation replaces the baby boom.

Even though the number of children is believed to be a major driver of demand, many of the children in the current under-5 age group are second or third children in the family. Since toys, clothes, books, and furniture can be handed down from one child to the next, parents do not spend as much money on second and third children as they did on the first. Furthermore, a large percentage of the children under 5 are in low-income families that lack the resources to spend on toys. Households headed by young adults under the age of 34 either experienced level or falling household incomes between 1980 and 1990. These younger parents have less disposable income than in the past.

(2) *More money to spend on toys.*   Some parents are having children after their households are formed and careers are established, so family incomes are higher. In many families, both parents are employed full time. The higher family incomes mean there is more money for discretionary items such as toys. In 1990, parents spent an average of around $400 on each child, which is three times more than was spent in 1960 even after adjustments are made for inflation.

(3) *Broader market appeal of toy stores.*   The toy market has joined with the video games and home electronics markets to form a broader category of "toys." The objective is to appeal to the teen and young adult market segment and draw this new group of buyers into the toy stores. While the industry was hurt badly by the decline in the video game market in 1984 and 1985, industry forecasters correctly predicted a resurgence of interest in the video game segment in the early 1990s.

Exhibit 13.2   Characteristics of households (census counts in thousands)

	1990	1980	Percent change
All households	93,920	80,467	16.7
Family households	66,542	59,190	12.4
Married couples	52,837	48,990	7.9
Without children < 18 yr	28,315	24,210	17.0
With children < 18 yr	24,522	24,780	−1.0
Other family, female head	11,130	8,205	35.6
Other family, male head	2,575	1,995	29.1
Non-family households	27,378	21,277	28.7
By age			
Under 25	4,683	6,709	−30.2
25 to 34	21,191	18,351	15.5
35 to 44	21,059	13,948	51.0
45 to 54	14,330	12,630	13.5
By income ($)			
All households	$29,317	$28,554	2.7
Under 25	17,405	19,430	−10.4
25 to 34	30,408	30,356	0.2
35 to 44	39,298	37,811	3.9
45 to 54	42,218	40,361	4.6

Source: Judith Waldrop and Thomas Exter, "What the 1990 Census Will Show," *American Demographics*, January 1990, p. 23.

The revival of the video game market was led by a Japanese company, Nintendo, with 70 percent of the market.

(4) *Licensing.*   Licensing, or basing a product on a motion picture, television program, or comic strip character, accelerated in importance in the eighties and continues to play a significant role in toy sales. According to manufacturers, toys based on popular characters appeal to an already established market. In late 1980s, toy retailers criticized manufacturers for relying too heavily on licensed toys. They argued that there were too many licenses in the market and too much variation in quality among them. At that time, many retailers cut back their stock of licensed products by as much as 10 to 30 percent, characterizing many licensed toys as "junk with stickers on it."

In the 1990s, licensing regained respectability. Toys based on the Disney animated films – *The Little Mermaid, Beauty and the Beast*, and *Aladdin* – have been very successful. The challenge for toy retailers is to stock the correct quantity of the licensed products at just the right time.

Toys 'R' Us

The aim of Toys'R'Us is to be the customer's only place of purchase for toys and related products. Management says it is proud that TRU attracts the least-affluent purchasers because of the everyday discount prices and also attracts the most-affluent purchasers because of the extensive product selection. In order to provide total service to all customer segments, the company maintains tight operating procedures and a strong customer orientation.

Virtually all Toys'R'Us stores are located on an important traffic artery leading to a major shopping mall. A location of this type serves two purposes: it allows TRU to attract mall patrons without paying high mall rents, and it gives TRU the space to do business the way it wants to – as a large "supermarket" for toys, complete with grocery-type shopping carts.

Retailing operations

According to Charles Lazarus, "Nothing is done in the stores."[4] What he means is that all buying and pricing decisions are made at corporate headquarters in Rochelle Park, New Jersey. The corporate buying and pricing decisions are made using an elaborate computerized inventory control system where sales by item and sales by store are monitored daily. Those actual sales numbers are compared to forecasts, and when substantial differences exist, the slow items are marked down to get them out of the stores and the fast-selling items are reordered in larger quantities.

By closely following the buying habits of the consumer, TRU is able to pick up on trends before the crucial Christmas buying season and maintain more flexibility than competitors. The overwhelming significance of this capability was first demonstrated in 1980. When sales of hand-held video games fell off sharply before Christmas that year, Toys'R'Us was forewarned by its extensive monitoring system and moved much of its stock of video games, at reduced prices, before the Christmas season. TRU was fully stocked with the big Christmas items that year – the Rubik's Cube and Strawberry Shortcake – unlike virtually all its competitors.

Toys'R'Us has a formidable reputation with toy manufacturers because of management's ability to predict the success or failure of new toys. Before the 1988 Christmas season, Toys'R'Us executives informed Hasbro that its $20 million new product, Nemo, aimed at the Nintendo market, was dull and too expensive. Hasbro canceled the Nemo line and took a $10 million write-off. In August of 1988, TRU used its market-by-market sales data to show Ohio Arts Co. that its newly developed commercial for its new plastic building set was ineffective. Ohio Arts pulled the new commercial and substituted an older one that had been tried in Canada. Sales increased by 30 percent.

To support its efficient operations and monitor its product sales, TRU makes extensive use of electronics technology in its stores and warehouses. Sales clerks in all stores use hand-held scanners which provide point-of-sale (POS) information at all registers. The sales information is transmitted among stores, distribution centers, and the home office via satellite and then processed using custom-developed software. TRU transmits 75 percent of its invoices to suppliers electronically, which cuts down on paperwork, errors, and delays. Within the next few years, TRU plans to have all of its warehouses converted from partial manual to fully automated systems.

In 1992, Toys'R'Us addressed one criticism by employing a technological

Exhibit 13.3   Toys 'R' Us stores in each of the company's 22 US regions in 1988

Warehouse/distribution region	Number of stores
Washington, DC, Virginia, Maryland	19
Southern California 1	13
Southern California 2	13
Northern California 1	9
Northern California 2	10
Illinois-Indiana	23
Wisconsin-Illinois	9
New York-New Jersey	30
Southern Texas-Louisiana	19
Michigan	19
New England	15
Northern Texas-Oklahoma	14
Pacific Northwest	11
Philadelphia	17
Northern Florida	9
Southern Florida	10
Georgia-Alabama-Tennessee	18
Western Ohio-Kentucky	18
Upstate New York	7
Carolinas	11
Cleveland-Pittsburgh	14
Phoenix	5

Source: Company Form 10K, 1988.

solution. Although TRU stores are designed around a self-serve, warehouse style concept, customers often complain that they can not get help from store personnel when needed. To help correct the problem, TRU installed paging boxes throughout its stores. When a customer pushes a button on the paging box, the service desk receives the signal and pages an employee to go help the customer in that area. The company is also testing a new telephone service enhancement. When customers call the store, a recorded message tells the caller where the store is located and the hours of operation, which satisfies the concerns of about 50 percent of customers who call. For customers who need additional assistance, the system forwards the call to an employee on the floor wearing a head-set and battery pack. The employee can determine immediately whether an item is in stock. The head-sets are also useful in managing stock on the store floor. One employee patrolling the store can identify shelves which need restocking and pinpoint areas needing clean-up, then tie-in to the paging system to make the appropriate arrangements.

The TRU stores are regionally clustered with a warehouse within one day's driving distance of every store. Exhibit 13.3 illustrates the clustering approach used by TRU in 1988. The company also owns a fleet of trucks to support its warehousing operations. The regional warehouses allow TRU to keep the stores well stocked and make it possible for TRU to order large quantities of merchandise early in the year, when manufacturers are eager to ship. Since most manufacturers will defer payments for 12 months on shipments made in the months immediately following Christmas, TRU is able to defer payment on about two-thirds of its inventory each year. TRU's competitors typically buy closer to Christmas, when buying terms are tighter.

All TRU stores have the same layout with the same items arranged on exactly the same shelves – according to blueprints sent from the corporate office. A TRU store is typically 43,000 square feet and is characterized by wide aisles and warehouse-style shelving stocked to the ceiling with over 18,000 different items. A substantial percent of the floor space is devoted to computers and computer-related products, and to non-toy items such as diapers, furniture, and clothing. However, toys, games, books, puzzles, and sports equipment are the major focus of the stores.

Each store is jointly managed by a merchandise manager and an operations manager. The merchandise manager has full responsibility for the merchandising effort in the store: content, stock level, and display. The operations manager is responsible for the building, personnel, cash control, customer service, and everything else that is not directly related to merchandise. Area supervisors oversee the total operations of three or four stores in a given area, and area general managers are responsible for the performance and profitability of all the TRU stores in a given market.

Toys'R'Us has little turnover among its middle and upper managers. In the past 10 years, more than 40 employees have become millionaires through the company's employee stock option plan. According to one executive manager, the company wants people who want to work. He says, "Toys'R'Us is not a 9-to-5 but an 8-to-faint job."[5]

Marketing

As indicated earlier, each Toys'R'Us store carries over 18,000 items. In addition to a broad selection of products, TRU emphasizes stock availability and easy return policies. Product availability is virtually guaranteed. Because of extensive inventory monitoring and attention to consumer buying habits, TRU rarely has a "stock out." Also, TRU boasts of a liberal return policy. The company claims it will accept all returns with no questions asked – even if a toy with no defect is broken by a child after several months of play.

Although toys represent, by far, the majority of the items stocked, other products include baby furniture, diapers, and children's clothing. Toys'R'Us offers deeply discounted prices on diapers to draw parents of children into the store on a regular basis. The feeling at TRU is that the parent will go to the store to buy a necessity or nonseasonal item and will leave with at least one toy purchase. The average TRU customer spends over $40 per visit.

The product line at TRU includes game computers and software as well as traditional toys. This serves to broaden the company's customer base to include teenagers and adults, and to create add-on business at each retail unit. According to company statistics, products for these "older children" account for more than 15 percent of sales. TRU feels strongly these products do not represent a change in its basic business – game computers and software are toys for adults. This strategy of carrying a wide selection of merchandise has benefited TRU in another way. The company has been successful in encouraging year-round buying at its stores. In 1980, 7.5 percent of profits were made in the nine months of January through September compared with 25 percent or more in subsequent years.

In 1992, TRU began testing three new store-within-a-store concepts, which are intended to further broaden and stabilize store demand patterns. At 30 of its toy stores, TRU created special Books'R'Us departments with carpeting, comfortable chairs, and a selection of books expanded from the typical 500 titles to over 1900 titles. The Books'R'Us concept is managed as a partnership between TRU and Western Publishing, the publisher of Little Golden Books. Under the agreement, Western Publishing provides an in-store sales person, selects the books, and serves as the wholesaler between TRU and other book publishers. If the new concept is successful, it will be rolled out for the whole toy chain. Since the children's book market is approximately $1 billion and growing faster than many other product categories, the sales prospects are significant if TRU can make a strong showing. Some analysts expect TRU to have 20 percent of the market ($200 million in sales) within two years. TRU is also testing store-within-a-store concepts with its trial Movies'R'Us and Parties 'R'Us departments in a few stores. The Movies'R'Us departments, which carry 600–700 titles, are racked by Visual Expressions, a video tape wholesaler.

TRU has a strong policy of year-round discount prices. Because TRU buys most of its merchandise during the off-season when manufacturers are offering discounts, the company is able to pass the discounts on to the customer. For several years, TRU maintained a policy of not having store sales. Individual items were marked down if they were not selling, but TRU did not have sales that were category-wide or store-wide. However, in 1991, faced with increased price competition from Wal-Mart, Kmart, and Child World, TRU published 20 million copies of an in-store catalog with $173 worth of coupons. Since then, TRU has offered coupons on toys, diapers, and baby supplies on a regular basis.

Whereas TRU's prices are lower than those of smaller specialty stores, the discounters undercut TRU's prices on some high volume items in 1990 and 1991 (see exhibit 13.4). In response, TRU renewed its commitment to everyday low prices, promised to match its competitors' advertised prices, and encouraged customers to bring in advertisements. The severe price competition has hurt profitability, however. Domestic toy stores account for 90 per cent of TRU's operating income. The aggressive price competition among TRU, Child World (bankrupt in 1992), and the discount chains has eroded TRU's operating income from over 12 percent to 10 percent recent years.

Toys'R'Us generally does no national advertising. Before entering a new region, TRU promotes the opening of the new stores through heavy television and newspaper advertising. Once the stores are open, TRU continues some very limited television and newspaper advertising, particularly around the holiday season. In the last few years, TRU has participated in joint promotions, for example, with MasterCard and Kentucky Fried Chicken. TRU considered signing an agreement with Soccer USA Partners to sponsor the World Cup in 1994. The sponsorship

Exhibit 13.4   Toys 'R' Us and Wal-Mart price comparisons, Wisconsin market (dollars)

Item	Toys'R'Us	Wal-Mart
Scattergories	19.99	19.97
Scrabble-Deluxe	21.99	24.86
Life	12.99	9.48
Candyland	4.99	3.97
Monopoly	9.99	8.97
Pictionary	21.99	21.74
Trivial Pursuit	24.99	24.94
Clue	8.99	8.93
Ninja Action Figures	3.99	4.76
Ninja Sewer Playset	39.99	37.84
Ninja Technodrome	49.99	44.87
Barbie:		
All American doll	8.99	7.93
Happy Birthday doll	24.99	24.94
Magical Motor Home	42.99	38.96
PJ Sparkles	24.99	24.97
Crayola Crayons	0.99	0.93
Nintendo 16-bit hardware	199.99	197.87
Gradius software	54.99	51.86
Tonka Mighty Dump	9.99	9.93
Dolls:		
Baby Face	16.99	16.86
Baby Alive	22.99	21.96

Source: Prudential Securities.

would require that TRU pay $2–2.5 million for the rights to use the US team logos. Approximately 16 million children and teenagers, ages 6 to 17, participate in soccer activities in the USA.

Domestic and foreign expansion

Toys'R'Us pursues a corporate objective of 18 percent expansion of retail space per year. In order to meet this objective, each year for several years TRU has opened more than 40–50 new toy stores in the USA, 20–25 new clothing stores in the USA, and 15–20 new international toy stores. Exhibit 13.5 shows TRU's store growth since 1980.

All of the expansions are made as a total entry into a new region. First, TRU builds a warehouse, then it clusters several stores within one day's driving distance of the warehouse so that prompt merchandise delivery is ensured. Typically, the warehouse and all the stores are up and running within the same fiscal year and in time for the Christmas season. Once TRU enters a local market with more than one store, it immediately becomes the low-price leader in the area, which forces competitors to bring down their prices.

Exhibit 13.5 Number of stores at fiscal year end (January)

	1993	1992	1991	1990	1989	1988	1987	1986	1985	1984	1983	1982	1981	1980
Toys 'R' Us United States	540	497	451	404	358	313	271	233	198	169	144	120	101	85
Toys 'R' Us International	167	126	97	74	52	37	24	13	5					
Kids'R'Us	213	189	164	137	112	74	43	23	10	2				

Source: Company Annual Reports.

Charles Lazarus keeps a file of locations that have already been selected as potential sites for future US stores. The regions are selected on the basis of demographic patterns and toy buying statistics. The individual store locations are decided after an analysis is completed of the area shopping malls, traffic patterns, and local retail toy competition. Charles Lazarus believes there is sufficient market demand for Toys'R'Us to build and operate a total of 900 stores in the United States.

In the last several years, TRU has focused much of its expansion efforts overseas using the same strategy of approximately five stores per nation per year (exhibit 13.6). In 1984, TRU constructed four stores in Canada and one, through a joint venture, in Singapore. The next year the company built five stores in the United Kingdom and three more in Canada. TRU entered West Germany in 1987, France in 1989, and Japan and Spain in 1991. Stores in Hong Kong, Malaysia, Singapore, and Japan were built with the assistance of joint venture partners.

Although stores in Germany have been very successful, TRU met with serious resistance when it first entered the market. Local toymakers warned of the danger of buying toys in a self-service environment with no one to describe a toy's potential for injury. However, despite the resistance by the local business community, the opening of a new outlet in Germany caused a 14-mile backup on the local autobahn.

Toys'R'Us met with even more resistance in Japan. One of the largest barriers to entry into the Japanese market is the "large-scale retail law." In Japan, a retailer who wants to open a store with more than 5400 square feet of floor space must obtain the approval of other retailers in the area. In some instances, local stores have stalled for as long as 10 years before giving approval. Other barriers to the Japanese market include the very high real estate prices and rents as well as a complicated distribution system which requires that retailers satisfy local laws and work with several layers of distributors and wholesalers.

Toys'R'Us spent three years negotiating with the Japanese bureaucracy including the Ministry of International Trade & Industry (MITI). In 1990, MITI agreed to limit the approval process for large scale stores to 18 months and a few months later TRU received approval to build a store as part of a joint venture with McDonald's Co. of Japan. TRU agreed to close the store one month each year, in compliance with the local custom. Since the custom in Japan is to sell through wholesalers and distributors, the company has experienced some difficulty in making arrangements to

Exhibit 13.6   Toys 'R' Us international stores

	1996E*	1995E*	1994E*	1993	1992	1991	1990	1989	1988	1987	1986	1985
Total store count	359	309	259	211	167	126	97	74	52	37	24	13
Canada	57	54	51	48	43	38	32	27	23	17	13	7
Singapore	4	4	3	3	3	2	2	2	2	2	2	1
United Kingdom	56	52	48	44	38	33	28	23	18	13	8	5
Hong Kong	5	5	4	3	3	3	3	1	1	1	1	
Germany	52	47	42	38	30	24	18	13	7	4		
Malaysia	2	2	2	2	2	2	2	2	1			
Taiwan	4	4	3	3	2	2	2	1				
France	37	32	27	22	16	11	10	5				
Spain	25	23	21	18	13	8						
Japan	42	32	22	14	5	1						
Portugal	7	6	5	4	2							
Austria	10	9	8	6	2							
Switzerland	9	7	5	3	3							
Benelux	10	9	6	5	2							
Italy	8	6	4									
Australia	9	5	3									
Mexico	8	6	3									
Hungary/Eastern Europe	7	4	2									
Korea	4	2										
Scandinavia	3											

*   Estimate.

Source: Estimated by Prudential Securities.

purchase toys directly from Japanese manufacturers. Japanese manufacturers have been reluctant to sell directly to Toys'R'Us for fear of offending their existing customers.

So far, the international stores have not been as profitable as the domestic stores. The major reason is the cost of establishing the infrastructure and distribution network to support the stores in each separate nation. For each nation. TRU creates a purchasing organization including a merchandise manager and several buyers, a managing director, and managers of operations, human resources, and real estate development. With the high costs of start-up, it usually takes 2 or 3 years to break even with an international store. In Japan, it may take even longer to make the stores profitable. Even though Japanese toy retailing is very fragmented and high cost – a perfect target for the TRU approach – Japan's economy has slowed considerably lately and is expected to stay in a slow growth/no growth phase for several years. In France, hypermarket chains, which are similar to US discount chains, control 60 percent of toy sales and are prepared to fight on price to keep TRU from taking too much of the market.

On the brighter side, however, future expansions overseas should not carry such

Exhibit 13.7   Location of all Toys 'R' Us properties in 1992

Toys'R'Us stores:			
Alabama	6	Puerto Rico	2
Arizona	9	Canada	38
Arkansas	2	France	11
California	63	Germany	24
Colorado	8	Hong Kong	3
Connecticut	6	Japan	2
Delaware	1	Malaysia	2
Florida	32	Singapore	2
Georgia	11	Spain	8
Hawaii	1	Taiwan	3
Idaho	1	United Kingdom	33
Illinois	29		
Indiana	11	Kids'R'Us Stores:	
Iowa	4	Alabama	1
Kansas	4	Arizona	3
Kentucky	6	California	29
Louisiana	7	Connecticut	5
Maine	2	Delaware	1
Maryland	14	Florida	8
Massachusetts	11	Georgia	2
Michigan	19	Illinois	19
Minnesota	8	Indiana	7
Mississippi	3	Iowa	1
Missouri	9	Kansas	1
Nebraska	1	Maine	1
Nevada	3	Maryland	6
New Hampshire	4	Massachusetts	1
New Jersey	18	Michigan	15
New Mexico	1	Minnesota	5
New York	32	Missouri	5
North Carolina	14	Nebraska	1
Ohio	26	New Hampshire	2
Oklahoma	4	New Jersey	14
Oregon	5	New York	15
Pennsylvania	23	Ohio	18
Rhode Island	1	Pennsylvania	13
South Carolina	8	Rhode Island	1
Tennessee	9	Texas	3
Texas	39	Utah	3
Utah	5	Virginia	6
Virginia	14	Wisconsin	3
Washington	9		
West Virginia	2		
Wisconsin	10		

high costs. With distribution and administration already set up in France, Germany, and Spain, TRU will be able to support stores in Italy, Switzerland, Portugal, and Austria through existing networks. Although TRU opened only one store in Japan in 1991, the company expects to open as many as 100 stores there over the next several years which will take full advantage of the existing infrastructure.

Kids'R'Us, too

TRU's only venture outside of toy retailing has been into children's clothing – a more than $6 billion industry in the United States alone. The corporate objective in creating Kids'R'Us was to "provide one-stop shopping with an overwhelming selection of first quality, designer and brand name children's clothing in the season's latest styles at everyday prices. . . . We have taken the knowledge and systems we have refined for our toy stores over the past 30 years and applied some of these principles to our Kids'R'Us stores."[6]

In 1983, TRU opened its first two Kids'R'Us stores in the New York area. As of January 1993 the company operated 213 Kids'R'Us stores in various markets in the USA with plans for even more in the future. Each store offers a full assortment of first-quality, discount-priced clothing and accessories for children up to age 12. The surroundings are spacious and well decorated with neon signs, color-coded departments, fitting rooms with platforms for small children, changing areas for infants, play areas for children, and color-coded store maps.

Some observers felt TRU would meet more resilient competition in children's clothing than it did in toys. Department and discount stores make more money on children's clothing than they do on toys and are not willing to give up that market easily. "Department stores fight when it comes to soft goods. That's their bread and butter, it's the guts of their business."[7] Some department store managers feel the purchase of children's clothing sets a family's buying patterns for years so the implication of losing the children's department as a way to draw in families goes beyond the immediate loss of profits in that area.

After five years, the Kids'R'Us move finally began to show a profit. Kids'R'Us sells 85 percent of its clothing at a profit with 15 percent marked down to clear inventory. The industry average for markdowns is 22 percent. Kids'R'Us sales in fiscal 1993 were roughly $745 million with estimated operating profits of $45 million. Prospects for improved profits are good. When the Kids'R'Us chain first opened, it was not large enough to exercise power over apparel manufacturers. It was forced to purchase odd lots and live with uneven delivery arrangements. With size, Kids'R'Us has gained respectability and negotiating power. It is able to negotiate for higher value brand-name apparel and arrange for more convenient and efficient deliveries. Consequently, inventories are lower and more even, and store sales and profits are up.

Reputation

TRU has an excellent reputation with consumers – a reputation that precedes the company into new market areas. Toys'R'Us also is feared and respected by its toy store competitors. Examples of comments from competitors include:

Exhibit 13.8   Toys 'R' Us financial statements 1

Balance sheet ($000)	FYE Feb. 1, 1992	FYE Feb. 2, 1991
ASSETS		
Cash	$ 444,539	$ 35,005
Marketable securities	N/A	N/A
Receivables	64,078	73,170
Inventory	1,390,605	1,275,169
Raw materials	N/A	N/A
Work-in-progress	N/A	N/A
Finished goods	N/A	N/A
Notes receivable	N/A	N/A
Other current assets	27,577	20,981
Total current assets	1,926,853	1,404,325
Property, plant & equipment	2,558,087	2,141,341
Accumulated depreciation	N/A	N/A
Net property, plant & equipment	2,558,087	2,141,341
Investment & advances to subsidiaries	N/A	N/A
Other non-current assets	N/A	N/A
Deferred charges	N/A	N/A
Intangibles	N/A	N/A
Deposits & other assets	63,336	36,777
Total assets	4,548,276	3,582,443
LIABILITIES		
Notes payable	$ 291,659	$ 386,470
Accounts payable	858,777	483,948
Current long-term debt	0	0
Current portion of capital leases	N/A	N/A
Accrued expenses	N/A	N/A
Income taxes	80,314	81,591
Other current liabilities	363,534	275,579
Total current liabilities	1,594,284	1,227,588
Mortgages	N/A	N/A
Deferred charges	136,626	113,405
Convertible debt	N/A	N/A
Long-term debt	379,880	182,695
Non-current capital leases	11,418	12,462
Other long-term liabilities	N/A	N/A
Total liabilities	2,122,208	1,536,150
Minority interest (liabilities)	N/A	N/A
Preferred stock	N/A	N/A
Common stock net	29,794	29,794
Capital surplus	384,803	353,924
Retained earnings	2,092,329	1,752,800
Treasury stock	127,717	129,340
Other liabilities	46,859	39,115
Shareholders' equity	2,426,068	2,046,293
Total liabilities & net worth	4,548,276	3,582,443

Exhibit 13.9 Toys 'R' Us financial statements 2

Income statement ($000)	FYE 92	FYE 91	FYE 90	FYE 89	FYE 88
Net sales	$6,124,209	$5,510,001	$4,787,830	$4,000,192	$3,136,568
Cost of goods	4,286,639	3,820,840	3,309,653	2,766,543	2,157,017
Gross profit	1,837,570	1,689,161	1,478,177	1,233,649	979,551
Research & development expense	N/A	N/A	N/A	N/A	N/A
Selling, general & administrative expenses	1,153,576	1,024,809	866,399	736,329	584,120
Income before depreciation & amortization	683,994	664,352	611,778	497,320	395,431
Depreciation & amortization	100,701	79,093	65,839	54,564	43,716
Non-operating income	13,521	11,233	12,050	11,880	8,056
Interest expense	57,885	73,304	44,309	25,812	13,849
Income before tax	538,929	523,188	513,680	428,824	345,922
Provision for income taxes	199,400	197,200	192,600	160,800	142,000
Minority interest (income)	N/A	N/A	N/A	N/A	N/A
Investment gains/losses	N/A	N/A	N/A	N/A	N/A
Other income	N/A	N/A	N/A	N/A	N/A
Net income before extraordinary items	339,529	325,988	321,080	268,024	203,922
Extraordinary income & discontinued operations	N/A	N/A	N/A	N/A	N/A
Net income	339,529	325,988	321,080	268,024	203,922

Toy store owner
We were going, "oh, nooo," because they were coming in right across the street from us.[8]

President of a buying guild about a children's store owner
All I can tell you is his face turned white. You come up against a giant like this, with every major line discounted, and where do you go? If you're the average kiddy shop next door, do you take gas or cut your throat?[9]

Manufacturer about a buyer
One department store buyer, arriving at the [TRU] store, said it caused her instant depression.[10]

Atlanta toy retailers about TRU's entry into the Atlanta market
I admire Toys 'R' Us. They will own the town.

I hope they take the business from Zayre, Richway, Lionel and not us. We may have to start looking outside Atlanta for locations.

The new Toys 'R' Us will saturate the market.[11]

Michael Vastola, chairman of the board of Lionel Corporation
They have paid a lot of attention to real estate and location, and it has paid off. You have got to say that they have a very disciplined, well-managed operation.[12]

NOTES AND REFERENCES

1 Stratford P. Sherman, "Where the dollars 'R'," *Fortune*, June 1, 1981, pp. 45–47.

2 Dan Fesperman, "Toys'R'Us is a giant in kids' business," *The Miami Herald*, November 22, 1982.

3 Subrata N. Chakravarty, "Toys 'r' fun," Forbes, March 28, 1983, pp. 58–60.

4 Sherman, op. cit., note 1.

5 Joseph Pereira, "Toys'R'Us, Big kid on the block, won't stop growing," *Wall Street Journal*, August 11, 1988, p. B1.

6 "Kids'R'Us – the children's clothing store both parents and kids will choose," press release from Toys'R'Us, July 1983.

7 Claudia Ricci, "Children's wear retailers brace for competition from Toys'R'Us," *The Wall Street Journal*, August 25, 1983.

8 Fesperman, op. cit., note 2.

9 Ricci, op. cit., note 7.

10 Ibid.

11 "A new hat in Atlanta's toy ring," *Toys, Hobbies & Crafts*, May 1983, pp. 5–8.

12 Peter Kerr, "The new game at Toys 'R'Us," *The New York Times*, July 4, 1983.

Wal-Mart, 1992

Walter E. Greene

Growth in sales . . . growth in profitability . . . growth in customers . . . growth in number of stores . . . growth in distribution centers . . . growth in markets . . . growth in associates . . . growth in market share . . . growth in shareholders . . . growth in suppliers . . . growth in financial strength . . .

History

No word better describes Wal-Mart than growth. Wal-Mart Stores, Inc. had its beginning in the small-town variety store business in 1945, when Sam Walton opened his first Ben Franklin franchise operating in Newport, Arkansas. Based in rural Bentonville, Arkansas, Walton, his wife, Helen, and brother, Bud, were the nation's most successful Ben Franklin franchisees. "We were a small chain," says Walton of his 16-store operation. "Things were running so smoothly we even had time for our families."[1] What more could a man want? A great deal, as it turned out.

Sam Walton felt he wasn't as secure as he seemed to be. "I could see that the variety store was gradually dying, because there were giant supermarkets and then discounters coming into the picture," explains Walton.[2] Far from being secure, Sam Walton knew he was under siege. He decided to counterattack. Walton first tried to convince the top management of Ben Franklin to enter discounting. After their refusal, Walton made a quick trip around the country in search of ideas. Walton then began opening his own discount stores in small Arkansas towns like Bentonville and Rogers.

As of February 2, 1991, Sam's Clubs merged the 28 wholesale clubs of The Wholesale Club, Inc., of Indianapolis, Indiana, into its operations. These new partners have 28 units located in six states in the Midwest. Also as of December 10, 1990, Wal-Mart completed the acquisition of the McLane Company, Inc., a provider of retail and grocery distribution services with 14 national distribution centers in 11 states.[3] In late 1991, Wal-Mart announced plans to open five warehouse clubs in Mexico, called Club Aurrera, a joint venture with Cifra (Mexico's biggest retailer) sometime in 1991–2.[4]

The company did not open its first discount department store (Wal-Mart) until November 1962. In 1974 at his induction ceremony with the business fraternity Alpha Kappa Psi (Beta Zeta Chapter at the University of Arkansas), he announced the opening of his fiftieth store. The early stores had bare tile floors and pipe racks and Wal-Mart did not begin to revamp its image significantly until the mid-1970s.

Growth in the early years was slow. However, once the company went public in 1970, sales began to increase rapidly. If one had purchased 100 shares of the stock in 1970, they would have been worth $350,000 in 1985. The stock traded between $25.13 and $33.75 in the fiscal year ending January 31, 1989, and was split two for one on July 6, 1990.

Such retailers as Target, Venture, and K-Mart provided the examples that Wal-Mart sought to emulate in its growth. The old Wal-Mart store colors, dark blue and white (too harsh), were dumped in favor of a three-tone combination of light beige, soft blue, and burnt orange. Carpeting, which had been long discarded on apparel sales floors, was put back. New racks were put into use that displayed the entire garment instead of only an edge of it. In 1987, Sam Walton named David D. Glass as the new CEO of Wal-Mart Stores Inc., while he remained Chairman of the Board.

Growth in Profitability

As of the end of their 1990 fiscal year (January 31, 1991) Wal-Mart had 1573 discount stores in 34 states, 148 Sam's Wholesale Clubs, 3 hypermarkets, 14 McLane's distribution centers, and 13 distribution centers. However, they sold their 14 Dot Discount Drug Stores in February 1990. Wal-Mart, with $32.6 billion in annual revenues, was one of the most profitable companies in all of US retailing and second only to Sears Roebuck in retailing.[5] While most discounters would gladly settle for 2.5 percent net margins, Wal-Mart's run closer to 3.5 percent. Its earnings per share for fiscal year ending January 31, 1992, were estimated to be $1.40 per share, up about 25 percent from 1991. Profits were $1.291 billion for fiscal year ending January 31, 1991 (see exhibit 14.1).[6]

Growth? In 1981, Wal-Mart racked up 50 percent gains in sales and earnings. In part, the increases came from opening 69 new stores, but Wal-Mart's same-store sales were up a remarkable 15 percent as well. Through June 1982 – a brutal period for most retailers – same-store sales were ahead 12 percent while first-half earnings for 1983 rose by an estimated 35 percent. Same-store sales for fiscal year 1987–8 rose 11 percent over previous year. Sales growth of 35 percent per year is normal for Wal-Mart.[7]

Growth in Markets

Wal-Mart stores carry a variety of merchandise, including soft lines, hard lines, domestics, housewares, electronics, and leased departments. Soft lines consist of clothing for the whole family. Hard lines are comprised of hardware, paints, automotives, sporting goods, lawn and garden supplies, and pet supplies. Domestics include furniture, crafts, and linens. Housewares consist of small appliances, detergents, food, picnic supplies, health and beauty aids, and toys. Electronics are comprised of records, tapes, stereos, televisions, and accessories. Leased departments include jewelry and shoes.

In his larger Wal-Mart stores, Walton added other departments, including pharmacies, automotive centers, beauty shops, and restaurants. For example, in Bonham, Texas, which has a population of 8000, the Wal-Mart store includes a pharmacy.

Growth in Number of Stores

Of approximately 1573 stores spanning the Sunbelt from Florida through Texas and on to California, and in the Midwest and Northeast, most are located in towns of 5000 to 25,000, although a few are located in and around a metropolitan area within the chain's regional trade territory (see exhibit 14.2).[8] There are still smaller stores for communities of 5000 and under. The listing below shows the number of stores operated in January 31 for each of the following years:

Year	Wal-Mart	Sam's Discount	Hypermarkets
1974	78		
1975	104		
1976	125		
1977	153		
1978	195		
1979	229		
1980	276		
1981	330		
1982	491		
1983	551		
1984	642	3	
1985	745	11	
1986	859	23	
1987	980	49	
1988	1,114	84	
1989	1,259	105	
1990	1,402	123	3
1991	1,573	148	3

There is yet another way for Walton to expand: by taking over failing chains and "Waltonizing" them. In July 1981, Walton picked up ailing Kuhn's Big-K stores – one warehouse and 92 locations – in effect acquiring cheap leases at a discount

Exhibit 14.1   Wal-Mart ten-year financial summary (dollar amounts in thousands except per share data)

	1991	1990	1989	1988
EARNINGS				
Net sales	32,601,594	25,810,656	20,649,001	15,959,255
Net sales increase (%)	26	25	29	34
Comparative store sales increases (%)	10	11	12	11
Licensed department rentals and other income-net	261,814	174,644	136,867	104,783
Cost of sales	25,499,834	20,070,034	16,056,856	12,281,744
Operating, selling and general and administrative expenses	5,152,178	4,069,695	3,267,864	2,599,367
Interest costs:				
Debt	42,716	20,346	36,286	25,262
Capital leases	125,920	117,725	99,395	88,995
Taxes on income	751,736	631,600	488,246	441,027
Net income	1,291,024	1,075,900	837,221	627,643
Per share of common stock:				
Net income	1.14	0.95	0.74	0.55
Dividends	0.14	0.11	0.08	0.06
FINANCIAL POSITION				
Current assets	6,414,775	4,712,616	3,630,987	2,905,145
Inventories at replacement cost	6,207,852	4,750,619	3,642,696	2,854,556
Less LIFO reserve	399,436	322,546	291,329	202,796
Inventories at LIFO cost	5,808,416	4,428,073	3,351,367	2,651,760
Net property, plant, equipment and capital leases	4,712,039	3,430,059	2,661,954	2,144,852
Total assets	11,388,915	8,198,484	6,359,668	5,131,809
Current liabilities	3,990,414	2,845,315	2,065,909	1,743,763
Long-term debt	740,254	185,152	184,439	185,672
Long-term obligations under capital leases	1,158,621	1,087,403	1,009,046	866,972
Preferred stock with mandatory redemption provisions	–	–	–	–
Shareholders' equity	5,365,524	3,965,561	3,007,909	2,257,267
FINANCIAL RATIOS				
Current ratio	1.6	1.7	1.8	1.7
Inventories/working capital	2.4	2.4	2.1	2.3
Return on assets[a] (%)	15.7	16.9	16.3	15.5
Return on shareholders' equity[a] (%)	32.6	35.8	37.1	37.1
Other year-end data:				
Number of Wal-Mart stores	1,573	1,402	1,259	1,114
Number of Sam's Clubs	148	123	105	84
Average Wal-Mart store size	70,700	66,400	63,500	61,500
Number of associates	328,000	271,000	223,000	183,000
Number of shareholders	122,414	79,929	80,270	79,777

All per share data have been adjusted to reflect the two-for-one stock split on July 6, 1990.

[a]   On beginning of year balances.

1987	1986	1985	1984	1983	1982
11,909,076	8,451,489	6,400,861	4,666,909	3,376,252	2,444,997
41	32	37	38	38	49
13	9	15	15	11	15
84,623	55,127	52,167	36,031	22,435	17,650
9,053,219	6,361,271	4,722,440	3,418,025	2,458,235	1,787,496
2,007,645	1,485,210	1,181,455	892,887	677,029	495,010
10,442	1,903	5,207	4,935	20,297	16,053
76,367	54,640	42,506	29,946	18,570	15,351
395,940	276,119	230,653	160,903	100,416	65,943
450,086	327,473	270,767	196,244	124,140	82,794
0.40	0.29	0.24	0.17	0.11	0.08
0.0425	0.035	0.0263	0.0175	0.0113	0.0082
2,353,271	1,784,275	1,303,254	1,005,567	720,537	589,161
2,184,847	1,528,349	1,227,264	857,155	658,949	578,088
153,875	140,181	123,339	121,760	103,247	87,515
2,030,972	1,388,168	1,103,925	735,395	555,702	490,573
1,676,282	1,303,450	870,309	628,151	457,509	333,026
4,049,092	3,103,645	2,205,229	1,652,254	1,187,448	937,513
1,340,291	992,683	688,968	502,763	347,318	339,961
179,234	180,682	41,237	40,866	106,465	104,581
764,128	595,205	449,886	339,930	222,610	154,196
–	4,902	5,874	6,411	6,861	7,438
1,690,493	1,277,659	984,672	737,503	488,109	323,942
1.8	1.8	1.9	2.0	2.1	1.7
2.0	1.8	1.8	1.5	1.5	2.0
14.5	14.8	16.4	16.5	13.2	14.0
35.2	33.3	36.7	40.2	38.3	33.3
980	859	745	642	551	491
49	23	11	3		
59,000	57,000	55,000	53,000	50,000	49,000
141,000	104,000	81,000	62,000	46,000	41,000
32,896	21,828	14,799	14,172	4,855	2,698

Exhibit 14.2 Wal-Mart and Sam's: 35 states and growing (fiscal year ended January 31, 1991)

1573 Wal-Mart stores		148 Sam's Clubs	
Alabama	73	Alabama	5
Arizona	20	Arkansas	4
Arkansas	77	Colorado	2
California	10	Florida	15
Colorado	29	Georgia	8
Florida	113	Illinois	8
Georgia	79	Indiana	6
Illinois	80	Iowa	2
Indiana	49	Kansas	2
Iowa	37	Kentucky	3
Kansas	41	Louisiana	9
Kentucky	64	Michigan	2
Louisiana	74	Mississippi	2
Michigan	9	Missouri	8
Minnesota	9	Nebraska	1
Mississippi	56	New Jersey	2
Missouri	105	North Carolina	5
Nebraska	14	North Dakota	1
Nevada	3	Ohio	4
New Mexico	19	Oklahoma	5
North Carolina	58	Pennsylvania	2
North Dakota	5	South Carolina	4
Ohio	28	South Dakota	1
Oklahoma	80	Tennessee	7
Pennsylvania	3	Texas	34
South Carolina	47	Virginia	1
South Dakota	7	West Virginia	1
Tennessee	85	Wisconsin	4
Texas	230		
Utah	5		
Virginia	18		
West Virginia	6		
Wisconsin	33		
Wyoming	7		

price. Wal-Mart assumed $19 million in debt and issued $7.5 million worth of preferred stock. Now Kuhn's has a new management team and $60 million in cash for a major facelift. Profits may pour in, as they did after Wal-Mart's only previous acquisition – the 1977 purchase of Mohr Value Stores. "We fixed them up and retrained the people, and now they're our best group," says Walton.[9] On December 10, 1990, Wal-Mart completed the acquisition of the 14 centers of McLane Company, Inc., a national distribution system in 11 states providing over 12,500 types of grocery and non-grocery products. As of February 2, 1991, Sam's Clubs merged the 28 wholesale clubs of The Whole Club, Inc., of Indianapolis, Indiana, into its operations.[10]

In 1987, Wal-Mart implemented their hypermarkets, 200,000 square foot stores that sell everything including food. Wal-Mart also introduced "Super Centers" (a scaled-down supermarket) in 1988.[11]

Growth in Sales

Growth in administrative and support functions was required to maintain sales growth through new stores and existing stores. However, a strong rein was held on operations and expense controls to permit required flexibility in reacting to change in sales trends. Wal-Mart's expense structure, measured as a percentage of sales, continued to be among the lowest in the industry, as reported in Cornell University's annual study on discount retailers. Within the expense constraints imposed by the company's strategy of selling merchandise at low margins, these support functions have grown at a controlled rate. Again, Sam's management ability came through with a sales volume of $20.65 billion in 1989, up from $15.9 billion in 1988, and from $11.9 billion in 1987 (see exhibit 14.3).[12]

Though Walton watches expenses, he didn't stint on rewarding sales managers. Sales figures were available to every employee. Monthly figures for each department were ranked and made available throughout the organization.[13] Employees who were "doing better than average, they get rewarded with raises, bonuses, and a pat on the back. If they're doing poorer, we have to talk with them to find out why and correct it. This leads to greater productivity." Repeated failure will not likely result in dismissal, although demotions are possible.

All employees (called associates) have a stake in the financial performance of the company. Store managers could earn as much as $100,000–150,000 per year. Part-time clerks even qualified for profit sharing and stock purchase plans. Millionaires among middle managers were not uncommon. Ideas were also solicited from all employees. Executives frequently asked employees if they had ideas for improving the organization. These ideas were noted and often put into use.

Growth in Financial Strength

With his stock selling at 20–30 times earnings – an almost incredible price – Walton presided over a sizable fortune. Wal-Mart stock was 39 percent held by the Walton family. Analysts projected the family holdings to be worth nearly $8 billion. Wal-Mart's long-term debt of $1,052,644,000 included $867 million of capital lease obligations. New stores were funded primarily through the sale of common stock and retained earnings or leaseback arrangements.

Like most discounters, Wal-Mart fills the aisles with tables displaying sales items backed by heavy promotion – an Electronic Bug Killer for $44.96, for example, or an RCA black-and-white 12-inch TV for $79.88. Here, however, was where the chain's competitive edge came in. According to a survey by *Discount Store News*, each Wal-Mart sale table generated twice as much revenue as competitors' (see exhibits 14.4, 14.5, and 14.6).[14]

Exhibit 14.3   Wal-Mart consolidated statements of income

(Amounts in thousands except per share data)	Fiscal year ended January 31		
	1991	1990	1989
Revenues:			
Net sales	$32,601,594	$25,810,656	$20,649,001
Rentals from licensed departments	22,362	16,685	12,961
Other income-net	239,452	157,959	123,906
	32,863,408	25,985,300	20,785,868
Costs and expenses:			
Cost of sales	25,499,834	20,070,034	16,056,856
Operating, selling and general and administrative expenses	5,152,178	4,069,695	3,267,864
Interest costs:			
Debt	42,716	20,346	36,286
Capital leases	125,920	117,725	99,395
	30,820,648	24,277,800	19,460,401
Income before income taxes	2,042,760	1,707,500	1,325,467
Provision for federal and state income taxes:			
Current	737,020	608,912	474,016
Deferred	14,716	22,688	14,230
	751,736	631,600	488,246
Net income	$ 1,291,024	$ 1,075,900	$ 837,221
Net income per share	$ 1.14	$ 0.95[a]	$ 0.74[a]

[a]   Adjusted to reflect the two-for-one stock split on July 6, 1990.

Annual report 1988.

Growth in Shareholders

Original investors have been rewarded spectacularly. Those 1970 Wal-Mart shares cost $16.50 and were worth some $900 in 1982. Since then, Walton had tapped the equity markets five times, raised a total of $123 million and kept his overall capital costs well below those of competitors. In December 1981, Wal-Mart sold $60 million worth of convertible debentures at 9.5 percent. Wal-Mart, in July 1982, announced its intention to sell 2 million shares of additional common. During periods of high interest rates, it's a lot cheaper to sell stock at a 20-times-earnings multiple than borrowing – and it's money you never have to pay back. Their stock has split numerous times, the last split before July 6, 1990 was in 1987.

Wal-Mart became a Wall Street darling, with the number of stockholders on January 31, 1989, totaling approximately 80,270 with over 565 million shares.

Exhibit 14.4   Wal-Mart consolidated balance sheets

	January 31	
(Amounts in thousands)	1991	1990
ASSETS		
Current assets:		
Cash and cash equivalents	$ 13,014	$ 12,790
Receivables	305,070	155,811
Recoverable costs from sale/leaseback	239,867	78,727
Inventories:		
At replacement cost	6,207,852	4,750,619
Less LIFO reserve	399,436	322,546
LIFO	5,808,416	4,428,073
Prepaid expenses	48,408	37,215
TOTAL CURRENT ASSETS	6,414,775	4,712,616
Property, plant and equipment, at cost:		
Land	833,344	463,110
Buildings and improvements	1,764,155	1,227,519
Fixtures and equipment	2,037,476	1,441,752
Transportation equipment	63,237	57,215
	4,698,212	3,189,596
Less accumulated depreciation	974,060	711,763
Net property, plant and equipment	3,724,152	2,477,833
Property under capital leases	1,298,452	1,212,169
Less accumulated amortization	310,565	259,943
Net property under capital leases	987,887	952,226
Other assets and deferred charges	262,101	55,809
Total assets	$11,388,915	$8,198,484
LIABILITIES AND SHAREHOLDERS' EQUITY		
Current liabilities:		
Commercial paper	$ 395,179	$ 184,774
Accounts payable	2,651,315	1,826,720
Accrued liabilities:		
Salaries	189,535	157,216
Other	539,020	473,677
Accrued federal and state income taxes	184,512	179,049
Long-term debt due within one year	6,394	1,581
Obligations under capital leases due within		
one year	24,459	22,298
TOTAL CURRENT LIABILITIES	3,990,414	2,845,315
Long-term debt	740,254	185,152
Long-term obligations under capital leases	1,158,621	1,087,403
Deferred income taxes	134,102	115,053
Shareholders' equity:		
Common stock (shares outstanding,		
1,142,282 in 1991 and 566,135 in 1990)	114,228	56,614
Capital in excess of par value	415,586	180,465
Retained earnings	4,835,710	3,728,482
TOTAL SHAREHOLDERS' EQUITY	5,365,524	3,965,561
Total liabilities and shareholders' equity	$11,388,915	$8,198,484

Exhibit 14.5 Wal-Mart consolidated statements of shareholders' equity

(Amounts in thousands except per share data)	Number of shares	Common stock	Capital in excess of par value	Retained earnings	Total
Balance January 31, 1988	565,112	$56,511	$170,440	$2,030,316	$2,257,267
Net income				837,221	837,221
Cash dividends ($0.08[a] per share)				(90,464)	(90,464)
Exercise of stock options	609	61	2,974		3,035
Tax benefit from stock options			4,778		4,778
Other	(130)	(13)	(3,915)		(3,928)
Balance January 31, 1989	565,591	56,559	174,277	2,777,073	3,007,909
Net income				1,075,900	1,075,900
Cash dividends ($0.11[a] per share)				(124,491)	(124,491)
Exercise of stock options	679	68	3,876		3,944
Tax benefit from stock options			7,000		7,000
Other	(135)	(13)	(4,688)		(4,701)
Balance January 31, 1990	566,135	56,614	180,465	3,728,482	3,965,561
Net income				1,291,024	1,291,024
Cash dividends ($0.14[a] per share)				(158,889)	(158,889)
Exercise of stock options	156	15	1,327		1,342
Other	(34)	(4)	(1,626)		(1,630)
Two-for-one stock split	566,257	56,625	(56,625)		
Exercise of stock options	506	51	2,427		2,478
Shares issued for McLane acquisition	10,366	1,037	273,659		274,696
Tax benefit from stock options			6,075		6,075
Purchase of stock	(1,000)	(100)	(819)	(24,907)	(25,826)
Walton Enterprises, Inc. stock exchange			14,000		14,000
Other	(104)	(10)	(3,297)		(3,307)
Balance January 31, 1991	1,142,282	$114,228	$415,586	$4,835,710	$5,365,524

[a] Cash dividends per share on stock prior to July 6, 1990, have been adjusted to reflect the two-for-one stock split on that date.

During the period 1982–3, its stock price tripled, going as high as $78. This reflected how Sam Walton merchandised his company's stock as skillfully as he does his store. As of April 1989, 33 percent of its shares were held by institutions, and each year he invited over a hundred analysts and institutional investors to the fieldhouse at the University of Arkansas for his annual meeting. The mid-June occasion is a day-and-a-half session where investors meet top executives, as well as Wal-Mart district managers, buyers, and 200,000 hourly salespeople (called associates). Investors see a give-and-take meeting between buyers and district managers. "Walton also introduces his employees. They shout his name and extol him. It's a sight to behold," says a regular attendee.[15]

Exhibit 14.6   Wal-Mart consolidated statements of cash flows

(Amounts in thousands)	Fiscal year ended January 31		
	1991	1990	1989
Cash flows from operating activities:			
Net income	$1,291,024	$1,075,900	$837,221
Adjustments to reconcile net income to net cash provided by operating activities:			
Depreciation and amortization	346,614	269,406	213,629
Loss from sale of assets	3,378	5,039	1,073
Increase in accounts receivable	(58,324)	(29,173)	(30,710)
Increase in inventories	(1,087,520)	(1,076,706)	(699,607)
Decrease (increase) in prepaid expenses	11,823	(11,439)	(6,561)
Increase in accounts payable	689,435	436,990	289,769
Increase in accrued liabilities	84,739	174,112	114,954
Increase in deferred income tax	14,716	22,688	14,230
Net cash provided by operating activities	1,295,885	866,817	733,998
Cash flows from investing activities:			
Payments for property, plant and equipment	(1,388,298)	(954,602)	(592,756)
Recoverable sale/leaseback expenditures	(235,894)	(131,464)	(204,262)
Sale/leaseback arrangements and other property sales	91,000	184,900	246,797
Decrease in other assets	7,058	7,375	9,087
Net cash used in investing activities	(1,526,134)	(893,791)	(541,134)
Cash flows from financing activities:			
Increase (decrease) in commercial paper	30,405	165,774	(85,382)
Proceeds from issuance of long-term debt	500,306	4,763	1,624
Proceeds from Walton Enterprises, Inc. stock exchange	14,000	–	–
Exercise of stock options	4,958	243	3,885
Payments for purchase of common stock	(25,826)	–	–
Dividends paid	(158,889)	(124,491)	(90,464)
Payment of long-term debt	(109,304)	(4,149)	(3,213)
Payment of capital lease obligation	(25,177)	(20,919)	(18,086)
Net cash provided by (used in) financing activities	230,473	27,211	(191,636)
Net increase in cash and cash equivalents	224	237	1,228
Cash and cash equivalents at beginning of year	12,790	12,553	11,325
Cash and cash equivalents at end of year	$ 13,014	$ 12,790	$ 12,553
Supplemental disclosure of cash flow information:			
Income tax paid	$ 721,036	$ 551,021	$473,631
Interest paid	166,134	136,762	134,048
Capital lease obligations incurred	100,972	104,122	164,845
McLane Company, Inc. liabilities at acquisition date	513,000	–	–

Growth in Employee Benefits

The single growth characteristic in which Wal-Mart management has taken the most pride is continued development of their people. Training was seen as critical to outstanding performance, and new programs were implemented on an ongoing basis in all areas of the company. The combination of grass roots meetings, the open door policy, video, printed material, classroom, homestudy, year-end management meetings, and on-the-job training has enabled employees to prepare themselves for assigned advancement and added responsibilities.

Wal-Mart managers also try to stay current with new developments and needed changes. Wal-Mart executives each spend one week per year in hourly jobs in various stores. Walton himself traveled at least three days per week, visiting competitors' stores and attending the opening of new stores, leading the Wal-Mart cheer, "Give me a W, give me an A . . ."[16]

Wal-Mart also encouraged employee stock purchases – about 8 percent of Wal-Mart stock was owned by employees. As of January 31, 1989, 5,336,822 shares of common stock were reserved for issuance under stock option plans. Under the Stock Purchase Plan, stock could be purchased by two different methods. First, an amount was deducted from each check with a maximum of $62.50 per check. An additional 15 percent of the amount deducted is contributed by Wal-Mart, Inc. through the Merrill Lynch stock brokerage firm. Dividends were reinvested in Wal-Mart stock unless otherwise instructed. Second, a lump sum purchase was allowed in April with a maximum of $1500 with an additional 15 percent added by Wal-Mart. For either plan, withdrawal may be made at any time and fractional interest may be purchased because you are buying by the dollar's worth instead of by the share.[17]

At the same time, there was a corporate profit-sharing plan with contributions of $98,327,000 as of January 31, 1991.[18] The purposes of the profit-sharing plan was to furnish an incentive for increased efficiency, to provide progressive recognition of service, and to encourage careers with the company by Wal-Mart associates. This is a trustee-administered plan, which means that the company's contributions to it were made only out of net profits of the company and were held by a trustee. The company from time to time will contribute to the plan such amounts of its net profits, usually 10 percent, as its board of directors shall determine, but not in excess of limits imposed by law.

Company contributions could be withdrawn only upon termination. If you terminate employment with the company because of retirement, death, or total and permanent disability, your company contribution will be fully vested. "Fully vested" means that your entire account is nonforfeitable.

If termination of employment occurs for any other reason, the amount that is nonforfeitable depends upon the number of years of service with the company. After completion of the third year of service with the company, 20 percent of each participant's account will be nonforfeitable for each subsequent year of service so that after seven years of service, a participant's account will be 100 percent vested. This is shown in the following table:

Completed years of service as an associate	Nonforfeitable percentages of company contributions accounts
Less than 3	0
3	20
4	40
5	60
6	80
7	100

For vesting purposes, a year of service credit will not be granted for any plan year during which a participant fails to work at least 1000 hours of service.

Walton is admittedly old-fashioned in many respects. Since Walton exercised considerable control over the culture of Wal-Mart Stores, store policies reflect many of Walton's values. One of the areas in which Walton could be considered particularly old-fashioned is in the area of women. Store policies forbid employees from dating other employees without prior approval of the executive committee. Similarly, women were rare in management positions. Annual manager meetings include sessions for wives to speak out on the problems of living with a Wal-Mart manager. No women were in the ranks of top management. Walton had also resisted placing women on the board of directors. Only 12 (17 percent) women have made it to the ranks of buyers. Walton is an EEOC/AA employer but has managed to get away with "apparent" discriminatory practices because most Wal-Marts were located in small rural towns in the Sun Belt States (open shop).

Growth in Marketing Strategies

Wal-Mart implemented many marketing strategies. Wal-Mart drew customers into the store by the use of radio and television advertising, a monthly circular, and weekly newspaper ads. Television advertising was used to convey an image of everyday low prices and quality merchandise. Radio was used to a lesser degree to promote specific products that were usually of high demand. Newspaper and monthly circulars were the major contributors to the program emphasizing deeply discounted items. They were effective at luring customers into the store.

Efforts were also made to discount corporate overhead. Visitors often mistook corporate headquarters for a warehouse owing to its limited decoration and "show." Wal-Mart executives were expected to share hotel rooms when traveling to reduce expenses. Walton also avoided spending money on consultants and marketing experts. He preferred instead to base decisions on intuitive judgments of employees and on his assessment of the strategies of other retail chains.

Walton entered into the ranks of the "deep" discounters with the opening of three Sam's Wholesale Clubs in 1984. As of January 31, 1991, there were 148 Sam's Wholesale Clubs, and three Hypermarts, with 15 distribution warehouses in operation; Walton had become the nation's largest deep discounter, passing K-Mart. As of February 2, 1991, Sam's Clubs merged the 28 wholesale clubs of The Wholesale Club, Inc., of Indianapolis, Indiana, into its operations. These new partners have 28 units located in six states in the Midwest. Also as of December 10,

1990, Wal-Mart completed the acquisition of the McLane Company, Inc., a provider of retail and grocery distribution services with 14 national distribution centers in 11 states. The "Super Center" was Wal-Mart's strategy to grow in smaller markets. Wal-Mart has been innovative in many of its marketing strategies. Since the mid-1980s Wal-Mart had advertised its "Buy American" policy in an effort to keep production at home. As such Wal-Mart buyers were constantly seeking vendors in grass roots America. As an example Wal-Mart dropped Fuji for 3M film. Additionally, Wal-Mart censors products it does not like. For example, Wal-Mart banned LPs, removed magazines, and pulled albums over graphics and lyric content as well as stopped marketing teen rock magazines.[19]

Growth in Distribution Centers

Close to 77 percent of the chain's merchandise passed through one of fifteen distribution warehouses. That percentage was more than K-Mart or Sears. Distributing, with the newest warehouse in late 1990, gave Wal-Mart a total of nearly 6 million square feet of storage space.

Wal-Mart's distribution operations were highly automated. Terminals at each store were used to wire merchandise requests to a warehouse, which in turn either shipped immediately or placed a reorder. Wal-Mart computers were linked directly with over 200 vendors, making deliveries even faster. "We spend a little over 2 cents for every dollar we ship out," says Walton. "For others it's around 4 cents. That's a 2 percent edge right there on gross margins."[20]

Wal-Mart owns a fleet of truck-tractors that could deliver goods to any store in 36 to 48 hours from the time the order is placed. "After our trucks drop off merchandise at our stores, they frequently pick up merchandise from manufacturers on the way back to the distribution center," says president Jack Shewmaker. "Our back-haul rate was currently running over 60 percent."[21] You don't need a computer to see this as yet another way of cutting costs.

Wal-Mart had one of the world's largest private satellite communication systems to control distribution. In addition Wal-Mart pledged to install POS bar-code scanning in all of its stores by 1990. Wal-Mart computers talked directly to vendors, trimming days off the ordering process.[22]

Management Succession

November 1987 was Wal-Mart's 25th anniversary. Sam Walton named David D. Glass president and CEO, and appointed himself as Chairman of the Board. For several years thereafter it was rumored that Mr Walton was suffering from bone cancer. This was confirmed, but in 1991, at age 73, Sam Walton is still active and visits most stores on a regular basis, flying his own private airplane. Mr Glass had continued the success of Wal-Mart Stores, and they had passed K-Mart in Sales in 1991, with only Sears Roebuck having greater annual sales. Can Mr Glass pass Sears in sales? (see exhibit 14.7). What strategies should Mr Glass initiate now that

Exhibit 14.7   Wal-Mart board of directors

		Committees of the board
David R. Banks	Chairman of the Board, President, and Chief Executive Officer Beverly Enterprises	Executive Committee
		Paul R. Carter
Paul R. Carter	Executive Vice President and Chief Financial Officer, Wal-Mart Stores, Inc.	David D. Glass
		A. L. Johnson
Hillary Rodham Clinton	Partner, Rose Law Firm, PA	R. Drayton McLane Jr
John A. Cooper Jr	Chairman of the Board, Cooper Communities, Inc.	Donald G. Soderquist
Robert H. Dedman	Chairman of the Board, Club Corporation International	James L. Walton
David D. Glass	President and Chief Executive Officer, Wal-Mart Stores, Inc.	Sam M. Walton
F. Kenneth Iverson	Chairman of the Board and Chief Executive Officer, Nucor Corporation	S. Robson Walton
A. L. Johnson	Vice Chairman, Wal-Mart Stores, Inc., Chief Executive Officer, Sam's Clubs, Division of Wal-Mart Stores, Inc.	Audit Committee
		F. Kenneth Iverson
James H. Jones	Chairman of the Board and Chief Executive Officer, Jameson Pharmaceutical Corp.	James H. Jones
		Robert Kahn
Robert Kahn	President, Robert Kahn and Associates Wal-Mart Stores, Inc. Consultant	
		Stock Option Committee
R. Drayton McLane Jr	Vice Chairman, Wal-Mart Stores, Inc.	David D. Glass
	President and Chief Executive Officer McLane Company, Inc., a wholly owned subsidiary of Wal-Mart Stores, Inc.	Donald G. Soderquist
		S. Robson Walton
Jack Shewmaker	Vice Chairman, Retired, Wal-Mart Stores, Inc. Consultant	Special Stock Option Committee
Donald G. Soderquist	Vice Chairman and Chief Operating Officer, Wal-Mart Stores, Inc.	John A. Cooper, Jr.
		F. Kenneth Iverson
John E. Tate	Executive Vice President, Retired, Wal-Mart Stores, Inc. Consultant	James H. Jones
James L. Walton	Senior Vice President, Wal-Mart Stores, Inc.	
Sam M. Walton	Chairman of the Board, Wal-Mart Stores, Inc.	
S. Robson Walton	Vice Chairman, Wal-Mart Stores, Inc.	

K-Mart has finally realized it is no longer the number one discount store in the USA? Wal-Mart plans to open five warehouse clubs, called Club Aurrera, a joint venture with Cifra (Mexico's largest retailer), before the end of 1992.[23] Will Wal-Mart's strategy work in Mexico?

NOTES AND REFERENCES

1 Howard Rudnitsky, "How Sam Walton does it," *Forbes*, August 1982, p. 42.

2 Op. cit.

3 Wal-Mart's Annual Report, January 31, 1991.

4 "Wal-Mart makes a savvy move," *Arkansas Gazette*, July 15, 1991, p. 18.

5 Nora E. Field and Richard Sookdeo, *Fortune*, August 26, 1991, p. 179.

6 Wal-Mart's Annual Report, January 31, 1988.

7 Jane Carmichael, "General Retailers," *Forbes*, January 1982, p. 226.

8 "Wal-Mart's relentless march to $100 Billion," *Arkansas Gazette*, June 1, 1991, p. 7.

9 Rudnitsky, op. cit., p. 44.

10 Wal-Mart's Annual Report, January 31, 1991.

11 Alice Bredin, "Hypermarkets: successful at last?" *Chain Store Age Executive*, 64, January 1988, p. 15.

12 Wal-Mart's Annual Report, January 31, 1988.

13 Rudnitsky, op. cit., p. 44.

14 Wal-Mart's Annual Report, January 31, 1988.

15 Breden, op. cit., p. 43.

16 John Huey, *Fortune*, September 23, 1991, p. 46.

17 "Summary plan description," *Profit Sharing Plan*, February 1980, p. 4.

18 Wal-Mart's Annual Report, January 31, 1991.

19 Arthur Markowitz, "Wal-Mart's super centers," *Discount Store News*, 27, March 28, 1988, p. 12 (2).

20 Rudnitsky, op. cit.

21 Op. cit.

22 Markowitz, op. cit.

23 Stephen Baker and Lynne Walker, *Business Week*, September 30, p. 102.

CADBURY SCHWEPPES PLC

*Franz Lohrke, James Combs,
and Gary J. Castrogiovanni*

All large [food] companies have broken out of their product boundaries. They are no longer the bread, beer, meat, milk or confectionery companies they were a relatively short time ago – they are food and drink companies. (Sir Adrian Cadbury, Chairman, (retired) Cadbury Schweppes plc, in Smith et al., 1990, p. 9)

In the early 1990s, Cadbury Schweppes plc embodied the archetypical modern food conglomerate. With extensive international operations in confectionery products and soft drinks, the company maintained a diversified global presence. Although Cadbury had enjoyed a relatively stable competitive environment through much of the company's history, contemporary developments in the international arena presented Cadbury management with many different and critical challenges.

The History of Cadbury

The company began in 1831 when John Cadbury began processing cocoa and chocolate in the United Kingdom (UK) to be used in beverages. In 1847, the company became Cadbury Brothers, and in 1866 it enjoyed its first major achievement when the second generation of Cadburys found a better way to process cocoa. By using an imported cocoa press to remove unpalatable cocoa butter from the company's hot cocoa drink mix instead of adding large quantities of sweeteners, Cadbury capitalized on a growing public concern for adulterated food.

The company further prospered when it later found that cocoa butter could be

Exhibit 15.1 Cadbury's foreign direct investment

1914–1918	1921	1930	1933	1937	1939–1945
First World War	Australia	New Zealand	Ireland	South Africa	Second World War

Source: Jones, 1986.

used in recipes for edible chocolates. In 1905, Cadbury introduced Cadbury Dairy Milk (CDM) as a challenge to Swiss firms' virtual monopoly in British milk chocolate sales. A year later, the firm scored another success with the introduction of a new hot chocolate drink mix, Bournville Cocoa. These two brands provided much of the impetus for Cadbury's early prosperity (Jones, 1986).

Cadbury faced rather benign competition throughout many of the firm's early years. In fact, at one point, Cadbury provided inputs for the UK operations of the American firm Mars, Inc. (Smith et al., 1990). Cadbury also formed trade associations with its UK counterparts, J. S. Fry and Rowntree & Co., for the purpose of, among other things, reducing uncertainty in cocoa prices. The company later merged financial interests with J. S. Fry, but spurned offers to consolidate with Rowntree in 1921 and 1930 (Jones, 1986).

Facing growing protectionist threats in overseas markets following the First World War, Cadbury began manufacturing outside the UK, primarily in Commonwealth countries (see exhibit 15.1). This international growth was also prompted by increasing competition. For example, by 1932 Cadbury management considered the Swiss company, Nestlé, as its primary competitor in the international arena (Jones, 1986).

In 1969, Cadbury merged with Schweppes, the worldwide maker of soft drinks and mixers. The merger offered both companies an array of advantages, both defensive and offensive. First of all, both companies faced potential takeover threats from larger firms, so the merger placed the new company in a better defensive posture to ward off unwanted suitors. On the offensive side, the marriage allowed the new company to compete better on a worldwide scale.

Cadbury had invested primarily in Commonwealth countries, and Schweppes had branched out into Europe and North America, so the new company enjoyed greater geographic dispersion. The increased international presence also allowed the company to defray product development costs over a wider geographic base. Furthermore, the new company enjoyed greater bargaining power from suppliers. For example, following the merger, Cadbury Schweppes became the largest UK purchaser of sugar (Smith et al., 1990).

The British confectionery companies historically pursued a different strategy than their American counterparts. While US companies, such as Mars, Inc., manufactured narrow product lines and employed centralized production, Cadbury maintained 237 confectionery products until the Second World War forced the company to scale back to 29. While faced with a lack of intense competition, Cadbury's brand proliferation strategy could be undertaken. As rivalry heated up in the mid-1970s, though, Cadbury's share of the UK chocolate market fell from 31.1 to 26.2 percent between 1975 and 1977. Management then began to realize that the lower cost, American-style strategy of rationalized product lines and centralized production provided the only viable means to compete (Child and Smith, 1987).

Cadbury had long been famous for its unique management style. "Cadburyism" drew influence from the founders' Quaker heritage, providing for worker welfare and harmonious community relations. Following Cadbury's reorientation toward core products and rationalized production, though, the company's old management style underwent a transformation. Confectionery manufacturing personnel were reduced from 8565 to 4508 between 1978 and 1985 (Child and Smith, 1987). In the process, management's traditional close relationship with workers, which had been built through years of maintaining employment stability, began to erode as worker reduction became a professed goal of Cadbury executives.

The Environment

As is the case with several products in the food industry, many of Cadbury's product lines enjoyed very long product life cycles. (See exhibit 15.2 for assorted confectionery products of Cadbury and its rivals.) Food and beverage companies derived substantial benefit from their long-established products, such as Cadbury's CDM bar, and the occasional new product introductions required little in the way of technological investment. The food companies, therefore, competed primarily by seeking cost reduction through process improvements such as automation, by finding alternative inputs to replace expensive cocoa, and by introducing creative packaging and marketing (Child and Smith, 1987).

Successful new product introductions remained sporadic, and many of the most successful confectionery products, such as Mars Bar and Rowntree's Kit Kat, had been around since the 1930s (Tisdall, 1982). Some unsatisfied demanded seemed to persist, however, as was evidenced by Rowntree's successful 1976 launch of its Yorkie bar, Mars' profitable introduction of Twix a few years later, Cadbury's notable 1984 launch in the UK of its Wispa bar, and Hershey's 1988 introduction of Bar None (Weber, 1989).

Nevertheless, new brand introductions required immense investments in development and marketing costs with only limited possibilities for success. For instance, various research suggests that approximately 60 percent of new food product introductions have been withdrawn inside of five years, and this figure may be an underestimate (Smith et al., 1990). Consequently, established brands with customer loyalty represented crucial assets for food and beverage companies.

Modern Cadbury-Schweppes

Expansion was key to Cadbury's plans to improve its international position. Chief Executive Officer Dominic Cadbury commented, "If you're not operating in terms

Exhibit 15.2   Assorted major brand names of Cadbury Schweppes and its confectionery
competition

Cadbury Schweppes:

Cadbury Dairy Milk (CDM)	Whole Nut
Milk Tray	Roses
Crunchie	Fruit and Nut
Wispa	Trebor

Nestlé:

Nestlé Crunch bar	Polo
Kit Kat	Quality Street
Smarties	Yorkie
After Eight	Aero
Rolo	Black Magic
Dairy Box	Fruit Pastilles
Butterfinger	Baby Ruth

M&M/Mars, Inc.:

Mars Bar	Galaxy
Twix	Maltesers
Bounty	Milky Way
M&Ms	Snickers

Hershey:

Hershey bars	Reese's Peanut Butter Cup
Hershey Kisses	Reese's Pieces
Mounds	Almond Joy

Phillip Morris:

Milka
Toblerone
E. J. Brachs candy

of world market share, you're unlikely to have the investment needed to support your brands" (Borrus et al., 1986, p. 132). In 1986, Cadbury shared third place in the world with Rowntree and Hershey, each having approximately 5 percent of the market. Nestlé held second place with about 7.5 percent, while Mars dominated internationally with approximately 13 percent (van de Vliet, 1986, pp. 44–5).

To generate its necessary worldwide expansion, Cadbury had two primary markets in which to gain positions. Enjoying a dominant position in its home market, the company realized that the United States and the remaining countries of the European Community (those besides the UK) provided critical markets for a worldwide standing. According to Terry Organ, director of international confectionery, "Rightly or wrongly . . . we decided to tackle the US first" (van de Vliet, 1986, p. 45). Earlier, Cadbury had taken steps toward competing more vigorously in the USA by acquiring Peter Paul in 1978. By 1980, however, the company still controlled only about 3.5 percent of the US confectionery market, far eclipsed by its bigger rivals, Hershey and Mars.

Cadbury did not have sufficient size to employ the sales force of its competitors. The company, therefore, had to rely on food brokers to push products to whole-salers, which left the firm far removed from the consumer. Further, the company could be easily outspent in advertising by its two larger rivals (Borrus et al., 1986).

To compound problems, the company also committed two marketing blunders in the US market. When Cadbury introduced Whispa, the company's marketing success of the decade in the UK, management did not realize that distribution channels in the USA were longer than in the UK. Consequently, the candy bars aged seven to nine months by the time they reached test markets in New England, and consumers reacted accordingly.

The company's second mistake occurred following an effort to standardize its candy bar size across countries. When Cadbury first introduced its CDM bar in the USA, the bar commanded a higher price than its US rivals. Since CDM was also larger than US competitors' regular bars, consumers were willing to pay a little extra. When Cadbury reduced the size, management discovered that given the choice between CDM and American confectionery products of equal size and price, US consumers usually chose the more familiar American products (van de Vliet, 1986). According to one former Cadbury executive, "What happened in the US was a gigantic, gargantuan cock-up, and the fact that London [Cadbury headquarters] did not know what was happening is a sheer disgrace" (Gofton, 1986, p. 20).

Not all the news from the other side of the Atlantic was bad for the UK com-pany, however. Although Peter Paul Cadbury only commanded a small slice of the market, some products, such as Coconut Mounds and York Peppermint Patties, dominated their segments. Cadbury's Creme Eggs also enjoyed seasonal success. Moreover, the company's acquisition of Canada Dry from R. J. Reynolds pro-vided Cadbury Schweppes with a strong position in the carbonated mixers mar-ket in the USA and many other countries (see exhibit 15.3 for US market shares). For example, although Cadbury Schweppes only commanded about a 3 percent market share in the $43 billion US soft drink industry, the company sold Canada Dry, the number one ginger ale and club soda in the USA, and Schweppes, the lead-ing tonic water in the American market (Winters, 1990). Additionally, the cola giants, Coca-Cola and PepsiCo, did not (as yet) vigorously market products in seg-ments dominated by Cadbury Schweppes. Overall, though, the company faced an uphill struggle in many segments of the US market.

In an effort to remedy some of the company's problems in the US confectionery market, Cadbury decided to sell its manufacturing assets to Hershey in 1988, cata-pulting the Pennsylvania company to the dominant position in the US market (see exhibit 15.4). Cadbury also granted Hershey licenses to manufacture and sell its Peter Paul products, including Mounds, Almond Joy, and York Peppermint Patties. Under this arrangement, Cadbury gained the benefit of Hershey's marketing muscle behind the Peter Paul products (Swarns and Toran, 1988).

Cadbury faced additional challenges to building market share in the European Community (EC). Schweppes' beverages enjoyed success on the Continent (Borrus et al., 1986), but Europe's confectionery industry proved difficult to break into since the market remained dominated by family-owned firms and suffered from overcapacity (van de Vliet, 1986). Successful expansion in the EC, however, was

Exhibit 15.3 Top five soft drink companies in the USA (percentage of total market)

	1986	1987	1988	1989	1990
Coca-Cola, Co.	39.8	39.9	39.8	40.0	40.4
Classic	19.1	19.8	19.9	19.5	19.4
Diet Coke	7.2	7.7	8.1	8.8	9.1
Sprite	3.6	3.6	3.6	3.6	3.6
PepsiCo	30.6	30.8	31.3	31.7	31.8
Pepsi-Cola	18.6	18.6	18.4	17.8	17.3
Diet Pepsi	4.4	4.8	5.2	5.7	6.2
Mountain Dew	3.0	3.3	3.4	3.6	3.8
Dr Pepper	4.8	5.0	5.3	5.6	5.8
Dr Pepper	3.9	4.0	4.3	4.6	4.8
Diet Dr Pepper	0.4	0.4	0.4	0.4	0.4
Seven-Up	5.0	5.1	4.7	4.3	4.0
7-Up	3.5	3.4	3.1	3.0	2.9
Diet 7-Up	1.4	1.0	1.0	0.9	0.9
Cadbury Schweppes	4.2	3.7	3.5	3.1	3.2
Canada Dry	1.4	1.4	1.4	1.3	1.2
Sunkist	0.9	0.7	0.7	0.7	0.7
Schweppes products	0.5	0.5	0.5	0.6	0.6
Crush	1.4	1.0	0.8	0.6	0.6
Total market share of top five	84.5	84.5	84.5	84.6	85.2

Source: Standard and Poor's Industry Surveys, 1991.

crucial to Cadbury's remaining a dominant player in the worldwide food and beverage industries.

Contemporary Challenges

The 1990s brought about radical shifts in the industries in which Cadbury Schweppes competed. First, corporate leaders (and stock markets) discovered that food and beverage enterprises with established brand names were not mundane investments offering only lackluster financial returns. Purchasing popular brands or taking over companies that had portfolios full of well known products often provided a safer and more economical avenue for growth than attempting to develop entirely new products. In 1985, for instance, Philip Morris acquired General Foods for $5.75 billion, approximately three times book value, while R. J. Reynolds laid out $4.9 billion for Nabisco Brands (van de Vliet, 1986).

These attempts to acquire popular brands were also dictated by dramatic industry-wide changes which altered the nature of competition faced by the international food and beverage enterprises. First, the push by the 12 countries of the EC to remove trade barriers among the member nations by 1992 sparked a buying frenzy

Exhibit 15.4   Top five companies in the $8 billion US confectionery market (percentage of total market)

1980		1988	
Company	Market share	Company	Market share
Mars	17.0	Hershey	20.5
Hershey	15.3	Mars	18.5
Nabisco	7.1	Jacobs Suchard	6.7
E. J. Brachs	6.4	Nestlé	6.7
Peter/Paul Cadbury	3.5	Leaf	5.6

Source: Weber, 1989.

Exhibit 15.5   The USA and the European Community (EC)

	USA	EC
Population	243.8 million	323.6 million
Gross national product (GNP) (in 1987 US$)	4.436 trillion	3.782 trillion
Per capita GNP (US$)	18,200	11,690
Inflation (%)	3.7	3.1
Unemployment (%)	6.1	11.0

Note: EC members include the UK (England, Scotland, Wales, Northern Ireland), Ireland, Denmark, Germany, France, Belgium, the Netherlands, Luxembourg, Portugal, Spain, Italy, and Greece, and more recently these were joined in the European Union by Austria, Finland, and Sweden.

Source: House, 1989.

of European food companies with established brand names (see exhibit 15.5 for a comparison of the North American and EC market). Many non-European companies feared that the EC would eventually increase tariff barriers for products from outside the Community, which could have effectively closed foreign companies out of the market. This anticipation of "Fortress Europe" sent companies without EC operations scurrying to acquire European enterprises.

Second, the common perception that only the largest companies in most industries would survive in Europe as well as internationally contributed to the takeover hysteria. To become big quickly, companies began aggressively acquiring rival food companies. For example, Nestlé scored a major victory in July 1988 when it outbid its Swiss counterpart, Jacob Suchard, to acquire Cadbury's long time UK competitor, Rowntree. In the process, Nestlé moved from a minor status in the EC confectionery market into a first place duel with Mars. In the UK market, Nestlé's acquisition positioned the company in a second place battle with Mars and within striking distance of first place Cadbury (*Mergers and Acquisitions*, 1989). In January 1992, Nestlé also attempted to continue its acquisition binge by launching a hostile takeover bid for the French mineral water company, Source Perrier.

Other major food conglomerates, such as Phillip Morris (USA) and Unilever

Exhibit 15.6   Food sales, Europe, including the UK (US$ billions)

Nestlé	15.1
Unilever	12.2
Phillip Morris[a]	8.0
BSN	7.8
Mars	4.1
Cadbury Schweppes	3.1

[a]   Includes Jacobs Suchard

Source: Templeman and Melcher, 1990.

Group (UK/Netherlands) were also rumored to be on the prowl for acquisitions in Europe (Browning and Studer, 1992). These heavyweights not only presented medium-sized food and beverage companies like Cadbury with increased competition in the marketplace, they also represented potential bidders in any acquisitions attempted by Cadbury. This increased competition threatened to drive up acquisition prices through cutthroat bidding for popular brand names. In fact, as the takeover battles became more heated, stock market analysts speculated that Cadbury and other medium-sized companies could find themselves targets of acquisition attempts (Browning and Studer, 1992).

The European food and beverage industries were undergoing other changes along with the acquisition binges. At the end of the food and beverage distribution pipeline, for example, many European supermarkets were also consolidating. In April 1990, eight EC grocery chains formed an alliance to combine buying power and promote house brands. As these supermarket companies combined forces, they greatly enhanced their bargaining power against the food and beverage companies. This increased power threatened future profits of food and beverage companies since the grocery chains' ability to demand price concessions from the companies was enhanced by the stores' consolidation. Furthermore, since supermarkets only wanted to carry the top two or three brands for each product type, food and beverage companies faced the option of acquiring popular brands or risking lost shelf space in stores (Templeman and Melcher, 1990).

In response to these massive changes in the industry, Cadbury also began acquiring name brand products and searching for strategic alliances. In 1986, for example, the company decided to end its bottling agreement with Pepsi to form a joint venture with Coke in the UK (Gofton, 1986). In 1990, Cadbury purchased the European soft drink operations of Source Perrier (Templeman and Melcher, 1990), and in 1991 the company formed a joint venture with Appolinarus Brunnen AG, a German bottler of sparkling water.

With the competitive environment heating up, Cadbury management faced a number of crucial questions. Could the company continue to compete independently against the food and beverage mega-corporations that were forming or should Cadbury merge with another company before being faced with a hostile takeover attempt? Did Cadbury have the resources to acquire more brand names or should management continue to investigate the joint venture route? Should the company reduce emphasis on Europe and instead attempt to exploit new opportunities in the underdeveloped Asian market? Whatever Cadbury Schweppes management decided to do, it had to move quickly. The choices of popular name brand food and beverage products on the table were being cleared away fast.

Exhibit 15.7 Cadbury Schweppes 1990 worldwide sales (UK£ millions)

Region	Total sales	Confectionery	Beverages
United Kingdom	1,476.0	715.4	760.6
Continental Europe	638.0	195.6	442.4
Americas	403.7	18.3	373.5
Pacific Rim	495.5[a]	n.a.	n.a.
Africa and other	132.9	91.2	38.8

Note: Total sales will not always equal confectionery plus beverages. In the USA (Americas region), for example, Cadbury Schweppes also generated sales from its Mott's subsidiary.

£1 = $1.93 in 1990.

[a] Sales primarily in Australia/New Zealand

Source: "Compact disclosure," Wall Street Journal.

Exhibit 15.8 Cadbury Schweppes financials (UK£ thousands)

	BALANCE SHEET		
Fiscal Year Ending	December 29, 1990	December 30, 1989	December 31, 1988
ASSETS			
Cash	62,600	57,400	41,300
Marketable securities	118,000	33,300	200,700
Receivables	554,100	548,200	434,500
Inventories	328,200	334,800	253,400
Total current assets	1,062,900	973,700	929,900
Net prop., plant, equip.	978,800	822,500	602,200
Other long-term assets	320,700	332,600	20,700
Total assets	2,362,400	2,128,800	1,552,800
LIABILITIES			
Notes payable	60,100	57,400	92,200
Accounts payable	272,100	263,900	409,500
Current capital leases	76,200	76,300	21,900
Accrued expenses	320,900	305,900	52,100
Income taxes	78,200	95,800	81,800
Other current liab.	154,700	143,600	118,800
Total current liab.	962,200	942,900	776,300
Long-term debt	407,900	381,400	124,700
Other long-term liab.	108,401	124,000	74,600
Total liabilities	1,478,500	1,448,300	975,600
Preferred stock	300	N/A	3,300
Net common stock	174,400	173,600	150,400
Capital surplus	95,800	36,700	33,000

Exhibit 15.8 (Cont'd)

Retained earnings	115,800	167,600	88,800
Miscellaneous	381,600	217,400	210,500
Total shareholders' equity	767,900	595,300	486,000
Minority interest	116,000	85,200	91,200
Tot. liab. & net worth	2,362,400	2,128,800	1,552,800

INCOME STATEMENT

Fiscal year ending	December 29, 1990	December 30, 1989	December 31, 1988
Net sales	3,146,100	2,766,700	2,381,600
Cost of goods sold	1,738,400	1,596,900	1,365,000
Gross profit	1,407,700	1,179,800	1,016,600
Sell gen. & admin. exp.	1,074,700	907,500	787,800
Income before int. & tax	333,000	272,300	228,800
Non-operating income	3,800	3,100	4,400
Interest expense	57,200	31,100	17,500
Income before taxes	279,600	244,300	215,700
Taxes & misc. expenses	100,200	85,500	75,200
Income before ex. items	179,400	157,800	140,500
Extraordinary items	N/A	15,200	28,400
Net income	179,400	173,000	168,900
£1=	$1.93	$1.61	$1.81

Source: "Compact disclosure," *Wall Street Journal*.

REFERENCES

Borrus, A., Sassen, J. and Harris, M. A. (1986) "Why Cadbury Schweppes looks sweet to the raiders," *Business Week*, January 13, 132–3.

Browning, E. S. and Studer, M. (1992) "Nestlé and Indosuez launch hostile bid for Perrier in contest with Agnellis," *Wall Street Journal*, January 21, A3.

Child, J. and Smith, C. (1987) "The context and process of organizational transformation – Cadbury Limited in its sector," *Journal of Management Studies*, 24, 565–93.

Gofton, K. (1986) "Has Cadbury got his finger on the button?," *Marketing*, July 31, 20–5.

House, K. E. (1989) "The 90's & beyond: the US stands to retain its global leadership," *Wall Street Journal*, January 23, A8.

Jones, G. (1986) "The chocolate multinationals: Cadbury, Fry and Rowntree 1918–1939," in G. Jones (ed.), *British Multinationals: Origins, Management and Performance*. Brookfield, VT: Gower Publishing Co, 96–118.

Mergers and Acquisitions (1989) "The Nestlé–Rowntree deal: bitter battle, sweet result," September/October, 66–7.

Smith, C., Child, J. and Rowlinson, M. (1990) *Reshaping Work: the Cadbury Experience*. Cambridge: Cambridge University Press.

Standard and Poor's Industry Surveys (1991) "Food, beverages, and tobacco," June 27, F23–F27.

Swarns, R. L. and Toran, B. (1988) "Hershey to buy US business from Cadbury," *Wall Street Journal*, July 25, 30.

Templeman, J. and Melcher, R. A. (1990) "Supermarket Darwinism: the survival of the fattest," *Business Week*, July 9, 42.

Tisdall, P. (1982) "Chocolate soldiers clash," *Marketing*, July 29, 30–4.

van de Vliet, A. (1986) "Bittersweet at Cadbury," *Management Today*, March, 42–9.

Wall Street Journal, Various issues.

Weber, J. (1989) "Why Hershey is smacking its lips," *Business Week*, October 30, 140.

Winters, P. (1990) "Cadbury Schweppes' plan: skirt cola giants," *Advertising Age*, August 13, 22–3.

KENTUCKY FRIED CHICKEN IN CHINA

Allen J. Morrison and Paul Beamish

In late September 1986, Tony Wang leaned back in his leather chair in his Singapore office and thought of the long road that lay ahead if Kentucky Fried Chicken (KFC) were ever to establish the first completely Western-style fast food joint venture in the People's Republic of China. Wang, an experienced entrepreneur and seven-year veteran of KFC had only two months previously accepted the position of company vice president for Southeast Asia with an option of bringing the world's largest chicken restaurant company into the world's most populous country. Yet, as he began exploring the opportunities facing KFC in Southeast Asia, Wang was beginning to wonder whether the company should attempt to enter the Chinese market at this time.

Without any industry track record, Wang wondered how to evaluate the attractiveness of the Chinese market within the context of KFC's Southeast Asia region. Compounding the challenge was the realization that although China was a huge, high profile market, it would demand precious managerial resources and could offer no real term prospects for significant hard currency profit repatriation – even in the medium term. Wang also realized that a decision to go into China necessitated

This case was prepared for the sole purpose of providing material for class discussion at the Western Business School. Certain names and other identifying information may have been disguised to protect confidentiality. It is not intended to illustrate either effective or ineffective handling of a managerial situation. Funding was provided by The Federation of Canadian Municipalities' Open City Project through a grant from the Canadian International Development Agency (CIDA) and by The University of Western Ontario. Copyright © The University of Western Ontario and CIDA, 1989.

selecting a particular investment location in the face of great uncertainty. It was equally clear that while opportunities and risks varied widely from city to city, the criteria for evaluating suitable locations remained unspecified. With limited information to go on, Wang realized that a positive decision on China would be inherently risky – both for the company and for his own reputation. And while Wang was intrigued by the enormous potential of the Chinese market, he also knew that many others had failed in similar ventures.

History

The origins of Kentucky Fried Chicken can be traced to Harland Sanders, who was born in 1890 in Henreyville, Indiana. When Sanders was a boy, he dropped out of the sixth grade and began a stream of odd jobs, concentrating eventually on cooking. In time he opened his own gas station with an adjoining restaurant. In the 1930s, Sanders developed a "secret" recipe for cooking chicken by first applying a coating containing a mixture of 11 herbs and spices and then frying the chicken under pressure. This "southern fried chicken" eventually became a hit at the gas station and in 1956 Sanders decided to franchise his novel concept. By 1964, he had sold almost 700 franchises. Much of Sanders' success in this pioneer industry lay in his near obsession with product quality and a commitment to maintaining a focused line of products.

In 1964, at the age of 74, Harland Sanders finally agreed to sell the business in exchange for US$ 2 million and a promise of a lifetime salary. The sale of the business to John Brown, a 29-year-old Kentucky lawyer, and his financial backer, Jack Massey, 60, was accompanied by the assurance that Sanders would maintain an active role in both product promotion and quality control of the new venture.

With new, aggressive managers and a rapidly evolving American fast food industry, KFC's growth soared. Over the next five years, sales grew by an average of 96 percent per year, topping $200 million by 1970. This same year almost 1000 new stores were built, the vast majority by franchisees.

A key element in this rapid growth was Brown's ability to select a group of hard-working entrepreneurial managers. Brown's philosophy was that every manager had the right to expect to become wealthy in the rapidly growing company. By relying heavily on franchising, the company was able to avoid the high capital costs associated with rapid expansion while maximizing returns to shareholders. Rapid sales growth provided promotion and opportunities to purchase stock for company managers as well as the opportunity for franchisees to improve margins by spreading administrative costs over a broader base of operations. This was critically important given the high fixed costs associated with each store. Volume, both at the individual store level and within a franchisee's territory, was thus essential in determining profitability. Profitability, in turn, assured the attractiveness of KFC to potential future franchisees.

In 1971, Brown and Massey sold KFC to Heublein Inc. for $275 million. Heublein, based in Farmington, Connecticut, was a packaged goods company which marketed such products as Smirnoff vodka, Black Velvet Canadian whisky, Grey Poupon mustard, and A1 steak sauce.

Challenges at home and abroad

The establishment of KFC's international operations began just prior to the company's acquisition by Heublein. KFC opened its first store in the Far East in Osaka, Japan in 1970 as part of Expo-70. By 1973, KFC had established 64 stores in Japan, mostly in the Tokyo area. KFC also moved quickly into Hong Kong, establishing 15 stores there by 1973. Other areas of expansion included Australia, the UK, and South Africa.

Shortly after the acquisition, KFC's small international staff was merged with Heublein's much larger international group in Connecticut. In spite of Heublein's efforts to impose rigid operational controls, KFC country managers were frustrated by the imposition of US store designs, menus, and marketing methods on culturally divergent host countries. Resistance to corporate control grew and led many stores to develop their own menus: fried fish and smoked chicken in Japan, hamburgers in South Africa, and roast chicken in Australia. In some cases, local managers seemed to know what they were doing; in other cases, they clearly did not. After heavy losses, KFC pulled out of Hong Kong entirely in 1975. In Japan, operations also began on shaky grounds with losses experienced throughout much of the 1970s.

In addition to poor relations between country managers and corporate staff, the 1970s presented a much more challenging environment for KFC in the United States. The fast food industry was becoming much more competitive with the national emergence of the Church's Fried Chicken franchise and the onset of several strong regional competitors. Important market share gains were also being made by McDonald's hamburgers.

With the Heublein acquisition, many top managers who had been hired by Brown and Massey were either fired or quit, resulting in much turmoil among the franchisees. By 1976, sales were off 8 percent and profits were decreasing by 26 percent per year. To make matters worse, rapid expansion had led to inconsistent quality, poor cleanliness and a burgeoning group of disenchanted franchisees who represented over 80 percent of total KFC sales. At one point, even white-haired Harland Sanders was publicly quoted admitting that many stores lacked adequate cleanliness while providing shoddy customer service and poor product quality.

Turning operations around

In the fall of 1975, with rapidly deteriorating operations both at home and abroad, Heublein tapped Michael Miles to salvage the chain. Miles was initially brought in to head up Heublein's international group, which by this point was dominated by KFC. Miles had come to Heublein after managing KFC's advertising account for ten years with the Leo Burnett agency. At Heublein, he had risen to vice-president in charge of the Grocery Products Division. While he had little international experience, he had developed a strong reputation for strategic planning. His challenge in late 1975 was to install consistency in international operations by increasing both corporate support and control. One of his first decisions was to move KFC International back to Louisville where it could begin to develop a degree of autonomy with the corporation. Within 18 months, Miles was asked to manage KFC's entire world-wide turnaround, including operations in the USA.

The basic thrust of Miles's strategy was a return to back-to-basics in terms of menu selection and commitment to quality, service, and cleanliness (QSC). The back-to-basics strategy was supported by a new series of staff training programs, random inspections of company-owned and franchisee stores, and a new "we do chicken right" advertising program. The goal was to focus consumer awareness on a sleeker, more customer-oriented KFC which would make one product – chicken – better than any of its competitors.

The results of the turnaround strategy were dramatic. By 1982, KFC had become Heublein's fastest growing division, with real growth of 2.3 percent. From 1978 to 1982, sales at company-owned stores jumped an average 73 percent, while franchise unit sales rose by almost 45 percent. Much of this growth came from KFC's international operations, where company units outnumbered even McDonald's outside the USA. While chicken is eaten almost everywhere in the world, the same is not true of beef, which has been poorly received in many countries. This provided KFC with a considerable advantage in penetrating foreign markets. Nowhere was this more true than in the Pacific Rim, where by 1982, KFC had nearly 400 stores in Japan. In Singapore alone, KFC had 23 franchised stores.

Acquisition by R. J. Reynolds

Although KFC had made dramatic progress, growth was limited by restricted expansion capital at Heublein. Most of the profits generated by KFC were being used to revive Heublein's spirits operations which were themselves facing flat sales and increased competition. By 1982, KFC was receiving only $50 million per year in expansion funds compared with the $400 million being spent by hamburger giant McDonald's. KFC also had one of the lowest ration of company-owned to franchisee stores in the industry. Many franchise stores were slow to upgrade facilities and it was understood that major investments would be required to assure the integrity of the overall KFC network.

In the late summer of 1982, R. J. Reynolds of Winston-Salem, NC, acquired Heublein for $1.4 billion. The acquisition was supported by Heublein directors fearful that the company might be taken over and sold in pieces. Reynolds had been seeking expansion possibilities in the consumer products industry where its marketing skills and huge cash flow could best be put to work. Although hugely profitable, Reynolds' tobacco operations were being attacked by soaring taxes and consumers' declining interest in smoking. The acquisition of Heublein was only part of a group of companies Reynolds acquired during the late 1970s and early 1980s, including Del-Monte Corp. in 1979, Canada Dry and Sunkist Soft Drinks in 1984, and Nabisco Brands in 1985.

Soon after the acquisition, Mike Miles left the company to become president of Dart and Kraft. He was succeeded as CEO of KFC by Richard Mayer who had worked with Miles on the turnaround. Mayer had put in a 10-year stint at General Foods where he rose to become head of the Jell-O product group. Mayer characterized the acquisition as "marvellous."

International expansion

The heavy financial backing of Reynolds resulted in further growth for KFC. Betting that health-consciousness consumers would increasingly shift consumption to chicken, Reynolds designed an ambitious worldwide expansion plan that promised $1 billion in funds over 5 years. Much of this expansion would come outside the USA where markets remained largely untapped.

As was the case with domestic operations, franchising played a major role in KFC's international growth. Franchising became the mode of choice in many markets where political risk and cultural unfamiliarity encouraged the use of locals. Another advantage with franchising was that KFC could be assured a flow of revenues with little investment, thus leveraging existing equity. This was a particularly attractive option internationally where potential deviations of franchisees from KFC operating procedures could be more easily isolated.

The downside of a reliance on franchisees was that it permitted an erosion of system integrity. Local franchisees typically controlled a portfolio of companies, with KFC sales representing only a portion of revenues. Local franchisees, driven by a desire to maximize profits, often cut corners or "milked" operations. While this type of strategy would generally not compromise short-term profitability, it often led to the deterioration of operations over the longer term. This problem was only exacerbated internationally where control was more difficult to maintain.

Southeast Asia operations

By 1983, KFC had established 85 franchise stores in southeast Asia, including 20 stores in Indonesia, 27 stores in Malaysia, and 23 stores in Singapore. This area was recognized as the Southeast Asia Region, one of five separate geographic regions within the corporation. Harry Schwab headed the Area office, where he served as a company vice-president. Schwab had been successful in managing KFC's South African operations where he eventually built a chain of 48 company-owned stores and 95 franchise stores. After returning to Louisville to assume the position of KFC vice-president for international franchising, he was given the added responsibility of supervising the company's Southeast Asia area.

The Chinese Market

After a 10-year absence, KFC moved back into Hong Kong in 1985. During KFC's long absence from Hong Kong, McDonald's, Burger King, Wendy's, and Pizza Hut had entered the market, providing the local population with a taste for Western fast food. After preparing a new Cantonese version of the "we do chicken right" advertising campaign, KFC opened the first of its 20 planned stores. During its first week of operation, the store sold more than 41,000 pieces of chicken, the most that any startup ever sold during its first week of operation. With renewed confidence that management had finally learned how to balance the need for corporate control with the demands for local responsiveness, the company began contemplating a much more ambitious move into the Chinese mainland.

The initial discussions over the feasibility of entering the huge Chinese market were held in early January 1985 between Richard Mayer and Ta-Tung (Tony)

Wang, a former executive of KFC. Tony Wang was born in Sichuan province in the People's Republic of China in 1944. When Tony was 5 years old, the family made its way to Taiwan where in 1968 he graduated from Chong-Yuan University with a degree in engineering. He later moved to the United States, and in 1973, completed a master's degree in management science from Stevens Institute of Technology in New Jersey. Wang then attended New York University where in 1975 he earned a post-master's certificate in international business management.

Upon completion of his studies in 1975, Wang accepted a position in Louisville with KFC. A series of promotions culminated with his assuming the position of Director of Business Development for the company. In this position, Wang reported directly to Mayer where the two developed a close personal relationship. Yet by 1982, Wang was feeling increasingly uneasy at KFC. Although KFC had completed a dramatic turnaround, Wang felt strongly that the company had been too conservative in penetrating international markets. Wang's conviction was that the company was afraid to take real investment risks, particularly in the Far East where American managers were culturally out of touch. In his capacity as director of business development, Wang also saw some of the enormous profits that many of his projects were generating for franchisees. In Wang's view he was merely a bureaucrat, "enriching a conservative, ethnocentric corporation." He plotted his departure. This eventually led to the establishment of QSR Management Company where Wang served as president. QSR was principally engaged in franchisee operations of Wendy's restaurants in Northern California. The company also provided management consulting to other franchisees of major fast food companies.

The Tianjin experience

In spite of QSR's highly profitable operations in California, Wang remained convinced of the enormous potential for American-style fast food in the Far East. In the summer of 1984, the mayor of Tianjin (the third largest city in China with a population of 7 million) visited San Francisco and spoke to a small group of Chinese-Americans about investment opportunities in his city. Wang attended the meeting and was alter invited by the mayor to serve as an advisor on improving the food service industry in Tianjin. Wang's counter-proposal was to serve not only as an advisor but as an investor in a joint Chinese–American style fast food restaurant. The major welcomed the idea. Primary backing for the project came from a group of Chinese-American investors in the San Francisco bay area; additional backing was provided by Don Stephens, the chairman of the Bank of San Francisco. With this support, Wang reached a 50–50 joint venture agreement with a local Tianjin partner to establish "Orchid Food," the first ever Chinese/US joint venture in the restaurant industry in China. The combination take-out/80-seat restaurant was hugely successful from its first day of operation with revenues averaging 100 percent above break even.

Buoyed by this success, Wang began reflecting on the tremendous potential that KFC had in China. Wang's interests were in bringing KFC into China through personally winning the franchise rights for key regions of the country. Barring this, he would try to convince his friend, Richard Mayer, to become a partner in a three-way deal involving Wang, KFC, and a local and as yet undetermined partner. In a letter to Mayer in mid-January 1985, Wang argued that the time was right for KFC to move "aggressively" into China.

> I am totally convinced that KFC has a definite competitive edge over any other major fast food chains in the US in developing the China market at the present time. In spite of the fact that McDonald's is trying to establish a relationship there, it will be a long while before beef could become feasibly available. On the other hand, the poultry industry is one of the top priority categories in China's agriculture modernization and it is highly encouraged by the government. It is my opinion that KFC can open the door in China and build an undisputable lead by first establishing a firm poultry-supply foundation.

Movement into China was also being encouraged by KFC's parent, R. J. Reynolds, itself interested in penetrating the vast Chinese market for cigarettes. Executives at RJR had long realized that, unlike North American demand, the demand for cigarettes was soaring in Third World and communist countries. American cigarettes, in particular, faced almost unlimited demand. China seemed like the perfect market for the company.

Mayer approached Wang's offer to bring KFC into China with great interest. On the one hand, Wang had a long and productive history with KFC; Mayer could trust him. He was aggressive and had a proven track record of successfully negotiating with the Chinese. He was also Chinese – he spoke perfect Mandarin and felt at ease in either Beijing or Louisville. If anyone could get KFC into China, it seemed that Tony Wang was the person. On the other hand, Mayer had considerable concerns about turning over such a strategically important market to a franchisee. Experiences in other international markets had shown the perils of relying on franchisees. The granting of franchise rights could also jeopardize KFC's ability to expand later in other regions of the country. According to Mayer, China was "too important to not be developed as a company operation."

Tony Wang himself was beginning to have serious doubts about his ability to move KFC into China by relying on his own resources. His experience in Tianjin had only reemphasized his conviction that major changes in the attitudes of Chinese employees would almost certainly be required for operation under the KFC banner. These changes could only be achieved through time consuming training programs, suggesting heavy pre-start-up costs which Wang could not adequately support. Wang was also concerned about the up-front money needed to find and negotiate a partnership, to sign a lease, and to gain operating permits. By late fall of 1985, it was becoming increasingly clear to Wang that "China is too big a market for individuals."

Changes in management

It was in April 1986 that Mayer decided to make his move. He telephoned Tony Wang with several announcements: Steve Fellingham was being promoted to head up all of KFC's international operations. Fellingham had over 10 years' experience in KFC-International and was widely respected as someone who would move much more aggressively internationally by relying less on franchisees and more on joint ventures with local partners. This observation was confirmed by Mayer. Mayer also announced that KFC was buying up its Singapore franchisee which now operated 29 KFC stores. This would result in considerably more administrative responsibilities for KFC's Southeast Asia regional office. Finally, Mayer was

Exhibit 16.1   Selected country statistics for Southeast Asia and China, 1986

	Population (Millions)	Life expectancy	GNP per Capita (US$)	Annual real GNP growth rate (%)	No. of KFC units	KFC sales (US$,000,000)
Thailand	52.6	64	790	5.3	4	1.5
Singapore	2.6	73	7,450	7.3	26	15.0
Malaysia	16.1	68	1,830	1.8	53	27.0
Indonesia	166.6	55	500	1.2	25	6.8
Hong Kong	5.4	76	7,030	12.1	4	2.7
PRC	1,054.0	69	300	7.9	–	–

moving Harry Schwab out of Singapore, and restructuring the Southeast Asia region. The job of running the region was Tony's, if he wanted it. Mayer also expressed his encouragement that Wang pursue the China option according to his best judgment and efforts.

After some soul-searching, Wang accepted the position and, in the summer of 1986, officially became vice president of KFC Southeast Asia with headquarters in Singapore. According to Wang, he accepted the job because of the "personal challenge to develop KFC in China." Wang viewed this opportunity of establishing the first Western-style fast food operation in China as a historic opportunity – both personally and for the company as a whole. He also realized that with this very visible challenge came high personal risks should the venture fail.

With the assumption of responsibility for all KFC operations in Southeast Asia, Wang began to see the decision to invest in China in a different light. The singular objective of getting into China would now have to be balanced with other investment opportunities in the region. KFC had enormous growth potential throughout Southeast Asia. The national markets of the region, while together smaller than the entire Chinese market, had already been exposed to Western-style fast food; patterns of demand for KFC's products were well understood. Compared to China, targeting these markets for growth had certain appeal. Control over partners and employees would be rather simple to maintain, leading to rapid growth and higher returns. Hard currency was also readily available. China, in contrast, would demand a huge amount of scarce managerial resources. The primary constraint was the limited number of Chinese-speaking KFC managers – many of whom were already being pushed to the limits in Hong Kong and Singapore. As a consequence, by the late summer of 1986, Wang was beginning to wonder whether committing these resources to China would be in the best interests of the region for which he was now responsible. Exhibit 16.1 presents selected national economic and population statistics for the Southeast Asia region as well as KFC location and sales figures.

The China option: investigating alternatives

Wang's reaction to the ambiguity surrounding the China option was to investigate the Chinese market more thoroughly. Here, the principal question facing Wang was the intended geographic location of the first Chinese store. The location decision would potentially have a dramatic effect on profitability, future expansion elsewhere in China, and managerial resource commitments – all vital considerations in a go/no-go decision.

In considering where to establish the first store, Wang initially thought of Tianjin. Through his earlier experiences, he had developed excellent contacts within the municipal government of Tianjin and he appreciated that Tianjin was one of three municipal governments in China that were administered directly by the Central Government in Beijing. (The other two were Shanghai and Beijing.) Yet, he also recognized that the city had several shortcomings. First, Tianjin lacked a convenient supply of grain-fed chickens. Experience in Hong Kong – where in 1973 KFC had entered the market using fish meal-fed chickens – suggested that Chinese consumers placed a high value on freshness and taste. This would be particularly important with a product prepared in a way which was unfamiliar to the Chinese. Another problem with Tianjin was that the city was not generally frequented by Western tourists. While Wang anticipated that most sales would be from soft currency renminbi (RMB), some hard foreign currency sales would be essential for profit repatriation and/or the purchase of critical supplies such as chicken coating, packaging, promotion materials, and so on.[1] Finally, and perhaps most importantly, Tianjin would be unable to provide KFC with the profile necessary to facilitate eventual national market penetration. In fact, Tianjin was generally regarded in China as a gateway to its larger sister, Beijing, only 85 miles to the northwest.

Other cities presenting viable alternative locations for KFC's entry into China included Shanghai, Guangzhou, and Beijing.

Shanghai

As China's largest city, Shanghai is home to some 11 million people, almost 9000 factories, and the country's busiest harbour. Metropolitan Shanghai is widely regarded as China's most prosperous business centre. The city alone accounts for approximately 11 percent of China's total industrial output and almost 17 percent of the country's exports. It is also one of three self-administered municipalities.

Shanghai has a long history of involvement with Westerners. The Treaty of Nanking, thrust upon the Chinese by the British during the middle of the nineteenth century, set Shanghai aside as one of five Chinese port cities open to foreign trade. Western commerce and cultural influence flourished. Foreign gunboats continued to patrol the river until well into the twentieth century. Complete expulsion of foreigners came in 1949 with the communist victory over the Nationalist Chinese army. However, since then the city has maintained an interest in international business and trade. Today, the city is the home of a large variety of Western hotels, business facilities, and tourists.

Shanghai also had the benefit of providing easy access to a seemingly ample supply of quality chickens. In fact, through joint ventures a Thailand-based company – the Chia Tai Group – had established ten feed mills and poultry operations in the region and was the largest poultry supplier in Shanghai. KFC's Southeast Asia office had good relations with Chia Tai and was currently negotiating with one of the company's divisions as a potential franchisee in Bangkok.

While Shanghai remains a major centre for business, its noise and pollution

have discouraged tourists. For KFC, the sheer population of a host city is important, although less so than the mix of potential customers. While Shanghai could
provide KFC with eagerly sought-after media exposure, the operation would also
need to promise an adequate return in FEC before an investment could be justified.
Here, the concern was whether or not Western business people would be attracted
to KFC or would prefer to frequent more fashionable restaurants. Clearly, no one
knew.

Guangzhou

Another alternative was the city of Guangzhou, located in southeast China only a
short distance from Hong Kong. Guangzhou, historically known as Canton, is one
of 14 special coastal cities set apart in 1984 as preferential treatment centres for
foreign investment. As such, Guangzhou was given greater autonomy in approving foreign investment projects, reducing tax rates, and encouraging technological
development. By the end of 1986, about 80 percent of the almost $6 billion US for-
eign investment in China had been located in these open coastal cities. In addition,
Guangzhou is the capital of Guangdong Province, which contains three of the
country's four "Special Economic Zones" (SEZs), designed specifically to attract foreign investment. The SEZs were initially set up as part of the broad economic reforms
that were launched in China in the late 1970s.

Guangzhou was frequented by Western business people as well as by tourists
who visited the city on one-day excursions from Hong Kong. Due to its proximity to
Hong Kong – less than 75 miles away and easily accessible by road or train – an
operation in Guangzhou could easily be serviced out of the company's Hong Kong
office. The Chinese in this region were also more familiar with Western management practices and culture. In fact, the people in Guangzhou speak Cantonese –
the same language spoken in Hong Kong. Cantonese Chinese is quite different from
the Mandarin Chinese spoken elsewhere in China. Preliminary investigations also
indicated that little difficulty would be anticipated in locating an adequate supplier
of chickens.

Beijing

Another location that warranted closer inspection was Beijing, China's second
most populous city (after Shanghai) with 9 million citizens. Since its establishment
as the Chinese capital by the Mongols in the thirteenth century, Beijing has remained
the political and cultural centre of China. For example, although China spans a
breath of 3000 miles, the entire nation runs according to Beijing time – an indication of the power of the central government. As the nation's capital, Beijing also
sports a subway and freeway system and an international airport complete with
air conditioning and a moving sidewalk.

Chinese citizens from all over the country pour into Beijing eager to attend
meetings or to represent their factories or districts before the authorities of the central government. The city is also the educational capital in the country with university campuses ringing the city. These factors all contribute to the relatively high
levels of affluence and the intellectual enlightenment of the population – critically
important in generating RMB sales. Beijing is also a tourist centre for Western visitors

anxious to see the Forbidden City, Summer Palace, and nearby Ming Tombs and Great Wall. This would mean a ready supply of FEC currency. Finally, without a doubt a start-up in Beijing would grab the people's attention and would communicate the tacit approval of the central authorities, thus facilitating future expansion outside the city.

Beijing could provide considerable advantages to a company eager to expand throughout China. A preliminary investigation indicated that several poultry producers were operating just outside the city. Yet, politically and operationally, Beijing would be more of a gamble than alternative locations. High profile operations heightened the possibility of government interference for political purposes.

Weighing the decision

In his heart, Tony Wang knew he was a man who liked taking risks, and clearly, China qualified as the risk of a lifetime. However, it was also clear that the location of the first store could mitigate much of the obvious risk of moving into China. Left undetermined was whether the low risk alternatives were worth pursuing. What was needed was to weigh the possibility of reducing the risks against the potential benefits that could be achieved through the investment.

Clearly, Wang had staked out a position as the person who could bring KFC into China. However, he now had different responsibilities which also demanded his attention and for which he would surely be evaluated. He was certain that there would be little second guessing by Richard Mayer if he recommended that after careful consideration, KFC should hold off for the present from China. He also realized that, because there were no competitors as yet in China, the present time could be the most opportune time for making the move. Indeed, even if a Chinese location were selected, it would likely take years of negotiations before operations could start. To delay any further risked ceding the market to others. The challenge to Wang would be in balancing these possible risks with the possible returns.

NOTE

1 Like virtually all communist economies, the Chinese economy operates through two separate currencies; renminbi, or the "People's currency", which is used by local Chinese for the purchase of goods and services; and FEC (Foreign Exchange Certificate), which is used by foreigners to represent the value of hard currency while in China. FEC is required at all hotels, taxis, restaurants, and shops which cater to foreigners. A black market for FEC existed in most large Chinese cities.

LABATT BREWERIES OF EUROPE (with Industry Note: Italy and Its Beer Industry)

Arthur Sharplin

At the start of May 1989, Labatt Breweries of Europe, London-based unit of Toronto's John Labatt Limited, was in the final stages of negotiations to purchase Italian brewers Birra Moretti, SpA, and Prinz Brau Brewing Company. Adam Humphries, finance chief for LBOE, recalled, "Moretti and Prinz were seen as strategic acquisitions to enable Labatt to start the process of becoming a key player internationally and, specifically, in the Italian and European beer markets." Acquisition team leader John Morgan added, "And they were priced right." Both purchases were set to close by the middle of the month, although just-discovered irregularities at Prinz gave Labatt the apparent right to abort that deal, if not both.

By Arthur Sharplin, Institute for International Business Studies, NEOS Consortium MBA, Pordenone, Italy and Waltham Associates Inc., Austin, Texas. Management assisted in the research for this case, which was written for research purposes and to stimulate scholarly discussion. Special thanks go to Richard Beveridge, Yasmin Ferrari, Adam Humphries, William G. Bourne, Sidney M. Oland, and John Morgan as well as to the editor and anonymous reviewers for the *Case Research Journal*. Copyright © the *Case Research Journal* and Arthur Sharplin, 1995.

Background

John Labatt Limited had two principal divisions, Labatt Brewing Company, headed by life-long brewer Sidney M. Oland, and Labatt Food Company, headed by George S. Taylor, a former finance specialist. Brewing had fiscal year 1989 (ending April 30) earnings before interest and taxes (EBIT) of C$158 million on sales of C$1.8 billion (the exchange rate as of March 31, 1989 was C$1 = US$0.8378). The Food Company's EBIT was C$106 million on sales of C$3.6 billion. About 15 percent of Food Company revenue came from "other investments," which included a Canadian sports broadcaster, an agricultural biotechnology company, and 45 percent ownership of the Toronto Blue Jays baseball club. Labatt had begun exporting its beer to England in 1982 and formed LBOE in 1987. Oland explained his strategy:

> We had won the battle in Canada. We were making lots of money in brewing and had to decide what to do with it. We surveyed the world looking for good places to invest. England was our first choice, mainly because of the language. Spain and France came next. But Italy was within our sights.

Humphries, a young Englishman who had moved up from Labatt's UK operation to LBOE, added, "Labatt's comfortable domestic market position [42.3 percent in 1988] was under threat from the US–Canada free trade agreement, and the diversification process outside brewing was not going well."

In fact, the USA was preparing a formal complaint against Canadian brewers under the General Agreement on Tariffs and Trade (GATT). A Canadian news-magazine soon concluded,

> The stage is set for cheap, tariff-free brew from the United States to flood Canada. . . . For the past sixty years, the domestic brewing industry has been governed by a host of interprovincial barriers that have angered foreign competitors. A particular sore spot is the time-honored rule forcing companies to brew beer in every province where they want to sell their brands. The result is a fragmented Canadian industry that has spawned many small, inefficient plants at a time when breweries in other countries have been producing cheaper beer by building huge megabreweries and consolidating smaller plants.[1]

Labatt, for example, had twelve breweries strung across Canada. The import treat intensified Labatt's competition with Molson Companies Ltd, which had merged its beer operations with Carling O'Keefe Breweries of Canada Ltd, giving Molson a 53 percent domestic share. But Oland pooh-poohed the impact of the Molson merger, saying, "Our weaker competitor combined with our weakest one." In the meantime, Canada's beer consumption declined from 86 liters per person in 1981 to 80 liters in 1989.[2]

Labatt sold several businesses in 1988, ostensibly due to their lack of "strategic relevance." According to Morgan, another reason for the divestments was pressure from Brascan Ltd to "maximize cash coming up [Labatt's] corporate chain." Brascan, owner of 42.3 percent of Labatt's outstanding common stock, was part of the troubled Peter F. and Edward F. Bronfman financial empire (headquartered in Toronto but with interests worldwide). Labatt's 23 directors included Peter Bronfman and two Brascan executives. In the winter of 1989, a new director slot had been added, filled by Dr Maurice J. LeClair, vice chairman of Canadian Imperial

Bank of Commerce, who also joined Labatt's audit committee. And Edwin A. Goodman, a director for 23 years and a business consultant, resigned and was replaced by Melvin M. Hawkrigg, Chairman of Trilon Financial Corporation. Morgan said Labatt was being "actively marketed" during this period, although Oland disputed that. "Actually," Oland added, "Our plan was to separate the company into brewing and entertainment divisions, both publicly traded. Labatt would own 51 percent of Brewing and 50 percent of Entertainment."

Seeking Major European Acquisitions

As Oland had instructed, Morgan pushed forward in Europe. The UK operation was shifted from importing to "toll brewing," employing regional brewers with excess capacity to brew the beer. The product was then marketed through joint venture arrangements. Morgan said Labatt's UK sales had expanded rapidly, characterizing the move as "the most successful lager launch ever in the UK."

In early 1988, Michael Hurst, a marketing executive from Labatt Canada, was transferred to LBOE as vice president, marketing. And in September that year, Humphries recruited Richard Beveridge, a recent graduate of the London Business School, as financial analyst.

Humphries said, "There was a window of opportunity to take a major position in Europe." He continued:

Our first choice was Grand Met's brewing assets, mostly in the UK. But we were offering cash, and Grand Met opted for a swap-type arrangement with another partner. We then looked at opportunities in Germany and Switzerland. When that seemed a dead end, we turned to La Cruz del Campo in Spain, but that deal wasn't ready to do either.

The Grand Met sale was valued at US$600 million. La Cruz del Campo was acquired by London-based Guinness plc in 1990 for US$1.15 billion. One former LBOE official said "pussyfooting" by recalcitrant Labatt directors had nixed the deals for the Canadians. Humphries acknowledged, "At corporate there were those who saw European expansion as risky and who needed to be convinced." But Morgan disputed the pussyfooting charge, saying, "Brascan's cash needs were the reason."

Turning to Italy

In the second quarter of 1988, the team turned its full attention to Italy. Humphries said, "It was important at the time to show results, and Moretti and Prinz were the only acquisitions which seemed doable." The acquisition team believed that Italy offered the following advantages:

1 It was one of the few growing beer markets in the world, averaging 2.5 percent annual growth over the previous 10 years.
2 It was ripe territory for branding, image-building strategies.
3 Operations could be distribution driven, through relations with small vendors.
4 The beer target group (males 18 to 35) was growing.
5 Italy had one of the lowest per capita beer consumption rates in Europe.

Exhibit 17.1   Per capita beer consumption, 1988, and 1980–1989 growth in per capita beer consumption for selected European countries

	1988 liters/capita	1980–89 growth (%)
Belgium/Luxembourg	121.0	−12.0
Denmark	125.2	−2.6
France	38.9	−7.9
Holland	86.0	1.4
Ireland	109.0	−25.8
Italy	24.2	30.5
Portugal	47.0	n/a
Spain	66.8	n/a
UK	110.5	−5.7
West Germany	118.0	−1.9

Source: Databank SpA.

Morgan said that these characteristics were similar to those that had preceded "the growth of beer in Canada." However, data then available from Assobirra, the Italian brewing industry association, revealed that all the growth in beer consumption in Italy noted above had occurred before 1986. And what Assobirra labeled the "formative beer drinking category," the 15 to 34 age bracket, was projected to peak at 18 million in 1990 and fall to 16 million in 2000. Italy's population in 1989 was 57.5 million.

Italy's beer industry

In Italy, 5000 or so "concessionaires" took large shipments of beer from brewers and delivered it to tens of thousands of small retailers. Concessionaires usually represented only one brewer and were given specific territories. They paid brewers deposits on bottles and crates and collected similar deposits from retailers. Brewers installed and serviced draught equipment, further tying retailers and concessionaires to brewers. Assobirra administered a cooperative advertising program, which used television, radio, and posters to advertise the beer category.[3]

Exhibit 17.1 provides statistics on beer drinking for selected European countries. According to Humphries, it was widely assumed that Italian beer consumption would grow to at least match that of Spain, Portugal, or France, if not of other European countries. The assumption was buttressed by the continuing decline in wine sales in Italy, which was believed to mean that Italians were switching to beer.

Exhibit 17.2 shows estimated shares of Italian beer production for all nine significant producers in 1988. About 2 percent of production was exported that year, up from about 1 percent in 1980 (imports were about 18 percent of consumption in the late 1980s). Peroni and Dreher had six plants each, Prinz and Poretti two each, and the others one each.

Multinational companies bought up most of the Italian brewing industry during the 1980s. Foreign ownership of the top four brewers in 1988 was as follows:

Exhibit 17.2   Estimated 1988 market shares of major Italian brewers

Brewer	Market share (%)
Peroni	38
Dreher	31
Poretti	9
Interbrew	7
Forst	6
Moretti	4
Prinz	3
Castelberg	1
Menabrea	1

Source: Assobirra.

- Dreher, Heineken, Dutch brewer (100 percent);
- Interbrew, Stella Artois, Belgian brewer (100 percent);
- Peroni, BSN Danone, French food group (percentage not known);
- Poretti, Carlsberg, Danish brewer (50 percent).

Sidney Oland said brewing was distinguished from other process industries by the need for sanitation and temperature control. "In fact," said Oland, "in brewing, we don't *make* beer. God does. And you know He never does the same thing twice. We just try to provide an environment which dampens the natural variations." Exhibit 17.3 describes how beer is made.

Moretti and Prinz

Moretti was headquartered in Udine, northeast of Venice, and Prinz in Crespellano, near Bologna. Each had a brewery at its headquarters and Prinz had a southern brewery, in Baragiano. Moretti's annual brewing capacity was 450,00 hectoliters (a hectoliter is 100 liters, or 26.4 US gallons) and Prinz's was about 700,000 at Crespellano and 75,000 at Bariagiano. Moretti was financially weak in 1989 but was still owned by Luigi Moretti, whose family had founded the brewery in 1859. Beveridge said the brewery had "a strong brand image, stable sales, and a well-established distribution network in northern Italy." It had agreed to stay out of southern Italy for 10 years in connection with an asset sale in mid-1980. Moretti's brewery, near Udine's central traffic circle, was operating near capacity, and cars in the area were often dusted with a sticky, white substance coming from the brewery's brew kettles. In the headquarters building were a restaurant and bar. Local citizens often gathered there to socialize and consume a special unfiltered, nonpasteurized draught brew sold nowhere else. There was also a museum containing memorabilia, pictures, and films from Moretti's 130-year history. Oland recalled:

The essential attraction of Moretti was that you had a good brand which had been constrained to a small area of Italy for legal, financial, and other reasons. That area happened to be home to most of

Exhibit 17.3   How beer is made

A modern brewery at first glance appears to be a simple process plant, consisting mainly of stainless steel tanks, hoppers, dryers, filters, pumps, and so forth, connected by pipes and valves. Temperatures, pressures, and product chemistry are tightly controlled throughout, and the system is sealed off from the atmosphere. An on-site laboratory uses spectrographic analysis and chemical methods to test raw materials and to check the product at various points. Brewery products are also tasted regularly. Few workers are required and only an occasional technician may be observed taking a sample, recording data, or adjusting machinery.

Primary raw materials for brewing beer are water, barley malt (which provides starch for conversion to alcohol), about a fourth as much of other cereal grain (such as rice or corn), a much smaller amount of hops (which impart bitterness and aroma), and yeast (to promote fermentation). The cereals and hops are cooked in large steam-jacketed kettles to produce wort, an amber sugar solution. This takes from 2.5 to 3.5 hours, allowing seven to nine batches per day. The residue is usually sold as animal feed.

The wort is fermented in large tanks for about four days and the resulting beer aged for about 16 days. Product characteristic – color, taste, alcohol content – are varied by adjusting the variety and amount of malt, grain, and hops used and by modifying the fermentation and aging regimens.

Italy's military. Young soldiers would learn to like Moretti beer, then not be able to find it when they got back home.

Prinz was virtually bankrupt in 1989, and had been since its purchase for L1000 (about US$1.00) by an Italian prince and another investor in 1985. Prinz leased its breweries but had the right to purchase them in the event that the company was sold. Most managers and many experienced operators and administrative people had left Prinz, and the company's distribution system was collapsing. According to Beveridge, the scant crew "made beer whenever suppliers could be talked into shipping raw materials and then attempted to sell the product." Oland added, "Prinz offered a chance to buy capacity very cheaply."

Making the Deals

Morgan and his team contacted the respective owners, set up confidentiality arrangements, and obtained data though necessary to value each company. Few executives in domestic Italian firms spoke English and even fewer workers did. No one on the acquisition team spoke much Italian, and most information and conversation had to be translated. Despite this, the team was able to prepare a report, including financial data and valuation estimates, and dispatch it to Oland.

In August 1988, Oland traveled to Udine and met with Luigi Moretti. Oland recalled, "The final negotiation took just a day. This was actually the second time I had met Moretti. The first was just a 'beauty contest," to get acquainted." Humphries said the two were initially far apart on price but quickly came to terms "at a price at the top end of the team's recommended maximum." He added, "Sid started high, which was a surprise, but this removed the block in negotiations, which could have dragged on for some time. And we were just very pleased to have the deal done." Oland confirmed Humphries's account in general, but said the deal was hardly "done" at this point. Oland added, "I put a great deal of weight on the financial projections and present value analysis the acquisition team had done. And the final price was in their recommended range – barely so, but within the range." The price for Moretti was never disclosed but was estimated by outsiders at US$75 million, including assumption of specified liabilities. One observer said Luigi Moretti asked that the price not be disclosed because, "In Sardinia [where Moretti vacationed], you let people know how much money you have and you end up with a sack over you head."

In September 1988, the team began negotiations with the owners of Prinz. In November that year, Morgan, Humphries, Hurst, and Beveridge flew to Canada to seek board approval to buy Moretti alone or to buy both Moretti and Prinz. Beveridge recalled, "We could never make a Prinz-only acquisition work in our model, at any purchase price." According to Oland, the combined operation was projected to become profitable "on an EBIT level" in the third year after acquisition. The board of directors gave authority to buy Moretti and Prinz, but not to buy either one alone. Oland said the board's consideration of this "was not controversial."

In December 1988, a letter of intent was signed with Moretti, subject to *due diligence* (audits ordinarily employed to verify seller representations). A purchase price for Prinz, estimated at US$25 million, was agreed upon in February 1989, also subject to due diligence. Oland said the cost of new construction would have been about US$150 per hectoliter of capacity, and the real cost of the Prinz capacity was about US$30 per hectoliter.

How Bad Can It Be?

The Moretti deal was ready to close by April, but delay was necessary because of concerns about problems discovered at Prinz during the due diligence audits. Beginning in early 1988, Prinz had apparently inflated its sales figures, failing to account for returns, billing some product that would not be delivered until later, and even delivering presold production, for cash, to different customers than those who had initially ordered and paid for it. In December 1988, Prinz's recorded sales began to plummet. By May 1989, prepaid customers were threatening to sue, and unpaid suppliers were refusing to ship. Beveridge recalled,

> The principals had a severely inflated sense of their own, and their company's, worth. Most of the good managers had left Prinz long before, and there wasn't enough of an information system in place to allow auditing. Beyond the standard financial reports submitted to the government and accumulated by industry analysts, we simply did not trust any information we were given. At one point, the Labatt team was even locked out of the brewery. They just stayed holed up in their hotel for days. All the "Italian" negotiating tricks were used against us.

No one on the acquisition team had even seen the Baragiano brewery. Oland said he wanted to go himself, but government officials in Baragiano would not permit it. "Kidnapping," said Oland. "They were afraid I would be kidnapped." An

Oland aide finally was flown from Canada to Baragiano and back the same day on the prince's private jet. "He was the only Labatt employee to see the brewery," said Oland.

During the first week of May 1989, Oland was briefed on the situation at Prinz. He remarked, "Okay, fellows, how bad can it be? Does it justify canning both deals?" It was then explained to an increasingly impatient Luigi Moretti that neither deal could be done without the other. Beveridge said this increased the pressure on the acquisition team to make a quick decision, because he felt the Prinz owners would ruthlessly exploit their position if they were to learn of the linkage with Moretti.

NOTES AND REFERENCES

1   John Demont, "A global brew," *Madean's*, vol. 102, no. 30 (July 24, 1989), p. 28.

2   Deirdre McMurdy, "Brewing struggle," *Maclean's*, vol. 104, no. 7 (February 18, 1991), p. 39.

3   Canadean Ltd, *The Beer Service Basic Report: Italy*. Basingstoke, UK: Canadean Ltd, 1992, sec. 8.

Italy's budget deficit for 1992 was 11 percent of GDP and its public debt *exceeded* GDP. The Economist Intelligence Unit, of London, summarized the country's economic and political situation in November of that year:

> *The prospects for growth have worsened as a result of the government's austerity measures. Consumer prices will rise following the devaluation of the lira [officially 7 percent, but more than 30 percent on international currency markets]. Salary increases should moderate, although the wage accord is under stress. Interest rates will stay high, affecting both the fiscal deficit and investment. The trade balance and the current-account position will improve. The government is proving resilient but the threat of political instability is ever present.*

The head of the ruling socialist party and the government's justice minister resigned in early 1993 under charges of corruption, as did two top Fiat officials. Over 150 Members of Parliament had been named in corruption inquiries, and 850 regional and municipal politicians and business people were arrested for corruption in 1992. Professor Franco Cazzola, of the University of Florence, wrote, "An entire political system, faced with a crisis of legitimacy, is now falling to pieces."[a]

Economic and demographic statistics

Exhibit 17.4 provides selected statistics for Italy through 1991. Population growth was expected to turn negative around the year 2000. The 15–34 age bracket, the "formative beer drinking category," peaked at 18 million in 1990 and was falling toward a projected 16 million in 2000 and 12 million in 2010. Unemployment had been stable for several years at about 10 percent.[b] But it was estimated at 11.2 percent in January 1993 and Censis, Italy's social research institute, said at least 700,000 jobs would be lost during the year. Industrial production had fallen 3.7 percent from a year earlier, employment in heavy industry was down 6.8 percent,

Exhibit 17.4　Selected statistics for Italy

	1987	1988	1989	1990	1991
GDP (L thousand billion)	984	1092	1194	1307	1427
Real GDP growth (%)	3.1	4.1	3.0	2.2	1.4
Consumer price inflation	4.7	5.1	6.3	6.5	6.3
Population (million)	57.3	57.4	57.5	57.7	57.8
Ave exchnge rate L/US$1	1296	1302	1372	1198	1241[a]

[a]　November 16, 1992, L1,393/US$1; February 25, 1993, L1,573/US$1.

Source of data: The Economist Intelligence Unit.

Nor for reproduction or distribution. Dated March 17, 1993. This country and industry note was written for research purposes and to stimulate scholarly discussion.

and the number of workers on temporary layoff and not counted in the jobless figures was up 36,000 from a year earlier. Italy's president, Oscar Scalfaro, wrote that unemployment had reached levels "an industrial democracy could not tolerate in the long term" and urged immediate action to solve the problem.[c]

Aspects of culture

Expatriate managers in Italy, especially those from North America, had usually found the Italian business culture, at best, disconcerting. Power distance, the degree to which employees accept unequal distributions of power, was high, as was "masculinity." And Hofstede's research indicated that organization culture seldom reduced, let alone overwhelmed, country cultures. In fact, Hofstede found that national cultures explained 50 percent of the variation in attitudes and behaviors in his sample of multinational divisions.[d] Such a belief in the intractability of country cultures led companies like Electrolux (Zanussi) and Heineken (Dreher) to employ mainly Italian managers in Italy and to focus on cultural adaptation rather than cultural change.

But massive cultural change seemed imminent in 1993, as evidenced by the following excerpts from news articles and guides. From *The Economist*:

> It is no accident that the demise of the Italian system has coincided with the collapse of communism. Democratic Italy resembled communist East Germany, or Hungary, or Bulgaria, in that nothing was so important as a party connection. Patronage was king. Access to jobs, pensions, hospital beds was eased by raccomandazioni – the favours of a local politician. Bigger jobs, bigger pensions, industrial companies, television stations – all were parcelled out by lottizzazione, the practice of rewarding parties according to their support at the most recent election.[e]

Prime Minister Giuliano Amato described Parliament as an "archipelago," continuing, "Everything has to be negotiated and everyone has to negotiate with everyone else. Every procedural step is a negotiation, and at each negotiation either one stops or one loses a part of what one is proposing."[f]

This excerpt from *The Economist Country Guide: Italy* suggested the Italian attitude toward business negotiation:

> Negotiating is an art in Italy: to the Italian way of thinking, the key management art . . . Studied nonchalance is often the style . . . Dramatically "changing the cards on the table" – for example, when an agreement seems near, suddenly bringing in a broad new set of demands – is another often-used technique . . . Unexpected closing of the meeting is another ploy . . . They are, however, only pretending . . . Just when the visitor is finally resigned to letting the whole thing slip away, the agreement can come together with amazing speed . . . [Also], the Italian concept of a "contract" does not grow out of the Anglo-Saxon legal tradition . . . An attempt to establish the "intentions" in the mind of contracting parties is of very limited importance. What holds is the text of the agreement, right down to the last comma or semicolon.

An Italian social scientist explained the roots of 1990s culture, and a possible solution:

> The 1980s saw the ascendancy of "yuppyism", the culture of the individual by which everyone was expected to use their office or position for their own exclusive advantage to make money. It coincided with the dismantling of the rules governing the business conducted between individuals and the public sector.
> A plethora of new legislation was passed to reduce the delays inherent in all state transactions.

There were "special" and "emergency" decrees passed to fund rebuilding in the Campania region after the 1980 Irpinia earthquake, to underwrite the cost of the 1990 World Soccer Championships and the 500th anniversary celebrations of Christopher Columbus's discovery of the New World.

To make way for governabilità *there was a breakdown of the established public law in favour of corruption. Slowly but surely, the faithful party politicians were replaced by greedy speculators who built their political careers on an ability to transform money into power and vice versa. Their relationship with politics was based more on convenience than party loyalty.*

The gradual spiral of decline was exacerbated by a public administration which still responds most effectively to the lure of public favour, of financial reward rather than the internal needs of the state.

It is not too difficult to identify the result of these developments: the creation of a grey zone between the legal and the illegal, the corrupter and the corrupted, the citizen and the politician. . . .

But will new rules alone help Italy escape its current crisis? There remains the need for fresh ethics to govern individual behavior – a new "legality" to guide society through this period of transition, not simply to clean up the market but to provide a new set of personal values.[g]

Beer consumption

Beverage consumption in Italy increased by about 2.4 percent a year from 1982 to 1991, to an average 378 liters per person. Wine use fell steadily by about 4.5 percent a year to 68 liters a person in 1991. Beer drinking increased during the first half of the eighties, but fell by 0.3 percent from 1985 to 1990, and by an additional 2.2 percent in 1991, to 22.6 liters per person. Of that, 19.5 liters was "normal beer" (not less than 3 percent alcohol by volume), 2.1 liters "special beer" (not less than 3.5 percent), 0.7 liters "double malt/red beer" (not less than 4 percent) etc., and 0.3 liters non-alcohol/low alcohol beer (less than 1 percent).

Beer's "share of the throat" (percentage of total beverage consumption) had fallen to 6 percent, its 1981 level, while soft drink consumption had climbed to 46 percent, up from 26 percent in 1981. Like other European countries, Italy had seen a shift from alcoholic to non-alcoholic beverages – with alcoholic drinks at 25 percent of total beverage consumption in Italy, down from 39 percent in 1981.[h] Canadean Limited, which studied the industry, concluded,

The alleged replacement of wine by beer is a concept in which hardly anyone believed anymore (Italians who do not drink wine during meals have turned massively to bottled water), and beer is hardly perceived as an in-between meals and/or after dinner drink or late night drink.[i]

In the 1980s, it was widely assumed that domestic beer consumption (24.2 liters per capita in 1988) would grow to at least match that of Spain (66.8), Portugal (47.0), or France (38.9), if not other European countries (e.g. Denmark, 125.2; Great Britain, 110.5; Holland, 86.0; Ireland, 109.0; Belgium/Luxembourg, 121).[j] The assumption was buttressed by the continuing decline in wine consumption in Italy, which was believed to mean Italians were switching to beer. Growth totals in per capita beer consumption for several countries for 1980–9 were: Belgium/Luxembourg, –12 percent; Denmark, –2.6 percent; France, –7.9 percent; West Germany, –1.9 percent; UK, –5.7 percent; Ireland, –25.8 percent; Holland, 1.4 percent; and Italy, 30.5 percent.[k]

Industry structure and competition

The beer industry in Italy was restructured and consolidated during the late 1980s. Of seven producers, only two small breweries were Italian controlled by 1993. Principal owners of the foreign-controlled brewers were as follows.

Exhibit 17.5 Brewers and reported production in Italy for years ended 30 september (thousands of hectoliters and percentage of total)

	1990		1991		1992	
Peroni	4117	38.3	3928	36.6	3936	36.0
Dreher	3243	30.2	3040	28.3	3266	29.8
Moretti	790	7.4	969	9.0	1116	10.2
Poretti	983	9.2	1081	10.1	1095	10.0
Interbrew	749	7.0	817	7.6	736	6.7
Forst	676	6.3	695	6.5	647	5.9
Castelberg[a]	134	1.2	157	1.5	109	1.0
Menabrea	43	0.4	43	0.4	45	0.4
Total	10,735	100.0	10,733	100.0	10,951	100.0

[a] Shut down in summer 1992.

Totals may not check, due to rounding.

Source of data: Assobirra.

Exhibit 17.6 Italy's monthly beer production, 1990–1992 (thousands of hectoliters)

	Jan.	Feb.	Mar.	Apr.	May.	Jun.	Jul.	Aug.	Sep.	Oct.	Nov.	Dec.
1990	762	832	1037	886	1245	1195	1292	1014	918	688	760	436
1991	846	904	970	992	1159	1077	1212	882	810	720	620	481
1992	707	965	1127	996	1114	1339	1350	736	775	n.a.	n.a.	n.a.

Source of data: Assobirra.

Peroni: BSN Danone, French food group.
Dreher: Heineken, Dutch brewer.
Moretti: Labatt, Canadian brewer.
Poretti: Carlsberg, Danish brewer.
Interbrew: Stella Artois, French conglomerate.

Exhibit 17.5 shows each brewer's reported production and percent of the total for years ended September 30, 1990–2. Peroni and Dreher had six plants each, Moretti three, Poretti two, and the others one each.[1]

Beer consumption in Italy, as elsewhere, varied through the year. Exhibit 17.6 shows monthly beer production in Italy for 1990–2. Exhibit 17.7 shows monthly imports. About 2 percent of production was exported in 1992, up from about 1 percent in 1981.[m] Beer imports were 17.5 percent of consumption in 1991, up from 11.7 percent in 1981 (imports were subject to a 25 percent value added tax, compared to a 19 percent value added tax on domestically produced beer). Exhibit 17.8 shows imports by country of origin for 1990–2.

Though several competitors had tried to "rationalize" production of beer by

Exhibit 17.7 Monthly beer imports to Italy, 1990–1992 (thousands of hectoliers)

	Jan.	Feb.	Mar.	Apr.	May.	Jun.	Jul.	Aug.	Sep.	Oct.	Nov.	Dec.
1990	139	144	201	211	275	326	323	242	178	119	141	120
1991	175	154	164	242	241	260	371	245	201	152	134	138
1992	182	198	202	224	290	343	360	251	223	n.a.	n.a.	n.a.

Source of data: Assobirra.

Exhibit 17.8 Imports to Italy by country of origin for years ended September 30, 1990–1992 (thousands of hectoliters and percentage of total)

	1990		1991		1992	
Germany	927	39.3	969	39.8	996	36.9
Denmark	338	14.3	372	15.3	438	16.2
Belgium/Luxembourg	212	9.0	264	10.9	322	11.9
Holland	302	12.8	225	9.2	219	8.1
France	241	10.2	170	7.0	177	6.6
Austria	133	5.6	137	5.6	147	5.4
Great Britain	73	3.1	90	3.7	108	4.0
Mexico	6	0.3	43	1.8	100	3.7
Czechoslovakia	34	1.4	34	1.4	43	1.6
Yugoslavia	27	1.1	36	1.5	40	1.5
Switzerland	27	1.1	30	1.2	26	1.0
Ireland	16	0.7	21	0.9	26	1.0
China	9	0.4	10	0.4	16	0.6
USA	4	0.2	6	0.3	15	0.6
Spain	9	0.4	7	0.3	14	0.5
Other countries	7	0.3	22	0.9	17	0.6
Total	2361	100.0	2434	100.0	2703	100.0
As % of consumption		18.0		18.5		19.8

Totals may not check, due to rounding.

Source of data: Assobirra.

closing down some plants and modernizing others, overall industry profits were negative throughout 1988–91, with only one small brewer reporting significant net income. Exhibit 17.9 shows the estimated distribution of the retail price of bottled beer in 1992. Retail prices for bottles, cans, and draught beer in May 1992 averaged L1600–2000 per liter for normal beers, and L2300–2500 for premium ones.[n]

Exhibit 17.10 shows the types of beer packaging in Italy in 1992. Refillable

Exhibit 17.9 Distribution of retail price of bottled beer, 1992 (percent)

Acquisition of prime materials and packing	7	(stable)
Overall cost of bottles	10	(increasing)
Production costs[a]	24	(increasing)
Promotion costs	5	(increasing)
Selling and administrative costs	7	(stable)
Manufacturer's margin	2	(stable)
Distributor's margins	45	(increasing)

[a]   Includes 19 percent value added tax (VAT), raised from 9 percent in July 1990.

Source of data: Databank.

Exhibit 17.10 Types of packaging used for beer sold in Italy, 1992

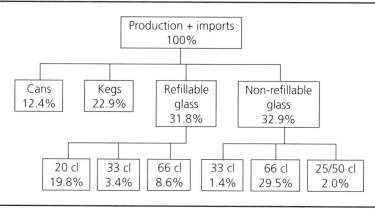

Source of data: *Il Mondo Della Birra*, December 1992, 30.

bottles were declining in use. Of the EC standard size bottles (25, 50 and 75cl), 25 and 50 cl ones had been introduced by Dreher and were being test marketed by Moretti. Practically all the cans used in Italy were 33 cl size and practically all the kegs were sold for draught installations. Twist-off caps had not been introduced by domestic producers, nor had flip-in tabs for cans.[o]

Television accounted for 84 percent of media advertising expenditures in 1991, and "trade press/magazines" another 8 percent. Posters had a small share of advertising budgets. An earlier collective ad campaign, managed by Assobirra (the Italian beer industry association), was restarted in 1990, with a budget of about L10 billion a year. Peroni reportedly spent L22 billion on advertising in 1991, Dreher L27 billion, and Moretti L19 billion.[p]

Exhibit 17.11 illustrates the distribution channel for beer sold in Italy in 1992.

Exhibit 17.11   Distribution channel for beer sold in Italy, 1992

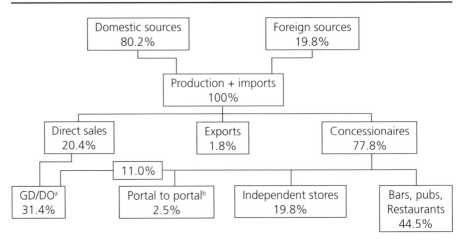

^a   *Grande Distribuzione/Distribuzione Organizzata* (large chains and purchasing groups).
^b   Sales directly to consumers from route trucks.

Source of data: *Il Mondo Della Birra*, December 1992, 30.

The 5000 or so "concessionaires" took large shipments of beer and delivered it to the tens of thousands of small retailers which distinguished Italy from most other markets. Some concessionaires also sold to other wholesalers, who delivered mixed loads of beer and other products to the tiniest outlets. And some beer was sold directly to consumers from route trucks.

Concessionaires were usually given specific territories. They paid deposits on bottles and crates and collected similar deposits from retailers. These deposits would be at risk if the concessionaire or retailer were to switch brewers. Brewers also installed and serviced draught equipment, further tying retailers and concessionaires to the brewer. An increasing percentage of beer was being purchased by Grande Distribuzione and Distribuzione Organizzata (centralized buying offices for chain stores and buying groups made up of large supermarkets).[q] The concessionaire system seemed to be slowly disintegrating in the early nineties.

The industry association

Assobirra, Italy's beer industry association, administered a "cooperative" advertising program, supported the industry's political agenda, and encouraged observance of certain "ethical" principles. For example, it was considered "unethical" for a brewer to try to entice another's draught customers on the basis of price or to attempt to hire another's employees. When the European Community adopted 25, 50, and 75 cl containers as standard in about 1982, Assobirra decided the Italian industry would continue using 33 and 66 cl packaging.

The beer making process

The primary raw materials for brewing beer are malt barley (which imparts bitterness), a small amount of other cereal grain, hops, and water. Yeast is used as a fermentation agent.

Birra Moretti SpA's San Giorgio facility was typical of Italian breweries in 1993. It was a simple process plant, consisting essentially of stainless steel tanks, hoppers, driers, filters, pumps, and so forth, connected by pipes and valves. Temperatures, pressures, and product chemistry were tightly controlled throughout and the system was closed from the atmosphere. An on-site laboratory used spectrographic analysis and chemical methods to test raw materials and to check the product at various points. The products were also tasted regularly. Such a plant requires few workers and only an occasional technician could be observed taking a sample, recording data, or adjusting machinery.

At one end of the plant, malt barley, about a fourth as much cereal grain (such as rice or corn), and a much smaller amount of hops were delivered on trucks and stored in silos. The "heart" of the brewery was a large room crowded with tanks, hoppers, and two large, gas-fired "kettles", where the grain was processed along with hops and yeast to produce wort, a tan fermenting liquid. The grain residue was dried for sale as animal feed and the wort piped to large tanks where fermentation and aging occurred. Processing time to this point was about 3.5 hours, allowing seven batches per day. The most modern plants in other countries required only 2.5 hours before fermentation began, allowing nine batches a day.

The wort was fermented for about four days and the resulting beer aged for about 16 days. Product characteristics were varied mainly by adjusting the amounts of malt, grain, and hops used and by changing the fermentation and aging times. The carbon dioxide produced during fermentation was taken off and liquefied for reintroduction to the beer after aging. The finished beer was pasteurized and discharged to the packaging building. There, modern, German-made machinery washed and sterilized containers (bottles, cans, and stainless steel kegs); filled them with beer; labeled the bottles; packaged the bottles and cans in cartons and the cartons in boxes; stacked the boxes and kegs on wood pallets; and shrink-wrapped the palletized products for shipment.

Fork truck operators moved pallets of empty packaging materials to the packaging area and shrink-wrapped pallets of product to a small storage area (which held about a day's production). But a mile or more of automatic conveyers transported the materials through the packaging process.

Large amounts of waste water, containing yeast and other solids, was generated in the brewing process. The water was treated to remove solids and volatile substances, leaving it clear and odorless. It was then discharged to the municipal sewer system under contract with the town of San Giorgio. City, provincial, and national health and environmental officials regularly checked the effluents from the plant and professors and students from a nearby university ran tests from time to time. The San Giorgio plant was well lighted and reasonably clean throughout. Only the bottling area was particularly noisy, averaging about 80 decibels.

NOTES AND REFERENCES

a Franco Cazzola, "Clean hands dip into the Tangentopoli," *The European*, February 25–28, 1993, p. 9.

b Canadean Limited, chart 1.1.2.

c Robert Graham, "Italy faces threat of big rise in unemployment," *Financial Times*, January 27, 1993, p. 2.

d Geert Hofstede, *Culture's Consequences: International Differences in Work Related Values* (Beverly Hills: Sage Publications, 1980).

e "The tangle in Italy," *The Economist*, February 20, 1993, pp. 13–14.

f "A sinking ship in Amato's archipelago," *The European*, February 25–28, 1993, p. 7.

g Cazzola, loc. cit.

h Canadean Ltd, *The Beer Service Basic Report Italy* (Basingstoke, UK: Canadean Ltd., 1992), section 1.

i Ibid., sections 2–3.

j Ibid., p. 62.

k Databank SpA, *Competitors Birra: Management Highlights* (Milan: Databank SpA, 1992), pp. 62–3.

l Ibid., sections 5–6.

m Ibid., section 3.

n Databank SpA, *Competitors Birra*, 7.

o Canadean Limited, section 9, and "Dossier," *Il Mondo Della Birra*, December 1992, 30.

p Ibid., section 7.

q Ibid., section 8.

DIBRELL BROTHERS, INC.

David W. Grigsby and Lester A. Hudson

By any measure, 1994 would have been considered a difficult time for any firm in the US tobacco industry. Congress was considering passage of the broadest ever ban on smoking in public places, the Clinton administration had proposed a stiff new excise tax on cigarettes to fund its health care reform bill, and militant anti-smoking groups were pushing for the regulation of tobacco, as a drug, by the Food and Drug Administration. On top of all this, world markets for leaf tobacco, which were already oversupplied, had been thrown into a tailspin by a new law limiting the foreign-grown tobacco leaf content of US-made cigarettes to 25 percent.

Despite the industry's rather bleak outlook, Claude B. Owen, Jr, President and CEO of Dibrell Brothers, Inc., one of the world's largest suppliers of leaf tobacco, remained extremely optimistic about his business: "Although the business is declining here in the States, expanding markets in the Far East and other parts of the world are making up for it. It so happens that Dibrell Brothers markets in leaf tobacco are expanding all over the world. It is also important to note that our company provides what is currently the most highly desired type of tobacco, light blends composed primarily of flue-cured and burley varieties."

Dibrell Brothers, Inc., a Fortune 500 company headquartered in Danville, Virginia, was actually engaged in two international businesses: the purchasing, processing, and selling of leaf tobacco and the purchasing and selling of fresh

The Dibrell Brothers, Inc. case is based on field research, interviews, and documents supplied by the subject company. It was written to serve as a basis for classroom discussion, and not to illustrate either effective or ineffective handling of administrative situations. Research was supported by a grant from the United States Department of Education, through the International Management Center of the University of Tulsa; Tulsa, Oklahoma, USA. The authors would like to thank Claude B. Owen, Jr. and other officials of Dibrell Brothers, Inc. for their cooperation. Copyright © David W. Grigsby, 1996.

Exhibit 18.1 Dibrell Brothers, Inc.: net sales, operating profit, and identifiable assets by line of business (US$ thousands)

	1992			1993			1994		
	Net sales	Operating profit[a]	Identifiable assets	Net sales	Operating profit[a]	Identifiable assets	Net sales	Operating profit[a]	Identifiable assets
Tobacco:									
United States	249,694	4,987	86,337	279,053	16,133	81,113	244,131	8,429	80,979
South America	317,854	53,718	339,734	268,551	53,490	341,934	162,567	(3,807)	345,112
Asia	27,028	1,447	9,756	37,987	4,961	13,337	22,633	511	8,686
Other	126,857	7,487	48,293	102,445	4,941	72,027	122,249	10,155	68,095
Worldwide supply center			15,879			14,660			12,000
Total tobacco	721,433	67,639	499,999	688,036	79,525	523,071	551,580	15,288	514,872
Flowers:									
Europe	294,818	9,676	95,676	312,888	5,471	83,273	294,094	3,989	89,241
United States	38,233	(1,834)	9,830	39,612	476	8,765	42,304	(2,109)	10,290
Other	26,605	689	3,742	24,903	534	3,324	31,137	681	3,409
Total flowers	359,656	8,531	109,248	377,403	6,481	95,362	367,535	2,561	102,940
Total	1,081,089	76,170	609,247	1,065,439	86,006	618,433	919,115	17,849	617,812

[a] As defined by FAS 14.

Source: Dibrell Brothers, Inc., 1994 annual report.

cut flowers. Tobacco operations accounted for the largest part of its sales (see exhibit 18.1). In addition to its substantial US domestic operations, Dibrell was the second largest exporter of US tobacco as well as a dominant supplier of tobacco from other countries to the world market. The company sold tobacco from over 60 countries totalling over 500 million pounds annually. This was enough to make approximately 250 billion cigarettes, or 5 percent of the world's total production. Dibrell's cut flower business, which it entered in 1987 through acquisitions, sourced flowers from virtually all over the world, primarily for distribution in Europe and North America. Considering the size and scope of all its flower operations, Dibrell Brothers was the world's largest importer and exporter of fresh cut flowers.

Although the long-range outlook for Dibrell's businesses was somewhat optimistic, Owen and his company faced several critical decisions in the summer of 1994. First of all, turmoil in the global leaf tobacco market had resulted in the company's poorest financial performance in many years. Following record profits in 1993, net sales declined 14 percent and the company posted a net loss of $9.1 million for the fiscal year that had ended on June 30, 1994. Given that the disruptions in the industry were expected to take several years to settle out, Owen needed a plan for avoiding losses in the meantime. Dibrell's cut flower business was not performing up to expectations, either. Persistent weaknesses in the European market and other factors had depressed sales and profits over the past three years. Moving that business along toward greater profitability would also require a significant management effort over the next few years. A number of very difficult questions would need to be answered during the coming year. What was the best plan for managing the two businesses? How should the company's resources be divided between them? Should Dibrell consider diversifying into new lines of business to lessen its dependence on tobacco and flowers?

As Dibrell management wrestled with these problems, a merger was proposed by Monk-Austin, Inc., a North Carolina-based leaf tobacco processor. Although the proposed combination was very attractive, Owen wondered if this was the right time to pursue it. On the positive side, the combination would result in increased operating efficiency as the companies combined their operations, and it would make Dibrell the second largest US tobacco leaf processing company. On the negative side, management wondered if it made good strategic sense to become more concentrated in tobacco, given the problems in that industry.

Company History

Dibrell Brothers was founded in 1873, when Richard H. Dibrell, a tobacco commission agent in Richmond, Virginia, sent his two sons to Danville to buy tobacco from local farmers. The sons, Alphonso and Richard Louis, quickly established themselves as able tobacco resellers, buying tobacco on warehouse floors, redrying and packing it into hogsheads, and shipping it to the ordering customers. The business grew and prospered as Danville became the largest loose-leaf tobacco market in the world, and one of the leading centers of the "New South". It was during this period that the well-known method of "chanting" during the process of the tobacco auction originated at the Danville market.

After the death of his brother in the late 1890s, Richard Louis Dibrell brought into the firm as partners two men who were to be instrumental in developing the business into one of the leading companies in the industry – Alexander Berkeley Carrington and Herbert L. Boatwright. The group of three proved to have a unique blend of abilities and skills. Carrington was the financial expert; Boatwright was an excellent judge of tobacco quality, types, and applications; and Dibrell was very effective at developing new markets and new customers, and identifying new opportunities. With this team in place, the company expanded rapidly during the first third of the twentieth century. Richard Louis Dibrell attributed the company's success to two factors: extensive travel to find new tobacco markets and customers, and timely acquisition of smaller subsidiary companies. Another factor in the firm's success was its membership, beginning in 1902, in the American Tobacco Trust led by James Biddle Duke.

The Dibrell Brothers strategy of seeking business through travel led it to be the first US leaf tobacco company to establish international business connections. An expansion into Canada in the 1880s added customers in Montreal and Halifax, and provided a base for later expansion. In the early 1890s, the business was expanded to Great Britain with sales to tobacco manufacturers in Scotland and England. This represented "the first direct connection [by Americans] with English manufacturers in buying leaf tobacco on direct order." In the 1890s, foreign operations were expanded by locating markets in Norway, Sweden, Belgium, China, and Japan. In time, overseas offices were set up to handle Dibrell's far-flung customer base. Offices were opened in London in 1911 and in Antwerp in 1927. Expansion into South America in the 1920s necessitated the opening of an office in New York in 1928 to oversee the Latin American market. The addition to its customer list in the 1930s of the Belgium Congo's Tabacongo Co. and other buyers firmly established the company in Africa. By 1935, Dibrell listed five international subsidiaries among its organizational units – Shanghai, London, Antwerp, Manila, and New York (for Latin America).

Expansion of US operations was also accomplished during this period. Following Dibrell's policy of "timely acquisition of smaller subsidiary companies" between 1900 and 1935, Dibrell Brothers in 1935 owned 15 subsidiaries, affiliates or branches in the southeastern United States. Tobacco purchasing, drying, processing, and storage facilities were located in Virginia, the Carolinas, Tennessee, Kentucky, and Georgia. Acquisition and market expansion paid off for Dibrell Brothers. The annual volume of business increased from 65 million pounds of tobacco in 1919 to almost 93 million pounds by 1931.

As the use automation in the production of tobacco products increased, manufacturers demanded more consistency in the raw product. To provide a more consistent product, Dibrell and other leaf providers began doing more of the processing that tobacco leaf needed before shipping it to the cigarette manufacturers. Tobacco processing at Dibrell entailed: (1) classification of leaf tobacco into several grades for different applications; (2) cleaning, curing, and aging for maximum value; (3) threshing, which was removing stalks and stems; (4) separating different types of leaf for different uses; and (5) storing the prepared product until it was shipped to the tobacco products company.

The Great Depression of the 1930s, was, ironically, a time of relative prosperity for Dibrell Brothers. Although earnings were down for a few years, the company posted profits throughout the period. Total processing capacity for the company in 1934 was 200 million pounds annually. During this time, ties were strengthened with US producers of tobacco products. Prior to the 1930s only P. Lorillard among the major US cigarette makers gave Dibrell much business. In the Depression years of the 1930s, American Tobacco Co. found a ready market for its new "roll-your-own" Bull Durham brand, and Dibrell Brothers was called upon to supply the low grade tobacco required for the product. This opportunity provided a base on which the company subsequently expanded its sales to all of the major US cigarette producers.

As the Second World War broke out in 1939, disruption of normal trade patterns caused the company's leadership to rethink its international business. Trade with Japan was curtailed, and Dibrell Brothers had to write off uncollectible debts in Nazi-controlled countries. Despite wartime controls on the homefront, however, the company posted handsome profits to offset losses abroad. Following the war, reconstruction of markets abroad offered opportunities for the company to further expand its international presence. By 1952, Dibrell Brothers had re-established its operations in Europe and the Far East, and had customers in forty-five separate countries. In 1959, Charles A. "Buck" Carr became President of Dibrell Brothers. This change represented the end of control by the three founding families and the beginning of control by the entire board of directors.

The late 1950s also brought a stepped-up effort in international acquisitions, primarily in Africa, and in expanding the company's international customer base. The 1960s were a time of consolidation and modernization of domestic processing facilities. Advanced processing equipment enabled the company to better respond to cigarette manufacturers demands for strip, versus leaf, tobacco. (Stripping is the first step in the manufacturing process, where the tobacco leaf is cut into strips before being introduced into the cigarette making machine.) Marginal operations were consolidated, and a modern processing plant was built near the company's headquarters in Danville which boosted Dibrell's per-day capacity to 950,000 pounds and achieved quality control unsurpassed in the industry.

Dibrell Brothers' first diversification outside the tobacco industry came with the purchase of Richmond Cedar Works, a manufacturer of ice cream freezers, in 1967. This was followed by the acquisition of American Interiors, a home lighting company, in 1969, and a restaurant chain shortly thereafter. Although all of these businesses were subsequently divested, according to Owen they provided valuable experience for senior managers in operating and evaluating businesses other than tobacco. Owen himself was responsible for the American Interiors business, and was very involved in the restaurant chain. He felt that these experiences prepared him well for Dibrell's later acquisitions in the cut flower industry.

In the 1970s and 1980s, under the leadership of Richard B. Bridgforth, Dibrell became a dominant supplier of tobacco from other countries, while maintaining its position as the second largest exporter of US leaf tobacco. Claude B. Owen Jr became Chairman of the Board of Directors and Chief Executive Officer of the company in 1990, and was subsequently appointed President.

Owen stated that Dibrell's principal objective is the creation of substantial long-term shareholder wealth. Specific goals are a long-term average annual total return to shareholders of 30 percent and a long-term average annual return on equity of at least 20 percent. Aligning management actions with shareholder's interests is a stated top management priority. Incentive compensation programs and a strategic decision-making process are tools used to accomplish this.

Organization and Top Management

Dibrell Brothers' history of growth through acquisition is reflected in its current organization. As of 1994, the company could best be described as a holding company. Its operations in both tobacco and cut flowers were conducted through a network of subsidiaries and affiliates spread throughout the world. Most subsidiaries were wholly owned by the parent company based in Danville, Virginia. Exhibit 18.2 depicts the principal subsidiaries as of June 30, 1993.

The top management team of Dibrell Brothers consisted of Claude B. Owen Jr and five senior vice presidents: Louis N. Dibrell III, Thomas H. Faucett, H. Peyton Green II, T. Wayne Oakes, and Richard A. Lassiter. As a group, they were a relatively young team (the oldest was 54). According to Owen "We've got expected continuity in management, and on the other hand, all of us have spent most of our careers at Dibrell." The only member of the team recruited from outside was Faucett, the Chief Financial Officer, who had been with the company for eight years. Within the top management team, responsibility was divided, primarily, by line of

Exhibit 18.2   Dibrell brothers Inc.: subsidiaries

Name	Jurisdiction in which organized	Percentage of voting securities owned	
		By registrant	By affiliate
Dibrell Brothers International BV	The Netherlands[a]	100.00	
Carolina Leaf Tobacco Company, Incorporated	Virginia[a]	100.00	
Commonwealth Tobacco Company, Inc.	Virginia[a]	100.00	
Dibrell Brothers Tobacco Company, Incorporated	Virginia[a]	100.00	
Dibrell Brothers of Canada Ltd	Canada[a]	100.00	
Dibrell Brothers International SA	Switzerland[a]	100.00	
Tobacco Export & Import Company, Inc.	Virginia[a]	100.00	
Rohtabakvergaerungs Aktiengesellschaft	Germany[a]		100.00[c]
Dibrell Do Brasil Tabacos Ltda	Brazil[a]		100.00[d]
Dibrell International BV	The Netherlands[a]	100.00	
Dibrell Brothers GmbH	Germany[a]	100.00	
Florimex Verwaltungs GmbH	Germany[a]		100.00[c]
Africa Holding, SA	Luxembourg[b]		49.00[e]
Dibrell Flowers BV	The Netherlands[a]	100.00	
Eastern Carolina Leaf Processing Company	North Carolina[b]		50.00[f]

[a]   Included in the consolidated financial statements.
[b]   Equity in net income included in the consolidated financial statements.
[c]   Owned by Dibrell Brothers GmbH.
[d]   Owned by Tobacco Export & Import Company, Inc.
[e]   Owned by Dibrell Brothers International SA.
[f]   Owned by Carolina Leaf Tobacco Company, Incorporated.

Source: Dibrell Brothers, Inc., 1993, Form 10-K.

business. The entire team, however, participated in strategic decisions concerning any line of business that affected the company. Continuing the Dibrell tradition of travel to support business development, each member of the management team spent a significant portion of his time overseeing the company's operations throughout the world.

Owen, a Danville native who was 48 years old in 1994, had worked at Dibrell since 1971. "The only job I've ever had is with Dibrell Brothers," says Owen. A graduate of Davidson College, where he was a varsity football and baseball player, Owen joined the company after receiving his MBA from the University of Maryland and serving two years as an officer in the army. His interest in sports dictates much of his leisure activities. Owen is an avid golfer and skier and an admitted "baseball nut." He follows his beloved Atlanta Braves faithfully, and participates in the

Braves annual executive camp. Owen's early assignments at Dibrell included conducting financial analyses of various operations, assessing opportunities, and developing recommendations for changes in the strategic plan. Owen travelled extensively around the world learning the tobacco business and developing strong relationships with major customers and suppliers – activities that had long been considered key success factors at Dibrell. Based on his own analysis, he promoted the cut flower business as a good diversification opportunity for Dibrell, and when the business was acquired, Owen was its first manager.

Tobacco Operations

Tobacco operations formed the majority of Dibrell's business activity. In fiscal year 1993, approximately 65 percent of Dibrell's revenues and over 92 percent of its profits were derived from tobacco operations. The basic relationships in the leaf tobacco industry in the United States had not changed much since the company's founding. Wholesalers such as Dibrell still bought tobacco at auction, processed it into the forms needed by the manufacturers of tobacco consumer products, then sold it to those manufacturers at a profit. The types of operations performed by leaf processors for the tobacco product companies had undergone dramatic changes, however. Leaf processing firms did much more preparation of the product than in the past.

Sourcing and processing

The range of activities for a company such as Dibrell included buying leaf tobacco at reasonable prices, conducting processing operations efficiently, supplying processed tobacco of a consistent quality, making it easy and efficient for customers to use its tobacco, and maintaining good relationships with customers. In the US market, Dibrell had little control over the first of these, since leaf tobacco was a non-differentiated commodity product, and prices were generally stabilized through US government price support programs. The processing and quality assurance steps were therefore the critical value-adding activities.

An important part of the quality expected by Dibrell's customers, the cigarette manufacturers, was consistency of blend. The more tobacco was processed, the better was the opportunity to maintain consistent blends and to reduce variation. Quality also resulted from reducing variation within each lot, as well as across lots. Different grades of tobacco were blended by the cigarette manufacturer to obtain maximum value, taste, and other characteristics. In order to produce a consistent product, any variation in the raw material (leaf tobacco) which was the result of differences in growing conditions, farming methods, and curing time had to be adjusted for in processing operations. Dibrell provided that consistency to the manufacturer through tightly controlled processing operations.

Dibrell's value to the manufacturer of cigarettes and other products depended on its ability to supply the kind and amount of tobacco that the manufacturer required on a timely basis. With product coming from virtually every corner of the globe, that required coordination of a very complicated network. Handling arrangements, international transfers, currency exchanges, documentation, and transportation all were critical skills for the leaf processor. Global sourcing of tobacco leaf was the best way to ensure that high quality and low cost tobacco was available for selected blending. Also, being able to tap multiple sources enhanced the company's ability to achieve high quality and minimize the variation in the processed tobacco it supplied to manufacturers.

With its ability to tap markets in virtually every part of the world, Dibrell was also able to take full advantage of changing prices for all the major types of raw product. Because of this growing complexity of world markets, US cigarette producers had come to depend less on their own vertically integrated buying units, and more on wholesalers such as Dibrell over the previous ten years.

While raw tobacco prices were not easily controllable, processing activities were. These activities, which included cleaning, threshing, blending, and sizing tobacco leaves, were important value-added activities for leaf suppliers the world over, since prices ultimately depended upon the quality of tobacco supplied to the manufacturers. Dibrell's state-of-the-art facilities had allowed it to provide for the increasingly stricter quality requirements of its customers. Cigarette manufacturers in particular had become more efficient through the use of very high-speed machinery. That had translated into a lower tolerance for substandard product, since the specifications of the leaf tobacco they bought had to be very consistent to accommodate their new equipment. To provide a more consistent product, processors such as Dibrell had taken on more of the operations to prepare tobacco for the final product. As Owen put it: "We're really now doing the first stages of manufacture. That has increased our investment in plant here in the United States and abroad. We have, however, been able to get a good return on that equipment, because we're offering a better service."

Customers

Dibrell's customers were manufacturers of cigarettes and tobacco products located in about 43 countries worldwide. Despite this dispersion, however, large customers were the rule in the leaf tobacco business. More than half of the company's consolidated tobacco sales (53 percent in 1993) were made to subsidiaries of three holding companies, each of which accounted for over 10 percent of Dibrell's total tobacco sales. These companies were Phillip Morris Companies, Inc., Japan Tobacco Co. (the state-run monopoly), and RJR Nabisco Holdings, Inc. Another 17 percent of tobacco sales were made to subsidiaries of three other large companies.

In 1993, 65 percent of Dibrell's consolidated tobacco revenues were derived from sales and services to foreign customers, or to foreign subsidiaries of US holding companies. Of these revenues, 55 percent were derived from sales of foreign grown tobacco, primarily flue-cured and burley varieties. Sales to foreign customers are made by the company's sales force, and also through agents. Substantially all sales were made in US dollars. The percentage of export sales of US-grown tobacco going to buyers in the Far East underwent significant growth in 1993, while sales to European customers declined significantly. Totals for 1991 through 1993 are shown in exhibit 18.3.

While relations with tobacco manufacturers were crucial to the success of the business, the number of major potential accounts was limited. As Owen put it:

Exhibit 18.3   Dibrell Brothers, Inc.: export sales of US origin (US$ thousands)

	1991	1992	1993	1994
Europe	124,535	99,801	87,388	61,438
Far East	80,969	97,009	105,937	104,516
Other	4,769	5,893	6,224	2,497
Total	210,273	202,703	199,549	168,451

Source: Dibrell Brothers, Inc., 1993 and 1994 annual reports.

> *In the tobacco business, there are relatively few major manufacturers around the world. They're either basically multinational manufacturers such as Phillip Morris, RJR, and B.A.T., or state-owned monopolies such as in Japan, France, and Italy. So, you've really got just a handful of customers.*

Dibrell strove to develop partnerships with these major customers, focusing on the customer and exceeding the customer's expectations. According to Owen:

> *Our goal is to make our customers successful on a repetitive basis, because Dibrell's success is based on their success. Strategic partnerships are the centerpiece of our approach to the international market. Our goal is to be the preferred supplier of our strategic customers around the world. We provide efficiency, reliability, and flexibility that surpasses our customers' expectations. Our hands-on approach is crucial in providing quality leaf tobacco and superior service to customers in over fifty countries.*

In 1993, Dibrell's tobacco division generated record operating profits despite declining prices brought on by an excess world supply. In the company's favor was its expertise in handling the types of tobacco most in demand on world markets. Light blended cigarette tobaccos were taking over more and more of the customer base as smokers abroad began to prefer American imports, and local companies began imitating their blends. These tobaccos, primarily flue-cured and burley varieties, were sourced from growers in the USA and abroad. Most processing occurred in the country of origin. Processed tobacco was then sold and shipped to manufacturers in various parts of the world. Where a particular grower's product ended up was a function of grading differences, relative market prices, supply levels, currency exchange rates, and other factors. Although Dibrell's operating efficiencies continued in 1994, world market oversupplies resulted in losses for the company's tobacco business, since the company's concentration on foreign sources made it especially vulnerable to the new US trade restriction capping the foreign content of US-made cigarettes at 25 percent.

Global sourcing

Dibrell Brothers used the country of origin as the basis for tracking costs and profits. In all, the company sourced tobacco directly from 15 different countries. Approximately 40 percent of the company's dollar volume of tobacco originated in the United States – bought at auctions of flue-cured, burley, and air-dried tobacco in the southeast. Another 33 percent of Dibrell's revenue was from Brazilian tobacco. In contrast to the US auction arrangement, Dibrell bought directly from growers in

Brazil and prefinanced some 25,000 individual tobacco farmers there. Owen estimated that his company bought over 20 percent of the total Brazilian tobacco crop each year, making it one of the largest buyers in the Brazilian market. In 1993, Dibrell's Brazilian subsidiary, Dibrell do Basil, accounted for 70 percent of the company's tobacco division profits. In spite of a $15 million expansion in 1992, Dibrell's Brazilian processing facilities were operating at capacity in 1993.

The balance of the company's tobacco purchases, 27 percent in all, were made in Argentina, Canada, China, Germany, Greece, India, Italy, Malawi, Mexico, Turkey, and Zimbabwe. The rising stars in this group were Argentina, Malawi, Zimbabwe, and, more significantly, China. According to Owen:

> I think China is already the largest producer and consumer of tobacco in the world. We're just now working with the Chinese State enterprises to improve the quality of tobacco, and to improve their techniques and handling of tobacco, both at the farm level and at the processing factory level, and we work with them on their shipping patterns so that we can get the tobacco.

Overall, Dibrell was considered the most "internationalized" of the four leading US leaf-processing companies. It sourced from a greater number of countries than any of its competitors, and its foreign sales were second in the industry, close behind those of Universal Corporation.

Taking into account all of the company's operations in more than fifty countries worldwide, Dibrell was believed to be the world's second largest processor of tobacco, behind Universal, as of early 1993. Moreover, a higher proportion of Dibrell's business was done overseas as compared to its competitors. "Our international business today is larger than the whole company was in 1989," stated Owen. Dibrell's dominant position in the Brazilian market was especially important, since Brazil was the second largest source of export, behind the USA, and gaining fast. Industry experts generally agreed with Owen's market share estimates. Wheat First Securities analyst John C. Maxwell Jr estimated in 1994 that Dibrell's shares in the world's flue-cured tobacco markets were: USA 10 percent, Brazil 19 percent, Malawi 18 percent, Argentina 14 percent, and Zimbabwe 8 percent. In burley tobaccos, Maxwell estimated the company's market shares to be: USA 7 percent, Brazil 15 percent, Argentina 24 percent, Malawi 15 percent.

The labor force and seasonality

Dibrell's consolidated tobacco operations were not labor intensive. Worldwide employment totals approximately 1700, excluding seasonal workers. Of these, 1200 were employed in foreign operations, and 500 in the USA. In the USA, flue-cured tobacco was purchased from July to November. Because of its semiperishable quality, most tobacco was cured and processed during those months. Other markets around the world had similar seasonality, but the periods were different. This resulted in less overall seasonality for Dibrell than for producers that were strictly domestic in their operations. Nevertheless, the company had always depended on sizable seasonal labor force to process the crop. In the USA, approximately 500 workers were hired on a seasonal basis to supplement the company's regular work force during the peak season. US seasonal workers were, for the most part, covered by collective bargaining agreements with several labor unions.

Facilities

Besides its Danville plant and storage facility, Dibrell operated tobacco processing and storage facilities in Greenville, North Carolina, through its Eastern Leaf Processors subsidiary. The Danville plant also included a modern laboratory to assist in the technical aspects of tobacco processing. A plant expansion and modernization program was completed at Danville in 1989 at a cost of over $10 million, and renovations to corporate headquarters were completed in 1991 at a cost of approximately $1.4 million. The company also operated processing facilities in Brazil, Germany, Turkey, Zimbabwe, and Malawi. The company's largest facility was located in Vera Cruz, Brazil.

Competitors

Although a number of domestic and foreign tobacco companies were structured vertically to buy and/or process leaf tobacco, principal competition in the leaf tobacco business was among the four significant US competitors who were not manufacturers. These four companies were located within 200 miles of each other in Virginia and North Carolina along what is known as "Tobacco Road." Among the four, Dibrell ranked third in sales in 1993. Given below are short profiles of the other three companies. The profits and revenues of all four companies for the years 1991 to 1993 are presented in exhibit 18.4.

Universal Corporation

Based in Richmond, Virginia, Universal was the largest of the group by far, with annual revenues of approximately $3 billion. While its total volume of US-sourced and foreign tobacco far exceeded Dibrell's, its foreign operations were estimated to be more nearly equivalent to Dibrell's in size. Universal operated in most of the same markets as Dibrell, and in 1993 acquired the European-based Casalee Group, the world's fifth largest tobacco dealer. The company believed that the Casaleê acquisition would enhance its chances for growth in China, Russia, and Eastern Europe. Universal's non-tobacco subsidiaries, which accounted for approximately one-quarter of its revenues, were equally divided between lumber and building products, and agriproducts (tea, sunflower seed, nuts, and dried fruit). Both of these business also had significant international operations. In 1994, Universal launched a global restructuring program designed to make its operations more efficient. Management expected annual cost savings of approximately $19 million to result from this effort.

Standard Commercial Corporation

Standard Commercial, based in Wilson, North Carolina was the closest competitor in size to Dibrell in 1994. Standard competed in both the domestic and foreign sectors of the leaf tobacco business, operating in substantially the same foreign markets as Dibrell and Universal. Brazil was the primary non-US source of all three firms. Although the company did not report its tobacco sales by market area, its foreign operations were believed to be smaller than those of Dibrell. Standard Commercial's major diversification was in the wholesale wool industry. The company acquired wool in Australia, New Zealand, South America, and South Africa

Exhibit 18.4   United States leaf tobacco industry, competitor profiles (dollar amounts in thousands)

	1991	1992	1993	1994
Universal Corporation				
Total revenue	2,896,464	2,989,018	3,047,213	2,975,050
% revenue from tobacco	78.4	74.8	75.0	73.1
Operating profit[a]	143,275	160,638	173,524	110,514
% operating profit from tobacco	85.7	83.8	84.3	74.7
Standard Commercial Corporation				
Total revenue	1,031,992	1,178,143	1,239,478	1,042,014
% revenue from tobacco	78.4	70.3	70.3	64.4
Operating profit[a]	56,227	76,688	78,443	12,153
% operating profit from tobacco	94.1	84.2	86.4	22.9
Dibrell Brothers, Incorporated				
Total revenue	1,003,022	1,081,089	1,065,439	919,114
% revenue from tobacco	65.5	66.7	64.6	60.0
Operating profit[a]	67,399	76,170	86,006	17,849
% operating profit from tobacco	80.58	88.80	92.46	85.70
Monk-Austin, Incorporated				
Total revenue	629,997	617,225	611,433	528,256
% revenue from tobacco	100.0	100.0	100.0	100.0
Operating profit[a]	45,278	44,473	43,934	21,287
% operating profit from tobacco	100.0	100.0	100.0	100.0

[a]   Operating profit as defined by FAS 14.

Source: 1993 and 1994 annual reports.

and processed it for distribution to woolen manufacturers. Smaller subsidiaries included a duty-free import/export business in Germany, a wholesale nursery and a wholesale/retail building materials company in North Carolina, and land investments in Manitoba, Canada.

Monk-Austin, Inc.

The smallest of the "big four" leaf processors, Monk-Austin, of Farmville, North Carolina, was founded in 1990 as a result of a merger between A. C. Monk and Co. and The Austin Company, Inc., and became a public company in November of 1992. As of 1994, Monk-Austin was the only major US leaf processor focused solely on the leaf tobacco business. Although most of its facilities were located in the United States, Monk-Austin was aggressively increasing its international business. It had operating facilities in five countries, and purchased tobacco in a total of 22 countries. Two significant acquisitions in 1993 were Centraleaf Ltd, a processing company in Malawi, and T. S. Ragsdale, Inc., a privately owned leaf dealer in South

Carolina. In 1994, Monk-Austin completed an agreement with R. J. Reynolds to purchase all of Reynolds' US tobacco needs from the auction markets. This arrangement was expected to produce an annual revenue boost, starting in 1995, of $200 to $300 million.

Dibrell's attempted merger with standard commercial

On March 28, 1993 Dibrell Brothers and Standard Commercial Corporation announced plans to merge, pending shareholder and government approval. Both companies' boards approved an agreement in principle, in which Dibrell shareholders would control 60 percent of the new company and Standard Commercial shareholders the remaining 40 percent. The transaction was expected to be tax-free, and would be concluded within three to four months. The combined companies would control about $1.5 billion in tobacco revenues and $720 million in non-tobacco sales. Spokepersons for both companies emphasized that synergistic effects of the merger would push combined net income well above the 1992 combined total of $58.8 million. The merger plan called for Claude B. Owen Jr to be the new company's president and CEO, and Alec G. Murray of Standard Commercial to serve as executive vice president. A Dibrell spokesperson said that the new company might retain the Dibrell name, but that a final decision had not been reached. In the wake of the announcement, Dibrell shares fell 50 cents to $33.25 and Standard Commercial shares fell 25 cents to $19.50.

A month later, on April 27, Standard Commercial announced that it was cancelling plans for the merger. The reason given was that, following a board meeting on due diligence, the stockholders determined that the merger was not in the company's best interest. Dibrell management felt that the merger had been stopped by the actions of a few powerful Standard Commercial stockholders who feared the loss of autonomy resulting from Standard's minority position in the proposed deal.

Flower Operations

Dibrell's cut flower operations consisted of buying flowers around the world and transporting them to its operating units to await resale to wholesale customers, and, increasingly, to supermarket chains for direct distribution. The company's diversification into the cut flower business began in 1987 with the acquisition of the Nuremberg-based Florimex Verwaltungs GmbH group (Florimex). Florimex distributed cut flowers through its network of 51 branch offices in 18 countries. Flowers were acquired from more than 300 suppliers located in 50 countries on five continents. Its primary sources of supply were located in the Netherlands, under the auction system, and in Kenya under contract arrangements. Latin America was also an important sourcing point for Florimex operations, particularly for exotic flower varieties. More direct links to Latin American markets were being developed by Florimex and the other flower dealers, a move which was directed at eventually lessening the industry's dependence on the Amsterdam auction. Most flowers were transported by commercial and cargo jet planes, and within hours of cutting had passed through distribution channels to flower vendors around the world.

In 1988, Dibrell acquired a controlling interest in Baardse BV, the second largest Dutch exporter of flowers, giving Dibrell a significant presence in Amsterdam, the world's largest flower market, where approximately two-thirds of the world's supply of flowers is sold. Both Florimex and Baardse maintained fleets of refrigerated trucks for transporting flowers throughout Europe, where the average consumption of fresh cut flowers was over twice that of the USA. Air shipment of cut flowers usually did not require refrigeration, as the cargo compartments of commercial airplanes flying at high altitudes had very low temperatures. Airport delivery and pickup were carefully coordinated to protect the fragile cargo.

Unlike the tobacco business, the market for cut flowers was a highly fragmented business. No single customer accounted for a significant amount of the volume of either Florimex or Baardse, who sold to thousands of wholesalers in Europe, North America, and Asia. Wholesalers placed their orders in advance, then took delivery of the product at market rates. Florimex also sold directly to retailers in Germany. Although together the two companies comprised the largest cut flower business in the world, no single competitor, including Dibrell's group, had a significant share of the worldwide market. Dibrell's total share was estimated at about 5 percent of the market. The high degree of fragmentation, coupled with the perishable nature of the product, and the fact that there were many substitutes for fresh flower purchases, meant that competition for market share was quite intense. Furthermore, profits had suffered in the early 1990s as European operations were hit hard by unfavorable currency exchange rates and rising costs in the Amsterdam market.

Sales of flowers were highly seasonal and, to a great degree, a function of holiday buying. The effect of special buying days, such as Valentine's Day and Mother's Day, also had a dramatic effect on flower volumes. An advantage of Dibrell's worldwide structure was that seasonal purchases in one part of the world tended to offset lags in other parts. Europe, Asia, and the United States tended to buy flowers at different times, as the emphasis on different holidays dictated. Even Mother's Day is celebrated on different dates around the world.

Dibrell management considered the development of strategic partnerships in the flower business just as important as in the tobacco business. According to Owen:

> *We have developed partnerships around the world to provide the varieties and qualities our customers demand. We avoided the historical "stem peddler" mentality in favor of an integrated marketing approach that makes us partners with our strategic customers and suppliers. Florimex is forging partnerships with key customers to become their preferred supplier of fresh-cut flowers, bouquets, and arrangements.*

Dibrell management was optimistic about the future of the cut flower business. Unlike the tobacco business, where world demand was essentially flat and the company's market share had to be gained through penetration, the flower industry had what Owen referred to as "organic growth."

> *Flowers are one of the fastest-growing consumer products in Europe and North America. There is more product moving all the time. Eighty percent of our business today is in europe, especially Northern Europe where the consumption patterns are very high. The rest of Europe is quickly following suit, and*

now the emerging democracies of Eastern Europe present even greater opportunities. With Florimex in Nuremberg, we're well positioned to take advantage of these emerging markets.

Although the USA was the largest single flower market in the world, industry experts estimated that Americans in 1993 bought only half as many cut flowers per capita as the Japanese and Italians, and only one-third as many as the Swiss and Germans. Less than 5 percent of the flowers passing through Alsmeer, the giant flower center in the Netherlands, were bound for US markets. Owen, Florimex, and Baardse were out to change that.

Florimex Worldwide, Inc., a wholly owned subsidiary of Dibrell Brothers, was an importer, exporter, and distributor of cut flowers in Europe, Asia, and North America. Flower wholesalers were the largest customers; however, mass retail merchants, whom Florimex supplies directly, are the fastest-growing customer segment. In North America, the focus is on direct supply of fresh floral arrangements to supermarkets, which is the fastest-growing retail outlet for fresh flowers.

The size and scope of Florimex's network were expected play a role in the expansion of the industry. According to Owen:

We do not see any move afoot for any competitor getting organized in the way that we are organized. Therefore, we think that the logistical advantages, which will translate into better product, fresher product, and more carefully handled product, will continue to allow us to grow in the business.

From 1990 to 1992, Dibrell's flower sales increased by 45 percent, with less than a 10 percent increase in assets employed in the business.

The recession in Europe and Japan slowed the sales growth in Dibrell's flower business to 5 percent in 1993, an increase of $18 million. During the year, the company restructured its Dutch export operation, Baardse, as a result of studies by consultants Alexander Proudfoot and McKinsey and Company. A new management team was installed and new methods and systems were adopted. Further restructuring of US flower operations in 1994 resulted in a $2.1 million operating loss.

Perhaps the most significant trend in the flower business, according to Owen, was the shift toward more sales through supermarket outlets. "It is ready to undergo a boom here in the United States and in Japan," said Owen. With ready availability of fresh cut flowers in their local supermarkets, shoppers were expected to buy them as a regular part of their weekly shopping instead of reserving the purchase of flowers for special occasions.

Reorganizing a business that has traditionally utilized long chains of middlemen would not be easy, but the potential profit margins were there. In traditional supply channels, flowers were marked up approximately 15 percent by Florimex and other wholesalers. The importing wholesaler, who was next in line, typically marked the product up another 20 percent before passing them along to the retail florist. The florist, who was the most likely middleman to be stuck with wilted flowers, marked them up again at an average 100 percent. A shipment of flowers that Florimex bought at auction in Amsterdam for $1000 therefore had a final selling value in the florist shop of about $2760. Exhibit 18.1 contains the 1992 to 1994 net sales, operating profits, and identifiable assets for Dibrell's flower businesses.

Unlike its tobacco operations, in which profit and loss centers are based on the origin of product, Dibrell's flower revenues and profits are tracked by final markets.

Shortly after entering the flower business, Dibrell experimented briefly with backward integration. Said Owen:

> We invested in flower-growing operations in Southern Spain, and it was a disaster. We should have known better than that. We got in and we got out, and thank goodness it only cost us a modest amount. We had been in the tobacco business for over 100 years, and we never thought we had to grow tobacco. We should have used that understanding as we analyzed why we were going to grow flowers. I use that as an example of how forgetting the lessons that got you here can cause you to go off in the wrong directions and make mistakes, and we've just got to avoid that.

Human Resources Management

Dibrell's consolidated companies employed approximately 3000 full-time workers. These included approximately 500 employed in the company's US tobacco operations, 1200 in non-US tobacco operations, and 1300 in flower subsidiaries around the world. The company also employed approximately 500 seasonal workers in its US tobacco operations and 3400 seasonal workers in its non-US tobacco subsidiaries. Benefits were, in general, above industry standards. Full-time employees in the USA were covered for health and life insurance, and were enrolled in a defined benefits pension plan. Retirees of the company continued to receive health and life insurance coverage. Benefit plans for non-US employees varied substantially from country to country, and were administered at the local subsidiary level.

The company's policy for promotions was generally a "promote-from-within" system, with current employees having first consideration for positions as they became open. Employees tended to stay with the company for their entire careers, and loyalty and morale were generally considered to be quite high.

Financial Management

Following record profits in 1993, Dibrell experienced a net loss of $9.1 million in 1994. Sales in the tobacco segment were down 19.8 percent, and operating profits from tobacco declined by over 80 percent. Oversupplied markets, the restrictions of the new US content law, and threats of increased excise taxes all combined to cause buyers to cut their orders of leaf tobacco. The resulting decreased demand caused significant decreases in world prices as well. Although these demand and pricing problems were showing improvement by June 1994, and were expected to correct within two years, Dibrell began shifting its investment focus away from expansion toward projects aimed at streamlining present operations to enhance efficiency.

Flower sales were down by 2.4 percent in 1994, and operating profits from flowers declined from $6.5 million in 1993 to just $2.6 million in 1994. Continued recession in Europe was the major cause for the poor showing, but the economy showed signs of beginning a rapid recovery. For 1995, the company planned to continue emphasizing cost reduction in its European operations, and aggressive promotion of its US and Japanese markets.

Overall, the effects of exchange rate fluctuations on Dibrell's financial statements tended to be neutral. Most tobacco sales were transacted in US dollars, and flower operations employed what are known as "natural hedges," which simply means that assets and liabilities were spread across complementary markets. Because of the company's widespread operations, exchange rate losses in one market were usually offset by gains in another. Two exceptions to this rule occurred in recent years. In 1993, the company profited by nearly $5 million due to currency exchange gains in Brazil and the United Kingdom. In 1994, however, Dibrell was hit with exchange rate losses on dollar sales of flowers.

The company's long-term debt consisted primarily of revolving credit notes. Historically, the company had needed sources of this type to provide capital in excess of cash flow at various time of the year, primarily to finance inventory and accounts receivable, and more recently, for financing costs related to acquisitions. In 1993, extraordinary items included a $2.1 million gain associated with the settlement of prior claims against R. J. Reynolds Tobacco Co. This was partially offset by the charges incurred in 1993 on the failed merger with Standard Commercial Corporation. For further analysis, exhibit 18.5 contains financial highlights of the company for the years 1992 through 1994.

Strategic Issues

The oversupply problem in the tobacco industry in 1993 and 1994 was primarily due to the persistent glut of flue-cured and burley varieties. As markets in Eastern Europe and the former Soviet republics began opening up in the 1990s, tobacco exporting countries saw opportunities there and began increasing their production. When these markets did not expand as rapidly as was expected, the result was excess supply. By 1993, overproduction of these tobacco types worldwide began causing an overall significant depressing effect on prices, a problem that was expected to take up to two years to resolve as market supplies adjusted. Reduced plantings of tobacco in 1994, however, were a good indication that oversupplies would be short-lived.

The unexpected passage, in 1993, of a 25 percent foreign content cap on US-produced cigarettes further exacerbated the situation for Dibrell and the other leaf processors. The measure, which was attached to the Omnibus Budget Reconciliation Act of 1993, was aimed at protecting US tobacco farmers from competing with low-cost foreign tobacco, although some industry observers believed it was offered as mitigation for the effects of increased tobacco excise taxes. When it passed, new purchases of imported leaf tobacco by cigarette manufacturers fell precipitously as each manufacturer adjusted its inventory level in response to the lower level of imported tobacco allowed. This loss of the US market, which had previously become the single most important export destination for most tobacco-producing nations, brought on intensive price competition among producers for the remaining markets in Europe and Asia. The average price for foreign-sourced leaf tobacco fell 18 percent in late 1993 and another 25 percent in early 1994. The law was rescinded in October 1994. There were various reasons for rescinding, but chief among them was that the law was in violation of the GATT agreement signed by the United States that year. Although the effects on the leaf tobacco industry

Exhibit 18.5 Dibrell Brothers, Inc.: selected consolidated financial data, 1992–1994 (US$ thousands, except shares and per share data)

	1992	1993	1994
STATEMENT OF INCOME DATA			
Net revenues	$1,081,089	$1,065,439	$919,114
Less: Cost of revenues	937,100	914,404	836,905
Gross Profit	143,989	151,035	82,209
Less: Selling and administrative expenses	77,670	81,875	78,576
Operating income	66,319	69,160	3,633
Interest income	3,787	4,076	5,551
Miscellaneous other income	2,918	8,338	3,805
Less: Interest expense	26,566	20,691	21,204
Less: Miscellaneous other deductions	3,211	2,623	413
Income (loss) before income taxes and other items	43,246	58,259	(8,628)
Income taxes	16,623	20,085	1,342
Income (loss) after taxes	26,623	38,174	(9,970)
Income applicable to minority interest	214	486	466
Income (loss) after minority interest	26,409	37,688	(10,436)
Equity in net income of investee companies	4,206	590	1,292
Net Income (loss) before extraordinary items	30,615	38,278	(9,144)
Extraordinary items (net)	(327)	–	–
Cumulative effect of accounting changes (net)	–	1,070	–
Net income (loss)	$30,288	$39,348	($9,144)
SHARE AND PER SHARE DATA			
Net income (loss) primary	$2.28	$2.95	($0.69)
Net income (loss) fully diluted	$2.05	$2.61	–
Dividends per share	$0.51	$0.63	$0.74
Weighted avg. common shares outstanding:			
Primary	13,257,011	13,326,117	13,318,113
Assuming full dilution	16,105,579	16,152,343	16,122,234
BALANCE SHEET DATA			
Current assets	$414,171	$405,092	$400,186
Current liabilities	292,404	279,498	277,136
Working capital	121,767	125,594	123,050
Fixed assets – property, plant & equipment	130,465	135,371	138,164
Total assets	630,460	639,778	651,457
Long-term debt	201,982	177,228	211,636
Total shareholder's equity	120,403	152,585	132,358

Source: Dibrell Brothers, Inc., 1993 and 1994 annual reports.

were devastating in the short run, the market was expected to adjust and be back in balance by the end of 1995.

Despite its intentions to protect US producers, if the 25 percent cap had been retained, it could eventually have caused cigarette production to shift off shore to escape the necessity of using the higher priced American tobacco. With the declining consumption of cigarettes by Americans, an increasing share of the US tobacco industry's production was being exported anyway. Despite such efforts by the US Congress and other trade restrictions around the world, a great deal of very compelling evidence pointed toward the inevitability of lower cost foreign tobaccos winning out on world markets – trends which favored Dibrell's international sourcing strategy. For example, in 1994, US exports of leaf tobacco accounted for only 20 percent of the world's supply, as opposed to 60 percent just thirty years previously.

Another development that had not been anticipated was the development of price wars between US private branded cigarettes in 1993 and 1994. Although the profits of cigarette producers were being squeezed by the continuation of this trend, its effect on the leaf processors was uncertain. Leaf prices were, for the most part, a function of world supplies and quality considerations. Any attempts by the cigarette makers to have suppliers assume some of this price pressure would therefore not likely be successful. If the price wars deepened, however, it could be predicted that cigarette producers might consider integrating backward in an attempt to lower their costs. Owen and others in the industry felt that was unlikely however. The leaf processors were better positioned to buy, sort, classify, and blend the large number of varieties that modern products used, and better able to maintain quality and handle complicated international arrangements.

Another force to be reckoned with was the growing success of antismoking campaigns. By 1994, various anti-smoking groups were beginning to have a significant effect on public policy in the United States. New taxes on cigarettes and other tobacco products were being proposed as a way of offsetting the costs of a national health care system, and in 1994, Congress was considering the passage of an act that would, in effect, ban smoking in practically every public building in the country. The government's attention focused on cigarette manufacturers.

The courts had also handed down several rulings in favor of anti-smoking forces. Whereas lower court decisions had restricted the tobacco companies' liabilities in cancer-related death cases because of their compliance with government warning label regulations, these were reversed by the Supreme Court in June of 1992. Some tort claims were therefore not pre-empted. There was speculation that this could throw open the door once again to a flood of claims against the cigarette manufacturers. Since Dibrell did not manufacture tobacco products or sell tobacco to consumers, it had avoided these legal issues and the potential liabilities associated with tobacco. However, the company had no control over adverse market reactions caused by public responses to its customer's businesses, and the reactions had been very negative.

Although the increased pressure on the smoking public had spread to other Western countries, smoking in other parts of the world was expected to continue to increase for another 20 years. Some countries, however, were beginning to react to the health concerns surrounding tobacco use. Alarmed at the meteoric increase in the popularity of smoking, some Asian governments had begun to regulate tobacco advertising for the first time.

Meanwhile, restrictions in Europe got tougher. The European Parliament voted in 1992 to impose a ban on all tobacco advertising throughout the European Union. Although still not approved by 1994, the proposed ban would apply to magazines, billboards, newspapers, and cinema screens as well as television – and sports events could not be sponsored by tobacco companies.

Perhaps more significant for Dibrell was the growing popularity of the light blended tobaccos in which the company specialized. Not only were American-style cigarettes preferred for their taste, but the tar content tended to be lower as well. European Union regulations which went into effect in January 1993 called for limiting the tar content of cigarettes sold to 15 milligrams, a level far below the US one. To comply, European producers began switching blends to the lighter ones, in which Dibrell specialized. It should be noted that competitors could not act quickly to change the composition of their products to match Dibrell's advantage in light flue-cured and burley products. Tobacco varieties were specific to various regions of the world, and a company's investments, as well as its sources and contacts, took time to develop within the source country. Dibrell, for example, contracted several years in advance with growers in Brazil and other countries to grow specific types of tobacco.

Developing low cost sources requires Dibrell to constantly assess its operations in developing nations, and to be ready to invest in new sourcing opportunities. Although its operations in Brazil, Zimbabwe, Malawi, and Argentina produced high-quality tobacco leaf at low cost, future low-cost sources were being evaluated. Opportunities to expand into China were especially intriguing to Dibrell management. As of 1993, leaf tobacco costs in China were less than one-half of those in Brazil. If the infrastructure and market arrangements could be mastered, China represented a vast supply source as well as a huge market for leaf tobacco.

Issues in the flower industry mostly revolved around how to operate the business more efficiently. Dibrell Brothers management believed that the best way to do this was to sell flowers directly to retailers, concentrating on large supermarket chains. The flower business was not without its regulatory issues, either. In 1994, US rose producers, whose market share had been eroding over the past two decades, managed to convince trade officials to place restrictions on imported roses, most of which came from Colombia and Ecuador.

Dibrell management believed that, in the long run, attention to two basic themes would lead to profitability in both of the company's businesses. These were (1) service to customer, and (2) cost efficiency. The service aspect was summarized by Owen as follows:

> *Dibrell was a service company long before that became a buzz word in business, and the kinds of principles we've used here have been a factor for a long time, particularly in our tobacco business. Understanding our customer, anticipating his needs, organizing our business to serve those needs rather than organizing our business to suit ourselves and then trying to push our product down his throat. I think we need to be awfully keen to preserve those real key characteristics that represent the history and success of our company.*

At Dibrell Brothers, cost efficiency was addressed by continuously developing low cost sources of supply and continuously finding new ways to leverage the company's investments effectively.

While diversification outside of the tobacco industry continued to be the rule for most companies, Owen saw no reason for Dibrell to expand beyond the two businesses that the company was in. "We have a lot to do yet in developing what we have. While we don't rule out further diversification efforts, we would be very careful in choosing what that would be."

The Proposed Merger with Monk-Austin

The possibility of a merger with Monk-Austin, Inc. was first raised by Thomas Faucett, Chief Financial Officer of Dibrell, early in the spring of 1994 in a conversation with Monk-Austin's CFO, John M. Hines. Although Monk-Austin did not pursue the idea at that time, the idea did spark interest at Monk-Austin headquarters. Later that spring, when another leaf tobacco company approached Monk-Austin management about merging, Monk's CEO, Albert C. Monk III, retained the services of an investment firm to assist the company in evaluating all potential partners in the industry. The analysis identified Dibrell as a desirable and feasible potential partner. On September 16, Monk-Austin initiated contact with Dibrell through intermediaries, and the first meeting between the two management groups was held in Raleigh, North Carolina on September 22, 1994. During that fall, Claude Owen and other Dibrell officers met with the management team of Monk-Austin, Inc. on several occasions to explore the possibility of merging the two companies.

Although Dibrell Brothers was larger overall than Monk-Austin, the two companies' tobacco operations were approximately equal in terms of sales volumes. Their strengths, however, lay in different areas. Dibrell's greatest strength was its market position in foreign tobacco, especially in the very important Brazilian market. This was important because global sourcing capability would continue to be a critical success factor in the industry. Monk-Austin, on the other hand, had a larger share of the domestic tobacco business. Given the new requirement for greater domestic content and the likelihood that some form of protectionism would be used to shield US growers from foreign competition, domestic sourcing ability would also continue to be a critical success factor in the business. Despite recent down years, both companies were financially sound at the time of the talks. (Exhibits 18.1, 18.3, and 18.5 presented earlier detail the financial position and performance of Dibrell Brothers. Exhibit 18.6 contains Monk-Austin's selected financial information for the years 1992 through 1994, Exhibit 18.7 displays Monk-Austin's market segment data for the same period, and exhibit 18.8 shows Monk-Austin's export sales of US origin tobacco.)

As the merger analysis progressed, Dibrell management began to see a number of possible advantages in a merger with Monk-Austin. (1) The combined companies would be able to take advantage of improved operating efficiencies by combining operations and eliminating duplicated efforts. (2) The economies of scale that could be achieved by combining leaf processing facilities in several key markets around the world would allow the new company to compete more effectively

Exhibit 18.6 Monk-Austin, Inc.: selected consolidated financial data, 1992–1994 (US$ thousands, except shares and per share data)

	1992	1993	1994
STATEMENT OF INCOME DATA			
Net revenues	$617,225	$611,433	$528,256
Less: Cost of revenues	544,220	538,061	472,130
Gross Profit	73,005	73,372	56,126
Less: Selling and administrative expenses	33,068	34,286	40,940
Operating income	39,937	39,086	15,186
Other (income) expenses:			
Interest expense	16,271	17,437	13,913
Foreign exchange (gain) loss	(4,222)	(5,159)	(965)
(Gain) loss on disposition of foreign operations	–	–	(1,792)
Interest and dividend income	(1,286)	(1,640)	(1,474)
Other, net	(2,058)	(6,465)	(2,113)
Income before income taxes and other items	31,214	34,913	7,617
Provision for income taxes	7,008	6,995	3,334
Income after taxes	24,206	27,918	4,283
Equity in (income) loss of unconsolidated affiliates	(640)	(774)	1,719
Income from continuing operations before			
extra. item & accounting changes	24,846	28,692	2,564
Extraordinary gain	2,900	–	–
Cumulative effect of accounting changes	–	–	(1,634)
Net income	$27,746	$28,692	$930
SHARE AND PER SHARE DATA			
Net income	$1.71	$1.68	$0.05
Dividends per share (rounded)	$0.04	$0.08	$0.18
Common shares outstanding, year end	15,422,208	18,113,614	18,113,614
BALANCE SHEET DATA			
Current assets	$244,626	$263,154	$299,476
Current liabilities	143,820	147,189	204,232
Working capital	91,800	115,965	95,244
Fixed assets – property, plant, & equipment	33,200	54,178	73,019
Total assets	311,043	365,486	414,400
Long-term debt	54,412	53,085	39,156
Total shareholder's equity	101,455	157,995	158,663

Source: Monk-Austin, Inc., 1993 and 1994 annual reports.

Exhibit 18.7 Monk-Austin, Inc.: net sales, operating profit, and identifiable assets by geographic area (US$ thousands)

	1992			1993			1994		
	Net revenues	Operating income[a]	Identifiable assets	Net revenues	Operating income[a]	Identifiable assets	Net revenues	Operating income[a]	Identifiable assets
Tobacco									
United States	$350,575	$9,882	$125,080	$359,193	$11,072	$129,512	$341,029	$9,926	$229,913
Central & South America	172,779	21,838	168,733	224,580	24,527	177,629	180,244	6,062	145,432
Africa	67,486	6,519	43,933	50,422	5,295	58,048	122,233	6,300	74,965
Other	77,861	7,060	29,596	56,442	3,712	17,782	45,700	(351)	18,853
Intersegment eliminations	(51,476)	(826)	(80,148)	(79,204)	(672)	(43,732)	(160,950)	(650)	(72,188)
Total	617,225	44,473	287,194	611,433	43,934	339,239	528,256	21,287	396,975
Corporate		(4,536)	2,462		(4,848)	2,185		(6,101)	1,958
Equity in net assets of unconsolidated affiliates			21,387			24,062			15,467
Total assets			311,043			365,486			3,324

[a] As defined by FAS 14.

Source: Monk-Austin, Inc., 1994 annual report.

Exhibit 18.8 Monk-Austin, Inc.: Export sales of US origin (US$ thousands)

	1991	1992	1993	1994
Europe	57,351	44,602	66,713	58,212
Far East	140,549	140,930	133,307	135,365
Other	28,103	23,736	24,650	7,014
Total	226,003	209,268	224,670	200,591

Source: Monk-Austin, Inc., 1993 and 1994 annual reports.

with the industry leader, Universal. (3) The merged company's larger sales base would allow more support for growth in emerging markets. (4) With a size almost double Dibrell's present one, the new company would be better able to fend off large competitors in the global tobacco industry. (5) Customer service could be improved by combining sales forces and concentrating each sales representative on a smaller set of customers and smaller region. (6) Overall asset utilization could be improved, as the duplication of processing capacity and warehouse facilities was eliminated. (7) Cost savings would be significant, also. Dibrell estimated that the two companies could save approximately $15 million annually as a result of the elimination of duplicate offices, staff, and support; improved processing efficiencies, combining purchasing and and administrative support in the USA, Africa, South America, Europe, and Asia. (8) Increased size would afford more "clout" in dealing with regulatory agencies and influencing Congress. (9) Combining sales and marketing strengths would enable the merged company to penetrate new markets quicker. (10) The increased size would make the new company a more attractive strategic partner for principal cigarette manufacturers of the world. (11) The merger would allow members of the combined management teams to concentrate on their individual (and complementary) areas of expertise, thereby resulting in more effective overall management. (12) If the merger were handled correctly, the combined company's stock price could be expected to reflect all of the efficiencies noted above, thereby enhancing stockholder value.

As the talks between the two companies progressed, the plan that developed called for a "merger of equals" rather than an acquisition of one company by the other. The proposal called for a new parent company to be formed which would be named DiMon, Inc. (pronounced DIE-mun). Dibrell and Monk-Austin would be wholly owned subsidiaries of DiMon. If approved by the two existing corporate boards and ratified by a majority of each company's shareholders, the new company would be formed as early as the first quarter of 1995. Dibrell shareholders would receive 1.5 shares of stock in DiMon for each share of Dibrell, while Monk-Austin shareholders would receive one share of DiMon stock for each of their shares. (At the time, Dibrell stock was trading on the Nasdaq exchange at approximately $20.75 per share and Monk-Austin was listed on the New York Stock Exchange at approximately $15.50). DiMon, Inc. would be headquartered in Danville, Virginia, the home of Dibrell Brothers. Claude Owen would become chairman and chief executive officer of the new company and Albert C. Monk, III the CEO of Monk-Austin, would serve as DiMon's President and Chief Operating Officer as well as chief executive of the company's tobacco division. The board of directors would be made up of twelve members, six of whom would be designated by Dibrell and six by Monk-Austin.

Owen and his team pondered the proposal and speculated about the short and long term strategic implications of the deal for their business. Merging with Monk-Austin would mean that the company would become even more deeply committed to the tobacco industry. Given recent problems in that industry, could that increased commitment be justified? If so, was this the best time to consider a merger, and was Monk-Austin the best potential partner?

Owen and his officers also considered the possible consequences of the proposal on their flower business. If the deal went through, would management's attention and corporate funding have to be diverted away from flowers at this critical point in the business' development? They had worked hard to develop this business, but it was still a few years away from maturing into the profitable venture they believed it could be. After a merger, they would be faced with having to convince the new board of directors, half of whom would be coming from Monk-Austin, to support their long-term growth plan for flowers. That would be difficult, unless a secure commitment to the future of the flower business could be negotiated as part of the merger agreement.

By rejecting the merger and "going it alone" Dibrell could continue to set its own course, whether that meant simply continuing the expansion of the flower business, or moving toward becoming a more diversified business by entering other new businesses. On the other hand, more efficient tobacco operations, such as those envisioned in the merger plan, could provide additional profits for pursuing growth businesses. In that sense, the flower business and other growth opportunities might have a better chance of succeeding.

Dibrell's decision on whether to accept the merger proposal, reject it, or push for additional concessions was due by October 22, when the negotiating team was scheduled to meet with the team from Monk-Austin for a final session.

LIZ CLAIBORNE, INC., 1994

David W. Grigsby, Linda O. Smith,
and Jane Crews

In 1993, Liz Claiborne, Inc. had topped $2 billion in sales for the third year in a row, a remarkable feat in the apparel industry. Financial success and industry dominance characterized the company. Since going public in 1981, the company had become the largest US industrial firm headed by a woman and, in 1985, had been declared the second-most-admired corporation in America by *Fortune* magazine. It was the undisputed darling of Seventh Avenue. By 1993 the company was facing multiple problems: a maturing brand name, a sluggish retail environment, and a 42 percent drop in net income. Moreover, retailers claimed that Claiborne fashions lacked the eye-catching freshness that was needed to lure shoppers, and they had lost confidence in the brand. Department store sales were abysmal. The closing price of Liz common stock fell from $42 at year-end in 1992 to $21 at the end of 1993. Institutional investors were gasping for air. Chairman Jerome Chazen, sitting in his office overlooking New York City's garment district, was in a very difficult position. "I knew they thought we walked on water," said Chazen, "but I never knew how deep it was."[1]

Prepared by Professor David W. Grigsby and graduate students Linda O. Smith and Jane Crews of Clemson University, as a basis for classroom discussion and not to illustrate either effective or ineffective handling of administrative situations. Copyright © David W. Grigsby, 1995.

Elisabeth Claiborne Ortenberg

The company's founder and namesake was the daughter of a European banker and, as such, spent much of her early childhood in Europe. Her family later moved from Brussels to New Orleans and then to Baltimore, giving the young Claiborne a wide exposure to culturally diverse societies and experiences, which had a lasting affect on her sense of style. Before finishing her high school education, Claiborne left the United States and returned to Brussels to pursue her interest in the fine arts. At the age of 20, she won a *Harper's Bazaar* design contest that fueled her ambition to become a leading designer. Against the wishes of her parents, she continued to pursue this interest and went to work as a sketcher and model in a New York design firm. Discovering her self-identity, Claiborne decided to change her image and cut her long dark hair into the shorter style that became her trademark.

In the mid-1950s Claiborne became a designer for a large women's sportswear company. Shortly thereafter, she and her boss, Arthur Ortenberg, were married. Claiborne's success in design eventually landed her the position of chief designer at Youth Guild, a junior dress division of Jonathan Logan, Inc. She remained at Logan until Liz Claiborne, Inc. was born in 1976.

By 1988, her popularity had surpassed that of all other American designers. Few chief executives were as recognizable as Liz Claiborne, whose appearance at the age of 59 reflected her success and personality. The image was a familiar one in the fashion world: close-cropped black hair, sculptured face, and her trademark oversized glasses.

Since their retirement in 1988, Liz and her husband have embarked on a personal campaign to protect wildlife and promote conservation in the Third World and the American West. They currently live on Tranquility Ranch in Montana. They have also gradually sold back their 6 percent equity share of common stock to the company.[2]

From Start-up to Industry Leadership: 1976–1985

Liz Claiborne, Inc. was founded in 1976 by Claiborne, her husband Arthur Ortenberg, and manufacturing expert Leonard Boxer. Marketing specialist Jerome Chazen was added to the firm a year later. Launched with an investment of $255,000, the company's mission was to provide an alternative to the stuffy business suits that career women were wearing to the office. Claiborne perceived a more casual trend in women's business wear. She designed a classic line of related components both for business and for leisure that were designed around a "more feminine look" concept, offered at affordable prices. With experienced management and some of the best designers in the business, the company had an immediate impact in the apparel industry. By September of the first year, the firm was already running in the black.

Claiborne's initial designs were in sportswear and priced in the "better" price range. They were targeted to be just below other well known designers such as

Ralph Lauren and just above mass-market designers such as Bernard Chaus. The company grew rapidly over the first five years. In 1981 the firm decided to go public with an offering at $19 a share and raised $6.5 million. At the time of the stock offering, earnings had increased ten-fold since 1976 and the company boasted an average compounded annual rate of sales growth of more than 40 percent.

In 1982 a Petites Division was created to offer fashions designed for the smaller figure. A new line of career dresses was also added. This line turned out to be one of the company's most successful segments, grossing $10 million in its first year. That same year, the company licensed its name for the production of accessories, including belts, scarves, and gloves. In 1983 the company added the new label LizKids, a better sportswear line for children. The company's product categories are shown in exhibit 19.1. In 1984, the company concentrated on building its reputation as a fashion merchandiser and solidifying its markets instead of introducing any new products.

In 1985 retail sales were flat and the apparel industry was experiencing skyrocketing production costs. However, Claiborne made some timely decisions that proved successful. The accessories line, previously licensed to outside companies, was bought outright. Claiborne realized that accessories have greater appeal during down cycles because they allow women who purchase fewer individual pieces of clothing to add more variety to their wardrobes. The accessories line brought in an additional $50 million in sales revenue. Claiborne fashions for men, composed of sweaters, shirts, and slacks designed to be worn as complete outfits, was added as a new line. LizWear, a fashionable denim line, was added to the sportswear division. In 1985, sales rose to over $550 million, a 10.9 percent return on sales was earned, and the company had one of the highest net profit margins in the industry.

Further Growth and Diversification: 1986–1989

The year 1986 brought more success to Liz Claiborne, Inc. The new men's collection hit the market and earned $40 million in sales its first year. The accessories line brought in $82 million. Claiborne also distributed a new fragrance as a joint venture with Avon. The company promoted the fragrance as a light, "workday" scent, with its first national advertising campaign costing $5 million. That year Liz Claiborne, Inc. was listed in the Fortune 500 for the first time (437). Total revenues for 1986 jumped to $813 million, $100 million over projections. It led all firms in the apparel industry on net profit margin (10.6 percent), return on equity (34.8 percent), and return on investment (25.7 percent). It led all Fortune 500 firms in return on investment.

Claiborne's stated objectives for continued growth in 1987 were twofold: to improve the product and to train sales personnel in the "Claiborne way," which was to understand the customer and see the clothing through Claiborne eyes. [3] The Petites Division strengthened its position by making changes in its operations. A new designer was hired, and the division's offices and showroom space were expanded. The Claiborne menswear segment posted a sales increase of 79

Exhibit 19.1   Liz Claiborne, Inc.: divisional sales (US$ millions)

	1993	1992	1991	1990	1989
Sportswear					
Total Misses Sportswear	$878.0	$947.7	$903.7	$782.4	$682.7
Petite Sportswear	253.5	268.5	250.7	216.6	164.8
Total women's sportswear	1,131.5	1,216.2	1,154.4	999.0	847.5
Dresses		158.6	180.3	164.4	143.4
Suits		12.7[a]	0.0	0.0	0.0
Total dresses and suits	130.0	171.3	180.3	164.4	143.4
Liz & Co.	91.9	96.4	75.9	58.8	8.5
Dana Buchman	90.2	73.5	28.9	16.8	15.3
Elisabeth	143.5	161.0	130.5	53.4	10.9
Claiborne	80.7	94.0	124.6	122.3	123.8
Crazy Horse[b]	0.0	0.0[a]	0.0	0.0	0.0
Russ	78.7	21.2[a]	0.0	0.0	0.0
The Villager[b]	0.0	0.0[a]	0.0	0.0	0.0
Accessories	172.4	144.9	129.9	159.4	167.5
Shoes	55.5	46.4	39.9	13.2[a]	0.0
Jewelry	25.0	18.3	6.2	8.6[a]	0.0
Cosmetics	88.4	72.7	75.0	73.6	60.2
Licensees	3.0	2.9	2.4	3.5	3.7
Retail stores	114.4	92.9	77.4	58.7	32.9
Outlet stores	122.4	113.9	84.7	62.1	39.1
Net Sales before inter-company sales eliminations	2,327.6	2,325.6	2,110.1	1,793.8	1,452.8
Inter-company sales eliminations	(123.3)	(131.3)	(102.9)	(64.9)	(42.1)
Net Sales	$2,204.3	$2,194.3	$2,007.2	$1,728.9	$1,410.7

[a] Denotes the first year of existence.
[b] The Crazy Horse and Villager labels were acquired in 1992 but product lines were not developed.

Source: Liz Claiborne, Inc., 1991, 1992, and 1993 Annual Reports to Stockholders.

percent, bringing in $75 million. Encouraged by the line's early success, Claiborne decided to expand it to include men's furnishings – dress shirts, hosiery, ties, and underwear. The accessories line posted a 66 percent increase over 1986 sales at $136 million. Handbags proved to be the best seller. The dresses line continued growing and brought in $141 million. The Cosmetics Division had sales of $26 million and gained significant market share. Its fragrance was one of the top five sold in the USA. Claiborne planned to continue this line, but Avon decided to discontinue the joint venture and seek another supplier for the product. A new line of sportswear, offering sophisticated styles at prices above better sportswear but below designer merchandise, was introduced under the Dana Buchman label. Although the venture was recognized as somewhat risky, the firm felt confident that it could capture a reasonable market share in this niche.

A number of problems were corrected in 1987. Customers complained that the men's pants fit poorly and were basically too baggy. New pants designs were tried for the following season. LizKids sales, at $15 million, were disappointing. The main problem was that the fashions were merely scaled-down versions of women's' styles – too sophisticated for children. Moreover, retail stores had no system for effectively displaying "better" children's fashions. Since the clothes are displayed by size and not price, Claiborne found her children's sportswear hanging next to lower-quality, lower-priced styles. To correct this problem, Claiborne began working directly with retailers to set up LizKids boutiques.

In 1988, four "stores-within-a-store" were operational. This concept is a jointly planned, department store area of 7000 square feet of Liz Claiborne apparel collections and coordinated accessories, shoes, hosiery, eyewear, and fragrances staffed with specially trained sales personnel and a shop manager. During the year, virtually all of the company's sales were made to over 5000 customer accounts operating 10,000 department and specialty store locations in the USA and Canada. Sales were also made to direct-mail catalog companies.[4]

Even so, the company was experiencing some fallout from the slump in the apparel industry. There was a general problem of overstocking, and too many stores carried similar items, which caused customers to stop buying. The company followed the industry trend and designed miniskirts into their designs. Loyal, middle-aged customers rebelled against baring their thighs. The line was a disaster, but an important lesson was reemphasized – listen to the customer.[5] The company also discontinued the failing LizKids line.[6] Although sales rose to $1.18 billion, profits declined for the first time.

As the company's growth began to level off in its primary markets, Jay Meltzer, industrial analyst at Goldman Sachs & Co., said that if the firm were to continue to grow, "they'll have to diversify." He also noted the inherent risk in diversification if management gets farther and farther away from doing what it knows best. Diversification plans commenced for Claiborne in 1988 with the opening of 13 of its own retail stores, First Issue, located in high-traffic shopping mall locations in major cities. A new sportswear line, sold exclusively through these stores, placed it in direct competition with The Limited, The Gap, and Banana Republic. The cost of opening a store was estimated to be $150,000, with no projected profit until 1990.

In 1989 the company achieved record sales and earnings, and three new divisions were introduced. The Elisabeth collection was designed specifically for larger-sized women. Liz & Co. offered the first collection of casual knitwear and had its own separate selling area in department stores. A Claiborne for Men fragrance was introduced, but men's hosiery and underwear was discontinued. Sales of Petites increased 22 percent, but the market for better dresses softened. Five Liz Claiborne retail stores and two Claiborne stores for men were placed into operation, though they did not generate a profit. These stores carried new styles under the Liz Claiborne label and were used mainly as a laboratory for consumer feedback. Against the backdrop of a record year, Liz Claiborne and Art Ortenberg announced their retirement.[7]

Top Management and Organization

The mission of management, as seen through Liz Claiborne's eyes, was to "generate meaningful work by creating products of integrity – to share the rewards of success amply, at all levels."[8] Brenda Gall, vice president at Merrill Lynch, attributed Liz Claiborne's success to the fact that it had four key individuals with complementary strengths in different areas of the business. From its inception, Claiborne has embodied the concept of team management. Liz Claiborne herself was responsible for the designing function; Arthur Ortenberg's strengths were finance, administration, and organization; Jerome Chazen was the sales and marketing expert; and Leonard Boxer was in charge of production and operations. These four individuals shared responsibility for long-range planning and strategic decisions.

By 1986, however, the top management team had become aware of the need to train successors for their jobs. Liz Claiborne began to delegate more and more of her own designing duties to staff members, and by 1988 had stepped back to perform only editing functions. Robert Abajian, a senior vice president, was groomed personally by Liz to take over her design duties.[9] Because competitive pressures for larger, more coordinated lines of products increased, Claiborne found less and less time for actual designing. Ortenberg, continuing his team approach to management, spent much of his time training a new group of managers to take over the business.

In 1987 some organizational restructuring occurred. Three new positions were created. Jay Margolis assumed the titles of executive vice president and president of the Women's Sportswear Group. An executive vice president of operations and corporate planning was added, whose primary functions were to oversee production planning, resource acquisition, and manufacturing distribution. Harvey Falk, who succeeded Leonard Boxer, assumed this title. Falk, a certified public accountant, had previously been executive vice president, finance. A senior vice president of corporate sales and marketing, responsible for coordinating marketing efforts among the current nine divisions, was created. Robert Bernard was appointed to fill this position. Bernard previously served as head of sportswear sales.

In February 1989, Liz Claiborne and Art Ortenberg announced their retirement. They planned to remain as board members of the firms. But in August, they resigned from the board of the firm they founded because of "growing pressures" on their time.[10] The couple expressed confidence in the strategy of the company's chairman, Jerome Chazen, another founder and the largest inside shareholder of the company. Liz assured stockholders that her values would remain at the core of the company's culture. Exhibit 19.2 contains Liz Claiborne's farewell to the stockholders, published in the 1988 Annual Report.

In July 1993, Jay Margolis resigned. His departure added speculation that Liz

Exhibit 19.2   Liz Claiborne, Inc.: president's letter, 1988 annual report

As I get ready to close the door behind myself, I find myself compelled to look once more over my shoulder and let my eyes and mind inventory the company I leave. There's Bob Abajian, the new Liz of sportswear, an extraordinary amalgam of talent, integrity, and professional know-how. There's Jay Margolis, the merchant supreme who perfectly synthesizes within himself who we are and what we stand for. There's Harvey Falk, who Jerry, Art, and I feel privileged to have worked with, whose knowledge of operations and whose unsurpassed credibility assures me that our supply base and engineering capabilities will only get better. I am reassured as I bring up mental pictures of our extraordinary team, so many players we love and respect. So many players I owe so much to.

These are the things that are important to me, the things I urge my colleagues to engrave deeply in their memories – that product and engineering are primary; that we are dedicated to coherent, consistent design; that we have the character to bypass fad and trend and live or die by a taste level we can be proud of; that we all learn and relearn the fundamentals of the game – fit, stitching, color matching, fabric evaluation; that top quality makes us proud and shoddy quality is intolerable.

I want all of us to remember that this company was started with pennies and a vision. And respect for our craft. And respect for our suppliers. And a firm regard for the intelligence and good discriminating sense of our ultimate consumer. And let's never forget that what we have demonstrated is that individuals working as a team can bring elegance and vitality to any endeavor.

I have done what I set out to do. I have participated in the building of a company that is certain of successful perpetuation. I thank you for having been, with me, part of a grand adventure.

Signed,

Liz Claiborne
Chairman, President and Chief Executive Officer

had lost its fashion edge.[11] In December, Robert Bernard moved from his position as senior vice president of domestic sales to become president of Claiborne's International Division. A month later he resigned to become president and CEO of J. Crew Group.[12]

The Apparel Industry

The US apparel manufacturing industry is an aggressive, labor-intensive business. Competition among US firms and with foreign competitors is, in a word, fierce. Intense price pressure has historically kept prices, operating margins, and wage rates low compared with other manufacturing industries. Most of the smaller companies produce a very narrow range of products, often under contract for a larger firm or a retailer.

Three types of manufacturing operations predominate in the industry: manufacturers, jobbers, and contractors. Manufacturers purchase the material from tex-

Exhibit 19.3 Liz Claiborne, Inc.: schedule of imports, exports, and trade imbalance

	1989	1990	1991
EXPORTS			
Textile Yarn Fabrics	3,897	4,922	5,457
Apparel	2,087	2,479	3,212
Total	5,984	7,401	8,669
IMPORTS			
Textile Yarn Fabrics	6,094	6,398	6,991
Apparel	24,559	25,533	26,206
Total	30,653	31,931	33,197
TRADE DEFICIT			
Textile Yarn Fabrics	(2,197)	(1,476)	(1,534)
Apparel	(22,472)	(23,054)	(22,994)
Total	(24,669)	(24,530)	(24,528)

Source: US Bureau of the Census, *US Merchandise Trade: Exports, General Imports, and Imports for Consumption,* Report FT925, monthly.

tile companies and then cut, sew, and sell the finished product to retailers. Jobbers typically buy material and sell the finished product but "job out" the manufacture to outside factory operations, or contractors, who receive the material and make the product according to specifications.

More than half of all production workers in the apparel industry are unionized. The two major unions are the Amalgamated Clothing and Textile Workers Union (ACTWU) and the International Ladies Garment Workers (ILGWU). Both major unions actively support and lobby for increased quota restrictions on imported goods. Increased production abroad has led to loss of jobs in the USA, and has kept wage levels below other manufacturing wages. The incentive to outsource is not all due to low wages in the Far East. Apparel importers have stated that they cannot get the quality and reliability from domestic sources that is available overseas.

In recent years, production of apparel goods in the USA has increased. As shown in exhibit 19.3, exports and imports have increased, while the overall trade deficit has remained constant.[13]

International Production and Operations

Although the company employs over 8700 people worldwide,[14] it has no manufacturing facilities. Its entire production is contracted out. Manufacturing overseas, primarily in the Far East, significantly reduces overhead. By keeping its capital investments low, Liz Claiborne, Inc. can post higher returns on equity than its competitors.

The production administration staff, headquartered in the North Bergen, New

Jersey, plant, is primarily responsible for maintaining cost and quality among the contractors. Staff duties range from production engineering and supplier allocation to quality control. Most of the suppliers to the firm are located in Hong Kong, Taiwan, South Korea, the Philippines, and China. Purchases are made through short-term purchase orders rather than formal long-term contracts. Approximately one-half of the supply of raw materials comes from overseas, specifically Hong Kong, Taiwan, and Japan.

Production is also spread between suppliers to such an extent that no single supplier of finished products accounted for more than 5 percent of the company's purchases. Liz Claiborne, Inc. also strives to lower reliance on top producers to guard against supply problems and price fluctuations. In 1990, only 31 percent of finished products were purchased from their top ten producers. Because of these practices, Liz Claiborne, Inc. has been able to achieve gross margins between 35 and 40 percent.[15]

In the apparel industry production lead times (from the time the order is placed to the time the piece arrives for sale) can be quite long. Manufacturing commitments need to reflect up-to-date consumer tastes. Therefore it is necessary to maintain good relationships with the overseas suppliers that have been reliable. At Claiborne, domestic suppliers' activities are monitored by staff specialists at the North Bergen plant, while overseas offices monitor its foreign suppliers.

Distribution channels are extensive worldwide. Warehouses and reprocessing factories are located in the USA and England.[16] The company ships merchandise weekly while most others ship monthly. This weekly supply ensures that styles in the stores change constantly and encourages consumers to buy when they see something they like. The quantity shipped to retailers is also restricted so that there isn't a flood of the same item available to everyone. For these reasons, loyal customers buy at full price because they know an item usually will not be around long enough to go on sale. This also means that the company rarely has to accept returns of unsold merchandise.[17]

Political and economic conditions abroad are always uncertain. All incoming merchandise is subject to US customs duties, and import quotas apply to certain classifications of merchandise, a result of bilateral agreements between the USA and exporting countries. Recognizing that escalation of these restrictions could harm the firm, Claiborne tried to allocate as much merchandise as possible to categories not covered by quota regulations.

With the increased knowledge of trade deficits and import laws, many companies have increased their production within the USA. This has not been the case with Liz Claiborne. Until it can get low prices and good quality that it currently has, the company plans to utilize mainly overseas production. Jerome Chazen criticized US textile executives in 1990, charging that "the industry was not doing enough to compete in foreign markets. He branded the industry as protectionist, sloppy, and uncreative."[18]

In response to charges of using loose US import quotas to boost financial success from cheap costs, Mr Chazen responded that the firm's job was not to redirect the textile industry but rather "to turn out the best product possible and be responsive to the consumer." He did add that all overseas operations dealt with are decent and honorable.[19]

Legislation which would restrict imports and increase costs is periodically introduced in Congress. The trading status of certain countries, including Most Favored Nation (MFN), is constantly being reevaluated. Import restrictions on suppliers located in countries without MFN status would adversely affect costs to manufacturers.[20]

In December 1994, the GATT treaty was passed by Congress and was expected to be signed by President Clinton. This agreement would reduce foreign tariffs and import quotas for all participating countries worldwide. It is unknown how this will ultimately affect apparel manufacturers.[21]

Marketing Strategy

The Claiborne marketing strategy is straightforward: know your customer. Claiborne's customer is about 43 years old "and not a perfect size 8."[22] Important to the company's success is the way Claiborne clothes fit its customers, whose figures are rarely those of fashion models. Capitalizing on the trend of increasing numbers of women entering the workforce, Claiborne offers stylish, comfortable clothes tailored for the working woman. Its marketing strategy is to sell clothes through leading department stores and specialty stores. The selections must be designed with a designer look, but at prices a working woman can afford. The working woman, said Liz Claiborne, "isn't going to spend $2,000 on a suit."[23]

Claiborne's vision for her corporation has always been to outfit the working woman from head to toe. Chazen identifies the Claiborne customer as the "executive, professional career woman who is updated in her taste level, as opposed to the traditional customer who wears structured suits." The fashions are up-to-date, but not avant-garde.[24] "The company's development of a competitive head-to-toe wardrobe gives it an edge in persuading retailers to rely on them more," according to Jay Meltzer, apparel analyst with Goodman, Sachs, and Co.[25] Because of the demand, retailers normally give Liz Claiborne products more floor space than any other label. These areas were designed by Claiborne managers and are the same in every store where products are sold.

The company prides itself on its close working relationship with its retailers, which is considered to be the best in the industry. Different from other firms in the industry, Claiborne's marketing technique centered on the New York showroom. Refusing to operate a road sales force, Claiborne forced retailers to make initial contact with her in her own showroom. Costs are reduced by eliminating unnecessary travel.

Claiborne provides wonderful on-site support to its retailers. Fashion specialists travel to all the stores, talking to customers, taking photographs of displays, and giving seminars to the sales people. They take time to discuss the company's goals and fashion point of view. In addition, all retailers receive copies of the "Claiborne Receiving Guide," which categorizes names and style numbers by style group and provides buyers with a management tool for keeping up with orders and shipments. Claiborne personnel also help to organize the in-store boutiques so that items that go together are displayed properly.

Store displays and groupings are important in the Liz Claiborne marketing system. Clothes are grouped by common fabrics and colors. A typical group might consist of a sweater, skirt, pants, and two or more coordinated blouses and T-shirts. Retailers are encouraged to show the items together. The marketing efforts of the firm reflect Claiborne and Ortenberg's personalities: intense and somewhat arrogant, driven by a mission of product quality and service.

There are six seasons in a Claiborne year: pre-spring, spring one, spring two, fall one, fall two, and holiday. Claiborne bases its production on the number of garments it expects to sell in the two-month period. Most items are sellouts, but no matter how successful, garments are never repeated in a subsequent season.[26] Marketing efforts and sales growth are monitored by a system call SURF (Systematic Updated Retail Feedback). Data are gathered on a cross-section of stores. Managers receive weekly data to get a good feel of consumer spending habits.

Under "Project Consumer," implemented in 1988, the number of dedicated in-store specialists and fashion consultants was expanded. The fashion consultants are Liz Claiborne employees who present product information seminars for store sales personnel, while the retail specialists are employed by the stores in which they work. These specialists are trained by Liz Claiborne, Inc. to get an in-depth knowledge of both product and presentation. They offer product information to consumers, and provide feedback on trends and customer preferences.[27]

Advertising and Pricing

The company has always participated in joint advertising with department stores for Liz Claiborne items. In 1991, the first advertising campaign for clothing and accessories promoted strictly by the company was initiated. The recession in the USA caused retailers to drastically cut orders in order to keep inventory levels down. The Liz Claiborne brand was also maturing. The average life of apparel firms is 15 to 20 years, and by this point the Claiborne label was 15 years old. The company initiated this ad campaign in an effort to recruit new customers and to expand its products and market share.[28]

The 1994 ad campaign has been cancelled due to disappointing retail sales in 1993. Instead management has decided to "allocate their marketing dollars to increased retail support, including improved store fixtures and some strategic direct mail pieces." The next campaign will probably be done in-house to minimize costs.[29]

In order to generate revenues during tough times, department stores began discounting prices. Discounting involves marking down current styles for short periods to attract customers. As this practice grew in frequency, customers grew to expect it and stopped buying many items at full price. Mr Chazen felt that the stores were "cannibalizing themselves" because they would not be able to return to full pricing in the future. He also felt this hurt the company's reputation for styles that were normally sold at full price. In 1992, the company sold approximately

Exhibit 19.4   Liz Claiborne, Inc.: listing of competitors

Ten largest apparel makers	1992 sales (US$ millions)
1 VF Corp.	3824
2 Liz Claiborne, Inc.	2194
3 Fruit of the Loom	1855
4 Kellwood	1078
5 Phillips-Van Heusen	1043
6 Russell Corp.	931
7 Leslie Fay	772
8 Hartmarx	732
9 Warnaco	625
10 Crystal Brands	589

Source: Standard and Poor's Industry Surveys, April 1994.

55 percent of its products at full price, compared to the industry average of 40 percent.[30]

Competition

When the company began in 1976, there was a definite need for career clothing for women. As a natural extension, other related lines were added as the company developed and gained a loyal customer base. As this demand increased, many other companies began to enter this market. Clothing in the same price range was introduced by firms and labels such as Jones New York, Adrienne Vittadini, Evan-Picone, Anne Klein II, and Chaus. All of these wanted a share of Liz Claiborne's market.[31] Exhibit 19.4 shows the ten largest apparel makers as of 1992.

Liz Claiborne without Liz: 1990–1992

The year 1990 was the best in its history. Sales rose 22.6 percent and net income was up 25 percent. Earnings per share climbed 26.7 percent. First Issue stores averaged sales of $400 per square foot. The average for specialty stores in the USA was $158 per square foot for the same period according to the National Federation of Retailers.[32] The company attributed its success to a company-wide commitment to quality, the value of putting consumers first, the depth of the company's management, and its design and manufacturing expertise. It stated that its four highest priorities were innovative ideas, team effort, commitment, and consumer satisfaction.[33]

But the picture was not completely rosy. Sales of accessories fell slightly, and mens' furnishings sales dropped nearly 30 percent. There were heavy costs associated with the debut of its new women's fragrance, Realities, and sales of its men's fragrance fell short of expectations. New retail store ventures were more costly than anticipated.[34] The company announced that it would raise its standard trade discount on Liz Claiborne sportswear and dresses from 8 to 10 percent the following year in an effort to help retailers improve their margins without raising prices to consumers.[35]

The company called 1991 a year of exceptional challenges, tribulations, and uncertainties. Retailers struggled with debt and recession.[36] Claiborne introduced its first athletic shoes for women. In its effort to access new markets, Claiborne was introduced in Great Britain, and in the fall of that year moved into Spain. The timing of the expansion was chosen to capitalize on the 1992 Olympics.[37] It also sold to stores in Ireland, Denmark, Switzerland, the Netherlands, and established retail licensees in Singapore, St Maartin, Hong Kong, and Japan. It announced plans to relocate its European distribution center to a warehouse near Rotterdam, with expansion into Belgium, Holland, Scandinavia, and Germany. Sales and net income for the company set records. Its free cash flow – a fundamental sign of financial health – was very strong, but the uncertainties of the economy were troubling.[38]

In 1992 Liz Claiborne, Inc. made its first acquisition, purchasing the operating assets of four women's apparel brands from Russ Togs (Crazy Horse, The Villager, and Russ), which filed for protection under Chapter 11 a few months earlier. It paid $31 million to acquire the trademarks, presold inventory, accounts receivable, and leases. Chazen, aware of the danger that the Claiborne image could be sullied by Russ designs created for the masses, said that his first priority was to improve the quality of the Russ sportswear line that sells for 20 to 30 percent less than Liz's. "The trick is to separate Liz Claiborne the fashion label from Liz Claiborne the corporation," he said. "They won't market [Russ Togs] under the Liz Claiborne name," says Frank Doroff, a Bloomingdale's executive vice president. "And I don't think the public will make the association." Chazen planned to treat Liz Claiborne and Russ Togs as independent companies, putting the right people in charge to develop each line. This acquisition extended Liz from department and specialty stores into mass merchandising chains.[39]

Because of changes in buying patterns, brand loyalty has not been passed on to the generation of women currently purchasing clothing and accessories. Baby boomers in the 1980s swore by Liz clothes.[40] Women in the 1990s do not have this mind set. They spend less per outfit and replace items in their wardrobes more often. Many 20 year olds think of Liz Claiborne as a brand for older women.

Although the recession continued in the USA throughout 1992, the company pursued a long-term growth strategy. It expanded its global manufacturing base, with independent suppliers in 50 countries. Through a joint venture in Augusta, Georgia, it dyed and finished high-quality knitted cotton fabrics for use in knitwear. This arrangement strengthened its control of the flow of fabric to Western Hemisphere apparel makers. Outside the USA, sales strategies included marketing through a mail-order catalog in Japan. Management felt it was just beginning to tap the potential of overseas markets. This was important because sales and earnings had come to a virtual standstill.[41]

Designing the Future: 1993 and Beyond

The year 1993 was marked by financial disappointment. Women's wear had not pulled out of its slump, and Christmas sales brought no cheer. The lower-priced Russ operation, still in the throes of reorganization, remained in the red. There were 55 First Issue stores operating throughout the USA, but none had shown a profit. Rumor had it that the Claiborne empire had branched so much that management had lost its focus on core merchandise. Headlines blared, "Liz loses some luster" and "The fashion giant faces a midlife crisis."[42] Analysts speculated whether the troubled designer that was the high-flier of the 1980s could achieve a turnaround. In addition, recent demographic figures show that women are not currently entering the workforce in as great a number as they did during the 1980s. Consumers were also more frugal in their spending according to recent studies.[43]

Moreover, nervous directors were hit with a class-action lawsuit from stockholders, who claimed that top Claiborne executives had lied to them. Stockholders charged that when the executives realized the company was in trouble and would have a hard time sustaining the kind of growth that had made them rich, they consistently told securities analysts that the problems were small and short term. This has raised serious legal questions about full disclosure, breach of fiduciary duty, and corporate cover-up. Management had hundreds of thousands of options of Claiborne stock that would have been worthless if the full truth came out. But one rosy report after another came out while top management sold its stock and made millions. At lavish expense, the company has hired the most prestigious law firm in Manhattan to fight the charges.[44]

Fortune reported, "Chairman Jerome Chazen must now prove he can win back Claiborne's star status."[45] Chazen has a plan: he is setting up clear identities by allocating specific types of merchandise to each line to establish distinction between brands. Everything considered basic – jeans, T-shirts, and turtlenecks – will now come from LizWear. LizSport will handle casual clothes like cotton pants, sweaters, and vests. Career-oriented skirts, jackets, and tailored pants will be in Collection. With its department store base shrinking, Chazen is expanding into Sears Roebuck, J. C. Penney, and Montgomery Ward with its Russ brands. Claiborne is also racking up tremendous growth with Dana Buchman, its sportswear line priced between moderate and designer lines. Rose Marie Bravo, president of Saks Fifth Avenue, says Buchman is the top seller of all its bridge lines and attributes its popularity to meticulous styling, fit, and quality. Six month ago Saks dropped nearly all other Claiborne merchandise to focus on the Buchman brand.[46]

International sales have more than doubled as a percentage of net sale since 1990 (see exhibit 19.5). The 1993 annual report states, "Our goal is to become the number one fashion brand throughout the world . . . Our balance sheet is virtually debt-free. We ended the year with cash and marketable securities of $309 million, which gives us great latitude in making acquisitions and other growth-oriented investments." Indeed, the company has upgraded computer systems and showrooms, purchased and equipped a distribution center in Montgomery, Alabama,

Exhibit 19.5   Liz Claiborne, Inc.: net sales by geographic areas

US$ thousands	1993	1992	1991	1990	1989
Domestic	2,091.0	2,092.5	1,923.6	1,672.5	1,377.7
International	113.3	101.8	83.6	56.4	33.0
Total net sales	2,204.3	2,194.3	2,007.2	1,728.9	1,410.7

Net sales by geographic areas as a percentage of total net sales

	1993	1992	1991	1990	1989
Domestic	94.86	95.36	95.83	96.74	97.66
International	5.14	4.64	4.17	3.26	2.34
Total net sales	100.00	100.00	100.00	100.00	100.00

Source: Liz Claiborne, Inc., 1991, 1992, and 1993 Annual Reports to Stockholders.

opened 20 new First Issue stores, and plans to add at least 20 more in 1994. To enable it to receive near-instantaneous information on market trends and obtain more accurate and timely customer feedback, the company has established 19 Liz Claiborne Stores and four Elisabeth Stores.[47]

On April 22, 1994 the company announced that Paul R. Charron, 51, who was passed over for chief executive at VF Corporation (Lee, Wrangler, and Vanity Fair), had been hired as Liz Claiborne's vice chairman. Claiborne CEO Chazen, 67, says he has no plans to retire. But sources say that Charron will assume that CEO post in 18 months.[48] "Mr Charron holds an MBA from Harvard University and has worked in various marketing positions at Cannon Mills Co., General Foods Corp. and Proctor & Gamble Co. At VF he repositioned its Vassarette lingerie business from a brand sold at department stores to one sold by mass merchants, moved half of its production overseas and acquired European lingerie brands to integrate into Vassarette."[49] Laurence Leeds, who follows the apparel industry as managing director of Buckingham Research Group, suggested that, "Common sense would say that he wouldn't leave a major executive position at VF, where he was in charge of over $2 billion in sales, unless he had assurance that, barring any major incompatibility, he would be the next chief executive."[50]

The company has gone out of its way to emphasize that three men, Harvey Falk, Jerome Chazen, and Paul Charron, would be at its helm. Mr Charron's arrival may signal interest among retailers like Sears and J. C. Penney, and even to discounters like Target. Mr Charron knows the mass market well. "This brings a new, innovative style of management to a company that has started to improve its business."[51] Others wonder whether a marketing wizard is the antidote to Liz Claiborne's problems.

Exhibit 19.6 Liz Claiborne, Inc.: divisional sales (as a percentage of total sales)

	1993	1992	1991	1990	1989
Sportswear					
Total Misses Sportswear	39.83	43.19	45.02	45.25	48.39
Petite Sportswear	11.50	12.24	12.49	12.53	11.68
Total women's sportswear	51.33	55.43	57.51	57.78	60.08
Dresses		7.23	8.98	9.51	10.17
Suits		0.58	0.00	0.00	0.00
Total dresses and suits	5.90	7.81	8.98	9.51	10.17
Liz & Co.	4.17	4.39	3.78	3.40	0.60
Dana Buchman	4.09	3.35	1.44	0.97	1.08
Elisabeth	6.51	7.34	6.50	3.09	0.77
Claiborne	3.66	4.28	6.21	7.07	8.78
Crazy Horse[b]	0.00	0.00	0.00	0.00	0.00
Russ	3.57	0.97[a]	0.00	0.00	0.00
The Villager[b]	0.00	0.00	0.00	0.00	0.00
Accessories	7.82	6.60	6.47	9.22	11.87
Shoes	2.52	2.11	1.99[a]	0.76	0.00
Jewelry	1.13	0.83	0.31[a]	0.50	0.00
Cosmetics	4.01	3.31	3.74	4.26	4.27
Licensees	0.14	0.13	0.12	0.20	0.26
Retail stores	5.19	4.23	3.86	3.40	2.33
Outlet stores	5.55	5.19	4.22	3.59	2.77
Net sales before inter-company sales eliminations	105.59	105.98	105.13	103.75	102.98
Inter-company sales eliminations	−5.59	−5.98	−5.13	−3.75	−2.98
Net sales	100.00	100.00	100.00	100.00	100.00

[a] Denotes the first year of existence.
[b] The Crazy Horse and Villager labels were acquired in 1992 but product lines were not developed.

Source: Liz Claiborne, Inc., 1991, 1992, and 1993 Annual Reports to Stockholders.

Exhibit 19.7 Liz Claiborne, Inc.: consolidated balance sheet (US$ thousands)

	1993	1992	1991	1990	1989
ASSETS					
Current assets:					
Cash and cash equivalent	104,720	130,721	189,195	143,717	82,182
Marketable securities	204,571	294,892	282,335	288,094	290,703
Accounts receivable – trade	174,435	200,183	145,910	100,196	131,470
Inventories	436,593	385,879	321,992	265,727	198,164
Deferred income tax benefits	15,065	21,050	12,174	12,196	10,625
Other current assets	69,055	77,240	62,075	42,937	33,273
Total current assets	1,004,439	1,109,965	1,013,681	852,867	746,417
Property and equipment – net	202,068	145,695	148,261	118,174	99,914
Other assets	29,831	29,647	13,003	13,464	2,192
TOTAL	1,236,338	1,285,307	1,174,945	984,505	848,523
LIABILITIES AND STOCKHOLDERS' EQUITY					
Current liabilities:					
Accounts payable	141,126	138,738	140,151	118,395	86,625
Accrued expenses	97,765	109,186	86,111	96,048	95,723
Long-term debt due within 1 year	15,547	0	0	0	443
Income taxes payable	0	22,109	23,568	29,706	26,519
Total current liabilities	254,438	270,033	249,830	244,149	209,310
Long-term debt	1,334	1,434	1,615	15,131	15,643
Deferred income taxes	2,275	16,065	13,901	12,076	11,908
Stockholders' equity					
Preferred stock	0	0	0	0	0
Common stock ($1 par value), 250,000,000 shares authorized	88,219	88,219	88,219	88,219	88,202
Capital in excess of par value	56,699	55,528	50,493	43,913	41,353
Retained earnings	1,123,413	1,034,280	854,003	664,211	482,496
Cumulative translation adjustment	(1,279)	(1,410)	0	0	0
	1,267,052	1,176,617	992,715	796,343	612,051
Treasury stock (at cost)	(288,761)	(178,842)	(83,116)	(83,194)	(389)
Total stockholders' equity	978,291	997,775	909,599	713,149	611,662
TOTAL	1,236,338	1,285,307	1,174,945	984,505	848,523

Source: Liz Claiborne, Inc., 1991, 1992, and 1993 Annual Report to Stockholders.

Exhibit 19.8 Liz Claiborne, Inc.: consolidated statements of income (US$ thousands)

	1993	1992	1991	1990	1989
Net sales	2,204,297	2,194,330	2,007,177	1,728,868	1,410,677
Cost of goods sold	1,453,381	1,364,214	1,207,502	1,030,835	841,736
Gross profit	750,916	830,116	799,675	698,033	568,941
Selling, general & admin expenses	568,286	507,541	471,060	393,061	321,882
Operating income	182,630	322,575	328,615	304,972	247,059
Investment and other income – net	16,151	19,349	22,133	24,328	22,832
Income before provision for income taxes and cumulative effect of a change in accounting principle	198,781	341,924	350,748	329,300	269,891
Provision for income taxes	73,500	123,100	128,000	123,500	105,300
Income before cumulative effect of a change in accounting principle	125,281	218,824	222,748	205,800	164,591
Cumulative effect of a change in the method of accounting for income taxes	1,643	0	0	0	0
Net income	126,924	218,824	222,748	205,800	164,591

Source: Liz Claiborne, Inc., 1991, 1992, and 1993 Annual Reports to Stockholders.

Exhibit 19.9 Liz Claiborne, Inc.: consolidated statements of income (percentage of sales comparisons)

	1993	1992	1991	1990	1989
Net sales	100.00	100.00	100.00	100.00	100.00
Cost of goods sold	65.93	62.17	60.16	59.62	59.67
Gross profit	34.07	37.83	39.84	40.38	40.33
Selling, general & admin expenses	25.78	23.13	23.47	22.74	22.82
Operating Income	8.29	14.70	16.37	17.64	17.51
Investment and other income – net	0.73	0.88	1.10	1.41	1.62
Income before provision for income taxes and cumulative effect of a change in accounting principle	9.02	15.58	17.47	19.05	19.13
Provision for income taxes	3.33	5.61	6.38	7.14	7.46
Income before cumulative effect of a change in accounting principle	5.68	9.97	11.10	11.90	11.67
Cumulative effect of a change in the method of accounting for income taxes	0.07	0.00	0.00	0.00	0.00
Net income	5.76	9.97	11.10	11.90	11.67

Source: Liz Claiborne, Inc., 1991, 1992, and 1993 Annual Reports to Stockholders.

NOTES AND REFERENCES

1 Nancy Hass, "Like a rock," *Financial World*, February 4, 1992, p. 22.

2 Laura Zinn, "Liz Claiborne without Liz: steady as she goes," *Business Week*, September 17, 1990, p. 70.

3 Liz Claiborne, Inc., *1987 Annual Report to Stockholders*, p. 6.

4 Nina Darnton, "The joy of polyester," *Newsweek*, August 3, 1992, p. 81.

5 Hass, p. 24.

6 Liz Claiborne, Inc., *1988 Annual Report to Stockholders*, pp. 15–20.

7 Liz Claiborne, Inc., *1989 Annual Report to Stockholders*, pp. 3–16.

8 Liz Claiborne, Inc., *1987 Annual Report to Stockholders*, p. 6.

9 Teri Agins, "At Liz Claiborne, Chazen remains as inquisitive as ever," *Wall Street Journal*, May 30, 1989, p. B16.

10 Thomas Ciampi, "Liz Claiborne: a $2 billion phenomenon," *Women's Wear Daily*, May 8, 1991, p. 6.

11 Teri Agins, "Liz Claiborne seems to be losing its invincible armor," *Wall Street Journal*, July 19, 1993, p. B4.

12 "Claiborne official to join J. Crew," *Wall Street Journal*, January 25, 1994, p. B10.

13 United States Department of Commerce, *Statistical Abstract of the United States*, 113rd edn. Washington, DC: Government Printing Office, 1993, p. 759.

14 Liz Claiborne, Inc., *1993 Annual Report to Stockholders*, p. 6.

15 Ciampi, p. 6.

16 James Fallon, "Claiborne speeding up its invasion of Europe," *Women's Wear Daily*, February 5, 1991, p. 18.

17 Zinn, p. 74.

18 Ciampi, p. 6.

19 Ibid., p. 6.

20 Liz Claiborne, Inc., *1993 Annual Report to Stockholders*, p. 15.

21 Dan Hoover, "Senate easily OKs trade pact," *The Greenville News*, December 2, 1994, p. 1.

22 Deveny, "Can Ms Fashion bounce back?", p. 64.

23 Ibid.

24 Skolnik, R., "Liz the Wiz," *Sales and Marketing Management*, September 9, 1985, pp. 173–6.

25 Ciampi, p. 6.

26 Lardner, J., 'Annals of business: the sweater trade – 1," *New Yorker*, January 11, 1988, p. 45.

27 Liz Claiborne, Inc., *1988 Annual Report to Stockholders*, pp. 3–8.

28 Teri Agins, "Claiborne Unveils Its First Big Campaign," *Wall Street Journal*, September 26, 1991, p. B1.

29 Pat Sloan, "Claiborne zaps 'bad' ads: hurting marketers halts '94 campaign," *Advertising Age*, December 6, 1993, p. 5.

30 Hass, pp. 22–3.

31 Nancy Marx Better, "The secret of Liz Claiborne's success," *Working Woman*, April 1992, p. 70.

32 Stephanie Strom, "Alarm is set off by Liz Claiborne," *The New York Times*, September 6, 1991.

33 Liz Claiborne, Inc., *1990 Annual Report to Stockholders*, pp. 6–10.

34 Ibid., pp. 6–10.

35 "Liz Claiborne sets discount increase," *The New York Times*, July 28, 1990, p. N19.

36 Liz Claiborne, Inc., *1991 Annual Report to Stockholders*, pp. 4–13.

37 Strom.

38 Liz Claiborne, Inc., *1991 Annual Report to Stockholders*, pp. 4–13.

39 Darnton, p. 81.

40 Zinn, p. 70.

41 Liz Claiborne, Inc., *1992 Annual Report to Stockholders*, pp. 6–10.

42 Laura Zinn, "A sagging bottom line at Liz Claiborne," *Business Week*, May 16, 1994, pp. 56–7.

43 Standard and Poor's, *Industry Surveys, Volume 2*, April 1994, p. 89.

44 Ben Stein, "Cashing in at Liz Claiborne," *New York*, April 25, 1994, pp. 28–9.

45 Susan Caminiti, "Liz Claiborne: how to get focused again," *Fortune*, January 24, 1994, p. 85.

46 Ibid., p. 86.

47 Liz Claiborne, Inc., *Public Relations Publication*, January 1994, p. 2.

48 Zinn, p. 56.

49 Teri Agins, "Liz Claiborne picks outside executive as vice chairman and potential CEO," *Wall Street Journal*, April 25, 1994, p. B6.

50 Ibid., p. B6.

51 Stephanie Strom, "Liz Claiborne names (anoints?) operating chief," *The New York Times*, April 23, 1994, p. 19N.

NIKE, INC.

David W. Grigsby, Susan Gaertner,
and Karen Roach

From its humble beginnings to its current status as the market leader of the $6 billion athletic shoe industry, Nike, Inc.'s business purpose has been "to enhance people's lives through sports and fitness."[1] The company's paramount brand recognition is proof that they have lived up to it. Through its innovative products, athletic spokespersons, and sponsorships of various sporting and civic events, Nike has established itself as a household name.

Nike designs, develops, and markets a broad array of athletic footwear and apparel, as well as, casual footwear in both domestic and international markets. The company's 900 or so products, representing 20 different sports, are sold through roughly 15,000 domestic retail accounts and in 80 different countries worldwide.

But with all of the successes Nike has experienced over the past twenty years, it is still feeling the pressures of a changing marketplace. The company's current domestic growth rates are approximately 5 percent annually, down from the double digit figures it experienced during the industry's golden years between 1980 and 1988. The US athletic footwear industry is entering the mature stage of its product life cycle, while the international market is going through a recessional period. Furthermore, the changing demographics, a trend toward a more casual lifestyle, and a shift away from status products to value products has Nike and its maverick CEO, Philip H. Knight, rethinking its present strategies so that it can continue to remain at the top of its industry.

History

The Nike company as we know it today began its legendary climb to the top of the sneaker industry as a company called Blue Ribbon Sports. Blue Ribbon Sports was founded in 1964 by William J. Bowerman, a University of Oregon track coach, and Philip H. Knight, one of Bill's athletes, out of a desire for a better American running shoe. Bill's obsession to find a shoe that was light, comfortable, and could "go the distance" led him to design his own shoe. The two men contracted with a Japanese shoe manufacturer, Onitsuka Tiger, to make 1000 pairs of a high-quality, low-cost shoe called the Cortez. Their initial investment of $500 each and "track-to-track" sales techniques paid off with the first year's sales reaching $8000. The shoes were stored in Phil Knight's parents' basement and sold out of the trunk of his 1964 Plymouth Valiant at track meets.

In 1968 the partners decided to come up with a distinctive trademark and a new name. Nike, Inc., named after the Greek goddess of victory, was born. The Nike symbol, or "Swoosh", as it has come to be known, was created by a local Portland student who was paid only $35 for her curious design. The new Nike shoes debuted at the 1972 Olympics Trials held in Eugene, Oregon, and contributed to the year's $3.2 million in sales. Also, during the same year, the company severed its already shaky ties with Tiger after an argument over distribution rights.

During the last half of the 1970s, Nike's sales grew from $10 million to $270 million. These sales were spawned by the creation of the patented waffle sole and the cushioning system, known as Nike Air. These innovations brought Nike into the forefront of the athletic shoe industry, so much so that over half of the running shoes sold in the United States were Nikes.

The early 1980s saw Nike replace the German footwear empire, Adidas, as the number one athletic shoe company in the American market. Not long ago the Adidas representatives laughed at Phil Knight as he peddled his new running shoes out of his car at track meets. Now the joke was on them. In the *Forbes* 1982 Annual Report on American Industry, Nike was listed as the most profitable organization in America over the past five years. It was also during the 1980s that Nike became a publicly traded company, making Knight one of the richest men in the world. In 1985, Nike introduced the Air Jordan, named after basketball superstar Michael Jordan. Later, in a move to diversify the products of the company, Nike acquired substantially all the stock of Cole Haan Holdings, Inc. for $80 million plus repayment of a $15 million debt. Cole Haan manufactures and markets high-quality, high-priced men's and women's dress and casual shoes.

The 1990s have brought on further acquisitions including Tetra Plastic Inc., purchased in 1991, and Sports Specialties Inc., purchased in 1993. Tetra is a manufacturer of plastic film which is used as an ingredient in the manufacture of Nike's Air-Sole cushioning components. Sports Specialties is a distributor of licensed headwear. Both companies operate as subsidiaries of Nike. In a continuing effort to become a truly global company, Nike recently acquired its Chilean distributor, secured 100 percent ownership of Nike Japan and Nike Korea, and entered into a joint venture with Alpargatas CTE to establish a distributorship in Argentina. And in a move that shocked the nation and Nike, their most effective and highest paid spokesperson, Michael Jordan, announced in October 1993 his retirement from professional basketball. Because of Jordan's hero appeal, his endorsements have brought in approximately $200 million annually in sales. His retirement could not have come at a more critical time though for Nike. The company's once booming basketball business appears to be declining. (Jordan later returned to basketball.)

Business Breakdown

Athletic footwear

Nike is the worldwide leader in athletic footwear with a US market share of 32 percent (appendix C). The US athletic footwear industry is one of the great growth stories of the past decade. Industry sales grew from $2.2 billion in 1984 to over $6 billion in 1993, largely as a result of the nation's increased emphasis on staying fit and a shift towards more casual dress styles. Nike both contributed to and benefited from this athletic craze. The company's sales grew from $270 million in 1980 to almost $4 billion in 1993 (appendix A). Ironically, only 20 percent of all athletic footwear purchased is actually used for athletic activities. The other 80 percent is purchased to be worn as casual attire.

The basketball market is the core of Nike's business, accounting for almost 30 percent of its footwear sales. This market is critical to Nike and the industry as a whole because it is one of the most popular sports among teen males, especially those in the inner cities, and because it has a universal following. Nike's dominance in basketball is being challenged by several of its competitors, particularly Reebok and Fila.

Nike is now positioned to pursue soccer, another sport that is growing in its international appeal. Many of the world's best soccer athletes are wearing the Nike Tiempo Premier shoe, including World Cup players Bebeto and Romario. Nike is gearing itself for a notable presence in the 1998 World Cup to be held in France.

Running is where it all started and where it continues to be. Nike's original market continues to hold opportunities for this market leader. This business has been fairly stable over the last several years in spite of decreased participation. Running currently holds a 9 percent share of Nike's footwear sales. Latin America promises opportunities in this market and Nike is already there due to its most recent acquisition in Chile and the joint venture in Argentina. In addition, the recent signing of the NAFTA agreement will help to secure Nike's competitive position in the Latin American countries.

Other athletic footwear offerings provided by Nike include aerobics, cross-training, baseball, tennis, and golf shoes. Nike has been slow to get into aerobics, a predominately female market led by rival marketer Reebok. But when the company modified its marketing approach and added some detailing to its designs, market share rose from 10 percent in 1991 to 17 percent in 1992. In the golf arena, Nike bought out the struggling Ben Hogan golf tour to gain access to the golf market. On the courts, Nikes can be seen on such famous feet as Andre Agassi and John McEnroe. But no matter what the sport, Nike can be counted on to have its best foot forward with the most innovative designs and clever marketing.

Athletic apparel

Nike began marketing athletic apparel as a logical extension to its already successful footwear business. Approximately 18 percent of annual sales come from the manufacture and marketing of men's and women's athletic clothing, including running shorts and shirts, tennis apparel, warm-up suits, and team licensed apparel. Given the trend toward more casual dress codes, it would appear that this business would offer important growth opportunities. Unfortunately, the apparel business, down almost 2 percent in 1993, has not been as easy for Nike to cultivate as was the footwear business. Nike's brand appeal is only one factor in apparel purchase decisions. Style, fit, and fabric play a far greater role. Also, Nike's clothing has been criticized as being too expensive. To spur apparel sales, Nike has contracted with several department stores, including Macy's and Dayton Hudson, to showcase its apparel and footwear in Nike Concept Shops.

Casual and dress footwear

Nike entered the casual and dress shoe market through its 1988 acquisition of Cole Haan Holdings, Inc. Cole Haan, representing 5 percent of Nike's revenues, manufactures and sells top-quality men's, women's, and children's footwear in eight different lifestyle categories, as well as men's and women's leather accessories. Like Nike, Cole Haan's success rests in its quality and innovative products. The company maintains three specific market strategies: to create products that are distinct in both style and quality, to service the various aspects of the consumer's lifestyle, and to stay in touch with the customer. The company operates 23 factories in seven countries worldwide, runs 15 retail stores in the USA, and has international offices in Italy, Japan, Canada, and Hong Kong. For the future, Cole Haan offers Nike strong growth potential because the brand is considered "much more than just a shoe – it is a key element of contemporary style."[2]

Retail operations

One of Nike's key strengths lies in its successful retail operations. Nike has estimated that 66 percent of its customers' purchase decisions are made at the point of sale, making its merchandising efforts all the more important. Nike has started a program, called "EKIN" (Nike spelled backward), that provides retailers with training in sales and merchandising. Its spirited concept shops located in department stores around the country help to promote the Nike product and image.

Taking its concept shops one step further, Nike has opened several Nike Town stores featuring its whole array of current products, as well as future products. The stated goal of the Nike Town stores is surprisingly not to sell merchandise but to increase consumer awareness and demand for its products. The stores also provide critical feedback for what consumers want and for what point-of-purchase techniques work best in the retail setting. Some retailers, however, fear these new showcase stores will cut into their sales. Nike contends that these claims are unfounded because Nike Town sells everything at full price, causing shoppers to go elsewhere for discounted products.

Outdoor footwear

One of the brightest areas in Nike's operations is the outdoor footwear category. Capitalizing on the back-to-basics lifestyle trend, Nike has come up with several innovative entries, incorporating Nike's renowned running shoe technology. Light-weight hiking boots, land and water sandals, and its outdoor cross-trainers or "access" shoes are just a few of the products offered. All of the company's outdoor footwear products sport soles consisting of 10 to 15 percent reground rubber. Sales in 1993 of outdoor footwear were up 39 percent over the previous year and CEO Knight predicts this category will reach the same proportions as its basketball business, eventually reaching $400 million.

Nike is deviating from its traditional marketing because the outdoor appeal is centered around individualism rather than the competitive spirit found in most Nike promotions. The outward branding found on the majority of Nike's products has also been suppressed for the outdoors. Many of the outdoor shoes have no "swoosh" or just a small one to compensate for the anti-brand attitude found in the market's young consumers. Average pricing among these products is 20 percent less than that of basketball shoes, which average around $60 a pair.

The Athletic Footwear Industry

Current market issues

Shifting trends are affecting the very lucrative athletic footwear industry. In 1992 it was estimated that two out of every five shoe purchases was for athletic shoes. But now the trend is moving away from the traditional sneaker and getting into other categories, especially the outdoor footwear category, which, in 1992, accounted for approximately $650 million in wholesale sales. The athletic shoe industry is also experiencing a lack of pricing power. Competition is being centered on price, with the newer footwear styles priced below the $60 average of the past few years.

Another problem facing the industry is the fact that overall participation in fitness activities has declined. Surveys show that the percentage of adults who exercise dropped from 22 percent in 1985 to 18 percent in 1990. It appears that people are beginning to view that being and looking athletic is not as important as it once was. Competition is also increasing in the athletic footwear category, another indicator that the category has possibly reached its maturity point. This fact has caused some of the major players such as Nike and Reebok to take a second look at their businesses. Both companies have already begun diversification efforts to alleviate the pressures of the industry.

Competitors

Reebok

Reebok is currently number two in the athletic footwear industry, with approximately 21 percent in market share (appendix C). While Nike has been dominant in the men's footwear category, Reebok has excelled in the women's category, which accounts for 50 percent of its domestic sales. Reebok's keen understanding of what women want has given the company a strong brand name. Reebok is very percept-ive to women's need for variety in their fitness activities and creates new shoes to go along with each of the different activities. The company has been in the forefront of sponsoring fitness activities such as step aerobics and slide.

The men's category has been tough for Reebok to break into. It was slow to realize that its strategy in the women's business was not effective in the men's busi-ness. Because women's fitness is more an individual endeavor and men's is more team-oriented and competitive, Reebok felt the need to assimilate Nike's successful marketing approach of using athletic heros to promote footwear products. So, in 1992, the company decided to aggressively seek endorsements from male athletes, most notably Shaquille O'Neal. While the company has been slow to catch on to the right marketing strategy for men, it has proven to be a leader in athletic shoe technology. Some of its creations include The Pump, Energy Return System (ERS), Hexalite, Energaire, and Instapump.

Reebok's entry in the casual footwear category is its Rockport brand of foot-wear. Purchased as an acquisition in 1985, Rockport has been a solid player for Reebok, holding a market share of 2.5 percent and a third place position in its mar-ket. But building Rockport has been somewhat of a challenge for Reebok because the casual footwear business is not as brand-conscious as the athletic business. Also, sneakers brands tend to cut across demographic lines while casual shoe brands do not. In 1992, Reebok introduced its own line of casual footwear under the Boks brand name.

LA Gear, Inc.

LA Gear, Inc. is currently third and holds a 5 percent market share in its race to be the top athletic footwear marketer (appendix C). LA Gear's products are moder-ately priced, with 90 percent of all its styles priced below $65 suggested retail. The company has taken the lead in catering to the changing demand by offering fashionable quality footwear at affordable prices. Recently, LA Gear entered into an agreement with Wal-Mart, a low-price distributor, where the retailer will pur-chase $80 million worth of footwear per year for the next three years.

The company offers products in over 60 countries under three different divi-sions, each representing one-third of the company: lifestyle, which centers on fash-ion; Athletic, which features innovation and performance; and Children's, which emphasizes innovation and fashion appeal for the younger set. Some of its product innovations include Light Gear, Leap Gear, LA Lights, and the Donzis Flak cush-ioning system, which could be 1994s hot new product.

In 1991, the company went through a total reorganization. The new manage-ment reduced expenses and inventory levels, improved relations with retailers and distributors, reduced staff by 45 percent, and discontinued its apparel marketing and design operations. LA Gear Worldwide Properties Group was then developed to license the LA Gear trademark on apparel and other non-footwear products. As part of the restructuring, the company also reduced the number of product styles from 335 to 225 and reduced its logos from twenty to three.

Because the international market for athletic footwear is growing faster than the domestic market, LA Gear has committed itself to global growth. Estimates show that within the next five years, LA Gear's international sales will exceed its domestic sales. The company has just recently acquired exclusive distributors in the Netherlands, Belgium, Luxembourg, the United Kingdom, and Germany. It has also established wholly owned subsidiaries in both Italy and France.

Converse, Inc.

In 1993, Converse, Inc. was tied for fourth in the industry with a 4 percent market share (appendix C). Converse is a wholly owned subsidiary of Interco Incorporated, a manufacturer and marketer of both furniture and footwear, including Broyhill Furniture, The Lane Company, and The Florsheim Shoe Co. The Converse manufacturing plants are located in Mexico and Lumberton, NC. The company operates a distribution facility in Charlotte, NC, and sales offices in three states and five countries.

In January 1991, its parent company filed for reorganization under Chapter 11, which, unfortunately, included the profitable Converse subsidiary. But by August 1992, the company came out of bankruptcy to get back into the business of selling athletic shoes.

To get back on track, the company has increased its advertising budget almost threefold, predominately targeting the younger market through such avenues as MTV Networks, Inc. Converse's goal is to become the third largest athletic shoe marketer by 1996. As part of its quest to become number three, Converse undertook sponsorship of the NBA 3-on-3 World Tour, which gave the company exposure in such places as Barcelona, Athens, Paris, London, Munich, Milan, and Rome. Currently, the company's products, the TAR MAX, All-Star, One Star, Run N Slam, and Aerojet to name a few, are sold in over 90 countries worldwide.

Fila

Fila is a foreign-owned footwear company that is making big strides in the US footwear market. The Italian company, Fila, established itself in Europe as a sports apparel manufacturer. Apparel sales are centered on tennis (51 percent) and skiwear (42 percent), with 25 percent of the product lines still sourced in Italy. The remainder of their products are manufactured in the Far East.

In the footwear market, Fila targets the male, high-performance segment. While only currently possessing a 4 percent market share, Fila is aiming for the auspicious number three spot in the US athletic footwear market (appendix C). Its shoe sales jumped almost 25 percent from 1992 to 1993. Fila's big advantage over its competitors is its reputation for fashionable styling and its command in the trendsetting inner-city market. Narrow product lines are the company's biggest weakness and it is not well established in certain markets, such as women, running, and the outdoor market.

All of Fila's footwear lines are designed in the USA but sourcing is done in the Far East, particularly South Korea, Indonesia, and China. US products are distributed primarily (50 percent) through Kinney's Footlocker stores. Fila's concentrated focus on the US market has left it falling behind in its homefront of Europe, where the demand for American-styled products is rising. Currently, the company's market share is less than 1 percent versus Adidas, Nike, and Reebok, which hold market shares of 30 percent, 25 percent, and 22 percent, respectively.

Suppliers

All of Nike's footwear products are sourced overseas, particularly in the Far East, to take advantage of the low production costs found in these areas. Thirty-two factories throughout the Asia-Pacific region produce Nike shoes. Nike began having most of its shoes made in South Korea. But when labor rates rose, the company looked to China and Indonesia. Vietnam, with its low wages, will be the next top manufacturing sight. Unlike footwear, Nike's apparel is manufactured by both domestic companies (57 percent) and contracted foreign companies (43 percent).

Because manufacturing lead times tend to be rather long, the company can have a difficult time predicting production needs for a constantly changing retail environment. To combat its ordering problems, Nike has devised its Futures inventory-control system to minimize ordering risks. Approximately 80 percent of domestic sales and 50 percent of international sales are made through Futures. With the Futures program, retailers are required to place orders with Nike six to eight months in advance. This allows retailers to take advantage of discounts and guaranteed delivery times. Nike is able to avoid excess inventory costs and assures better prices from its suppliers. Still, Nike has had a few problems with its ordering process because of the constantly changing retail trends. Nike's Air Deschutz line of sport sandals completely sold out in 1993 and the company could not produce more to satisfy the demand.

Management and Organizational Structure

Top management

Philip Knight has succeeded in reaching his initial goal to make Nike a "global megabrand." The chairman and founder of Nike is the epitome of a sportsfan and his enthusiasm flows through his organization right down to the lowest level. With his unconventional management style, Knight has often been criticized as being too brash. But obviously he knows how to run a successful company. Knight's constant refusals to be interviewed add to his enigmatic aura. It has been said about Knight that "the Nike chairman's reticence comprises the man's fervid determination to win each and every game he plays."[3]

Other top officials at Nike include: William Bowerman, co-founder and deputy chairman, who at 85 is still active in the company; Thomas Clarke, president and COO; Delbert Hayes, executive VP; Harry Carsh, VP of footwear division; Robert Falcone, who joined Nike as director of acquisitions and is currently Chief Financial Officer; Marsha Stillwell, Treasurer; and John Jaqua, a practicing attorney serving as corporate secretary.

Organizational structure

Nike follows a matrix organizational structure, but with a little twist. Nike's structure has been described as "a rangy structure designed – and constantly redesigned – so as to retain the romance and collegiality of an entrepreneurial past within the context of a big corporation forever being chased from behind."[4] The company's footwear division is broken down into smaller units based on each particular sports category. These are then linked together through a "team" system to production processes, sales, and advertising. By separating the company into these sport divisions, the company is able to focus on market penetration, product excellence, and athlete endorsement activity, which is the crux of Nike's marketing strategy. Nike's matrix structure is not without fault though. Communication can get confused and the creativity on which Nike was founded can get lost within the matrix.

Nike's marketing manager for its running shoe division complained that "too many bright ideas die inside the matrix."[5]

Corporate culture

Nike employs approximately 9600 employees. Nike has been criticized as being a cult organization and reasonably so. Some of the company's employees are so devoted to the Nike cause that they even get tattooed with the Nike swoosh. Nike's World Headquarters, located in Beaverton, Oregon, is called the Nike World Campus and encompasses 74 acres with six buildings and a seven-acre man-made lake. On campus, employees can get haircuts, do laundry, take advantage of day care facilities, and make purchases from a company store. Almost every Nike employee is fit and healthy and is an avid sports fan.

The company tends to project a macho attitude, reflected in its hard core athletic image as well as in its predominately male management team. Difficulties in marketing the women's category stem from this corporate perspective.

Marketing Strategies

Products

Nike's products fall into two divisions: footwear and apparel. Each of these divisions is broken down into categories by sport. Some of the major categories include: basketball, cross-training, tennis, golf, aerobics, walking, running, golf, and kids. The newest category is Outdoor, which includes such products as hiking boots, sport sandals, the Aqua Sock, the "potato shoe," and the appropriate apparel to wear with them.

Nike is famous for its high-tech product designs. But this position is not achieved by happenstance. Research and development is one of the most important activities of the company. In a typical 12-month period, Nike spends approximately $22.6 million on research, product development, and product testing. Its Sports Research Lab is assigned the task of developing the most comfortable and aesthetically pleasing shoe that allows the athlete to reach his or her highest performance level. Nike's shoes are made with the athlete in mind, but statistics show that only 20 percent are actually used for their intended sport.

Because the other 80 percent of Nike's consumers wear their footwear for casual purposes, product styling is also important. The company's high-end shoes form a "styling umbrella" over the entire line. And because they are produced in limited quantities, they are made even more desirable to consumers, thus preserving Nike's exclusivity.

Promotion

Branding

The Nike brand is the company's greatest asset. It is perhaps the most widely recognized brand in the world and symbolizes "sports, performance, and the free-flowing spirit of the athlete."[6] In the USA, the Nike "Swoosh" can be seen on one out of every three pairs of sneakers sold.

Branding is extremely important in the athletic footwear business. Athletic footwear is the only footwear or apparel category that is outward branded, meaning the brand is displayed on the outside of the product. By wearing a particular brand, the consumer is providing free advertising for the company. Nike has taken this industry characteristic and exploited it to the fullest by differentiating its brand from its competitors and conveying a uniqueness about its product.

Advertising

Through creative and memorable advertising, Nike has positioned itself as a hip brand. In 1993, Nike spend $250 million promoting its products and the Nike brand name. Its products are primarily endorsed by talented, high-profile athletes who are seen as heroes by consumers wanting to emulate their achievements. This hero-based advertising phenomenon is now being imitated by Nike's competitors.

Two of Nike's most successful advertising campaigns have been the "Bo knows" campaign featuring Heisman winner Bo Jackson and rock-and-roller Bo Diddley and the "Just do it" campaign. The "Bo knows" ad for Nike's cross-trainers was widely praised by critics for its "wit and intelligence" and earned Nike an 80 percent share in the new market. "Just do it" was first run in 1988 and featured Craig Blanchette, a wheelchair racer. This ad demonstrated that nothing was impossible while wearing Nikes.

The most important relationship between Nike and one of its spokespersons has been with Michael Jordan. Nike picked Jordan up when he was just a promising rookie for the Chicago Bulls basketball team. Jordan's charm and hero appeal rocketed the sales of his namesake shoe, the Air Jordan, to $200 million. Jordan also benefited from his association with the footwear giant. On top of his annual $18 million contract, Jordan receives a 5 percent royalty on the wholesale price of every pair of Air Jordans sold. Other top endorsers for Nike include basketballers Charles Barkley and Alonzo Mourning, baseball and football player Deion Sanders, tennis stars Andre Agassi and John McEnroe, and Olympic runner Jackie Joyner Kersee.

Nike had to change its advertising strategies in its women's and outdoor markets. Both of these markets are centered on individualism so the hero concept is not an effective marketing tool. Nike came from behind in its women's category with the help of some ingenious advertising. Its "dialogue" ad campaign presented athletics as a personal growth experience instead of "a path to glory and physical power." These ads also touched on non-athletic themes, such as emotions, inspiration, and relationships. Nike's outdoor advertising focuses on self-empowerment and the back-to-basics lifestyle that is becoming so popular in today's footwear market.

Distribution

Nike products are sold through more than 15,000 domestic retail accounts. The company's biggest retail customer is Foot Locker, accounting for 14 percent of its 1992 sales. Other customers include department stores, Lady Foot Locker, Sports Authority, shoe stores, and various sports specialty stores across the country. To gain more control of its international distribution systems, Nike is moving away from independent distributorships and is in the process of acquiring many of its distributorships in Europe, the Far East, Australia, and Latin America.

The company's US distribution centers are located in Wilsonville, Oregon, and two separate centers for footwear and apparel in Memphis, Tennessee. Nike's newest distribution center lies in Memphis and handles all of the products in the apparel line. The center's projected daily throughput is 270,000 items in one eight-hour shift, with total inventory capacity at almost 21 million items. Employees at the distribution center inspect 100 percent of all incoming merchandise to ensure accuracy and the center also guarantees overnight delivery. Nike's attention to accuracy and speedy delivery helps it stay ahead of the competition.

Financial Highlights

Nike's financial statements for the fiscal years ended 1989 through 1994 are shown in appendix A. In fiscal 1994 revenues decreased for the first time in seven years, dropping 4 percent from its record $3.93 billion earned in 1993. Nike did, however, achieve a company record of hitting $1 billion in sales for two quarters during 1994. Net income also decreased for the first time in seven years, dropping 18 percent to $299 million from 1993's record $365 million. Decreased revenues and increased selling and administrative expenses were the primary factors. Fiscal 1994 was the second-best revenue year and the third-best net income year in the company's history. A 10 percent increase in Futures orders indicates renewed growth heading into the first six months of fiscal 1995. (Taken from Nike, Inc. 1994 Annual Report.)

Future Opportunities

Nike plans to continue its efforts in the Outdoor footwear category. This category is relatively new and holds many opportunities for growth which is what Nike does best. Nike has taken a different approach to marketing this category and it appears to be putting the pressure on the market leader, Timberland. Nike is currently in the number two position but sales of its sport sandal, the Air Deschutz, are higher than any other Nike shoe. Also, Nike predicts that its new hiking boot, the Air Mada, will help Outdoor sales to exceed $200 million by fiscal yearend 1995.

Nike also plans to take on the international market at full force in 1995. This is the area with the biggest growth potential for Nike. Already, Nike has established itself in China, a country with a population of over one billion. Currently, the penetration rate for athletic footwear in China is the lowest at 11,821, persons per pair versus four persons per pair in the USA (appendix C). The high cost of athletic shoes sold abroad coupled with diverse cultural factors has contributed to these low penetration rates.

Mexico and Latin America also offer Nike growth potential. With its recent acquisitions in Chile and Argentina, Nike is positioning itself to take hold of this market. The passing of the NAFTA agreement will also open doors for Nike in the Latin countries.

Europe continues to hold opportunities for Nike. Its largest retailer, Foot Locker, has planned expansion in Europe and will help Nike to compete with the market leader and its long-time rival, Adidas, which has seen its market share drop from 46 to 33 percent in the past four years. Eastern European countries, in particular, will be looked at for potential market penetration opportunities.

APPENDIX A: NIKE, INC. FINANCIAL STATEMENTS

Nike Inc. consolidated statements of income ($millions)
Fiscal year ends May 31

	1989	1990	1991	1992	1993	1994
Net revenues	1,711	2,235	3,004	3,405	3,931	3,790
Cost of sales	1,075	1,384	1,851	2,089	2,387	2,302
Gross income	636	851	1,153	1,316	1,544	1,488
Sales, genl & admin. exp.	355	455	664	762	922	974
EBIT	281	397	489	555	622	514
Net interest	14	11	27	31	26	15
Other income	3	7	0	−2	−2	−8
Pretax income	271	393	462	522	595	491
Income taxes	104	150	175	193	230	192
Net income	167	243	287	329	365	299

Nike Inc. consolidated Balance sheet ($millions)
Fiscal year ends May 31

	1989	1990	1991	1992	1993	1994
Assets						
Cash & equivalents	86	90	120	260	291	519
Receivables	296	401	522	596	668	704
Inventories	223	310	587	471	593	470
Other current assets	33	37	52	61	69	78
Total current assets	638	838	1,280	1,388	1,621	1,771
Net plant & equipment	90	160	293	346	378	406
Goodwill	82	81	115	110	158	157
Other long-term assets	15	16	21	29	31	40
Total assets	825	1,095	1,708	1,873	2,188	2,374
Liabilities and shareholder's equity						
Current liabilities						
Current debt	41	40	301	109	161	132
Payables & accruals	175	233	328	335	291	430
Total current liabilities	216	273	629	444	453	562

	1989	1990	1991	1992	1993	1994
Long-term debt	34	26	30	70	15	12
Deferred taxes & other	13	11	17	27	74	59
Preferred stock	0	0	0	0	0	0
Common equity	562	784	1,033	1,332	1,646	1,741
Total liabilities & equity	825	1,095	1,708	1,873	2,188	2,374

Nike, Inc. sales by segments ($millions)

Fiscal year	1991	1992	1993	1994	1995E
US athletic footwear	1,676	1,748	1,967	1,869	1,791
US athletic apparel	326	361	357	339	349
Total US athletic	2,002	2,109	2,324	2,208	2,140
International footwear	652	867	1,049	998	951
International apparel	211	267	353	359	360
Total international	863	1,134	1,402	1,357	1,312
Other brands	139	162	205	225	253
Total	3,004	3,405	3,931	3,790	3,705

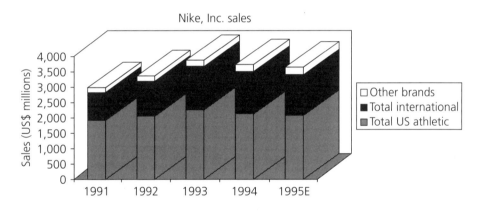

Nike, Inc. sales

APPENDIX B: REEBOK INTERNATIONAL LTD FINANCIAL STATEMENTS

Reebok International Ltd consolidated statements of income ($millions)
Fiscal year ends December 31

	1990	1991	1992	1993
Net revenues	2,159	2,735	2,944	2,894
Cost of sales	1,288	1,645	1,742	1,720
Gross income	871	1,090	1,202	1,174
Sales, genl & admin. exp.	572	683	791	778
EBIT	299	407	411	396
Net interest	3	19	11	17

	1990	1991	1992	1993
Other income	−1	2	8	−12
Pretax income	295	390	408	367
Income taxes	118	155	159	140
Net income	177	235	249	226

Reebok International Ltd. consolidated balance sheet ($millions)
Fiscal year ends December 31

	1990	1991	1992	1993
Assets				
Cash & equivalents	227	85	105	79
Receivables	391	404	418	457
Inventories	367	414	434	514
Other current assets	44	79	103	76
Total current assets	1,030	981	1,060	1,127
Net plant & equipment	111	122	128	131
Goodwill	255	215	103	94
Other long-term assets	7	104	55	40
Total assets	1,403	1,422	1,345	1,391
Liabilities and shareholders' equity				
Current liabilities				
Current debt	69	12	4	24
Payables & accruals	225	405	381	372
Total current liabilities	294	417	385	396
Long-term debt	106	170	116	134
Deferred taxes & other	7	12	5	15
Preferred stock	0	0	0	0
Common equity	997	824	839	846
Total liabilities & equity	1,403	1,422	1,345	1,391

Reebok International Ltd. sales by segments ($millions)

Fiscal year	1991	1992	1993	1994E	1995E
US athletic footwear	1,336	1,472	1,300	1,311	1,337
US athletic apparel	53	60	122	171	206
Total US athletic	1,389	1,532	1,422	1,482	1,543
Total international	833	1,008	1,077	1,166	1,259
Other brands	513	404	416	443	473
Total	2,735	2,944	2,915	3,091	3,275

APPENDIX C: ATHLETIC FOOTWEAR INDUSTRY

US athletic footwear market ($millions)

	1991	1992	1993
Nike	1,693	1,817	1,958
Reebok	1,336	1,472	1,320
Converse	187	215	265

Fila	77	201	250
LA Gear	492	311	290
Total top 5	3,785	4,016	4,083
Other	2,015	1,984	2,117
Est. total market	5,800	6,000	6,200

US athletic footwear market share (percent)

	1991	1992	1993
Nike	29	30	32
Reebok	23	25	21
Converse	3	4	4
Fila	1	3	4
LA Gear	8	5	5
Total top 5	65	67	66
Other	35	33	34
Est. total market	100	100	100

Athletic footwear penetration by country

	Population (millions)	Pop./pair
USA	248	4
France	55	11
UK	56	14
Germany	77	23
Spain	40	33
China	1,123	11,821
Korea	45	121
Japan	124	50
Argentina	33	24
Brazil	150	88
Mexico	89	212

US athletic footwear sales

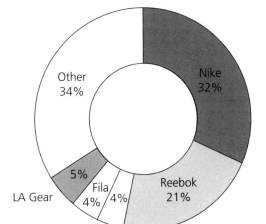

NOTES AND REFERENCES

1 Donald Katz, *Just Do It*, p. 25.

2 J. R. Esquival et al., "Cole-Haan – company report", *Lehman Brothers, Inc.*, November 18, 1993.

3 *Just Do It*, p. 18.

4 *Just Do It*, p. 154.

5 *Just Do It*, p. 280.

6 Doris J. Yang and Michael Oneal, "Can Nike just do it?", *Business Week*, April 18, 1994, p. 88.

Lee Jing Textile Company Ltd

Sue Greenfeld and Shun-Ching Horng

Introduction

In 1993, Lee Jing Textile Company Ltd had sales of $3860 million New Taiwan (NT) dollars (about US $148 million), assets of NT $10,917 million (about US $420 million) and about 2500 employees. Lee Jing basically purchases raw cotton from its suppliers, then spins, weaves, and creates dyed fabric. Its primary products are cotton fabric and denim that are sold to customers in Taiwan, Hong Kong, USA, Germany, Singapore, Malaysia, the United Kingdom, Japan, the Netherlands, and other parts of the world. Lee Jing is a first generation company of the Kuo Lee Group, a Taiwanese conglomerate.

Recently, Lee Jing has been downsizing as it is caught in a price squeeze. Like the USA, Japan, and Europe, Taiwan is having fundamental problems with its textile industry because fabric tends to be an undifferentiated product. This means that price is often an overriding consideration; hence, textiles constantly search for areas where wages are low. Rising wage costs coupled with chronic labor shortages are making the production of fabric at competitive prices very difficult. The

Prepared by Professors Sue Greenfeld of California State University, San Bernardino, and Shun-Ching Horng of National Chengchi University (Taiwan) as the basis for education discussion rather than to illustrate either effective or ineffective handling of an administrative situation. The names of various participants, the actual company, and its various mill locations have been disguised. Copyright © Sue Greenfeld, 1995.

company for the past eight years has been losing a significant amount of money, and it needs a strategy to position itself in the world market.

The major challenges facing Lee Jing mean nothing less than the survival of the company. Lee Jing must determine how to best organize itself to tackle this painful transition. Lee Jing hopes that a change in strategy toward high value-added products, superior on-time delivery, and service will distinguish itself from its competitors.

Background of Taiwan

The Republic of China (ROC) on Taiwan is the formal name for the country of Taiwan, an island southeast of mainland China. Some economics statistics in 1993 sketch the achievement of Taiwan. First, the gross domestic product (GDP) was $206 billion for a population size of 21 million people, with a per capita income figure of $10,000, as compared to 1982, when GDP stood at $71.5 billion for 18 million and per capita income was $2710. The economic growth rate has averaged around 8.7 percent annually for more than 30 years. So dramatic has been the improvement in living conditions, industrial structure and trade that many call this "Taiwan's economic miracle."

After the Second World War, Taiwan embarked upon an industrial policy which guided its economic development. Specifically, the transition of Taiwan toward becoming a developed country can be broken into six stages. The 1940s witnessed the economic reconstruction of the island, including land reform and the cultivation of emerging industries such as textiles and fertilizers. In the 1950s, Taiwan began an import substitution strategy. This meant that high tariffs were placed on consumer commodity imported goods, and Taiwanese firms were encouraged to begin exporting goods.

The 1960s saw the continued rapid growth of light industries. Both textiles and electronics flourished during this period. The 1970s saw a major structural change toward the development of capital- and technology-intensive industries. The government initiated and completed ten national construction projects, which benefited steel, ship-building, petrochemical, electrical power, telecommunication, transportation, and utilities.

The 1980s again saw a shift in industrial policy toward government-supported development of high-tech industries. The Hsinchu science-based Industrial Park was modeled on the Silicon Valley concept in northern California. The government at this time also took a strong stand on reducing industrial pollution.

The 1990s present new opportunities and challenges for Taiwan. Specifically, in 1991, the ROC government adopted the Six-Year National Development plan for improving Taiwan's infrastructure and transportation systems. This creates more jobs and upgrades the developing environment for strategic industries. On the other hand, problems facing Taiwan include the 40 percent appreciation of NT dollars since the late 1980s, rising wage costs, insufficient labor force, high cost of land, ecological concerns, and competition from other developing countries. Refer to exhibit 21.1 for a guide to doing business in Taiwan.

Exhibit 21.1   Guide to doing business in Taiwan

1   *Develop a relationship*. Relationships are a very important element of an Oriental cul-
    ture. This relationship or *guanxi* can be instrumental in doing business. While Western
    cultures emphasize a contract as legally binding, Chinese rely on mutual trust and
    friendship. Personal friends and business friends are often the same.

2   *Respect another's "face"*. Chinese care very much about harmony, and to cause
    another to "lose face" can mean "losing business." One does not usually criticize
    another person directly. Thus, there is no disagreement in public. Consensus is import-
    ant. A straightforward disagreement in public is considered to be an attack. Try to
    express opinions indirectly or in private.

3   *Look for a longer time horizon*. Business decisions are based on the long term. Chin-
    ese are reluctant to give a big order immediately. They are likely to handle a small
    order first, even if they lose money. They expect more business in the future. The first
    several deals provide a good opportunity to develop *guanxi*: do not miss it.

4   *Don't be surprised at Chinese hospitality*. The Chinese show tremendous grace and
    hospitality when they meet people for the first time. Guests are entertained well, and
    usually are given a gift of the occasion. Because of this hospitality, Westerners some-
    times become too optimistic about the cooperation that is to follow.

5   *Inquiries about one's background are common*. Chinese people like to inquire about
    each other's background. They will be very happy to know they have something in
    common. Unfortunately, some inquiries can make Westerners feel uncomfortable and
    they think their privacy has been invaded.

6   *Negotiations may be unclear*. The Chinese tend not to make clear what they really
    want. They believe that with mutual trust and friendship, friends know instinctively
    what the other is thinking. This can be confusing to Westerners. Negotiation sched-
    ules can be delayed, and different conclusions reached.

Adapted by Sue Greenfeld from: Dah Hsian William Seetoo, "Communication, negotiation and management system: the Chinese style," unpublished paper, National Chengchi
University, April 1994.

The Textile Industry

The word textile comes from the Latin *textere*, which means to weave, interlace, or
intertwine. Earliest known records show that some type of clothing existed in
prehistoric times, but weaving dates back only to 5000 BC. Textile fibers can be natural (from animal or plant sources), mineral (such as glass or metallic), man-made
(such as rayon or nylon), or a modification or combination of these. Linen is believed
to be the oldest textile fabric. Silk dates back to 2640 BC with the Chinese, while
wool is mentioned in biblical sources. The Crusades and world exploration spread
the knowledge of cotton throughout Europe, as cotton was found extensively in
Mexico, Central, and South America. In 1641, the cotton-based textile industry in
England was established, and it rapidly became competitive with wool.

Early civilizations, like the Egyptian, Greek, Roman, and Chinese, all had systems for producing clothes, including hand looms and the hand spindle, but the
Middle Ages transformed the industry with the development of the spinning wheel,

the horizontal loom, and a process to remove the natural grease in wool to make the fibers.

The Industrial Revolution dramatically expanded the cotton textile industry, especially in Great Britain, from a home operation into a large-scale enterprise consisting of huge mills with mechanized mass production employing a million and a half people. British cotton mills were supplied by raw material from the United States, and by 1850 these mills were producing over 2025 million yards per year.

In the early 1800s, US textile mills began operations, mostly in New England, New York, and Pennsylvania, where they flourished until the 1920s. The US textile industry then migrated to the Southern states. In 1925, the man-made fibers of acetate, rayon, and nylon made their first appearance, and became increasingly popular. After the Second World War, rapid progress in transportation, telecommunications, mass retailing, production, and distribution of clothing again changed the textile industry into a global endeavor. Rotor spinning and shuttleless looms were introduced, which greatly increased automation.

The 1960s marked the enormous movement of textile and apparel operations to developing countries, such as Taiwan. While employment in textiles declined in Europe, the USA, and Japan during the past thirty years, the textile industry became a leading employer for many developing countries.

By 1991, the ten leading exporters of textiles and clothing were Hong Kong, Italy, China, Germany, South Korea, Taiwan, France, the USA, Belgium/Luxembourg, and the UK. The top five importers were the USA, Germany, Hong Kong, France, and the UK. From 1980 to 1990, the fastest growing exporter of clothing was mainland China.

Yet the textile industry has also sometimes suffered from a poor image. Besides low wages, even as early as the seventeenth century the industry realized that its workers had health problems. The most serious is byssinosis, also known as brown lung. This is a respiratory disorder caused by the dust from cotton and other fibers. Over time (usually several years), breathing becomes more difficult and the lungs develop a brownish tint. Persons with mild cases experience a chest tightness and shortness of breath on the first day of work after a break (e.g. weekend). More serious cases involve chronic, irreversible lung damage. For some textile manufacturers, there have also been union-management problems, and labor strikes. The movie *Norma Rae* about worker grievances and union-organizing is based on a true incident at J. P. Stevens.

The global textile industry has become extremely competitive, with supply exceeding demand. Japan, for example, has realized that it can no longer compete in the basic low-end fabric line, and has adopted a value-added product strategy. The Germans have invested heavily in new technologies and labor-saving machinery, while the Italians are developing close collaborations with well-known designers. The Taiwan Textile Federation (TTF), established in 1975 and authorized by the Taiwanese Ministry of Economic Affairs, attempts to monitor trends in the industry, and provide Taiwanese firms with this information. TTF has a computerized data bank and design center to serve those interested in buying Taiwan textile products. It also negotiates with foreign authorities, administers textile export quotas, and promotes Taiwan textile products internationally.

Numerous Taiwanese textiles firms have already moved part of their operations off the island, frequently to mainland China. To curb this outflow of investment to mainland China, the ROC President Lee Teng-Hui has encouraged Taiwanese businesses to adopt a "southern investment" strategy into Singapore, the Philippines, or Indonesia instead.

According to Bruno D. C. Huang, marketing research assistant at Taiwan's World Trade Center, in 1993 more than 1000 Taiwanese firms were engaged in the textile industry, employing about 288,427 workers, down from 459,321 in 1987. In 1993, textiles were still Taiwan's leading export product, followed by electronics in a very close second. In 1992, Far Eastern Textile Ltd was the leading Taiwanese textile firm in the cotton industry.

History of Lee Jing Textiles

The company was established in 1949 by Shih-Tei Kuo and Siang-Chun Chang when they migrated from mainland China to Taiwan. The two men brought old equipment from Shanghai and some thirty people who worked for them and set up their first factory in Taoyuan. The original capacity of the plant was 7508 spindles.

In 1956, Lee Jing built another plant, this one for spinning, and for the next thirty years, Lee Jing alternated between building spinning and weaving plants until it had six spinning, six weaving, and two dyeing mills.

In 1980, Lee Jing made a strategic change in its product orientation by adding a higher value-added product. It started the production of denim fabric, including a dyeing and finishing mill. Through the 1980s, the company added new capacity, but closed down older facilities. The number of employees grew slowly to a high of 5500 reached in the late 1980s.

Since 1988, the company has been downsizing through increased automation, through the natural attrition of 20 percent from employee turnover, and from layoffs. Laid-off workers receive one month's severance pay for each year of service to Lee Jing. In 1993, Lee Jing employed about 2500 employees. Until 1986, Lee Jing was quite profitable, but since 1987, Lee Jing has been losing money. For years 1991 through 1993, operating costs alone exceeded net revenue. Between the years 1992 and 1993, Lee Jing changed its accounting procedures. Refer to exhibits 21.2, 21.3, and 21.4 balance sheet and income statements.

Due to industry overcapacity and increasing labor costs, Lee Jing began in 1988 to consider moving some operations to other locales. During one three-year period, top executives visited Indonesia, Thailand, Vietnam, Mexico, and Nicaragua. Enlei Lu, one of the company's general managers, went to Nicaragua many times for discussion purposes, including dinner with the president of the country, but too many problems were encountered. For all their joint ventures, President Chih Nen Wang believes it is necessary for Lee Jing to have 51 percent of the stock for controlling purposes. President Wang has been CEO of Lee Jing for the past three years.

Production and Products

Lee Jing has its headquarters in Taipei, with factory operations in Taoyuan, Hsinchu, and Kaohsiung, but the last was closed in 1993. Total land space is 602,489 square

Exhibit 21.2   Balance sheet, assets (thousands of new Taiwan dollars, NT$)

Current assets	1991	1992	1993
Cash	102,270	63,425	151,925
Short investment	1,098,922	1,118,811	1,294,153
Notes receivable	434,322	197,737	151,543
Accounts receivable	279,099	260,656	162,325
Inventory	1,857,155	1,349,727	1,093,133
Prepaid items	280,766	108,882	59,661
Other current assets	101,166	114,255	67,951
Total current assets	4,153,700	3,213,493	2,980,691
Long-term investment	3,282,276	3,893,120	4,239,978
Fixed assets			
Land	377,849	381,006	381,006
Plant & equipment	1,873,917	1,818,643	1,911,309
Machine equipment	7,013,020	6,629,838	6,072,387
Transportation equip.	114,542	113,725	108,781
Other equipment	105,414	109,602	111,410
	9,484,742	9,052,814	8,584,893
Replacement	109,678	109,679	109,679
Total	9,594,420	9,162,493	8,694,572
Accum. deprec.	(5,233,258)	(5,387,411)	(5,332,028)
Unfinished construction	24,868	26,926	231,630
Net fixed assets	4,386,030	3,802,008	3,594,174
Other assets	1,754	118,414	102,975
Total assets	11,823,761	11,027,035	10,917,818

Note: Exchange rate 1994: 26 NT dollars = US $1.

meters (about 149 acres), with most land designated for Taoyuan, 405,342 square meters (about 100 acres). Taoyuan has six spinning plants, three weaving plants, and one denim dyeing and finishing plant. The other plant is in Hsinchu, and there is an arrangement for production in mainland China. In 1993, total monthly production was 29,000 bales of yarn, 12 million yards of greige and finished fabrics, including 4 million yards of denim, 300,000 kilograms of knitted fabric, and 30,000 dozen knitted garments, eighty percent of which is for export.

The head office employs about 124 people, with the rest located in the Taoyuan and Hsinchu. Lee Jing had been organized functionally, but is moving toward an SBU structure. The organizational chart is shown in exhibit 21.5.

Lee Jing has four main product lines: yarn, grade piece goods, denim, and finished goods. Yarn and grade piece goods are about 25 and 14 percent of the business, while denim and finished cloth are 32 and 28 percent respectively. Of the

Exhibit 21.3   Balance sheet, liabilities (NT$ thousands)

Current liabilities	1991	1992	1993
Bank loans	1,549,670	1,284,093	503,214
Accounts payable	177,092	95,232	62,713
Other current liabilities	1,169,319	953,558	1,728,974
Total current liabilities	2,896,080	2,332,883	2,294,901
Long-term debt	478,810	251,090	89,210
Reserves for employee retirement	80,000	23,997	14,939
Other liabilities	88,413	88,413	164,594
Total liabilities	3,543,303	2,696,383	2,563,643
Owner equity			
Capital stock	4,400,000	4,400,000	4,400,000
Capital surplus	418,993	487,300	376,520
Retained earnings	3,461,465	3,443,352	3,576,256
Total owner equity	8,280,458	8,330,652	8,354,176
Liabilities & equity	11,823,761	11,027,035	10,917,818

Note: Exchange rate 1994: 26 NT dollars = US $1.

yarn, almost 40 percent is differentiated. Grade piece goods are totally undifferentiated. Denim is 50 percent differentiated. The two to three year goal is to have 70 percent of the yarn differentiated, 100 percent of grade piece goods differentiated, and 80 percent of the denim differentiated. Eventually, all the undifferentiated fabric will be produced in mainland China, and all the specialized, differentiated goods, R&D, and marketing will be in Taiwan. President Wang wants to make Lee Jing the most profitable textile firm in Taiwan, not necessarily the largest.

As one of the oldest textile firms in Taiwan, the reputation of Lee Jing is very good. Lee Jing could be considered the Ford of the industry – moderate prices, high quality, and wide range of products. According to Margaret Li, General Merchandising Manager for Liz Claiborne International in Taiwan, "Lee Jing is one of our fourteen piece goods suppliers because they have reasonable prices, their quality of dyeing is good, their shrinkage is consistent, their inspection is very good, they correct defects, and they are very cooperative. . . . Liz Claiborne has very high standards, and if they are one of our suppliers, they have to be good." Other Lee Jing customers include The Gap, Van Heusen, Oxford, Biermann, Mark Spence, and Crew Peabody.

By 1994, Lee Jing had successfully applied for and attained ISO 9000. It had also won more than fifteen awards from the government for excellence in exporting. In 1981 and 1982, it received the Isikawa award for quality control, and in 1987, received an industry pollution protection award from Taiwan's Environmental Protection Agency (EPA).

Exhibit 21.4   Income statement   (NT$ thousands)

	1991	1992	1993**
Operating revenue	$5,410,316	4,472,972	3,880,554
Sales returns & allow.	(16,007)	(28,822)	(19,805)
Net revenue	5,394,309	4,444,150	3,860,749
Operating cost	5,640,718	4,824,313	3,868,494
Operating gross	(246,409)	(380,162)	(7,745)
Operating expenses	395,764	362,025	360,069
Operating income	(642,173)	(742,187)	(367,814)
Non-operating income			
Investment revenue	743,874	822,542	693,591
Financial revenue	–	–	33,904
Gain from inventory checking	–	–	2,932
Diff. est. raw material	–	–	1,490
Dividend revenue	688	69,888	–
Gain on sale fixed assets	1,028	68,059	–
Rent revenue	23,093	25,452	–
Exchange revenue	37,405	20,484	–
Recovery/loss of investment	–	19,890	–
Recovery/loss of inventory	20,000	11,000	–
Sales of by-products	16,762	9,752	–
Gain/sale of LT investment	14,851	4,070	–
Interest revenue	32,462	3,091	–
Recovery/deferred revenue	551,178	–	–
Recovery/exporting loss	38,255	–	–
Other	40,830	19,974	95,787
Total non-oper. income	1,520,426	1,074,202	827,704
Non-operating expense			
Financial expense	–	–	166,297
Loss/selling assets	–	–	1,343
Loss checking inventory	–	–	42
Loss/inventory price red.	–	–	24,500
Interest expense	286,752	184,295	–
Loss of shutdown	54,031	74,204	–
Loss/selling fixed assets	169,841	4,545	57
Loss/investment	19,890	–	21
Other loss	–	–	1,549
Other expense	6,054	6,137	242,557
Total non-oper. exp.	536,568	269,181	436,366
Income before tax	341,685	62,834	23,524
Tax	–	–	–
Net income after tax	341,685	62,834	23,524

[a]   Reporting changed in 1993. Exchange rate 1994: 26 NT dollars = US $1.

Exhibit 21.5 Organizational chart, 1994

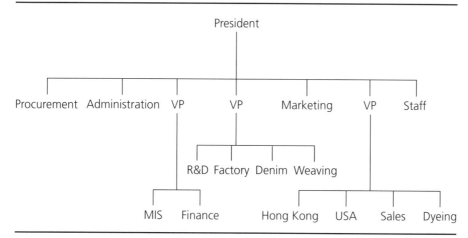

Lee Jing is guided by its three statements: (1) people-based permanent operation; (2) quality is first; and (3) kindness and goodwill to all people.

Marketing of Lee Jing Products

According to President Chih Nen Wang, Lee Jing is in a turnaround situation, and faces a lot of competition from Third World countries, such as mainland China, Pakistan, and Indonesia. Cost is a big factor, and due to accelerating labor costs, Lee Jing cannot make the fabric as cheaply as these other countries. Lee Jing must import its raw material, while mainland China and Pakistan produce their own cotton. Also, in 1994, world prices for traditional undifferentiated fabric were 30 percent lower than in 1984. This was due to industry overcapacity. President Wang indicated that supply runs about 17 percent higher than demand, and he expects the problem of oversupply to continue until 1999.

Hence, Lee Jing in the past three years has adopted a strategy of product differentiation. President Wang acknowledged that Lee Jing should have begun this new strategy even earlier "about seven or eight years ago when the NT dollar was appreciated." However, he also believes that in 1994, Lee Jing will break even or make a small profit. With this new strategy, President Wang established in 1993 a research and development department of six textile engineers to create differentiated products. Even for differentiated products, the life cycle is only four to six months before a competitor will "copy" the product.

Also in 1993 President Wang created for the first time a marketing department of three people. Richard Tsai, Vice General Manager, was assigned to head up this department. His focus is both external and internal. Externally, Lee Jing will strengthen its system of gathering market information to assess customer trends and demands. Data will be gathered from papers, magazines, government, TTF, and visiting customers. Additional activities, such as sales promotions, will be performed, such as an upcoming business trip to New York to visit twenty piece goods customers, and to emphasize Lee Jing's denim goods items. Lee Jing has two branch offices, one at 6th Avenue near the fashion area in New York, and the other in Hong Kong.

Lee Jing has always attended international exhibitions, and will continue this activity. It usually attends five to six exhibitions per year in the world's major fashion centers. Lee Jing advertises in *Women's Wear Daily* and other major trade publications, but Richard Tsai believes the benefits of such endeavors are hard to evaluate. TTF also introduces customers to Lee Jing, but "developing new customers is very difficult."

Internally, the marketing department started a series of seminars whereby the members of the R&D department from the plant in Taoyuan give presentations to the Lee Jing sales representatives in the Taipei headquarters. These seminars are scheduled every two weeks. The R&D department was described as "in the kitchen." The sales personnel were unaware of a number of new Lee Jing products. Lee Jing does have its own trademark.

With the establishment of the R&D and marketing departments, the culture of Lee Jing appears to be changing from a production-driven company to one that is marketing-oriented under the leadership of President Wang. One outside source described the culture of Lee Jing as "very conservative."

Quality Circles

Lee Jing has been engaged in quality circles since 1981. Initially, sixty quality circles were established, but the number was later reduced to twenty. Quality circles are partly voluntary, and partly assigned. Each circle has six to ten people who meet twice a year for a quality control campaign that lasts three to four months. Each circle competes to make the best suggestions. Each team makes a presentation, with NT12,000 (US $480) awarded to the first place team. All participants will each receive NT600 (US $24) for the entire campaign.

One quality control project included buying a machine that cost US $100,000. The machine's purpose involved measuring "nips" in a piece of fabric. "Nips" are the tiny balls of thread on the fabric's surface. The ideal fabric has no or few "nips." A multiple regression model was developed, and a ten-week experiment was drawn up. The results showed the optimal drawing length of the cotton to satisfy customers' needs while also reducing the amount of waste. One positive outcome was the reduction of customer complaints.

MIS and the Use of Computers

In terms of its use of computers, Edward Huang, one of Lee Jing's three Vice Presidents, expressed his opinion that the integration of the system could be improved. Currently, more than twenty people staff the computer department. He stated that too many unnecessary reports are generated. A consultant will be looking at how to integrate the computer system. Management believes that the current system is too expensive to maintain, and too complicated. Managers are contemplating a major revision of both hardware and software, but do not plan to outsource their MIS needs.

Systems that are computerized include purchasing material, payroll, personnel, accounting, financing, and warehousing. Production operations are only partly computerized. International Business Machines (IBM) is the current main computer vendor. Lee Jing has had a computer network system for the past ten years. Prior to the network, communication between headquarters and the plants was carried on via telephone.

Industrial Safety

At Lee Jing, there is a formal Labor Safety and Hygiene Committee composed of nine managers and seven union workers who meet four times a year. The head of the committee is Edward Huang. The Committee has been operating since the plant opened in 1951, but it became formally established in 1975. The committee discusses plant safety and hygiene issues.

From the committee, smaller groups of five people go on two-day inspections, and give scores for every Lee Jing plant on a grading sheet. The team checks to see that safety lights are operational, stairs are cleared, and hoses for fires are functional. Workers are checked to see that long hair is curled, and that no one is wearing slippers. Pavements have to be intact. No cigarette butts or cups are to be around. Water fountains and restrooms must be clean. Individuals are rewarded monetarily or punished through fees in the range of NT500 to 3000 (about US $20 to 120).

There has been one issue bothering managers for quite a while, but they feel somewhat helpless to remedy the situation. Although managers are aware of the noise level in the plant, they have been unable to get the workers to wear earplugs. About once a year, a government official conducts a safety training program in the plant to discuss the problems associated with damage to the eardrum, but the program so far appears to be unsuccessful. Management stated that only about 10 percent of the workers wear earplugs, but that 80–90 percent wear face masks (especially those working in the denim dyeing plant). Management asserted that workers think the earplugs are uncomfortable, and that they prevent conversations.

External visits from Taiwanese government agencies include a once-a-year inspection of the boiler, and several visits from the county fire department. The Environmental Protection Agency (EPA) checks randomly for air pollution. The highest fine experienced by Lee Jing was for NT100,000 (US $4000) for water pollution.

In the history of Lee Jing, only one fatality occurred in the mid-1980s when a factory roof crashed during a seasonal typhoon. In accordance with the Taiwanese Labor Safety and Health Act of 1974 (revised 1991), Lee Jing (like other Taiwanese firms) keeps monthly safety records.

At the Taoyuan plant, there is one medical doctor, Dr Shu Woei Jan and five other medical personnel. Dr Jan stated that his facility was established in 1961. He cares not only for the workers, but the workers' families as well. Daily he sees many complaints for head colds and stomach aches. The most frequent industrial accidents are cuts to the hand, mostly the fingers. After four days of absenteeism, industrial cases must be reported to the Bureau of Labor Insurance for compensation. Lee Jing reports about nine to ten cases a year.

Every two years, all plant workers must undergo a minor physical examination. They are checked for their weight, height, ears, eyes, blood pressure, and 11 items in their blood, including hemoglobin and hepatitis A virus. They are also given a X-ray examination for their lungs. Those individuals over 45 years of age and those overweight, with elevated blood pressure, problems with their eyes, ears, or lungs are rechecked on an annual basis. In 1993, over a one-week period, about 2215 people participated in the examinations conducted by a local hospital. Between 400 to 600 individuals fell into the annual recheck category.

Dr Jan showed that in a group of 320 workers, 27 of them had suspicious lung problems and should be monitored for the possibility of "brown lung." He also indicated that these people might be changed to another job within the plant. In the same group, there were about 63 people who had some type of hearing defect. Dr Jan wonders what he should say to management to encourage a higher usage of protective gear. Overall, accidents have decreased at Lee Jing due to three factors: (1) workers are more experienced (they have been at the plant longer); (2) there are better equipment and more training; and (3) the quarterly meeting has helped to heighten awareness about industrial safety and hygiene.

Pollution and Waste Minimization in Taiwan

In the 1990s, the issue of pollution has come to the forefront in Taiwan. The west coast of the Taiwan island has one of the highest population densities in the world. The crowded conditions mean many industrial areas are too close to residential areas, and that managing wastes is problematic.

According to Tin-Bai Pan, Deputy General Director of the Industrial Development Bureau of the Ministry of Economic Affairs, in 1991 Taiwan's waste reached 12,000,000 tons per year, 5 percent of which is hazardous. He stated that by 1998 Taiwan needs to build 22 more garbage incinerators, and that Taiwan has aggressively adopted the strategy of industrial waste minimization to "make possible both economic growth and environmental protection."

In the textile industry, a major issue is how to deal with and treat dye and finishing wastewater. The discharge water may be colored, and high or low in pH. Lee Jing already has made two major investments in waste water treatment in 1982 and 1988. The first cost approximately NT 60 million (US $240,000) while the second ran NT 50 million (US $200,000). For other waste (scraps of yarn and cotton), Lee Jing has two large incinerators. According to management, maintenance of this equipment is very expensive. In terms of steam, about 30 percent can be reclaimed and recycled.

In Taiwan, Edward Huang believes that Lee Jing is an industry leader in pollution control. Most small- and medium-sized firms do not have such waste minimization equipment, and they rely on the government to pick up and dispose of waste. Management believes it has done as much as it can for environmental protection.

Exhibit 21.6   Average score for worker satisfaction

1	Work	1.28
2	Supervision	1.54
3	Pay	0.89
4	Co-workers	2.17
5	Overall satisfaction	1.48

$n = 235$.

Personnel Practices and Employee Satisfaction

One issue that concerns Lee Jing has been the changing work ethic of the Taiwanese people. According to Enlei Lu, Taiwan's raising affluence has decreased young people's desire to work in a factory. According to Department of Health documents, the median age in Taiwan is almost 28, but for Lee Jing, the average worker ranges in age between 38 and 40 years old. For the past four years, Lee Jing has not been able to hire any college graduates to work in the factory.

Problems of this nature concerned Chih Nen Wang when he assumed the presidency of Lee Jing in 1992. He initiated a major job satisfaction study on 2275 factory workers in November 1993. This study used the Minnesota Employee Job Satisfaction Inventory as the research tool, which includes five dimensions of jobs, namely work, pay, promotion, supervision, and coworkers. Since promotion is very rare, this dimension was deleted from the survey. If a respondent's answer for a positive statement is "yes," the score for the question is 3. If the answer is "no," the score is 0, while 1 means "don't know." Using a stratified random sample, 247 questionnaires were distributed with 235 completed. The results are shown as exhibit 21.6.

Another issue of concern to President Wang is the lack of cross-training. For example, there is no system to rotate the people through different areas. People stay in the factory for twenty years in the same job. In terms of education for managers, recently President Wang and two other top managers began participating in the executive MBA program at the National Chengchi University (NCU). According to President Wang, his involvement with the university has been invaluable to him, and has allowed him to think more "strategically." He plans to send more middle-line managers to NCU in the next five years.

Future Challenges

One of the biggest challenges has been the transition of the company from its traditional production focus to a more marketing focus. For example, President Wang wonders: to what extent should Lee Jing use outsourcing? Traditionally, Lee Jing yarn has been its own supplier for its product lines, but in 1992, this began to change. Lee Jing now faces a "make or buy" question. Which is better? Which will be more profitable for the company?

VP Cheng wonders: how can Lee Jing attract young college graduates to work in the plant, and gain experience? Who are going to be their next generation of managers? Others recognize that the textile volume in Taiwan will probably reduce to one-third. Is Lee Jing positioned to maintain its share of this decreasing market? Lee Jing appears concerned about worker safety and the environment, but given Taiwan's growing quality-of-life movement, could Lee Jing do an even better job for worker safety and health, and for the environment?

Another challenge for Lee Jing is the development of the land following the closing of the Kaohsiung factory. Lee Jing is looking for opportunities for this piece of property, but is not quite sure what it should do. Lee Jing also owns property (about 54,000 square meters) in Kaohsiung that has potential for development. The current price of this land is NT 10 billion (or US $400 million).

As President Chih Nen Wang looks toward the future, he wonders: what can he do to turn this company around and make it profitable? Or should he just recommend to the board that they leave the textile industry altogether?

AMTRAK: IS THIS ANY WAY TO RUN A RAILROAD?

David W. Grigsby, Steven Harshbarger, and Jeffrey West

Early in 1994, as he prepared to petition the Congress of the United States for additional funds, Thomas Downs, the President of Amtrak, contemplated his company's recent run of bad luck. Midwest floods during the summer of 1993 had caused the company to incur huge unexpected expenses for refurbishing hundred of miles of tracks that were destroyed. Amtrak had also experienced several recent derailments, the latest of which had occurred in September 1993, killing 42 passengers. Although 20 percent of the railroad's operations were still subsidized by the federal budget, its financial performance remained dismal and passenger ridership was falling. A growing number of the members of Congress had expressed their reluctance to continue Amtrak's funding into the future.

Downs' vision was to convince Congress that Amtrak needed one final boost to be able to put its operations on a for-profit basis once and for all. He was preparing a presentation to ask for appropriations for new ICE 2000 locomotives. Downs was

Prepared by Professor David W. Grigsby and graduate students Steven Harshbarger and Jeffrey West of Clemson University from secondary sources as a basis for classroom discussion and not to illustrate either effective or ineffective handling of administrative situations. Copyright © David W. Grigsby, 1996.

convinced that the new engines were desperately needed. They would be very expensive, however, and Amtrak could not afford to purchase new engines without Congress's help. As Downs put the finishing touches on his presentation, he felt the weight of Amtrak's 23 year history on his shoulders.

Background

Before the Second World War, rail was the principal mode of transportation between cities. By 1958, railroads had been displaced by the automobile, and the rail passenger service had fallen to 4 percent of all intercity transportation. The rail companies, most of which carried both passengers and freight, began reducing their new capital investments in passenger cars and facilities. Consequently, the passenger service began to deteriorate in the 1960s. In a country that was dominated by airlines, airports, super-highways, and private automobiles, freight companies could no longer make the passenger rail service pay its way. Passenger train losses seemed an unacceptable handicap in the highly competitive world of freight transportation, but federal regulations required the railroads to operate passenger services.

The companies began looking to Congress for help, where, for some time, there had been interest in having the government establish a for-profit rail service company. In 1970, following heavy lobbying from the rail companies, Congress decided to attempt to preserve and revive the national rail passenger system with the passage of the Rail Passenger Service Act. This act created Amtrak, a private company incorporated under the laws of the District of Columbia. The new company was officially named the National Railroad Passenger Corporation, but its nickname, Amtrak, caught on quickly. Following passage of the act, Congress appropriated funds for the first two years of operation, and pressured the company to be profitable as soon as possible. Amtrak began full operations, managing a national passenger transportation system, on May 1, 1971.

Operating problems beset the new company from the beginning. Although Amtrak had responsibility for scheduling and operating all passenger trains, the ownership of the stations, terminals, yards, engines, and maintenance facilities remained with individual railroads. This left Amtrak at the mercy of the railroad companies, which were now only in the freight business. Amtrak rented right of way on the rails from these companies, but its passengers often had to take a back seat to freight cargoes. The commercial railroads were accused of treating Amtrak trains the same as freight, often extending run times and enraging customers. For example, railroad lines were in the habit of leaving their freight cars alone in the stations without power for hours at a time, and they often treated passenger trains the same way – a practice that was unacceptable to passengers. The on-time performance among railroads across the country ranged from 50 percent to slightly over 90 percent. Amtrak needed to do much better in order to revitalize rail travel in America.

During its first years of service, the company received approximately 75 percent of its operating revenues in the form of subsidies from the government. Nevertheless, Amtrak experienced difficulty raising its revenues. Antiquated equipment kept passengers away. Low ridership, in turn, meant that little in the way of capital reserves could be accumulated. With little capital to upgrade equipment, and declining support in Congress, the company found it next to impossible to operate high-quality rail service while complying with the regulations imposed upon it.

Some relief came with the passage of the Regional Rail Reorganization Act of 1973 and the Revitalization and Regulatory Reform Act of 1976. These acts gave more autonomy to Amtrak. Amtrak acquired the rights to the Northeast corridor from a bankrupt Pennsylvania Central Railroad. It also gained control over some terminals and stations. These stations could become another avenue of income for the company, by being upgraded into commercial malls and operated for profit. The government hoped this legislation would permit Amtrak to run without subsidies. However, by 1981 Amtrak was still receiving approximately 50 percent of its operating funds in subsidies from the government. At that time, the government mandated Amtrak to maximize the use of all resources – employees, facilities, and real estate – to enter into agreements with the private sector, and to undertake initiatives designed to minimize federal financial support. Amtrak then found a new CEO, Mr W. Graham Claytor, who they hoped would turn Amtrak into a profitable operation. His vision for the future of Amtrak was summarized in a document called AMTRAK 2000.

AMTRAK 2000

President W. Graham Claytor, in an effort to appease government criticism, initiated a strategic plan known as AMTRAK 2000. The plan contained the following major points:

- continue to improve the quality of its service to attract and retain customers;
- continue to improve productivity, via modernization of facilities, labor work rules, and benefits plans;
- become a for-profit company by the year 2000 by cutting costs.

When the plan was implemented, quality improvements were made and the public's image of Amtrak was improved. Government subsidies were decreased from over 40 percent in 1985 to 20 percent in 1993 (see exhibit 22.1). However, these numbers were inflated. Some creative accounting was performed in 1991, exempting the railroad pension fund expense from the government subsidy numbers.

Amtrak in 1994

In 1994, Amtrak operated 250 intercity trains per day over 24,000 miles of rail line and served 525 communities in every state but four in the continental United States. Amtrak carried more than 40 million passengers per year – about 22 million intercity passengers and 18 million metropolitan commuters.

Conflicts and scheduling problems with the freight railroads continued to exacerbate Amtrak's rather dismal on-time performance. In financial year (FY)

Exhibit 22.1   Government subsidy

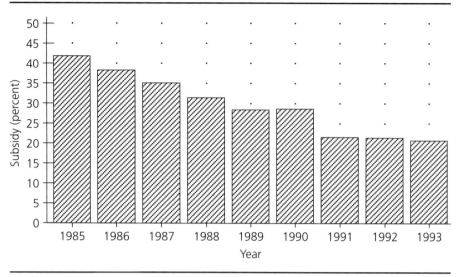

Source: Amtrak Annual Reports, 1988–1993.

1993, Amtrak paid $14.7 million on hotels, meals, and alternate transportation for passengers who missed their connections. Passenger complaints about late trains doubled from 1992 to 1993. Impossible to measure was the cost in loss business. In FY 1993 a study showed that 36 percent of the delay time suffered by Amtrak trains was attributable to factors that were wholly controlled by the freight carriers. Amtrak claimed that the freight lines were not abiding by the agreements set when Amtrak started operations.

As part of the Rail Passenger Service Act of 1970, the freight companies had been relieved of all responsibility for providing passenger service in exchange for contract performance in the area of moving Amtrak passengers across the country. Amtrak and the freight companies had fought over this point for years. The freight companies argued that since Amtrak received direct government subsidies, it was not a for-profit company, and that the government unfairly subsidized its operations at the expense of their own. Amtrak, according to the freight railroads, should therefore pay a higher percentage of roadbed maintenance and other costs. The Amtrak response was that the Department of Transportation is responsible for setting appropriations for all modes of passenger transportation. The airline and automobile systems received indirect subsidies. The airlines received indirect funds when the government paid the salaries of air traffic controllers. Also, the state governments paid a major portion of the costs of building airports. The highways received indirect subsidies from state taxes for the upgrade of the roadways. Therefore, all US transportation was directly or indirectly subsidized. As of 1994,

Exhibit 22.2   Ridership in millions of passengers

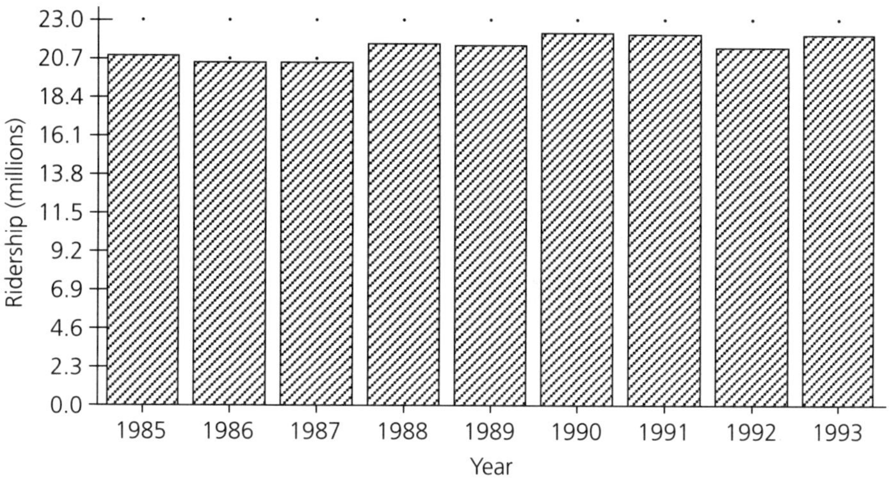

Source: Amtrak Annual Reports, 1988–1993.

these conflict had still not been resolved, and continued to exacerbate Amtrak's often poor relationship with the freight companies.

Ridership

Amtrak identifies four separate types of service: short distance, long distance, Northeast corridor, and special trains. In 1985, 20.8 million passengers traveled on Amtrak for 4,825,000 miles. By 1993 the number had increased to 22.1 million passengers for 6,199,000 miles (see exhibits 22.2 and 22.3). In 1993, the Northeast corridor carried 46.5 percent of total passengers. The short and long distance routes carried 25.5 percent and 26.6 percent respectively, leaving the special trains like the AutoTrain for 0.2 percent. The distinguishing point between "short" and "long" is approximately 600 one-way miles; each of the broad categories is further subdivided.

These percentages were quite different in regard to passenger miles. The Northeast corridor was responsible for 23.1 percent of the passenger miles. The short and long distance routes encompass 12.6 percent and 64.1 percent of passenger miles, respectively. The special trains remained the same, with 0.2 percent of the miles. Focusing on passenger miles also casts light on another important characteristic of Amtrak performance. Over time, Amtrak's growth in passenger miles improved at a much better rate than its growth as measured simply by passenger boardings (see exhibits 22.2 and 22.3). Goals for the future included increasing passenger boardings while increasing service.

Exhibit 22.3 Passenger miles in millions

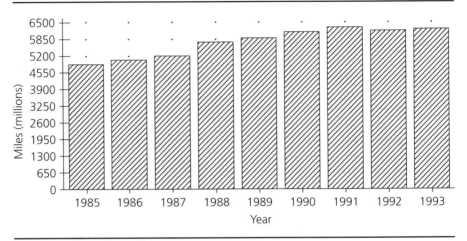

Source: Amtrak Annual Reports, 1988–1993.

Equipment for a New Century

Amtrak realized that it would be extremely difficult to increase reliable service given the age of its locomotives. When Amtrak was formed, it received cars and engines from many different rail companies; thus Amtrak coined the name "rainbow train." When Amtrak began operations in 1971, its most basic asset – the passenger equipment necessary to transport people – already was old. Amtrak inherited passenger cars and locomotives from the freight railroads, most of which were built during the 1950s. Although Amtrak acquired free engines at its inception, they were already over a decade old. This equipment, which should have been close to retirement at the time, was still in service, and adding hundreds of thousands of additional miles to its tallies. The age of the trains increased from 14.8 years in 1985 to 22.4 years in 1993 (see exhibit 22.4). These older trains were not easily serviced. Some parts actually had to be fabricated at Amtrak yards. This method of keeping the trains running was proving to be very costly. Equipment could only be rebuilt or overhauled a limited number of times before it became unsafe and unreliable. Each time a train was repaired it was more difficult and expensive to keep it consistent with the comfort, image, and reliability demanded by business and pleasure travelers. This crippled ridership and revenues, imposed excessive maintenance and overhaul costs, and severely undermined efforts to position rail passenger service as a mode of the future.

In Down's opinion, Amtrak's future depended on being able to upgrade its trains. The feature comforts incorporated in new passenger designs – improved accessibility, ergonomic lighting and information systems, and advanced on-board telecommunications and conference facilities – would greatly enhance the quality of

Exhibit 22.4 Average age of rail cars

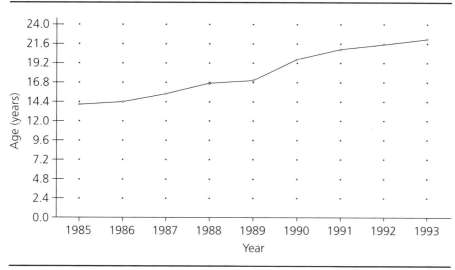

Source: Amtrak Annual Reports, 1988–1993.

service for business and discretionary travelers alike and enable Amtrak to offer a product that was comparable to other travel alternatives. State-of-the-art mechanical systems, in both passenger cars and locomotives, would mean far more reliable and consistent service that would be less expensive and easier to maintain. The acquisition of new equipment could change the nature of Amtrak's product from basic, low-cost transportation to a preferred means of travel between cities.

Some improvement in equipment had been made, however, and others were scheduled. One hundred and forty new bilevel Superliner cars had been acquired in 1993. These cars doubled the existing capacity when they replaced the older single level Heritage cars. The Superliners were able to generate higher returns on investment, and service on them proved extremely marketable. The new cars incorporated state-of-the-art on-board air quality control systems, and improved accessibility for all passengers as well as meeting all requirements under the 1990 Americans with Disabilities Act. The cars featured modular design for ease of repair and enhanced ergonomics. Amtrak expected to exercise options for more Superliners as funding became available.

Amtrak also had plans to upgrade its long distance service by acquiring new sleeping cars known as "Viewliners." Viewliners would replace the 40-year-old Heritage sleepers then in use, and would generate nearly 50 percent more revenue. Passengers would enjoy enhanced accommodations, including on-board showers and music and lighting systems. Delivery of the first 50 cars was expected to be completed during 1996.

In 1993 and 1994, Amtrak took delivery on a fleet of new diesel electric passenger locomotives. The AMD-103 "Genesis" units from GE Transportation systems were the first Amtrak locomotives designed and built solely for passenger service and not a derivative of freight designs. Amtrak ordered 54 of these new GE locomotives and by 1994 had taken delivery of the first 26. Amtrak also expected to benefit from the availability of passenger cars being built for and financed by the state of California. Delivery of these cars was expected to begin in late 1994.

High-speed Service

Amtrak management was committed to the concept of bringing high-speed service (greater than 80 m.p.h.) to US rails. The first objective was to build a high-speed system which would compete with airlines and automobiles for the commuter dollar in the New York–Boston market. Amtrak's Northeast High Speed Railroad Improvement Project (NHRRIP) included plans for the purchase of 26 or more high-speed trains. In 1994, it was the only North American high-speed rail project making measurable progress. Amtrak had successfully tested two European high-speed trains (the Swedish X2000, and the German Inter City Express, ICE) and was expected to award a contract to procure its own high-speed equipment by 1996.

The ability to compete with airlines and automobiles between New York and Boston – the second largest business travel market in the continental United States – had long been a goal of Amtrak. Amtrak felt that in that market rail routes could be a viable alternative to the congested highways and busy airports. Between New York and Washington, where rail travel times are competitive with air travel, Amtrak controlled 43 percent of the market and carried more passengers than either of the two air shuttles. With its four to five hour Boston to New York schedules, however, Amtrak was rarely an alternative for the business traveler.

Beginning in 1997, that was expected to change. Electrification and upgrading of the New York to Boston line were expected to be completed so that new high-speed trains could begin operations. In 1994, work had begun on the electrification design and on significant track and signal work that would permit speeds of up to 150 m.p.h. along portions of the route. Amtrak was working with a number of companies to develop new technology that would represent the standard for high speed rail programs in America. These included development of 80 m.p.h. high-speed track switches, advanced track equipment for installing lengthy and heavy high speed crossovers, self-powered track inspection and catenary maintenance vehicles, and signal, cab, and traffic control systems for safe and reliable high-speed operations. Amtrak completed a successful revenue test in 1993 of a Swedish X2000 tilting high-speed trainset and a German ICE high-speed trainset. Both operated in revenue service at 135 m.p.h., 10 m.p.h. above the limit for existing Metroliners.

Because Amtrak was subject to "Buy America" provisions and strict United States safety standards, it could not acquire off-the-shelf European high-speed rail equipment, however. Nevertheless, Amtrak was gearing up for high-speed operation of the full Northeast corridor by 1997, and was positioning itself for an incremental approach to operating high-speed trains in other new corridors.

Once again, conflicts arose with the freight carriers. Freight operators could not exceed 65 m.p.h. on their trains, but the tracks needed to be upgraded for the faster passenger cars. These railroads, who owned the majority of the rails, did not want to spend the additional capital to upgrade their rails or keep them maintained. The high-speed cars needed to have a higher outside rail to accommodate the centrifugal forces on the turns. The rail companies' traffic was freight, but the curve modifications would be done solely for the benefit of Amtrak's passenger trains. Further, the freight carriers would need to worry about safety concerns on the higher elevation rails. They pointed out that these rails could cause cargo to shift, especially on double stacked loads, and that could cause derailments. But the most difficult issue of all would be the liability issue. Freight railroads were greatly concerned about the possibility of catastrophic accidents and the issue of potential charges of gross negligence, and wanted the government to guarantee them relief from punitive damage settlements.

Diversification

In 1981, Amtrak created the Corporate Development Department to explore, develop, and more fully utilize Amtrak's corporate assets to increase revenue and help reduce the dependence on federal support. Several profitable ventures have resulted. Amtrak entered into agreements with MCI and AT&T, leasing its right-of-way for these companies to install fiber optic lines. Amtrak's maintenance facilities and skilled employees also proved to be very marketable assets. The company overhauled commuter cars for various intracity transit authorities. A steady source of revenue was also provided by Amtrak's maintenance division. Amtrak performed track maintenance for several commuter agencies in the Northeast and leased a wide variety of its equipment to contractors, other railroads, and government agencies.

Amtrak also capitalized on its expertise in planning and designing rail service by acting as a consultant to other rail companies. Additional revenues are generated from Railfones – a phone system used by passengers which averages over 5000 calls per week. Amtrak also contracted with the Federal Railroad Administration, acting as an agent for the US Air Force, to develop a training program for the Peacekeeper Rail Garrison MX Missile System. Amtrak was also involved in upgrading the FRA's terminals and stations.

Terminals

When Amtrak was created in 1971, it inherited outmoded and dilapidated passenger stations. To correct this situation, the company began working with state and local communities to replace and rebuild many stations. Washington Union Station, Chicago Union Station, LA Union Station, Cincinnati Union Station, Boston's South Station, and Philadelphia's 30th Street Station were all modernized with the help of local governments. Station upgrades not only served to attract additional passengers, but benefited Amtrak by providing additional direct revenue. Amtrak received rental income from businesses located in its stations and from from air rights above the stations, and under some agreements the company also received a share of revenues generated by the business. In 1994, Amtrak earmarked $90 million for improvements to New York's Penn Station. The upgrade was to include shops, restaurants, and movie theaters, which would not only serve the needs of travelers, but bring in additional patrons from the surrounding area.

Amtrak's success in real estate management can be traced in annual revenues. Prior to 1976 there were virtually none. By 1981 real estate revenues generated approximately $9 million a year. By 1991 it was $31 million, and it is expected to reach $100 million a year by the year 2000.

Disasters

On September 22, 1993, Amtrak's Sunset Limited enroute from Los Angeles to Miami derailed over Big Bayou Canot near Mobile, Alabama, causing the worst accident in Amtrak's history. The bridge collapsed as the train sped onto it, causing three engines and four cars to plunge into the bayou below. The accident killed 42 passengers and five crew members, and injured 103. The bridge had been struck by a barge minutes before the train was to cross. The National Transportation Safety Board placed blame for the accident on the tow boat pilot's lack of radar skills and recommended more stringent training and licensing for barge companies. However, the company's public safety image was tainted. To play down the disaster, as Amtrak does for all accidents, the company pulled its advertisements in the local area.

On August 3, 1994, a Chicago bound passenger train derailed near Batavia, NY, sending nine cars hurtling down an embankment. Twenty-nine people were hospitalized and 92 injured when a faulty wheel unit on a mail car jumped the track 3.1 miles before the rest of the train derailed. These two unfortunate accidents should, however, be evaluated in contrast to an overall improved safety performance for the industry as a whole over the previous four years (see exhibit 22.5).

Stockholders

Although Amtrak was, in 1994, a semi-private company, subsidized by the federal government, it had stockholders. Its stockholders consisted of the rail companies whose passenger services were taken over by Amtrak in 1971. Consolidated Rail Corporation, the largest holder of Amtrak stock, holds 55.8 percent of the shares. Burlington Northern, Soo Line Corporation, and The Grand Trunk Western Railroad own 35.6, 6, and 2.6 percent, respectively. Amtrak's common stock is not traded on any exchange.

Amtrak's preferred shares were all held by the US Secretary of Transportation for the benefit of the US government. Preferred stock was issued in the amount of the government subsidy each year. Amtrak's stockholders wield little power in the company's strategic decisions, however. Because the company was so dependent on the political situation in Washington, true power lay in the hands of Amtrak's board of directors.

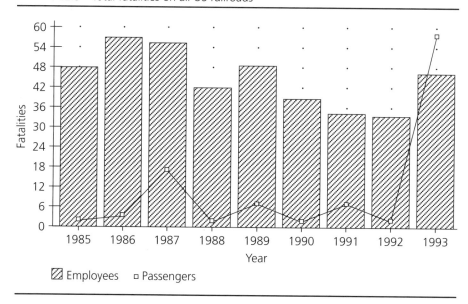

Exhibit 22.5 Total fatalities on all US railroads

Source: Amtrak Annual Reports, 1988–1993.

Board of Directors

Amtrak's Board of Directors changes frequently. Seats are held by the present Secretary of Transportation, former Amtrak presidents and governors of key Amtrak states. In 1994, the seven member board consisted of:

- Haley Barbour, chairman of Republican National Committee, who was serving his fourth year;
- W. Graham Claytor Jr, former president of Amtrak, who was serving his fourth year (Mr Claytor died May 14, 1994);
- Robert R. Kiley, CEO of Fischbach Corporation, who was serving his first year;
- Leon J. Lombardi, partner of a Boston law firm, who was serving his first year;
- Don J. Pease, former US Congressman from Ohio, who was serving his first year;
- Frederico Pena, present Secretary of Transportation, who was serving his first year;
- Tommy G. Thompson, governor of Wisconsin, who was serving his fourth year.

The Downs Era

Thomas M. Downs, 50, the CEO of Amtrak in 1994, was a native of Kansas City. He began his career as administrative assistant to the city manager of Little Rock,

Arkansas, in 1970, becoming assistant city manager in 1972 and leaving in 1974 for the city manager's job in Leavenworth, Kansas. His career took a sharp turn in 1977 when he was selected as a White House Fellow under President Jimmy Carter and assigned as special assistant to Transportation Secretary Brock Adams. He rose through suceedingly higher level jobs in the Carter administration, becoming associate administrator for planning and policy development in the Federal Highway Administration and the executive director of the Urban Mass Transit Administration. When President Carter lost his re-election bid in 1980, Downs was asked to become Transportation Director for the District of Columbia. In 1983, he became DC city administrator under Mayor Marion Barry. Despite the difficulty of running an impossible city under an often-impossible mayor, Downs lasted longer than any DC administrator had in recent years. Downs next became President of the Triborough Bridge and Tunnel Authority in New York, and in 1990 he was named New Jersey Transportation Commissioner.

When New Jersey Governor Jim Florio lost the 1993 election, Downs was available to come back to Washington. He had supporters in the Clinton administration, one of whom was Deputy Transportation Secretary Mort Downey, who emerged as a key executive in the Transportation Department. Downey and Downs had known each other for many years, their relationship dating back to the Carter administration and later in the New York area. Transportation Secretary Federico Pena suggested Downs, and President Clinton appointed him shortly after the November 1992 election.

Upon taking over the helm of Amtrak in December 1993, Downs realized that he must take action, and quickly. During the previous eight years, Amtrak had lost over $700 million per year (see exhibit 22.6), and was faced with pressing problems: a shortage of reliable equipment (compounded by an overabundance of old, worn out rolling stock that needed replacement rather than refurbishment), a long history of less-than-adequate capital and operating funding, an inefficient management structure, chronically late trains (a problem sometimes exacerbated by less than cooperative host freight railroads), and train personnel who often felt overworked and came across as rude to customers.

Downs set out to "re-engineer" Amtrak toward a customer service-oriented approach to business. He briefed Congress on Amtrak's dire need for capital investment, and took it upon himself to get out on the system, ride the trains, and talk to his new charges. As a result of the time that Downs spent riding the trains, he decided to hold a first-ever management/employee leadership conference. During this conference, Downs spoke about what he encountered out in the field. His main concern was that "for a growing number of passengers, the Amtrak experience is not what it should be." Downs found a number of employees who loved railroading but felt that passengers got in the way. He told the Conference attendees that this was "related to the fact that we have systems that don't work, we have management structures that don't work, and we sure as hell have equipment that doesn't work." Downs went on to say that he felt "these problems were symptoms of the carrier's emphasis on survival over growth. Under Graham Claytor's stewardship – and through two Presidential administrations that frequently sought to eliminate financial support – Amtrak focused on keeping costs down and on getting by

Exhibit 22.6 Revenues and losses (US$ millions)

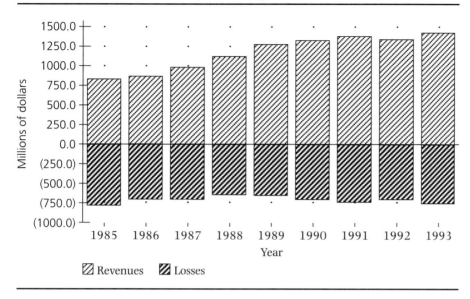

Source: Amtrak Annual Reports, 1988–1993.

with limited resources." Although this approach worked for a time, Downs felt that it could not continue.

Amtrak's cost recovery ratio of approximately 80 percent is as high as any national rail passenger operation in the world. However, Downs felt that Amtrak had pushed itself as far as it could go in that area and that the next step was capital return on investment – improving Amtrak and technology to obtain better efficiencies. Amtrak had been decapitalized at the rate of about $250 million per year, and was now paying the price. Downs stated that "Amtrak has the potential to become a world-class passenger railroad." Under Graham Claytor, the re-engineering process had begun with its roots in a Continuous Quality Improvement program. However, like many of the railroads, Amtrak is structured as a functional organization. Downs felt that Amtrak should reorganize around lines of business to focus better on the customer, and customer demands, not on the functions. Downs stated that "rethinking Amtrak starts with building a series of smaller businesses within Amtrak. Intercity passenger service is one. Medium-range commuter business, like the Northeast, is another. Contract commuter operations is another. California may be a business all by itself because of the nature of the capital investment."

The issues that had to be addressed first involved changing the functional way Amtrak is managed, which Downs described as "currently a series of 'stovepipes' that run from top to bottom." Free-standing local business units that have control over everything they need to be accountable for must be established. "Our people

Exhibit 22.7   Percentage on-time performance

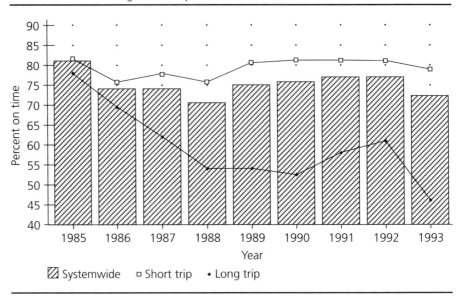

Source: Amtrak Annual Reports, 1988–1993.

need to be able to make decisions about service interruptions, baggage, fare adjustment, on time performance, food quality – everything that goes into that business," says Downs. "It has to be managed at a local level – you can't manage the
entire Amtrak system out of Union Station in Washington, DC."

Another area of concern for Amtrak was improving host-railroad relations.
"Often, the commercial railroads will treat an Amtrak train the same as freight,"
said Downs. "They'll just park it on a siding and say, 'We'll get back to you.' That's
very frustrating for our customers." As a national system, Amtrak's experience
with its host railroads can best be described as inconsistent, he says. "Our on time
performance with some railroads right now is absolutely miserable" (see exhibit
22.7). "I don't expect them to tell us about the status of every train operating in
their territory – that's part of our responsibility, and our customers are paying for
it. What I expect from the railroads is this. We have a contract with them to get
across their territory on a schedule that we have agreed to. We negotiate a price
that includes a fixed cost plus performance criteria – and we pay the railroads
almost $80 million a year for that."

Were freight carriers living up to their part of the agreement? Not always,
said Downs. "In some cases, we're not getting what we pay for. I want our host
railroads to be more accountable for what they're doing to thousands of railroad
passengers by not delivering them on time. But the variations in on-time performance among railroads across our system range anywhere from 50 percent to a
little more than 90 percent." Downs's game plan was to start publishing on-time

performance of their commercial carriers and using these data as a communication tool with their CEOs. Downs states that, "contract performance is an area that I want to hold them accountable for. They're bound by law. It was part of the agreements they entered into as a condition for being relieved of all responsibility for providing passenger service. Now, to some of them, we are merely a nuisance, and that can't be allowed. We have too much at stake to let that happen. I'm willing to contract with railroads like Conrail for a total potential payment, even in excess of what they're demanding on a fixed-formula basis, but with a substantial portion of it tied to performance. We're not asking for a free ride. If some railroads can deliver in the 90 percent margin, then they all can. Many railroads have lost sight of the fundamental agreement they they made with the US government in 1971 when they made the decision to abandon rail passenger service." Downs stated his job over the next few years would be to make sure that Amtrak's interest are not overlooked.

Downs's three-step approach for the future was as follows: "First, we have to establish as a foundation that Amtrak is a viable national entity that serves a useful national purpose. Second, we have to convince people that they can make a capital investment in Amtrak that will have a long-term payoff. Third, if we can make that argument successfully, then we will need a dedicated capital fund to make that objective a reality. At the end, we can argue where the revenue is going to come from and how much it will be."

Downs continued, "in its last two decades, Amtrak has entirely reversed the decline of rail passenger service in this country and demonstrated over and over again the enormous role that rail service can play in the national transportation system. The nation must decide whether it will support the capital investment required to meet the existing and future needs of high-quality passenger service, or whether the Amtrak system must be modified in order to live within the funding levels that Congress reasonably believes it can provide."

Exhibit 22.8 National Railroad Passenger Corporation and subsidiaries (Amtrak): consolidated statements of operations (US$ thousands)

	For the years ended September 30		
	1993	1992	1991
REVENUES			
Transportation related	1,267,791	1,195,568	1,208,682
Other	135,189	129,228	150,268
Total revenue	1,402,980	1,324,796	1,358, 950
EXPENSES			
Train operations	491,712	462,050	449,585
Maintenance of equipment	422,900	440,924	443,481
Maintenance of way	220,561	203,022	204,511
On-board services	181,844	171,224	169,733
Stations	143,402	134,690	125,464
Marketing and reservations	185,595	177,177	184,457

Exhibit 22.8   (cont'd)

| | For the years ended September 30 | | |
	1993	1992	1991
General Support	131,838	112,216	147,293
Taxes and Insurance	79,113	61,943	63,368
Depreciation and amortization	206,325	205,800	202,643
General and administrative	50,104	49,672	49,531
Special charges	0	0	27,165
Interest	20,560	17,858	13,307
Total expenses	2,133,954	2,036,576	2,080,538
Net profit (loss)	(730,974)	(711,780)	(721,588)

Source: NRPC (Amtrak) 1993 and 1992 Annual Reports.

Exhibit 22.9   National Railroad Passenger Corporation and subsidiaries (Amtrak): consolidated balance sheets (US$ thousands)

ASSETS	SEPTEMBER 30, 1993	SEPTEMBER 30, 1992	SEPTEMBER 30, 1991
CURRENT ASSETS			
Cash and cash equivalents	24,991	35,638	30,937
Short-term cash investments			3,164
Accounts receivable	65,035	58,230	76,033
Materials and supplies	134,571	146,572	148,651
Other current assets	6,219	5,464	11,075
Total current assets	230,816	245,904	269,860
PROPERTY AND EQUIPMENT			
Passenger cars and locomotives	2,028, 382	1,907, 643	1,824, 259
Northeast corridor	3,532, 631	3,422,572	3,099,027
Other	485,676	418,273	412,163
	6,046,689	5,748,488	5,335,449
Less: accumulated depreciation	(2,011,534)	(1,863,812)	(1,701,102)
	4,035,155	3,884,676	3,634,347
OTHER ASSETS AND DEFERRED CHARGES			
Escrowed proceeds from sale of tax benefits	51,093	57,812	65,072
Deferred charges and other	73,394	115,480	107,958
	124,487	173,292	173,030
TOTAL ASSETS	4,390,458	4,303,872	4,077,237

Exhibit 22.9   (Cont'd)

ASSETS	SEPTEMBER 30, 1993	SEPTEMBER 30, 1992	SEPTEMBER 30, 1991
LIABILITIES AND CAPITALIZATION			
CURRENT LIABILITIES			
Accounts payable	146,780	139,095	138,101
Accrued expenses and other current liabilities	124,975	118,290	145,046
Current debt and capital lease obligations	51,806	43,500	12,755
Deferred ticket revenue	12,740	12,240	9,632
Total current liabilities	336,301	313,125	305,534
LONG-TERM DEBT AND CAPITAL LEASE OBLIGATIONS			
Capital lease obligations	268,442	196,721	170,848
Equipment and other debt	172,053	178,603	107,487
	440,495	375,324	278,335
OTHER LIABILITIES AND DEFERRED CREDITS			
Causalty reserves	58,501	62,115	77,137
Deferred revenue, sale of tax benefits	51,093	57,812	65,072
Deferred revenue, Penn Station joint venture	13,702	21,518	28,077
Advances from railroads and commuter agencies	49,345	50,602	44,008
Other	4,110	4,669	5,506
	176,751	196,716	219,800
Total liabilities	953,547	885,165	803,669
COMMITMENTS AND CONTINGENCIES			
Capitalization	3,436,911	3,418,707	3,273,568
TOTAL LIABILITIES AND CAPITALIZATION	4,390,458	4,303,872	4,077,237

Source: NRPC (Amtrak) 1993 and 1992 Annual Reports.

UNICRE SA AND THE CREDIT CARD INDUSTRY IN PORTUGAL

David W. Grigsby and Vitor F. C. Gonçalves

Seated in a conference room on the ninth floor of UNICRE headquarters overlooking Edward VII Park in downtown Lisbon, Sebastião Lancastre reviewed the recent performance of his company. As founding Director General of Portugal's largest credit card company, Lancastre felt he had reasons to be pleased with its performance. UNICRE's revenues had reached their highest-ever levels in 1990, and an improving Portuguese economy showed signs of continuing to boost the company's profits ever higher as the company entered its eighteenth year of operations. A number of critical strategic issues faced the company, however. Lancastre wondered how to deal with rapid changes in the Portuguese banking system and how to react to increased competitive threats on several fronts.

UNICRE (formally known as UNICRE-Cartão International de Crédito, SA) was a principal member of eight international credit card organizations, including

By David W. Grigsby, of Clemson University, and Vitor F. C. Gonçalves, of the Technical University of Lisbon. Originally presented at a meeting of the North American Case Research Association, November, 1991. Management cooperated in the field research for this case, which was written solely for the purpose of stimulating student discussion. All incidents and events are real. Copyright © the *Case Research Journal* and David W. Grigsby, 1992.

Visa, MasterCard, American Express, Diner's Club, Carte Blanche, JCB, DKV, and AirPlus. It was a jointly owned subsidiary of Portugal's eighteen largest commercial banks, which together controlled over 95 percent of the country's total deposits. UNICRE was formed in 1971 to issue credit cards and to process credit card charges in Portugal. Six banks originally formed the company through a consortium arrangement, with each member bank holding one-sixth of the capital stock. By 1991, UNICRE had over 220,000 Visa cards in circulation under the name UNIBANCO and maintained an exclusive arrangement which processed all credit card purchases for a network of over 18,500 merchants.

History of the Company

The concept of UNICRE came about in 1969, as two banks that would later be founding members, Banco Totta & Açores (BTA), and Banco Português do Atlântico (BPA), began to investigate the possibility of issuing bank credit cards under one of the two existing major systems, BankAmericard (later Visa), or Interbank/MasterCharge, both of which were based in the United States. At the time, only T&E (travel and entertainment) cards were operating in Portugal. Diner's Club, operating through Banco do Alentejo, had 2000 cards in circulation, and American Express was set up to process charges on its cards through Banco Borges & Irmão.

By 1917, the bank credit card business had grown rapidly throughout the world, and cards were in widespread use in most of Western Europe. Interest in starting a bank card network in Portugal spread from the original two banks to others. A meeting of the major banks was held to discuss the oncoming credit card revolution and how the Portuguese banking system might respond to it. Subsequent to the meeting, several banks agreed to set up a bank card network to serve the whole country. The concept was to charter the operation as a separate corporation, jointly owned by the banks. This would provide a means of avoiding the intense competition which had typified credit card systems in some other European countries.

A single event the previous year had underscored the necessity of moving quickly. Banco Pinto & Sotto Mayor (BPSM) had struck a deal on its own with BankAmericard (Visa) and launched the first Portuguese bank card in February of 1970. Since BankAmericard's policy was to grant a license to only one organization per country, the bank group then decided to seek an arrangement through Interbank/Master Charge, BankAmericard's primary rival.

The name UNICRE was chosen for the venture. It is an acronym for Unido Credito (United Credit). The next step was to set aside start-up capital and hire an executive to found the new company. Unable to agree on any internal candidates from the banks themselves, UNICRE directors decided to seek a chief executive from outside.

"I never thought I would be involved in the banking business. I was trained as a mining engineer," said Lancastre. Following his university training, Lancastre had worked in a family-owned gold mining company in the northern region of Portugal, a rural area known as Tras-as-Montes (literally, "behind the mountains"). After 12 years working there as an engineer, he had moved to Lisbon to assume duties in the mining company's home office. In 1971, Lancastre, who had become dissatisfied with his job, saw a newspaper advertisement that simply stated that a new company was being formed and sought an executive to head up its operations. "If I had known that the company was in banking, I might never have answered the ad, but the idea of being involved in a totally new venture intrigued me. So, I applied."

The primary qualification UNICRE sought in its Director General was the ability to make decisions in an uncertain environment. According to Lancastre, "This was something for which I was well qualified by virtue of my experience in the mining industry. There we made many decisions daily, often ones of a life-and-death nature." The directors of UNICRE agreed, and Lancastre was hired to head up the new company. So in 1971, the venture was begun. With no experience in the credit card field and no employees, Lancastre had much to do. Hiring staff, buying equipment, finding office space, and hundreds of other details consumed a three-year start-up period before actual credit card operations could begin. Lancastre traveled extensively, visiting other credit card companies and studying successful operations in the United States and in other European countries.

UNICRE's credit card was named UNIBANCO, an acronym for "unido banco" (united bank), in reference to the cooperative nature of the venture. The founders had originally intended to use UNIBANCO as the company's name, but government officials had objected to the word "banco" in the title since the organization was not to be a chartered bank.

After putting together a working organization in Lisbon, Lancastre established a merchant network and began issuing credit cards. Operations actually began on April 17, 1974. Eight days later, the Portuguese "revolution" changed everything.

Background

On the April 25, 1974, a democratic left-wing government, supported by the military, overthrew the Portuguese "premier for life" in a swift, nearly bloodless coup, ending 48 years of authoritarian rule and establishing widespread civil and political liberties in Portugal.

Within a year, Portugal's African colonies had declared their independence and plunged into civil wars. Seeking asylum from the new African regimes and prosperity under Portugal's newly granted civil liberties, nearly one million overseas Portuguese, most of whom had been born in the colonies and lived their entire lives there, streamed into Portugal, increasing its population by nearly 15 percent.

The influx of these "*retornados*" brought additional problems to the economy, which was already in disarray. The new socialist government had instituted wholesale economic reforms, including the country's first ever broad-based social assistance programs, and announced plans to nationalize Portugal's major industries and all Portuguese financial institutions. Despite the radically changed business environment and heavy controls placed on almost every aspect of the banking industry, UNICRE officials decided to continue operating. According to Lancastre, "For five years, we just survived."

Portuguese banks and other financial institutions were nationalized in March 1975. All systems in the industry were centralized, and complete authority for all decisions was vested in the Ministry of Finance. In order to mitigate outflows of badly needed foreign exchange, the Finance Ministry prohibited the use of Portuguese credit cards outside the country. In December of that year, the ministry went a step further and announced intentions to begin a process that would eventually dissolve all independent credit card operations then in existence and give one organization the sole responsibility for issuing bank credit cards and maintaining the country's merchant network. A period of indefiniteness followed, which was finally relieved in 1979 when a law was enacted which officially gave UNICRE the sole responsibility for bank credit cards in Portugal. The resulting single operation was, ironically, what the consortium of banks had in mind when it established UNICRE.

The government was slow in enforcing the new law. Diner's Club continued issuing cards until 1977, and finally ceased all operations in 1979. In the meantime, Visa International had relaxed its restriction against dual operations. This gave UNICRE the opportunity to switch its own card, the UNIBANCO card, to Visa in 1981. BPSM continued to operate its Visa business until 1984, when it was finally forced to abandon it and join UNICRE as a member/stockholder. From that point until 1988 when restrictions were relaxed, UNICRE operated as the sole entity representing international credit card organizations in the country.

Beginning in the mid-1980s, the country entered a period of rapid economic growth and credit expansion. Portugal's entry into the European Community in 1986, which was accompanied by a substantial aid package for infrastructure development, added greatly to its improved economic position. (For more information concerning Portugal and the Portuguese economy, refer to the statistics in the appendix at the conclusion of the case.)

The UNICRE concept

The decision to form one company to launch the credit card era in Portugal was a fortunate one, not only for UNICRE, which enjoyed a unique position, but also in terms of overall market efficiency. In larger markets, competing card companies often operated parallel merchant networks, which vied for the right to process credit card purchases in return for a percentage of the merchant's credit sales. This percentage, known as the "discount," varied from 2 to 5 percent depending on the volume of the merchant's credit sales and the intensity of competition between the companies.

In a country the size of Portugal, where the total volume of credit sales was small, operational economies of scale were much more difficult to achieve. Under these conditions, competition among credit card networks would probably have resulted in the erosion of profit margins below the breakeven level, making it impossible for the networks to survive.

The Competitive Environment

Bank regulation and credit reform

In 1988, the Portuguese government relaxed its controls on the banking and credit industry. The major banks that had been nationalized after the 1974 revolution, all of which were member stockholders in UNICRE, were slated to be reprivatized beginning in 1991. The gradual process of reprivatization, which involved selling the stock of public banks on the open market, began with some of the stronger banks. Eventually all 18 members of UNICRE would be in private hands, with the exception of Caixa Geral de Depósitos (CGD), which is the national savings bank. This meant that for a number of years, UNICRE could expect to have a mixture of private and public banks as its stockholders.

As of 1991, the Portuguese banking system was still highly regulated. In order to protect the nationalized banks from competition for deposits from the private banks, maximum interest rates on deposits were set by the government. Lending rates had, however, been deregulated. This situation kept intermediation margins in the banking industry quite high. Consequently, the country's few private banks and several of its national banks had a series of very profitable years beginning in 1988. By 1991, the high profit margins had led to vigorous competition among the banks for deposits, which were still at the relatively low regulated rates around 15 percent.

As the European Community countries, including Portugal, approached the deadline for economic consolidation in 1992, reforms were being installed rapidly. Deregulation of interest rates on deposits was scheduled to be a part of the overall plan, but government officials delayed that action, fearing that the public banks, which in mid-1991 still controlled a majority of the total bank deposits in Portugal, would be hard-pressed to compete in a completely deregulated banking market, and that the consequent loss of earnings would depress the value of their stocks upon privatization.

As a part of its 1988 reforms, the government also relaxed its regulation of credit cards. For the first time, Portuguese citizens were permitted to hold more than one bank credit card. Also, beginning in 1988, banks were permitted to issue their own cards. Some of the banks quickly made arrangements to do so, either in association with UNICRE or as independent members of an international system. UNICRE, however, still held the largest share of the cards in the country by far with its original UNIBANCO card, a standard Visa card, and continued to control the merchant network through which all other card charges were processed.

UNIBANCO

In 1991, UNICRE's regular UNIBANCO card was being issued to qualified applicants for an annual fee of 3500 escudos (approximately $23), which entitled them to receive two cards. Interest rate charges in 1991 were 3.5 percent per month on unpaid balances (about 42 percent annually). The interest rates consisted of three components: a mandatory rate, a flexible rate, and a government tax on credit balances. The mandatory rate, which was 12 percent in 1991, was a minimum rate imposed by the government. The flexible rate was an additional amount, with no limits, that could be imposed by creditors. UNICRE used a formula of the prime rate plus 1.5 percent to set the flexible portion. With prime rates at approximately 18.5 percent in 1991, the flexible rate was 20 percent. Taxes of 10 percent were imposed on credit balances in 1991. Total interest charges in 1991 were therefore equal to an annual rate of 42 percent (the 12 percent mandatory rate plus the 20 percent flexible rate, plus the 10 percent tax). UNICRE realized revenues of 32 percent APR on account balances (the total rate minus the 10 percent tax, which was simply passed on to the government).

The high prime rate of interest was attributable to the country's overall inflation rate, which in 1991 stood at about 13.5 percent annually. Credit card operations were able to charge rates well above prime for a number of reasons. First of all, the structure of the industry was not conducive to interest rate competition. Since UNICRE controlled most of the credit cards issued, the ordinary market forces that would inspire price competition were not active. Also, since UNICRE was a subsidiary of the banks, there was little incentive for banks to engage in direct competition with it. The situation was therefore one in which UNICRE acted as price leader, and implicit price setting prevailed. The banks simply followed UNICRE's rates.

In Portugal, most customers paid off credit card balances monthly and did not incur interest charges. This was not entirely due to the high interest rates. In fact, studies conducted by Visa International had shown cardholders to be extremely price inelastic when it came to using credit cards as a source of consumer debt. A large part of the phenomenon was due to a national characteristic; Portuguese consumers avoided accumulating debt. Despite high inflation rates and relatively low average income, the Portuguese savings rate was the highest in Europe – approximately 20 percent of disposable income.

Another factor that contributed to the lack of carryover balances was UNICRE's very conservative policies for approving credit card applications. Unicre had a practice of granting accounts to only the best risks. Qualification restrictions based on income level and occupation kept many Portuguese citizens from obtaining a card. Also, individual credit limits were set quite low for most customers, a practice which discouraged them from using the card for large purchases and carrying over balances.

Only 220,000 total UNIBANCO cards were outstanding in 1991. It was estimated that there were fewer than 300,000 total credit cards held in the country, despite studies which indicated that present income levels could justify expanding the number to over 500,000 without changing substantially the conservative credit policies then in effect. A 1990 survey revealed that while 84.5 percent of individuals in Portugal between the ages of 15 and 70 had bank accounts, only 10.3 percent had credit cards.

In addition to its standard card, UNICRE also offered a Premier Visa ("gold") card to the top 15 percent of income earners. Launched in 1991, the UNIBANCO gold card offered a comprehensive package of benefits and services to cardholders including health, travel, and accident insurance, and discounts on rental cars and hotel rooms. Annual fees for Premier Card accounts were 10,000 escudos for the first card and 5000 escudos for a second card (approximately $67 and $33, respectively). Interest rates and the terms and conditions for paying account balances were identical to those of the regular UNIBANCO card, but credit limits were considerably higher for the preferred gold card customers.

The competitors

When financial reforms finally allowed banks to issue their own credit cards in 1988, UNICRE faced the paradoxical situation of being forced into competition with its own stockholders. Realizing that this situation could lead to the eventual demise of the UNIBANCO card as banks pushed their own cards, or to cutthroat competition for credit card customers among the member banks, Lancastre and his staff decided that rather than resist the competition, UNICRE would offer its expertise to banks that wanted to issue their own cards. Four options were devised and agreed to by the stockholder banks:

1 Banks could issue their own credit cards as principal members of an international credit card organization. UNICRE would offer assistance in making contacts and provide technical assistance. As of 1991, three banks had become principal members of Visa. One of these was BPSM, which had been the first bank to issue a card before the revolution. In addition to regular cards, all three offered gold cards which had features similar to UNIBANCO's, but carried higher annual fees.
2 A second option was for banks to continue to issue "debit" cards, a practice which had been permitted prior to credit card liberalization. These cards were used primarily as a convenience to replace the necessity of check writing, with charges automatically withdrawn from members' checking accounts. A number of banks had chosen this option and issued the cards as associate members of Visa, sponsored by UNICRE. Most debit cards were issued as gold cards, which, in addition to gold card benefits, carried the extra attraction of the "prestige" cachet.
3 Banks could also issue regular credit cards as associate members of Visa sponsored by UNICRE. These cards carried the same rates and annual fees as the UNIBANCO card, and could be issued as either standard cards or premier cards. Of the banks that had chosen this option, all had originally issued debit cards before the law was changed.
4 A final option was available for banks that chose not to enter the credit card business. The bank could offer a special UNIBANCO card to its customers which carried both the bank's logo and UNICRE's. The member bank received a fee from UNICRE for distributing the card. Also, banks that issued their own cards could offer UNIBANCO as a second card to their customers.

Before 1991, most banks had not begun to compete directly with UNICRE for credit card customers, and those that issued cards offered only debit cards. That was beginning to change, however. As the private banks grew and formerly state-owned banks were privatized, both began to seek out new sources of revenue offered by the credit card business. Although as of 1991 there was still an implicit agreement among the banks to not compete on interest rates, the banks were beginning to compete on annual card fees, especially in the gold card segment.

Compared to other European countries, credit card purchases as a percentage of all retail sales were quite low in Portugal. The country's economy was expanding rapidly, however, and credit purchases were rising along with it. Exhibit 23.1

Exhibit 23.1   Value of credit card transactions in Portugal, 1987–1990 (millions of Escudos)

Credit card	1990	1989	1988	1987
UNIBANCO Visa Card	46,210	29,963	21,110	14,046
Other Portuguese bank cards	34,881	14,234	5,162	1,376
Foreign bank cards[a]	43,373	31,200	21,675	15,717
T&E cards[b]	15,186	14,244	12,118	10,330
Total	139,650	89,641	60,155	41,469

[a]   Visa, MasterCard, and EuroCard.
[b]   JCB, Carte Blanche, Diner's Club, American Express, and DKV.
Note: Figures are not adjusted for inflation. The consumer price inflation rate in Portugal was 13.5 percent in 1990, 11.8 percent in 1989, 9.6 percent in 1988, and 9.3 percent in 1987.

Source: UNICRE internal document.

Exhibit 23.2   Number of credit card transactions in Portugal, 1987–1990

Credit card	1990	1989	1988	1987
UNIBANCO Visa Card	4,928,861	3,143,712	2,833,584	2,260,000
Other Portuguese bank cards	2,895,228	1,077,151	333,044	100,579
Foreign bank cards	2,698,056	2,095,329	1,558,906	1,248,865
T&E cards	515,675	519,282	489,321	459,517
Total	11,037,820	6,835,474	5,214,855	4,068,961

Source: UNICRE internal document.

details the total value of credit purchases by card type, and exhibit 23.2 shows the number of transactions by type.

Revenues and Industry Dynamics

Revenues

Bank credit card companies such as UNICRE generate revenue from merchant discount fees, annual card fees, revolving credit charges, and cash advance fees. Each of these is explained below.

Merchant discount fees

In return for processing credit card charges, UNICRE charged each participating merchant in the network a discount fee, regardless of the type of credit card used in the transaction or who issued the card that was used. The fee was determined by the type of business and the merchant's total annual volume, and ranged from 2 to 5 percent of the total amount charged. Merchant fees were subtracted directly

Exhibit 23.3   UNICRE financial and organizational summary, 1987–1990

	1990	1989	1988	1987
Financial Data (in 1000 escudos)				
Total volume, incl. cash advances	139,650,000	89,641,000	60,155,000	41,469,000
Total revenue (all sources)	5,326,187	3,438,141	2,137,258	1,487,832
Distributions to stockholders	800,000	800,000	600,000	400,000
Net income (after taxes)	238,919	217,648	187,746	144,076
Dividends	100,000	80,000	75,000	70,000
Effective cash flow (including distributions to stockholders)	1,504,094	1,695,664	1,205,635	860,799
Reserve for contingencies:				
Additions	. . .	464,613	246,593	139,718
Balance	833,750	931,481	554,275	375,481
Depreciation/Amortization	143,168	92,495	59,000	43,617
Bad Debts:				
Additions	95,500	82,016	49,161	20,137
Balance	395,304	299,804	132,214	168,627
Leasehold payments	425,495	171,201	43,875	33,275
Provision for pension fund	125,000	80,000	120,000	100,000
Total personnel costs	1,362,244	919,233	723,292	565,120
Capital stock	1,000,000	500,000	500,000	500,000
Total stockholder's equity	1,559,612	916,318	769,601	601,335
Non-financial data				
Number of stockholders	18	13	12	10
Cards issued and in circulation	220,000	205,000	180,000	150,000
Merchants in network	19,500	16,214	13,736	11,638
No. of transactions processed	11,300,000	7,006,000	5,221,000	4,066,000
UNICRE employees	279	213	184	150

Note: Figures are not adjusted for inflation. The consumer price inflation rate in Portugal was 13.5 percent in 1990, 11.8 percent in 1989, 9.6 percent in 1988, and 9.3 percent in 1987.

Source: UNICRE internal document.

when credit charges were deposited in the merchant's bank. When banks began issuing their own cards in 1988, UNICRE adopted a plan for rebating portions of the merchant fees to them. For charges made using the UNIBANCO card, UNICRE continued to retain the entire discount. On charges made with independently issued cards, the issuing bank received 80 percent of the discount if it was a UNICRE stockholder, 50 percent if not. For charges made using cards issued by stockholder banks in association with UNICRE, the banks received 50 percent of the discount. Merchant discounts represented the largest portion of UNICRE's total revenues. Exhibit 23.3 presents a financial and organizational summary of the company,

Exhibit 23.4   UNICRE revenues by source, 1988–1991

Source of revenue	1991	1990	1989	1988
Merchant discounts	5,136,556	3,782,046	2,519,428	1,500,338
Annual card fees	604,689	396,659	265,172	167,032
Interest on card balances	1,595,832	988,119	653,541	469,888
Cash advance fees	269,876	159,363	–	–
Total revenues	7,606,953	5,326,187	3,438,141	2,137,258

Source: UNICRE internal document.

and exhibit 23.4 presents a breakdown of the sources of revenue for the years 1988 through 1991. Note that the totals shown include the entire discount before rebates to the card-issuing banks.

Annual fees

Annual card fees were paid by cardholders directly to the issuing bank. The revenues from annual fees shown in exhibit 23.4 represent the fees collected by UNICRE for its regular and premiere UNIBANCO Visa cards.

Revolving credit charges

Interest payments are retained by the card-issuing bank, which collects payments from the cardholders on accounts. Totals shown in exhibit 24.4 are the interest charges paid by UNIBANCO customers.

Cash advance fees

Cash advances were handled differently from regular merchandise charges. A cash advance fee of 3.33 percent was charged to the cardholder on the total amount of the advance. Before 1990, cash advances were simply passed on to Visa International. Starting in 1990, UNICRE retained the bulk of the fee, 3 percent, and the remaining 0.33 percent went directly to Visa International.

Seasonality

Transactions from foreign bank cards, which represent approximately 31 percent of all credit card purchases, are concentrated in the months of June, July, August, and September, the most active months for tourism in Portugal. This traditional seasonality has been offset somewhat in recent years by two developments. Winter tourism to the Algarve, Portugal's southern coast, had been increasing as the area's popularity with foreign visitors, particularly northern Europeans, increased. Also, the increasing popularity of Formula 1 automobile racing in Portugal has increased tourism during its season in October.

Bank credit card activity from Portuguese-issued cards follows patterns similar to those in the United States, with December being by far the heaviest month because of Christmas buying. Domestic credit card activity also increases in the months of July, August, and September, which is the vacation season for Portuguese schools and businesses.

Exhibit 23.5 Visa International highlights, 1987–1990

	1990	1989	1988	1987
Payment service volume (purchases and cash advances) ($000)	345,557,150	270,229,866	212,048,010	168,500,964
% change	27.9	27.4	25.8	22.7
Number of accounts	201,909,561	171,037,749	139,663,944	121,196,967
% change	18.0	22.5	15.2	11.1
Number of cards	256,774,000	220,558,000	186,568,000	163,798,000
% change	16.4	18.2	13.9	10.4
Number of member offices	332,843	278,981	249,070	215,584
% change	19.3	12.0	15.5	11.1
Total outstanding ($000)	119,480,969	98,616,094	82,111,652	68,085,947
% change	21.2	20.1	20.6	17.7
Percent of dollars delinquent	5.99	4.86	4.59	4.48
Net Charge-offs as % of payment service volume				
Credit	1.07	1.14	1.21	1.34
Fraud	0.12	0.10	0.09	0.10
Total	1.19	1.24	1.30	1.44

Source: Visa International Statistical Reports, 1990.

VISA International

Visa International, the world's largest credit card network, is operated through a nonprofit "membership" arrangement: banks pay a membership fee to join and then pay fees for services and operations offered by the company. Any residual profits are redistributed to banks annually in proportion to their volumes of business. As of 1900, Visa International had over 265 million cards in circulation, generating an annual sales volume of more than $345 billion. Exhibit 23.5 lists the financial and organizational highlights of Visa International for the years 1987 to 1990, and exhibit 23.6 lists the number of cards and payment volumes in each of Visa's operating areas around the world for the same time period.

The fees UNICRE pays to Visa International are based on the number of cards in circulation and the total volume of credit business transacted. In 1991, the fees paid to Visa International totaled about $35,000 per quarter, plus cash advance fees and authorization fees. In return, Visa International operates its worldwide credit processing network and offers card membership services.

Organization, Management, and the Environment

Stockholders and board of directors

Three members, elected by the banks on a rotating basis, served on the company's board of directors. The board had a very close relationship with UNICRE, meeting

Exhibit 23.6 Visa International cards in circulation (millions) and payment service volume by region (US$ millions), 1987–1990

Region	1990	1989	1988	1987
United States				
Cards in circulation	135.6	121.9	114.4	106.1
Card volume	158,100	134,000	115,300	97,400
Travelers checks	17,100	3,000	3,100	2,600
Total	175,200	137,000	118,200	100,000
Canada				
Cards in circulation	15.2	14.0	13.2	12.0
Card volume	24,900	21,800	18,500	16,000
Travelers checks	2,400	1,300	1,000	900
Total	26,500	23,100	19,500	16,900
Europe, Middle East, and Africa				
Cards in circulation	56.0	46.1	36.8	31.3
Card volume	125,800	90,900	62,700	43,900
Travelers checks	4,300	3,900	3,900	3,200
Total	130,100	94,800	66,600	47,100
Asia-Pacific				
Cards in circulation	39.2	29.0	15.2	9.5
Card volume	28,400	19,000	13,000	9,600
Travelers checks	4,300	3,100	2,300	1,700
Total	32,700	22,100	15,300	11,300
Latin America				
Cards in circulation	10.8	9.6	7.0	4.9
Card volume	8,300	4,500	2,700	1,400
Travelers checks	400	300	300	300
Total	8,700	4,800	3,000	1,700
Visa International (total)				
Cards in circulation	265.8	220.6	186.6	163.8
Card volume	346,000	270,000	212,000	168,000
Travelers checks	13,000	12,000	11,000	9,000
Total	359,000	282,000	223,000	177,000

Source: Visa International Statistical Reports, 1990.

every two weeks at UNICRE headquarters. Its relationship to management was an unusual one for Portugal, where strong boards normally dominate and managers act as administrators. Because of his experience and expertise in the industry, Lancastre's relationship to the board of directors was similar to that found in US corporations. He was the chief strategist for the company, and the board usually supported his decisions.

In 1991, 18 banks held stock in UNICRE, with 10 of these holding over 90 percent of the capital stock. Banks may be added to the list of stockholders by approval of

Exhibit 23.7   Member bank stockholders of UNICRE in 1991

Member bank (abbreviation)	Year joined (F = founder)	Legal status	Capital stock (000 esc.)
Banco Totta & Açores (BTA)	F	State-owned	90,675
Banco Português do Atlântico (BPA)	F	Reprivatized	90,675
Banco Nacional Ultramarino (BNU)	F	State-owned	90,675
Banco Espirito Santo Comercial de Lisboa (BESCL)	F	Reprivatized	90,675
Banco Borges & Irmão (BBI)	F	State-owned	90,675
Banco Fonsecas & Burnay (BFB)	F	State-owned	90,675
Crédito Predial Português (CPP)	1981	State-owned	90,675
União de Bancos Portugueses (UBP)	1983	State-owned	90,675
Caixa Geral de Depósitos (CGD)	1983	State-owned[a]	90,675
Banco Pinto & Sotto Mayor (BPSM)	1984	Reprivatized	90,675
Montepio Geral (MG)	1988	State-owned	29,250
Banco Comercial Português (BCP)	1988	Private[b]	29,250
Banco Internacional do Funchal (BANIF)	1989	State-owned	9,750
Banco Comercial dos Açores (BCA)	1990	State-owned	5,000
Banco Comercial de Macau (BCM)	1990	State-owned	5,000
Banco Comércio e Indústria (BCI)	1990	Private[b]	5,000
Credit Lyonnais Portugal (CLP)	1990	Private[b]	5,000
Banco Bilbao y Vizcaya (BBV) (formerly Lloyd's Bank)	1990	Private[b]	5,000

[a]   Exempt from eventual privatization.
[b]   Established as a private bank after 1988 bank reforms.

Source: UNICRE internal document.

the board of directors. In some cases, the existing banks simply sell a portion of their share holdings to the new member. In other cases, the amount of capital stock is increased to allow the new members to buy in. In 1990, five new banks joined UNICRE. This was the largest addition of bank members since the company's founding. UNICRE voted at that time to double its capital stock to one billion escudos. Exhibit 23.7 lists the member banks and their shares as of January of 1991. The newest member bank was Banco Bilbao y Vizcaya (BBV), a Spanish bank that took over the Portuguese operations of Lloyd's Bank in June of 1991, which had joined as one of the group of five in 1990. As of 1991, two additional banks had applied for membership and were awaiting approval: Banco Fomento Exterior (BFE) and Barclay's Bank (BAR).

Membership in UNICRE was a profitable proposition for the banks. In 1990, 800 million escudos were distributed to the banks before taxes, and 100 million in dividends were paid (a total of approximately $6 million). Both types of distributions were made on the basis of the shares of stock held in the company.

Organization and management
UNICRE employees were divided into an administrative staff and eight functional divisions. Exhibit 23.8 shows UNICRE's organization chart.

Exhibit 23.8   UNICR Cartão International de Credito SA: organization chart, 1991

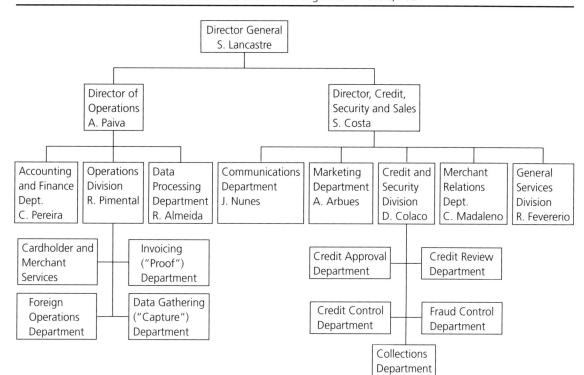

Operations, data processing, and accounting and finance were the responsibility of Director Amadeu Paiva, who was a recent addition to the UNICRE management team. Paiva, 37 years old, was a former executive of Banco Comercial dos Açores (BCA), one of the member bank stockholders of UNICRE. He was a graduate of The Technical University of Lisbon's Higher Institute of Economics and Management, one of the foremost business schools in Portugal. A growing part of Paiva's responsibilities was bank support services, which included UNICRE's assistance to member banks who were setting up and administering their own credit cards through the UNICRE system.

Operations was the largest division in the company, employing 88 employees in four departments: Cardholder and Merchant Services, Foreign Operations, Invoicing (Proof), and Data Gathering (Capture). Managing the division was Assistant Director Ricardo Pimental, 47.

Cardholder and Merchant Services, which employed 34 persons, handled requests and answered questions from clients and merchants in the UNICRE network. The department was also responsible for preparing reports from accounting data.

The Foreign Operations Department had the responsibility for preparing and processing invoices for charges made in Portugal with foreign credit cards, and processing payments to foreign countries for charges made by UNIBANCO cardholders traveling abroad. Ten employees were assigned to the department.

The Invoicing, or Proof, Department prepared batches of accounts from drafts received from merchants – the familiar carbon sets prepared by the merchant when a cardholder makes a charge. The ten employees in this department also checked the carbons for errors and looked for duplication of charges. They also checked for the prohibited "splitting" of orders, which merchants sometimes resorted to in an effort to avoid the necessity of calling UNICRE for credit authorization on charges exceeding 12,000 escudos.

The Data Gathering, or Capture, Department, which employed 34 people, was responsible for entering each manually generated transaction into the computer. In 1991, approximately 61 percent of all credit card charges were still being handled by manual methods. The number of point-of-sale (POS) transactions (those automatically entered by on-line computers in the store) was, however, increasing each year.

The Accounting and Finance Department, which employed 12, was headed by Costa Pereira, 46. The Data Processing Department, with 28 employees, was headed by Antonio Almeida, 42.

Director Santos Costa had responsibility for the Credit and Security Division, Communications, Marketing, Merchant Relations, and General Services. Costa had more years of experience in the business than any member of the management team besides Lancastre. He was 50 years old and had been with UNICRE since 1974.

The Credit Security Division, which was headed by Daniel Colaço, 43, was divided into five Departments: Credit Approval, Credit Review, Credit Control, Fraud Control, and Collections. The Credit Approval Department, which employed 20 persons, was responsible for handling telephone calls for credit approval from merchants that used the manual system. Operators checked for card validity and the customer's credit limit via computer and issued verbal authorization for the charge. Credit Security also produced a "card recovery bulletin" for the merchants which listed invalid card numbers.

The Credit Review Department, which employed four persons, reviewed applications for UNIBANCO card accounts, ran credit checks, and approved new accounts. Credit Control, with eight employees, was responsible for monitoring credit limits, changing the status of card accounts that were in arrears, and canceling cards. The department also handled requests for extension of credit limits.

Fraud Control was responsible for preventing and controlling the unauthorized use of UNIBANCO cards. This department had the authority to cancel cards that had been fraudulently used or stolen. The Collections Department sent out letters and made telephone calls to account holders whose payments were in arrears, attempting to get the customer to make the account current. If they were unsuccessful, the accounts were turned over to legal authorities. Nine employees were assigned to the Fraud Department and four to Collections.

Communications and Marketing were both small departments. Communications, with only two employees, was responsible for handling public relations and also published a magazine for cardholders which promoted the company's services. Marketing, with four employees, handled advertising and also contacted prospective customers for the UNIBANCO Gold Card.

The Merchant Relations Department handled contacts with all merchants in the UNICRE network. This department was responsible for soliciting new merchants to join the network and also for routine tasks such as seeing that merchants were stocked with forms and materials. The 31 members of the department were divided into regional groups serving Lisbon, Porto, and The Algarve, and a headquarters staff that took care of the rest of the country. Merchant Services was headed up by Carlos Madaleno, 42. The General Services Division was responsible for general office functions, technical services, microfilm, mail, and records. It employed 30 people and was managed by Rui Fevereiro, 36.

According to Paiva, some features of the organizational structure caused confusion. For example, the Operations Division was traditionally considered "back office," but it had some responsibility for dealing directly with cardholders through its cardholder services department. Because the other offices that dealt directly with cardholders were located in the Credit and Security Division, cardholders were sometimes passed from one office to another when they contacted the company about their accounts.

Another aspect of the organizational arrangement was that both the granting and the control of credit were vested in the same part of the organization, the Credit and Security Division. Although they were handled by different departments of the division, further separation of these functions could serve to increase credit security.

Human Resources Management

Human resources management at UNICRE was handled informally. Although employee records and payroll services were centralized, recruiting and selection were the responsibility of each department head. As position vacancies occurred, the department heads conducted their own internal and external searches, interviewed applicants, and hired new employees. For positions within the top four management levels, Director General Lancastre approved all promotions and new hires. For most positions, formal written job descriptions were not used, nor were formal training programs in place. As of 1991, UNICRE did not have a formal performance evaluation system for its 300 employees.

Pay and benefits for most administrative and secretarial positions within the company were kept equivalent to similar jobs in the banking industry. For specialized positions, management attempted to keep pay and benefits equal to or above other organizations, but UNICRE had lost a number of key technical employees to other companies. One source of competition for specialized technical skills had been the banks. When some of the banks started their own credit card operations following the 1988 relaxation of controls, they lured away key UNICRE employees with high salary offers.

While managers at UNICRE were well paid in comparison to those in similar positions at the banks, they were normally given more responsibility and authority at an earlier age than were their banking counterparts. The growth of UNICRE over the years provided ample opportunity for managerial advancement, and vacancies in most positions had been filled from within the organization. An exception to that policy was the recent addition of Amadeu Paiva as Director of Operations. Paiva had been hired from a member bank of UNICRE, Banco Comercial dos Açores (BCA).

Operations and the Technological Environment

For the 61 percent of all credit card transactions that were still being handled by manual methods, carbon copies of charge slips were the originating documents. These were delivered to UNICRE headquarters after being collected at the banks where they had been deposited by network merchants.

At each bank, UNICRE maintained an account through which charges were cleared. When a merchant deposited charge slips, the merchant's account was credited with the total immediately and UNICRE's account was debited. This provided a means of eliminating long clearing times for the merchants. As UNICRE officials pointed out, this feature was unique to their network system, and could serve as a competitive advantage if a rival processing network ever came into being.

After arriving at the UNICRE operations center, batches of charge slips were cleared and bunched. Operators then entered the charge slips into the computer. Totals were prepared, by bank, for each day's charges. Because most of these operations were entered manually, they had to be checked often to insure accuracy. Since the merchant had already been paid, time was money in this part of the business. As of 1991, "float time" – the number of days between the time a charge was incurred and the time payment was received by UNICRE – averaged 35 days for manual charges.

For charges that entered the system through POS computer terminals, all of these operations occurred automatically. The tedious "proof and capture" of each individual transaction by keyboard operators was circumvented, thereby saving many hours of labor and avoiding errors in the process. Another advantage of POS terminals was their ability to provide instantaneous checks for card validity, even on the smallest purchases. UNICRE officials estimated that POS charges averaged 12 to 13 days less float time in the system than manual charges, which represented a substantial saving in short-term cash-flow charges.

UNICRE was, for these reasons, interested in stepping up the adoption of POS equipment in Portugal. The larger merchants had their own POS equipment, which was often connected to bar-code scanning equipment for checkout speed and inventory control. Smaller merchants did not, and because of cost, had no plans for purchasing the equipment. Therefore, in 1990 UNICRE initiated a program of purchasing and installing POS equipment for members of its merchant network at no cost. By 1991, 4000 POS terminals had been installed, with another 2000 slated for installation in 1991 and 1992. Each POS terminal cost UNICRE

90,000 escudos (approximately $600). According to Paiva, "The POS terminals are a good investment for us."

In 1991, POS credit card charges made in large stores were mostly handled through Portugal's automatic teller machine (ATM) system, an integrated system called MultiBanco. The MultiBanco network, like UNICRE, was owned and operated by a consortium of major banks. The ATM system was linked to POS terminals in major chain stores so that customers could charge purchases directly to their checking account balances by using their ATM cards and entering a four-digit personal identification number (PIN). Although it proved to be very efficient for the merchants, the system required that UNICRE's own POS equipment be tied into the MultiBanco system and that processing charges be paid to MultiBanco for system maintenance.

The merchant network

By virtue of the original noncompetitive agreement among the banks and legal protection until 1988, UNICRE had enjoyed a unique situation with respect to its merchant network. As of 1991, UNICRE still processed all credit card purchases made in the country, including those made with Visa and MasterCard as well as those made with T&E cards such as Diner's Club, Carte Blanche, and American Express.

Although under its virtual monopoly UNICRE could have adopted a take-it-to-leave-it attitude in its relationships with members of the network, it chose not to do so. UNICRE management realized from the outset that a strong merchant network would be important for success in the credit card business, and that for merchants to encourage the use of cards, UNICRE had to provide exceptional service. In addition to supplying all of the paper products needed to record charges, providing arrangements for immediate credit on deposits of card receipts, and purchasing POS terminals, UNICRE also offered direct consultation services to network merchants.

By 1991, growth in the merchant network had, for the previous five years, exceeded overall economic growth in Portugal. Travel and tourism, long an important industry for the country, had grown rapidly. This growth in the tourism sector, while increasing overall credit card purchases, also added substantially to the merchant network. New businesses sprang up in tourist areas, and existing businesses adopted credit cards in order to capture more of the tourist trade. Recent growth in disposable incomes in Portugal also provided a major impetus to the expanded use of credit cards and thereby added to the growth of the merchant network. Exhibit 23.9 shows the number of merchants in the UNICRE network, as of 1989 and 1990, by merchant type and geographical area. Exhibit 23.10 lists the value of credit card purchases by merchant type and geographical area for the same two years.

Fraud control

Losses from fraudulent use of credit cards, including unauthorized use of cards and charges made with stolen cards, were extremely low in Portugal. The total

Exhibit 23.9   UNICRE merchant network: number of merchants by type and
geographic area

	1990	1989
Merchant type		
Hotels	989	895
Restaurants	3,259	2,599
Car rental agencies	425	384
Travel agencies	476	405
Retail stores and shops	12,286	10,324
Services	2,008	1,607
Total	19,443	16,214
Geographic area		
Lisbon and suburban area	7,624	6,611
Porto and suburban area	3,320	2,630
Algarve	2,826	2,405
Northern provinces	1,598	1,261
Central and southern provinces	2,795	2,294
Madeira	826	690
The Azores	454	323
Total	19,443	16,214

Source: UNICRE internal document.

percentage of fraudulent transactions was just over 0.08 percent of all transactions in 1990 (see exhibit 23.11). This represents a decrease from approximately 0.09 percent in the previous year. By comparison, Visa International reported fraud rates of approximately 0.12 percent worldwide.

Recent improvement in UNICRE's fraud rate had been credited to the installation of the new POS machines, which afforded an instantaneous validity check via on-line computer. According to Director General Lancastre: "Our consistently low rate of fraud is due to the efforts of a conscientious merchant network and also, in part, to the conservative card-issuing policy of UNICRE in the past." Also, with fewer cards in circulation per capita than in, for example, the United States, fewer were apt to be mislaid or not reported stolen.

Authentication of credit card validity is the responsibility of the merchant. Before accepting a card, the merchant is required to check the card's number against a list of invalid card numbers in the card recovery bulletin which is provided by UNICRE on a regular basis to all merchants in the network. On purchases of greater than 12,000 escudos, merchants are required to telephone UNICRE headquarters for specific credit approval. For POS terminal transactions, card validity and credit limits are checked automatically, regardless of the amount of the purchase.

Losses through fraudulent use are borne primarily by the institution that issued the card. If merchants fail to follow the required procedures to authenticate a card's

Exhibit 23.10 UNICRE merchant network: value of transactions by merchant type and geographic area (millions of escudos)

	1990	1989
Merchant type		
Hotels	26,659	20,932
Restaurants	21,195	13,424
Car rental agencies	4,575	3,722
Travel agencies	5,558	3,100
Retail stores and shops	48,335	27,894
Services	16,037	8,985
Total	122,359	78,057
Geographic area		
Lisbon and suburban area	70,488	43,875
Porto and suburban area	16,634	9,416
Algarve	17,917	13,582
Northern provinces	3,754	2,235
Central and southern provinces	7,587	4,711
Madeira	4,894	3,616
The Azores	1,085	622
Total	122,359	78,057

Note: Figures are not adjusted for inflation.

Source: UNICRE internal document.

validity, either by neglecting to call UNICRE or failing to check the card recovery bulletin, they may also be liable for fraudulent charges.

Financial Performance

UNICRE's growth rate over the period 1987 to 1990 was exceptional. Total volume of charges processed more than tripled during that time, and the number of UNIBANCO cards rose by nearly 50 percent. The merchant network, which UNICRE officials felt was the key to expanded volume, grew rapidly. Net income also rose over the period, even after increases were made in the levels of distributions to stockholders and of dividends.

UNICRE and the Future

Market expansion

The Portuguese economy was expected to continue to grow rapidly throughout the 1990s. UNICRE officials expected credit expansion to keep pace with this growth. According to Director of Operations Paiva, "The credit granting policies of the banks will probably be relaxed, and competition over rates and annual fees will be likely."

Exhibit 23.11 Fraudulent bank credit card transactions in Portugal, 1990

Card type	No. of transactions	Value (000 esc.)	UNICRE loss (000 esc.)
UNIBANCO Visa Card	996	20,694	8,965
Other Portuguese bank cards in circulation	865	26,279	520
Foreign cards			
Visa	3,401	40,917	1,393
MasterCard	2,761	35,549	1,258
T&E cards	108	1,825	8
Total	8,131	125,264	12,144

Source: UNICRE internal document.

As of 1991, credit sales as a proportion of total retail sales were still quite low. UNICRE officials looked for lower inflation and interest rates to spur credit sales in Portugal, encouraging more cardholders to use their credit cards for large purchases.

Merchant network relations

In the summer of 1991, a debate was going on in the European Community over the types of merchant network arrangements that would be permitted under economic consolidation. "American-style" systems of payment, such as that employed by UNICRE, were the norm. In these, banks owned the system, took risks against nonpayment of accounts, and made profits, while merchant discounts provided the revenues. Other arrangements, such as merchant-controlled networks (so-called "European" systems) were favored in a few countries. In Great Britain, there was sentiment for abolishing merchant discounts entirely. The contention was that, since the banks profited from the system, they should bear all of the costs. According to UNICRE officials, some accommodation might have to be made eventually, especially if the tide in European Community regulatory bodies turned toward merchant-based systems. One alternative mentioned was the adoption of a system like that of Finland, where the country's single network was owned by a cooperative association of both merchants and banks.

Of more immediate concern to UNICRE's management was the increased militancy among Portuguese merchants. In a meeting held in July of 1991, The Confederation of Independent Merchants declared that UNICRE's sliding scale of merchant discounts based on volume was discriminatory, and demanded that it be replaced by a single discount rate for all. Contributing to this upsurge in merchant militancy was the rapid growth of large "hypermarket" chain stores throughout the country. Government agencies estimated that the hypermarkets, most of which were owned and controlled by foreign interests, would eventually displace up to 45,000 small merchants. Because of their large volumes, hypermarkets qualified for UNICRE's lowest rate of 2.0 percent. Countering the merchant's demands, UNICRE officials pointed out that there were increased costs associated with serving small accounts, most of whom still used manual charge forms, which justified the higher discount rates charged. Here, as in the debate over the European Community network options, UNICRE management anticipated that some accoummodation might have to be made eventually.

Following the 1988 reforms, UNICRE no longer enjoyed immunity from competition for its merchant network, which generated, through merchant discount payments, the majority of the company's revenues. The probability of a bank or group of banks starting a rival network, however, was considered to be remote at best. Potential returns for a second network in a country the size of Portugal would probably be quite low, especially in what could be expected to be a long start-up period. Besides, under the agreements that were in force in 1991, banks which had their own independent credit cards already received 80 percent of the merchant discounts generated with those cards through rebates from UNICRE. Moreover, most of UNICRE's profits were being returned to the banks. Thus there was little incentive to justify the huge fixed cost investment required for a new merchant network.

Despite these seemingly poor potential returns, however, one company, American Express, which ran its own networks in other European countries, was discussing the establishment of a separate network in Portugal. Total charges by American Express cardholders in Portugal were approximately 200 million escudos annually ($1.35 million).

Currency consolidation in the European Community

One component of the income on foreign card sales is exchange revenues. For example, when an English tourist uses a Visa card in Portugal, UNICRE charges the cardholder's issuing company for the purchase in British pounds sterling. By "bunching" all charges involving British cards in a single payment through Visa International, UNICRE receives very favorable exchange rate treatment, as do all members of the Visa network in similar cases.

The first steps toward currency consolidation in the European Community were being taken in 1991. Although the problems of consolidating the 12 currencies were considerable, EC officials hoped to have a single monetary system by the year 2000. If the hope materialized, the exchange rate revenues described above would disappear on all international purchases within the EC, and UNICRE would lose this source of revenue.

Stockholder relations

Since 1975, UNICRE has been, essentially, the subsidiary of a group of national banks. As privatization of the country's major banks began in 1991, UNICRE suddenly became the subsidiary of a *mixture* of private and public institutions. As could be expected, the orientation of its privatized stockholders was very different from that of its public bank members, and the managers of the privates, under pressure from their own stockholders to show profits, began to question a number of the company's policies.

A debate over the handling of UNICRE's expansion and the distribution of earnings to stockholders was beginning to surface in mid-1991. This dispute, in the opinion of some UNICRE managers, could eventually require the company to rethink its membership and capital structure. Membership expansion of UNICRE had been handled in two ways in the past – through adjusting existing members' shares or by increasing total capitalization. In either case, the shares, and inevitably the earnings, of existing members were diluted. Prior to 1991, when all of the banks were state-owned, earnings dilution posed few problems since bank performance was not evaluated in profit-and-loss terms. With privatization pending for most of the larger banks, they had begun to question the process, since their UNICRE earnings distributions were adversely affected every time a new member was admitted. Private banks favored a change that would recognize the potential earnings being acquired by the new members and, conversely, that lost by existing members. UNICRE management felt that an open-market exchange of shares was not the answer, however, since it would make capital expansion more difficult.

A few of the members had also begun to question the policy of distributing earnings to member banks solely on the basis of their shares. They pointed out that some banks, primarily those that had large numbers of active cards in circulation and serviced large numbers of merchant accounts, actually contributed much more to the earnings of UNICRE than did some of the others. Caixa Geral de Depositos (the state savings bank), for instance, was one of the Largest members, but originated little of that type of income-generating activity. The banks that were questioning the policy pointed out that while this policy might make sense for dividend distribution, before-tax distributions, which had been 800 million escudos in 1990 ($5.3 million), should be made on some more equitable basis.

Defining the Business
According to Director General Lancastre,

> We are not in one business, but four. First, there is the business of representing international credit card associations in Portugal. Second, there is the business of operating the country's merchant network and processing credit card charges. Third is the business of granting credit, issuing Visa cards under the UNIBANCO name, and collecting payments from customers. The fourth business is offering services to member banks.

Prior to the financial reforms that were instituted beginning in 1988, UNICRE enjoyed protection under the law from competition in the first three of these business. The fourth business did not exist before the reform, but arose as a response to the new situation. In the context of the changes that were going on in Portugal and throughout Europe in 1991, each of the four businesses was being redefined.

Concerning the first of these four, UNICRE was no longer the sole representative of international credit card operations in Portugal. Three of its own bank members had recently become principal members of Visa International in order to issue their own independent cards, and one other was making preparations to join MasterCard/Eurocard. Other independent relationships were expected to develop under deregulation.

UNICRE's second business was, in most respects, its most profitable. Any threat to its dominance in the merchant network business would have to be taken very seriously. According to Paiva, the merchant network seemed safe at least for the next five years. If the economy continued to grow, increased economies of scale might favor a new entry at some point. Even if that happened, Paiva felt that UNICRE could compete very effectively on the basis of service to merchants. A greater threat was the possible loss of revenues if a European-style payment system was forced on the company under EC consolidation, or if the small merchants' demand for a single rate on discounts was enacted into law.

UNICRE's own credit card business was still strong. The company had the number one credit card in the country, its UNIBANCO card. Competition for new credit card customers was increasing among all card-issuing institutions, however, including UNICRE's own member banks. UNICRE planned to continue to promote both its regular and gold cards in their respective target markets. Another strategy was to encourage banks to offer the UNIBANCO card as a second card, along with their own cards. Despite the inevitability of increasing competition in the market, UNICRE officials remained optimistic about the future of the UNIBANCO card. The possibility remained, however, that at some point, UNICRE's stockholders could insist that it phase out its credit card business.

The fourth and newest business, banking services, was still in its infancy. The present focus of assisting members in starting and managing their own credit card operations was seen by some, including Paiva, as only a beginning. With its expertise in data processing and POS technology, its credibility and respect among members of the merchant community, and its contacts with a wide range of international organizations, UNICRE had a wealth of opportunities that could be exploited within the bank services industry. A strategic decision to push this business had not been made by 1991, however. To do so would first require the approval of its member stockholder banks and then increased investments for developing the organizational framework to emphasize that side of the business.

Overall, the company's businesses were undergoing fundamental changes as new competitive forces were brought to bear on this previously protected industry. There was a feeling of optimism in the company about its chances of prospering in the new climate, however, and an eagerness to take on the new challenges. As Director General Lancastre stated, "Now we must compete with our own shareholders, but there is room enough for all."

APPENDIX: A PROFILE OF THE REPUBLIC OF PORTUGAL

Geography
Area: 94,276 sq. km (36,390 sq. mi.), including the Azores and Madeira Islands; about the size of Indiana. Cities: capital, Lisbon (pop. 2.1 million in the metropolitan district); other city, Oporto (1.7 million in metropolitan district). Terrain: mountainous in the north; rolling in central south, Climate: maritime temperature.

People
Nationality: noun and adjective Portuguese (sing. and pl.). Population (1989): 10.3 million. Annual growth rate (1989): 3 percent. Ethnic groups: homogeneous

Mediterranean stock with small black African minority. Religion: Roman Catholic 97 percent. Language: Portuguese. Education: years compulsory 6; attendance 60 percent; literacy (1985) 83.3 percent. Health: infant mortality rate (1987) 14.2/1000; life expectancy (1985) 73 years. Work force (4.7 million, 1989): agriculture 19 percent; industry 35 percent; government, commerce, and services 46 percent.

Government

Type: parliamentary democracy. Constitution: entered into effect April 25, 1976; revised October 30, 1982 and June 1, 1989.

Branches: Executive, president (chief of state), Council of State (presidential advisory body), prime minister (head of government), Council of Ministers; legislative, unicameral Assembly of the Republic (between 230 and 235 deputies); judicial, Supreme Court, district courts, appeals courts, Constitutional Tribunal.

Major political parties: Social Democratic Party (PSD), Socialist Party (PS), Portuguese Communist Party (PCP), Center Social Democratic Party (CDS), Democratic Renewal Party (PRD), Popular Monarchist Party (PPM). Suffrage: universal over 18.

Subdivisions: 18 districts, two autonomous regions, and one dependency.

Central government budget (1990): $23.2 billion (expenditures).

Defense (1990): 2.2 percent of GDP.

Flag: a vertically divided field, one-third green along the staff, two-thirds red; centered on the dividing line is the Portuguese coat of arms encircled in gold.

Economy

GDP (1989): $45 billion. Annual growth rate (1989): 5.4 percent. Per capita GDP (1989): $4,363. Avg. inflation rate (1989): 12.6 percent.

Natural resources: fish, cork, tungsten, iron, copper, tin, and uranium ores.

Production (percentages of 1988 total gross value added): agriculture, forestry, fisheries (7 percent).

Industry (44 percent of GDP): types textiles, clothing, footwear (9 percent); construction (7 percent); food, beverages, tobacco (6 percent).

Services (49 percent): main branches commerce (20 percent), government and nonmarketable services (15 percent), housing and other marketable services (10 percent), banking and finance (8 percent).

Trade (1989). Exports ($12.7 billion): clothing, footware, electrical machinery and appliances, automobiles. Imports ($18.9 billion): electrical and nonelectrical machinery, automobiles, fuel, appliances. Partners: European Community, USA, European Free Trade Association (EFTA).

Official exchange rate (May 1990): 149 escudos = US$1.

Membership in international organizations

UN and its specialized agencies, Council of Europe, North Atlantic Treaty Organization (NATO), European Community (EC), Western European Union (WEU), Organization for Economic Cooperation and Development (OECD), International Energy Agency (IEA), INTELSAT, African Development Bank (ADB), African Development Fund (ADF), Coordinating Committee for Multi-Lateral Export Controls (COCOM).

Source: Background Notes, Portugal. United States Department of State, Bureau of Public Affairs May 1990.

CASE

TWENTY-FOUR

TRANSVIT OF NOVGOROD, RUSSIA

Joseph Wolfe

Alexander Kolesjonkov, an assistant director and head of Transvit's newly created marketing department, is currently facing a number of problems associated with the restructuring of Russia's economy. With the simultaneous fall of communism and the Berlin Wall and the disintegration of the Soviet Union as a relatively homogeneous economic bloc, rapid inflation has ensued, demand for certain domestically produced products has fallen markedly, and superior foreign and nervous domestic producers are entering once well protected markets. For the superior foreign competitiors the spur is the quest for new profits and first-mover advantages, while for the nervous domestic producers it is bare survival. Transvit itself is in the process of a restructuring, although its near-term goals are to protect its current market share, consisting primarily of Russian manufacturers of home electronic equipment, increase its sales in Western markets, and capture a greater amount of value-added from its manufacturing operations by obtaining IEC 65 standards for its products.

The case writer wishes to express his deepest appreciation to Yuri Kirpichenko and Eric Romanov for help during this study's field research stage and especially to the former for his comments on draft versions of the final case presentation. Funding for this case research project was provided by Portland State University's Free Market Business Development Institute in conjunction with its Russian–American School of Business Administration. The case itself has been created to highlight various issues involved and to encourage an intelligent discussion of managerial actions which might be taken, and should not be considered a judgment of the subject company's management skills or of the wisdom of past actions or decisions.

Exhibit 24.1   Sales proportions by general product line

Product line	Percent of total
Power transformers	67.5
Throttles	22.5
Reeled magnetic cores	2.5
Printed circuit boards	2.5
Electronic units	2.5
Consumer goods	2.5

Source: Company estimates.

The Transvit Company

The Transvit Company was founded in Novgorod, Russia, in 1961 by the nation's Ministry of Radio and Electronics. Anatolii Nesterov headed a manufacturing consortium and an electronics research institute as well as serving as Transvit's general manager. Upon his retirement he was succeeded in the late 1980s by Igor Susanin, the company's chosen successor and present head.

Transvit specializes in making some of the electronic parts found in such consumer durables as television sets, radios, record players, and audio and video cassette recorders (VCRs). Its main products are power transformers in the 1.5 to 350 volt range with outputs up to 300 watts, throttles, and reeled magnetic cores for radio electronic utility and industrial equipment. Exhibit 24.1 presents what Alexander Kolesjonkov believes has been his firm's typical product mix for the past few years, with an annual variation in the four smaller product lines based on specific contracts obtained within the year.

The Small Electrical Transformer Industry

The transformer itself was invented in 1831 by Michael Faraday and serves in the typical home entertainment product to "step down" domestic power supply voltages of 110/120 volts in the United States (220 volts in Europe) to voltages typically in the 4 to 12 volt range. Because transformers of this type are a known and mature technology and have become almost commodities within the electronics industry, manufacturers have limited alternatives at their disposal. Some have created highly automated manufacturing processes and mass produce these units in large numbers. To insure quality control standards and to obtain as much unit profit as possible, vertical integrations or supplier joint ventures sometimes occur. May & Christe GmbH, a German producer of transformers as well as lighting ballasts and other electrical equipment, integrated its operations in early 1992 with MagneTeck Inc., an electric equipment manufacturer. Some transformer manufacturers have become almost captive, in-house suppliers to their customers. Other manufacturers have attempted to create in-use value-added by employing unique, proprietory raw materials or materials that are highly reliable or overspecified. These make their products either highly dependable or functional under extremely severe and/or divergent operating conditions. Armco Inc. and Canadian steelmaker Dofasco Inc. finish specialty steels that are particularly appropriate for transformer applications, while Japan's NKK Corporation has created a new less-brittle 6.5 percent silicon electromagnetic steel designed for the special transformers found only in audio-visual equipment.

Another profit source comes from capitalizing on the new electrical products requiring modest modifications in transformer technology. The coming of the personal computer, as well as the highly automated business office with both its free-standing work stations and local area networks (LANs), has provided new growth areas for the transformer. Today's offices require more electrical outlets and connections, and all their electrical components, such as power, lighting, heating, ventilating, and air conditioning, must be designed as a total, integrated system. The office's computers need an uninterrupted and non-variable power supply, and surge suppression devices, such as voltage regulators and line conditioners, use transformers to provide constant output voltage over a wide range of input voltages.

Through various fresh designs, transformers have also found new applications within both standing systems and new electrical devices. Through the use of a highly efficient transformer that interfaces balanced and unbalanced signal lines, Tut Systems Inc. has created an Ethernet implementation that employs ordinary and less-expensive flat telephone wire or twisted-pair in-wall telephone wire. The need for high-volume portable disk drives that support graphics programs and PC-based presentations has increased the need for the transformers found in those units. And Diablo Engineering's state-of-the art, electrode-less light bulb uses a high-frequency electric transformer to light a phosphor-coated glass bulb. The bulb emits little or no heat, is dimmable, reduces energy use by 70–75 percent, and lasts over 20,000 hours in normal use.

Although certain developments have maintained or even increased the demand for the small transformer as a piece of technology, other developments may reduce its overall importance or eliminate it completely in certain applications. Sonic Systems Inc.'s MicroSCSI Ethernet adapter is small, lightweight and does not need an AC transformer, and some fluorescent fixture manufacturers have switched to electronic ballasts. These ballasts provide quick starts for the tubes, thereby increasing their life, and completely eliminates the core-and-coil transformer and its annoying humming sound.

Transvit's Markets

For many years the company sold its products only to Russian manufacturers and exhibit 24.2 displays the various consumer home entertainment products in which its output could currently be found. Based on company estimates, the firm has a 30.0 percent market share of the audio tape-recorder market, an 11.0 percent share of the radio set market, a 100.0 percent share of Electronika's (Russia's only VCR manufacturer) BM-12 production, and an 8.0 percent share of the television

Exhibit 24.2   Russian-made home entertainment equipment

Video cassette recorders: Electronika BM-12, BM-18 BM-20, and BM-32.

Television sets: Rubin, Temp, Sadko, Raduga, Record, Gorezont, Foton, Shiljalis, Slavutich, and Electron.

Radios: VEF, Okean, Selga, Tourist, Sonata, Alpinist Leningrad, and Vega.

Audio Tape players: Dnepr, Nota, Sonata, Vega, Mayak, and Orel.

Record players: Berdsk, Amphiton, Rigonda, Electronica, Vega, and Aria.

Exhibit 24.3   Unit sales by general market area (millions of units)

Year	Domestic	Export	Total
1981	6.56		6.56
1982	6.78		6.78
1983	6.79		6.79
1984	7.06		7.06
1985	6.67		6.67
1986	6.04	0.05	6.09
1987	4.26	0.16	4.42
1988	4.35	0.2^	4.55
1989	4.23	0.20	4.43
1990	3.69	0.24	3.93
1991	3.13	0.43	3.56
1992	1.45	0.96	2.41
1993	1.09	1.87*	2.96

Note: No distinction has been made between West European sales and sales to former USSR republics.

Source: Company records.

set market. Kolesjonkov noted, however, that Transvit's transformers were used only in the television set's remote control circuits, thereby missing out on many of that product's other transformer applications.

Although it was once a supplier to only Russian firms, Transvit's export sales have increased in the past few years. Exhibit 24.3 presents the company's domestic and export sales in millions of units since 1980. Foreign sales are now being made in Germany and Italy, and until recently Transvit had supplied the Thompson Company of France with parts. That relationship was discontinued, however, when Thompson phased out its television set that used Transvit's TP-60-8 transformer. Kolesjonkov notes that a buyer's market exists in the Western markets but that his firm has been price competitive over the years. Exhibit 24.4 shows what has been the 1985-90 historical degrees of wealth and market growth rates

Exhibit 24.4 Target market wealth and growth

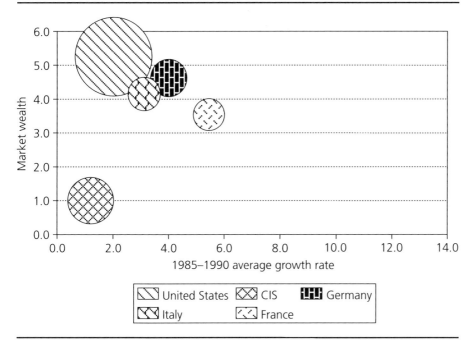

Source: "BI Market Indexes, 1980, 1985, 1990," *Business International*, July 6, 1992, p. 216.

associated with the countries in which Transvit has been competing or is targeting for future sales growth. Exhibit 24.5 displays current data on the near-past and expected near-future growth rates and per capita wealth for these targeted countries.

Domestic Demand and the Marketing of Electronic Components

Within the past two years major inroads into Russia's consumer electronics market have been made by such Pacific Rim companies as Sony, Panasonic, Sharp, Technics, Samsung, Shivaki, Funai, and Aiwa. Only minor penetrations, however, have been made by Western Europe's manufacturers, such as Philips and Grundig, as the Pacific Rim's products feature more attractive designs and offer more value. The extent of Japan's penetration into the Russian market can be sensed from examining the number of distributors in exhibit 24.6 operating in mid-1994 in Moscow, the country's Russia's largest wholesale electronics center.

In the face of these falling sales for Russian-made products, Alexander Kolesjonkov lays the blame for his marketing problems on the low actual or perceived quality of his country's home entertainment devices. As Japan's products entered the Russian market the demand for Russia's domestically produced equipment fell

Exhibit 24.5   Growth rates and per capita wealth of target markets

Country	Year 1993	Year 1994	Wealth ($)
France	−0.9	1.3	22,995
Germany	−1.3	0.7	25,793
Italy	−0.2	1.4	20,675
Russia	−14.0	−9.8	7,050
United States	2.8	3.1	23,438

Sources: Blue chip economic indicators and "Emerging-market indicators," *The Economist*, May 7, 1994, p. 118, for market growth rates. Vienna Institute for Comparative Economic Studies for Russian GDP data and OECD Economic Surveys for GDP data on remaining countries.

drastically, as has also been clearly the case in the United States and to a lesser degree in Western Europe. Japan's products were more fully featured, were well made, and presented good value, although higher priced by Russian standards. For comparative purposes, when the Russian-made Electronika BM-27 VCR was in production it sold for $100.00 or 300,00 rubles each, while a comparably-featured Sony unit sold for $320.00 or 960,000 rubles. The major difference between the two products, however, resided in the Sony unit's superior quality and reliability. For Kolesjonkov's company to do well, he believes, Russia's own manufacturers must improve the quality of their products, but he does not believe this will happen very soon. In the meantime he recognizes he must deal with the products being manufactured closer to home. New competition has come from from the Vega Radio Equipment Factory of Berdsk in Siberia and within the Commonwealth of Independent States (CIS) from the newly formed 50th Jubilee of Lenin Comsomol Factory of Nikovaev in Ukraine. Some of Transvit's major customers in Western Siberia have also begun to produce transformers in-house to eliminate the transportation costs associated with working with Transvit. Closer to home, in the Novgorod region Kometa has begun making electronic components and Transvit has lost about 10.0 percent of its sales to Kometa. The electronics research institute, although in the process of being privatized and desirous of new profit-making opportunities, does not possess enough production capacity to pose a competitive threat to Transvit. Moreover, Transvit has begun to design its own products rather than relying on the product development skills of the research institute.

The Production and Product Development Cycle

During the Soviet Union's planned economy days Transvit faced few problems in estimating production and sales levels. Little seasonal demand existed, although a large amount of production-related "storming" occurred at the end of each quarter and year as the company struggled to meet its production goals and quotas. Three shifts plus Saturday and Sunday overtime were normal during these periods until

Exhibit 24.6 Number of wholesale distributors in the Moscow home entertainment center market by company brand

Company and brand	Distributors
Television sets	
Panasonic 14L3R	56
Funai 2000MK7	144
Sony 2100	133
Sony 1400	94
Sony 2185	64
Sony 2530	55
Sony 1485	54
Sony 14DK1	38
JVC 21Z	41
JVC 14Z	41
Video cassette recorders	
Panasonic SD-25AM	69
Panasonic SD-11AM	57
Funai V8008CM	45
Sony X57	69
Sony X37	48
Sony 426	42
Sony 226	34
JVC 1200	29
Aiwa 925	36
Supra 21	25
Video cassette players	
Panasonic P04	71
Funai 5000 HC	86
Funai 5000 LR	39
Sony P51	38
Sony X130	37
JVC P28	69
Akai 120	143
Samsung 31R	32
Orion 688	30
Orion 388	30

Source: Appendix, *Komsomol Pravda*, April 22, 1994, p. 12.

the early 1990s. Since then, due to falling demand and the need to lower labor costs, Transvit has basically been a two-shift, straight-time operation. Overall employment has fluctuated around the 3000 level since 1971. Through the combined effects of falling demand and automation the company has projected an employment level of 2500 in the near future.

Although Kolesjonkov has a mandate to preserve domestic market share and to increase sales in Western Europe, much of the company's business has been obtained through contacts and personal relationships rather than direct marketing campaigns. An electronic equipment manufacturer will typically design a new product and will then contact past suppliers to make specially engineered components for the new final product. Depending on how unusual the component is, the prospective supplier may work closely with the final user in designing the component, often making suggestions regarding changes in the component's configuration or specifications. Should the component manufacturer become an authorized supplier, a sales contract is created and sales will ensue for the component, depending on the ultimate demand for the end-product. Repeat business has been the rule for Transvit as it has a good reputation within the industry and it has never lost a customer due to quality control or delivery conditions under its direct influence.

A period lasting from one to six months or more can elapse between the component solicitation stage and its initial manufacturing run. The development cycle's length itself depends on the new product's compatibility and "know-how" associated with previously developed products. Kolesjonkov has found that a high degree of knowledge transfer has prevailed in the past and that the rate of technological advance has slowed over the years in the electronic parts industry. Moreover, Transvit has learned how to develop new products faster by using existing parts for successor products more intelligently and unifying the firm's design and development stages.

Once the product has been launched certain experience curve effects take hold and these cost-saving effects are built into the product's quoted selling price. The length of the component's production run may last from one to five or more years, based on the end-product's commercial life and/or the component's transferability to successor end-user products. Breakeven profits typically occur when production levels amount to 10,000 units per month, with manufacturing markups of 20 to 28 percent typically employed. Unfortunately, Kolesjonkov notes that high inflation rates, which effect raw material costs, combined with lagging customer payments have recently resulted in zero or negligible unit profits. Transvit's financial results in the form of balance sheets and income statements can be found in exhibits 24.7 and 24.8.

Value-added recovery

Due to a lack of international certification on its products, Transvit has often sold them to others, such as the Neotype Company, as semi-finished goods. These companies, in turn, alter the products slightly by installing plugs or connectors, subjecting the finished component to a certification test which certain customers require, and embossing the revised product with their logotype. Based on these actions they charge a price that is 5 to 10 percent over Transvit's price. To obtain this markup for itself Transvit has completed phase 1 of the IEC 65 Standards certification process and a decision on product certification should be made in May 1994 in Geneva, Switzerland. Should this certification be obtained, Transvit could offer its products in August or September 1994. Although the additional markup

Exhibit 24.7 Transvit income statements (thousands of rubles)

	1992	1993
Sales	1,368,767	6,832,142
Cost of goods sold	750,122	5,118,754
Gross profit	618,645	1,713,388
Expenses		
Depreciation	58,462	83,083
Personnel	56,039	388,439
Telephone and utilities	52,706	427,509
Freight	31,011	175,636
Advertising and auditing	18,952	1,119,868
Interest	9,288	424,918
Services	3,623	23,322
Travel and entertainment	1,126	9,593
Miscellaneous	18,142	149,725
Profit before tax	369,296	(1,088,705)
Value-added tax	180,917	1,092,630
Profit after tax	188,379	(2,181,335)

Source: Constructed by the case writer from unaudited internal company records.

percentage is a welcome feature of this activity, Kolesjonkov observed that certification will also serve to increase the company's target customer base by 20 percent. Exhibit 24.9 provides a breakdown of the company's most recent cost of goods sold components.

Organization Structure

For over twenty years Transvit has operated with the organization structure shown in exhibit 24.10. Although not completely formalized, it is believed that the structure shown in exhibit 24.11, primarily necessitated by the fact that Transvit has become a joint-stock corporation, will be implemented within the year. In addition to fulfilling the governance requirements for a joint-stock company, Alexander Kolesjonkov believes that this structure's virtues lie in its emphasis on his company's need for a serious marketing effort.

With his company's new marketing emphasis, Alexander brings to his job a number of years of engineering experience. He graduated from the Novgorod Technical Institute as a tests and measurements engineer and served as another local company's main statistical engineer for seven years. For eight succeeding years he functioned as Transvit's metrology department chief before heading its new marketing department. Kolesjonkov has been exposed to marketing concepts and theories through his participation in Portland State University's Russian–American School of Business Administration (RASBA) program in Novgorod and

Exhibit 24.8 Transvit balance sheets (thousands of rubles)

	1990	1991	1992	1993
ASSETS				
Current assets				
Cash	1	1	1,172	74,581
Deposits and other cash	541	93	48,806	251,167
Accounts receivable	6,446	13,862	315,442	1,303,766
Raw material	14,732	34,065	290,499	1,009,872
Parts and supplies	2,400	3,868	25,820	18,190
Goods in progress	3,511	7,838	35,814	148,289
Finished goods	3,160	4,575	54,962	400,061
Budget payments	0	0	68,294	144,843
Total current assets	30,791	64,302	840,809	3,350,769
Fixed Plant and Equipment				
Current plant and equipment	55,316	55,084	1,083,106	1,133,815
Less depreciation	26,374	23,123	584,337	644,480
Net current plant and equipment	28,374	31,961	498,769	489,335
New equipment purchased	0	1,473	10	11,443
Capital in progress	0	3,704	32,985	62,094
New plant fund	0	1,000	6,227	631,389
Total Plant and Equipment	28,942	38,138	537,991	1,194,261
TOTAL ASSETS	59,733	102,440	1,378,800	4,545,030
LIABILITIES				
Current Liabilities				
Short term loan	12,501	26,380	112,384	287,901
Employee bank credit	45	44	22	1
Accounts payable:				
Salaries and wages	2,331	5,610	147,696	858,744
Social security	772	2,544	21,206	312,206
Insurance	30	938	7,961	73,029
Budget	0	19	161	4,604
Other creditors	68	3,205	76,103	268,975
Total accounts payable	3,201	12,316	253,127	1,517,558
Total Current Liabilities	15,747	38,740	365,533	1,805,460
Long Term Loan	0	2,000	1,927	1,877
Total debt	15,747	40,740	367,460	1,807,337
Special purpose funds	1,674	10,594	655,744	767,005
Ministry support	0	0	42,150	46,100
Advance payments	97	513	136,756	884,975
Earnings of future periods	0	0	0	567,913
Anticipated expenses and payments	697	264	19,338	42,306
Bad debt allowance	0	0	523	435
Owner's equity				
Paid-in capital	41,475	50,329	50,329	115,559
Retained earnings	43	0	106,500	313,400
Total equity	41,518	50,329	156,829	428,959
TOTAL LIABILITIES	59,733	102,440	1,378,800	4,545,030

Source: Constructed by the case writer from unaudited internal company records.

Exhibit 24.9 Transvit's cost of goods sold components (thousands of rubles)

	1992	1993
Labor	145,260	1,004,081
Raw materials and components	4,761	46,710
Purchased components and subassemblies	563,735	3,885,647
Subcontracting	36,366	182,316
Cost of goods sold	750,122	5,118,754

Source: Constructed by the case writer from unaudited internal company records.

Exhibit 24.10 Transvit's current organization structure

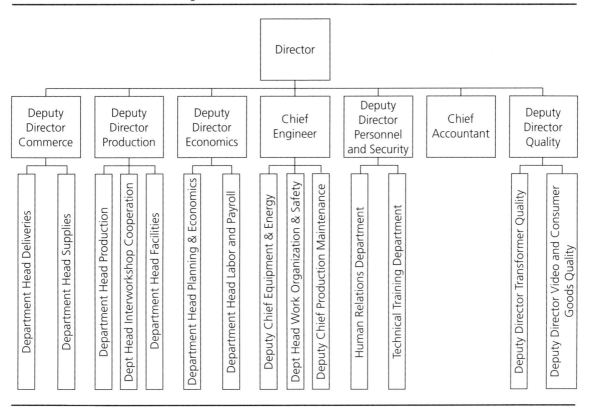

he has near his desk a Russian version of America's most popular marketing text-book. As a result of this formal education in marketing he says, "My present knowledge is deficient both professionally and personally and the only training I've received in marketing is what I've learned at RASBA. But I think I know the preliminaries and that's good enough for now."

Exhibit 24.11   Transvit's proposed organization structure

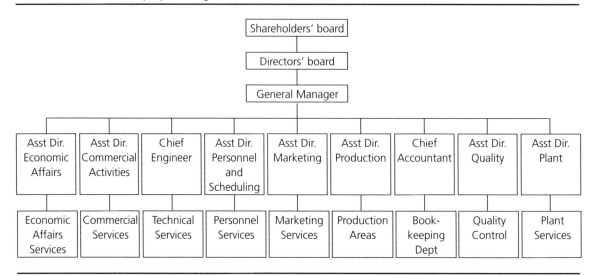

Future Marketing Efforts

In looking for new applications for his company's transformer manufacturing capabilities, Kolesjonkov is thinking about selling transformers to computer printer manufacturers in the United States, as well as for components in halogen lighting installations in the CIS. Transvit does not have reliable information on the demand for halogen installations but they are being made throughout the country, although most products come from the West. Should CIS companies enter this market Kolesjonkov believes his main competitors would be Elecon of Kasan, Promelectro of Moscow, and Lisma of Saransk. Transvit is also doing product development research for applications in automobile service centers as well as automobile recharging devices. Given Russia's fleet of aging automobiles, and the fact that the nearby Novgorod State University has an automobile service center education program, Transvit is optimistic about the success of these endeavors, for which production will begin in September 1994.

INDEX